On Sensations from Pressure and Impact: With Special Reference to the Intensity, Area and Time of Stimulation

Harold Griffing

Psychological Review

EDITED BY

J. MARK BALDWIN
PRINCETON UNIVERSITY

AND

J. McKEEN CATTELL
COLUMBIA UNIVERSITY

WITH THE CO-OPERATION OF

ALFRED BINET, ÉCOLE DES HAUTES-ÉTUDES, PARIS; JOHN DEWEY, UNIVERSITY OF CHICAGO; H. H. DONALDSON, UNIVERSITY OF CHICAGO; G. S. FULLERTON, UNIVERSITY OF PENNSYLVANIA; JOSEPH JASTROW, UNIVERSITY OF WISCONSIN; G. T. LADD, YALE UNIVERSITY; HUGO MÜNSTERBERG, HARVARD UNIVERSITY; M. ALLEN STARR, COLLEGE OF PHYSICIANS AND SURGEONS, NEW YORK; CARL STUMPF, UNIVERSITY, BERLIN; JAMES SULLY, UNIVERSITY COLLEGE, LONDON.

MONOGRAPH SUPPLEMENTS.

Vol. I, 1895–96.

PUBLISHED BI-MONTHLY BY
THE MACMILLAN COMPANY,
66 FIFTH AVENUE, NEW YORK; AND LONDON.

MONOGRAPH SUPPLEMENTS.

VOLUME I.

CONTENTS.

1. *On Sensations from Pressure and Impact:* HAROLD GRIFFING, Pp. 88.

2. *Association. An Essay Analytic and Experimental:* MARY WHITON CALKINS, Pp. 56.

3. *The Mental Development of a Child:* KATHLEEN CARTER MOORE, Pp. 150.

4. *A Study of Kant's Psychology with Reference to the Critical Philosophy:* EDWARD FRANKLIN BUCHNER, Pp. 208.

CONTENTS.

PAGE

Introduction, ...   1

CHAPTER I.

THE QUALITY OF THE STIMULUS.

Sec. 1. Semi-organic Sensations and their Stimuli   3
Sec. 2. Sensations of Touch and Temperature   4
Sec. 3. Active Touch   7
Sec. 4. Passive Touch   8
Sec. 5. The Classification of Dermal Sensations   9

CHAPTER II.

THE INTENSITY OF THE STIMULUS.

Sec. 1. The Concept Intensity 10
Sec. 2. Touch and Pressure 11
Sec. 3. The Threshold for Pain 14
Sec. 4. The Range of Pressure Sensations 16
Sec. 5. The Intensity of Sensation and the Intensity of the Stimulus . . . 20
Sec. 6. Haptic Sensations and Dermal Pain 24
Sec. 7. The Quality and Intensity of Sensation 27

CHAPTER III.

THE DISCRIMINATION OF WEIGHTS WITHOUT EFFORT AND THE INTENSITY OF THE STIMULUS.

Sec. 1. Preceding Investigations 29
Sec. 2. Further Experiments: Method of Procedure 31
Sec. 3. Results 38
Sec. 4. The Constant Error 43
Sec. 5. The Confidence of the Observer 44

CHAPTER IV.

THE PLACE OF STIMULATION.

PAGE.

Sec. 1. Previous Investigations   47
Sec. 2. Further Experiments: the Accuracy of Discrimination   50
Sec. 3. The Intensity of the Sensation   51
Sec. 4. The Threshold for Pain   52

CHAPTER V.

SENSATIONS OF IMPACT.

Sec. 1. The Threshold for Touch   54
Sec. 2. The Threshold for Pain   55
Sec. 3. The Analysis of Mass and Velocity in Impact Stimuli   57
Sec. 4. The Discrimination of Mass and Velocity   59

CHAPTER VI.

THE AREA OF STIMULATION.

Sec. 1. The Area of Stimulation and Judgments of the Intensity of the
         Stimulus   65
Sec. 2. The Threshold for Touch   68
Sec. 3. The Threshold for Pain . , ...   69
Sec. 4. Theoretic Interpretation of Experiments on the Intensive Effect of
         the Area   71
Sec. 5. The Area and the Discrimination of Intensity   73
Sec. 6. The Intensity of Stimulation and the Discrimination of Areas . .   74

CHAPTER VII.

THE TIME OF STIMULATION.

Sec. 1. The Intensity of Haptic Sensations in Relation to the Time: Low
         Intensities   77
Sec. 2. High Intensities   80

Summary   84

INTRODUCTION.

The extent to which mental phenomena can be measured is not the least important of the many problems before Experimental Psychology. If one mental process is functionally related to another, it is possible for Psychology to become an exact science. If, however, the only measurable attribute of Mind is Time, Psychology can never hope to attain to the exactness of the physical sciences.

The solution of this problem will be found only by experience. The psychologist should not, moreover, be discouraged because Herbart's heroic attempt to apply to Psychology the methods of Mechanics was an ultimate failure, nor yet because Fechner's famous logarithmic law is not now generally accepted. Even if the measurement of mental relations be yet an open question, exact methods may be applied to the investigation of the subjective correlatives of measurable physical phenomena. The most obvious problem of the kind is the relation between the intensity of stimulation and the corresponding sensation. But stimuli may vary in the time and area of application as well as in the intensity. If intensity be a measurable attribute of sensation, and if the time and area of stimulation be also related to the intensity of sensation, the relation of the four quantities may be expressed in the form of an equation:

$$S = f(i, a, t).$$

Only when such an equation is determined will the foundation be laid for the mathematical investigation of mental phenomena. For it is doubtful if exact methods can be applied to the study of mental relations, independent of physical phenomena, until the much simpler problems of Psycho-physics have been solved.

In the following pages we will discuss systematically the relations existing between the intensity, area and time of dermal stimuli, and the resultant sensations and perceptions. We will first, however, treat of dermal sensations with reference to the quality of the stimulus. In this way we shall be in a position to appreciate more fully the significance of the effects of variations of the stimulus in quantity.

CHAPTER I.

DERMAL SENSATIONS AND THE QUALITY OF THE STIMULUS.

SEC. 1. *Semi-Organic Sensations and their Stimuli.*

Unlike the end-organs of the other senses, that of touch shows traces of the primitive sensibility of the entire periphery. Instead of being specialized in structure and function, the skin has many different and independent functions. Even its sensory functions are quite distinct. Not only are tactile and temperature sensations utterly disparate, but equally distinct are many obscure sensations which, though apparently of dermal origin, seem allied in their vagueness and diffusiveness rather to the group of general or organic sensations. These may be called *semi-organic* sensations, since they represent the transition stage from those sensations which refer to the outer world and those which refer only to the activities of the organism. Nevertheless, we are not justified in considering all dermal sensations as members of the organic group, as has been attempted by some. For temperature and pressure sensations are clearly the data for cognitions of the environment and not of the activities of the organism.

In the case of many of these sensations the stimuli are clearly some peripheral or other physiological processes independent of external agency. Where the sensation appears to be induced by external stimulus, physiologists have endeavored to explain the quality of the sensation by intermediate processes which are considered the true stimuli in such sensations. Among such processes are irradiation, summation, vaso-motor disturbances, and sympathetic nervous action. The resultant *Mitempfindungen* are considered as the subjective effects of heterogeneous sensory excita-

3

tions.[1] In the case of the tickle sensation, however, which is induced only by external pressure, such pressure must be considered as the stimulus, since it is the physical antecedent of a sensation. The intermediate neural processes may not, moreover, contribute so much to the quality of the sensation as may functional peculiarities of sensory cells. According to Bronson, indeed, the tickle sensation is a relic of a primitive contact sense which existed long before touch proper, and which is, therefore, closely related to the activities of self-preservation and reproduction.[2]

Another state of consciousness, frequently of dermal origin, is pain. If pain be a sensation, it must belong to the organic or semi-organic group; and, in fact, is so classified by Weber, Funke, Wundt and others.[3] As it is not claimed that dermal pain is caused only by secondary nervous excitations, its relation to the stimulus will be discussed in another chapter.

SEC. 2. *Sensations of Touch and Temperature.*

In spite of the universal agreement that the tactile and temperature senses are utterly disparate, it has been claimed on experimental grounds that sensations of touch and temperature are causally related. Weber found that a cold coin was judged heavier than a warm one;[4] and Szabadföldi found, conversely, that a hot wooden cylinder seemed heavier than one of the temperature of the skin.[5] Szabadföldi experimented only on himself; but Weber's experiments were conclusive, and have been corroborated by Dessoir.[6] This writer questions Szabadföldi's results, but we have confirmed them in the following manner:

[1] Quincke, *Zeit. für Klin. Med.*, Bd. xvii. 1890, 429; Goldscheider, *Berlin. Physiol. Gesell.*, 1890–91, no. 1, 5; Külpe, *Grundriss der Psy.*, 92; Wundt, *Grundzüge der Phys. Psy.*, iv.ᵗᵉ Auf., 1, 408; Dessoir, *Archiv. für Anat. und Physiol.*, 1892, 324.

[2] Bronson, *The Medical Record*, xxviii. 425.

[3] Weber, *Wagner's Handbuch der Physiol.*, iii. 2ᵗᵉ Abth.; Funke, *Hermann's Physiologie*, iii. 292; Wundt, *op. cit.*, i. 544.

[4] Weber, *op. cit.*, 512.

[5] Szabadföldi, *Moleschott's Untersuchungen*, IX, 624.

[6] Dessoir, *op. cit.*, 305.

A 25-cent silver coin was heated in water to a temperature of from 50° to 55° C., and then placed carefully upon the palm of the observer's hand, the eyes being closed. It was then removed, and a similar coin heated to about the temperature of the skin was placed upon the hand. This was repeated a number of times, though occasionally the hot stimulus was the second to be applied. Four observers judged the hot coin heavier, and one showed no marked constant tendency. With one observer the writer applied two coins simultaneously, one over the other, the pressure of the two being compared with that of the hot coin. The one hot coin was judged heavier five times in ten trials, some of the observer's answers being guesses. From these experiments we conclude that pressure stimuli of low intensity and high temperature are judged heavier than those having the temperature of the skin.

It does not follow, however, that all stimuli thus differing in temperature will give rise to such illusions. In order to ascertain whether hot or cold weights of high intensity are judged heavier, the writer applied to the palm of the hand a brass kilogram weight heated to about 50° C. This was removed and placed again upon the hand, but not in contact, a circular card-board of the area of the base lying between the weight and the skin. The hand of the observer was comfortably supported. Different persons served as subjects, and all were ignorant of the purpose of the experiment. As in the preceding experiment, a number of trials were made for each observer. Similar experiments were made with a cold weight and one which had no appreciable temperature effect on the skin. The cold weight generally had a temperature equal to that of the room, about 20° C., and at times much below this, so that from the area of stimulation, 16 sq. cm., and the conductivity of the metal, a marked sensation of cold was produced. It was found, as shown in the table of results given below, that stimuli of very high or low temperature are not judged heavier at 1000 g. In fact, the hot weight is rather judged lighter. In the table here given the figures denote the number of times the cold and hot weights were judged heavier or lighter than those of moderate temperature.

Observer.	Cold weight, 1 kg		Hot weight, 1 kg	
	Heavier.	Lighter.	Heavier.	Lighter.
L. F.	2	6	2	8
S. F.	–	–	0	10
K.	2	3	2	5
M. G.	7	3	4	6
J. G.	5	5	4	6
Total,	16	17	12	35

The results above given go to show that tactile and temperature sensations are not related, as Weber[1] and Szabadföldi[2] inferred. Dessoir's explanation is that the illusion is due to the contraction of the skin from the lower temperature, and consequent increase in the number of sensory nerves that are affected.[3] But heated coins are overestimated, and according to this hypothesis they should be underestimated. A more satisfactory explanation is that an illusion of judgment is involved.[4] This is rendered plausible by the fact that stimuli of high intensities are not overestimated. We may suppose that the mind tends to infer from the intensity of the temperature sensation that the corresponding stimulus is of greater magnitude, and therefore heavier than the stimulus causing a purely haptic[5] sensation of but little intensity. For heavy weights we should on this hypothesis expect underestimation rather than overestimation, of hot or cold stimuli, and that there is some such tendency, at least for hot weights, the experiments seem to show. The objection of Dessoir against such an explanation is, we think, inconclusive. A difference in dis-

[1] Weber, *op. cit.*, 551.
[2] Szabadföldi, *op. cit.*
[3] Dessoir, *op. cit.*, 306.
[4] *Cf.* Funke, *op. cit.*, 321.
[5] We use the term *haptic* (Greek ἅπτομαι) of all sensations of contact, touch, pressure or impact. For this term we are indebted to Dessoir.

crimination-time for weight and temperature when only the quantity judged is variable, does not preclude such an illusion when the conditions are different.

The other experimental evidence in favor of any fundamental relation between haptic and temperature sensations is equally inconclusive. The fact that heavy weights seem hotter or colder than lighter weights, as stated by Nothnagel,[1] may be due to differences in conduction arising from differences in contact. Wunderli found that observers had difficulty in distinguishing tactile from temperature stimuli of low intensity.[2] But the errors occurred only when the back was the surface stimulated, and though temperature stimuli were confused with tactile stimuli, the reverse error did not occur. As we are not accustomed to temperature sensations in the back, such a confusion is but natural, especially when the stimuli are of such low intensity that the process of perception is obscured.

SEC. 3. *Active Touch.*

The great majority of so-called tactile sensations are in reality results of complex kinaesthetic and haptic sensory elements. In fact, many have distinguished between active and passive touch. Dessoir opposes contact sensations to those of pselaphesia,[3] and Bronson goes so far as to consider contact sensations and those of active touch not only as quite distinct but as having different end organs.[4] It is clear, however, that active touch may involve movement with or without muscular effort, or, conversely, muscular effort with or without movement. We have, therefore, a triple set of sensory impulses to consider as the physiological antecedents of the sensation of active touch.

Many psychologists have explained the sensation of movement by alterations in the tension of the skin and by atmospheric pressure.[5] This view is apparently corroborated

---

[1] Nothnagel, *Deutsches Archiv. für Klin. Med.*, II, 298.

[2] Wunderli, *Moleschott's Untersuchungen*, VII, 393.

[3] Dessoir, *op. cit.*, 242.

[4] Bronson, *op. cit.*

[5] For references see the works of Wundt and James, and Delabarre, *Ueber Bewegungsempfindungen*, Freiburg, 1891.

by the influence of dermal anaesthesia or hyperaesthesia on the perception of movement. The pathological evidence proves that dermal sensations enter into those of movement, but that is all. Other well authenticated observations show that anaesthesia does not necessarily affect the perception of movement. In complexes of tactile and kinaesthetic sensations we must, therefore, assume different sensory processes.

But active touch is possible without movement either of the stimulus or the sense organ. If through an act of volition we exert pressure upon an external object, we have in addition to the sensation of dermal pressure that of effort. In fact, all the feelings of strain and tension are felt which enter into the muscular consciousness. As pathological observations and experiments on lifted weights prove the muscular sense to be independent of touch,[1] it is evident that where pressure is exerted voluntarily the resultant sensation is complex, and not a haptic sensation proper. We have, therefore, to distinguish between what we might call subjective pressure, or pressure with effort, and objective pressure, or pressure without effort.

SEC. 4. *Passive Touch.*

Having analysed the various elements entering into tactile complexes, we turn to those sensations in which the subject is passive and the stimulus acts only upon a definite area. The stimulus may then be pressure exerted upon the skin, the energy of a body striking the skin, or traction tending to separate the dermal end organ from the organism to which it belongs. These stimuli are qualitatively different, as are the corresponding sensations, though for traction these are less distinct than would be supposed.[2] The blow of a moving object upon the periphery gives rise to a sensation distinct from that of a motionless weight. This difference increases with the velocity of the moving mass. The stimulus in such sensations, therefore, is to be considered the product of the mass and its velocity, or some function of its velocity. The resulting sensation may be called a sensation of impact, as distinguished from one of pressure.

---

[1] See Wundt, *op. cit.*, 427; Delabarre, *op. cit.*, 37, 38.
[2] See Hall and Motora, *Am. Journal of Psy.*, I, 72.

But is not this difference between pressure and impact only a difference in degree? When a weight is applied to the hand there must be some impact, whatever be the velocity at which the weight be applied. If a weight of low intensity, as 100g or less, be applied, and the area of stimulation be not too small, the sensation is one of impact; but if a stimulus of moderate intensity be used, a distinct pressure sensation will be observed in addition to that of impact. This is due to the effect of the weight in overcoming the elasticity of the skin and depressing the dermal tissues. The stimulus in pressure sensations may, therefore, be considered not momentum or kinetic energy, but rather as mechanical force exerted through the object in contact with the skin, or more accurately, the work done by this force in displacing the dermal tissues. In reality, however, the process of stimulation is often more complex. When the pressure is sufficiently great to produce motion, kinaesthetic elements will affect the sensory result. When movement is prevented by opposing forces, a double process of dermal stimulation will result, since action and reaction are equal and opposite.

SEC. 5. *The Classification of Dermal Sensations.*

The general results of the analysis above given may be summarized in a classification of dermal sensations with special reference to the quality of the stimulus:

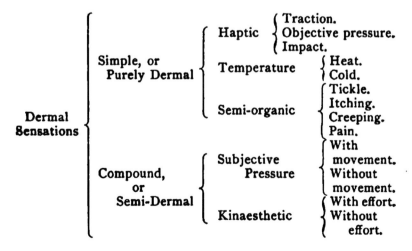

CHAPTER II.

THE INTENSITY OF STIMULATION.

SEC. 1. *The Concept Intensity.*

The term intensity, as applied to neural stimuli, has long been in universal use among psychologists, but frequently in a manner that is far from exact. In physical science the term is used as the quantitative predicate of force. But many stimuli, as those of smell and taste, cannot be measured in terms of force. To avoid ambiguity in the use of this term, we would suggest as a working definition of intensity, as used in Psychology, the following, which is based upon obvious psychological grounds: that quantitative property of neural stimuli, the magnitude of which determines whether or not they give rise to a sensation; and, if so, whether that sensation be painful, or have only the particular quality due to the quality of the stimulus.

From this point of view the intensity of visual and auditory stimuli may be measured by the energy of motion transmitted to the end organ in a given time. The intensity of gustatory and olfactory stimuli may be measured for a given substance by the quantity which is applied to the end organ. But with temperature stimuli the measure of intensity is more complex. Then, too, as heat and cold are physically the same, the absolute measure of heat is not the measure of the intensity of heat, as regards its physiological and psychological effects. Passing from the temperature sense to that of effort, the work done by muscular contraction in a given time is clearly the measure of intensity; but when no motion takes place the criterion is different, as such units cannot be used. In this case the measure of intensity is clearly the force which is exerted.

The measurement of the intensity of haptic stimuli is, fortunately for our purpose, comparatively simple. When impact may be neglected, the intensity of the stimulus is measured by the weight that is applied; for the work done in depressing and displacing the dermal tissues will be proportionate to the impressed force. When, however, appreciable movement occurs before the full pressure is exerted, the matter is more complex, since the subjective effect is dependent not only on the mass but also on its velocity. We might suppose that the measure of the intensity of an impact stimulus would be the product of the mass and the square of the velocity, since this quantity represents the energy of the blow. But, as we shall find in the chapter on Sensations of Impact, the square of the velocity does not appear to have as intensive an effect as does the mass.

SEC. 2. *Touch and Pressure.*

It was shown by Aubert and Kammler that pressure and impact stimuli, below a certain intensity, are not perceived.[1] The sensations from stimuli of low intensity are sensations of passive touch, the element of pressure being apparently absent. From such data Meissner inferred that pressure sensations are absolutely distinct from those of touch proper, *einfache Tastempfindungen*, and that these have special end organs, the tactile corpuscles.[2] Meissner's distinction between touch and pressure is accepted by Aubert and Kammler, Bronson and Dessoir, but is rejected by Funke, Wundt and Külpe. We shall now consider in detail the evidence that has been brought forward to support this view.

According to Meissner, touch furnishes the data for the concept of externality, and accompanies all pressure sensations, though not necessarily accompanied by them.[3] Clearly, however, this is but an hypothesis to account for what is assumed, that is, the difference between touch and pressure. Aubert and Kammler reject Meissner's hypothesis, basing their distinction upon their alleged observation that contact sensations are subjective modalities. This does not accord

[1] Aubert and Kammler, *Moleschott's Untersuchungen*, v. 145.
[2] Meissner, *Zeitschrift für Rat. Med.*, 2ᵗᵉ R., iv. ; also, *Beiträge zur Anatomie und Physiol. der Haut*, Leipzig, 1853.
[3] Meissner, *op. cit.*, 272.

with the introspection of the writer. The apparent difference observed may be due to the fact that stimuli of low intensity do not give rise to sensations of sufficient clearness for the mind to perceive the quality of the stimulus. We certainly do refer a tactile sensation to an external *something*, though what that may be we may not know.

Dessoir gives as the characteristic of pressure sensations the feeling of effort which is involved.[1] But Dessoir undoubtedly refers to subjective pressure, or pressure with effort; and as sensations of pressure are possible without effort, the criterion is not applicable.

Bronson bases his separation from pure contact of *pselaphesia*, or perceptive touch, partly upon the above facts of introspection and partly upon the apparent relationship of sensations of contact to semi-organic sensations.[2] According to Bronson, sensations of contact require as their peripheral antecedents only the stimulation of the epidermal fibrillæ, and are, therefore, to be considered distinct and primitive sensations.

However conclusive be Bronson's arguments as to the biological theory of dermal sensations, they do not prove touch to be distinct from pressure, because the tickle sensation does not necessarily accompany that of contact. It is a distinct state of consciousness independent of the tactile sensation, and the same may be said of the aphrodisiac sense. We conclude, therefore, that there is no psychological basis for the distinction, unless there be other evidence than that which we have discussed. If touch and pressure were distinct, we should look for such evidence in pathology; but the writer knows of none. Bronson states that hyperaesthesia and apselaphesia may coexist. But it is probable that he really refers to hyperalgesia, which is quite irrelevant. According to Richet, tactile hyperaesthesia is unknown.[3] There have been instances of anæsthesia for pressure stimuli of low intensity without anæsthesia for those of high inten-

---

[1] Dessoir, *op. cit.*, 242.

[2] Bronson, *op. cit.* Bronson does not state these arguments categorically, but the above appears to be his position.

[3] Richet, *Récherches sur la Sensibilité*, 219.

sity.[1] But, as Richet observes, this may be explained by the fact that the nerves die first at their extremities.

Apart, however, from these negative considerations, it must be admitted that the classification of one group of sensations, as distinct from another group, logically implies our inability in introspection to pass gradually from one to the other. By this criterion the sense of touch and that of pressure must be identical. It is impossible to tell where one begins and the other ends. Stimuli that are barely perceptible may be judged with reference to their weight.[2] On the other hand, individuals differ as to what they call pressure. In the course of experiments on the threshold of pain, to be described in the next section, one observer said he began to feel pressure at 3.5k., pain appearing at 8.5k. The writer would call that sensation one of pressure when the instrument used registered only 1.0k.

Even if touch and pressure be indistinguishable, the apparent change of quality requires an explanation. That generally given is that different physiological processes are induced by intense stimuli. Aubert and Kammler explain the distinction by the displacement of the skin. But this displacement varies with the intensity of the stimulus.[3] Külpe mentions the effect of intense pressure upon the muscular tissues,[4] but we have pressure sensations where there are no muscles. Meissner's hypothesis, to which that of Bronson is similar, that the sensory cells in the dermis are the anatomical basis of pressure sensations, is inadequate, since these cells appear to be absent on parts that are sensitive to pressure.[5] Goldscheider found special pressure spots,[6] but his results, both histological and psychological, are disputed.[7] The writer's own observation does not enable him to detect the existence of points that give pressure or contact sensations only. Certain spots may be more sensitive

[1] Richet, *op. cit.*, 227.
[2] See Chapter III., Section 3.
[3] For measurements of this, see Hall and Motora, *op. cit.*
[4] Külpe, *op. cit.*, 91.
[5] Cf. Wundt, *op. cit.*, i. 302 ; Dessoir, *op. cit.*, 275.
[6] Goldscheider, *Archiv. für Anat. und Physiol.*, 1885 Supp. Bd., 76.
[7] Cf. Dessoir, *op. cit.*, 251.

than others, but this would throw no light on the question. Besides, it is difficult to obtain a distinct sensation of pressure when so small an area is stimulated as is necessary in such experiments, since the sensation of pressure passes so quickly into that of pain or other semi-organic sensations.

But if there is no additional process of sensory excitation in pressure sensations, in what way may the apparent difference be explained? Our answer is that there is no difference in sensation, but only in perception. What we mean by a sensation of pressure is one of such a quality that we can ascribe the subjective effect to some definite objective cause and one exerting such pressure that its removal would involve appreciable muscular work. The apparent difference may, we think, be thus explained, for it is impossible to analyse in consciousness the mental reaction in perception out of the total sensational and perceptive complex.

3. *The Threshold of Pain.*

For the purpose of measuring the intensity of pressure causing pain a spring dynamometer was used by which a given pressure could be exerted upon any surface.[1]

FIG. I.

Attached to the lower end of the spring was a sliding cylindrical piece of brass. This was capped with hard rubber (A), which was applied to the surface to be stimulated. The cap which came in contact with the skin was hemispherical, and about 8mm. in diameter. The pressure was exerted by the hand of the experimenter, and the amount of pressure was registered in kilograms by the movable piece (B) attached to the spring. The scale was tested by an accurate balance adapted to heavy weights, and was found to be free from appreciable error. The stimulus was applied by the writer to the volar surface of the left hand of the subject over the fifth meta-

[1] This instrument was devised by Prof. J. McK. Cattell. He has suggested the term *algometer* by which to designate it, and this expression will be used hereafter.

carpal. The pressure was increased as nearly as possible at the same rate for different observers, about 1.4k. per sec. If we take .3 sec.[1] as the double reaction-time, we have to subtract $1.4 \times .3 = .4k.$ from the reading of the instrument. The observers were asked to speak when the instrument began to hurt at all or be uncomfortable; for it was found that individuals differed as to what they called 'pain.' The subjects tested were students in Columbia and Barnard Colleges and in private schools.[2] Below we give the average in kilograms as well as the maxima and minima corrected for the constant error above referred to. The approximate ages are also given.

Ob-servers.	50 Boys.	40 College Students. (Men.)	38 Law Students.	58 Women.	40 College Students. (Women.)
Ages,	12 to 15	16 to 21	19 to 25	16 to 20	17 to 22
Av.,	4.8	5.1	7.8	3.6	3.6
Max.,	8.4	13.6	15+	7.6	8.6
Min.,	2.1	1.9	3.9	1.8	1.7

From the above results it appears that although individuals differ greatly in sensitiveness to pain, on the whole women and boys are more sensitive than men. The variations in those of the same age and sex are not due to chance, since any one person when tested gives fairly constant results. Nor are they due to individual differences in perception and judgment, though doubtless these affect the results to some extent; for it is very easy to tell when the pressure begins to be uncomfortable, and the 'imagination' does not seem to be a disturbing factor. Indeed, the pain seems often to come with greater suddenness. These variations are rather to be ascribed to constitutional nervous differences, and in part, perhaps, to differences in the thickness of the skin.

[1] This was verified by chronoscopic measurements.

[2] The writer takes pleasure in acknowledging his indebtedness to Registrar Mrs. N. F. Liggett and Principals Miss Brown and Mr. Cutler for furnishing him the opportunity of making the tests on young women and boys.

SEC 4. *The Range of Pressure Sensations.*

If the *minimum tangible*, or tactile threshold (T), were measurable, as is the threshold of pain (P), and if the sensation of pressure ceased as soon as that of pain appeared, we could determine the range of haptic sensations (R) by the formula:

$$R = \frac{P^1}{T}.$$

Since the haptic sensation does not cease when pain begins, but rather decreases gradually as the pain increases, the so-called range cannot be measured. We may, however, use the term to indicate the extent of haptic sensations up to the pain threshold. But are we justified in assuming the pain threshold to be a quantity? According to the algedonic[2] tone theory we are not so justified. And, even assuming that a stimulus becomes painful at a certain point, the one sensation is at first so obscured by the other that it is not immediately appreciable. Nevertheless, the appearance of pain is generally so sudden when the stimulus is increasing in intensity, that we treat the threshold of pain as approximately a quantity.

Assuming then that the range, and therefore the thresholds of touch and pain, can be measured, it is evident that in determining them the conditions of stimulation should be constant. Not only the time and space conditions, but also the mode of applying the stimulus, must be constant.

In the measurements of the tactile threshold made by Aubert and Kammler the element of impact was involved, and their results could not be compared with our own measurements of the pain threshold, since in these impact was excluded. Bloch employed the same method, that of pure pressure,[3] but his experiments were made on himself, and we judge them, therefore, inconclusive. We found that results are obtained under such circumstances quite different from those obtained when the stimulus is applied by another

[1] *Cf.* Wundt, *op. cit.*, I, 335.
[2] We have borrowed this translation of *Gefühlston* from Marshall, *Pain, Pleasure and Æsthetics.*
[3] Bloch, *Archives de Physiologie*, 1891, 322.

person and the observer is ignorant of the time of application. Bloch gives .0005g to .0015g as the smallest appreciable pressure. Aubert and Kammler found for an area of 9mm, .005g as the *minimum tangibile*. The results above given are much more discordant than they might at first seem, since the greater value for the threshold is obtained for the smaller area,[1] and since impact is clearly involved rather than pressure.[2]

In order to make further experiments on the smallest perceptible haptic stimuli, the writer constructed an instrument similar to that used by Bloch.

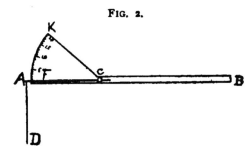

FIG. 2.

To a wooden handle (B) was attached by wax a horizontal bristle (AC), taken from an ordinary broom. At the end (A) was fastened by wax a vertical piece (AD) of the same material, the point of which was applied to the part stimulated. The pressure was exerted by the hand of the experimenter. The degree of pressure was shown by the elevation of the bristle, which was read off on a scale (FK). The readings on this scale were in grams, the elevations corresponding to different pressures having been found by a balance. The pressure was applied upon a circular card board about .9cm in area. This card was so light, .05g, that its weight could be neglected after the moment of application, as it rested on the skin during the experiments. The observer's eyes were closed, and he did not know when the stimulus was applied. The rate of application of the pressure was kept as constant as possible. It was as rapid as was consistent with taking the readings, about .3g per sec.

[1] See chapter V, sec. 2.
[2] See chapter VI, sec. 2.

We subtract, therefore .3×.3=.1g from the reading obtained. Ten experiments were made on S. F., and also on
G., the writer, for the smallest perceptible pressure, T.
The same number were made for the threshold of pain, P,
by means of the dynamometer already described. The area
of stimulation for the pain measurements was also .9cm.
The results are given in grams. The values of the Range,
R, are found by dividing the average values of P by the
average values of T.

	T.			P.			$R = \dfrac{P}{T}$
	Av.	Max.	Min.	Av.	Max.	Min.	
F.	1.9	2.7	1.	3230	4300	2700	1700
G.	2.6	2.5	.4	4400	5700	3800	1697

According to these results the haptic range is about 1700.
The great variation in the values obtained for the threshold renders these figures necessarily very inexact. The
values of the threshold here given are very much greater
than those obtained by previous investigations. The elimination of the element of impact[1] and of the knowledge of
the observer would tend to give far greater values than those
obtained by Bloch and by Aubert and Kammler. Then, too,
the area and time of stimulation are factors not to be neglected; but these differences are not such as to affect the
results appreciably.[2]

It is generally assumed that the threshold is a definite
quantity.[3] In the case of sensations of pain, the results
obtained for any individual are sufficiently constant to justify
this assumption as a working hypothesis. The results given
above for the tactile threshold are, however, so variable
that we are led to doubt the validity of such an assumption.
In fact, the very conception of a threshold involves a logical
contradiction. If by this we mean a quantity that we can
always perceive under moderately constant conditions of

[1] See Chapter V, Sec. 1.
[2] See Chapter VI, Sec. 2; Chapter VII, Sec. 1.
[3] Wundt, *op. cit.*, I, 334; Külpe, *op. cit.*, 51; Ladd, *Elements of Phys. Psy.*, 363.

attention, we shall have to assume a quantity much larger than what we often perceive. In the course of experiments on the perception of differences in weights, the application of a stimulus of 5g was unobserved several times, and that, too, by an excellent subject, who was expecting the stimulus at the time of application.[1] Even a stimulus of 100g has been unobserved by good observers in experiments by the method of right and wrong cases. We must conclude, then, that stimuli of a given intensity will be observed a certain proportion of times and no more, if a sufficient number of experiments be made. We may also infer that stimuli far below the so-called threshold will be observed, some times, at least, in an infinite number of trials. What, then, shall we call the threshold? It is not the quantity that is always observed, for this would involve a contradiction. It is not that which is observed a certain percentage of trials, for this could not be called the least perceptible intensity. We can only say that the probability that a given stimulus will be perceived by the observer is functionally related to the intensity of the stimulus. In fact, the so-called threshold is no more a definite quantity than the so-called least noticeable difference, which we think leads, when discussed from the standpoint of probabilities, to a similar *reductio ad absurdum*.[2] Indeed, the processes involved are much the same. Not the least important of the factors entering into the measurement of one as well as the other, is the confidence of the observer, which varies from extreme doubt to absolute certainty.[3] The wrong cases, or mistakes due to errors of observation, which occur when different stimuli are compared, have their counterpart in tactile hallucinations, a number of which occurred in the course of our experiments on the threshold.[4]

[1] See Chapter III, Secs. 2 and 3.
[2] Fullerton and Cattell, *On the Perception of Small Differences*, 10; Pierce and Jastrow, *National Academy of Sciences*, 1884, III, 75.
[3] See Chapter III, Sec. 5.
[4] *Cf.* Krohn, *Journal of Mental and Nervous Diseases*, March, 1893, 14.

SEC. 5. *The Intensity of Sensation and the Intensity of the Stimulus.*

This relation has generally been investigated by deductions from the relation of the least noticeable differences to the absolute intensity of the stimulus. But, as is shown by the application of the method of right and wrong cases, there is no such quantity, and therefore the deductions based upon it are invalid. Of the other psycho-physical methods, two have been applied by Merkel to the investigation of haptic sensations.[1] By the method of double stimuli it was found that the ratio of the normal to the estimated double stimulus was approximately 1 : 2 for from 100g to 2000g. By the method of mean gradation Merkel found that the values of the estimated arithmetic mean of two stimuli was but slightly less than the true arithmetic mean. Merkel's experiments were, however, made only on himself, and the muscular sense was not excluded, so that his results are not conclusive.

In the hope of throwing some light on the much discussed psycho-physical problem in pressure sensations, experiments were made by a method different from those generally used, the observer being required to judge of two stimuli how much greater one was than the other. The method of experiment in detail was as follows. A wax mould having been constructed to fit the left hand, the hand was placed in this, the palm being upward under the pan of a balance. The pressure was given by weights placed upon the pan of the balance. The pressure was transmitted to the hand by means of a piece of wood glued to the pan. A circular cap of cardboard attached to the end of the stick, and about 4 mm in diameter, came in contact with the skin. The observer having closed his eyes, and the cardboard cap being barely in contact with the skin, a weight was carefully placed in the pan, and after about two seconds was removed and replaced by a weight very much heavier, the observer being asked to judge the ratio of the weights. But few experiments were made at one sitting, so that memory

[1] Merkel, *Philosophische Studien*, v. 253.

could not affect the results. For purposes of convenience the lowest stimulus was applied first, the next higher following; but the reverse order was at times adopted without perceptible difference. The observers were, of course, ignorant of the objective relations of the weights as well as of the purpose of the experiment. They were all students of Psychology. In the table appended are given the results. The first horizontal column denotes the stimuli in grams. The numbers in the vertical columns, under those denoting the stimuli, indicate the average judgments as to how many times the given stimulus was greater than the stimulus preceding. Thus S. F. judged 50 g., 3.1 times as heavy as 10 g, and 250 g., 4.2 times as heavy as 50 g. The figures preceded by the sign $\pm$ denote the probable error of the given average.[1]

But few experiments were made on each observer, for not only were the mean variations small, but the individual differences were very great.

Observer.	No. expts.	2 g.	10 g.	50 g.	250 g.	1250 g.	1800 g.
S. F.	10×4	—	—	3.1±.01	4.2±.03	7.1±.04	3.8±.04
L. F.	6×4	—	—	2.0±.00	2.7±.00	4.9±.01	3.9[2]±.01
P.	5×5	—	2.2±.00	2.5±.01	3.0±.00	5.6±.03	3.4±.01
K.	5×5	—	1.9±.00	1.9±.00	2.1±.00	3.4±.00	1.7±.00
Av.	—	—	2.0	2.4	3.0	5.2	3.0[3]

In order to represent the relation between the stimulus and the estimate of the stimulus, let us take the number 2 as representing the estimated weight at 2 g. Multiplying this by the estimated values of 10 g. in terms of 2 g., the number obtained will represent the increase of the estimate of the stimulus as the stimulus increases from 2 to 10. In like manner, by taking this result and multiplying it by the esti-

---

[1] This is such an error (or deviation from the average) that half of the errors would be smaller and half would be larger. It is here obtained by the briefer formula,

$$P = \frac{.845 \; \Sigma v}{n \sqrt{n-1}}$$

See Merriman, Airy and other writers on the theory of probabilities and the method of least squares.

[2] This number refers to 2500 g., not to 1800 g., as do the others in this column.

[3] This average is based upon 3 values, 3.8, 3.4 and 1.7. See note 1.

mated values of 50 g. in terms of 10 g., we obtain the increase of the estimate as the stimulus increases from 10 g. to 50 g. In the case of S. F. and L. F., as no measurements were made of the estimate of 10 g. in terms of 2 g., we take as the unit of estimated weight at 10 g. 4.4, which is the value obtained for P., with whose results those of S. F. and L. F. fairly agree.[1] In this way the relative increase of the estimate of weights is obtained. The increase of the stimulus is shown by the intensities used, these being, with the exception of the highest, in geometrical progression. Below are given the calculated values of the estimates of the stimuli:

Observer.	2 g.	10 g.	50 g.	250 g.	1250 g.	1800 g.
S. F.	—	4.4[2]	13.	57.	404.	1535.
L. F.	—	4.4[2]	9.	23.	112.	433.[4]
P.	2	4.4	11.	33.	185.	629.
K.	2	3.8	7.2	15.	51.	86.
Av. estimate of stimulus,	2	4.2	10.	32.	188.	750.[4]

The relations here expressed are graphically represented in the accompanying curves. The ordinates express the estimates of the intensity of the stimulus, and the abscissae the true intensities in grams.

In interpreting these results we may assume that the intensity of sensation increases in proportion to the estimated increase of the stimulus. Such an assumption would be illegitimate, if the stimuli were such that the observers could judge them by some means other than their effect on sensation. But where the muscular sense is excluded, as in these experiments, association cannot very well influence the

---

[1] 2 g. was found to be so often inappreciable by S. F. that the determination based upon it was difficult. The experiments on L. F. were made before it was decided what weights had best be used.

[2] These are taken as units, as explained above.

[3] This number refers to 2500 g. instead of 1800 g.

[4] Based upon three values. See note 3.

results; for the concept of weight is based upon sensations of effort. Assuming, then, that a relation is obtained between the intensity of the stimulus and that of the sensation,

FIG. 3.

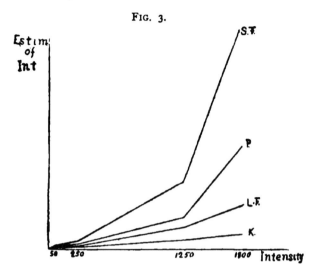

it is evident that for moderate intensities the sensation increases much more slowly than in direct proportion to the stimulus. As the stimulus approaches the pain threshold, the sensation appears to increase at a much greater rate than before. The individual variations are so great as to render impossible an analytical expression of the relation. Nevertheless, the shapes of the different curves are similar. It is clear, moreover, that a logarithmic relation as demanded by Fechner's law does not hold, even within narrow limits, for any one of the observers. If such were the case, the estimates of the stimulus would increase arithmetically, since the stimulus increases geometrically.

It is, however, possible that this relatively rapid increase for high intensities is due to processes of perception and judgment, and not to real differences in the rate of increase of the sensation. As stimuli approach the pain threshold, the consciousness of impending pain may cause us to overestimate the magnitude of the stimulus. This might happen in either of two ways. In the first place, since the sensation of pain and that of pressure are heterogeneous, we might suppose that the mind would unconsciously assume great

objective differences in quantity as causally related to subjective differences in quality. Another possible explanation
is that the sensation of pain, tending to occupy the field of
consciousness to the exclusion of other presentations, is to
be considered as essentially a sensation of great intensity;
from which it follows that stimuli causing pain, or approaching the pain threshold, are estimated as relatively of greater
intensity than those into the perception of which the element
of pain does not enter.

SEC. 6. *Haptic Sensations and Dermal Pain.*

We have already found, in Chapter I, that the peculiar
quality of the tickle sensation is not logically ascribable to
the quality of the stimulus. We may state, therefore, that
sensations differing in quality may be caused by stimuli differing in quantity. It is not, however, near the lower limit of
haptic stimulation that this qualitative transition is most
marked. If pain be considered a sensation, two disparate
sensations are induced by high as well as low intensities of
dermal stimuli. If, however, pain be considered but an
intensive form of an element existing in all sensational states
of consciousness, such a generalization is impossible.

According to the commonly accepted view, the algedonic[1]
tone of a sensation is negative, that is, unpleasant, for very
low intensities, but upon increase in the stimulus becomes
positive. As the stimulus is further increased, a maximum
of the positive values is reached, after which the algedonic
tone rapidly decreases. This doctrine has, undoubtedly,
many theoretic advantages. But it does not seem to accord
with the observed phenomena of dermal sensation. In the
experiments on pain already described, the appearance of
pain was generally quite sudden. If the pain consciousness
were merely an intensive form of what accompanies all
dermal stimulation, we should not expect such sudden transitions. Then, too, in the writer's experience, at least, there
is no pleasurable element whatsoever in a haptic sensation
of moderate intensity. It may be said that we prefer certain

---

[1] Wundt, *op. cit.* I, 558; Külpe, *Grundriss der Psychologie*, 256. See also the
writings of Ward, Sully, and Bain.

intensities to others.   But this is not necessarily due to differences in their algedonic tone.   The very fact that one
stimulus may be preferred to another when there is no conscious pleasure or pain, tends to show that the phenomenon
is due to complex processes of association.[1]   The pressure
acting on a small area will, on this hypothesis, be judged
unpleasant because we tend to think of the pain that would
result if the area were much diminished, or the intensity of
the stimulus much increased.   In like manner, a stimulus of
moderate intensity is preferable to one of very low intensity,
because for low intensities perception is less distinct, and we
tend, as a rule, to prefer things that we can understand.   At
least such appears to be the process in judgments of low
dermal stimuli, so far as the writer's introspection justifies
any *à priori* hypothesis.

But there are also positive as well as negative reasons for
considering the phenomena of dermal pain to be most readily
intelligible on the hypothesis which regards pain as a distinct
sensation rather than as a *quale* or a psychic element of all
states of consciousness.   In the first place, pain has a
peculiar quality of its own, and may occur unaccompanied
by any other sensory element.   When induced by haptic
stimulation the consciousness of pain in the part stimulated
may continue some time after the removal of the stimulus.[2]

But there are other points of difference in the time phenomena of pain and dermal sensations.   If we touch a hot
object the sensation of contact precedes that of pain.[3]   Lehmann explains this by the difference in the reaction-times for
sensations of touch and temperature.[4]   The same phenomena,
however, occur when the pain producing stimulus is not
heat but pressure.[5]   If a needle be suddenly pressed into the
skin a secondary pain will appear after the sensation of pressure.   In our experiments on the pain threshold for impact

---

[1] *Cf.* Dessoir, *op. cit.*, 186.
[2] See Chap. VII, Sec. 2.
[3] *Cf.* Dessoir, *op. cit.*, 201, 324.
[4] Lehmann, *Die Hauptgesetze des mensch. Gefühlsleben*, 44, 45.
[5] *Cf.* Goldscheider, *Physiol. Gesell.*, Oct., 1890; Die Lehre der Specif. Energien
der Sinnesorgane, 1881.

stimuli the same time relation was observed.[1] Marshall argues that the pain consciousness appearing under these conditions is not necessarily a new sensation, but a sensation x in a painful phase.[2] But is this not to reduce a known state of consciousness to one that is unknown and only assumed? The same criticism, we will remark, may be made of the explanation generally given of pains arising from pathological processes in the internal organs and in the muscular and nervous tissues.

Apart from introspective and experimental evidence, the sensation theory of pain is strongly corroborated by dermal pathology. It has been known for many years that tactile anaesthesia may exist without analgesia, and analgesia without anaesthesia;[3] and, although hyperalgesia may be so acute that the slighest mechanical jar causes pain, true tactile hyperaesthesia is unknown.[4]

The different facts we have noted above certainly go to show that pain and haptic sensations are utterly disparate states of consciousness, and that in all probability there is a corresponding difference between the physiological processes. In fact, from the time when Schiff made his celebrated experiments many physiologists have believed that impulses for pain and touch pass to the brain by different paths. Goldscheider claims even to have discovered special nerves for pain; but his results have been questioned.[5] Wundt explains the physiological and pathological experiments by the altered excitability of the sensory nerves after passing through the gray matter of the cord.[6] It is possible that at least a partial cause of the delay in the appearance of pain is the development of pathological processes in the dermal tissues incited by intense stimulation. That the process of dermal pain stimulation is somewhat of this nature is made

[1] See Chap. V, Sec. 2.

[2] Marshall, *op. cit.*, 18.

[3] Wundt, *op. cit.*, I, iii; Funke, *op. cit.*, 297. Other references are given by these writers.

[4] Richet, *op. cit.*, 219.

[5] Goldscheider, *Archiv für Anat. und Physiol.*, 1885, Supp. Bd., 87. For criticism of G., *cf.* Lehmann, *op. cit.*; also Dessoir, *op. cit.*

[6] Wundt, *op. cit.*, I, 110, 437, 596; Funke, *op. cit.*, 297.

probable by an observation of Goldscheider. According to this writer the delay in the appearance of pain upon stimulation of the foot of a person afflicted with some disturbance of the circulation in that part decreased appreciably as the diseased tissues were recovering to their normal condition.[1]

That the delay is due, at least in part, to peripheral processes is also borne out by our own observations. In the course of experiments on the pain threshold for impact stimuli, the writer has observed pain in the part stimulated nearly an hour after the completion of the experiments. And again, when pain was induced only after long continued pressure, it would continue several seconds after the removal of the stimulus.[2] But whatever physiological hypothesis be accepted, there seems no doubt that there is a qualitative physical difference in function corresponding to the qualitative psychical difference in sensation.

SEC. 7. *The Quality and Intensity of Sensation.*

In the above discussion we have used the terms quality and intensity as applied to sensation. These terms have been almost universally used to denote fundamental attributes of sensation.[3] They are, however, seldom defined. The term intensity is generally used in the sense of that property of sensation which is functionally related to the intensity of the stimulus. If, as some have been led to believe, states of consciousness cannot be treated quantitatively, the term as applied to sensation clearly cannot be used in such a sense. Such a use is, however, implied in the word, since it carries with it the idea of physical quantity measurable in terms of space, to which all physical measurements are reducible. But if we reject the term altogether, applying only the predicate *qualitative* to sensational changes, in what way shall we describe subjective changes that are discontinuous, as opposed to those which are continuous? On the other hand, it may be said that, if the term quality be thus restricted, we shall have no means

---

[1] Goldscheider, *Deutsch. Med. Wochenschrift*, 1890, no 31.
[2] See Chap. VII. Sec. 2.
[3] *Cf.* Wundt, *op. cit.*, I, 332; Ladd, *op. cit.*, 356; Stumpf, *Tonpsychologie*, I, 350.

of distinguishing continuous sensational changes due to intensive variations from those due to non-intensive variations in the stimulus. But we do not think that there is necessarily such a difference in these modes of subjective change. The difference may be rather one of perception. The sensational change as haptic stimuli are altered in area, or as auditory stimuli are altered in pitch, is as much a continuous, and, we think, quantitative, change as is that caused by intensive variations in haptic and auditory stimuli. We are, perhaps, accustomed to think of intensive sensational differences as being measurable, rather than non-intensive differences, simply because it is a matter of familiar experience that the corresponding changes in the stimulus are quantitative changes, and we are accustomed to estimate the magnitude of the stimulus by the changes in sensation. If this view be correct, we have no term to apply universally to those changes in sensation that are continuous, as opposed to those that are discontinuous. For from the use of the term intensity in physical science it would be difficult to extend its meaning so as to cover those changes in sensation that are independent of the intensity of the stimulus.

CHAPTER III.

THE DISCRIMINATION OF WEIGHTS WITHOUT EFFORT AND THE INTENSITY OF THE STIMULUS.

SEC. 1. *Preceding Investigations.*

The comparative ease with which the intensity of haptic stimuli can be measured renders the relation between the accuracy of discrimination and the intensity of the stimulus an attractive field for investigation. In fact, it was upon experiments with weights that E. H. Weber based his famous generalization. These experiments were, however, too few and inaccurate to base a quantitative conclusion upon them. By simultaneous pressure stimulations Weber found the least noticeable difference for 32 oz. to be 15 oz. and 10 oz., or about ½ and ⅓ of the stimulus, for the two observers. For 32 dr. the least noticeable difference for the same observers was found to be 8 dr. and 10 dr. or about ⅓ of the stimulus. When the stimuli were applied in succession, the least noticeable difference was found to be $\frac{1}{29}$ to $\frac{1}{44}$ of the stimulus, but Weber does not say what intensities were used.[1]

The next research of importance is that of Dohrn, who applied the method of least noticeable difference to the investigation of the discrimination of weights of low intensities.[2] Dohrn found that for the volar surface of the right hand a weight of 1 g. had to be doubled in order for a difference to be perceived. These experiments were made on himself, and also on a boy of eleven, and must, therefore, be considered as of little quantitative value.

A series of experiments with impact stimuli conducted by Biedermann and Löwit is described by Hering, who

---

[1] An account of these experiments in more detail is found in G. E. Müller, *Grundlegung der Psycho-physik*, 189. Weber's original work is inaccessible to the writer.

[2] Dohrn, *Zeitschrift für Rat. Med.*, 3ᵗᵉ R., X, 339.

states that they do not conform to Weber's law.[1] The method of least noticeable difference was used, and this is sufficient to discredit the results, not to speak of the absence of information as to the other details of the experiment. In experiments on lifted weights by the same experimenters, the least noticeable difference for 450 g. is stated to be $\frac{1}{4}$ g., whereas for 500 g. it is given as $\frac{1}{30}$ of the stimulus, a result that throws suspicion on the accuracy of these as well as the other experiments.

The most systematic investigation of the subject is that of Merkel, who found the least noticeable difference at 50 g. to be $\frac{1}{14}$ of the stimulus, and to be fairly constant up to 2000 g.[2] In these experiments the pressure was exerted upon the finger by the arm of a balance constructed for the purpose. The muscular reaction of the finger may, therefore, have affected the judgment. That this was the case is extremely probable, since Merkel's results closely correspond with those of the most accurate researches on lifted weights.[3] Then, too, Merkel's experiments were made on himself, and, as in all such experiments, the knowledge of the objective relations of the weights could not but have influenced the observer.

In an interesting series of experiments by Hall and Motora, the least noticeable difference was found for from 5 g. to 200 g. by changing the pressure at the rate of $\frac{4}{111}$ of the stimulus per second.[4] From 5 g. to 30 g. this quantity was about $\frac{1}{3}$ the stimulus, after which it increased considerably. In these experiments the time relations were such that the results could not be compared with those based on experiments in which successive stimulation is applied. The fact that the intensity of pressure sensations decreases rapidly, at least for low intensities, after the application of the weight, makes the problem one of considerable perplexity.[5]

We know of no other work on the subject to the record

[1] Hering, *Sitzungsber. der Wiener Acad.*, 3ᵗᵉ Abth., LXXII, 342, as given in Müller, *op. cit.*, 200.
[2] Merkel, *Philosophische Studien*, V, 253.
[3] *Cf.* Fullerton and Cattell, *op. cit.*, 122; Merkel, *op. cit.*, 261.
[4] Hall and Motora, *Amer. Journ. of Psy.*, I, 72.
[5] See Chapter VII, Sec. 1.

of which we have access,[1] except that of Pierce and Jastrow.[2] In this research the probable error for 250 g. was found to be $\frac{1}{30}$ of the stimulus, and to be further decreased by practice. The relation of the probable error to the magnitude of the stimulus was not considered. In these experiments the pressure was exerted through the muscles, and therefore it is probable that, as in Merkel's experiments, the discrimination for effort is what is measured.

SEC. 2. *Further Experiments: Method of Procedure.*

There being no satisfactory determination of the accuracy of discrimination for objective, as opposed to subjective pressure, a series of experiments was made in the following way. The left hand of the observer was placed on the table, comfortably supported, and in such a manner that the palm, which was turned upward, was fairly level. The eyes of the observer being closed, two weights were placed successively upon the hand, and the observer was required to judge which was heavier by the method of right and wrong cases. When no difference was perceived the observer was required to guess. The stimuli with the smaller areas were placed on different parts of the region covered by the large area. The place was constant, however, for every two compared. The degree of confidence was recorded by having the observer use four letters, *a*, *b*, *c* and *d*, according to his confidence. The apparatus used is shown in the accompanying cut.

The weights used were cylindrical boxes, B, filled with shot, the sides being built up when necessary by stiff paper. To the bottom of the box was affixed a projecting piece of the shape of a fustrum of a cone, N, the base of which came in contact with the skin. In this way a small area of stimulation could be obtained. The material in contact with the skin was thick cardboard, so that the influence of temperature was practically excluded. Projecting upward from the centre of the box was an iron rod, AC, which, on being inserted within the glass support, M, of a chemist's stand, S,

[1] We have not access to the dissertation of Bastelberger, *Exper. Prüf. der su Drucksinn angewandten Methoden*, Stuttgart, 1879.
[2] Pierce and Jastrow, *National Academy of Sciences*, 1884, III, 75.

prevented the weight from tipping over, as it would otherwise have done when the smaller area of stimulation was
used.   The weights were, of course, always placed so as to
be as nearly as possible perpendicular to the hand.   In order
to obviate slight differences in the surface applied, the same

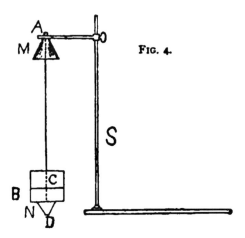

FIG. 4.

box was used to give the variable and the standard stimulus.
The increment of weight consisted of a bag of shot which
could be placed in the box without being noticed by the
observer.   The stimuli applied were as described above,
except that having a weight of 3200 g.   This consisted of
three cylindrical kilogram weights placed one over the other.
Through these weights ran an iron rod, which served as a
support as with the other weights.   To the base was affixed
a small box loaded with shot, so as to make a total weight of
3200 g.   The base consisted of circular cardboard.   The
time relations were fairly constant.   The careful application
and removal of the weights by the experimenter made it impossible to have the times of application and the intervals
between the stimulations as constant as might be desired.
It was found, however, by having the observer note these
times, that they did not vary appreciably from 2 sec. and
3 sec. respectively.   Moreover, the judgment of weight
seems to be easiest as soon as the hand receives the full
force of the weight, and the accuracy of discrimination does
not vary appreciably when the interval between the applica-

tion of the two stimuli is not greater than 10 sec.[1] No fixed order was used in applying the stimuli, the only requirement being that for a series of 100 experiments in 50 the second weight should be heavier, and in the other 50 lighter. About 10 sec. intervened between two successive experiments, but no effort was made to have this constant. At one sitting 20 or 25 experiments in a given series were made. Then the observer rested a few minutes, and another set of experiments was made. The time devoted to the experiments at one sitting varied generally from an hour to an hour and a half. In order that the influence of fatigue might be the same for the different intensities used, the order in which the different sets of experiments for the different series was made was varied, so that a given intensity would be used as much in the first as in the latter part of the sittings. The observers were students of Psychology, with some previous practice in experimental work.[2] The experiments were begun in March, 1892, and completed in June, 1893.

With regard to possible sources of error, most of them, we think, were eliminated. In applying the weights with the hand, it is impossible to control properly the velocity of impact. The writer endeavored to obviate this difficulty by applying the weights slowly and carefully. In this way the error may be neglected for weights of sufficient intensity to cause a distinct sensation of pressure apart from one of impact. For weights of 100 g. and 200 g., however, the depression of the skin due to the pressure is so slight that impact cannot be entirely neglected. The rate of application was, however, kept as constant as practicable. Then, as is shown in Chapter V., the discrimination of weights by impact is about the same as by pressure.[3]

Another source of error lies in the slight variations of the weight from a perpendicular position and consequent pressure upon the glass support. For the purpose of inves-

[1] Cf. Weber, *op. cit.*, 545, where it is stated that there is no appreciable difference in the accuracy of discrimination after an interval of 30 sec. A far more accurate investigation of the matter is that of Fullerton and Cattell, *op. cit.*, 148.

[2] The writer would take this occasion to express his appreciation of the kindness of those who have devoted so much time to these and other experiments, and to express his gratitude for the assistance so generously given.

[3] See Ch. V., Sec. 4.

tigating this source of error, a formula was deduced for the decrease in the amount of pressure exerted upon the hand when the weight was not perpendicular. If C be the centre of gravity of the mass, D the point of application, the area being, for convenience, considered inappreciable, A the point of application of the rod upon the glass support, W the weight, and S the angular deviation from the perpendicular of the line through C, D and A; then for the loss of weight at D, which we shall call x, we shall have,

$$x = W \sin^2 \phi \frac{C\,D}{A\,D}$$

In this formula it is assumed that at the point A there is such friction that the mass is not free to move. By observing what appeared to be approximately the maximum value of ϕ in the experiments, the corresponding value of x for a weight of 500 g. was found by the formula to be 1.2 g. An experimental determination of this quality was also made by means of the balance. A 500 g. box with sharpened base was placed in the pan, so that the rod in contact with the glass support deviated from the perpendicular to about the same extent as that which was found to be the maximum deviation in the experiments. The loss of weight was found to be 1.5 g. Inasmuch as the measurement was rendered inexact by the horizontal component of the pressure exerted, the result corresponded as closely as was expected with that obtained by calculation. The true loss of weight was, however, much less than this for the stimuli used; for the place of application having considerable area, it is evident that the weight will tend to be in more stable equilibrium. Then the true error is not the average loss of weight, but the variation from this average, which is of course much less. We may, therefore, neglect this source of error entirely.

In every set of 100 experiments, in 50 of which the second weight was lighter and in 50 heavier, the percentage of right answers was calculated for both groups of 50 answers. The accuracy of discrimination, h, was determined from these data by tables based upon the well-known formula:

$$\frac{r}{n} = \frac{1}{2} + \frac{1}{\sqrt{\pi}} \int_0^{h \triangle} e^{-t^2} dt$$

In the tables used[1] the values of $\frac{\Delta}{P.E.}$ were given, instead of those of hΔ, P.E. being the probable error, or that error which would be equal to Δ, when the percentage of right cases is 75. Tables giving the values of hΔ may be readily changed so as to give the values of $\frac{\Delta}{P.E.}$ by substituting for h the expression $\frac{.477}{P.E.}$. In some of the series it was found that the constant error, or tendency to overestimate the second stimulus, was so great that the use of a larger increment was necessary when the second weight was lighter. For otherwise the second weight would have been judged heavier the great majority of trials; and the observer, therefore, would have acquired the habit of judging the second weight the heavier, which would have vitiated the experiments. This involved the use of special formulae, which we now give. C.E. is the constant error, P.E. the probable error, T_1 the value in the table for $\frac{\Delta}{P.E.}$ when the second weight is lighter, T_h the value when it is heavier, and Δ_h and Δ_1 are the increments used when the second weight is heavier or lighter.

CASE I.

When no constant error occurs, real or apparent, $\Delta_h = \Delta_1 = \Delta$, and $T_h = T_1 = T$. Then

$$\frac{\Delta}{P.E.} = T,$$

whence,

$$P.E. = \frac{\Delta}{T}.$$

CASE II.

When a constant error occurs, and only one increment is used, we have,

[1] Given by Fullerton and Cattell, *op. cit.*, 16. They will also be found, in different form, in *Philosoph. Studien*, IX, 145; and in Fechner, *Elemente der Psychophysik*, II* Auf., Leipzig, 1889, 108.

$$\frac{\Delta + \text{C.E.}}{\text{P.E.}} = T_{\text{h}} \text{ and } \frac{\Delta - \text{C.E.}}{\text{P.E.}} = T_{\text{l}},$$

whence,

$$\text{P.E.} = \frac{2\,\Delta}{T_{\text{h}} + T_{\text{l}}}, \text{ and C.E.} = T_{\text{h}}\,\text{P.E.} - \Delta$$

Case III.

If a constant error occurs, and Δ_{h} is $> \Delta_{\text{l}}$ or $< \Delta_{\text{l}}$, we have,

$$\text{P.E.} = \frac{\Delta_{\text{h}} + \Delta_{\text{l}}}{T_{\text{h}} + T_{\text{l}}}, \text{ and C.E.} = T_{\text{h}}\,\text{P.E.} - \Delta_{\text{h}}.$$

Case IV.

If both stimuli are equal when the second is judged heavier, *i. e.*, if $\Delta_{\text{h}} = 0$, we have,

$$\text{P.E.} = \frac{\Delta_{\text{l}}}{T_{\text{h}} + T_{\text{l}}}$$

and

$$C = \text{P.E.}\ T_{\text{l}}.$$

Case V.

If the first stimulus is greater than the second, when the second is judged heavier, Δ_{h} is minus, and we have,

$$\frac{-\Delta_{\text{h}} + \text{C.E.}}{\text{P.E.}} = T_{\text{h}},$$

and

$$\frac{\Delta_{\text{l}} - \text{C.E.}}{\text{P.E.}} = T_{\text{l}};$$

whence,

$$\text{P.E.} = \frac{\Delta_{\text{l}} - \Delta_{\text{h}}}{T_{\text{h}} + T_{\text{l}}},$$

and

$$\text{C.E.} = \text{P.E.}\ T_{\text{h}} + \Delta_{\text{h}}.$$

Case VI.

If the conditions are the same as in Case V., but $\frac{r}{n} < \frac{50}{100}$ when the second weight is judged lighter, calling the value of the probability integral corresponding to $100 - \frac{r}{n}$, T_{l}^{1}, we have

$$\frac{\text{C.E.} - \Delta_{\text{h}}}{\text{P.E.}} = T_{\text{h}},$$

and

$$\frac{C.E. - \Delta_1}{P.E.} = T_1{}^1;$$

whence,

$$P.E. = \frac{\Delta_1 - \Delta_2}{T_2 - T_1{}^1}$$

and

$$C.E. = P.E. \, T_2 + \Delta_2.$$

CASE VII.

If the conditions are the same as in Case VI., except that no increment is used when the second weight is judged heavier, we have

$$P.E. = \frac{\Delta_1}{T_2 - T_1{}^1}$$

and

$$C.E. = T_2 \, P.E.$$

CASE VIII.

If the conditions are the same as in Cases VI. and VII., except that for the second to be judged heavier, an increment is used, $+ \Delta_2$, we have

$$P.E. = \frac{\Delta_1 + \Delta_2}{T_2 - T_1{}^1},$$

and

$$C.E. = P.E. \, T_2 - \Delta_2.$$

By the above formulæ were calculated the values of P.E. and C.E. for each set of 100 experiments.[1] That under Case II. was used in the great majority of the calculations. Such increments were generally used as would give a percentage of right cases as near as possible to 84 per cent., since fewer observations are needed for such a value of Δ in order to calculate the value of P.E.

The value of P.E. thus found is not strictly that for the standard stimulus, but is compounded of this and its value

[1] In order to test the approximate accuracy of the formulæ, the value for C.E. thus found was added to the second stimulus, and it was noted whether the conditions were such as to give about the value of $\frac{r}{n}$ as expected from the value calculated for P.E.

for the variable stimulus.[1] When the increment is very
small this error may be neglected. But in some of our experiments, on account of the magnitude of the constant
error, an increment was used of from $\frac{1}{4}$ to $\frac{1}{3}$ of the stimulus.
This difficulty cannot be overcome unless the relation of the
probable error to the stimulus is known. Inasmuch as we
found that this relation was approximately that demanded
by Weber's law, at least within certain limits, we corrected
the values of P.E. on this assumption. The result will at
least be more correct than it would if such a correction were
not made, even if the probable error increased more slowly
than is assumed. To make such a correction, let S be the
standard stimulus, P.E. the probable error obtained from
the formulæ above given, and P.E.$_2$ the value of P.E. corrected for the standard stimulus. Then P.E. may be considered as approximately the arithmetic mean of the probable errors for the stimuli used. We shall have, therefore,

$$P.E. = \frac{2\,P.E._2 + P.E._2\,\dfrac{(S + \Delta_1)}{S} + P.E._2\,\dfrac{(S + \Delta_2)}{S}}{4}$$

whence,

$$P.E._2 = P.E.\left(\frac{4S}{4S + \Delta_1 + \Delta_2}\right).$$

SEC. 3. *Results.*

The values of P.E. given in the tables below are the corrected values. In the majority of cases they do not differ
appreciably from the uncorrected values, but at times the
difference is considerable. No correction was made for the
constant error, since its relation to the magnitude of the
stimulus is more complex.

In the appended tables the standard stimuli used are
given in the first column. Then follow the different probable errors for each set of 100 experiments,[2] P$_1$, P$_2$, etc., and
their averages and mean variations. The other columns
give the different constant errors, C$_1$, C$_2$, etc.

[1] Cf. Müller, *op. cit.*, 21

[2] The probable errors for N. F. and J. S. are based upon 80 experiments.

Observer, N. F.; area, 8 cm.

S	P_1	P_2	P_3	P_4	Av.	M. V.	C_1	C_2	C_3	C_4	Av.	M. V.
200	31	21	16	21	22	4.	17	17	16	17	17	0.
800	255	138	72	86	137	59	120	164	176	159	155	17
1600	191	221	185	175	193	18	157	143	280	200	195	43
3200	341	474	—	—	408	44	119	222	—	—	170	57

Observer, J. S.; area, 8 cm.

S	P_1	P_2	Av.	M. V.	C_1	C_2	Av.	M. V.
800	134	97	115	18	11	30	20	9
1600	148	207	177	28	51	100	75	24
3200	244	261	252	8	149	121	135	14

Observer, R.; area, 8 cm.

S	P_1	P_2	P_3	Av.	M. V.	C_1	C_2	C_3	Av.	M. V.
100	25	27	19	23	3	17	16	37	23	9
500	102	121	83	102	13	70	120	166	119	32
1500	248	337	229	271	43	631	799	682	704	63

Observer, McW.; area, 8 cm.

S	P_1	P_2	P_3	P_4	P_5	Av.	M. V.	C_1	C_2	C_3	C_4	C_5	Av.	M. V.
100	20	24	24	14	16	19	3	1	0	15	5	2	4	4
500	33	42	31	40	33	36	4	-13	-13	2	-24	2	-9	9
1500	110	130	110	100	109	112	7	6	9	6	18	12	10	4
3200	233	183	156	196	197	193	19	96	286	200	233	285	218	56

Observer, L. S.; area, 8 cm.

S	P_1	P_2	P_3	P_4	P_5	Av.	M. V.	C_1	C_2	C_3	C_4	C_5	Av.	M. V.
100	17	20	17	19	16	18	1	-4	-3	1	6	0	0	3
500	37	29	39	42	47	39	4	-12	-2	-6	0	-11	-6	3
1500	114	100	114	103	111	108	5	0	67	13	57	69	41	28
3200	243	217	256	206	243	233	17	85	195	125	70	239	143	59

Observer, L. S.; area, $\frac{8}{64}$ cm.

S	P_1	P_2	P_3	P_4	P_5	Av.	M. V.	C_1	C_2	C_3	C_4	C_5	Av.	M. V.
100	9	14	13	16	16	13	2	1	-1	1	1	4	1	1
500	43	29	35	57	41	41	7	0	-2	-14	17	19	4	8
1500	124	91	127	105	105	110	11	59	49	111	74	74	73	15

Observer, N. F.; area, $\frac{8}{64}$ cm.

S	P_1	P_2	P_3	P_4	Av.	M. V.	C_1	C_2	C_3	C_4	Av.	M. V.
200	36	77	—	—	56	20	48	30	—	—	39	9
800	87	121	120	125	113	12	195	146	65	70	119	51
1600	227	231	196	158	203	26	259	263	215	133	217	44

Observer, J. S.; area, $\frac{8}{64}$ cm.

S	P_1	P_2	Av.	M. V.	C_1	C_2	Av.	M. V.
800	104	103	103	0	-26	-26	-26	0
1600	221	171	196	25	94	0	47	47

These results are graphically represented in the accompanying curves.

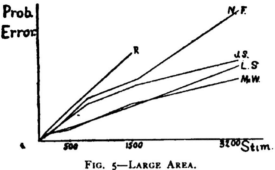

FIG. 5—LARGE AREA.

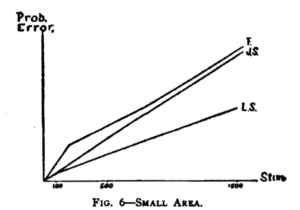

FIG. 6—SMALL AREA.

In the above experiments no stimuli were used less than 100 g. Less extended experiments were made on S. F., an excellent observer, for a standard stimulus of 5 g., the variable stimulus being 7 g. The stimuli used were cylindrical pieces of lead. To the bottom was fastened a circular piece of cardboard, having a diameter of 1.5 cm. The weights were carefully lowered upon the palm of the hand by iron rings projecting from the tops. Below are the values of the three probable errors obtained for each set of 100 experiments, and also the value of the average divided by the mean of the stimuli used.

Observer, S. F.

Stimulus.	P_1	P_2	P_3	Av. P.	$\frac{S}{P}$
5 g. and 7 g.	3.7	1.8	2.0	2.5	.4

These results may be taken as representative for good observers, since the probable error for S. F. at 1000 g., and with the same area, was found by 200 experiments to be about $\frac{1}{16}$ of the stimulus, which is fairly typical.

It is evident from the above results that Weber's law holds fairly well between the approximate limits, 300 g. and 3000 g. For very low stimuli the probable error increases much more slowly than the stimulus. For high intensities it increases somewhat more slowly, though the deviation is not very marked. It is probable that observers differ somewhat not only in their absolute accuracy of discrimination, but even in the relation of this accuracy to the magnitude of the stimulus. This is shown in the curves for L. S., J. S., and McW. (Figure 2), that of J. S. clearly departing from the straight line demanded by Weber's law. The irregular shape of N. F.'s curve is perhaps to be explained by the decided variation in his accuracy of discrimination, as shown in the tables. If it be assumed that such variation is the cause of the irregularity of the curve, it is evident that for this observer the probable error increases in direct proportion to the stimulus within the limits used.

Summarizing the quantitative results obtained, the maximum value of $\frac{P.E.}{S}$ for a set of 100 experiments was $\frac{1}{3}$,[1] the minimum $\frac{1}{16}$,[1] and the average for all observers and all intensities above 100 g. was $\frac{1}{5}$.

It is evident that individuals of about the same age and social class differ somewhat in their discrimination. Of the eight observers tested only two showed much variation from the average, N. F. and R. having as their relative probable errors $\frac{1}{3}$ and $\frac{1}{4}$. From both of these observers the writer would have expected at least as good results as from others. Both complained of a tendency to drowsiness in the course of the experiments, and to this their low accuracy may perhaps be ascribed.

[1] Calculations based upon only 100 experiments are, of course, somewhat affected by the variable error.

Sec. 4. *The Constant Error.*

It has for many years been known that in comparing two stimuli applied successively, there is in general a tendency to overestimate the second. In no instance known to the writer has a constant error of such magnitude been observed as those shown in the records of R. and N. F., which were for some stimuli as great as $\frac{1}{8}$ of the stimulus. The value of C. E. seems to increase with the stimulus, but not in direct proportion. It is very small or even negative for low intensities, but increases rapidly, apparently soon reaching a maximum. Some persons do not show any constant error except for very high intensities. Experiments on L. F. showed no constant error for 1000 g.,[1] but at 3200 g. it was appreciable.

Persons having a large constant error tend to have a large probable error. This is shown by the following average values, in round numbers, of $\frac{P.E.}{S}$ and $\frac{C.E.}{S}$ for 8 persons.

	L. F.[1]	S. F.[2]	McW.	L. S.	J. S.	W.[2]	N. F.	R.
Av. $\frac{P.E.}{S}$	$\frac{1}{16}$	$\frac{1}{16}$	$\frac{1}{16}$	$\frac{1}{16}$	$\frac{1}{8}$	$\frac{1}{8}$	$\frac{1}{7}$	$\frac{1}{8}$
Av. $\frac{C.E.}{S}$	[zero]	[zero]	$\frac{1}{33}$	$\frac{1}{33}$	$\frac{1}{33}$	$\frac{1}{16}$	$\frac{1}{16}$	$\frac{1}{8}$

Whether the constant error influences the probable error or *vice versa*, we cannot say. Possibly these magnitudes are causally related to some process affecting them both.

The constant error appears to vary more than the probable error. Below are given the relative mean variations of the probable and constant error. They are calculated by taking the mean of the values of the mean variation divided by the probable or constant error, as the case may be. We give also, for the sake of comparison, the average value of $\frac{P.E.}{S}$ for the different observers.

---

[1] See Chapter V, Sec. 5.

[2] The experiments on W., L. F. and S. F. will be given in Chap. V., Sec. 4, and Chap. VI., Sec. 5. The standard stimulus was not varied, being 200 g. for W. and 1000 g. for L. F. and S. F.

	N.F.	J.S.	R.	L.S.	McW.	W.
$\frac{M.V.}{P.E.}$	$\frac{1}{6}$	$\frac{1}{10}$	$\frac{1}{7}$	$\frac{1}{10}$	$\frac{1}{10}$	$\frac{2}{3}$
$\frac{M.V.}{C.E.}$	$\frac{1}{6}$	$\frac{1}{8}$	$\frac{1}{4}$	$\frac{2}{3}$	$\frac{2}{3}$	$\frac{2}{3}$
$\frac{P.E.}{S}$	$\frac{1}{7}$	$\frac{1}{9}$	$\frac{1}{6}$	$\frac{1}{10}$	$\frac{1}{10}$	$\frac{1}{8}$

Since there is in general greater variation in C.E. than in P.E., we conclude that these variations are to some extent true variations rather than chance variations due to the conditions of the experiment. The variation of the constant error was most noticeable in the case of an observer, E. G., on whom in two weeks over 500 experiments were made. In these experiments the value of C.E. increased so rapidly that no calculations could be made. At first it was inappreciable for 100 g., 500 g. and 1500 g.; but it increased with practice until for 100 g. it was apparently as great as the stimulus, and for the higher intensities from $\frac{1}{2}$ to $\frac{1}{3}$ as great. The theoretical importance of these variations lies in the application of the probability integral to the method of right and wrong cases, for in this integral P.E. and C.E. are assumed to be constant.

If the constant error be due to central processes, we should expect individuals having a great error for pressure to have a similarly great error for lifted weights. But this is not the case. R., who had the greatest C.E. of all the observers, failed to show the slightest trace of any overestimation in forty experiments with lifted weights. L. S. and McW. likewise had no appreciable C.E. for lifted weights of high intensity, though they had for pressure stimuli of high intensity. Not only this, but a constant error for pressure does not apparently involve one for impact. At least in 25 experiments on R., no C.E. was appreciable for 50 g. falling 20 cm.

SEC. 5. *The Confidence of the Observer.*

The confidence of an observer in estimating stimuli not differing greatly, varies from complete doubt to complete certainty. The degree of confidence depends upon the magnitude of the difference of the stimuli, and consequently upon the probability of correctness.[1]

In the experiments on the discrimination of weights, observers were requested to say *a* when certain, *b* when fairly confident, *c* when less confident and almost doubtful, and *d* when unable to decide except by guessing. The results for different observers are now given. The figures indicate the percentages of times the different letters were used when the observer was right and also when he was wrong.

McW.

	a.	*b.*	*c.*	*d.*
r.	14 per cent.	44 per cent.	37 per cent.	5 per cent.
w.	4 "	29 "	55 "	12 "

L. S.

r.	1 per cent.	17 per cent.	73 per cent.	9 per cent.
w.	—	3 "	70 "	27 "

R.

r.	—	13 per cent.	78 per cent.	9 per cent.
w.	—	6 "	78 "	16 "

J. S.

r.	—	77 per cent.	92 per cent.	1 per cent.
w.	—	22 "	98 "	—

N. F.

r.	2 per cent.	24 per cent.	66 per cent.	18 per cent.
w.	8 "	27 "	59 "	6 "

As the percentage of right cases varied for different observers, we cannot express their degree of confidence by the percentage of times *a* and *b* were used. We may, however, use as a rough indication of individual differences the fraction $\frac{c}{w}$, that is, the ratio of the number of times he was confident when wrong to the total number of times he was wrong. This fraction is for L. S. only $\frac{3}{100}$; for R., $\frac{6}{100}$; for McW., $\frac{33}{100}$; for J. S., $\frac{22}{100}$; and for N. F., $\frac{35}{100}$. By com-

[1] In experiments on lifted weights described by Fullerton and Cattell, the degree of confidence varies nearly as the percentage of right cases. *Op. cit.*, 126.

paring these numbers with the relative probable errors,[1] we see that there is no relation between the two quantities.[2] As will be seen from the above results, the observers were seldom certain. It is remarkable, however, that two observers were certain 4 per cent. and 8 per cent. of the time respectively when they were wrong. We might suppose that the probability of correctness when confident would be inversely related to the degree of confidence, as shown by the fraction $\frac{c}{w}$ above mentioned. This does not appear to be the case. For McW. and J. S. the probability of correctness when confident was $\frac{9}{10}$[3]; but the values of $\frac{c}{w}$ for the two observers were quite different.

The number of times the observers were correct when guessing was greater than could be explained by chance. By taking the number of d's in ten separate sets, of from 100 to 150 each, and computing the percentage of right cases, it was found that in all of these ten sets this percentage was over 50 per cent., the average being 59 per cent.[4] From this it follows that to halve the number of doubtful answers and add this to the number of right cases, as has generally been done, is an illegitimate method of procedure, since based on an erroneous assumption. In the case of some observers whose confidence was small, this percentage ran as high as 65 per cent. and 70 per cent. The bearing of this on the method of least noticeable differences is, we think, quite obvious. F., about 70 per cent. of whose guesses were correct, stated explicitly that when guessing he felt no difference whatsoever, and that his judgment was entirely a guess. But apart from problems of method, such facts are of not a little theoretic importance, since they show clearly the possible accuracy of unconscious mental processes.

---

[1] See Sec. 4 of this chapter.

[2] Fullerton and Cattell found, contrary to this, that observers having the largest probable errors had the greatest confidence. *Op. cit.*, 126.

[3] This corresponds with the results of Fullerton and Cattell for lifted weights, $\frac{44}{100}$ being the average probability of correctness when confident for ten observers.

[4] Sixty per cent. is that given by Pierce and Jastrow, *op. cit.*; Fullerton and Cattell give 60 and 65 per cent. for two observers, *op. cit.*, 132.

CHAPTER IV.

THE PLACE OF STIMULATION.

SEC. 1. *Previous Investigations.*

In our study of the accuracy of discrimination we confined our experiments to a definite area. It has, however, been asserted on experimental grounds that the accuracy of discrimination varies for different parts of the body. We shall now turn to this aspect of the question.

The so-called tactile sensibility of different parts has generally been determined by Weber's æsthesiometer. But by this method the spatial sensibility only is measured, and we are not justified in assuming that this represents the general delicacy of the peripheral end organs. Perhaps the simplest method of testing the sensibility of different parts is to determine the threshold at these parts. The fact that the threshold is not a fixed quantity does not render this method impracticable. Aubert and Kammler[1] found by this method that there was but little difference between the different parts of the body. The face was somewhat more sensitive and the foot less sensitive than other regions, and no appreciable difference appeared between the sensitiveness of dorsal and volar surfaces. The results were quite different for parts where the hairs were shaved. Similar results were obtained by Bloch,[2] according to whom the face and palm of the hand were more sensitive than the trunk, arms and legs when shaved.

A quite different method was used by Goltz,[3] who applied to the place of stimulation the end of a rubber tube filled with water, the other end being applied to the radial artery. The stimulus was the periodic pressure from the arterial

[1] Aubert and Kammler, *op. cit.* (See Chap. II, Sec. 4.)
[2] Bloch, *op. cit.* (See Chap. II, Sec. 4.)
[3] Goltz, *Centralblatt für die Med. Wiss.*, 1863, 273.

pulsations. Goltz concluded that the sensitiveness of the skin to pressure stimuli varied in general in the same way as the discriminative sensibility for space. The method used is, however, extremely unsatisfactory. Not only was no quantitative determination made, but possible preconceptions could not but influence the process of judgment. Goltz was led to the use of such a method by observing that a branch of the temporal artery can be easily felt with the finger, but not with the hand. This apparent difference in sensitiveness is, we think, at least partly due to differences in the manner of applying the pressure. It is much more difficult to feel the arterial pulsations with the dorsal than with the volar surface of the finger, but Aubert and Kammler, as well as Bloch, found that there is no appreciable difference in the sensitiveness of the dorsal and volar regions.

A still more novel method is that of Funke,[1] who tested the sensitiveness of the skin by applying glycerine solutions of different proportions. That solution was determined the adhesiveness of which could be just distinguished from that of pure glycerine. It is clear that the accuracy of discrimination is here tested, not the threshold, and that, too, in such an inexact manner that accurate quantitative results would be impossible. Besides, the stimulus used is traction and not pressure, and as would be expected, the results are quite different from those obtained by others for pressure. Considering the inaccuracy of the method employed, Funke's results agree fairly with those of Bloch,[2] for traction stimuli, the order of sensitiveness of the principal parts of the body being: finger tips, palm of the hand, back of the hand, forearms, breast, thigh, feet and back.

Results quite different from those of the threshold investigators were found by Schwaner[3] and also by Sergi,[4] who determined the rate of vibration of a tuning fork at which

[1] Funke, *Fischer's Med. Buchhandlung*, 1891, 29, as quoted in *Zeit. für Psy.*, Vol. 2, 399.

[2] Bloch, *op. cit.*

[3] Schwaner, *Die Prüfung der Hautsensibilität*, Dissert., Marburg, 1890, as quoted in *Zeit. für Psy.*, II, 398.

[4] Sergi, *Revista di Filosofia Scientifica*, 1891, as quoted in *Zeit. für Psy.*, III, 175.

the tactile sensations began to fuse.   Schwaner's results are criticised by Sergi, who points out that the amplitude of vibration, and consequently the intensity of the stimulus, is much greater for forks at low pitch.   Sergi concludes that we measure the sensitiveness of the different parts of the skin by differences in the intensity of the stimulus necessary to cause a distinct sensation.   It is probable that the threshold element enters into the experiment, as Sergi holds; but as the results are quite different from those of Bloch and Aubert and Kammler, it is not improbable that local differences in the duration and fusion of tactile sensations affect the results. Krohn[1] states that dermal after-images last much longer for some parts than for others.

The accuracy of discrimination for different regions was investigated by Weber[2] and also by Dohrn.[3]   Weber applied weights to the forearm, and found that the increment necessary in order to be appreciated was twice as great as when the same weight was applied to the hand.   Weber does not, however, mention the magnitude of the stimuli used.   According to Dohrn's researches, the method of which has been described, the least noticeable difference for a stimulus of 1 g. was smallest for the thumb and fingers.   Then follow the hand, forearm, breast, knee pan and feet.   But, as we have already noted, these experiments are of little exact value, since not only is the method open to serious objections, but the experiments were made by the observer on himself. Then, too, according to Aubert and Kammler, individuals differ not a little in the relative sensitiveness of different parts.   We cannot assume, however, even if these results are accepted, that the absolute accuracy of discrimination is measured for different places.   As we have seen, the relative accuracy of discrimination is much greater for stimuli of moderate intensity; consequently, the lower the threshold for a given region, the greater would be the accuracy of discrimination at this region for low intensities.

[1] Krohn, *Journal of Mental and Nervous Diseases*, March, 1893, 11.
[2] Weber, *op. cit.*, 548.   See Chap. I, Sec. 1.
[3] Dohrn, *op. cit.*   See Chap. III, Sec. 1.

SEC. 2. *Further Experiments: the Accuracy of Discrimination.*

The writer made a few rough experiments on the threshold sensibility of the hand, arm and face, by the instrument already described,[1] and the results corroborated those given by Bloch, Aubert and Kammler, as well as Dohrn, assuming that the latter's results were due to the threshold differences. Experiments were also made on the discrimination of weights by the method of right and wrong cases, the probable error being determined for different parts. Six hundred experiments were made on N. F., the volar surface of the left index finger, third phalanx, being the place of stimulation. The stimuli used were 50 g., 200 g. and 800 g. The average of the six values of $\frac{P.E.}{S.}$ obtained was $\frac{1}{10}$, which was approximately the same as that obtained for the palm of the hand of the same observer.[2] Experiments were also made on L. S. The stimulus was 100 g., and the places of application were the volar surface of the left index finger and the back of the hand. The probable error for each set of 100 experiments is given below, as well as that obtained for the palm of the hand at the same time.

Observer.	P.E. for finger.	P.E. for palm of hand.	P.E. for back of the hand.
L. S.,	9.	16.	17.

On account of the comparatively small number of experiments the probable errors given are considerably affected by the variable error. Making allowance for the variable error, the results for L. S., taken together with those for N. F., indicate that apart from individual variations there is no very marked difference in the accuracy of discrimination for moderate intensities at different parts of the hand.

A further series of experiments was made on S. F. with 5 g. and 7 g. as the stimuli. The volar surface of the index finger and the hand, and the dorsal surface of the forearm, were the places of stimulation. In these experiments the error due to impact is constant for the different places, and

[1] See Chap. II, Sec. 4.
[2] See Chap. III, Sec. 3. Av. $\frac{P.E.}{S.}$ for N. F. is $\frac{1}{7}$.

does·not, ·therefore, ·affect the ʻrelative results. Below are given the probable errors for the different sets of 100 experiments.

Stimuli.	Finger.				Hand.				Wrist.			
	P_1	P_2	P_3	Av.	P_1	P_2	P_3	Av.	P_1	P_2	P_3	Av.
5 g. and 7 g.	1.3	1.5	1.5	1.4	3.7	1.8	2.	2.5	9.1	3.3	2.3	4.9

These experiments show that for 5.g.–7.g. the discrimination is somewhat more accurate for ʻthe tip of the finger than for the palm of·the hand, and much more so·than for the back of the fore arm. The observer improved, however, greatly from practice in the experiments on the wrist. As the threshold sensitiveness is here much less, and we are not accustomed to judging stimuli thus placed, the difference was to be expected.

SEC. 3. *The Intensity of the Sensation.*

Another method of investigating the sensitiveness of different places is by comparing the intensive effect of a given stimulus with that of the stimulus applied to another region. Weber found that 5 oz. placed on the finger was judged greater than 4 oz. on the arm, but when the weights were reversed they were judged equal.[1] In order to obtain more accurate results, a weight of 5, 100, or 1000 g. was applied to the finger, and upon removal applied to the dorsal surface of the wrist, the observer being required to judge which seemed heavier. The observers were ignorant of the fact that the stimuli applied were the same. If in 10 experiments no underestimation of the stimulus was appreciable at one of the two places of stimulation, as compared to the other, we concluded that any difference in sensitiveness was too slight to be considered. When, however, the answers were such that the weight when applied to the wrist was considered much lighter, increments were added to it until it seemed equal to the standard weight applied to the finger. When 5 g. was used, increments could not be conveniently

[1] Weber, *op. cit.*

added, so 7 g. and 10 g. weights of the same area were used as comparison stimuli. Below are the results for four observers. The values of the increments given are based on five experiments.

Stimulus.	Increments added on wrist.			
	P	K	L	F
1000g - - -	0	0	0	300
100g - - -	50	0	0	90
5g - - -	>5	0	>2<5	>2<5

The above results seem to show that there is, at least for low intensities, a marked underestimation of stimuli applied to the arm, in comparison with stimuli applied to the finger. Observers differ greatly, however, that this cannot be stated as a universal law, K. not showing any appreciable underestimation. Possibly these individual differences may be due to central processes, such as unconscious allowance for sensory difference in comparing the stimuli. The fact that the underestimation tends to diminish for high intensities goes to show that different regions of the periphery do not have an intensity coefficient as Weber concluded.

SEC. 4. *The Pain Threshold.*

By the algometer already described the writer made five measurements of the pain threshold for different parts of the body. But one measurement for a given place was made at a time.. Below are the results in kilograms, with the probable errors of the averages.

Top of the head, parietal region. -   -   -   1.8 ±.005
Forehead, frontal region. -   -   -   -   -   1.3 ±.008
Breast, over sternum. -   -   -   -   -   2.4 ±.006
Abdomen. -   -   -   -   -   -   -   1.7 ±.006
Back. -   -   -   -   -   -   -   8.0 ±.010
Right temporal region of head. -   -   -   -   1.0 ±.003
Left   "   "   "   -   -   -   -   1.3 ±.004

Right thigh, ventral region. - - - - 4.3 ±.01
Left " " " - - - - 3.2 ±.007
Right foot, plantar surface. - - - - 3.5 ±.009
Left " " " - - - - - 3.4 ±.005
Right heel. " " - - - - - 7.0 ±.006
Left " " " - - - - - 5.9 ±.01
Right hand, volar surface. - - - - - 7.3[1] ±.007
Left " " " - - - - - 6.2 ±.007
Right hand, dorsal surface.[1] - - - - 3.3 ±.006
Left " " " - - - - 3.6 ±.01
Right index finger, volar surface, 3d phalanx. - 3.5 ±.006
Left " " " " " " 3.3 ±.006

From this it appears that the regions over the frontal and temporal bones are most sensitive to pressure, and the heel, the back, and the muscular regions of the leg and hand the least sensitive. The sensitiveness to pain seems, then, to depend largely upon the thickness of the skin and the extent of subcutaneous tissues. The left side of the body is perhaps slightly more sensitive than the right side, but the difference, if any exists, is hardly appreciable.

[1] The measurements on the hand were carried on simultaneously with the others. But quite a number of experiments had been made on the hand before, and it seemed to have become less sensitive by about 2 k. than when it was first tested.

CHAPTER V.

SENSATIONS OF IMPACT.

SEC. 1. *The Threshold[1] for Touch.*

We should expect *a priori* that a given weight would have greater effect if applied with appreciable impact than if impact were excluded. In order to find if such were the case, a circular piece of cardboard was placed carefully upon the hand of the observer, being suspended by a delicate brass wire about 1 cm. long. The whole weighed .01g. S. F. and the writer served as observers, the one not acting as observer placing the stimulus. The observer's eyes were closed, and he did not know when the stimulus was applied. Fifty experiments were made on both observers, and the number of times they perceived the stimulus was recorded. In order to compare the results with those obtained when impact was excluded, the pressure was applied by means of the instrument described in Chap. II, Sec. 4. In order to have the area of stimulation constant, the pressure was exerted upon the card piece to which reference has just been made, the projecting wire handle having been removed. The pressure thus applied was .4 g. Below are given the percentage of times the stimuli was felt in 50 experiments.

	Impact.	Pressure.
	.01g	.4 g
F. - -	56%	66%
G. - -	52%	30%
AV. - -	54%	48%

---

[1] We retain this term for purposes of convenience, there being no other to denote stimuli that are perceived with difficulty.

It is evident from the above that a pressure stimulus has a much less intensive effect than one of impact, even if the velocity of the weight applied be very small. If the pressure were applied more rapidly (between 1 and 2 sec. was the time), the effect upon the dermal end organs would be more marked. But the quicker the increase of pressure the more would its effect resemble that of impact.

SEC. 2. *The Threshold of Pain.*

To find the threshold for impact stimuli a wooden upright frame was constructed 1 m. in height. A box containing a weight, of lead or brass, could slide in an open groove without appreciable friction. A scale showed the height in centimetres through which the box fell. The part of the stimulus in contact with the skin was of wood and circular in shape, the diameter being 1 cm. The box was allowed to fall by the hand, after being raised to the height desired. A wax model was made to fit the hand of the observer, so that when the hand was once placed under the movable stimulus its position could not be changed. The palm of the hand was the place of stimulation. By means of this instrument the height causing pain was found for different weights.

The experiment was conducted as follows. The required height having been previously found very roughly, the weight was allowed to fall from a height somewhat below this point. It was then allowed to fall from a height 5 cm. greater, and this was continued until pain was caused by the blow. From two to five experiments were generally made before the pain threshold was recorded. As it was found that repeated trials made the tissues more sensitive, an interval of about half a minute elapsed between the experiments.[1] Four weights were used, and with two or three exceptions but one measurement was made at one sitting for each weight. The order in which the heights for the different weights were found was the reverse in half of the experiments from that which was followed in the other half. Ten experiments for

[1] This precaution was all the more necessary because of the difference in times of the appearance of pain and the sensation of impact. This difference was occasionally very marked.

each weight were made by the writer upon himself and five upon L., an advanced student of psychology. We give below the average values in centimeters of the height necessary to cause pain for the different weights used. The probable errors of the averages are also given, being preceded by the sign ±.

Observer.	25 g.	50 g.	100 g.	300 g.
L.	32.8± .5	18.6±.4	10.6±.3	3.1±.03
G.	69.4±1.1	34.2±.3	16.8±.1	5.4± .2

If we multiply the above values for the height by the corresponding weights, we obtain the following results:[1]

	25 g.	50 g.	100 g.	300 g.
L.	820.±12.	930.±20.	1060.±30.	930.±9.
G.	1730.±27.	1710.±15.	1680.±10.	1620.±60

From this it appears that the product of the weight and the height necessary to cause pain is fairly constant. Expressing this in the form of an equation we have,

$$Wh = k,$$

which is the equation of an hyperbola. If for Wh we substitute its value, $\frac{1}{2} m v^2$, we have,

$$\tfrac{1}{2} m v^2 = k,$$

which expresses the relation between the mass and velocity necessary to cause pain. If we substitute $\frac{1}{m}$ for m, we have,

$$v^2 = 2k\, m.$$

This equation expresses the relation of the velocity and the mass, considered as factors determining the intensity of the stimulus. The equation is that of a parabola. Its meaning is that an increase of the square of the velocity has the same intensive effect on pain sensations as a corresponding increase in the mass.

[1] The probable errors of these results are found by multiplying the original probable errors by the weights.

By taking the average values of the product Wh for the two observers, and comparing these with the average values of the pressure threshold for the same area, we find that for L. a pressure of about 2300 g. is equivalent to a blow of the same mass through a height of 4 mm., and therefore a velocity of 28 cm. per sec.[1] For G., in like manner, the pressure of 4500 g. is equivalent to a blow of the same mass having a velocity 27 cm. per sec. For velocities less than these greater masses would, according to theory, be required for impact than for pressure. It is probable, therefore, that the equation does not hold for very low velocities. This we might naturally expect, since as the velocity decreases the less is the difference between impact and pressure stimulation.

SEC. 3. *The Analysis of Mass and Velocity in Impact Stimuli.*

When the same weight falls upon the skin from different heights, different sensations are aroused. In order to investigate the subjective effects of mass and velocity in haptic sensations proper, as opposed to those of pain, the writer allowed a weight of 100 g. to fall upon the palm of the observer's hand from a height of 5 cm., in the manner already described, and then found the approximate height at which a weight of 25 g., and the same area, seemed to give rise to a sensation of equal intensity. That height was considered the height required, at which, in ten or more trials, about half of the observer's judgments were 'heavier' and half 'lighter.' When the experiments were begun, the observers were asked to judge which weight seemed heavier or lighter rather than which seemed to give the more intense sensation. It was, however, evident from the statements made by the observers that they judged the intensity of the blow. Some spoke of a difference in the quality of the sensations, and two said that the weights fell with different velocities. We give below the heights determined for different observers at which the blow of 25 g. seemed equal to that of 100 g. at 5 cm.

---

[1] The velocity is readily calculated from the height by the formula, $h = \dfrac{v^2}{2g}$

We give also the square roots of the heights, since these may be taken to represent the velocities.

Observer.	S. F.	L. F.	L.	K.	P.
h.	40	40	58	33	20
$\sqrt{h}$.	6.3	6.3	7.6	5.7	4.5

The individual differences are so great that an exact inference is impossible. It is, however, evident that in order that blows be judged of equal intensity, the height, or the square of the velocity, has in general much less effect than the weight. For if this were not the case, the average height for 25 g., to cause a blow judged equal to that from 100 g. at 5 cm. would be not far from 20 cm.[1] On the other hand the velocity appears to have a relatively greater effect than the mass. Otherwise the average values of $\sqrt{h}$ for 25 g. would be approximately 8.8 cm. or more.[2] If we assume that the above judgments are based upon equality of sensory intensity, we may conclude that to cause an intensive effect equal to that of the velocity, the mass must increase faster than the velocity, but more slowly than the square of the velocity. The great individual variations make it probable, however, that the process of judgment is somewhat complex. Possibly the fact that we are more accustomed to judge weights than velocities, may partly account for the difficulty observers have in forming a judgment. Then, too, the change in sensation due to velocity is of different modality from that due to weight. But although we cannot assume that a relation is obtained between the intensive effects of mass and velocity, this is extremely probable. The complexity of the processes of comparison is such that great individual variations are to be expected; but to whatever extent the judgments be affected by non-peripheral processes, they are doubtless based upon differences in sensory intensity.

[1] 100 g. × 5 cm. = 25 g. × 20 cm.
[2] 100 g. × 2.2 cm. = 25 g. × 8.8 cm.

Sec. 4. *The Discrimination of Mass and Velocity.*

In order to investigate the accuracy of discrimination for impact stimuli, an apparatus was used constructed as shown in the cut.

Fig. 7.

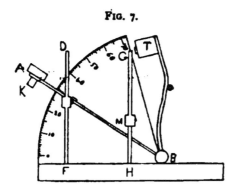

An aluminium bar, AB, movable vertically, was attached to a horizontal axis, B, so that it could fall from different angular elevations. At the extremity of the bar weights of brass or lead could be attached. Metallic upright bars, attached to the wooden base, DF, GH, were provided with movable clamps, L and M. On these clamps catches were fitted by which the experimenter could let the weight and bar fall from any desired angular elevation. When a constant height was used, it was more convenient to let fall the weight from an electro-magnet, T. A scale furnished the means of adjusting the angular elevations. The stimulus was applied to the palm of the left hand, which was placed in a wax rest made to fit the hand. The hand was in contact with the cylindrical piece, K, projecting from the extremity of the weighted aluminium bar when the bar was horizontal.

Two different sets of experiments were made. In one of these the mass applied was variable and the velocity constant. In the other the mass was constant, the observer being required to estimate differences in the intensity of the blow from increments in velocity due to height. If K denote the moment of inertia of the falling mass, ω the angular velocity, W the weight, v the linear velocity, h the height through which the centre of gravity falls, and r the distance from the axis to the centre of gravity, we have

$$\tfrac{1}{2} K \omega^2 = Wh^1$$

and

$$\tfrac{1}{2} K r^2 v^2 = Wh.$$

Since $K r^2$ is constant, when the height only is variable,

$$v = c \sqrt{h}.$$

Hence we may take $\sqrt{h}$ to represent the velocity when the height is varied. This quantity is taken as the stimulus when the mass is constant, the weight being allowed to fall successively from different heights, and the accuracy of discrimination being measured by the method of right and wrong cases. In order that the judgment might be based upon the sensation of impact only, the writer caught the lever arm of the weight by the hand the moment after it struck the observer's hand. As there was a slight rebound, it was thus comparatively easy to eliminate pressure sensations. The values of h for different values of the angular elevation of the lever arm, θ, were calculated by the formula deduced for the purpose,

$$h = r \sin (\theta + a) - l,$$

in which a represents the angle betwen the lever arm and the line passing from the axis of rotation to the centre of gravity of the lever arm and weight, C, and l represents the distance from C to the lever arm. The position of C was found by experiment. The above formula was roughly verified by measurements which, on account of the position of C, were too inexact to serve as a basis for calculations.

In the experiments the results of which are given below the standard weight was 50 g. Two standard heights were used, 5.4 cm. and 17.5 cm. The increments were for height 1.3 cm. and 3.5 cm., and for weight 10 g. The percentage of right answers varied generally between 70% and 90%. In the tables appended are given the probable errors

---

[1] For the deduction of this formula, the writer is indebted to Prof. R. S. Woodward, of Columbia College. If F be the impressed forces, r the lever arm, and θ the angular elevation, $K \dfrac{d^2 \theta}{dt^2} = Fr = Wr \cos \theta$. Hence,

$$K \int \frac{d^2 \theta}{dt^2} d\theta = Wr \sin \theta = Wh = \tfrac{1}{2} K \omega^2.$$

for the different sets of 100 experiments.[1] The second column indicates the nature of the variable stimulus, whether weight, W, or velocity, $\sqrt{h}$. When the variable stimulus is the weight, the probable error is, of course, in terms of weight. When the variable stimulus is velocity, the probable error is calculated in terms of $\sqrt{h}$.[2] In the sixth columns are given the values of $\dfrac{P}{S}$, the average probable error divided by the mean of the two stimuli compared. In the last columns are the values of $\dfrac{P}{S}$ for velocity, Rv, divided by $\dfrac{P}{S}$ for weight, Rw. This indicates the ratio of the accuracy of discrimination for velocity to that for weight.

H = 5.4 cm. H + ΔH = 6.7 cm.

$\sqrt{H}$ = 2.32 cm. $\sqrt{H + \Delta H}$ = 2.58 cm.

Observer.	Var. S.	P_1	P_2	Av. P.	$\dfrac{P}{S}$ = R.	$\dfrac{Rv}{Rw}$
S. F.	W = 50 g.	6.5	8.0	7.2	.13 = Rw.	.8
	$\sqrt{h}$ = 2.32 cm.	.33	.25	.29	.12 = Rv.	
L. F.	W = 50 g.	5.9	—	5.9	.11 = Rw.	.4
	$\sqrt{h}$ = 2.32 cm.	.12	—	.12	.05 = Rv.	

H = 17.5 cm. H + ΔH = 21. cm.

$\sqrt{H}$ = 4.19 cm. $\sqrt{H + \Delta H}$ = 4.58 cm.

Observer.	Var. S.	P_1	P_2	Av. P.	$\dfrac{P}{S}$ = R.	$\dfrac{Rv}{Rw}$
S. F.	W = 50 g.	4.2	6.7	5.4	.10 = Rw.	1.0
	$\sqrt{h}$ = 4.19 cm.	.43	.43	.43	.10 = Rv.	
L. F.	W = 50 g.	5.	3.9	4.4	.08 = Rw.	.7
	$\sqrt{h}$ = 4.19 cm.	.23	.27	.25	.06 = Rv.	
L.	W = 50 g.	6.3	7.7	7.0	.13 = Rw.	1.1
	$\sqrt{h}$ = 4.19 cm.	.73	.60	.66	.15 = Rv.	

[1] See Chap. III for method of calculation. The prob. errors are not here corrected as in Chap. III.

[2] When the weight is varied there is a slight change in the velocity. For a small increment of weight, however, this may be neglected, as will be seen from the formula, $\frac{1}{2} K\omega^2 = Wh$.

In order to compare the accuracy of discrimination for blows with that for pressure stimuli, 400 experiments on S. F. and L. F. were made with a weight of 1000 g. and an area approximately the same as that used in the impact experiments. We give below the mean of the two probable errors obtained for S. F. and for L. F., divided by the mean of the stimuli compared, $\frac{P}{S}$. The values of $\frac{P}{S}$ for 50 g. are also given for comparison. These are for the greater height 17.5 cm., since, in order to have a logical basis of comparison, it is necessary to compare the relative probable errors at intensities not greatly differing. Weber's law, we have seen, holds approximately only for moderately high intensities. This is moreover evident from the table since the relative probable errors at the two heights are appreciably different.

$\frac{P}{S}$ for pressure, $\frac{P}{S}$ for impact.

S. F. $\frac{1}{11}$ 1000 g. $\frac{1}{16}$ 50 g. × 17.5 cm.

L. F. $\frac{1}{14}$ $\frac{1}{11}$.

From the results given above we may conclude, first that there is no marked difference in the accuracy of discrimination for pressure and for impact, and second, that the discrimination for velocity tends to be more accurate than that of weight. If, however, instead of calculating the probable errors for the square root of the height, we had calculated them for the height, which represents the energy of the blow, we should have found that the discrimination was better for the mass than the height. This difference in the discrimination for mass and velocity may be due to processes of perception or to actual differences in the intensive effects of mass and velocity. If we assume that the latter explanation is the true one, we can say that in order to produce equal sensory effects the relative increments of mass and velocity are related as expressed by the equation,

$$\frac{\Delta v}{v} k = \frac{\Delta m}{m}$$

in which k is a constant, having the same value as $\frac{Rv}{Rw}$ in the tables. If this equation hold, whatever be the values of Δm, and Δv, we have,

$$\frac{dv}{v} = k \, \frac{dm}{m}$$

whence, by integration,

$$\log. \, C + \log. \, v = k \log. \, m,$$

in which log. C may be taken as the constant of integration. From this we have,

$$C \, v = m^k$$

or,

$$v = C'm^k.$$

Substituting for k the average of the values of $\frac{Rv}{Rw}$,

$$v = C'm^{\frac{3}{4}}.$$

That is, the velocity increases as $m^{\frac{3}{4}}$. As it is more convenient to take the mass as the most direct factor in the intensive effect of the stimulus, the above relation may be expressed,

$$m = C''v^{1.3}$$

We may, therefore, write as the intensive stimulus in impact, S,

$$S = mv^{1.3}$$

The quantity k is so difficult to determine, whether or not it be variable for individuals, that the above expression is only approximate. It is, however, clear that the stimulus is to be judged a quantity varying between the momentum mv, and the kinetic energy, mv^2. In other words the mass has greater intensive effect than the energy due to the velocity, but less effect than the velocity.

It is possible that the results obtained are dependent entirely on the processes of comparison and judgment. The conclusion at which we arrived, assuming this not to be the explanation, is the same as that which we reached in the experiments on the direct comparison of the intensive effects of mass and velocity. It seems, therefore, preferable to consider the complex central process involved as causally related only to the great individual variations. It is, nevertheless, not to be assumed that these variations are entirely of central origin. They may be due to differences in the sensitiveness of the dermal nerves to impact stimuli. The problem becomes still more complex in view of the fact that, as we have found, the pain threshold is determined, approximately at least, by the kinetic energy of the blow. This might be explained teleologically in that the injury done to the organism would tend to vary as the energy of the blow. If, as we think probable, dermal pain is a distinct sensation, with perhaps a distinct anatomical and physiological basis, it is not surprising that its stimulus should be different from that for impact sensations proper.

CHAPTER VI.

The Area of Stimulation.

SEC. 1. *The Area of Stimulation and Judgments of the Intensity of the Stimulus.*

It is a common experience that a needle or other stimulus acting on a small dermal area will cause pain, when the same pressure applied to a large area will not. The intensity of haptic sensations appears, therefore, inversely related to the area of stimulation. For the study of this problem different methods were used, the first of which will now be described.

Boxes constructed as described in Chapter III, Sec. 2, were applied successively to the volar surface of the left hand, and the observer was required to say which seemed the heavier. The area of one of the bases, which were circular, was 8 sq. cm., that of the other was .12 sq. cm. approximately, that is $\frac{1}{64}$ of the larger area. For convenience we shall speak of the larger area as A, and that of the smaller as a. Two sets of experiments by the method of right and wrong cases were carried on simultaneously. In one set an increment, which we shall call Δ_1, was added to the box A, weighted to 200 g., so that a, weighted to 200 g., was generally judged the lighter. In this set A was always the first to be applied. In the other set a different increment (Δ_2) was added to A, such that $A+\Delta_2$ was generally judged lighter than a. In this series a was always the first to be given. In this way the observer could not be influenced by the association of one area with an apparently greater intensity.

The method of calculating the overestimation of the intensity of a is as follows.

Let C.E. be the constant error due to overestimation of the second of two stimuli, P.E. the probable error, T_1 and

T_1 the values of the probability integral corresponding to the percentages the second stimulus is judged heavier and lighter, and N, the required constant overestimation of the stimulus acting on the smaller area. Then for the series $A+\Delta_1$ as first, and a as second stimulus, from the formula,

$$\frac{\Delta}{P.E.} = T_h,$$

we have,

$$\frac{C.E.+N-\Delta_1}{P.E.} = T_h$$

whence,

$$N = T_h\, P.E. + \Delta_1 - C.E.$$

For the series a as first, and $A+\Delta_2$ as second stimulus, we have,

$$\frac{N-C.E.-\Delta_2}{P.E.} = T_l,$$

whence,

$$N = T_l\, P.E + \Delta_2 + C.E.$$

The values of P.E. and C.E. having been found by experiments carried on simultaneously with these, the values of N were calculated from the above equations. With W., an advanced student of psychology, 400 experiments were made, and the values of N for each set of 100 were as follows:

Observer, W.	N_1	N_2	N_3	N_4	Av.N.	$\frac{N}{S}$
Stimulus, 200 g.,	65	68	75	69	69	1/3

The overestimation of the weight applied to about $\frac{1}{64}$ of the larger area was, therefore, approximately $\frac{1}{3}$ of the stimulus. Experiments were also made by another method, and on a number of observers. The method of right and wrong cases was used, but the relations of the stimuli were different. The first stimulus was constant, and had the smaller area. The second stimulus was part of the time $A+\Delta_1$, and part of the time $A+\Delta_2$, the values of Δ_1 and Δ_2 being such that $A+\Delta_1$ was judged heavier and $A+\Delta_2$ lighter than a, the constant first stimulus. By this method from twenty to fifty experiments were made on W., N. F., L. S., and McW., all being subjects in the experiments on discrimination of weights already described. Not enough experiments were made to base a calculation upon them, but enough to estimate roughly the overestimation. The results for W. were corroborative of those already obtained, both for 100 g. and 200 g. L. S. and McW. showed an overestimation at 500 g. of about ¼ the stimulus, closely corresponding to that of W. N. F. showed, however, an appreciable tendency to *underestimate* the weight of *a* at 100 g. and also at 200 g.

By a third method the increment added to a weight with area *A* pressing on the hand in order to make it appear equal to the same weight lifted was compared to the increment which had to be added when the area was *a* instead of *A*. Below are the values of the increments obtained for a 200 g. weight, each based upon five or more experiments. The observers were, of course, ignorant of the purpose of the experiment, as well as of the magnitude of the increments.

	P.	K.	L.F.	S.F.
A.	37	0	150	148
a.	0	0	0	140

In only two of the four observers does this overestimation due to the area appear very marked in these experiments. From this, and from the fact that by a different method there was not only no overestimation found for N. F., but even the reverse, we may conclude that this constant tendency is by no means universal.

The fact that individual variations are such that we cannot infer a relation between the area and the intensity of stimulation does not prove that such a relation does not exist. An observer may unconsciously allow for this overestimation in his judgment, though this was certainly not the case with N. F., since this observer supposed the larger area would seem heavier. It is difficult, moreover, to explain in this way the results obtained by the last method. But in the direct comparison of weights of different areas, great difficulty is experienced by some observers in forming a judgment. The sensations seem heterogeneous and therefore incomparable. It is only by abstraction that a judgment of intensity is possible; and in this process it is but natural that individuals should differ greatly.

SEC. 2. *The Tactile Threshold.*

If the intensity of haptic sensations is related to the area of stimulation, we should expect the tactile threshold to vary with the area. For the purpose of investigating this problem, the writer cut circular pieces of card board about 3.5 mm. and 10.7 mm. in diameter, their areas being, therefore, approximately in the ratio 1 : 9. The weights of the cards were about .01 g. and .05 g.; but this may be neglected, since only at the moment of application of the weight do pressure stimuli of low intensity have any sensory effect. When one or both of these cards had been placed on the palm of the hand of the observer, who was blindfolded, the pressure necessary to affect consciousness was found by the apparatus and methods described in Chapter II. The same corrections are also made. Ten experiments for each area were made on L. F. by the writer, and as many on the writer by S. F., who was carefully instructed as to the precautions necessary. A third set of experiments was made in which no card was used, the pressure being exerted directly upon the skin by the vertically projecting bristle of the instrument. The diameter of the bristle being about .4 mm. the area applied was about 1.2 mm. Below are the results in grams for each group of ten experiments.

Area.	S. F.			H. G.		
	Av.	Max.	Min.	Av.	Max.	Min.
1 mm.	.2	.5	.1	.5	1.	.2
10 mm.	.9	1.7	.3	1.4	3.2	.3
90 mm.	1.9	2.7	1.	1.6	2.5	.4

It appears from this that the tactile threshold varies with the area of stimulation, but that it increases much more slowly than in direct proportion. From what we have already said regarding the possibility of regarding the threshold as a definite quantity more exact results could hardly be expected. Strictly speaking we are not justified in using the term threshold, but it is convenient to do so, if we bear in mind that no absolute quantity is measured, but only the relative sensory effect of stimuli acting on different areas.

SEC. 3. *The Threshold of Pain.*

In order to investigate this relation with accuracy, wooden cones of hard wood were cut across vertically by a lathe at three points so determined by calculation that the diameters of the sections would be approximately 6.18 mm., 10.70 mm., and 18.54 mm. A still smaller circular base, about 3.56 mm. in diameter, was made by rotating a wooden cone cut by hand over sand paper until the diameter required was obtained. In this way areas were obtained of approximately 10, 30, 90, and 270 sq. mm. The diameters of the two smaller bases were measured a number of times on the dividing engine. The averages of five readings were 6.21 cm. and 3.58 cm., which shows that the areas are sufficiently accurate. In applying the pressure the algometer already described was used. The pressure was exerted upon the desired area by fitting the upper part of the wooden piece, the base of which had the area in question, into another wooden piece. Into this in turn could be fitted the projecting cap of the algometer. The rate of increase of the pressure was kept as constant as possible, and this was as great as was consistent with taking the readings accurately. The error due to the increase of pressure between the appearance of the pain and the taking of the reading is corrected as in Chapter II. It will, therefore, not affect the results. The place of stimulation was the palm of the hand. With F. the right hand was used, but the left hand was used in experiments on G. But four experiments were made on one day, one for each area. In half of the experiments the order in which the different areas were used was the reverse of that which was followed in the other half. Though the experiments made by the writer on himself were purposely extended over several weeks, a gradual decrease of sensitiveness to dermal pain was observed. This is not so noticeable in the results found for S. F. The averages, with their probable errors,[1] are given below, for each set of five experiments. The figures indicate kilograms.

---

[1] As the quantity determined increases appreciably for G., the use of the probable error is not justified, and it is not given.

Observer.	Group.	Area.			
		.1 cm.	.3 cm.	.9 cm.	2.7 cm.
S. F.	1st five.	1.4±.0	2.7.1±	3. ±.1	4.5±.2
	2nd five.	1.9±.1	2.7.±1	3.4±.1	4.8±.2
G.	1st five.	1.	2.6	4.6	7.3
	2nd five.	1.3	3.1	6.8	10.
Av.		1.4	2.8	4.4	6.6

These results are represented graphically in the accompanying curves.

FIGURE 8.

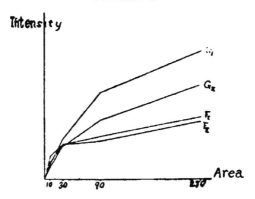

As the curves obtained differ somewhat, it is impossible to express the relations by a simple expression. They approximately are logarithmic curves, but for the largest area the increase of intensity is too great. As the stimuli are in geometrical progression, the logarithmic relation requires an arithmetical increase of the area. We may, therefore, test the results by finding the differences between the threshold at the different areas. These differences are as follows:

	10 and 30 mm.	30 and 90 mm.	90 and 270 mm.
S. F.	1.3	.3	1.5
S. F.	.8	.7	1.4
G.	1.6	2.0	2.7
G.	1.8	3.7	3.2
Av.	1.3	1.7	2.2

The increments appear to increase with the area, whereas an arithmetical progression requires that they be constant.

But as will be seen by inspection of the above figures, the increase is within the limit of individual and other variations.

SEC. 4. *Theoretic Interpretation of Experiments on the Intensive Effect of the Area.*

We have by three entirely different methods investigated the intensive effect of the area of stimulation. By each one of these methods we have arrived at the same result, that the intensity of pressure sensations is inversely related to the area of stimulation. We have seen that the intensity causing pain is approximately proportional to the logarithm of the area. Hence, as the intensity of the stimulus increases, its effect is the same as that from the decrease of the corresponding logarithm of the area. The experiments on the tactile threshold and on judgments of intensity, though not admitting of such an interpretation, nevertheless seem to show that the intensity threshold increases much more slowly than the area. Hence we may write as an approximate expression of the relation between the intensity and the area of the stimulus which must exist in order that equal subjective intensive effects be produced,

$$I = \frac{K}{\log A}$$

If we could assume Fechner's law we could substitute the value of I in the equation,

$$S = K_1 \log I,$$

in which S denotes intensity of sensation, and obtain,

$$S = K_1 \log \left(\frac{K}{\log A} \right).$$

That is, the intensity of the sensation increases as the logarithm of the reciprocal of the logarithm of the area multiplied by a constant. If, as Hering and some others hold, S is directly related to I, the relation between S and A would be an inverse logarithmic one. If, as the majority of psycho-physicists believe, S increases much more slowly than I, even though not in logarithmic proportion, it would increase correspondingly more slowly than the reciprocal of the logarithm of the area. The inverse relation here existing is contrary to what we might expect by the analogy of other senses. In the case of temperature sensations Weber showed that the intensity increased with the area.[1] Müller–Lyer found that the least noticeable difference for visual stimuli increased with the area of stimulation in about the same proportion as when the intensity was variable and the area constant.[2] With pressure stimuli the conditions are apparently the same; the larger the area the greater the number of nerve fibres stimulated.[3] If the stimulus were the physical pressure exerted, the intensity would, we think, increase with the area. For not only are more nerves acted on by larger areas, but the pressure increases in direct proportion to the area, provided the force applied be constant. As the exact reverse effect is produced upon the sensory end organs, the stimulus can not be considered mere pressure, but rather as work done upon the skin and subcutaneous tissues.

In sensations of impact the stimulus is, as we have seen, the energy of the moving mass or a quantity more approaching to the momentum.[4] In the case of impact stimuli, therefore, we should not expect the intensity of the sensation to increase, but rather to diminish with the area. For the greater the area the less the energy or momentum transferred to the dermal tissues within a given area. When no impact, but only pressure, is exerted, then the stimulus is the work expended in overcoming the resistance of the skin. The work done is independent of the area of stimulation, as it depends upon the impressed forces. Consequently, the greater the area the less is the work done at any one point in the region affected by the pressure; in other words, the less the intensity of stimulation. If, moreover, the function of the touch corpuscles be protective, as some suppose, the stimulus will meet with greater resistance, the greater the area upon which it acts.

[1] Weber, *op. cit.*, 553; also Dessoir, *op. cit.*, 297.
[2] Müller–Lyer, Archiv für Anat. und Physiol., 1889, Supp. Bd.
[3] Funke even states that the intensity increases with the area. *Op. cit.*, 331.
[4] The movement theory of haptic stimulation was, we believe, first advanced by Lotze, *Med. Psychologie*, 198.

This leads us to the consideration of the peculiar phenomena of dermal pressure from liquid or gaseous bodies. The atmosphere exerts a pressure upon the body of 1.03 k. per sq. centimeter, but has no effect upon consciousness. When the hand is placed in a fluid, even of considerable density, no pressure is felt except at the surface. These phenomena are intelligible, when we consider that the process of haptic stimulation involves a transference of energy. The element of time is of not a little importance, but will be considered later. The ring effect observed when the hand is plunged in mercury has its counterpart in the relatively great intensity of pressure sensations from solid stimuli in the region of the perimeter of the surface applied. A kilogram weight placed on the hand will be felt most distinctly at the edge. That the skin is more affected in this region is shown by the dark red line from vaso-motor disturbance that here appears when the stimulus is removed. It is not necessary, therefore, to explain the phenomena by such hypotheses as that of Meissner, who held that the process of pressure stimulation was an oscillatory action in the tactile corpuscles.[1]

SEC. 5. *The Area of Stimulation and the Discrimination of Intensity.*

In the chapter on the accuracy of discrimination for different intensities, two areas were used, 8 cm. and $\frac{8}{64}$ cm., approximately. In addition to the experiments there described, 1000 experiments were made on W. In 500 of these the larger area was used, and in the other 500 the smaller area. In the following table will be found the probable and constant errors based upon each set of 100 experiments.

Stimulus, 200 g.

Area.	P₁	P₂	P₃	P₄	P₅	Av. P.	C₁	C₂	C₃	C₄	C₅	Av.C.
8 cm.	37	19.	22.	20.	14.	22.	15	10	15	9	5	11
$\frac{8}{64}$ cm.	33	56	10.	14	16	25	32	8	9	3	12	13

[1] Meissner, *Zeit. für Rat. Med.*, 3ᵗᵉ R., VII. *Cf.* Funke, *op. cit.*, 328, for a criticism of Meissner's theory.

From these results it is evident that the accuracy of discrimination of this observer was not on the whole appreciably altered by the variation of the area. The same might be said of the constant error. The variation of the probable error for the smaller area is, however, so great that in spite of the large number of experiments, the results do not admit of an exact interpretation. By comparing the average values of $\frac{P}{S}$ for the observers S. F., J. S. and L. S., on whom experiments were made for both areas, we obtain somewhat more satisfactory results. By referring to the tables, Chap. III, Sec. 3, we see that although N. F.'s probable errors are very variable, especially for the smaller area, those of L. S. for both areas are fairly constant. The following table gives the average values of $\frac{P}{S}$, the probable error divided by the stimulus, for all intensities used.

Area.	Average values of $\frac{P}{S}$.			
	N. F.	J. S.	L. S.	W.
8 cm. . .	.13	.11	.10	.11
$\frac{8}{64}$ cm. . .	.18	.12	.10	.13

Although W. and N. F. appear to judge stimuli of the larger area more accurately, there is no appreciable difference for J. S. and L. S., the most constant of the four observers.

SEC. 6. *The Intensity of Stimulation and the Discrimination of Areas.*

It was not our purpose to enter into a discussion of the problem of tactile space perception. But having found that the discrimination of intensity was not uniformly affected by the area of stimulation, the question suggested itself whether the converse was true. For the purpose of finding if this were so, weights were used of 200 g. and 800 g. Two standard areas were used, being approximately 32 mm. and 11.3 mm. in diameter, and therefore 800 mm. and 100 mm. in area. The bases of the boxes applied were covered with stiff paper cut so as to be circular in shape. We were not investigating the absolute accuracy of discrimination of areas, nor yet the relation of this to the magnitude of the area; consequently any errors due to the method of obtaining the different areas may be neglected. The probable and constant errors given in the tables are, of course, in millimeters. They were obtained, as in other experiments, by the method of right and wrong cases, from the percentage of right answers in a hundred experiments. In these experiments the area is considered the stimulus, S, and the increment Δ, is the difference between the area of the standard, 100 or 800 mm., and that of the area to be compared. The magnitude of the increment is obtained by the equation,

$$\Delta = \pi (r^2 - r_1^2,) = \pi (r + r_1,) (r - r_1,),$$

in which r and r_1 are the radii of the bases. The first of the two tables gives the results for three observers, the smaller area being used. The second table gives corresponding results for the larger area. But 100 experiments were made upon N. F. and W. for each of the probable errors calculated. The probable errors for L. S., however, are each calculated from the results of 300 experiments.

Area, 100 mm.

Weight.	Probable Error.			
	L. S.	N. F.	W.	Av.
200 g.	43	40	21	31
800 g.	31[1]	—	47	39

Area, 800 mm.

| 200 g. | 73 | 47 | 41 | 53 |
| 800 g. | 91[1] | 70 | 69 | 73 |

[1] A weight of 1000 g., instead of 800 g., was used in experiments on L. S.

The figures above given show that the discrimination for areas is not as accurate for the high intensity, the probable errors for 800 g. being in four cases out of five much greater than for 200 g. The one exception appears in the experiments on L. S. for the smaller area. In conducting these experiments, however, it was found that the accuracy of discrimination for 800 g. increased to such an extent from practice that the variable area had to be changed in order that the increment might not be too great for accurate calculation of the probable error. In the first few experiments made, then, the accuracy of discrimination was undoubtedly much less for 800 g. than for 200 g. There was, however, no appreciable improvement from practice after thirty or forty experiments. The apparent exception, therefore, partially confirms the results obtained for the other observers.

If we compare the second table with the first, we note that the probable error for the larger area, although appreciably greater, does not increase in proportion to the areas. It is possible that in these experiments what is really discriminated is the linear relation, that is, the relative diameters of the circles. This is, however, not probable; for the difference felt seems to be a qualitative difference in the sensations from which that of space is inferred. The change in sensation corresponding to change in the area of stimulation might, indeed, be supposed to be merely a quantitative change in extensity. But the great difficulty observers have of comparing intensities of different areas confirms the results of the writer's introspection, that this change in sensation is not primarily a spatial change.

CHAPTER VII.

THE TIME OF STIMULATION.

SEC. 1. *The Intensity of Haptic Sensations in Relation to the Time: Low Intensities.*

The intensity of visual and temperature sensations is clearly related to the time of stimulation. But if a weight of low intensity, and of not too small an area, be applied to the skin, the resulting sensation will continue but a few seconds, and will not increase, as might be expected, with the time of application. It is largely on this principle that the phenomena of gaseous and liquid pressure may be explained. The pressure of the atmosphere is fairly constant, and is, therefore, not perceived. Meissner observed that melted wax allowed to harden on the hand had no sensory effect, although his explanation is different from that here given. When the hand is plunged in mercury and held in the same position, the pressure remains constant, and it is only when the hand is moved that the pressure sensation is distinct.[1] Hall and Motora found, contrary to what we might expect, that the discrimination of gradual pressure change was best for the slowest rate of change of stimulus that was used, $\frac{1}{110}$ of the stimulus per second.[2] In these experiments the observer had first to decide whether the stimulus was increasing or decreasing; and it is probable that, as suggested by the writers, the cause of the decrease in the accuracy of discrimination was the distracting effect of sudden changes upon the attention, and consequently upon the accuracy of perception.

We intended to make experiments on judgments of intensity in relation to the time of stimulation, but the appa-

[1] *Cf.* Meissner, *op. cit.*
[2] Hall and Motora, *Am. Journ. Psy.*, I, 87.

rent impossibility of eliminating the error arising from memory of the standard stimulus led us to confine ourselves to qualitative observations. We did, however, make experiments on the intensive effect of the time for stimuli of such low intensity as to be perceived with difficulty. The instrument used was that already described, by which pressure was exerted by the hand of the experimenter.[1] There was no means of regulating the rate of application of the pressure except the judgment of the experimenter, and the results must therefore be considered as inexact. The experimenter practised himself in increasing the pressure at such a rate that it took 8–10 sec. to reach a pressure of .4 g. In like manner a time of 1–2 sec. was obtained. The third time of application was the shortest, $\frac{1}{4}-\frac{1}{3}$ sec., the increase being as rapid as was consistent with accuracy. The rates of increase were, therefore, .05–.04 g., .4–.2 g. and 2.3–1.6 g. per sec. The maximum pressure, .4 g., was, of course, kept fairly constant. Fifty experiments were made for each rate by the writer on S. F., and as many by S. F. on the writer. In the tables below are the percentages of times the stimulus .4 g. was perceived at the different rates of increase.

		.05–.04 g. per sec.	.4–.2 g. per sec.	2.3–1.6 g. per sec.
S. F.	- -	10%	34%	82%
G.	- -	2%	30%	82%
Av.	- -	6%	32%	82%

From these results it is evident that the sensory effect of pressure stimuli increases with the rate of application. This is what we should expect on the assumption that the intensity of pressure sensations decreases rapidly with the time of application.

As for the theoretic interpretation of these results, we judge them corroborative of the movement theory of dermal stimulation. The stimulus is not to be considered mere pressure, but the energy expended upon the dermal tissues. From this point of view we are not justified in identifying the time of application of a pressure stimulus with the time

[1] See Chap. II, Sec. 3.

of actual stimulation. If a vibrating tuning-fork of sufficient amplitude to cause a distinct sensation be placed in contact with the skin, there is continued intermittent stimulation, and the sensation does not decrease as when a pressure stimulus is applied. The intermittent process of stimulation by the tuning-fork is similar to that of visual and auditory stimulation, for the physical stimuli are successive transformations of energy.

The time phenomena of pressure stimulation may also be brought under the general law that it is not static conditions, but changes in the environment that give rise to the 'nervous shock' of Spencerian psychology. It is such conditions of the environment that the organism needs to perceive in order to coördinate its motor activities for purposes of self-preservation and reproduction. The cataplectic shock so frequently experienced when one is unexpectedly addressed, shows how sensitive the central nervous system is to sudden peripheral changes. But we need not depend only upon observation for proofs of this principle. It is well known that motion on the skin may be perceived within the circumference of Weber's sensor circles; and Hall and Donaldson found that the perception of motion is independent of direction, and is clearest immediately after the motion begins.[1] In fact, the time phenomena of dermal sensations point clearly to the difference theory of sensation, according to which change in the objective environment and in the subjective mind is the *sine qua non* of sensation.[2] The psychological generalization has, moreover, a demonstrable physiological basis. Only on making or breaking an electric circuit is a motor nerve stimulated. More closely bearing on our problem are the experiments of Fontana, who found that pressure could be applied so gradually as to kill a motor nerve without inducing muscular contraction. Similar results have been obtained for temperature stimuli.[3]

[1] Hall and Donaldson, *Mind*, X, 556.
[2] Cf. Höffding, *op. cit.*, 138, 141 ; Dessoir, *op. cit.*, 188.
[3] Heinzmann, *Archiv. für gesammte Physiol.*, VI, 222.

SEC. 2. *High Intensities.*

When stimuli beyond a certain intensity are applied, the phenomena are quite different. If a kilogram weight be placed on the hand, the intensity of the sensation seems gradually to increase and to pass into pain. Müller observed that a sensation of pricking and of having a limb 'asleep' could be caused by long-continued pressure stimulation.[1] Similar observations on temperature stimuli were made by Weber. Thus it appears that heterogeneous sensations may be caused by variations in the time of application of dermal stimuli.

For the purpose of investigating the relation between the time of pressure causing pain and the intensive pain threshold, weights of different magnitudes were placed in a balance pan so as to act on a constant area of the palm of the hand, and the time was noted which elapsed before the appearance of pain. To the under side of the balance pan a wooden piece was fastened, the circular end of which, 1.5 mm. in diameter, came in contact with the palm of the hand. The longer times were recorded by a watch, and the shorter times by the Hipp chronoscope, a Morse key being so placed that the observer could close the circuit as he applied the weight without appreciable error. The place of stimulation was varied within a radius of about 1 cm.; otherwise there would have been danger of alterations in the condition of the skin at the place of stimulation as the experiments progressed. Ten experiments were made for each weight on two observers, S. F. and the writer.[2] But one experiment for a given weight was made on any one day, and not more than three or four times a week were these experiments made. The order of half of the experiments was the reverse of that of the other half. The figures below indicate the time in seconds for the various stimuli to cause pain. Only the averages are given, together with their probable errors.

[1] Quoted by Weber, *op. cit.*
[2] Experiments were begun on another observer, but were not completed. It was evident, however, that results would have been obtained similar to those obtained for G. and S. F.

Observer.	100 g.	200 g.	300 g.	500 g.
S. F. . . .	294 ± 30.	37 ± 3.6	8. ± .9	3.3 ± .2
G. . . .	167 ± 17.	34 ± 2.7	12 ± 1.5	6. ± .06

The results shown above are represented graphically in the accompanying curves.

FIGURE 9.

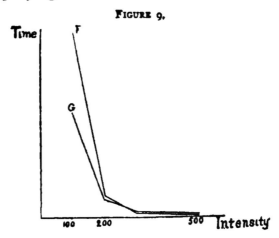

The experiments prove beyond question that the pain threshold is functionally related to the time as well as the intensity of stimulation. The results obtained are not sufficiently exact to admit of an analytical expression. It appears that the time curve approaches O as its limit for high intensities, and that for low intensities it either increases indefinitely or approaches as its limit an asympotic line parallel to the axis T. That the ascending branch does approach a limit is evident from introspective observation. Weights of low intensities soon cease to be perceptible, and never become painful. Thus the clothing we wear exerts continual pressure, but is never painful. The curves obtained may be said, therefore, to resemble rectangular hyperbolas. If the relation between the time and intensity causing pain could be thus represented, it would be expressed analytically by the equation,

$$(I—b) \, T = k,$$

in which h is a constant, being the intensity below which stimuli are never painful. To obtain the relation between the time and intensity having equal intensive effects as the sensation increases in intensity, we can substitute in the above equation the reciprocal of T, since the intensive effect would of course decrease as the threshold increases. We then have,

$$T = \frac{I}{k} - \frac{h}{k}.$$

From this equation, that of a straight line, we see that as regards their intensive effect on pain sensations, the intensity and time of the stimulus increase in direct proportion.

A striking feature of the above experiments is the great variation in the time before the pain appears. This is, however, only partially a true variation. It is generally difficult to decide, especially for low intensities, when the stimulus becomes painful. This is quite the contrary of what we found to be the case when the intensive threshold was being determined. There is, however, no constancy even in the manner of variation. At times for the 100 g. stimulus the pain would come very suddenly, only to cease and reappear, but generally the appearance of pain was very gradual. The sensation seemed to increase in intensity before the pain was distinctly felt. In the experiments on 100 g. a latent period seemed to elapse before any appreciable increase in intensity began. This latent period for S. F. seemed to be on the average about half of the total time. The two observers disagreed as to whether there was any appreciable decrease in intensity before the increase began.

We are not justified in assuming that the relation between the time of pressure and the intensity of pain holds also for pressure sensations. The gradual appearance of the dermal pain, preceded by an apparent increase of pressure intensity, undoubtedly points to such a conclusion. But the results admit of another interpretation. It is quite possible that the mind confuses the incipient pain with the pressure sensation. As we know dermal pain to be related to the intensity of the stimulus, and as we are not accustomed to think so much of the time as a factor, it is but natural that we should judge the change in sensation to be due to more intense stimulation. We should then consider this change an intensive change, until the painful element became so clear as to be distinct in consciousness. That it *is* difficult to distinguish heterogeneous sensations of very low intensity is shown by the experiments of Wunderli.[1]

Moreover, our experiments are, we think, corroborative of the theory that sensations of pain and pressure are utterly disparate. For, otherwise, how could we explain the fact that the intensity of pain increases with the time, whereas the intensity of pressure sensations, at least for low intensities, decreases rapidly with the time ? Equally difficult to account for on the algedonic tone theory is the continuation of the pain after the cessation of stimulation, which was very marked for 100 g.

But if pain be a distinct sensation, with a distinct physical basis, the results are quite intelligible. From this point of view, we can understand how pressure without appreciable transformation of energy can be considered a stimulus to pain. Unlike haptic sensations proper, dermal pain furnishes the sensory data for perceptions, not of the objective environment, but of the subjective self; and may, therefore, be induced by any stimulus of sufficient intensity. This view finds further support in teleological considerations. If pain exist for the purpose of warning the higher centres of injury done to the tissues, the intensity of pain would, we should expect, be related to the time of pressure; for the longer the time of pressure the greater the resultant injury to the tissues.

[1] See Ch. I, Sec. 2.

SUMMARY.

We shall now present a brief summary of the more important results of the investigations described in the preceding pages.

A.—EXPERIMENTAL.

1. Hot and cold stimuli are overestimated for low intensities, but not for high intensities.
2. The estimate of the intensity of haptic stimuli increases for low intensities much more slowly than the stimulus; but as the stimulus approaches the pain threshold, the estimate of intensity increases much faster.
3. The intensive pain threshold, for pressure acting on .5 cm. of the hand, varies greatly with individuals, the average being 5400 g. Age and sex appear to have less effect than individual differences.
4. The average value of the least perceptible pressure acting on an area of .9 cm., the rate of increase being about .3 g. per sec., was 1.9 g. for S. F. and 2.6 g. for G. The intensive range of haptic sensations for these observers, as based upon these measurements, was about 1700.
5. Weber's law holds approximately for weights greater than 100 to 500 g. For low intensities the probable error increases much more slowly than the stimulus.
6. The average value of the ratio of the probable error to the stimulus for stimuli of from 100 g. to 3000 g. is $\frac{1}{5}$.

7. The constant error is frequently very great for pressure stimuli. It increases with the stimulus, but the relation is complex, and is subject to great individual variations. Some observers have no constant error except for stimuli of very great intensity. The constant error is more variable than the probable error. Its magnitude seems inversely related to the accuracy of discrimination. A great constant error for pressure does not necessitate one for lifted weights.

8. The degree of confidence in the perception of intensive differences varies greatly for individuals, the proportion of wrong judgments of which observers were confident ranging from $\frac{1}{4}$ to $\frac{1}{30}$. The probability of correctness when confident was for most observers from .8 to .9. There is no relation between either of these quantities and the accuracy of discrimination. The percentage of correct guesses varied from 52% to 70%, the average being 59%.

9. The accuracy of discrimination for weights of 100 g. or more is, on the average, not appreciably different for the palm of the hand, the back of the hand and the volar surface of the index finger. For 5–7 g. the accuracy of discrimination, as found from one observer, for the palm of the hand and the back of the forearm, is less than for the index finger, but improves greatly by practice.

10. Stimuli of low intensity placed on the forearm, are judged lighter than when placed on the palm of the hand or the index finger.

11. The pain threshold for pressure varies with the place of stimulation, being greatest where the skin is thick and separated from the bone by muscular tissues. The temporal region of the head is the most sensitive, and the palm of the hand, the thigh, and the heel, are among the least sensitive parts.

12. Weights of .01 g. are about as easily perceived when impact is not entirely excluded, as weights of .4 g. when pressure only is applied, the time of application being 1–2 sec.

13. The pain threshold for impact stimuli is determined by the product of the mass and the square of the velocity.

14. In judgments of the intensity of impact stimuli the mass has in general more effect than the square of the velocity, but less than the velocity.

15. Differences in velocity are perceived, on the whole, more accurately than differences in mass, but much less accurately than differences in the square of velocity. Individuals differ greatly, however.

16. The discrimination for moving weights is about the same as for weights applied without appreciable impact.

17. The area of stimulation does not, on the whole, affect the accuracy of discrimination for weights. But individual peculiarities appear in the results obtained.

18. Pressure stimuli of small area are generally overestimated. The extent of overestimation of intensity for an area $\frac{1}{4}$ of 8 cm. was on the average $\frac{1}{3}$.

19. The probability that a stimulus of very low intensity will be perceived is inversely related to the area of stimulation.

20. The pain threshold increases with the area of stimulation in approximately a logarithmic proportion,

21. The discrimination of areas is much better for stimuli of 200 g. than for stimuli of 800 g.

22. The relative accuracy of discrimination for areas is not constant, but is greater for large areas.

23. The probability that pressure stimuli of very low intensity will be perceived increases with the rate of increase of the stimulus.

24. The relation between the time and intensity threshold of pain is approximately expressed by an hyper-

bolic curve. The appearance of pain as the time of stimulation is increased, is generally very gradual and difficult to determine. There is an intensive limit below which stimuli never cause pain.

B.—Theoretical.

1. There is no basis for the alleged identity of haptic and temperature sensations.

2. Pain, tickle and pressure sensations are heterogeneous sensations induced by quantitative changes in the intensity of the stimulus. Dermal pain itself is probably a sensation and not merely an intensive form of the algedonic tone.

3. Touch and pressure sensations are qualitatively the same. The apparent difference between them is really one of perceptive processes.

4. The so-called threshold is not a true quantity. This may be shown by the same arguments that are applied to the so-called least noticeable difference.

5. If the estimate of the intensity of the stimulus may be considered as indicative of a corresponding increase in the intensity of sensation, this quantity increases much more slowly than the stimulus. The apparent rapid increase for very high intensities may be due to perceptive processes and not be a true increase in sensation.

6. The variation of the probable and constant errors renders inexact the use of the probability integral in the method of right and wrong cases.

7. The variations in the confidence of observers and in the percentage of right cases in guessing, goes to prove that there is no such quantity as a least noticeable difference.

8. The accuracy of discrimination is in general probably independent of the place of stimulation, except for very low intensities, which have less intensive effect at some places than at others. Practice seems to aid the discrimination at places not accustomed to pressure stimuli.

9. The intensive effect of impact stimuli for pain is equally dependent upon the mass and the square of the velocity. The intensive effect for such stimuli causing only impact sensations apparently increases faster for the velocity than the mass, but more slowly for the square of velocity than for the mass. If this be true, the stimulus for impact sensations is different from that for pain sensations, the stimulus for pain being mv^2 and that for impact sensations being mv^k, in which k is somewhat greater than unity, and possibly subject to individual variations.

10. The intensity of dermal sensations, is inversely related to the area of stimulation. If we assume any of the psycho-physical laws deduced, the intensity of the sensation increases much more slowly than the reciprocal of the logarithm of the area.

11. The intensive effect of the area may be explained by the probable physiological process of stimulation, the effect upon the sensory nerves being dependent upon the energy expended upon the surrounding tissues. The stimulus in pressure sensations is not to be considered the force applied, but the work done by this force, or more strictly the energy lost by the mass applied.

12. The intensity of pressure sensations decreases for low intensities with the time of pressure. For high intensities causing pain, the intensity of the sensation of pain increases with the time of pressure. The relation of the intensive effects of the time and that of the intensity of stimulation for pain sensations is probably that of a direct proportion.

13. The time phenomena of dermal stimulation support the theory advanced as to the process of stimulation. They also tend to show that dermal pain is a distinct sensation.

Monograph Supplement.   No. 2.   February, 1896.

THE
Psychological Review

EDITED BY

J. McKEEN CATTELL   J. MARK BALDWIN
COLUMBIA COLLEGE   AND   PRINCETON UNIVERSITY

WITH THE CO-OPERATION OF

ALFRED BINET, ÉCOLE DES HAUTES-ÉTUDES, PARIS; JOHN DEWEY, UNIVERSITY OF
CHICAGO; H. H. DONALDSON, UNIVERSITY OF CHICAGO; G. S. FULLERTON,
UNIVERSITY OF PENNSYLVANIA; WILLIAM JAMES, HARVARD UNIVERSITY;
JOSEPH JASTROW, UNIVERSITY OF WISCONSIN; G. T. LADD, YALE
UNIVERSITY; HUGO MÜNSTERBERG, HARVARD UNIVERSITY;
M. ALLEN STARR, COLLEGE OF PHYSICIANS AND SURGEONS,
NEW YORK; CARL STUMPF, UNIVERSITY, BERLIN;
JAMES SULLY, UNIVERSITY COLLEGE, LONDON.

ASSOCIATION.

AN ESSAY ANALYTIC AND EXPERIMENTAL.

BY

MARY WHITON CALKINS.

PUBLISHED BI-MONTHLY BY

MACMILLAN AND CO.,

66 FIFTH AVENUE, NEW YORK; AND LONDON.

PREFATORY NOTE.

The tables and most of the text of Part II. of this monograph are reprinted from the PSYCHOLOGICAL REVIEW of January, 1896. The additions, of which some are quotations from an article in the REVIEW of January, 1895, include comments and statements of detail, so that the record in its present form is the only complete report of the experiments described. Some of the conclusions reached by the analysis attempted in Part I. were formulated in a paper printed in the *Philosophical Review* of June, 1892, but the present discussion is an independent one.

The writer takes this occasion to acknowledge gratefully the inspiration and direction in psychological study, received from her teachers and friends, Professors Hugo Münsterberg and William James, of Harvard University, and Professor Edmund C. Sanford, of Clark University.

WELLESLEY COLLEGE, January, 1896.

SUMMARY OF CONTENTS.

PART I.

THE NATURE OF ASSOCIATION.

I. PRELIMINARY ANALYSIS.   PAGE
    a. *Provisional Definition*............................... 1

Association is the observable connection between succeeding objects or elements of consciousness of which the second is not an object of perception.

    b. *The Associationist and the Spiritualist theory of Association*....................................... 2

Association is neither a 'psychic force' nor an 'activity of the self.'

II. DETAILED ANALYSIS.
    a. *Assumed identity of the associated objects with connected past objects of consciousness.* 5

Association can be psychologically 'accounted for,' only in that its terms are assumed to be identical with continuous past objects of consciousness.

    b. *The implication of 'assumed identity.'*.................. 10

Both the Spiritualist and the Associationist theory are more than psychological; and the latter is, besides, metaphysically invalid.

    c. *Discussion of 'association by similarity' and 'by contiguity.'*.. 12

'Association by Similarity' is reducible to 'Association by Contiguity'; but both terms are misleading.

III. THE CLASSIFICATION OF CASES OF ASSOCIATION.
    a. *Total, partial and focalized association*................... 15

Cases of association are best distinguished according as the first term is a concrete whole; or a group of persisting elements of such a whole; or a single persisting element.

b. *Simultaneous Association*..................................... 19

> Cases of simultaneous association are those of the reflectively-observed connection of the parts of total objects of consciousness, when there has been no re-membered succession.

c. *So-called Voluntary Association*............................ 21

> ' Voluntary Association' is really no form of association.

IV. A MODERN FORM OF ASSOCIATION BY SIMILARITY.

a. *The sequence upon a percept of images like itself is not association*.. 22

b. *The Associationist argument for this so-called ' associ-ation.'*... 24

> The Associationist theory of revivable images is un-true to fact and metaphysically invalid.

c. *Höffding's theory of this so-called ' association' (or ' assimilation.')* 25

1. *The possibility of ' immediate recognition.'*............. 25

> Immediate recognition may occur.

2. *The relation of this so-called association to imme-diate recognition.....* 27

> Immediate recognition neither requires nor admits this so-called association as explanation.

V. THE PHYSIOLOGICAL EXPLANATION OF ASSOCIATION.   32

> The physiological explanation of association, through habitual connection between brain-tracts and between sensory and motor activities, must not be confused with the psychological analysis.

PART II.

EXPERIMENTAL INVESTIGATION OF CONDITIONS OF SUGGESTI-BILITY.

INTRODUCTION.

Classification of cases of suggestiveness and of sug-gestibility.. 35

I. SIMPLE SERIES.

a. *Visual series.*

1. *Successive arrangement*.................................... 37

The 'frequent' numeral is remembered in 63.7 % of the possible cases... 40

The 'vivid' numeral is remembered in 52.2 % of the possible cases.. 43

The 'recent' numeral is remembered in 53.7 % of possible cases............................ 44

2. *Simultaneous arrangement*................................. 46

    The results are parallel with those of the 'successive' experiments.

b. *Auditory series.*

    The 'frequent' numeral is remembered in 80 % of the cases.. 48

    The 'vivid' numeral is remembered in 56.5 % of the cases.. 49

    The 'recent' numeral is remembered in 82.5 % of the cases.. 50

II. Comparative Series... 51

    The 'frequent' numeral is associated more often than by

    The 'vivid' by 19.7 % of the cases........ 52

    The 'recent' by 7.6 of the cases...................... 54

    The 'vivid' numeral is associated more often than the 'recent' by 10.5 % of the cases.................... 54

ASSOCIATION.

PART I.

THE NATURE OF ASSOCIATION.

I. Preliminary Analysis.

a. Provisional Definition.

Association may be provisionally defined as the observable connection between successive objects or partial objects of consciousness, of which the second is not an object of perception. The expression 'object of consciousness' is proposed as an equivalent for that most useful term of the Germans, *Vorstellung*. It is used in order to avoid the inadequacy of the statement, 'association is of things, not thoughts,'[1] which is open to misrepresentation as a theory of extra-mental connection, and which, besides, leaves out of account the cases in which sense qualities, not concrete things, are the associated terms; like the expression 'association of ideas' it also ignores the possibility clearly shown by experiments in free association,[2] that the factors of an associative series may be emotions or motor impulses. The condition that the second object of consciousness shall be representation, not percept, excludes from association not only the sequence of one percept upon another, or the intrusion of a presentation upon a train of thought, but also that combination of several present sense qualities into an object which Wundt[3] calls fusion (*Verschmelzung*) and incorrectly enumerates under the head of association.

This definition may stand as the starting point of discussion because it assumes no more than everybody grants, so that every

---

[1] Cf. James, *Principles of Psychology* I., p. 554.
[2] Cf. Scripture, *Vorstellung und Gefühl.* Philos. Stud., 1890.
[3] *Grundzüge der physiologischen Psychologie* 4ᵗᵉ Aufl. II., p. 437.

other definition merely supplements without supplanting it. As a matter of fact, writers of the two schools—the Spiritualist and the Associationist—which hold a different theory of association, often define it in exactly these terms. So Wundt says: "Association is the connection of one object of consciousness with a preceding memory-image or sense impression."[1] And, on the other side, Hobbes may be supposed to have this meaning, when he says of the 'consequence or trayn of thoughts,'[2] that "when a man thinketh on anything whatsoever his next thought after is not altogether so casual as it seems to be;" Hume embodies this view, in describing association[3] as 'a connection between the different thoughts and ideas of the mind;' and James Mill expressly repudiates the more dynamic theory in the words:[4] "In successive order of ideas that which precedes is sometimes called the suggesting, that which succeeds the suggested idea; not that any power is supposed to reside in the antecedent over the consequent; [the words] mean only antecedent and consequent with the additional idea that such order is not casual but to a degree permanent."

b. The Associationist and the Spiritualist theory of association.

But from this safe and simple recognition of association as the observable connection of facts of consciousness, the Associationists pass swiftly to the unwarrantable assertion that association is the complete explanation, and the adequate philosophy of psychic phenomena. "Every mental affection and operation," Priestley says,[5] "are but different modes or cases of the association of ideas." Here association is evidently something more than phenomenal, and turns out to be a force, or power, belonging to the facts of consciousness, or ideas, by virtue of which they associate each other. So Hume[6] calls association a 'gentle force' as well as 'a principle of connection.' Hartley

---

[1] *op. cit.*, II., p. 453. "Die Association ist [der] Zusammenhang einer Vorstellung mit einem vorausgegangenen Erinnerungsbild oder Sinneseindruck."

[2] *Leviathan*, Part I., c. 3.

[3] *Essay*, Section III.

[4] *Analysis of the Phenomena of Human Mind*, ed. by J. S. Mill, p. 81.

[5] In *Essay II.* of Introduction to Priestley's edition of Hartley.

[6] *Treatise*, Sect. IV.

says :[1] "Any sensations, A, B, C, by being associated with one another a sufficient number of times, get such a power over the corresponding ideas, a, b and c, etc., that any one of the sensations, A when impressed alone shall be able to excite in the mind b, c, etc., the Ideas of the Rest." Spencer repeats in slightly varying form the statement,[2] " each feeling as it arises associates itself instantly not with its class only, but with its sub-class."

The underlying dogma of this conception of association as a force or function of ideas, is a theory of ideas which makes of them single, psychic entities or realities, soul-things, as it were, each with an independent existence of its own, each possessing a mysterious force, called association, by which to summon others to its side. In this view, indeed, as Lehmann says, ideas become " glatte Atome, mit Haken angestaltet so dass sie sich einander einheften können."

Now the relative independence of mental phenomena is a necessary hypothesis of psychological investigation, for psychical facts must be studied as if ultimate, must be abstracted from all implications of a deeper reality and must be correlated with definable physical and physiological facts. Such independent ideas, are, however, mere abstractions, corresponding with no reality directly known, but inferred for purposes of scientific or metaphysical utility. And the Associationist theory, since it gains all its persuasiveness by just this assumption, that we are immediately aware of independent ' ideas,' is obviously a metaphysical hypothesis masquerading as a description of phenomena.

The simple definition of association is abandoned also, by writers quite antagonistic to Associationist doctrine. Their conception, too, is a dynamic one; they describe association as a ' process,'[3] an ' activity,'[4] ' eine unterstützende Funktion,'[5] ' eine zusammen-fassende, vereinende Thätigkeit.'[6] This doc-

[1] *Observations on Man*, Sect. II., Prop. X.
[2] *Principles of Psychology*, I. p. 254.
[3] Murray, *Psychology*, p. 75 (cf. Dewey, *Psychology*, and Höffding, *Vierteljahrschrift für Wissenschaftliche Philosophie*, XIV., p. 204).
[4] Dewey, *Psychology*, p. 92.
[5] Wundt, *op. cit.*, II., p. 457.
[6] Höffding, *op. cit.*, p. 190.

trine of association as process is opposed, as we have seen, to the teaching of the English school, in that it conceives of association as a function of a self, rather than as a sort of psychic energy inherent in primarily unrelated elements. Höffding, to be sure, with his definition of association as ' comprehending, unifying activity,' purports to oppose not merely the atomistic conception, but also the spiritualistic tendency to distinguish between association and a higher activity. He ends, however, by identifying, almost explicitly, association and thought, concluding that there is ' no reason to assume a thought capacity entirely distinct from the association capacity.'[1] Virtually, therefore, so far from opposing the spiritualist theory he adopts it, pointing out, with admirable insight, that it has no room for any real distinction of thought from association.

But to the ordinary consciousness, association means something other than thought or unifying activity. The bare observation that objects of consciousness are connected is not a consciousness of a process which connects them. Therefore simplicity, at least, and conformity with the admitted phenomena are gained by rejecting altogether expressions with such dynamical, and therefore either realistic or else idealistic, implications as ' process,' ' force' or ' activity.'

The objection to this spiritualist interpretation of the nature of association is by no means a denial of the totality underlying the manifold facts of consciousness, or a rejection of the doctrine of the unity of self-consciousness. On the other hand, such a totality and such a continuous self seem to the writer to be an inevitable presupposition of psychic phenomena of every kind. But the identification of this unity with association is a manifestation of an unhappy passion for simplicity at all hazards. In the rigid resolve not to multiply realities *praeter necessitatem,* Occam's razor has cut too deeply, and real distinctions have been ruthlessly pruned away. The term association has been wrested from its present use as description of a perfectly obvious, even if psychologically inexplicable, relation of conscious elements, and has been freighted with a weight of epistemological truth which it cannot carry. What we mean

[1] Höffding, *op. cit.*, XIV.

by association is just a certain observable connection between contents of consciousness. When we begin to reflect upon the implications of this connection then indeed we find ourselves driven to the presupposition of this ' higher unity ' of the self, but the reflection leads us at once from the matter-of-fact plane of psychology, into the domain of metaphysics. Höffding, though he usually treats the subject, as has been said, from the spiritualistic standpoint, in one interesting passage correctly formulates the relation of association to the activity of the self : ' Die Einheit des Bewusstsein's,' he says, ' [ist] gerade eine Voraussetzung aller Association.'

This examination of the two theories, which propose in place of the simple description of association a deeper analysis of its nature, has therefore verified the provisional definition by showing in the one case an unwarrantable metaphysical assumption, and in the other a needless confusion of the philosophical with the scientific point of view.

II. Detailed Analysis of Association.

a. *Assumed identity of the associated objects with connected past objects of consciousness.*

Granting, then, that association is an observable connection between contents of consciousness, the question rises whether this connection may not be more closely described. One does in fact, account for any given case of association by referring to the connection in actual past experience of certain objects of consciousness with which the associated objects are assumed to be respectively identical. If, for instance, a vivid image of a temple in Olympia follows upon the glimpse, to-day, of a friend's face in a crowd, I explain this as due to the fact that I once saw her standing at the eastern porch of the Heraion. One recognizes at once that this is no chance relation, but rather an essential feature of admitted cases of association. A presentation-sequence of percept upon percept, or of percept upon image, does not at all require us to assume this parallel sequence in the past : a steam whistle may interrupt my revery without requiring me to suppose that the same interruption ever before occurred, or I may have a first experience of out-of-door roses in winter; but an object of imagination can not be associated with another, unless in my immediate, perceptual experience, such a sequence has before occurred. It is true that this is not in any ultimate sense an explanation of association; the concurrence of past objects of consciousness—the percept of friend and of temple, for instance—does not necessarily involve a present connection of percept and image; but unquestionably the nature of associated connection is described by this reference to the connection in experience of these past objects.

It is not, however, evident without further investigation, that this description applies to every sort of association; indeed, at first sight it seems to leave one class of cases out of account. To test its adequacy, therefore, a preliminary classification is necessary, and the most obvious, every-day distinction is that between similarity association, better named intrinsic, and contiguity, or extrinsic,[1] association. Certain objects or events which are associated are connected in what we call their essential or inner nature, others are externally or accidentally related. Between 'love' and the 'star to every wandering bark' there is a more intimate relation than between the star and the sky; between Daniel Deronda and Michael Angelo's David there is a subtler connection than that between the words and the paper on which they are written, or than that between the marble and the chisel. Now the external sort of association is evidently described and explained as fully as possible by the reference to the past, related objects of experience. The connection between a present, psychic phenomenon (X or x) and that which follows it (y)—for instance, between the sight of a volume of Wundt's *Philosophische Studien* and the image of the library shelf on which it belongs, is simply the relation implied in the fact that these objects of consciousness are 'the same' as former ones, X^n and Y^n, which were successive or coexistent. That is, in this supposed case, the association implies that I had seen the *Studien* on the shelf.

[1] Wundt's terms, *op. cit.* II., p. 455.

The relation may be symbolized thus:

$$\begin{array}{cc} X^a & Y^a \\ | & | \\ x & <\!\!-\!\!>y \end{array}$$

Here the small letter represents an image, the capitals stand for percept or image, and the indexes refer to past time.

But suppose instead, that Höffding's article at which the volume lies open reminds me of the figure of St. George in Raphael's picture. Now I have certainly had no simultaneous or immediately successive experience of the book and the painting, so that at first blush this seems to be a case of association which cannot be described by an assumed identity of the connected terms with past objects of consciousness occurring together. This case, therefore, must be carefully analyzed. The connection between the sight of the psychological essay and the following image of the pictured warrior is, evidently, the polemic attitude of both. But this observed hostility is an element of the earlier object of consciousness persisting in the later. None of the other qualities of the printed article—its material, its form, its technical statements—have any connection whatever with the picture; the element of hostility in the essay is not associated with anything in the picture, for it is itself one of the factors of the picture; in fine, the only association involved is that between the element 'hostility,' on the one hand, common both to essay and to picture, and on the other the remaining qualities of the picture, its material, color and form. Compared with the other instance, the characteristic feature of this one is readily seen to be the narrow starting point of the association. There, the connection was between the sight of a concrete thing, a book, and an image of its environment; here, the first of the associated terms is a single, highly abstract quality; and the connection is between this quality (hostility, X) and the sum of the remaining qualities which make up the complex object of consciousness, a picture ($y = m + n + o$). Or, to illustrate by a concreter example: If a pair of new shoes reminds me of a hand organ, the association is *not* between shoes and hand organ as total complex objects, but between the inexorable squeak, common to both instruments of torture, and the other qualities of the hand organ. In symbolic terms once more, the object of consciousness WX is followed by Xy; the formula in full is somewhat as follows:

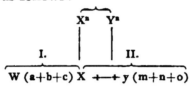

$$X^n \quad Y^n$$

$$\text{I.} \qquad \qquad \text{II.}$$

$$W\,(a+b+c)\,X \longleftrightarrow y\,(m+n+o)$$

Here the Roman numerals, I. and II., represent the present total objects of consciousness, that is, in this case (if we ignore the environment to which attention is not directed),[1] the shoes and the hand organ. X is one quality (the squeak) of the percept I., while the other qualities, color, shape, texture (a, b, c), which have no part in the association, are grouped together and represented by the letter W. But the perceived quality X, the squeak, is also a part of the second complex object of consciousness (II., the hand organ), that is, X is connected with the imagined qualities of the hand organ, the shape, color, surface, (m, n, o, grouped together under y). This intrinsic association really then consists in the connection of one quality with a group of qualities, and it proves to be perfectly parallel with extrinsic association, and describable by reference to connected past elements of objects of consciousness. I account for the fact that squeaky shoes remind me of a hand organ by the fact that I have had previous experience of a hand organ, that is of the connection of squeakiness with the remaining qualities of the hand organ; in other words, the X^n and the Y^n with which the X and the y are assumed to be identical have coexisted before in my experience.

Not only is this a possible explanation of such cases of association, but it is the only consistent one. This is shown by consideration of the alternatives. According to the ordinary view, the earlier concrete object of consciousness is associated as a whole with a later concrete object. But this is impossible here, for most of the elements of the earlier object, in this case the shoes, have nothing to do with the later object, the hand organ, and in themselves would never have suggested it.

[1] The braces ⌒ mark the union of qualities into concrete wholes; the indexes mark the past objects of consciousness, with which the associated terms are parallel.

More plausibly, it is urged that the connecting element is slightly different in the two objects associated. That is, squeakiness in the boots is different from squeakiness in the hand organ, and the association is between these two. But, unless one can disprove the ordinary conception of similarity as presence of identical elements, the supposition that there are two sorts of squeakiness indicates simply that these have a common element which is then the first term of the association, so that boots and hand organ have a more subtle connection than we have supposed. In this way Höffding's chief argument against the theory of persisting elements may be met. He calls attention to the fact that sensations, which are recognized, he says, as unanalyzable units of consciousness are nevertheless similar and so suggest each other. "Yellow and orange", he says, "have no common element and yet recall each other."[1] But it is incorrect to assert that any given sensations are absolutely ultimate. The existence of such *unanalyzable* elements is a convenient postulate of psychological science, but the name sensation is given to certain merely *unanalyzed* partial contents of our consciousness, and nothing forbids the assumption of unnamed elements even more simple than some of these.

Höffding objects, in the second place, to the theory of persistence of elements, that it renews the old realistic abstraction fallacy. The thinness common to the leaf on the tree and the leaf of paper is no identical element of the two, because thinness in and for itself does not exist.[2] This objection, however, clearly reveals Höffding's misunderstanding of the theory; the element, or elements, forming the first term of such an association are not regarded as 'independent middle terms,' or as qualities existing in and for themselves. For purposes of discussion only, they are treated as if they possessed this fictitious

[1] *Op. cit.* XIV., p. 161. "Gelb und Orange, oder die verschiedenen Nuancen des Roth haben kein gemeinschaftliches Element und doch erinneren sie an einander."

[2] *op. cit.* p. 168. "Zwischen diesen beiden Vorstellungen sollte also eine Vorstellung der Dünne, aber, wohl zu merken *weder* von der Dünne des Pflanzenplattes *noch* von der des Papiers, sondern von der Dünne an und für sich liegen? Man kann diese Auffassung nicht vertheidigen, ohne die alte Abstractions theorie zu erneuern, welche die gemeinschaftlichen Elemente unserer Vorstellungen genügen lässt um neue, selbständige Vorstellungen zu bilden."

and abstract sort of independence, but they actually exist only as emphasized portions of complex contents of consciousness. Such 'implicate' elements, which are all that the theory demands cannot possibly be denied by Höffding without an odd inconsistency with his own doctrine of immediate recognition.[1]

The consideration of these objections demonstrates the validity of the parallel treatment of internal and external association, and verifies the complete definition of association which may now be formulated somewhat as follows: *Association is the connection between objects or elements of consciousness (of which the second is not perceptual), assumed to be respectively identical with preceding objects, or elements, of consciousness which have stood to each other in a relation of simultaneity or of succession.*

The relation may be symbolically expressed by the proportion $X : y : : X^n : Y^n$. The 'persisting element' and the suggested elements are not necessarily cognitive sense qualities, but may be emotional or motor. Musical associations, for instance, are almost invariably either through persisting emotions or through self perpetuating rhythmic activities, and many of the most striking abnormal associations in cases of colored hearing are clearly emotional. On the other hand, many instances of what Baldwin calls 'sensori-motor association or assimilation' are through the presence of the motor elements involved in attention.

b. *The implication of assumed identity.*

The fact that associated objects of consciousness are 'assumed to be identical' with past objects has offered a tempting chance for metaphysical discussion, and the opportunity has been promptly embraced. Associationists, of course, have found no difficulty with this apparent identity of present with past. The early writers content themselves for the most part with explanations which are no more than metaphorical descriptions. The 'recurring' experience is called a 'miniature vibration'[2] and a 'copy.'[3] So far there is little advance

---

[1] Cf. page 27 *seq.*

[2] Hartley. *Observations on Man*, II, Prop. IX.

[3] Hartley, *op. cit.* II, Prop. VIII; and Hume, *Treatise* I, 1, and *Inquiry* II; and James Mill, *Analysis* I.

upon Plato and Aristotle who spoke of the stamp (σῆμα, τύπον)[1] upon the mind of that which has passed out of consciousness. But the later and more consistent Associationists, especially the Herbartians, recognize the need of explanation. The identity of present with past object of consciousness is for them an actual and complete identity. To-day's idea, which seems like yesterday's, is the same idea reëmerging from the ocean of temporary unconsciousness. So Spencer speaks of the 'revivability of feelings'[2] exactly as Wahle talks of the 'Auftauchen der Vorstellungen'[3] and Herbart says, " so soon as the object of consciousness P is unhindered, it lifts itself up into consciousness."[4]

The rejection of the Associationist philosophy, that is the denial of the independent existence of ideas, of course requires the abandonment of this crude doctrine of their revivability, since no state of consciousness, regarded as a single event in time, ever reappears. Nevertheless the actually assumed identity, the observed sameness, requires explanation, and spiritualists in psychology have usually reconciled the entire impotence of states of consciousness once vanished to reinstate themselves and the evident presence, on the other hand, of an identical element in experience, by means of a distinction between 'universal' and 'particular' or between 'form' and 'content'. The identity is predicated of the universal forms of consciousness, while the momentary sensations are allowed to be perishable. But all this is a mere repetition, in stately, yet rather unmeaning phraseology, of the old paradox. Truth to tell, there is no recourse here save in the recognition of that ' inexpugnable assumption'[5] of the permanent self beneath the changing phenomena. One can never have the same states of consciousness, in successive hours or moments, but one may be conscious in the same way at different times, and in that sense only the succeedings objects of one's consciousness may be called 'the same.'

---

[1] Cf. Plato, *Theataitos*, 194, 195; and Aristotle, *De Memoria, Bek.* 95, 25.

[2] *Principles of Psychology*, I. c. 5, *et alt.*

[3] *Vierteljahrschr. f. wiss. Phil.*, IX., p. 85. Cf. the statement (ib., p. 405), ' eine Vorstellung [besteht] aus alte Elemente.'

[4] *Psychologie als Wissenschaft* I., 3, 4. "Auf einmal verschwindet für [Vorstellung] P alles Hinderniss, so richtet sich P. ins Bewusstsein auf."

[5] Ward *Enc. Brit.*, Vol. XX., p. 39.

For this reason, because the connected objects must be defined as in some sense identical with the preceding ones, the fact of association, though in itself an observed, objective connection, has, as has been said already, for its presupposition the existence of a self in some sense continuous, whose methods of activity may recur.

This entire discussion of the implication of the identity assumed in association is nevertheless an intrusion of metaphysics upon science. Psychology is the study of the immediate facts of consciousness and the simply psychological standpoint, which avowedly is not an ultimate one, requires the bare acceptance of the predicates ' same ' and ' identical ' as facts of consciousness, without a further attempt to probe their meaning.

It should be added that the assertion of an assumed identity of associated contents with past objects of consciousness must not be supposed to imply that the individual subject in every case recognizes the associated objects as identical with certain preceding ones. Everyday observation and experimental studies, like those of Dr. Scripture,[1] include repeated instances of association in which the associater has completely forgotten his former experience of the associated objects. In these cases, however, the subject does not even realize the existence of the association which appears to him as a chance sequence; and the observer recognizes it as association only when he discovers the continuity of the ' identical ' past objects.

c. Discussion of association ' by similarity ' and ' by contiguity.'

Up to this point, the expressions association ' by contiguity ' and ' by similarity ' have been used, as synonyms for ' extrinsic ' and ' intrinsic ' association, to characterize broadly a common distinction which however has been shown, strictly speaking, to lie outside the limits of association. Since nevertheless not even a slight innovation of psychological doctrine can claim support, unless accompanied by a serious consideration of the traditional view which it replaces, the ordinary classification must next be more carefully studied. The statement, ' association is by contiguity ' or ' by similarity ' clearly indicates that

[1] Cf. Scripture. *Über den associativen Verlauf,* p. 90 seq.

the contiguity or the similarity is supposed to be itself the agent of the association. But this is evidently impossible. In any case of similarity, that, for instance, in which the first vivid streak of light on the eastern horizon is followed in the poet's mind by the image of a ' blade of gold flashed on the horizon's rim,' the similar objects are the perceived light and the imaged blade, and this imaged blade evidently cannot be similar to the flashing light until it comes into existence, but it does not exist until the poet thinks of it, and yet by the time he thinks of it, it is already associated with the percept of the light. The similarity so far from explaining the association requires and involves the sequence, and so the association. As Dr. James says[1] : " The similarity of two things does not exist till both things are there—it is meaningless to talk of it as an agent of production of anything. It is a relation which the mind perceives after the fact."

It is even more apparent that the contiguity of the associated objects themselves does not explain their association. The opposite view derives some of its force from the unwarranted assumption that the contiguity in question is spatial, a view which easily leaps to the error of supposing that the association is of extra-mental things. But association is of objects of consciousness, and their contiguity is evidently what Rabier calls ' *contiguité de la conscience*' and Ward names ' continuity.' Now this continuity of the associated objects does not precede association, but is involved in it. The contiguity is not there until the second object of consciousness actually has followed upon the first, but now—and not till now—the connection between first and second is there too. As Bradley says, " If they are contiguous, then they must both be there, and how can one call in the other?"

It is perfectly clear, therefore, that neither the contiguity nor the similarity can be regarded, after the manner of the old,

---

[1] *Op. cit.*, I. p. 591. Cf. Bradley, *Principles of Logic*, p. 294 : " Similarity is a relation, which, strictly speaking does not exist until both terms are before the mind." Cf. Rabier, *Psychologie* : " S'il n'y a pas moyen de percevoir une ressemblance entre un état de conscience et un autre qui n'existe pas dans la pensée, comment la perception pourra-t-elle susciter ce second état dans la pensée."

naive realism, as agents of the association. But the possibility remains that the expressions may have a descriptive value, and that, dropping the old preposition, we may legitimately speak of the 'association *of* the similar' and '*of* the contiguous.' Regarding first the associated objects themselves, it certainly is true that they are contiguous in the sense already explained of 'continuous.' But this continuity is true not only of all kinds of association, but even of the sequence in consciousness of percept upon percept; it cannot therefore be a peculiarity of trains of association. On the other hand, the similarity of associated objects seems to be a significant mark of the association. To recur to our old examples, the squeaky shoes are like the hand organ, love is like 'the star to every wandering bark' and one copy of a book is like another. But even if we admit the preëminence of similarity among the relations observed between associated terms, it has no right to an exclusive place. Things may remind us of their opposites as well as of their similars, as when 'imperial Rome' recalls to Hilda her native village. Causes may recall effects or wholes bring parts to mind. The old multiplicity of so-called laws, indeed, seems truer to the facts than this partiality for a single one. As Dr. James says,[1] "If perceived relations among objects are to be treated as grounds for their appearance before the mind, similarity has of course no right to an exclusive, or even to a predominant place."

Moreover the analysis of associations of the similar, which are really synonymous with what we have called internal associations, would show us, as before, that the association is not strictly speaking between the whole, concrete, 'similar' objects, but between elements common to both, and the combination of remaining elements of the second object of association. Therefore, though two so-called objects of association are certainly often similar, similarity is surely not a distinguishing principle of association.

Finally, then, we may inquire whether similarity and contiguity should be predicated, not of the objects of association, but of past objects of experience with which these are assumed to be identical. It at once appears that such identical objects of

[1] *Op. cit.* p. 591.

past experience are not even necessarily assumed in the case of so-called similarity association. Shelley need never even have seen a sky-lark before the moment when he conceived its likeness to the 'high-born maiden,' 'the glow worm golden' and the 'rose embowered.' On the other hand, the continuity of past objects of consciousness with which the associated objects are assumed to be identical has been found already to be the common assumption of every instance of association.

In terms of traditional psychology, 'association by contiguity' is therefore the only actual form of association, and means ' association explained by the continuity of past objects of consciousness with which the associated contents are assumed to be identical.' But the universality of this sort of association seems to excuse it from the requirement of a particular name; and the ambiguity of the expression makes it desirable to reject ' association by contiguity' along with ' association by similarity,' which has been abandoned for more vital reasons, both because it is not the only observed relation between associated phenomena and because it really reduces itself to 'association by contiguity.' Neither principle is in any sense a causative explanation of association.

III. THE CLASSIFICATION OF CASES OF ASSOCIATION,

a. Total, partial and focalized association.

The analysis of extreme cases of external (so-called contiguity) and internal (or similarity) association has shown that the fundamental principle is the same in both cases and that both reduce themselves to the suggested law of association, which is merely a generalized statement of the continuity in earlier experience of elements or objects corresponding with the associated ones.

In the course of this analysis, however, it has appeared that the provisional distinction of cases of association, as ' external' and ' internal,' is inadequate. For the supposed objects of internal association have turned out to be, strictly speaking, not associated at all, and the association, in these cases, has been observed to lie between an element common to two objects and a group of qualities in the second one.   Yet the old distinction is one which we unquestionably do recognize; in some sense, therefore, it must be retained, only its place may be shifted and its boundaries newly surveyed.

The principle of the revised classification may best be gained by considering other instances of association which lie midway between those cases in which the starting point is a single accentuated element, and those whose first term is a whole, concrete thing.   Between these extremes there is a whole series of gradations.   The Höffding article might remind me, for instance, of one of Weissman's papers on the 'Acquired Character' distinction; here the starting point would be a combination of the many common qualities of polemical, scientific monographs.[1]   Or the shoes might recall the sabots of a little Breton peasant, and here again the first term of the association would include a complex of qualities, not a single element. Yet both these would be recognized as examples of internal (or similarity) association; and even the connection between this copy and another of the volume of the *Philosophische Studien* or between this pair, and another, of shoes is an internal, not an external, relation, and thus quite different from the case of external association in which the book recalls the shelf on which it belongs.

Our distinction is really, therefore, between cases in which the first term of the association—the X—is a particular, concrete thing, and those in which this first term is any element or combination of elements, cognitive, emotional or impulsive.   It will be readily allowed that the distinction may be made in most cases: the association between book and shelf, between perceived thing and imagined environment, corresponds with what is called external association; the association between shrillness and other

---

[1] The formula here is:

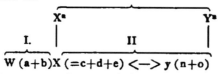

indicating that X, the common factor, includes several elements, the material qualities of magazine articles, scientific character, etc.

qualities corresponds with what we have known as internal association.

When, however, one book reminds me of another, the association is an internal one (of so-called similarity), yet the first term seems to be a concrete thing, and if this is so, the distinction just drawn is not perfectly parallel with the ordinary one. As a matter of fact however, in such a case as this, the association is not between two concrete things—in this case between two copies of a book—but between the sum of the elements common to the perceived and to the imagined book, and the sum of the qualities, however few, which distinguish the imagined from the perceived book. If a red book remind me of a blue one, otherwise exactly like it, the first term of the association is the sum of the qualities of the books except the color, and the second term is the blueness of the second book. The distinction between the succeeding objects of consciousness may be indefinitely less than a pronounced contrast of color, but always there is some difference between this thing and another, however similar, and the point of difference forms the second term of the association.

The most significant system of classification distinguishes, therefore, between concrete association of things, and the association of elements or qualities. In the first case, the earlier term of the association possesses the completeness and the relative isolation which constitute the concreteness of a comparatively permanent combination of qualities; in the second case the starting point of the association lacks concreteness and forms a part, larger or smaller, of some including total. The various possibilities are enumerated in the following summary:

Classification of Cases of Association.
I. Total or Concrete association of concrete objects of conciousness.
      a. Without appreciable persistence.
      b. With persistence.
II. Partial association of elements of consciousness.
    Always with persistence.
      a. Successive association.

1. Multiple association (in which the starting point of the as
sociation is a large group of persisting elements).

2. Focalized association (in which the starting point is a
single element or a small group).

b. Simultaneous association (assimilation).[1]

The terms ' total,' ' partial' and ' focalized' are those proposed by Dr. James, but are used with somewhat altered meaning.
' Total Association' is an especially misleading expression, retained in default of a better one; it is not to be interpreted as if
it required that the entire object of consciousness of a given
moment be associated with a following one, for it covers instances in which the first term of the association is very narrow,
for instance a single word. The essential feature of these
cases is that the first term be concrete and complete in itself, a
single word or object or event, which can be treated independently of accompanying contents of consciousness. The
extreme forms—concrete and focalized association— are obviously characteristic of opposing types of intellect—of the literal
and prosaic, which proceeds by the sober path of recollection or
of concrete induction from one thing to another, so that the life
of the imagination is a close transcript of the life of experience,
and on the other hand, of the penetrative and creative mind,
which so singles out the remote and subtle elements and qualities of its gross contents that they then become the centres of
ever widening circles of revery or of thought.

The persistence of the earlier term is a significant accompaniment of many forms of association. The prominence of change
in the mental life has often been emphasized at the expense of
this opposite but equally fundamental factor. In all cases of
partial association, the second term is a group of elements or a
single one requiring, for concretion into a total object of consciousness, the persistence of the first term.

In an earlier discussion of the subject,[2] the writer made the
presence or absence of persistence the basis of the differentia-

[1] Cf. page 19. In the body of this paper ' association ' is treated as synonymous with successive association. The division is made here in order to indicate the proper place of ' simultaneous association ' if it be included.

[2] *Philosophical Review*, July, 1892.

tion of the two chief types of association, which were named respectively 'persistent' and 'desistent.' Wundt[1] suggests a classification in the main like this, except that he calls the persistence itself similarity association (*Gleichheitsassociation*) which is manifestly incorrect. Several considerations have led to the rejection of this principle of division. The term 'desistent' is objectionable because of the implication that the earlier of the associated objects entirely disappears before the occurrence of the second.[2] Certainly this often seems to happen, but it is probable that the earlier object, though unattended to, fades gradually away and persists, for at least an unappreciable moment, with the later one. The chief objection, however, to the classification of association as 'desistent' and 'persistent,' is the frequent triviality of the distinction. What essential difference is there between the 'persistent' association of the verbal image 'tariff reform' after the sound of the word 'tariff' in place of the 'desistent' image 'reform?' Or what basis of division lies in the fact that at sight of a rose I think of the friend who gave it to me with or without the rose in her hand? Evidently the significant distinction is the quantitative one. All the instances just enumerated are of concrete, total association, and are therefore to be opposed to connections of the subtler, more intensive kind.

b. *Simultaneous association.*

The ordinary distinction between simultaneous and successive association is unessential, for successive association which is 'observable connection' requires the 'simultaneous' presence of the associated terms, which, however, *have* succeeded each other in consciousness; while so-called simultaneous association is usually the familiar case of the observable persistence in consciousness of an earlier object of association with a later one. Wundt, who has a peculiarly elaborate theory of simultaneous association, distinguishes three forms, fusion (*Verschmelzung*), assimilation and complication.

---

[1] *Philosophische Studien*, VII., p. 341.
[2] This criticism was made by a reviewer in the *Zeitschrift der Psychologie und Physiologie der Sinnesorgane.*

Fusion is defined[1] as the connection of like or disparate sensations, making up a total percept: so one may perceive a rose, and in one and the same moment see it, smell it and touch its velvety petals. But the second term of an association is never an object of perception, so that these cases of fusion or connection of merely perceived qualities can never be cases of association. Wundt himself leaves them out of account in the essay in the *Philosophische Studien.*[2]

By assimilation, Wundt means the connection of *Vorstellungselemente*—that is of separable parts less elemental than sensations—within a single object of consciousness. All these must be of the same sense-order, and Wundt remarks that one is usually impression, and the rest images;[3] if associated they certainly are not all impressions. Wundt's examples are chiefly from the field of illusions—instances of reading words omitted by the printer, or of 'seeing' the rough blotches of theatre scenes as genuine landscapes. In these, the so-called simultaneous association is the connection between the actual sense impression and the imaged qualities belonging to a total percept, for instance, between the green daubs as seen, and the imaged qualities necessary to complete the percept 'forest.' Now such 'simultaneous association' certainly is not present in immediate perception, for there can be no association of parts within a total object, without a recognition of the existence of such parts; and the essence of perception is just this, that it ignores parts and grasps wholes. As Dr. Ward says,[4] "though the percept is complex, it is but a single whole, and the act of perception is single too." But the existence of these parts within the percept may later be reflected on, and then their observed connection may be called a case of simultaneous association. The sort of reflection here involved is, however, of a relatively rare and ar-

[1] *Grundzüge*, II., p. 437.
[2] *Philos. Stud.*, VII.
[3] *Op. cit.* II., pp. 439-448.. Wundt, however, sometimes uses assimilation, as Ward does, in the sense of Höffding's implicate association by similarity, to indicate that the presentation of a given object is followed by images of the same. The validity of this theory will be discussed later. Cf. *Philos. Stud.* VII., pp. 340 and 341. "[Ein Eindruck] wird eine Erinnerung nur immer insoweit erwecken können als er ihm gleich ist."
[4] *Enc. Brit.* XX., p. 57.

tificial sort; and Wundt's whole discussion gains its force by his constant incorrect assumption that assimilation is involved in mere perception.[1]

Complication, finally, is defined as the connection between sense impressions and images of a different sense order. For example, the sight of an apple at a distance may be followed by an image of its taste, or the sound of an electric car bell may suggest a visual image of the car. In these cases there is usually a separation in time: the visual image of the apple distinctly precedes the gustatory, the bell is heard before the car is imaged. Here we have a case of successive association, involving the observed persistence of the earlier percept, for instance, the clang, with the following image. Wundt remarks this frequent relation in the words:[2] "In der That * * * geschieht [es] wahrscheinlich sehr häufig dass die simultane Association einer gewissen Zeitdauer und zeitliche Folge zu ihrer Entstehung bedarf."

There certainly may be, therefore, within total objects of consciousness, a connection of imaged, or of perceptual with imaged elements which may be called simultaneous association, since its explanation is, of course, an ' assumed identity' with former elements which were continuous in actual experience. The simpler term ' assimilation' seems, however, to describe this situation equally well, and association has accordingly been used throughout this discussion to cover only cases of the successive kind.

c. *So-called voluntary association.*

Another ordinary distinction is that between involuntary or passive and voluntary or active association. Aristotle's pic-

---

[1] Baldwin makes the same assertion (*cf. Mental Development in the Child and The Race*, p. 311, *et. alt.*): "All perception is accordingly a case of assimilation." But assimilation is here used of a physiological combination of ' sensory processes' and ' motor reactions' and therefore does not refer to psychological association at all.

[2] *Philos. Stud.* VII., p. 334. The immediately following sentence seems to suggest that, similarly, successive association may be the result of simultaneous. ("Anderseits ist es nicht ausgeschlossen dass bei einer successiven Association die verbundenen Vorstellungen an sich gleichzeitig in das Bewusstsein treten, dass sie aber nur successiv appercipirt werden.") But the so-called case of simultaneous association is here very evidently a complex percept.

turesque expression θήρευσις, or the parallel terms of Hobbes, 'seeking' and 'hunting,' adequately characterize this strenuous stage of consciousness, in which we eagerly pursue the baffling solution of our problem and explore the recesses of memory for fleeting face or name.

But that which distinguishes this so-called voluntary association is evidently no characteristic of association itself. It is rather a complex of image, emotion and volition; the possession of a partial or a general image, the realization of its incompleteness, the desire to complete it and the successive emphasis of one part after another of this vague image of present consciousness in the hope that it may associate the unknown. Our rules of practice in the selection of the first term, as it were, for the desired association, are the so-called secondary laws of association; we accentuate the objects of our consciousness which we know to have been frequently, or recently, or impressively connected with the desired image; or we dwell upon a combination of these particularly suggestive elements. The discussion of these secondary laws is postponed to the later division of this paper.[1]

What is called voluntary association is therefore a very complex mode of consciousness of whose content association is but one factor. To speak of voluntary association is, indeed, to return to the old error of conceiving association as an operation, whereas it is really an observed content; voluntary imagination or recollection, or simply thought, are the proper names for this form of consciousness.

IV. A Modern Form of 'Association by Similarity.'

a. *The sequence upon a percept of images like itself is not association.*

Some modern psychologists believe that they find lurking among the phenomena of consciousness, still another kind of association. It is usually regarded as a sort of 'association by similarity,' and Bain and Spencer try to make the new sort more

---

[1] Cf. Part II.

plausible by illustrating it through many examples of the old, but Höffding,[1] with greater insight, recognizes and does not confuse the two varieties of so-called association by similarity.

The new kind of association ordinarily appears as a refutation of the attempted reduction of ' association by similarity' to ' association by contiguity.' Admitting that what is commonly called internal association is the connection of elements, rather than of objects, it is urged that there is a process of association still more elementary which is presupposed by every observed connection. This process is nothing less than the sequence upon a given present percept or image, X or x, of repeated images, x^1, x^2, x^3, x^4, like itself; and such a succession of images like itself is necessary, it is asserted, before the appearance of the different image, the y, of ordinary external association. My percept ' Mary' is, and must be, followed by a succession of images ' Mary,' before it can be followed by the image ' lamb;' I must recognize the Sistine Madonna before she can remind me of the portrait of Raphael, and this recognition is through a mental procession of images, standing for previous percepts of the picture.

The first comment on this entire construction is that, true or false, it is utterly misnamed when it is called Association. The fact of ' being reminded' has not the faintest resemblance to the fact of ' observing an association.' The reappearance of what we call an ' image of the same'—even a ghostly procession of such images, always growing fainter—is quite different from the observed connection of different contents. Such a process in which the purported similarity amounts to identity truly is as Dr. Ward says, ' more fundamental than association by contiguity, but then it is not a process of Association.' Even Höffding often questions the propriety of the expression ' association by similarity' in this use of it. '' If one sufficiently extend the conception of similarity association to include immediate recognition, * * *'' he says in one passage[2], with the evident infer-

---

[1] *Op. cit.* XIV., p. 49 seq.; *Psychology*, Eng. Tr. p. 151.

[2] *Vierteljahrschr. f. Wiss. Phil.* XIV, p. 190. '' Will man den Begriff der Aenlichkeits-association so weit ausdehnen dass er auch das unmittelbare Wiedererkennen umfasst.''

ence that the procedure is a doubtful one. On the other hand he indicates his satisfaction with the term ' assimilation,' which is sometimes used by Wundt in this sense.

The critic of association theories would be justified, therefore, in refusing to consider further this spurious sort of association between presentation and representations of the same, on the mere ground that such a phenomenon is not in any sense a variety of association. But the process in question has played so prominent a part in discussions, and does, in the later forms of the theory, oppose itself so strongly to what is really association, that the consideration of its significance and validity is hardly to be omitted.

The immediate question is, therefore, does this process, really exist? Is it requisite to the association of a percept X, with an image, y, that the percept should have been followed immediately by one or more images, x, x—, exactly corresponding with it, in fact identical except in time. Is the complete formula of an association $X–x^n <—> y$, instead of $X <—> y$?

b. The Associationist argument for this so-called ' association.'

The English psychologists offer an argument for this process, which is really a corollary of their well known theory. They admit that the present percept, X, by virtue of its perceptual nature, is something relatively new in consciousness; therefore, they insist, X cannot by itself suggest the image y of a past experience. So the image x, which has to do with the past, must appear before y, also a phenomenon of the past, can come to consciousness. "My present sensation," Stuart Mill says[1] "could not remind me of those former sensations unlike itself, unless by first reminding me of the sensation like itself which really did coexist with them." In the same fashion, Spencer writes,[2] "the primary association is between each feeling and the class, order * * * * and variety of preceding feelings like itself * * * *. The act of recognition and the act of association are two aspects of the same act. And the implication is that besides this law there is no other."

[1] Note to James Mill's *Analysis.* Cf. Bain, *Senses and Intellect,* p. 458.
[2] *Principles of Psychology,* I. 270.

But this is only the old Associationist fallacy. A present image is treated as identical with a past percept, whereas it is a new fact of consciousness. So the *image* of my Paris Baedeker is supposed to suggest my percept five years ago of the Sainte Chapelle, which the mere *sight* of my Baedeker could not, it is believed, associate. Of course this explanation is a tissue of impossibilities. In the first place, the supposed image of the Baedeker would be as much an affair of the present as the sight of it; the present image was not in existence at the time of that past percept, and is therefore no more able than the present percept, to explain the association; and, on the other hand, the past percept cannot reappear. "Ein gewesener Zustand," as Lehmann says, "kommt niemals wieder auf." In the second place, there is no earthly need of this impossible, present-past percept to explain the association, for the suggested object, the richly lighted church interior, is no past percept but is itself a present image. In symbolic terms then the Associationist construction may be pronounced incorrect, both because x is not X^n and because y not Y^n is associated. Nevertheless the Associationist theory will continue persistently to ignore the distinction between present and past, and its 'ideas,' however deeply buried, will always 'bob up serenely,' to paraphrase Herbart's own word *auftauchen*, whenever they are wanted.

c. *Höffding's theory of this so-called 'association' (or 'assimilation').*

This theory of assimilation finds its completest and most technical expression in Höffding's discussion. His starting point is the existence of immediate recognition, that is, recognition of objects, scenes or simple sense experiences, without any representation to ourselves of the attendant circumstances. He claims that this bare familiarity without detailed recollection can only be explained by an assimilation to the given presentation of like representations, that is, by a sequence of the x^1, x^2 * * * x^n upon the X.

1. *The possibility of immediate recognition.*

At this point, therefore, our problem is the validity of the concept of immediate recognition. Is there really any

' immediate recognition'? Do we recall things without any representation to ourselves of attendant circumstances (*Nebenvorstellungen*), which distinguished the former experience from the present? Höffding's examples[1] are the instant recognition of an unaccustomed and unnamed, yet familiar, tint in the sky, of a foreign word, which we are nevertheless unable to translate, of some unnamed and unlocated organic sensation. In all these cases, he says, we know nothing about the former setting of the experience; we know neither the time nor the circumstances of its former occurrence; we do not know even the name. The objects are, nevertheless, 'familiar,' though introspection shows 'no faintest trace of other representations, awakened by the recognized phenomenon.'[2] Lehmann's experimental observations corroborate the possibility of such familiarity. In a series of experiments on the recognition of odors[3], these appeared familiar in seven per cent. of the cases, though the subjects were unable to name them or in any way to connect them with other experiences.

Höffding concludes that this fact of being recognized is an immediate and distinguishing quality of the object, *Bekanntheitsqualität*, as simple and as indescribable as the difference 'between pain and pleasure or between yellow and blue.' Immediate recognition, as thus understood, is momentary and simple; it flashes upon a mind unprepared for it, and it is distinguished from mediate recognition just in that it does not involve association. This absence of association is the important point. In mediate recognition the sight of an object is followed by the memory of that object in the different environment of the past. The elements which make up this different environment are the attendant images (*Nebenvorstellungen*), which are associated with the percept of the object; these are the condition and the mark of mediate recognition, and must be proved to be entirely lacking in any case of immediate recognition.

The existence of immediate recognition is therefore disputed by those who believe that these *Nebenvorstellungen* must always be present, in however faint and fleeting a fashion, in every

[1] *Vierteljahrschr. f. wiss. Phil.* XIII., 425.
[2] *Op. cit.* XIII., p. 428. "Nicht die geringste Spur von anderen Vorstellungen die durch die erkannte Erscheinung erweckt wurden."
[3] *Philosophische Studien* VII., p. 190.

case of recognition. The accuracy of Höffding's self-observation is questioned; for instance it is urged[1] that an educated man 'not color-blind' could not recognize a tint, however unusual, without some consciousness of a more or less appropriate name. On this ground, Wundt and James deny rigorously the possibility of immediate recognition. "There certainly always is," Dr. James says[2], "[a] 'fringe of tendency' toward the arousal of extrinsic association." "Weder glaube ich," Wundt writes[3], 'dass diese [Bekanntheits] Qualität jemals ohne mitwirkende Vorstellungen vorkommt." It must be admitted, however, as Höffding, in his reply to Lehmann[4], does not fail to observe, that Wundt abandons this position and definitely contradicts himself by the theory, advanced in volume VII., of the *Philosophische Studien*, that every association is really made up of two processes[5], a combination of like elements and a later association of previously continuous elements. Even Dr. James seems to allow by two or three unguarded phrases[6], which Höffding triumphantly extracts, the occasional possibility within 'a couple of minutes interval' from the presentation of 'recognition of the immediate sort.' This must, in fact, be admitted as a possibility, however sceptical one is about particular instances. Undoubtedly most supposed cases of immediate recognition have really involved a recollection of a name or a faint background of imagery, yet familiarity, without real recollection, does not seem to be *a priori* impossible, and has experimental evidence on its side.

2. *The relation of this so-called association to immediate recognition.*

Granting the fact of immediate recognition, its bearing on the theory in question must next be discussed. Höffding

---

[1] Lehmann. *Wiedererkennen. Philos. Stud.*, VII., p. 180.

[2] *Op. cit.* I., p. 674. Note.

[3] *Philos. Stud.*, VII., p. 352; cf. pp. 360, 361.

[4] *Philos. Stud.*, VIII., p. 93.

[5] *Philos. Stud.*, VII. p. 343. " aus einer unmittelbaren Verbindung gleicher Elemente verschiedener Vorstellungen, und aus einer daran mittelbar sich anschliessenden Verbindung solcher Bestandtheile die in früheren Vorstellungen mit jenen gleichen Elementen in äusserlichen Berührung gewesen waren."

[6] *Op. cit.* I., p. 675. Note.

insists that immediate recognition is explained only by such an
assimilation of images to percept.[1] His theory, however, undergoes much modification as it proceeds, and includes physiological as well as psychological considerations. The fact to be
explained is the immediate recognition, and its physiological
condition, according to Höffding, is the neural habit which results from repetition (*Uebung*), that is, the cerebral ' disposition' to activity, the facility or readiness of neural response
to stimulation. The hypothesis of cerebral habit is greatly
emphasized in Höffding's later paper,[2] where he says : " Ich
wende also das einfache Gesetz der Uebung an." This physiological explanation of immediate recognition will at once
be admitted. It is, in fact, a commonplace of psychological theory that familiarity depends on the physiological facility
which results from repetition ; nobody doubts this assertion and
it can be fitted to any theory. The characteristic part of the
Höffding theory is, however, the hypothesis that the psychological correlate of physiological habit, the factor of consciousness
which explains the immediate recognition, is the occurrence,
along with the recognized percept (X) of a number of images
(x^1, x^2 ——) corresponding with it. The color is familiar because I have not only the percept of it, but a series of images of
former percepts (always without any distinguishing marks of
the former occurrences). These images explain, or rather they
are, the *Bekanntheitsqualität*. " In order that A may excite the
ideas of B, C, D, with which it usually arises simultaneously in
consciousness, it must first establish its identity. Thus A must
give rise to a, and only then will a bring with it b, c and d."[3]
The modification of the theory by which the similar ideas or
images are treated as merely possible will be later considered,
but the expression ' images ' is retained throughout.

In varying ways, Höffding argues the plausibility of this
view, by insisting that it involves no more than is admitted by
those who deny 'assimilation,' and assume the presence of association in all cases of recognition. The neural predisposition,

[1] *Vierteljahrschrift f. wiss. Phil.*, XIII., p. 431, *seq.*
[2] *Philos. Studien*, VIII., p. 87, *seq.*
[3] *Psychology* (Engl. ed.), p. 157.

he says[1], which is required for the sequence of image y upon percept X, is even more likely to bring about the appearance of image x after X. No argument, however, can establish a psychological hypothesis in the total lack of confirming experience. The addition made by the feeling of familiarity to a given percept, whatever it may be, certainly is not a series of images corresponding with the percept. The present image of the color we are this moment seeing, the image of the sound which is still sounding in our ears, the image of the present odor or taste—this is a baseless and a needless construction.

The theory of assimilation, in this form, has not even the merit of corresponding accurately with what has been admitted as a physiological explanation of familiarity—that is, with neural habit. For, as Lehmann has shown[2], it obliges us to suppose that the physiological equivalent of an image is nothing more than the ease *(Leichtigkeit)* of nervous discharge in an accustomed way. This, however, is incredible. For the neural accompaniment of image, no less than of percept, includes a certain definitely localized brain process; the mere increase of nervous plasticity cannot possibly, speaking physiologically, entirely account for an image. But just this would be demanded by the theory under consideration, for the only difference between the physiological condition accompanying bare perception, and that which accompanies immediate recognition, is the greater ease of nervous response in the latter case.

This is the objection which Dr. James urges[3] against this theory: "To say that the process *A* can only reach [the process *b*] by the help of a weaker process *a*, is like saying that we need a candle to see the sun by. *A* replaces *a*, does all that *a* does and more, and there is no intelligible meaning, to my mind, in saying that the weaker process coexists with the stronger." The last clause of the passage just quoted makes the assumption that the brain process accompanying an

---

[1] *Vierteljahrschr, f. wiss. Phil.*, XIV., p. 42. "Es scheint eine unvermeidliche Folgerung • • • dass die Disposition zur Vorstellung *a* in weit höherem. Grade erregt werden müsse wenn *A* selbst eintritt, als die Disposition zu *b* erregt wird, weil das von *B* verschiedene *A* eintritt."

[2] *Philos. Stud.*, VII., p. 181.

[3] *op. cit.*, I., p. 592, et. alt.

image differs from that accompanying a percept only in its lessened force. The argument, therefore, claims more than is necessary to the refutation of Höffding's theory. It urges that the bodily process accompanying the percept includes every element of the image process in greater intensity, so that no separate physiological correlate, belonging to the image only, can remain. To refute this assimilation theory, however, it is only necessary to show that image and percept process are so nearly the same that the physiological correlate which *distinguishes* the image (neural ease, according to the theory) is not, by itself, sufficient to *account for* the image.

Dr. James's supposition of the entire identity (except in degree), of the image and the percept process is, in fact, open to question. Dr. Ward opposes it warmly, and proposes a theory of the 'distinction of the seats' of perception and imagination, basing it chiefly on arguments drawn from cases of cerebral disturbance, in which "visual memory images are for the most part retained, so that old scenes can be recalled and familiar objects or persons accurately described, and yet the recognition of them is no longer possible."[1] The points at issue are less significant than they appear, The 'distinction of seats' which Ward proposes is no 'wide separation' but a mere difference of cortical layer. And he defends merely the fact of immediate recognition (which, however, he calls assimilation), and does not uphold Höffding's proposed explanation, that is the theory of 'implicate association by similarity' or association by a percept, of images like itself.

Höffding's answer to his critics involves, according to the fiercest of them, Lehmann, a restatement of the theory as it appeared in the Psychology, with a complete shifting of its position. Already, in the Psychology,[2] Höffding had called the assimilated images implicate (*gebundene*) and fused (*verschmolzen*), but nevertheless had treated them as possessing a certain faint and subordinate reality of their own. For instance, the assertion, "the reawakened state fuses immediately with the

---

[1] *Mind,* October, 1894.
[2] *Philos. Stud.,* VII., 173.
[3] *Engl. Tr.,* pp. 121–123 and 157.

given sensation, and does not stand out beside it as a free and independent representation "[1] clearly suggests that the representation has a certain life of its own; otherwise in what sense would it be 'reawakened;' and what would there be to 'fuse?' In the *Vierteljahrschrift*, however, and even more definitely in the latest paper of all, that of the *Philosophische Studien*, Höffding seems to rob these 'implicate images' or 'ideas' of all the actuality they had retained. Under this treatment they become mere possibilities, abstractions of thought, "Elemente die wir jedes für sich zu denken vermögen; theoretisch gedachte Faktoren." *Bekanntheitsqualität* is defined as a *Vorstellungspotentialität*.

Now this view undoubtedly avoids the difficulties of the theory of assimilation of images, but it does so by making the whole theory superfluous and by forfeiting all claim to the name similarity association. If the 'associated' images are not actual they should not be invoked at all; it is meaningless to say that they are present only in the sense that under other circumstances images[2] would be present. In other words the conception of 'possible images' has no significance except for metaphysics and for physiology. In this latter sense, as an abbreviated statement of the existence of neural activity without the corresponding accompaniment in consciousness, Höffding practically uses the term. More and more the explanation of familiarity is given in terms of physiology. It is a 'disposition;' it forms, with the sense stimulus, the condition of immediate recognition; it is that which would under other circumstances make a free representation possible. ("Beim unmittelbaren Wiedererkennen [wirkt] dasselbe was unter anderen Verhältnissen eine freie Repräsentation *a* möglich machen würde.")

The possibility of immediate recognition has been granted, and the probability that its physiological accompaniment is a certain neural habit. The hypothesis that such immediate recognition is through the association or assimilation of 'similar' ideas or images has been denied. If it is necessary to suggest

[1] *Psychology*, p. 123.
[2] Cf. the next quotation; and the statement that immediate recognition is an 'untrennbares Ganze.'

a psychological correlate in place of this one, an equivalent in consciousness for physiological ease or *Leichtigkeit*, one may follow Lehmann[1] and Wundt[2], and apparently James[3], in describing this as a certain emotional element (*Gefühlston*), a quality of ease or warmth, a certain *Lustgefühl;* or it may be defined, as by Baldwin, to be "readiness or ease * * * in the motor sensations of adjustment;" or finally, it may be no further definable than by the expression 'consciousness of identity.' It remains true, as has been noticed already, that recognition is usually of the mediate sort, involving the association of some environing circumstances, some reaction upon the object or some shade of feeling which does not recur in the present.

The result of the whole discussion is, therefore, first, to show that a sequence of like images upon a percept is not a form of association; second, to indicate that such a process does not occur at all, either to explain association, as the English psychologists assert, or to explain immediate recognition, as Höffding holds.[5]

V. THE PHYSIOLOGICAL EXPLANATION OF ASSOCIATION.

The present discussion is merely an introspective analysis of the full psychological meaning and assumption of association, not an attempted formulation of its causes. Psychologically, indeed, association is further inexplicable, but a suggestive physiological explanation may be discovered by the observation and the inference of characteristic bodily accompaniments. These are, of course, the varied forms of neural and muscular habit, the spread of bodily stimulations through paths already worn.

[1] *Philos. Stud.*, VII., p. 191.
[2] *Philos. Stud.*, VII., p. 345 ('Erkennungsgefühl').
[3] *Op. cit.*, I., p. 675. Note.
[4] *Op. cit.*, p. 318.
[5] Since this paper was sent to the press I have read *Ueber das Grundprincip der Association* (Berlin, 1895), by Arthur Allin, Ph. D., and two articles by the same author in the *American Journal of Psychology*, Vol. VII., 2. Dr. Allin presents in greater detail and with admirable clearness the theory of association, as related to immediate recognition and to assimilation, which I have here defended.

The quantitative distinctions between total, multiple and focalized association, and the difference between association with and without persistence, are easily stated in cerebral terms. The most significant advance of what may be called psychological physiology is, however, the application of the concept of habit not only to cerebral connections, but to connections between sensory and motor processes, or between motor processes alone. This principle, which has been particularly emphasized and developed by Münsterberg and by Baldwin, opens up rich fields of physiological explanation and of vivified psychological analysis. Not merely association, but perception, illusion, recognition and conception are susceptible of this sort of explanation. In so far, also, as these motor reactions are elements of conscious contents they are direct material of psychology; not the least value of the theories of 'dynamogenesis' is their accentuation of the constancy in our consciousness of these 'feelings of bodily behavior.' In cases of multiple, partial association, when an image follows upon a percept nearly like it, as in the puzzling instances when a thing thing reminds one of 'itself' in a similar environment, the second and differentiating term of the association may be an imaged bodily reaction; and often when the link between associated objects seems undiscoverable it may be found in the form of an unmarked motor adjustment.

This observation of bodily reactions and the study of physiological correlates should never, however, be mistaken for a psychological analysis of the nature of association, though the confusion does actually occur in the midst of the most brilliant and most effective psychological writing. "So far as association stands for a cause" Dr. James says, [1] "it is between processes of the brain," "These reactions," in the words of Dr. Baldwin,[2] "are reduced to orderly habitual discharges; *this is* association by assimilation." Both writers frequently formulate the correct view of the physiological connection as 'basis' or 'foundation' or 'organic side' of association, but the tendency to make the two synonymous is also noticeable. So Wundt's

[1] *Op. cit.*, I., p. 554.
[2] *Op. cit.*, p. 310. Italics mine.

theory of assimilation translated into physiological terms is a satisfactory one, but is untrue, as has been shown, to the facts of consciousness. So far, indeed, as the combination of sensory stimulations, or of motor effects, or of sensory with motor processes, is not known to the subject, it simply is no case of association at all, but is rather the physiological correlate of association.

PART II.

EXPERIMENTAL INVESTIGATION OF CONDITIONS OF ASSOCIATIVE SUGGESTIBILITY.

Experimental investigation may best supplement the purely introspective study of the nature of association by describing in relatively concrete terms the probable direction of trains of associated images. To this end there is necessary such a consideration of the so-called suggestibility of objects of consciousness as shall answer the question: what one of the numberless images which might conceivably follow upon the present percept or image will actually be associated with it?

Ordinary self-observation has long recognized that the readily associated objects are the 'interesting' ones, and has further enumerated frequency, recency, vividness or impressiveness, and primacy (the earliest position in a definite series of events) as the factors of interest, and therefore the conditions of association. A given object, then, is likely to be suggested by one with which it was frequently, recently or vividly connected, and by one with which it stood at the beginning of a series.

Logically prior to the discussion of suggestibility is the study of the suggestiveness of objects of consciousness, that is, the consideration of the question: what part of the present total content of consciousness will be associated with a following image? The suggesting object may, of course, be of varied extent. In the rare cases of 'total redintegration,' practically the entire present content is connected, as a whole, with what follows. Far more often, some one accentuated part of the total object of consciousness is the starting point of the association; and this emphasis of attention is once more upon the 'interesting' part of the entire content, that is upon some vivid, recent or repeated object, or upon one which has had the early place in a series. Finally, neither the total content of consciousness, nor a single accentuated portion of that total, but a group of these single factors or objects of consciousness may form the starting point of the association.

These distinctions may be summarized, somewhat as follows :

I. Contents of consciousness are 'suggestive.'
  a. As totals (Total Redintegration.)
  b. As complex.
    1. *Groups* of objects are suggestive (through 'constellation.')
    2. *Single* portions are suggestive, through their *interest*, due to
      (a) Repetition (Frequency.)
      (b) Vividness.
      (c) Recency.
      (d) Primacy.

II. Objects of consciousness are 'suggestible,' through their *interest*, due to
  a. Frequency of connection.
  b. Vividness   "   "
  c. Recency   "   "
  d. Primacy   "   "

The experimental investigation whose results are here reported concerned itself with the conditions of suggestibility.

The relative significance of frequency, recency, primacy and vividness, was studied in about 2,200 experiments. This number does not include the introductory experiments undertaken in order to select satisfactory methods nor the practice experiments of each subject. There were 17 subjects, no one of whom assisted in more than 275 nor in less than 40 experiments; and the average number was 130 for each subject. Most of the visual experiments were repeated with 40 members of the writer's Wellesley College class, with an average of 12 experiments each. The results coincide very closely with those of the more extended study in the Harvard laboratory; they are not included except in one or two instances which will be noticed. All the subjects were entirely or comparatively ignorant of the aims and the problems of the investigation, which was not discussed until the conclusion of the work. The results were twice set down, once in the books kept for the individual subjects, and again in the books which contained the grouped records of the different sorts of experiment. These experimental ledger pages have been balanced, and all the figures given in the tables represent the concurring results of both forms of record. Constant notes were kept of subjective experiences, but have not been reported, for none of them tended to modify the conclusions drawn from the experiments themselves except where the occurrence of natural associations made it necessary to reject entirely the results of particular experiments.

The experiments were of two main types, visual and auditory; the visual experiments are divided again into the successive and the simultaneous; finally, all the experiments may be classed, with reference to their purpose, as simple or comparative.

I. SIMPLE SERIES.

a. 1. Successive Arrangement. Visual Series.

The method of the visual experiments was as follows: the subjects, of whom two to eight were present at one time, sat before a white screen large enough to shield the conductor of the experiment. Through an opening, 10 cm. square, a color was shown for four seconds, followed immediately by a numeral, usually black on a white ground, for the same time. After a pause of about eight seconds, during which the subject looked steadily at the white background, another color was shown, succeeded at once by a second numeral, each exposed for four seconds. The pause of eight seconds followed, and the series of 7, 10 or 12 pairs of quickly succeeding color and numeral was continued in the same way. At the close a series was shown of the same colors in altered order, and the subject was asked, as each color appeared, to write down the suggested numerals if any such occurred. The pause between the combination-series, in which colors and numerals appeared together, and the test-series, in which the colors only were shown, was eight seconds in the case of the short series and four to six seconds in the case of the longer. Color and numeral were placed together in their position behind the opening of the screen, the numeral at first concealed by the color, which was then slipped out. There was thus a merely momentary pause between the appearance of color and of numeral. During the eight-second pauses the opening was filled by a white ground, ½ cm. behind the screen. The subject thus saw nothing in the opening except this white ground, or the color, which filled the whole square, or the printed numeral; the movements of the experimenter were entirely concealed. The time was at first kept by following the ticks of a watch suspended close to the experimenter's ear; but in the last 1,200 tests by listening to the beats of a metronome, which rung a bell every four seconds; the metronome was enclosed in a sound-proof box, so that the subjects were not disturbed by the beats, which reached the experimenter through a rubber tube. All the series were carefully placed in order beforehand.

In the first group of experiments, some one color appeared several times in each series, once in an unimportant position with any chance numeral, but also once or more in some emphasized connection—either repeatedly with the same numeral (a 'frequent' combination), or at the very beginning or very end of a series (cases of 'primacy' and of 'recency'), or with a numeral of unusual size or color (an instance of 'vividness').

The following are representative series:

Visual series 89.   Frequency (3: 12).

I. (Combination Series.)   Green, 47; brown, 73; *violet, 61 (f)*; light grey, 58; *violet, 61 (f)*; orange, 84; blue, 12; *violet, 61 (f)*; medium grey, 39; *violet, 26 (n)*; light green, 78; strawberry, 52.

II. (Test Series.)   Blue, light grey, strawberry, green, *violet (f)*, orange, brown, medium grey, light green.

Visual Series, 213.   Vividness.

I. Brown, 34; peacock, 65; orange, 51; *green, 792 (v)*; blue, 19; violet, 48; *green, 27 (n)*; grey, 36; strawberry, 87; dark red, 54.

II. Blue, grey, dark red, brown, *green (v)*, orange, strawberry, grey, peacock.

Visual Series, 127.   Recency.

I. Peacock, 46; *blue, 38 (n); * brown, 51; grey, 74; yellow, 29; *blue, 52 (r).*

II. Grey, *blue (r)*, peacock, yellow, strawberry, brown.

Visual Series, 69b.   Primacy.

I. *Light red, 48 (p);* strawberry, 13; violet, 60; grey, 82; orange, 29; *light red, 31 (n);* yellow, 53; green, 94; light violet, 17; blue, 69.

II. Green, gray, *light red (p)*, light violet, strawberry, orange, violet, yellow, blue.

The problem of the experiment is the discovery of the proportion of cases in which the accentuated color, *e. g.*, green (as in series 213, above), suggests the numeral—here 792—with which it was emphatically combined, instead of suggesting the other numeral with which also it was shown.

To gain a basis of comparison about 1,300 series of all types, and from the records of all the subjects, have been considered as a mere memory test, leaving out of account, for the time being, the emphasized combinations which they contain. About *one-fourth of the ordinary combinations in the longer series* (10 to 12 pairs), *and one-third in the shorter series* (7 pairs) *are remembered.*   This is shown in

TABLE I.   CORRECT ASSOCIATIONS.

Series.	Number of Series.	Possible Correct Associations.	Actual Correct Associations. Full.	Half.	%
Long	867	7672	1728	558	26.1
Short	444	2144	674	170	35.2

In this calculation, and in all similar ones, all cases were excluded in which any accidental association already existed between color (or syllable) and numeral.   If the color was thus naturally associated with the emphasized or the contrasted numeral, the whole series was excluded; otherwise, as in the cases included under this table, merely the combination thus connected was set aside.

The tabulated results of the experiments on frequency as a condition of association are as follows:

TABLE II. FREQUENCY, VISUAL.

Number of Series.	Both			Normal Only.			Frequent Only.		
	Full.	Half.	%	Full.	Half.	%	Full.	Half.	%
Freq. 3 : 12...... 200	37	3	19.2	7	9	5.7	83	12	44.5
Freq. 2 : 12...... 143	16	7	13.6	8	16	11.2	29	3	21.3

The table shows the number of those cases in which both numerals were recalled, then the number of cases in which the color suggested only the numeral with which it had been but once associated, and in the last group the number of times in which that numeral was recalled with which the color had been twice or three times combined.   Under the heading 'Half' are given those cases in which one digit of the numeral was recalled, and in estimating per cents. these cases are rated as half correct.   The comparison of the 'frequent' with the unemphasized, that is the 'normal,' shows that, with repetitions amounting to one in four, the *repeated numeral is associated in 63.7 % of the possible cases* (44.5+19.2 %), *the normal in only 24.9 % (5.7+19.2 %).*   When only one numeral is suggested, the 'frequent' appears more than seven times as often as the once combined numeral.

The comparison of both these per cents. with that representing the likelihood of recall for such long series (Table I.) leads to the same conclusion.   *The frequently combined numeral is associated more than twice as often* (63.7 % instead of 26.1 %), while *the unemphasized numeral is associated slightly less often, than the average* (24.9 % instead of 26.1 %).   This latter comparison, which, however, needs substantiation by a greater number of experiments, suggests the negative result of habit, since the effect of habitual combination with a given stimulus is seen to be a small decrease of the likelihood of ordinary connection with the same stimulus.   In the case of subjects with retentive memories—observe, for instance, the record which follows, of Sh. — 'both' numerals are likely to be recalled, the normal as well as the frequent.   This is easily explained when the normal comes late in the series for the occurrence of a color already accentuated by repetition may direct the attention to the following numeral even when that is not emphasized.   This fact makes the general lowering of the percentage of recall of the normal in the 'frequent' series the more striking.

It must be added that in the case of the frequent and the vivid series this influence of position was eliminated by constantly changing the place of the unemphasized pair of stimuli; thus, in the 'vivid' series the normal and the vivid combination alternated between the early middle and the late middle parts of the series; and in the 'frequent' series the normal was placed successively in the early, the early middle, the late middle or the late part of the series. From the results it appears that the normal combination is slightly more likely to be forgotten if placed in the early part of the series, but this does not alter the general tendency.

It is noticeable, also, that the influence of repetition is much lowered when the 'frequent' combination appears twice only instead of three times. The second line of Table II. gives the results; the 'frequent' numeral is recalled in 34.9% of the series (21.3+13.6%) which is only 8.8% more than the ordinary average of associations without repetition, and 28.8% less than the proportion of three times repeated associations. The table of individual records is therefore given only for the one-fourth frequency series; it shows that the results are not due to any misleading massing of the figures, for the preponderance of 'frequency' associations appears for each subject.

TABLE III. FREQUENCY (3:12), VISUAL.

Names.	Number of Series.	Both. Full.	Half.	%	Normal only. Full.	Half.	%	Frequent only. Full.	Half.	%
B.	20	4	1					5	2	
C.	24	3	1		2	3		9	1	
Ha.	13	2				2		6		
Ns.	5							3		
Pt.	22	3			1			14	1	
Shp.	6	2						2	1	
St.	17	2			1	1		12		
Lg.	11	3						5	1	
Mc.	6							3		
N.	11	3				1		2		
E.P.	6				1	2		2		
J.P.	12	1						2	2	
R.	12	3			1			5	1	
Sh.	12	8						3		
Si.	11		1		1			3	1	
So.	12	3						8		
Total,	200	37	3 (19.2%)		7	9 (5.7%)		84	10(44.5%)	

The greatest difficulty of these experiments was unquestionably in the study of vividness as a condition of suggestibility. The category is a vague and elusive one, seeming to include all those forms of the interesting which cannot be referred to the repetition, the recency or the primacy of the experience. In the main, therefore, the 'vivid' is either the 'unusual,' or it is the object of instinctive, and therefore of psychologically inexplicable, interest.

The following summary distinguishes the different devices used to make the combinations 'vivid.' Since the color was always repeated, this result could only be secured by varying the numeral, which was accordingly either black, of two digits, but much smaller than the other numerals (B_{2s}); or black, of usual size, but of three digits (B_3) ; or of usual size and of two digits, but red (R_2); or, finally, of usual size but of three digits and red (R_2), About 200 records obtained from experiments at Wellesley are added to the table.

Table IV. Vividness, Visual.

Nature of Vividness.	Number of Series.	Both. Full.	Half.	%	Normal Alone. Full.	Half.	%	Vivid Alone. Full.	Half.	%
B_1	147	9	6	8.2	11	2	8.2	63	4	44.2
B_2	102	7	2	7.8	12	6	14.7	21	3	22.1
R_1	132	11	5	14.7	11	0	8.3	39	18	36.3
R_2	159	18	6	13.2	12	4	8.8	53	21	39.9

The comparison of these different sorts of impressiveness shows an interesting preponderance of associating three place black numerals (52.4 %) over associating black numerals of only two digits (29.9 %). Since the latter were visually very striking, because so small, this difference is very likely due to the fact that the numerals of three places, introducing, if pronounced, the word 'hundred,' are helped by the articulatory memory. Only the Harvard records are used in the following table of individual results.

Table V. Vividness, Visual.

Names.	Number of Series.	Both. Full.	Half.	%	Normal Only. Full.	Half.	%	Vivid Only. Full.	Half.	%
B.	33				1			13	6	
C.	8				2	1		4		
Ha.	39	4			2			16	3	
Mi.	42	3			9	1		12	7	
Ns.	47	6	1		1			17	2	
Lg.	10	2			1			6	1	
Lh.	35	5	1					7	8	
Mc.	43	11			5	2		10	6	
N.	9					1		1	1	
E.P.	29	4						12	7	
J.P.	10				2			1	2	
R.	11	3						4	1	
Sh.	9	3						1	2	
Si.	10	1			1	1		3	1	
So.	11	1	1		1			6		
Total,	346	43	3	(12.8%)	25	6	(8%)	113	47	(39.4%)

Thus the vividly-associated numerals are remembered in about one-half (52.2 %) of the series, while the normal associations with the same colors are only one-fifth (20.8%) of the entire number. The lessened strength of these sorts of vividness, as compared with that of the three repetitions, is shown by the greater number of cases in which neither numeral is remembered. J. P., however, is the only one of the subjects whose records, only 10 in number, show no influence at all of vividness.

In the attempt to fix a rate of associative recency, series were used varying in length from 4 to 7 pairs. Only the series of 7 pairs proved suitable to the purpose, for in the shorter ones both numerals were usually recalled so that a comparison became impossible. The 'recent' color, which appeared last, of course, in the combination series was placed second, not first, in the test-series, in order that no after-image of the numeral might remain. The individual records which are grouped in the following table offer only one variation from the type, again in the case of J. P. They show that *the last numeral is recalled in 53.7% of the possible cases; the other numeral associated with the same color, only in 25.7%.*

TABLE VI. RECENCY, VISUAL.

Names.	Number of Series.	Both. Full.	Both. Half.	%	Normal Only. Full.	Normal Only. Half.	%	Recent Only. Full.	Recent Only. Half.	%
Hy.	4	1						1	1	
Lg.	9	2						3		
Lh.	19	3						11	1	
Mc.	27	6			1	1		8	3	
Nr.	9				1			3	2	
E.P.	18	2			3			9	1	
J.P.	18	2	1		4	1		3	1	
R.	17	2			2			8	1	
Sh.	12	4			1			4	3	
Si.	15				3	1		3		
So.	17	2			1	3		8	2	
Mi.	6				1			1	1	
B.	10	1			1	1		2	1	
Ha.	9				2			3	1	
Ns.	10	2				1		4		
Total,	200	27		1 (13.7%)	20	8	(12%)	71	18(40%)	

The influence of recency has been studied also in the series which were arranged without this immediate end in view, by recording all cases in which the last numeral was correctly associated with the color on which it had followed. In these cases the likelihood of recall does not surpass that of the average nu meral, though the 'recent' color was shown third in the second half-series: the recall of the recent numeral occurred only in 26.4% of 276 series. *The swiftly decreasing influence of recency*, well-known from such experiments as those of Ebbinghaus on memory, *is thus clearly indicated:* even the intervention of only two colors between the last combination of color and numeral and the reappearance of the color was sufficient to annihilate the effect of the recency.

Finally, the suggestibility of a numeral which had already appeared at the very beginning of a series was compared with that of another numeral combined with the same color midway in the series.

TABLE VII.   PRIMACY, VISUAL.

Names.	Number of Series.	Both. Full.	Half.	%	Normal Only. Full.	Half.	%	Primacy Only. Full.	Half.	%
Hy.	8				1			2		
Lg.	14				1					
Lh.	20	2			8	3		2	1	
Mc.	19	2			2	3		6	2	
Mi.	2				1	1				
N.	18	1			2			6	2	
E.P.	20	4			3	3		2	1	
J.P.	21				3	1		5		
R.	22	1			3	1		12	1	
Sh.	17	3			2	3		6	2	
Si.	17	2			1	2		4	1	
So.	22	3	2		4	1		3	2	
Total,	200	18	2	(9.5%)	31	18	(20%)	48	12	(27%)

The table shows very clearly that with long series, *primacy is a significant factor only in individual cases.* Thus, its influence is very marked on R.'s associations, and may be observed in the records of Mc. and Sh. Lh. on the other hand associates the later numeral, that is the 'normal,' much more often, and with four of the other subjects the normal has a slight advantage. A record of cases was also kept in which the first of the series was remembered, without special competition with any other numeral, but the proportion was barely the average one in the long series; *in the short series* on the other hand *the first numeral was associated in more than two-fifths of*

the cases—in 43%, that is 8% more often than the average numeral and only 8% less often than the recent.

The ineffectiveness of primacy in the long series seems at
first sight to contradict the testimony of common experience
and of experiment,[1] for, in committing long series to memory,
the learner is certainly very apt to remember the first presentation. This difference, however, is easily explained: in
memorizing, the subject sets himself to learn the series as a
whole, and he may not only accentuate the first presentation,
but recur to it while learning the rest of the series; moreover,
when he repeats the series, or records it in writing, he almost
invariably gives first the earliest presentation. In the association experiment, on the contrary, the first presentation was
always repeated toward the middle of the test-series, thus multiplying the chances that the combination would be crowded out
of the memory.

2. *Simultaneous Arrangement. Visual Series.*

These general results have been amplified, and at the same
time verified, by introducing series in which the connected
color and numeral were simultaneously shown. This method
might have been used more often, since the simultaneous combination of stimuli is perhaps more common in ordinary experience than the successive; but the experiments of the successive
type, in which the combination of color and numeral is emphasized
by the long pause between each pair, were employed as affording
a close comparison between the visual and the auditory series. So
far, however, as these subjects are concerned, the results of the
simultaneous series are so closely parallel with those of the successive ones that no characteristic differences appear. Color
and numeral were shown side by side in an opening 10x4 cm.,
by slipping them into double passe-partout frames, made for
the purpose. Each frame held a color and a numeral separated by a narrow band of white. The intervals of exposure
were six seconds, and in a few series four seconds; the pauses
were usually six seconds, occasionally four seconds. In each
of the three most important simple forms of the experiment, 50

[1] Cf. Dr. W. G. Smith, *Psychological Review*, III., p. 30.

tests were made. The average of recall, leaving out of account the emphasized numerals, was 25.4% for the 100 long series and 30% for the 50 short series, thus falling, as has been said, slightly below the average of recall in the successive series. Moreover the percentage of emphasized numerals which were associated was slightly greater than in the successive series, because of the larger number of cases in which *both* numerals were recalled. This result, however, may be due to the greater degree of practice when these simultaneous tests were made.

The number of experiments is so small that the individual records are not given, but they are *closely parallel with those of the successive series.* In the table which follows, the figures for the 'half' correct, which are small, are combined with those of the fully correct, and the corresponding per cents. of the successive series are added in parenthesis.

TABLE VIII. SIMULTANEOUS COMBINATION.

Nature of Series.	Number of Series.	Both.		Normal only.		Emphasized.	
		Sim. No. %	Suc. %	Sim. No. %	Suc. %	Sim. No. %	Suc. %
Freq.	50	11 22%	1½ 3%	(19%)	(5.7%)	24 48%	(44.5%)
Viv.	50	15 30 "	4½ 9 "	(12.8")	(8 ")	19 38 "	(39.4 ")
Rec.	50	10 21 "	5½ 11"	(13.7")	(12 ")	19 38 "	(40.7 ")

b. Auditory Series.

All the varieties of experiment which have so far been described, except those in primacy, were repeated with nonsense syllables and numerals, as the association-elements, both pronounced to the subjects. These series were arranged in pairs of a nonsense syllable and a numeral each, with four seconds allowed to the pronunciation of each pair, and four seconds interval both between the pairs and between the two parts of the series. One series will serve as illustration of all.

Series 335b. Vivid, Auditory.

I. Zet, 24; Kip, 62; Tox, 96; *Wez, 319 (v)*; Vit, 38; Lup, 45; Nuk, 29; *Wez, 73 (n)*; Vab, 57; Muv, 41.

II. Vit, Kip, Muv, Zet, *Wez,* Nuk, Lup, Vab, Tox.

The results of the *experiments are generally parallel with those of the visual tests*, with certain suggestive variations which will be noticed later. The general average of recall, disregarding the accentuated pairs is shown in

TABLE IX. CORRECT ASSOCIATIONS, AUDITORY.

Series.	Number of Series.	Possible Correct Associations.	Actual Correct Associations.		
			Full.	Half.	%
Long.	254	2405	498	22	(25.3%)
Short.	100	581	118	39	(23.6%)

The 'frequent' numeral is recalled twice as often as the unemphasized (in 80 % as against 40 % of the possible cases) as appears from

TABLE X. FREQUENCY (3:12) AUDITORY.

Names.	Number of Series.	Both.			Normal only.			Frequent only.		
		Full.	Half.	%	Full.	Half.	%	Full.	Half.	%
Hy.	5	1						1		
Lg.	14	8			1			3	1	
Lh.	12	3				1		5	2	
Mc.	15	9						4	2	
Nr.	14		1			1		7	2	
E.P.	14	5	1					5	2	
J.P.	14	9						2	3	
R.	15	4						7	3	
Sh.	17	8				1		6	2	
Si.	14	8						3	3	
So.	16	2				1		9	3	
Total,	150	57	2	(38%)	1	4	(2%)	52	23	(42%)

The position of the normal in the series was carefully varied, as in the visual experiments. The following table shows, however, that *whatever the position of the normal, associations with the repeated numeral are much in excess*, though they decrease where the normal is midway in the series so that the repetition affects it also.

TABLE XI. FREQUENCY, AUDITORY.

Position of Normal.	Number of Series.	Both.			Normal Only.			Frequent Only.		
		Full.	Half.	%	Full.	Half.	%	Full.	Half.	%
Early.	42	11		(26 %)				25	3	(63 %)
Middle.	57	26		(45.6")		3	(2.6%)	10	13	(28.9")
Late.	51	20	2	(41 ")	1	1	(3 ")	17	7	(40 ")
	150	57	2	(38 ")	1	4	(2 ")	52	23	(42 ")

Two methods of making a numeral impressive were employed. Sometimes, as in the example given, a numeral of three digits was used. At other times the emphasized numeral was read in a very loud tone. The next summary shows that both methods were effective, but that the voice-stress was a little more impressive.

TABLE XII. VIVID, AUDITORY.

Nature of Vivid.	Number of Series.	Both.			Normal Only.			Frequent Only.		
		Full.	Half.	%	Full.	Half.	%	Full.	Half.	%
Digits.	97	14	3	(15.9%)	4	9	(9.7%)	26	29	(41.7%)
Loud.	103	22	1	(21.8 ")	6	6	(8.7 ")	31	7	(33.4 ")
Total,	200	36	4	(19 %)	10	15	(8.7%)	57	36	(37.5%)

The individual records show *greater variation from the type than the reports of frequency-association.*

TABLE XIII. VIVID, AUDITORY.

Names.	Number of Series.	Both.			Normal only.			Vivid only.		
		Full.	Half.	%	Full.	Half.	%	Full.	Half.	%
Hy.	4							1		
Lg.	19	2				2		6	4	
Lh.	14	2	2			1		6	2	
Mc.	22	5	1		1	2		10	2	
Nr.	10					1			3	
E.P.	12	2			1			7	2	
J.P.	23	8	1		1			4	5	
R.	26	3			4	5		7	4	
Sh.	23	7				1		6	8	
Si.	20	3			3	1		2	3	
So.	27	4				2		8	3	
Total,	200	36	4	(19%)	10	15	(8.7%)	57	36	(37.5%)

The influence of the position of the normal shows itself, as in the other series, in the larger number of cases in which ' both ' are remembered, when the normal comes after the vivid combination.

TABLE XIV. VIVID, AUDITORY.

Position of Normal.	Number of Series.	Both.			Normal only			Vivid only.		
		Full.	Half.	%	Full.	Half.	%	Full.	Half.	%
Early.	108	13		(12%)	7	4	(8%)	40	22	(46%)
Late.	92	23	4	(27 ")	3	11	(9 ")	17	14	(26 ")
Total,	200	36	4	(19%)	10	15	(8.7%)	57	36	(37.5%)

The records of the recency experiments show *the very striking effect of auditory recency.* There are no individual variations from the general type, and *the number of cases in which the normal is remembered does not rise above one-eighth.* In about half the records the 'recent' is wholly or partially remembered in every case.

TABLE XV. RECENCY, AUDITORY.

Names.	Number of Series.	Both. Full.	Half.	%	Normal Only. Full.	Half.	%	Recent Only. Full.	Half.	%
Hy.	5							5		
Lg.	9	1						8		
Lh.	6							5	1	
Mc.	9	3						4	1	
N.	8							4	3	
E. P.	10							9	1	
J. P.	10	2				1		4	2	
R.	11	1			1			7	1	
Sh.	10	1						5	1	
Si.	11	2			1	1		5	2	
So.	11							10	1	
Total,	100	10		(10%)	2	2	(3%)	66	13	(72.5%)

Auditory experiments to determine the effectiveness of primacy were undertaken, but were soon discontinued because they showed from the beginning the insignificance of this factor in long series. In the short auditory series, however, as in the visual, the first position proved very important: the first numeral was associated in 38.4% of the possible cases, that is, in 14% more than the average number.

The general relations of the auditory to the visual series appear in the next table in which only per cents. are given:

XVI. COMPARISON OF VISUAL AND AUDITORY ASSOCIATIONS.

Type of Series.	Correct Ass.	Both.	Normal.	F, V or R.	Total F, V or R.	Total Normal.
F. Vis.	26%	19%	6 %	44.5%	63.5%	25 %
F. Aud.	25 "	38 "	2 "	42 "	80 "	40 "
Viv. Vis.	26 "	13 "	8 "	39.4 "	52 "	21 "
Viv. Aud.	25 "	19 "	8.7 "	37.5 "	56.5 "	27.7 "
Rec. Vis.	33 "	14 "	12 "	40 "	54 "	26 "
Rec. Aud.	23 "	10 "	3 "	72.5 "	82.5 "	13 "

These figures may seem to contradict Dr. Münsterberg's conclusion[1], from his memory experiments, that " when isolated the visual memory surpasses by far the aural." But the comparison of visual and aural memory in these association-experiments is, in the first place, an unfair one, since the suggesting stimuli differ so much in the two types of experiment, consisting in the one case of colors, in the other of syllables. Furthermore, the figures themselves (in the column of 'Correct Associations') show that the memory for ordinary combinations is rather stronger in the visual series. *The suggestiveness, not the reproduction, seems to be increased in the auditory series,* and this is very likely a case of the well-known associativeness of language. The preponderance, already noticed, of recency associations is also, perhaps, peculiar to verbal suggestions. At the very least, the auditory experiments corroborate the results of the visual by reproducing these in another sense-material.

II. Comparative Series.

In showing that frequency, vividness, primacy and recentness are conditions of association these experiments have so far, of course, merely substantiated ordinary observation. The real purpose of the investigation is attained only by a comparison of these factors. Already it has appeared that the per cent. of correct 'frequency' associations is slightly the largest, and that recency is the principle of the combination in the next greatest number of cases. In order, however, to carry out the comparison under like conditions, these principles of combination were compared within the same series. To this end, long ' successive' series were arranged in which the significance of frequency was contrasted with that of vividness by showing a color three times with the same two-digit numeral (f) and once with a three-digit numeral (v) ; others, in which the color three times shown with a numeral (f) appeared also at the first of the series with another numeral (p). Short 'successive' series were formed in which the last color (r) had appeared once before

[1] *Psychological Review*, I., p. 37.

with a three-digit numeral (v), or at the very beginning of the series (p), or twice before with a repeated numeral (f).

In the following summary of results of the comparison of frequency and primacy, half the records are those of Wellesley subjects. The individual records are not given because they are few in number and show no variation. The experiments were not continued further because their result was so unmistakable, verifying the conclusion already reached by the study of primacy alone, that this is evidently an unimportant feature of long series.

TABLE XVII. FREQUENCY AND PRIMACY.

Number of Series.	Both. Full. Half.	%	Prim. Only Full. Half.	%	Freq. Only Full. Half.	%
80	15 2	20%	3 2	5%	44 3	56.8%

The comparison of frequency with vividness shows far less inequality, and yet *there is a definite excess of correct associations with frequency.* In half the cases where there was any association at all, both the frequent and the vivid numeral were recalled. The records are these:

TABLE XVIII. FREQUENCY AND VIVIDNESS.

Names.	Number of Series.	Both. Full. Half.	%	Vivid Full. Half.	%	Frequent. Full. Half.	%
Hy.	7					2 2	
Lg.	13	8				2	
Lh.	23	15		1		3 4	
Mc.	26	12		3		6 4	
Na.	17	2		1 1		8 2	
E. P.	20	16		1		2 1	
J. P.	18	4		7		3 1	
R.	23	13		1		2 6	
Sh.	16	11		1		3	
Si.	14	4		3		6	
So.	23	6		1		9 5	
Total,	200	91	(45.5%)	16 4	(9%)	44 27	(28.7%)

This shows *a total of 74.2% (28.7+45.5) of associations with the numeral frequently combined* with the color presented, and *54.5% (9+45.5) of associations with the numeral vividly combined.* Frequency, however, is not invariably the more determining factor: the records of E. P., Lh., and Sh. show only a small difference between 'frequent' and 'vivid' associations, while J. P. has more with the vividly combined numeral.

The greater significance of frequency of combination was brought out more strongly by lengthening and filling the interval between the half-series. After the pairs of colors and numerals had been shown to the subjects, short anecdotes or news-items, of about one hundred and fifty words, were rapidly read aloud. The test series, of colors only, was then shown and the subjects tried as usual to associate the numerals. The table shows that the per cent. of association was a little lowered, but that the per cent. of frequency associations is greater than after the unfilled interlude. *The frequently combined numerals seem to be more tenaciously associated.* This method might with advantage have been extended to the other experiments.

TABLE XIX. FREQUENCY AND VIVIDNESS.

INFLUENCE OF FILLED INTERLUDE.

Inter-lude.	No. of Series.	Both.			Viv. Only.			Freq. Only.		
		Full.	Half.	%	Full.	Half.	%	Full.	Half.	%
Unfilled.	89	49	(55	%)	7	1	(8.4%)	16	10	(23.6%)
Filled.	111	42	(37.8	")	9	3	(9.4 ")	28	17	(32.8 ")
Total,	200	91	(45.5	")	16	4	(9 ")	44	27	(28.7 ")

The influence of position in the series does not alter the general relation of frequent and vivid associations, though the greatest number of 'frequent associations only' does occur where the vivid numeral is nearest the beginning of the first half-series and so at a relative disadvantage. The greatest likelihood of remembering 'both' occurs when the vivid is near the middle of the series so that it is influenced by the repetition and itself influences the remaining repetitions. All this appears in the following table:

TABLE XX. FREQUENCY AND VIVIDNESS.

INFLUENCE OF POSITION IN SERIES.

Position of Vivid.	Number of Series.	Both			Vivid.			Freq. Only.		
		Full.	Half.	%	Full.	Half.	%	Full.	Half.	%
Early.	68	25	(36.7%)		7	1	(11 %)	20	9	(36%)
Midway.	72	42	(58.3 ")		5	1	(7.6 ")	12	5	(20 ")
Late.	60	24	(40 ")		4	2	(8.3 ")	12	13	(30.8 ")
Total,	200	91	(45.5 ")		16	4	(9 ")	44	27	(28.7 ")

The results of the comparison of recency with the other conditions of suggestibility is made in the three following tables:

TABLE XXI. RECENCY AND VIVIDNESS.

Name.	Number of Series.	Both.			Vivid Only.			Rec. Only.		
		Full.	Half.	%	Full.	Half.	%	Full.	Half.	%
Hy.	5	1								
Lg.	9	6			1					
Lh.	26	6			5	7		2	3	
Mc.	22	4			7	4		2		
Mi.	10	2			2			2	1	
Nh.	10	3			4			1		
E.P.	24	13			4	1		3	1	
J.P.	17	3	1		2	1		1		
R.	17	8	1		2	3			1	
Sh.	11	6			3	2				
Si.	9							2		
So.	17	2			1	1		6	3	
B.	6				2	1				
Ha.	8	3			1	2				
Ns.	9	2			2	1		3		
Total,	200	59	2	(30%)	36	23	(23.7%)	22	9	(13.2%)

TABLE XXII. RECENCY AND FREQUENCY.

Name.	Number of Series.	Both.			Frequent Only.			Recent Only.		
		Full.	Half.	%	Full.	Half.	%	Full.	Half.	%
B.	6					2				
Ha.	8	2			3	2		1		
Lg.	9	6						1		
Lh.	11	2			1	2		2	1	
Mc.	17	7			5	2			1	
Mi.	10	6			3			1		
Nr.	3	1	1					1		
Ns.	9	3			2	2		1		
E.P.	8	3			1	2		2		
J.P.	7	3			1			1	1	
R.	10	7	2					1		
Sh.	10	6			2			1		
Si.	7				2			2	1	
So.	10	4			2	1		3		
Total,	125	50	3	(41.2%)	22	13	(22.8%)	17	4	(15.2%)

TABLE XXIII. RECENCY AND PRIMACY.

Name.	Number of Series.	Both. Full.	Half.	%	Primacy Only. Full.	Half.	%	Recent Only. Full.	Half.	%
Ha.	4	1						1	1	
Lg.	13	6			1	1		3		
Lh.	4	2			1					
Mc.	8	2			1	1		1	2	
Mj.	4	1						3		
Na.	8	1			2	1		1		
Ns.	3	1			1					
E.P	3	2								
J.P.	4							2	1	
R.	13	4				4		2	1	
Sh.	12	2	1		1	3		3	1	
Si.	10							3	1	
So.	14	3			3	1		6		
Total,	100	25	1 (25.5%)		10	11 (15.5%)		25	7 (28.5%)	

The discussion of these results will be facilitated by comparing the per cents. of the total number of the recent and of the contrasted associations in the different cases:

	RECENT ASSOC. %	CONTRASTED ASSOC. %
Rec. and Viv.	43.2%	(v) 53.7%
Rec. and Freq.	56.2 "	(F) 64 "
Rec. and Prim.	54 "	(P) 41 "

It appears that in *this direct competition recency yields both to frequency and to vividness as a condition of suggestibility.* The vivid numeral seems even to suppress the recent, for in the recent-vivid series the recent is recalled 10% less often than in the series where the recent is compared with an ordinary numeral (See Table VI.). On the other hand, the effect of recency is as usual, to raise the likelihood of the recall of the contrasted numeral, but not to the level of the frequent associations.

The associations with the first numeral of the series are decidedly less than those with the recent, though far more numerous than in the longer series. Individual differences, however, are to be noticed here, and would doubtless appear more strongly in a larger number of experiments; they may also be observed in a few records of the other short series, as in that of So., who has few vivid, and many recent, associations.

From this mass of figures a few conclusions emerge into prominence. Some of these have been already formulated, but the more important ones may be briefly stated again.

No one of these generalizations, it should be remarked, is proof against the caprice of the individual, who may have his own favorite type of association which resists opposition. Thus the preference of one of our subjects—So.—for the recent may be traced through almost all the series, often in contradiction of the general result.

Frequency has been the most constant condition of suggestibility. The proportion of the frequent as compared with the normal associations is one-tenth greater than that of the vivid or of the recent. When directly compared with the vivid and the recent the proportion is still greater, though the number of associations with the contrasted numeral is larger than that of the associations with an ordinary one, because of the tendency of the repetition to accentuate the compared factor.

This significance of frequency is rather surprising. For though everybody recognizes the importance of repetition in forming associations, we are yet more accustomed to 'account for' these by referring to recent or to impressive combinations. The possibility that the prominence of frequency in our results is not fairly representative of ordinary trains of association is strengthened by the fact that it is contrasted with forms of vividness which are only two or three of many, and which do not approach the impressiveness, for instance, of richly emotional experiences. But this does not affect the importance of frequency as a corrective influence. Granted a sufficient number of repetitions, it seems possible to supplement, if not actually to supplant, associations which have been formed through impressive or through recent experiences. Moreover, the trustworthiness of the ordinary observation, which relegates frequency to a comparatively unimportant place among the factors of suggestibility, may be seriously questioned: I have found many cases, during experiments in free association in which the subject, asked to explain the association, does not always mention repetition, even when it has obviously occurred, but seems, as it were, to take it for granted. The prominence of frequency is of course of grave importance, for it means the possibility of exercising some control over the life of the imagination and of definitely combating harmful or troublesome associations.

Monograph Supplement.　　No. 3, October, 1896.

THE

Psychological Review

EDITED BY

J. McKEEN CATTELL　　*AND*　　J. MARK BALDWIN
COLUMBIA UNIVERSITY　　　　　PRINCETON UNIVERSITY

WITH THE CO-OPERATION OF

ALFRED BINET, ÉCOLE DES HAUTES-ÉTUDES, PARIS; JOHN DEWEY, UNIVERSITY OF
CHICAGO; H. H. DONALDSON, UNIVERSITY OF CHICAGO; G. S. FULLERTON,
UNIVERSITY OF PENNSYLVANIA; WILLIAM JAMES, HARVARD UNIVERSITY;
JOSEPH JASTROW, UNIVERSITY OF WISCONSIN; G. T. LADD, YALE
UNIVERSITY; HUGO MÜNSTERBERG, HARVARD UNIVERSITY;
M. ALLEN STARR, COLLEGE OF PHYSICIANS AND SURGEONS,
NEW YORK; CARL STUMPF, UNIVERSITY, BERLIN;
JAMES SULLY, UNIVERSITY COLLEGE, LONDON.

The

Mental Development

of a

Child

By

Kathleen Carter Moore

PUBLISHED BI-MONTHLY BY
THE MACMILLAN COMPANY,
66 FIFTH AVENUE, NEW YORK; AND LONDON.

PREFATORY NOTE.

It is unavoidable, yet to be regretted, that fuller biblio-
graphical references do not accompany this work. In the
presence of such a defect I must not omit an acknowledgment
of indebtedness to Professor Preyer[1] and to Professor Wundt,[2]
from whose works, more than from anything else which I have
read, have been drawn the inspiration and enlightenment which
enabled me to carry out my observations.

Mr. Moore has given me many suggestions and much help
in the corroboration of observations—invaluable aids in the
collection of facts.

[1] Die Seele des Kindes, translated and condensed by Miss Emma Marwedel,
and appended to her book, Conscious Motherhood.

[2] Physiologische Psychologie.

TABLE OF CONTENTS.

Prefatory Note..iii
Introduction 1-7

PART I.—MOVEMENTS.

Preliminary 8-11
Section 1, Habits 12-23
    *A Personal Habit....'. *12-15
    *Grasping and allied Habits.............................*15-23
Section 2, Voluntary Movements 23-32
Section 3, Inhibitory Movements..............................32-35
Section 4, Automatic Movements........ 35-37
Section 5, Movements of Emotional Expression 37-42
Section 6, Reflex Movements..................................42-43
Summary 43-44

PART II.—SENSATIONS.

Section 1, Sight...45-60
    Observations on the Development of Visual Percep-
    tion 45-50
    Vision, general discussion...............................50-60
Section 2, Hearing 60-72
Section 3, Touch...72-82
Section 4, Taste..82-83
Section 5, Smell 83-84

PART III.—IDEAS.

Section 1, Mental Development.................................85-105
Section 2, Time...106-107
Section 3, Distance, Direction and Magnitude.....................107-112
Section 4, Notes on the Recognition and Interpretation of Pic-
    tures..112-114

PART IV.—LANGUAGE.

Section 1, Sounds. 115-120
Section 2, Words...120-131
Section 3, Sentences 131-137

With ten illustrative tables.

INTRODUCTION.

The attitude of mind in which an observer approaches the child must exert an important influence upon the interpretation of that which she observes. In imagination she may project herself into the infant's life, regarding him as a bit of humanity, potentially rich in thoughts and emotions whose manifestations are to be met with in any form of activity whatsoever. The unfolding germs of mental life, she may be inclined to identify as the seed leaves of a glorious plant. Such an attitude is not conducive to an impartial interpretation of facts. To read too much between the lines may obscure the true meaning of the text. On the other hand, an observer may watch the child with intelligent interest to learn what she can of the processes of development. She weighs, sifts and classifies; she regards the child as a child, and not as a diminutive man. It is obvious that a well proportioned mixture of two such positions would give a basis upon which to accomplish most. She who is so profoundly imbued with the love of her subject that nothing is too trivial to evoke a sympathetic response, yet in whom the habit of reflection is so strong that no observation can be allowed to pass unmeasured and unclassified, will be the one to gather the greatest harvest of facts, to estimate justly the value of each, and its relation to all.

A condition of equal moment to that of the observer is that of the observed—the subject. Everything must be subservient to the comfort and welfare of the child. Over-excitement and fatigue are injurious to the child; and, as much intercourse with people produces both excitement and fatigue, observations must sometimes be brought to a standstill when one feels oneself on the verge of important disclosures. Nor can the young child always be made to act under a given set of conditions. The chances are that he may not respond to one's cleverly arranged experiment.

Personally I have constantly been impressed by the extreme difficulty of making tests. Most of my attempts to obtain results through experiments have proved signal failures.[1] I early gave up the idea of obtaining the bulk of facts with the help of experiments, and occupied myself with the observation of the phenomena of development, as they one by one arose and assumed more generous proportions and complicated relations. Nor did I find any dearth of material. I can say now, with a vast quantity of classified facts at hand, that the method which I employed holds its own with any other. Every verified observation made under known and carefully noted conditions, is as valuable as an observation made under prearranged conditions. But the facts are more unwieldy to handle, and it requires endless patience to get them.

In brief, my method comprised :

I.
- *A.*—The observation of all manifestations of activity.
- *B.*—The observation of the conditions under which a given manifestation occurred.
- *C.*—The prompt recording of *A* and *B.*

II.
- *D.*—The observation of all manifestations of change.
- *E.*—The observation of the conditions under which a given manifestation of change occurred.
- *F.*—The prompt recording of *D* and *E.*

The facts obtained from I. gave data from which to study the formation of habits, the fixed lines of activity. Those obtained from II. afforded a basis for a study of expansion and development. Beside this, summaries were written out at stated intervals which described and reviewed the mental condition of the child at given periods. The first of such descriptions summarized the advancement in all lines of activity. Later, when there was so much to record, it was found more satisfactory to confine a summary within the limits of a definite set of activities.[2] Tendencies also were carefully noted.

---

[1] I do not wish to be understood to oppose the employment of the experimental method. Doubtless my own want of ingenuity in devising experiments had much to do with my lack of success.

[2] Language, association, etc.

No observation has been incorporated into the body of facts out of which this story of development is woven, which has not received corroboration from subsequent observations. Excepting those of the first seven days, in which I was greatly assisted by my husband, and twelve sentences recorded in the second year, all observations herein presented were made and recorded by myself. In one respect, my observations sometimes lacked completeness. As this has been the only infant mind whose unfolding I have carefully followed, I failed to recognize in all cases the first appearance of each advancing step; hence, my time record, though always approximately accurate, is sometimes at fault by a few days, or even a week; I have therefore adopted the custom of recording dates by weeks instead of by days, after the sixtieth day. Fortunately in such cases, in pursuance of the plan summed up in II., there existed in the journal a register of the gradations by which the higher plane had been reached.

Notes of the reactions of the child to the normal surroundings are the material most of value in such a study as the present one. But such material does not easily lend itself to the manufacture of quantitative tables. In writing out my results, I have, where tabulation was difficult, arranged series of typical observations in a progressive form. These have the advantage of placing before the reader facts from which, if he so choose, he may independently draw his own conclusions. They have a further advantage. I have ventured to hope that some mother wishing to understand her growing child, and eager to be in close sympathy with the pulsations of baby life, might seek assistance in these pages, and I knew that the record of concrete cases would be of help to her.

The course of my child's development has, I believe, been a normal one. He suffered but little from interference, and was never stimulated to premature action. He was accustomed to playing alone. Especial care was taken not to teach him the tricks which are commonly taught to babies; but some he did learn. He heard neither 'baby talk' nor any of the set phrases which are regarded as suitable to the comprehension of small children. When it was necessary that he should be taught habits essential to his welfare, no pains were spared. Regular hours of feeding, sleeping, etc., were maintained.   Good health and rapid growth have uniformly been his.

The period of infancy is said to extend over the first two years of life.   In order to give an introductory outline of the movement and direction of development, I have subdivided infancy into four periods, each of which is characterized by the vigorous growth of some form of activity.   These are no artificial divisions made for purposes of convenience.   The close of one period overlapped the beginning of its successor, but the respective high-water marks were clearly distinguishable.

The development, practice, and use of the sensory apparatus belonged primarily to the first year, while the formation of concepts and the acquirement of language were characteristic of the second year, as speech and action daily served to show. The four periods have been designated accordingly as those

1. Of seeing.
2. Of feeling.
3. Of examination.
4. Of speaking.

Three of the four periods were completed within the first year; the fourth extended over the entire second year.   The first was of four months' duration, beginning at birth.   Sight cannot be said to have been more active during this time than later, but it was certainly more active in proportion to the activity of the other senses than at any subsequent period.   The child was entertained almost exclusively by what he saw.   At the close of the fourth month, he had learned to distinguish some sounds and to localize them to a certain extent.   Muscle and skin sensation had also developed considerably during the four months, and he had acquired some control over his own body.   Concerning taste and smell, I found little to record.   The point which I wish to make in thus referring to the degrees of development which other senses had respectively attained is, that of all senses sight was the one whose objects engendered interest, engaged attention, stimulated effort and furnished material for a later growth of ideas.   I have called this period that of seeing, wishing to make a distinction between seeing and active looking, which latter term is too closely related to examination to express the mental attitude of the child during the four months in question.

At three months of age, the child for the first time was observed to follow with his eyes his own reaching and grasping hand. From this time, the ability to reach for and grasp objects developed rapidly. By the end of the fourth month he took pleasure in feeling of all sorts of things which came within his reach, from his clothing and parts of his own body to the balls of the first Froebelian gift. Gradually the desire to have and to finger things developed, until the pleasures of sight alone were no longer sufficient, but had to be supplemented by the satisfactions of touch. The second period has been called that of feeling. At first glance, the term may seem too general; but there is no other which fits so well. Either contact or touch would be too specific; for I wish to include in the term, sensations from the whole series of activities involving the use of muscles, bones and skin. All general bodily activity gave him pleasure so long as it fell short of fatigue. The ability to recognize and localize sounds increased in a marked degree. But feeling was undoubtedly the source from which the child derived most during his second period. When sitting became a habit, feeling gave place to examination.

The foundations of the more developed activities of the third period were laid by the continual looking and feeling of the first seven months. During the five months covered by the third period the child was developing along all lines. He was chiefly engaged in acquiring control of his own body, and in the examination of common objects. He gained considerable knowledge of familiar household objects through handling them, placing them in all sorts of positions, putting together and taking apart. He learned to sit alone, to raise himself to a sitting position, to pull himself upon his feet, to stand and to step forward with assistance in balancing, to roll, to get on his hands and knees, to creep, to feed himself from the bottle, and with bread also. He learned to use a few words and to understand a number. He showed himself capable of forming some abstractions. And the primary links were formed of that chain which, in later life, binds each of us in some measure to his social inheritance.

The acquirement of language was the conspicuous feature of the fourth period. At its beginning—at the close of the first year—the child had a vocabulary of but few words, though a language of gesture aided him in making known his wants; at its close he commanded enough of language to place him in intelligent communication with other persons. He learned during the fourth period to walk alone, to get upon his feet without pulling himself up by the arms, to run, to walk on knees, toes or heels, to go up and down the stairs or an inclined plane, to climb on the furniture and to take care of himself in all ordinary situations. He performed a number of acts requiring nice muscular adjustments. The range of perception became extended with astonishing rapidity. New ideas were formed and old ones modified. In short, change and progress occurred everywhere during the second year.

There are some other features of development which should be considered in such a general review as this. Progress, uninterrupted as its course was, still had seasons of noticeable acceleration and intervals of extraordinary slowness. I was unable to discover what causes governed the varying rate of advancement. A known physical cause acted as a retarding agent only once; namely, when a bad cold made it prudent to keep the child from the floor just as he was learning to walk. He suffered no real set-back then, merely a postponement of accomplishment.

The first of the seasons of rapid development began on the thirty-fifth day. It was ushered in by a day of awakening,[1] upon which the child seemed extraordinarily bright and intelligent. His face wore an expression of alertness and he evinced a new interest in objects. He looked continually at persons, smiled repeatedly at them, and responded to words addressed to him by various cooings and gurglings. When the child was three and a-half months old, another peculiarly bright day occurred. Upon this day also he seemed unusually alert. He appeared to understand what was being done for him, and fell naturally into the scheme of regularity which I had tried to maintain. From that day he composed himself for sleep when, at the hour for his nap, he was laid upon his bed.

[1] Preyer describes such a day.

The third period of rapid development occurred in the eleventh month. The ability to creep, acquired within a few days, ushered in another means of gaining perceptions, so that within two weeks the child seemed to have learned a great deal that was new.

The fourth period came with learning to walk (fourteenth month). During it, he gained much in the art of using his body to advantage, and acquired a new understanding of certain features of his surroundings which previously he could take in by sight only. Some words were added to his vocabulary.

An interval of six weeks separated the fourth and fifth seasons (sixteenth month). During the fifth period, which lasted for two weeks, the rate of development was a rapid one. The sixth and last season was observed in the twenty-first month, when words, hitherto added to the vocabulary so slowly, came into use at the rate of one to three daily.

It was difficult to estimate the length of one of these seasons, which seemed to wax suddenly, and to wane gradually. The gains made while they lasted, remained with the child to be incorporated into his daily life; no premonitory signs announced their approach, though he was slowly preparing for each during the interval which preceded it. In looking for an explanation of the periods these facts would seem to point away from a field of causation wholly external to the child. Perhaps like a clay modeller who works by turns upon each portion of the figure he is moulding, and finds his model finished as if by magic beneath his touch, the child, experimenting now here, now there, gaining control first in one direction then in another, one day surprises his elders by a display of knowledge and ability of which they had not supposed him possessed. The acquisition of new power then leads to an increase of knowledge and the growth of further ability along related lines. However this may be, the rate of progress apparently became more uniform after the sixth period, because the striking features of its course had been developed.

PART I.—MOVEMENTS.

PRELIMINARY.

All motor manifestations of the child, from the spontaneous physiological activities of nerve centers and muscles to the complex actions of later infancy, may be classified as movements. Hence, this has been selected as the most suitable term under which to subordinate the several divisions contained in Part I. of the present work. The materials for the study of the development of movements I have classified under eight heads, as follows:

1. Spontaneous
2. Instinctive
3. Habitual
4. Voluntary
5. Automatic } Movements.
6. Inhibitory
7. Expressive
8. Mechanical

The succession in which this enumeration of the classes of movements is arranged does not indicate, except in the roughest way, the order of their development.

According to the classification made by Preyer, which has been quoted and used by other authors,[1] the movements of a child have been arranged in four groups,[2] designated—

1. Impulsive
2. Instinctive } Movements.
3. Reflex
4. Voluntary

At birth, movements of the first class (spontaneous or impulsive) were the most conspicuous. Immediately after birth, the

[1] For example: *The Psychology of Childhood*, Tracy, 2nd edition, p. 92.
[2] *The Senses and the Will* (Preyer), pp. 195-201. Also *The Infant Mind* (Preyer), pp. 51-55.

child continued to lie in a position which closely resembled that of the fœtus. The early movements were generally conditioned in range and direction, by the maintenance of this position. Within an hour after birth the arms were waved towards the head and face; the legs were repeatedly straightened and flexed, the eye balls rolled continually beneath the closed lids, the muscles of the face were active. With the development of action, movements such as these gradually disappeared. The change was very noticeable in the case of the eye ball. With increased frequency and perfection in the visual coördinations of the eye muscles, the eyeballs ceased altogether to roll about (during the hours of wakefulness.) Preyer, observing (a) the number and variety of the early movements, (b) the occurrence of adaptive movements while the spontaneous movements were conspicuous, and (c) the gradual disappearance of the early movements as adaptations became habitual, was led to regard adaptive motor coördinations as combinations of the purposeless movements, fortunate in their results, and therefore selected and preserved. He then ascribed to them the function of progenitors to the succeeding generations of movements, whether these be habitual bodily activities (walking etc.), or voluntary actions. To movements standing in this ancestral relation the name impulsive might fitly be applied. But a consideration of the phenomena of movement, and in particular the observation of just what movements were selected for further development, have led me to the belief that the significance of these movements is not what Preyer supposed it to be, and that they are in consequence more correctly named spontaneous[1] movements. In this series of independent, but related studies, spontaneous movements are not treated in a separate division. They are often referred to and severally described from time to time during the course of the discussions.

The definition of instinct here adopted as a basis for the discrimination of certain classes of movements is this: An instinct is the ability to perform without previous individual experience, a given purposive act by which changes in con-

---

[1] As such they are designated by Bain, *The Emotions and the Will;* The WHl, Chap. I., and by Prof. Baldwin, *Mental Development,* p. 81.

scious states are induced. This definition does not permit of the inclusion in the class of instincts of the habitual actions called race instincts. One and all of the race instincts (sitting, walking, running, etc.), were acquired slowly, and their attainment was the result of a great number of previous trials, failures and partial successes. Herein they differed widely from actions which were at once performed without experience, such as sucking and clasping. In order to show by comparison that the manner of acquiring a habit common to the human race is in no wise different from the way in which a personal habit becomes fixed, I shall describe fully the rise of one habit of each class—grasping, and sucking the thumb.

The studies of these have moreover a three-fold purpose:

I. To give the history of the rise of the habit.

II. To ascertain the primitive, or simplest types of movement upon which were built up subsequent coördinations, complications, and modifications of movements.

III. To discover the principles upon which rested the development of the series from the types.

The movements described as habitual, voluntary, automatic and inhibitory are closely related forms of activity. In the chapters devoted to the discussion of these movements it will be more clearly shown what, and how close, the relationship is.

All my notes on movements might be called into requisition for a study of the development of automatism in the child. There is no doubt that the child at birth was a being less endowed than at two years of age with the ability to perform automatic acts, and possessed with fewer forms of the same. Without, however, pretending to cover the general question, I shall give the history of some automatic actions.

I could not in this study in individual psychology, discuss adequately the standpoint of modern psychologists on the question of emotional expression and development. The evidence obtained from a single individual may be sufficient to make one distrust general conclusions, and yet in itself lack the volume and detail upon which to base new ones. In the chapters on movements of expression and mechanical reflexes I have recorded facts which related to the development of the child, but the material, though suggestive, was somewhat too scanty to be used as the foundation of special studies within the respective fields.

Before bringing these preliminary remarks to a close it may be well to record examples of the survival and transformation of some spontaneous movements which were preserved in connection with forms of habitual actions. These, because of their relation to the subject of reaction time, belong to movements as a whole rather than to any one class. The spontaneous movements were quicker and often more jerky than voluntary movements. Thus many movements made within the first two months had an appearance of rapidity which was in curious contrast to the slow and trembling motions with which he made his first attempts at reaching and grasping. If the reaction time of the child were judged by sensori-motor standards (for example the hurt and the cry, the noise and the movement), the time of reaction always seemed long. Some rapid movements were preserved in grasping, however, as reference to the examples under that heading will serve to show. First, he grasped what came within the range of his sweeping arm. Then, he sometimes gained a sighted object by a rapid arm movement, a reproduction of the sweeping one, which was more likely to succeed than was reaching by his newly acquired method. When a strong desire to take everything in the hands had grown up, the child developed such quickness at seizing, with the same arm movement, what he passed or was near, that he often took an article from beneath one's eyes ere one realized that he had stirred. When he could sit upon the floor and had learned not to plunge forward so that he fell, rapidity of action was extended from arm to body movements, enabling him by a sudden lurch and recovery to regain what had rolled away, or to catch what approached him. At the close of the second year the rate of movement was generally more uniform; it was not varied by phenomenal slowness at the one extreme, nor by startling quickness at the other.

SECTION I.—HABITS.

A Personal Habit: Record.

First Day.—Within an hour after birth the child was seen to be sucking his thumb.

Fourth Day.—Sucking the thumb again occurred. Between the first and fourth days he often sucked his fists. During the first month he was not prevented from doing this, but his thumb was always taken out of his mouth.

Twenty-second Day.—He had not formed the habit of sucking his thumb, but, in the turning and twisting of the fists, the thumb sometimes found its way into the mouth.

Thirty-fifth Day.—In this manner he twice got the thumb in his mouth.

Forty-ninth Day.—By this day he often got the thumb into his mouth. If it was taken away from him, he sometimes, after an interval not exceeding twenty minutes, got it again. After a long interval he did not take his thumb, but sucked his fists. These would seem to have suggested the thumb, which by turning his hands, he soon obtained.

Tenth Week.—Holding the four fingers closed, the thumb extended, the child raised the thumb towards his face, no longer beginning with his fists. He was quite as likely to strike his forehead, eyes or cheek with his thumb as to place it in his mouth. Spontaneous arm movements interfered to prevent his holding the thumb in his mouth, and caused the hand to be jerked away. If this happened many times the child cried from vexation. In the excitement of crying the arm movements increased, and the less certain became his hold on the thumb. In spite of these obstacles the child usually persevered till he succeeded in getting the thumb firmly in his mouth.

In the tenth week he was vaccinated, and the doctor advised that the child, who was slightly feverish, be not worried by attempts to prevent his sucking the thumb. Doubtless thirst and feelings of general discomfort caused the child to suck more than usual. At any rate the habit became fixed in the two weeks during which the vaccination took its course.

Eleventh Week.—He no longer experienced difficulty in holding the thumb in the mouth. If his mother's breast was offered to the child while he was sucking his thumb, he made no attempt to take it, but sucked on contentedly, even though he lay quite close to the breast and was looking at it.

Sixteenth Week.—When he saw the breast he quickly dropped the thumb to seize it.

Eighteenth Week.—When both hands were free he sucked either thumb, but chiefly the left. If the left thumb was confined in a stall, he sucked neither the right nor left.

Twentieth Week.—The child began to suck the right thumb when the left was encased; but instead of holding his hand in a closed fist, he held it open, the palm turned downward.

Twenty-fourth Week.—When the stall was transferred from the left thumb to the right, he made no attempt to suck the left, but fretted for the right. One day, he put the thumb in his mouth, then took it out and looked at the stall. The next day he looked at his thumb, which wore no stall, then put it into his mouth. After the twenty-fourth week he learned to suck the free thumb of either hand. A stall was then put on each thumb.

Thirty-eighth Week.—He began to suck the forefinger of either hand when his thumbs were tied up, holding the palm of the hand upwards.

At the close of the second year, the child still sucked his thumb.

INTERPRETATION.

The habit of sucking the thumb is of wide occurrence among children, and a great diversity of opinion exists as to the possible effects of indulgence in it. All children who suck do not suck the thumb. Some suck a finger (usually the index or second) which may be held in various positions when in the the mouth; others suck a knuckle, and yet others a part of the flesh of the hand or arm. Nor does the habit of sucking so far as I have been able to learn from inquiry, appear to run in families, though tradition regarding it does, causing some mothers to teach it to their children, and others to try by every means to prevent its acquirement. It is generally conceded that it

' makes a good baby' of the little one to have this comforter amidst the trials of its young life. The possibility that the substitute may afford solace rests upon two significant facts : (*a*) the concentration of the early impressions around the satisfaction of hunger, and (*b*) the failure of the child to discriminate among his feelings.

It is probable that the thumb first found its way into the mouth by accident. The position of the hands and arms and their constant movement within a circumscribed limit, naturally brought them into juxtaposition with the mouth. Of all the fingers, the thumb because of its position on the hand was likely to be the one to get into the mouth, and was moreover the only one with an exposed free end.[1] The thumb, having come in contact with the lips, was, owing to the strong tendency to suck, taken into the mouth and at once made use of. Owing to the same strong tendency, the backs of the fists were sucked. But the size and shape of the thumb fitted it preëminently for the purpose. When a difference in its favor had been experienced a preference for it led to a repetition of those movements whereby it had been obtained. On the forty-ninth day we find the child getting hold of his thumb by a round-about method, the reproduction of early movements, whereas by the tenth week a direct method had been developed. By the forty-ninth day an associative link was established which connected, with the sucking complex, certain hand movements and feelings of satisfaction in favor of the thumb. By the tenth week thumb sensations had become differentiated from the sum of the hand sensations, thumb-perception and thumb-desire had been formed and thumb-habit formulated but not perfected.[2] It is noteworthy that an indisposition was instrumental in clinching the habit.

At first the thumb was used as a substitute for the mother's breast, evidence that he had as yet no idea of his own hands by which to distinguish them fully. After the tenth week sucking the hands no longer served as an expression of physical uneasi-

[1] Not more than three times was the child's thumb observed to be enclosed in the fist.

[2] Compare with stage of progress of grasping (tenth week.)

ness; but sucking the thumb became the means of obtaining comfort. The discussion of this personal habit has been carried to the point of its formation. Let us, before going further, pause to note the native elements which lay at its foundation.

1. Instinct of sucking.
2. Fœtal position of the hands.
3. Spontaneous movements of the hands and arms.
4. Peculiar fitness of the thumb.

These pertain especially to the thumb habit; to them must be added Nos. 2, 3 and 4 of the capabilities enumerated below under the interpretation of the facts relating to grasping. Such a form of activity as grasping might be declared to have developed through reflex action without intellectual accompaniment. The evidence here brought forward, bearing on the formation of the thumb sucking habit, points directly to a hedonic element at the foundation of its growth. While we may not designate this element as pleasure or pain, we may describe it as the recognition of feelings of comfort and discomfort.

RECORD OF HAND AND ARM MOVEMENTS.

First Day.—During the first hour the arms were waved about towards the head and face. Later the hands, usually held beneath the chin, were closed in a fist. They clasped a finger when it was introduced into the palm; they did not clasp what merely touched the hand.

Sixth Day.—The fingers, no longer continually flexed, were sometimes extended. When nursing, the open hands lay upon the mother's breast.

Seventh Day.—The hands were often open but held near the face.

Twenty-ninth Day.—A finger was placed in a hand which the child had been sucking. He clasped the finger and essayed twice to draw it towards his mouth.

Thirty-sixth Day.—The attitude of the fingers was now peculiar, the forefinger crooked, the other three extended, or flexed slightly at the distal phalanges. The elbows were still flexed. About this date he began to grasp the clothing of the person in whose arms he was held, and to maintain his hold upon it.

Thirty-eighth Day.—Grasping and holding became frequent. He repeatedly grasped and held a fold of the mother's gown—once maintaining his hold for fifteen minutes. When a finger was placed in the hand of an arm which was waving about, he took the finger firmly and carried it towards his face. The child no longer allowed his hands to be covered, but removed them from beneath the blanket even when asleep.

Fifty-fifth Day.—He grasped whatever came within the sweep of his active arms.

Tenth Week.—He fingered things a great deal as if feeling of them. Before the tenth week the child had worn only flannel dresses, but during this week a change was made to muslin dresses. He at once began to handle these, gathering the stuff up into bunches which he could see. When the flannel dresses were put on again he did not handle them.

Twelfth Week.—Sometimes grasped with the thumb opposing the fingers. Once grasped with the thumb and index finger. In his first attempt at reaching he fixed his gaze upon an *object*, pursed his lips in attention, and moved his hand gropingly towards it.

Thirteenth Week.—Was seen to watch his *hand*, as he stretched out his arm and grasped his mother's dress.

Fifteenth Week.—He reached with an uncertain, shaky hand for a pair of scissors which he obtained twice.

Sixteenth Week—In the beginning of the week two balls of the first gift were suspended by strings above the child's bed and within reach of his arms. At first he gave no heed to them, continuing to gather up his dress in bunches. Later in the week he did notice them, reached for them with open hands, and seemed annoyed that he could not hold them.

Seventeenth Week.—He began to play with his own fingers. Reaching became more frequent. Sometimes he struck the object with the back of the hand, thereupon he turned the hand over so that the palmar surface touched it. He did not try to get articles whose distance from him was greater than the length of his arm, or if he did, he attempted to move his body toward them.

Eighteenth Week.—Hand and arm movements in grasping

and reaching still very imperfect. The hand was sometimes outstretched with a trembling uncertain movement, when it often fell short of its goal; sometimes it caught the object by a rapid sweep of the arm and firm grasp. He frequently handled the balls without looking at them or his hands.

Twenty-first Week—His feet became a favored plaything.

Twenty-fifth Week.—He objected to having them covered by stockings or bed clothing.

Twenty-sixth Week.—They invariably supplemented the hands in feeling of objects; the hands grasped the object first, the feet then went up to feel of it. One hand, or one foot rarely acted alone, though the movements were not symmetrical. One sometimes initiated the movement, but the other, unless in the mouth, soon followed.

Twenty-seventh Week.—He attempted to hold with the feet. He touched an object with an open palm as one feels of a flat surface. But in taking hold of the balls he passed his fingers under them.

Thirtieth Week.—He drummed on the table of his chair, holding a spoon or 'gum ring' in his hand.

Thirty-first Week.—He amused himself by grasping between his first and second toes the leg supporting the table of his chair, which he alternately lifted and let fall so that it rapped upon the floor.

Thirty-second Week.—He tried for the first time to grasp with his whole hand a very small object—a fly. He reached for the fold of the table cloth which droops from the corner of the table, his hand conforming in its attitude to the form of the fold.

Thirty-third Week.—Before the thirty-third week the child had never been seen to use the two hands for different purposes at the same time, with the exception of the occasions upon which he sucked his thumb, when the other hand usually fingered something. One day in the thirty-third week he was holding a napkin ring up to his mouth, when a bearded face was thrust in front of his. He gazed upon this for a few moments, then, carefully taking the ring in one hand and slipping the other out, he reached for the beard, continuing to bite the ring. ,

In this week he ceased to use his feet for playthings, but

continued to use them in reaching and feeling. When given an orange he handled it much as he did the balls, with evident appreciation of its form.[1]

Thirty-fourth Week.—The separate use of the hands had become a habit, but he could be seen to show no preference for one hand over the other. He regarded his hands with a fresh interest, holding one before his eyes, opening and closing the fingers. The forefinger was separated from the other three and used independently; it was often held open when the rest were closed, as though in the attitude of pointing. In this week he used separately the index and thumb, and three other fingers; grasping the lips of a person with his whole hand, he maintained his hold with three fingers, while with thumb and index he reached after the nose, which he held also.

Thirty-sixth Week.—He failed to reach a dish, though he leaned forward as far as he could and stretched his arm to its full length. He then took up a spoon and succeeded by its help in touching the dish.

Thirty-eighth Week.—He twice imitated actions of his mother. Holding two spoons by their handles she clapped the bowls together till they rang. The child reached for the spoons and awkwardly copied the action. His mother then did it a second time, upon which he reached for one spoon which he took in his left hand. In order to get the second he passed the first on to the right hand, and took the second in the left. He now held them in such a way that the bowl of the second spoon projected beyond that of the first; he then raised the first spoon till the two were even, after which he clapped them together.

Thirty-ninth Week.—He now felt of objects with his forefinger, holding the other fingers flexed.

Forty-first Week.—Before taking hold of an object he looked it over carefully, then grasped the smaller part, which he could

[1] The study of the accommodation of hand movements and attitudes to the various objects handled is capable of far wider investigation than I have given it. Through it may be gained much insight into the growth of the perception of form. In my work I trusted to a series of instantaneous photographs, merely noting movements in the journal and not describing them fully. It is greatly to be regretted that the photographs, owing to a fault in the films, proved worthless. Hence this important subject cannot here receive the consideration which is its due.

easily hold in his hand (tail of a toy cat, handle of a dipper, etc.).

Forty-fourth Week.—In trying to pick up a small thing, such as a piece of thread or a bread crumb, he first pointed at and touched it with his forefinger, then withdrawing the flexed hand a short distance, he made a downward dart with the now open hand, which he closed over the object. Usually the first attempt was not crowned with success; but be repeated the action till its end was attained—often as many as six times. He occasionally picked up a small object with his thumb and forefinger; by the fifty-second week this method had entirely superseded the other.

Forty-seventh Week.—He reached after the coffee-pot with a spoon, which he hooked in the handle, and drew the pot towards him.

Fifty-sixth Week.—The forefinger used less markedly. The hand in general employed with more skill.

Seventy-second Week.—At this time he fed himself with the left hand.

Eighty-eighth Week.—The child was observed sitting on the floor, holding a magazine between his legs, and letting the pages slip from between his thumb and forefinger as he viewed the pictures. The forefinger was used in pointing out objects and persons.

Ninety-first Week.—He still looked at his outstretched hand. Upon one occasion, after pointing to an object, he regarded his hand reflectively and said, " see an !" (see hand).

Ninety-third and Ninety-fourth Weeks.—Observations and experiments failed to reveal a development of right-handedness. Experiments showed a slight but inconclusive preponderance of actions of a certain class in favor of the right hand.

Ninety-fifth Week.—He learned to throw a ball overhand, and to make marks with a pencil on paper. He experienced considerable difficulty in holding the first and second fingers together and separated from the rest.

One Hundred and Fifth Week.—In performing difficult actions with the right hand and arm, the child gave evidence of being right-handed.

INTERPRETATION.

Immediately after birth the baby's hands were not organs of prehension at all. They went forth to meet nothing and did not even close over what came into contact with them, unless it was actually thrust into the palm. In the twelfth week his hands became true organs of prehension; for they were then able to get what was perceived through the sense of sight. The steps by which the child gained the power to use his hands may be described as follows: As the first one, there was the inborn ability to clasp, or close the hand—the instinct of clasping. Sensations of touch and movement ensued upon the exercise of this inborn ability. By the alteration of the attitudes of the hand from pre-natal to post-natal ones, a larger surface was exposed, increasing the area for stimulation. Sensations of contact from all parts of the hand ensued. Spontaneous movements of the arms brought the hands into various situations and contacts. The change from pre- to post-natal arm attitudes gave a different quality to arm movements. A sweeping motion of the fully extended arm then became more common. Holding, or the continuation of the action in the presence of the stimulus, as opposed to mere clasping, was next developed.

He experienced new muscular sensations induced by resistance encountered when he tried to draw towards his mouth the object which he had clasped. Sensations of touch from all parts of the hand were bound by association to the act of clasping in such a way as to insure the clasping of anything touching any part of the hand. After this the hands clasped whatever they were brought into contact with by the activity of the arms, in other words, not only what came to them, but also that which they went out to meet. In the tenth week he reacted distinctly to differences in sensations of touch received through the hands.

In opening and closing his hands on the material which caused the change of sensation, and in flexing his elbows, he carried bunches of the material into his field of vision. Sensations of sight were then experienced in company with those of muscle and skin. At this time the child had already developed by other experiences some perceptions of things seen and some appreciation of direction and distance.[1]

[1] Consult Part III., Sec. 2, of this work.

Hereafter the child frequently saw his hands in conjunction with objects clasped, a constant element in every vision. In his first attempts at reaching, the child fixed his gaze on the object, and not on the hand, guiding the hand and arm entirely by standards of movement which were established before he could sit up, or had seen his body and limbs. In this connection it is interesting to note that as late as the sixth month he took pleasure in playing with objects that he did not see.

In the thirteenth week he began to watch his moving hand. After this he was able to reach after and grasp, though as yet very awkwardly, something held within a suitable distance.

If the foregoing interpretation of the process of the growth of reaching and grasping be the correct one, we may assume the following capabilities and conditions to have existed in the child as a basis which made the growth possible (but did not cause it), namely:

1. Instinct of clasping.

2. Capability of receiving sensations of touch and movement.

3. The tendency of one or more terms of a series composed of sensations which have been felt together, or in conjunction with the mental representative of a movement, to call up the other term or terms.

4. Physiological law of habit.

5. Range and variety of movements conditioned by the modification of the fœtal attitudes which were maintained by the child.

If we examine the later history of hand movements and a further development of the thumb-sucking habit, they are found to have, respectively and in common, some significant points.

Between the thirteenth and sixteenth weeks occurred the perception of the hand as distinct from other objects. By the sixteenth week his thumb no longer afforded satisfaction as a substitute for his mother's breast. In the seventeenth week he took an interest in the hands for themselves, using them as playthings. At this time he usually reached with both arms, though he sometimes, as when sucking, used one hand alone. Nevertheless, he was not aware of the number and separateness of the hands, as was shown by his actions when one thumb was tied up in a stall.

In the twenty-sixth week matters were further complicated by the addition of the feet as organs of touch. I was at first inclined to regard this peculiar feature of the use of the feet as a rudimentary instinct, inherited from the remote past, and suppressed in most children by the custom of keeping the feet encased. But later a review of the rise, continuance and decline of the practice led me to discard the earlier opinion. As soon as the weather permitted, the child ceased to wear stockings, and, dressed in light warm clothing, he was allowed every freedom of movement. His whole body was now in constant motion, so that in a short time he inevitably discovered his feet (21st week). The hand had then acquired no extraordinary skill, but was occupied in feeling objects of various kinds, so the feet were able to do their share, also coming in contact with numbers of things. It is true grasping still belonged to the hand; but it must be remembered how extremely imperfect a form of grasping it was. To have and to hold was not its purpose, nor had the child perceptions of objects upon which to base a desire for them. However, as the hands became more skillful the office of feeling was delegated to the feet, which invariably felt of that which the hands held. With the development of hand movements, and the acquirement of the habit of sitting erect, such use of the feet gradually ceased, till it had largely disappeared.

Development of hand movements after the twenty-fourth week may be summarized as follows:

The separation of the sensations of each thumb, and the formation, of a representation of each individual thumb, accompanied by increased dexterity in its use; the separation of the forefinger sensations, and the formation of a forefinger idea, accompanied by increasing dexterity; the differentation of hand and feet sensations, the growth of a hand-idea, accompanied by the growth of perceptions of things seen and handled, with consequent desire to get and to handle, and increased dexterity of hand and arm movement; the differentation of the sensations of each hand and arm, then of the index and thumb (for uses of grasping), and the growth of the corresponding ideas.

In the thirty-eighth week the first decisive acts of conscious imitation were observed. These showed a possible recognition of a likeness between his own hands and those of another person. In the thirty-ninth week came the concentration of the sensations of touch in the index finger, and (forty-fourth week) the consequent development of a peculiar method of picking up small objects. This method was finally superseded by another older and less awkward one. After the fifty-second week development was along the line of a greater perfection of the movements acquired, and was conditioned, nay called forth, by the child's experimentation with things and his attemps at conscious imitations of the actions of other persons.

SECTION II.—VOLUNTARY MOVEMENTS.

RECORD.

Fourth Day.—If some one kissed the hungry child, or touched him on the cheek, he turned his open mouth towards the side touched.

In the second week the child, when hungry or uncomfortable from any cause, opened his mouth and rolled his head from side to side, as when searching for food. This he did, also, if the breast slipped from his mouth.

Seventeenth Day.—Wishing to regain his hold of the breast he turned his head towards it, instead of rolling the head from side to side.

Thirty-seeond Day.—Turned the head in the direction whence sounds proceeded.

Thirty-seventh Day.—He held objects which he clasped.

Thirty-eighth Day.—Mr. C. called, and the baby looked attentively at him. When sitting on his mother's lap he made vigorous and repeated efforts to hold his head erect in order to see this visitor. His whole body quivered with the exertion.

Fifty-ninth Day.—If the child lost his hold upon the nipple, with open mouth and eyes fixed upon the breast, he made 'reaches' with his head and neck till he succeeded in regaining his hold.

Tenth Week.—Having learned to suck his thumb, he returned it to his mouth as repeatedly as it was taken away.

Twelfth Week.—Persistent attempts at reaching and grasping. Efforts to raise his body from a reclining to a sitting position became common.

Seventeenth Week.—Attempts at turning the body over.[1] He tried to get a ball to his mouth, and was annoyed at his failure to do so. He held his head erect, turned it to the side through an angle of 90°, and raised his eyes to the face of one who had spoken to him.

Twenty-second Week.—When he saw approaching, the spoon from which he received his water, he opened his mouth, then seized the spoon in his hand and pulled it towards his face.

Twenty-fifth Week.—In trying to draw the breast to his mouth he put his hand over the nipple. When he found that it was not the nipple which came to his lips, he drew back, looked at the breast for a few moments, then removed his hand and seized the nipple between his jaws as usual.

Twenty-ninth Week.—The child expressed his desire for food by pulling at his mother's dress.

Thirty-third Week.—At noon he derived great pleasure from playing with an orange which had been given him by his father who held the child on his lap. In the evening he saw some oranges in the fruit dish on the sideboard, and at once manifested excitement by the usual signs. He looked from the fruit to his father a number of times, making sundry little noises. The action was evidently expressive of desire, and he was much pleased to have an orange given to him.

Thirty-fourth Week.—The child had a spoon to play with, and was deeply interested when his father extended his hands to take him up from his chair. He looked at the hands, holding out one of his own; but when about to extend the other he turned away from his father to the spoon, withdrawing the one already given. Then he looked back at his father, and again started to give his hands, but once more turned away. This

---

[1] I refer to such actions here in order to show what the habitual actions were in the acquirement of which the child was occupied, or which when established entered into voluntary actions.

performance was repeated three times, until in a longer contemplation of the hands he seemed to forget the spoon.

Thirty-fifth Week.—He threw down a spoon, to which a string was attached. His mother put the string into the hand with which he was slapping the arm of a chair. The movement of his hand caused the spoon to rap upon the floor. The noise surprised him, and he continued to slap, seeming to think that his hand on the arm caused the sound. Afterwards he discovered that the noise could be made when his hand was extended beyond the chair, and holding the string in hand, he began to beat the air with a downward motion, as if hitting something hard. Only occasionally did the spoon rap upon the floor.

Thirty-sixth Week.—Conscious repetition of one of his own sounds quoted by an older person for his amusement.

Thirty-eighth Week.—Conscious imitation of an action, the result and not the act being the end in view, (see hand movements p. 18).

Fourtieth Week.—The spoon with which he was playing fell through the rounds of the back of a chair which was lying on its side in front of him. He was about to cry at its loss, but did not do so, and tried to get it. The first attempts were unsuccessful, for he put his arm through the wrong opening, and each time his hand was too far from the spoon. Finally he found the opening nearest to the spoon, which he recovered. The child succeeded a number of times in pulling himself to his feet by the aid of a chair, each successful attempt alternating with three or four unsuccessful ones.

Forty-first Week.—He now took hold of the far end of an object to pull it towards himself, instead of touching it with his finger tips and pushing it farther away.

Forty-second Week.—Intentional but unintelligent repetition of syllables and words.

Forty-sixth Week.—Creeping became a habit. When the child was carried into a room in which someone had hidden, he, when told to do so, went in search of the person, whom he located by the sound of a voice emanating from the hiding place. On the fourth trial his mother threw a wrapper over a chair, fastened it, and hid behind the chair. When the child reached the chair he tried to pull the wrapper down as he had previously done with a quilt, but found this impossible to him. He sat a few moments as if in thought, then crept around the chair.

Fifty-second Week.—Request for food expressed by extending first one hand and then the other.

Fifty-eighth Week.—The child, who was sitting beside the kitchen table while the vegetables were being prepared, was given pared potatoes to drop into a pan of water. He knew from past experiences that his mother would not permit him to put them into his mouth. He looked at his mother, and if her face was turned away, slyly put the potato up to his lips.

Sixty-first Week.—He succeeded in walking alone.

Sixty-fourth Week.—He took hold of the finger and led one to a door out of which he wished to pass, or went behind and tried to push one along. Expressed his desire to be taken up by pulling at ones clothing.

Seventy-third Week.—He was one day walking behind his parents as they were leaving the grounds in which the buildings of the U. S. Fish Commission stood. Four separate gates led into these grounds, two small ones on the foot paths, and two large ones on the carriage ways. The child in his carriage had passed in and out of each gate many times in two months. The path on which they were walking was separated from the roadway by a grass plot and gutter. His parents passed out of the gate and closed it. When he perceived that the gate was closed, the child started across the grass towards the large gate, which stood open. Arrived at the brink of the gutter, down to which the grass plot sloped in a short, steep incline, he hesitated while glancing from the incline to the small gate, then turned quickly and resolutely back across the grass to the path, and walked to the small gate which he opened and out of which he passed.

Seventy-fifth Week.—In an adjoining room he found two pins, things which had always been taken away from him. He hastened at once to his mother with them, calling, "mamma! mamma!" in a tone of excitement. He gave them up freely; but cried bitterly to have them taken away.

Seventy-eighth Week.—The acquirement and practice of new words occupied him at this time.

Eightieth Week.—The child stood his bottle on the floor, then tilted his doll over it to take a drink.

Eighty-second Week.—He accidentally broke the head of his wooden horse. He took the head to his mother, led her to the horse, pulled her down to the floor and awkardly put the head and body together as a sign that he wished her to mend it.

Ninetieth Week.—When called into the bath room, to get ready for a bath, the child invariably seated himself on the floor and held out his feet to have his shoes taken off.

Ninety-first Week.—He got a cloth and imitated his mother in polishing the piano. 'Contrary' actions became more common. They increased in frequency up to the beginning of the twenty-fourth month. At the close of the twenty-fourth month they became less frequent, the child, understanding language better, became more amenable to verbal suggestion.

Ninety-ninth Week.—Seeing his mother fitting a collar, he took a triangular piece of cloth, put it around his neck and said, 'fit!' Wiped his nose with the same and called it a handkerchief, spread it out and called it a table cloth.

One Hundred and First Week.—Sometimes he gave expression to his purpose before acting. Acts of conscious imitation began to predominate.

One Huudred and Fourth Week.—Actions suggested by association became very prominent, for example, when taken into the kitchen and placed on a certain chair, the child demanded a book which had been given to him but once, three weeks before, when sitting on the same chair.

INTERPRETATION.

If it be true, as I believe the evidence adduced in this paper proves, that voluntary action rises out of the performance of instinctive action, we should seek to find the first voluntary movement not in the first deliberative act, nor in the first act of conscious imitation, but in the repetition of an act which had originally caused either a cessation of discomfort or a sense of gratification. This act may have been performed from one to thirty times before it contained an element of volition. But

when an associative link had been established between some
mental representative of the movement and the feeling of satisfaction, so that the movement was made in the attainment of
satisfaction, the movement was to be regarded as a voluntary
one.   No idea of the effect of his movement considered as a
cause is to be imputed to the child.   On its intellectual side this
primitive act of volition must be divested of representation and
choice, and regarded, thus stripped of that which we are accustomed to think of as belonging to volition, as an extremely
simple response to a suggestion by which it was initiated.
To make this statement more clear I would refer the reader
to the record of voluntary actions.   On the fourth day it was
recorded of the child that if touched on the cheek he turned his
open mouth towards the side touched.   This the newly born
baby did not do.   Each time that he was to be fed the child was
laid in a certain position, and the nurse, taking his head between
her hands, turned it slightly to one side in order to put his lips
against the nipple.   On the fourth day the child had gone
through the experience some thirty times as a preliminary to the
satisfaction of hunger.   On the fourth day he repeated the act
of his own accord.   But he could not have had in mind a definite desire, impelling him to make efforts to obtain his mother's
breast, or even food, since, in the discussion of the thumb sucking habit, it was clearly shown that the child had no differentiated representation of his mother's breast prior to the sixteenth
week, and as he was satisfied to suck when hungry without receiving milk, it could have been no demand for food ,thought of
as such, which prompted him.   The act was the representative
of one of several contiguous links.   But this is not volition, it
may be argued.   What is volition but action under the stimulus
of an idea?   True, the associations were not ideas, nor connections between ideas.   But there were no real ideas existing thus
early in the life of the child; and it must never be lost to view
in this search for beginnings, that the words and definitions
framed to fit a psychology of the adult mind, must suffer a little
expansion if they are to be used at all in describing that which
is most primitive.   It must be borne in mind that these associations are, on the intellectual side, the forerunners of percep-

tions, representations and finally of concepts, to all of which they are genetically related.

I have called the first stage of the development of voluntary movements the associative stage. Certainly all actions of the first three weeks belonged to it exclusively, and throughout infancy, movements belonging to this class continued to be made every day. The perceptive stage was the next to be developed, and was ushered in, when, through reiterated experiences, it was possible for the child to have some perceptions of the objects which acted as stimuli to the various departments of sensation. The action recorded of the child on the thirty-eighth day belonged to the class of voluntary actions performed under the stimulus of a perception. To this class also belong those efforts of the child to reach and handle the many objects which he saw. When it was possible for him to form an abstraction, some idea, however incomplete, of a thing, an action or an experience, this idea without the mediation of a direct sensory stimulus, served to initiate action. Volition had then reached the representative stage.

According to this view the voluntary actions of a given period were made possible by the forms of activity already developed, and consisted in an application and extension of these forms to present conditions, which application and extension by no means implied an understanding of the conditions. Before going further, I wish to emphasize one point, namely, that nowhere did I find, through the whole series of observations, numbering hundreds, a single instance of an action of which it could be said, here entered a new force, for here was an action without antecedents. The only actions without antecedents were those movements for whose performance the nervous and muscular mechanism was prepared at birth.

In order to facilitate a comprehensive view of the actions recorded as voluntary they are divided into four classes :

1. Those which had their origin in an instinct or an instinctive desire, and their end in automatism (or habit) after the action had, by means of endeavor and experience, reached a degree of perfection. To this class belong such as balancing the head, standing, walking, etc.

2. Actions in which the child made use of acquired dexterity of movement to accomplish some aim. They may be considered characteristic of the individual on the one hand, and on the other, regarded as reactions to a personal environment. They do not necessarily become habitual. Within this class belonged those actions which involved inference, deliberation and choice.

3. Expressive actions, gestures which tend ultimately to become habitual. To this class belong such as the one in which he pulled his mother by the dress to get her to accompany him.

4. Actions reproduced upon suggestion. The suggestions proceeded either directly from another person, from an object or from earlier experiences called up by association. These actions became very common when the child had some command of language. They did or did not become habitual, according to the conditions in which the child was placed. Acts of conscious imitation should be included in this class.

The persistence everywhere displayed by the child was extraordinary, but most so when he was learning to perform movements belonging to the first class.

It is noteworthy that actions of the second class should have occurred *before* those of the third; the latter appeared towards the close of the first year and reached their largest numerical proportion before the child had acquired a command of language. It is profoundly significant to psychology and pedagogy that a child may be led to acts involving inference, deliberation and choice, through his experiences with himself and things. I was surprised upon being confronted with this fact, and when, at the close of the second year, the whole subject of voluntary actions was reviewed, it would seem that the child had performed acts of greater complexity at an earlier period. It occurred to me then that such might have passed unnoticed amid the multiplicity and diversity of the actions of later infancy. I therefore set for myself the task of looking for them. For days I did not observe one. The whole character of the child's performances had changed. Everywhere some suggestion from without or from within controlled the direction of activity. The difference was apparently in favor of the earlier performances; but not really so, for the later acts, in being the expression of thoughts or symbols, marked a great advance, while in the earlier ones inference and choice dealt, not in the symbols for things, but with the things themselves.

In the later half of the second year it became possible for a purely mental stimulus to arouse an inclination towards action. Then the strange period of perverseness, through which so many children pass, developed.[1] At the time of the appearance of this phase, the child acted almost entirely from suggestion through association. Hence when a certain course of action was proposed, the representation of the opposite course was at once called up and appealed to him with some force, since the ability to perceive the consequences of either act was as yet undeveloped. The child never expressed (in contrary mood) the mere negation or refusal; *he proposed an alternative.* Frequently, though not always, the representation did not prompt to action, and fell away upon the repetition of the suggestion. If, however, one agreed with him, saying: 'Well, we shall do as you wish,' he often burst into tears, demanding that the original plan be carried out, and thus showed the side on which the preponderance of desire hung.

The movements of expression arose almost without exception before the child had learned to express himself easily in language (between the sixth and twenty-second months); but after he was old enough to try to make his wishes known, and, persisting after he had learned to speak, they were frequently used to emphasize his demands. A description of the rise of one will elucidate the method by which all originated—a method analogous to that which obtained in the early stages of language development. In the twentieth month a gesture of dismissal which consisted in a lateral, chopping motion of one or both arms, became habitual. It was made in imitation of the sweep of the arm by which his mother brushed away the flies which came around the food. At first he copied the action, exclaiming " ly ! ly !" (fly, fly). Next he applied it to food which he wished to refuse, then used it to sweep away any unpleasant object or distasteful proposition, and finally added the words,

[1] Contrary suggestion, Baldwin, *op. cit.*, p. 145.

'take it away,' (object), or 'good bye,' (proposition). As associations between representations multiplied, the child daily performed a number of actions dependent thereon, and even performed them regularly in a mechanical sort of way after they had lost the power to entertain him.   He objected to slight deviations from the regular routine, such as washing the feet before the hands.

He was never given to that quality of conscious imitation which at once attempts to reproduce what others are seen to do. Acts of conscious imitation did not begin to play an extremely important part till he had gained some understanding of the meaning involved in the actions of others, then he was ever ready to do his share.

SECTION III.—INHIBITORY MOVEMENTS.

RECORD.

Third Day.—He frequently started at loud noises and ceased crying.

Twenty-fourth Day.—The striking of a clock caused him to stop crying.

Thirty-eighth Day.—The voice of his father caused him to stop crying.

Forty-first Day.—Interesting sights diverted the child's mind from personal discomforts, great enough to cause crying.

Forty-sixth Day.—The sound of rattling spoons caused the child to stop crying.

Fifty-fifth Day.—The child, who had been held more than usual during the second month, cried, on the fifty-fifth day, when laid down.   When no one responded, he ceased crying and became pleasant.

Tenth Week.—Inhibition of crying was of frequent occurrence ; the child often stopped with his face made up to cry, the cry being lost in the active contemplation of some interesting performance.

Eleventh Week.—If the hungry child was fretting, he stopped as soon as he saw his mother begin to unfasten her dress, looking at her with wide open eyes, and breathing quickly.

Eighteenth Week.—When his thumb was encased in a stall, and he had found that it was not good to suck thus, he held his hand quite still at his side.

Nineteenth Week.—Th child upon waking from a nap, twice raised his thumb almost to his mouth, then put his hand down.

Twenty-eighth Week.—For two days in succession the child who had before been held at the table during the meal, cried, and was taken to the dinner table. The third time he cried, (two days having intervened) this was not done; but he was permitted to cry until, of his own accord, he stopped. After this he did not cry again[1] upon seing others go to the table.

Seventh Month.—The child liked to play with a spoon, with which he pounded upon the table. When he became tired of this occupation he put the spoon in his mouth and invariably poked it so far down his throat that he choked. After he had played with a spoon for a month, and choked himself times without number, he in the thirty-sixth week learned not to do so any more, though he frequently put the spoon in his mouth.

Thirty-ninth Week.—Having acquired the habit of sitting alone, the child, sitting on a quilt on the floor, plunged forward after a toy and fell off the quilt on his face, severely bumping his nose. Thereafter he was never seen to plunge forward after a lost toy, though before he had been hurt in falling, this performance had been one of almost hourly occurrence.

Fifty-seventh Week.—The fear of falling having become associated with experience in a more general way, the child learned to take better care of himself by controlling his heedlessness; but a strong desire was still sufficient to submerge all prudence, as when seeing his cup on the floor, he would have plunged headlong off the bed after it.

Seventy-ninth Week.—His hand was extended to take from the wash-stand a mug, which he had never been allowed to have. The sight of his mother, who upon several occasions

---

[1] The question here arises as to whether crying is itself unpleasant to the child. There seems to be ground for believing it to be a direct source of discomfort.

had taken the mug away, was enough to cause him to withdraw his hand.

During the latter half of the second year the child learned to control himself in several directions. He could, and very frequently did, cease crying when told to do so. (No form of punishment had been inflicted upon him to teach him not to cry.)

When running at headlong speed he frequently failed to see a table or other piece of furniture till close upon it. Then he could draw up so shortly that one could see no space between his head and the table edge, yet escape the least blow. It was often a matter of surprise that he received so few real hurts. This was to be attributed partly to the ability to guide himself around dangerous places, partly to the power of control which enabled him to call a stop at instant notice.

Through training the child had acquired a certain amount of voluntary control, inasmuch as he often inhibited certain actions, though the desire to perform them must have been strong. In the twenty-third and twenty-fourth months, having learned to throw his ball overhand, he took delight in throwing everything which he could lift, from books to his little chair. At this time he was especially fond of sitting beside his mother's desk, playing with her letters, etc., while she was writing. He almost always threw each article away in a few moments. This practice could not be permitted; hence he was deprived of the pleasure of sitting in the high chair, a severe punishment, causing many tears to flow. He was often observed to stay his hand in the very act of throwing, and instead pass the things to his mother. When the child was enjoined not to touch something—the table set for a meal, for example—he could restrain himself if not too long exposed to the temptation. If, however, he yielded at all, it was altogether. He would then run around the table, taking everything within his reach, and finally pull off the cloth.

INTERPRETATION.

Inhibition was first induced by a sense stimulus, which in drawing attention into another channel caused a movement already in progress to cease. As other forms of inhibition arose this, the sensorial one, did not disappear. It was used by the persons who dealt with the child, who endeavored to stop his crying and prevent the performance of various acts, by bringing forward attractions by which to stimulate sensation. Thus it became related to suggestion. The inhibition of crying was the first conspicuous manifestation. Very soon (eleventh week) a perception in which was involved memory of an agreeable sensation induced the cessation of crying. Later the recollection of an unpleasant experience caused the child to pause in the performance of a voluntary movement. These were the steps by which inhibition, occurring first as a response to a counter stimulus, ultimately became, as it were, engrafted upon voluntary action. In its early stages inhibition did not occur with an extensive range of actions; but was developed along with special forms of activity. Experience taught the child what and when to inhibit. Sometimes the lesson of experience was learned only after a long course of training; sometimes a single hard lesson sufficed to define a boundary of control.

The cases cited in the record serve to show how intimate a relationship existed between inhibitions and the acquirement of bodily control and dexterity. If we consider them in connection with this relationship we find ourselves once more in the territory of habitual and voluntary movements.

SECTION IV.—SOME AUTOMATIC MOVEMENTS.

RECORD.

In the early weeks of life perfect repose during sleep was rare. Starting, movements of the hands and feet, low noises and brief fits of crying disturbed the slumber of the child, especially during the day, when the noises of the street exerted their influence also. About the sixth week sleep began to be more peaceful; gradually the child became a quiet sleeper, except when uncomfortable from some indisposition.

Thirty-ninth Day.—The child, by this time, objected to having his hands covered, and even when asleep removed them from beneath the covers.

Twenty-third Week.—When a steam siren blew, which had previously awakened him, the child cried out in his sleep without opening his eyes.

Twenty-fifth Week.—With eyes tightly shut, the sleeping child, lifted from his crib, could find the breast quickly and suckle as well as when awake. As soon as satisfied, he fell back, his body stiffened, as if prepared to be laid down. He objected to the covering on his feet, and invariably kicked it off when asleep.

Thirty-second Week.—Having, by dint of repeated efforts, learned to roll on the floor, the child in the thirty-second week began to roll in his crib during sleep.

Thirty-eighth Week.—When the thumbs were tied up the child sucked a forefinger. This he never did in sleep, though under the same circumstances he would have taken his thumb.

Fortieth Week.—The sleeping child, after having been fed, lay across his mother's knees while his clothing was arranged. A pair of slippers was on the bed beside them. He stretched out his hand and encountered a slipper, which he grasped and carried to his mouth, babbling as he did so. During the performance his eyes were closed. He then opened his eyes, looked for a moment at a light in the next room, let go of the slipper, closed his eyes and was immediately asleep.

Forty-fifth Week.—In the fortieth week he learned to suck milk from the bottle. In the forty-fifth week he was not able to fall asleep while doing this; but within a week it became possible to him to do so. Then the bottle was given to him at 10:30 P. M., when he was sleeping. Upon being disturbed he put up his hand as was his wont, to his mother's neck, but receiving the bottle he carried it to his mouth and drank the milk. This performance was the more noteworthy as the rubber nipple sometimes collapsed, making it necessary that the child should release it in order that it might be refilled by air and milk, a trick which he had learned only after some practice.

Fifty-fifth Week.—The child had acquired the habit of pulling his own ear or that of another person while sucking his thumb. When disturbed, but not awakened, he immediately put his thumb into his mouth and began to pull his ear.

SECTION V.—MOVEMENTS OF EMOTIONAL EX-PRESSION.

RECORD.

First Day.—When uncomfortable the child cried.

Sixth Day.—Smiled when comfortable.

Seventh Day—Smiled at his father four consecutive times, accompanying the smile with movements of the arms.

Tenth Day.—Tear secretion observed for the first time.

Seventeenth Day.—Fretting—a sort of cry—expressed discomfort.

Twentieth Day.—Smiling at persons became more frequent, and the smile more intelligent.

Forty-sixth Day.—Laughed aloud upon several occasions (at persons.) The laugh consisted of a smile accompanied by a sound caused by alternate expiration and inspiration; it did not resemble the coördinated laughter of the later months.

Fifty-fifth Day.—Displeasure indicated by hard crying and rigidity of the whole body, which was so complete that if taken by the hands he could be raised to his feet without having bent the vertebral column and lower limbs.

Sixty-first Day.—Pursing of the lips accompanied fixed attention.

Tenth Week.—Rapid, alternate flexions and extensions of the limbs in excitement were first observed in this week.

Twelfth Week.—Kicking and waving the arms became the habitual method of venting excitement, and were sometimes accompanied by pursing of the lips. While on a journey a phenomenon was noticed for the first time which afterwards occurred frequently; namely, the retention of the urine during an exciting experience. Six hours was the longest period during which the urine was retained, but throughout the journey the intervals were uniformly longer than they had hitherto been. From the twelfth week to the close of the second year the child never visited a new house, saw visitors at his own home, became deeply absorbed in any occupation or plaything without the occurrence of this phenomenon. After the ninth month excitement interfered with evacuation of the fæces also. By the twelfth week the voice had become more expressive of the child's states of feeling.

Thirteenth Week.—Expectancy (of food) accompanied by a quivering of the body and sundry little noises.

Sixteenth Week.—Tear secretion was established. When hurt he began his cry with a loud, explosive ' Mä-ä.' When getting hungry or sleepy he fretted, and gradually broke into a cry. Sometimes his eyes filled with tears preliminary to the utterance of a cry. Sometimes he first drew down the corners of his mouth and whimpered. Great excitement in novel experiences was accompanied by protrusion of the lips, wide opening of the eyes, during forward inclination of the body, reaching with the hands, rapid movements of the arms and legs, trembling of the body and especially of the arms and hands, and accelerated respiration. In surprise his eyes were widely opened.

Eighteenth Week.—When suddenly surprised the child started and threw out his hands. In a broad smile his whole scalp was seen to move. A broad smile, with wide opening of the mouth, expressed extreme pleasure. Frowning accompanied great effort. General repose of the face indicated bodily comfort. Grunts accompanied by a twisting and turning from side to side indicated bodily dissatisfaction. It is doubtful whether the child had ever felt fright.

Nineteenth Week.—Writhing and twisting of the body expressed delight.

Twenty-fourth Week.—Kicking and laughing accompanied pleasure. Good health and high spirits found vent in loud laughter and occasional screams.

Twenty-fifth Week.—Disappointment (when not taken out of doors) indicated by fretting and scolding. Vigorous kicking in which the feet were used alternately, indicated excitement. The rythmical striking of one foot against the other leg indicated displeasure. The rapidity of the movements seemed to be a measure of the strength of the feeling. In hard crying he rolled his body from side to side, or held his legs raised and rigid, but flexed slightly at the knees.

Thirtieth Week.—The movements made during displeasure became rythmical. They consisted in turning the body to the side, succeeded by the recovery of the first position, or throwing out and drawing in the arm, or in the flexion and extension of one leg. It was customary for him to repeat the action again and again at short and regular intervals. The child was observed to frown when slightly annoyed.

Thirty-third Week.—He acquired a new form of smile, which gradually but not entirely supplanted the broad, open-mouthed smile referred to above. The nose was wrinkled up, the eyes nearly closed, the angles of the slightly parted lips were drawn backward, and the jaws were approximated. This smile seemed to express an extreme and more conscious enjoyment. For a long time it was never observed in the presence of strangers.

Thirty-fourth Week.—When sitting had become a habit, vigorous kicking as the outlet of enjoyable excitement gave place to a jumping up and down of the whole body. Frowning as an expression of displeasure became frequent and persisted.

Forty-third Week.—Delight was expressed by a piercing scream, accompanied by flapping of the arms and rubbing of the feet back and forth upon the floor.

Forty-sixth Week.—Delight was expressed by a shiver such as might accompany a sudden chill.

Fifty-second Week.—He no longer shivered with pleasure; this habit he had gradually abandoned.

Fifty-fifth Week.—A mischievous look was seen for the first time. Thereafter it was frequently observed.

Seventy-eighth Week.—Shyness was indicated by hiding the head. The squarely open mouth in crying was observed. It had occurred earlier, but I neglected to record its first appearance.

Eighty-Seventh Week.—In fits of temper, which were provoked by attempts to force his clothing upon the child, and to make him go in a given direction, he struggled and bit. This practice lasted but a few weeks.

One Hundred and Fifth Week.—At the close of the second year, in the excitement of pleasure, the child stamped rapidly and alternately with each foot, his hands trembled, his eyes sparkled. Finally, as though he could contain himself no longer, he often ran round and round the room as fast as he was able. He smiled frequently; but loud laughter was not usual except when playing with other children, or his elders. In crying, the habit of drawing down the corners of the mouth had largely superseded that of opening the mouth squarely. Throughout infancy, as in adult life, the voice was the chief instrument of expression; but I have here omitted to treat of it because it would be impossible to transcribe its many indications of feeling changes; and for the further reason that the growth of the ability to use the voice is alluded to under Language.

INTERPRETATION.

In treating the subject of movements of expression my only aim is to describe the prominent features of the changes which took place during the development of the child. In the early weeks the facial expression varied greatly from hour to hour. The continual changes were not due to definite emotional causes, but resulted from spontaneous movements of the muscles of the face. When the child's attention was deeply engrossed, he was comparatively still, for the spontaneous movements then partially ceased. During profound sleep, also, the muscles of the face were more quiet than in a light sleep. While awakening, which sometimes required so long a time as half an hour, the changes in facial expression were most marked.

The question of the first smile is one which has led to much discussion. The popular belief seems to be that any smile occurring before the child is a month (some say six weeks) old is due to pain resulting from digestive disturbance. My observations point conclusively to the erroneousness of this belief (as applying to one individual.) Prior to the fifth week the child smiled but rarely. On and after the fifth week smiles were often to be observed. The first smiles were clearly different from the later ones. They were produced by the muscles around the mouth; the muscles around the eyes did not participate noticeably. They were extremely evanescent. They occurred under the following circumstances : (1) Almost invariably when the child, having been fed and laid in a comfortable position, was peacefully dropping to sleep; (2) During the light sleep which succeeded a deep and restful one, and occasionally during all sleep; (3) Occasionally at persons. They never occurred when the child was known to be in pain. The smile changed with the expression of the face, the two gaining in the appearance of intelligence. Finally the whole face, and even the scalp, seemed to unite in producing a smile. When the intelligent human smile had quite superseded the earlier form, it occurred like its predecessor, when the child, in perfect comfort, was sinking into sleep.

I may now briefly summarize a few other facts taught by the observations. 1 It will be seen that there existed at birth no well defined movements of pleasurable expression, for, even the smile, observed within the first week, has been challenged to prove its right to that office; on the other hand the method of expressing displeasure, discomfort and pain was perfected at birth. 2 The method of expressing pleasure or pleasurable excitement underwent many transformations; but the method of expressing displeasure did not pass through so many changes. 3 The method of expressing pleasure became clearly defined with the dawning of intelligence, and its transitions corresponded to features of mental and bodily development. 4 A method of expressing displeasure without crying was developed, peculiarly rythmical (resembling in this respect the rocking to and fro of a person in agony), as compared with the jerky or explosive nature of the method by which the child gave vent to feelings of pleasurable excitement. The prominent part taken by the feet and legs whenever a strong emotion of either kind was finding expression is well worthy of note.

SECTION VI.—REFLEX MOVEMENTS.

RECORD.

First Day.—First cry. He 'nestled' close to a person who held him.

Third Day.—He started at loud noises.

Twentieth Day.—When water was squeezed from a sponge over his head and face, he closed his eyes and mouth, which he did not do at six months of age. (The practice of pouring water over the head having in the meantime been discontinued.)

Twenty-second Day.—Upon exposure of the face to the rays of a bright light during sleep, tighter closing of the eyelids was observed.

Forty-ninth Day.—He threw out the arms when lowered into a bassinet. This occurred earlier, and was, by its first observer, ascribed to an instinctive fear of falling. I failed to note exactly the date of its disappearance, though by the sixth month it no longer took place.

Twelfth Week.—Each time the train stopped, started or jolted during a journey lasting twenty-four hours, whether the child was waking or asleep, he threw out his arms as when lowered into a bed. While driving over a rough road he clutched the clothing of the person holding him when the wagon lurched.

Eighteenth Week.—He turned away the head from a strong light. This action he did not perform after the sixth month, and as late as the twenty-fourth month he was often puzzled as to which way to turn his head to avoid the direct rays of the sun. He raised the hands as if to ward off something, if touched during sleep.

Twenty-second Week.—He appeared as if frightened when the train passed under bridges, even very short ones; but the loud noise of passing trains failed to disturb him.

Twenty-fifth Week.—He clutched the arm and clothing of a person lifting him during sleep. (He had never fallen.)

Thirty-second Week.—When lifted up during sleep he drew his feet close to his body as if their soles had been tickled. General restlessness in illness, activity in health.

INTERPRETATION.

For purposes of utility I have in this paper chosen a natural, rather than a philosophical definition of instinct. It is one which serves a two-fold purpose, designating a particular form of inherent activity and serving as a basis upon which to separate out allied forms which are called reflexes. Since my studies were in development and my records dealt in changes, I did not make reflexes the subject of a special investigation; but noted such as appeared from time to time during the early weeks of life. While the definition of instinct calls for an element of consciousness, it must not be supposed that any conclusive evidence is at hand showing such to be wanting in reflexes. So little of emotional expression was developed during the first few weeks of life, that it was difficult to decide whether the so-called reflexes were, or were not, accompanied by consciousness. I have, therefore, found the evidence of consciousness to lie, not in the action itself, but in the subsequent history of the act. If one of two acts performed at the same period should be repeated with little or no variation, only on the recurrence of the circumstances under which it was first performed; and if the other, continually changing and expanding, gave rise to new reactions in dissimilar circumstances, some justification may be found for ascribing an element of consciousness to the second which we withhold from the first.

SUMMARY.

The movements first selected for development were instinctive. Pleasure was not felt as such at birth. Feelings of discomfort were felt, but not distinguished one from another; they were strong. The first instinctive acts alleviated feelings of discomfort; and comfort (or satisfaction) was the result. Movements directed toward the attainment of comfort, replaced in a measure the mere expression of discomfort. Satisfaction or pleasure, as an end or goal, then emerged in consciousness; it corresponded to desire. After the growth of desires, development proceeded rapidly, in response to a demand for the satisfaction of them.

If we review the movements which have survived, we find them to have existed, (a) as instinctive movements alone; (b) as modifications of and additions to instinctive movements— direct accommodations to environment; (c) as instinctive plus spontaneous movements. No conclusive case is recorded of a spontaneous movement which alone has afforded a foundation for the development of further complex acts.

But the pleasurable feeling resulting from satisfaction is not enough to account for the reproduction of acts. It was necessary that an associative link should have been formed between a mental correlative of the act and the feeling, in order that a repetition of the act might be insured. Ample evidence is at hand of such links having been formed.

The development of the individual is thus seen to have depended upon three factors:

1. Upon inheritance as expressed (a) in instincts, (b) in the structure of the body, the relations of whose bony and muscular parts were such as to make possible only certain movements, and to exercise a control upon the range and direction of movements, (c) in the structure and functions of the nervous system, which rendered it capable of receiving forms of stimulation and responding to them, and which, moreover, was so constituted that paths once opened by stimulation and discharge, were thereby rendered the more pervious to the reiterated influences of like stimulations and discharges, and, (d) by the possession of consciousness.

2. Upon environment in a broad sense, comprising all things which might act as stimuli, from the food which the child took and the manner of taking it, to the objects which he handled and the persons who surrounded him; but especially upon those features of the environment which, by their persistence, acted as continued stimuli through whose instrumentality the fundamental movements of future activities became habitual.

3. Upon the plasticity of structures and functions.

PART II.—SENSATIONS.

SECTION I.—SIGHT.

Observations on the Development of Visual Perception.

First Day.—The eyes were opened by only a narrow crack. Sometimes they remained closed when the child was awake. The eye balls rolled constantly, whether the eyes were open or shut. Upon exposure to strong light the pupils underwent little alteration.

Second Day.—At twenty-nine hours the child looked intently at a bright light (of a lamp). At forty-four hours his eyes followed the movement of a pair of shining calipers, and he appeared to look, but without focusing the eyes, at his father who held them.

Third Day.—At seventy-five hours his eyes were wide open, and turned from one object to another. The eyes were not in focus. Convergence of the axes was marked.

Seventh Day.—Focus still imperfect. His eyes again followed a moving object. He looked successively at the faces of three persons who, standing in a row, bent over him.

Eighth Day.—He was seen to focus his eyes in looking at a hand. He looked fixedly at the hand when it was quiet, and followed it when moved.[1] He lay awake for half an hour looking at his surroundings.

Tenth Day.—His eyes were often in focus. His eyes followed the hand of a person beside whom he was lying, five times in its course back and forth across some sewing.

Twenty-sixth Day.—Attention and interest were excited by persons and light.

[1] Here unfortunately the notes have failed to record whether or not his eyes maintained their focus while following the hand, and the plane and direction in which the hand was moved.

Twenty-eight Day.—He turned his head (while lying down) in order to follow with his eyes the face of a person speaking to him.

Thirtieth Day.—At twilight he turned his eyes from a gas jet burning within a ground glass globe, to an adjacent twilight window, at which he looked fixedly.

Thirty-first Day.—His attention was engaged by a blue sacque (upon its first appearance), of a shade was similar to that of a blue piano scarf at which he had often looked.

Thirty-ninth Day.—As the child lay looking at the wall, which was illuminated by lamplight, his father's head was so interposed as to cut off his view. Thereupon he moved his eyes, and afterwards his head, in order to see again the wall behind the obstacle.

Forty-fourth Day.—Instead of dropping to sleep as he had previously done when taken for a walk, the child remained awake and interested himself in looking about.

Forty-seventh Day.—He watched the window as the light faded, keeping quiet and absorbed for half an hour. He continued to look with interest at the golden brown curtain which had held his gaze on the twentieth day. By this time he habitually kept awake when carried out of doors. He looked with interest at the beard of a male visitor.

Fifty-seventh Day.—He was amused by watching silent movements of the lips and tongue.

Fifty-ninth Day.—He was interested in looking out of the window at the trees, whose newly-opened leaves were constantly in gentle motion; also in watching an empty chair rocking before him, the separate movements of which his eyes did not follow.

Sixtieth Day.—He showed that he distinguished between a familiar and an unfamiliar face, by smiling at the former and regarding the latter seriously, with the pursed lips characteristic of attention.

Tenth Week.—The child at once noticed a stray lock of hair which was hanging at the side of his mother's face. When riding in the horse-car he tried to sit up and look around, and was annoyed by a shawl raised in front of his face to protect him from wind and dust. While crying he was laid upon a sofa above which a gas jet was burning. The moment he saw the light his crying ceased, and his whole body began to move in excitement. Interest and excitement were maintained without interruption for half an hour. The light was then put out.

Eleventh Week.—The child looked repeatedly, and as if comparing them, from the face of one person to that of another. Upon a journey, the lights on the ceiling of the sleeping car gave him entertainment. During the day he lay on a pillow and looked continually at the figured linen on the back of the seat, or at the ceiling of the car.

Twelfth Week.—When hungry, the child cried if his mother appeared. Most of his waking moments were spent in his bassinet on a porch, watching the trees moving in the wind against the sky. Thus occupied he often lay for an hour, quiet except for the movements which accompanied deep interest.

Fifteenth Week.—The child observed his own reflection in a mirror. After the tenth week he had looked at the image of the face of the person holding him, never at the reflection of himself. Later in the fifteenth week he smiled at his own image.

Sixteenth Week.—He looked at his own pink dress and occasionally at some swinging balls. A red and yellow ball were offered him, he took the yellow one once, but could not be induced to reach again.[1]

Seventeenth Week.—The child was taken for a drive (in the country) during which he was so much interested that he became neither sleepy nor hungry. He directed his gaze continually to all quarters. He observed a white cotton string which was stretched above his bed and parallel with it, and from which his balls were suspended. He made many efforts to turn himself in order to follow its course above and behind him. He looked at trees, etc., outside of the window ; but not at articles of furniture and movable objects within the room. He watched people. He recognized his mother as reflected in a mirror.

Nineteenth Week.—A box of blooming nasturtiums stood

[1] Thus did he baffle attempts at experiments.

within his field of vision. The child was never seen to give them more than a passing glance. One day a humming bird visited the flowers. He watched the bird with interest, and followed its flight with eyes and head. In the midst of a heavy shower the child watched a single stream of water which trickled from the roof and fell splashing upon the steps. He gazed out of the window, then turned his glance indoors, looking from one piece of furniture to another. After this he habitually regarded the furniture with interest. He began to notice flowers. He still enjoyed watching the fading light.

Twentieth Week.—Upon one occasion, in the eighteenth week, the child withdrew crying from contact with a person clad in black, who had also a loud voice. He afterwards saw persons so attired without evincing the least aversion to any one of them. A little kitten placed in his lap failed to elicit any response from him. He was interested in seeing his mother eat. He watched the cutting of the food and followed attentively the course of each bit from the plate to the mouth. Thus he was entertained during a meal.

Twenty-second Week.—When taken (in the city) for the first ride in his carriage, he looked at horses, carts and other passing objects, and at the parasol over his head.

Twenty-third Week.—After an absence of some twelve weeks the child was taken home. He at once observed the changed surroundings, and during the first day looked around the room continually. The golden brown curtain referred to above attracted the child's attention, and he watched it with as much interest as he had shown earlier. He laughed when he saw his mother don her hat. The association of the sight of the hat with going out was formed within ten days. In the country his mother had not worn her hat when out with the child.

Twenty-fourth Week.—Once again he would take no notice of a kitten. He did not notice, nor did he appear to see, a baby; but smiled at the woman who held her.

Twenty-seventh Week.—He observed a large picture of a boy on the wall of a strange house, and a landscape on the wall of his own room. He perceived a single human hair. He perceived people and wagons a block away, and watched their approach and disappearance.

Thirty-first Week.—He discovered the shadow of his carriage, and watched it for half a mile.

Thirty-third Week.—When riding in a horse-car, the straps swinging overhead interested the child. The other people in the car also interested him, and he observed the objects which they held in their hands. It became habitual with him to look after objects which had been dropped. He recognized an orange at a distance of several feet and in new surroundings.

Thirty-ninth Week.—A rubber cat and ball were given to the child. He took the ball and played with it; but the cat received no notice.

Fortieth Week.—He made fairly good estimations by the eye of size and distance.

Forty-third Week.—It gave the child delight to see a person leave the room and close the door, then suddenly open the door and reappear.

Forty-fourth Week.—He examined his nursing bottle with great interest.

Forty-fifth Week.—He distinguished between two bottles containing respectively milk and water, and chose the bottle of milk. He failed to follow the rapid movements of his father, who passed quickly in front of the child from one side to the other. Each time the child greeted his father in a new position with surprise, then looked to the one which he had just vacated. When his father ran quickly round and round the child, who sat upon the floor, he remained quite still, puzzled and unable to follow. When red and yellow balls were offered to him, he took the yellow 6 times out of 10; afterwards he would not reach for them.

Forty-ninth Week.—The child was greatly distressed to see a familiar object for the first time out of place. A clothes hamper, usually occupying a corner, was during his absence placed in the middle of the room. Upon his return he immediately perceived it and began to cry. His crying ceased when it had been returned to its proper position.

Fiftieth Week.—He stood before a mirror and made grimaces at his own reflection. He stopped the performance upon perceiving in the mirror that he was observed.

Fifty-first Week.—He observed another baby with interest.

Fifty-eighth Week.—He recognized a person whom he had seen but once, and for a few moments, three days before, but by whom he had been hurt. He was much interested in observing dogs, birds and a cow. He observed other children closely.

Sixty-fourth Week.—Caterpillars, bugs, beetles and worms became interesting to the child. He examined the feet and legs of some frogs.

Sixty-sixth Week.—He recognized the locality of the house in which he stayed, and of the laboratory in which his father worked.

Sixty-ninth Week.—Pictures, righted or reversed, interested him.

Seventy-sixth Week.—During a journey the child was entertained not only by what he saw within the car, but by looking out of the window and viewing the passing objects.

Seventy-seventh Week.—During three months the child had seldom looked in a mirror. When, at the end of this period, he was held before one, he at once recognized his own reflection as that of a baby.

Eighty-second Week.—He noticed the moon, and spontaneously called it a light.

Ninety-fourth Week.—He began to use the word 'big' in such a way as to reveal an appreciation of the size of objects seen.

One-hundredth Week.—He never evinced the least preference for colored over uncolored pictures. By this week he could distinguish the details of pictures whose area did not exceed ⅝ of an inch.

Vision.

In dividing my observations upon vision into three classes, I obtain series of facts from which to study some aspects of sensations in general, and from which to follow the course of the development of the ability to see.

Class I. includes all records relating to sensation proper; namely, those which reveal (a) the ability of the child to experience sensations of a given quality, and to react in a manner peculiar to them; and those which show (b) that it is possible to obtain through observation, data for the estimation of the intensities of sensations (or perceptions) relatively to one another.

Class II. includes observations pertaining to the muscular adjustments which were requisite to the accomplishment of clear vision.

Class III. contains observations illustrating the growth of the perception of things seen.

Sensations of light experienced during the first day were probably relatively insignificant; for very little light could have penetrated to the retina through the narrow chink of the nearly closed lids. The child was born at 3:20 P. M., on the 19th of March. He was therefore exposed to the light of day for but a brief time during the first sixteen hours. At night only a dim light was burned in the room. He slept during the greater part of the first 24 hours, and his eyes were often closed even when not asleep. Hence it was that the child, on the day following birth, was not continuously subjected to the influence of the rays of a bright light. At the beginning of the second day he opened his eyes more widely. At 29 hours he responded by a definite reaction to a retinal stimulus received from the full light of a Rochester lamp. The reaction consisted in resting the gaze upon the object of stimulation; it pointed to the occurrence of sensation, but gave no clue to its value in relation to the strength of the stimulus.

Simple as this reaction was, and inconclusive as it might be considered by one who had not closely observed the developing child, certain facts relating to the influence exerted upon attention by diverse objects at once help to place such a reaction in a position of importance, and give it the right to be considered a true concomitant of a sense impression of a definite kind.

Before going further in the subject of sensations I must digress slightly to explain what these facts were, and must ask the reader to bear them in mind as he proceeds. When the child was very young, only an extremely limited number of objects called forth reactions at all. This number increased with age and experience. It was possible to present to him one new

thing after another without eliciting the least perceptible response. Things were repeatedly shown to the child which,
though in the immediate field of vision, he appeared not to see.
Examples in the recorded observations which illustrate this are
to be found in records for the 15th, 19th, 20th and 39th weeks.

In the history of individual development there may be found
an unbroken chain of reactions which show more clearly than
words can describe, just what the course of unfolding was.
When a response followed the presentation of an object which
might act as a stimulus, and was repeated with the recurring
advent of the object, the response was to be regarded as a definite reaction, accompanying an impression made upon a sense
organ which was in the proper condition for its reception. I
would not be understood to claim that the objects which called
forth no reaction aroused no sensation; but that those which
called forth a reaction did cause a sensation, while others, such
as objects seen in indirect vision, frequently failed to arouse
that form of reaction which accompanied the stimulation of the
sense organ.

In the study of sensation as such, I have ruled out, so far as
possible, all cases in which the perceptive element was present.
This was an extremely difficult matter to accomplish in dealing
with records other than those of the earliest days. The early
sensations may have been accompanied by the conscious recognition of the objects causing them; but it is in a high degree
doubtful whether they were so accompanied. It is, however,
certain that they were not attended by those groups of associations which soon began to gather round experiences. When
a large surface, uniformly colored, engaged the attention
of the child and held it for perhaps fifteen minutes, an
example was given of stimulation and reaction which did not
necessitate a perception of the colored surface, as distinguished
from an illuminated one, nor did it inevitably involve any elements of association whatsoever.

In part I.[1] of this work it was pointed out that the child
might experience sensations without distinguishing them one
from another, and this fact must be again emphasized here.

[1] Movements, p. 14.

The study of the growth of the power to discriminate is closely associated with the development of the ability to perceive. That the child reacted in a peculiar manner to a certain form of stimulation is not a proof that he distinguished this from some other form, to which he had previously reacted in a different manner, or that the second stimulation and reaction called up the first. On the whole, I think we must admit that the first sensations at least approached somewhat closely to our notion of what extremely simple ones should be; to wit, feelings unattended by memory, anticipation or discrimination.

The order in which the child displayed the ability to experience qualities of visual sensation was as follows,

Light, undoubtedly the first retinal sensation, was experienced early in the second day. On the seventh day he gave evidence of having experienced sensations in indirect vision. On the fifteenth and twentieth days he possibly experienced color sensations, blue, golden-brown and red having been the colors which might have acted as stimuli (none pure tones of the colors, they represented). On the thirty-first day a white surface, receiving no direct illumination, acted as a stimulus, also a blue surface. On the thirty-fourth day a blue and white object and the golden-brown curtain arrested his attention. On the fifty-third day a plaid waist in which scarlet was the predominating color interested the child. In the sixteenth week he looked repeatedly at his pink dress. In the twenty-third week, after a long absence from home, the golden-brown curtain again attracted his attention. He did not give conclusive proof of the ability to recognize colors till the second year, when he showed that he recognized (without having received any instructions) the following colors: pink (eighty-fourth week), yellow (eighty-ninth week), black (ninety-fourth week), blue (ninety-seventh week), red (ninety-eighth week), light brown and gray (ninety-ninth week). Light always interested the child. After the thirtieth day he was pleased for some weeks to watch the window as daylight faded to darkness. On the thirty-sixth day, light reflected from eye-glasses called forth repeated expressions of pleasure. In the tenth week a burning gas jet proved deeply interesting, though the roaring and flickering of the flame doubtless influenced him also. In the eighty-sixth week he used words to point out distinctions of light and darkness.

Before the tenth week the child gave no evidence of having received impressions from objects smaller than the features of the human face. In the tenth week he looked attentively at a stray lock of dark hair hanging beside a familiar face. Large objects and surfaces, moving or illuminated, attracted his gaze in the early weeks. In the seventeenth week a single strand of white cotton string such as comes from the grocer's, interested the child. In the twenty-third week he watched some flies on the window pane. In the forty-fourth week small objects, such as bread crumbs, became interesting to the child.

The simplest test of the strength of a sensation was that it should be followed by a motor reaction. In order to get some data for comparisons we have to inquire whether there existed any well marked differences in the motor reactions themselves from which something might be learned, as to the relative value of the sensations which they accompanied respectively. Such differences were clearly present. They were to be found in the varying force of reactions. Reactions of greater force were of two kinds; the first of which consisted of impulses, prolonged and involving a few muscles; the second, of impulses, diffuse and involving a great many muscles, notably those used in the expression of attention, and of the feelings of pleasure and pain. For example, when experiencing a sensation, the child sometimes remained quiet for half an hour, his gaze rivetted upon the object, or again, by a quivering of the whole body, flexions and extensions of the members, acceleration of respiration, etc., gave every evidence of excitement. It was not observed that attention accompanied by signs of excitement endured for a shorter time than attention accompanied by bodily quiet;[1] it cannot, therefore, be inferred that sensations accompanied by the expression of excitement were of greater intensity than those not so accompanied. That they might have been so, is not to be

[1] This is not to be taken to mean complete repose, which with the young infant was to be observed only during sleep.

denied. But it was clearly shown in the history of development, that the marked expressions of excitement did not accompany the early sensations, which were characterized rather by a quiet, prolonged interest in the object; while the later sensations, in the main associated with perceptions, had involved in their concomitant reactions, those movements which revealed the diffusion of the motor impulse. That it was possible for a sensation to be felt without calling forth a definite reaction was shown by the evidence of indirect vision. An object seen in indirect vision failed to attract attention, while an interesting object seen in direct vision was present; but, when for any reason, the object of direct vision failed to hold attention, the eyes were frequently turned to the second object in such a way as to show that this, as well as its predecessor, had made an impression. There were, therefore, three somewhat rough measures of the comparative intensities, of sensations, which were: first, of sufficient intensity to be felt without immediately causing a reaction; or, second, of sufficient intensity to be followed by a transient motor reaction; or, third, of sufficient intensity to be followed by a reaction which endured often as long as half an hour, which reaction consisted sometimes of those movements which were the peculiar attendants upon the stimulation of a given sense organ, plus the signs of attention, sometimes in the said movements, plus the signs of excitement.

The ability to see small objects depended upon the acquirement of the muscular adjustments essential to monocular and binocular vision, and is therefore related to the subject of eye movements.

The development of eye movements might well have been treated along with movements in general in Part I. The questions which there arise as to the original forms of other movements, and the methods by which variety and skill grew up, arise here. Was the first successful eye movement a chance coördination, or a reaction to a simultaneous stimulation of two organs of sight? It would seem that the movements of the eye muscles which pertain to vision, originated like other movements in some such primitive reaction or coördination as has elsewhere been called an instinct;[1] and that the subsequent coördinations

[1]Movements, p. 9.

neccessary to focus, fixation, etc., were built up upon this basis. That the history of the development of other movements has suggested this view to me I must frankly state. Nevertheless the careful consideration of the evolution of eye-movements would seem to point to it independently.

On the second day the eyes followed the movement of a pair of calipers—a shining object illuminated by daylight. Therefore following with both eyes preceded focusing and occurred immediately after the first determinate reaction to light stimulus. Following with the eyes would thus appear to belong among the inherent reactions as clearly as do clasping, sucking, etc. Amid the spontaneous eye-movement of the first few days such a reaction stood out very conspicuously. A great many movements besides those of the eye muscles are associated with vision. There are movements of the eyelids which allow of the entrance of light, and of the extension upwards of the field of vision, and all the accessory neck and trunk movements by which the eyes, along with the head, are carried into a better positions for seeing. None of these accessory movements (except that of opening the eyes) were observed during the first three weeks.

The eyes were not seen to be in focus before the eighth day. On that day the child focused his eyes upon a hand which was held above him at a distance greater than one foot, but not exceeding two. After the tenth day the eyes were frequently in focus.

Spontaneous eye movements occurred more rarely as time passed. By the eighteenth week spontaneous movements had ceased to be noticeable, and the eyes were usually in focus.

By the twenty-seventh week he had acquired so nice an adjustment that he was able to perceive a single human hair. Earlier than the thirty-seventh day little was recorded as to the accommodation of the eyes to near and distant vision. It was, however, certain that the child perceived objects at distances varying from six inches to ten feet after the tenth day. On the thirty-first day his gaze followed the departing figure of his mother across the room, a distance of ten feet, and the accommodation to the slow increase of distance was fairly good. By the fifty-ninth day he could perceive from the second story window trees some fifteen feet away.

At twelve weeks he perceived moving objects at distances of 25 to 50 feet. In the twenty-seventh week he perceived objects in the street a block away and watched their approach. After the eighteenth week, when holding objects in his hands and looking at them, he usually held them at a distance for good vision.

In the second day, as has been said before, the eyes of the child followed the movement of an illuminated object. On the third day they again followed a moving object. On the seventh day they turned in succession towards each of a row of three objects, a phenomenon somewhat different from that of following movement, since it involved indirect vision, and movements made in response to sensations thus received. On and after the tenth day his gaze frequently followed a moving object. Active direction of the gaze towards an object of interest was not observed until the thirty-ninth day, and head as well as eye movements were involved in this direction. By the seventeenth week he was able to direct his gaze in all ways. In the tenth week he evinced a desire to sit up in order to see. In the seventeenth week he turned the body as well the head to extend the range of vision; in this week he held his head erect, turned it to the side, and raised his eyes to see the face of one who had spoken to him.

Previous to the nineteenth week he had followed only very slow movements; but in this week he made a distinct advance in being able to follow the flight of a humming bird as it passed from flower to flower, hovering for an instant at each. In the forty-fifth week he was utterly unable to follow rapid movements of a large body back and forth and round and round. Nor did he follow the course of a falling object, but discovered its position on the floor from the sound of the fall. In the sixty-sixth week, lying on his back, his eyes followed the flight of a fly which circled somewhat slowly above his bed. As late as the close of the second year he was rarely successful in perceiving the course of a projectile, (*i. e.*, a ball thrown by the hand).

He could perform more rapid movements of the body than

the eye could perceive when performed by objects or other persons.

The development of the perception of objects of vision is closely connected, on one side with an increasing sensibility to the influence of a greater variety of stimuli, and on the other with the development of the movements which pertain to vision. All study of sensations which extends beyond the territory of the first sense impressions, trespasses upon the confines of perception; and the consideration of the growth of the susceptibility to various qualities of sensation is so entangled with that of growth of the ability to perceive objects of sense, that it must be treated along with the discussion of the latter question.

I have explained above the manner in which the term sensation is used, and have pointed out that the child probably had but few pure sensations as compared with the number of perceptions, and that those nearest-to-pure sensations belonged to the early days. Nevertheless there must have been many occasions throughout infancy when a new experience, a new form of stimulus produced an effect closely allied in nature to those early sensations. There was, however, one significant difference which characterized the later sensations as partially perceptive—they were roughly classified and referred to their proper domain in the territory of sensation.

The confounding of sensations, (not the failure to localize them) which was conspicuous earlier in life, gave place to the ability to distinguish them one from another. New reactions arose, based upon differentiated sensations. These reactions showed the paths which the differentiation had pursued. The first perceptions were immediately the result of the first sensations and the reactions to them. The differentiation of sensation was accomplished by means of reactions, and it was not possible for perceptions to occur till sensations had undergone such differentiations.[1]

The term perception is here taken to mean the recognition of the presence of an object of sense. All objects possibly present to sense did not arouse reactions which showed them to have stimulated sensation, nor did all objects which stimulated

[1]For illustrations see Touch, below.

sensation, come to be immediately perceived. The requisites of perception were :

A. {
1. Sensation
   and
2. Reaction
3. A second sensation, or sensations, resulting from the reaction.

B. { The repetition of A a sufficient number of times to establish an associative connection of 1 and 2 with 3.

It will at once be seen, according to this view, that no perception could have occurred without a foundation in sensation and reaction; and that sensations and perceptions did not occur at haphazard upon the infant intelligence, an unassorted medley pouring in a steady volume upon it; but that the ability to receive and to perceive developed side by side along definite lines.

Visual preceptions, like muscular adjustments, were the result of the training received through experience. The early reactions were the instinctive movements which followed upon the stimulation of the retinae; but as seeing was replaced by looking, new reactions were manifested, and feature after feature of the surroundings grew through reiterated influence, to have some meaning for the child. The familiar, not the unfamiliar things then took on a deep interest for him. He watched them, and in following their changes, got perceptions of details, and of new objects in relation to the old. The history of perception tells of this steady advance, on the one hand, towards the perception of more in the familiar, on the other, towards the perception of change in the familiar.

To the twenty-eighth day the history consists in an enumeration of things which interested the child and engaged attention. On the twenty-eighth and thirty-first days in order to see more of an object, he put forth effort in the form of new adaptations of movement. After the thirty-first day there was steady progress in singling out features of the environment.

In the record several instances are noted of the failure of objects to elicit attention. The example of the cat was a good one. When a kitten was shown to the child in the twentieth

week he seemed not to see her. He had previously seen no
small animals whatsoever. In the thirty-ninth week a rubber
cat was given to him for a plaything, which proved equally un-
interesting. During the following summer he handled animals
of all sizes and often saw a cat and her family of kittens. The
rubber cat in the meantime had been left at home. After his
return it was immediately singled out as an object of special
affection. It was given a name, 'lum,' by which all cats were
then designated, and finally fell to pieces as a consequence of too
much handling.

He perceived adults before he noticed children (whom he
rarely saw closely during the first year), and was interested in
pictures of persons for months before he cared for illustrations
of other things. About the sixty-ninth week his interest in pictures increased greatly and he began to look at them himself.
Naturally he got them inverted. The reversal never seemed to
trouble him in the least, and until the ninety-third week, he continued to look at them either way with evident enjoyment. In
the eighty-third week he was able to point out the details of
familiar and unfamiliar pictures when looking at them inverted.
It was not until the ninetieth week that he became interested in
pictures representing a diversity of unfamiliar, as well as of
familiar objects. From such examples as the above it may be
gathered that much was to be learned from seemingly negative
results as to the child's knowledge of things at a given period.
In fact the record of what did not interest him taught almost as
much as the record of what did.

The growth of the ideas of size, distance and direction, and
his interpretations of pictures will be treated in Part III.

SECTION II.—HEARING.

RECORD OF OBSERVATIONS.

Second Day.—The child ceased crying several times when
nis father began to whistle.

Fourth Day.—He frequently looked at his father when
spoken to by him.

Seventh Day.—He looked intently into the face of a person who spoke to him.

Seventeenth Day.—During this day he was peculiarly sensitive to sound.

Twentieth Day.—He lay still for fifteen minutes while someone was singing to him.

Twenty-fourth Day.—The effect of the striking of the clock was observed. Twice he stopped crying while it struck, and once he was aroused from a light sleep by its gong.

Thirtieth Day.—Undoubtedly he turned his head in the direction whence sounds proceeded.

Forty-sixth Day.—To talking and singing he replied by cooing. At this time and later the effects were observed of noises from within and from without the room. Those from within frequently, though not always, disturbed him; those from without, though often loud, rarely aroused him.

Seventeenth Week.—He evinced pleasure in an action song, looking from the hands to the face of the singer.

Eighteenth Week.—Hearing the rain falling, he turned his head towards the open window and lay quiet listening. S and sh sounds had a soothing effect.

Twentieth Week.—The slightest sound served to interrupt his meal, and he looked in the direction whence it came.

Twenty-second Week.—In the beginning of a journey the child was continually startled by the shrill whistles of the trains; but after twelve hours they ceased to annoy him, and he even became oblivious of the loud noise of passing trains. Sounds in his sleeping room not loud enough to waken him, were followed by such movements as rolling the head, lifting the hands feet and legs, and by inarticulate murmurs. He took pleasure in a noise made by himself, but rendered articulate by the hand of another patting his mouth.

Twenty-sixth Week.—Noises which startled him when awake no longer caused crying, but the child displayed great curiosity as to their source.

Twenty-seventh Week.—Localization of sounds, with the exception of those from behind the head, was fairly well established.

Twenty-eighth Week.—He recognized the tune of the action song which had first given him pleasure in the seventeenth week.

Thirty-second Week.—His father's imitations of the voices of animals entertained the child and made him laugh.

Thirty-third Week.—The ringing of the door bell in a room caused great astonishment.

Thirty-eighth Week.—He drummed continually with some hard object upon the table of his high chair.

Forty-first Week.—He began to distinguish among spoken words. He enjoyed screaming, making each successive scream louder than the last, till he jumped with the effort.

Forty-third Week.—The sound of a blow upon the sterilizer frightened the child ; but after he had been shown the sterilizer, inside and out, he no longer objected to the noise.

Forty-eighth Week.—He recognized a second tune, belonging to an action song.

Fifty-second Week.—Any noise coming from the direction of the stairs, he associated with the coming of his father.

Fifty-fifth Week.—He understood a little language and possessed some words of his own.

Seventieth Week.—Words which he merely imitated, and which had no meaning for him, he did not afterwards repeat.

Seventy-second Week.—He struck a bell jar with a glass stopper. The sound which resulted caused him to start with surprise. He turned to a scrap basket and struck that with the stopper once, then returned to the bell jar and made it ring repeatedly.

Seventy-fourth Week.—He heard the tolling of the buoy bell 2½ miles out to sea, and said 'g'ling, g'ling,' a word used to indicate a bell.

Seventy-seven Week.—He called out 'baby' when one cried in another state-room.

Ninety-third Week.—He sometimes confused words which sounded alike if they were used together.

Ninety-seventh Week.—When singing he made a somewhat doleful noise, lacking the least semblance of a tune. At this time he easily recognized five tunes, and if they were hummed for him, was able to supply words at the right notes.

One-hundredth and fourth Week.—One day the oven door was slammed when the child was sitting in the kitchen. He began to cry, and putting his hands upon the epigastric region of his body said that he was hurt.

HEARING.

The first definite reactions to auditory sensations were observed on the second day, during which the child several times stopped crying when his father began to whistle. If a loud noise accompanied by a perceptible jar had thus affected the child, the reaction might have been attributed to the influence of the vibration upon the body, as well as to the sensation of sound. Such a noise as whistling, however, could scarcely induce a general bodily sensation, so the reactions must have occurred in consequence of auditory sensations experienced by the child on the second day.

Auditory sensations, unlike others, so far as could be ascertained, depended directly upon the physical condition of the child, who unquestionably had times of extreme sensibility to the impressions of sound. An apparent insensibility to noises was characteristic of the first month of infancy. During this period the child would sleep undisturbed in the family living room, while persons were conversing and moving about. And it was by variations in this apparent insensibility that much was learned concerning his ability to hear. On the third day loud noises, such as the slamming of a door, caused the child to start, or to cease crying; but the common sounds of the room called forth no reaction. On the fourth day he showed that he heard the human voice. On the seventeenth day the child was restless, and, owing to a slight indisposition, unlike his usual self. During the day he did not sleep well, and such noises as a footfall or a voice within the room aroused him. On the three succeeding days he was once more quiet and oblivious of sounds; but on the twenty-first day, after an attack of colic, the child was peculiarly sensitive to sounds, so that he could get but little sleep. Sudden noises, whether loud or low, were especially disturbing to him. On the twenty-second day he returned to a condition of normal indifference. It was, however, noteworthy that a slow but steady increase of irritability was taking place, which ultimately landed him in a condition of normal irritability, very similar to the abnormal one which had accompanied the early indispositions. In the sixteenth week, the child being to all appearances in perfect health, the least noise in his sleeping room (such as the rustling of a pillow case) aroused him from his nap. This was not true of his night sleep, which was probably heavier.

The increase of sensibility to the influence of sound was shown in another way; namely, by the effect of noises upon the child while eating. In the early weeks the child devoted himself to the task of satisfying his hunger regardless of what went on about him. He had to learn to accommodate himself to his supply of nutriment as well as to other features of his surroundings, and no doubt found the task of suckling thoroughly engrossing in its pre-automatic stages. It is therefore not surprising that noises, if he heard them while feeding, failed to attract his attention. In the sixteenth week sounds began to prove a real source of distraction, causing him to pause and to look around many times during his meal.

The possibility of becoming accustomed to the influence of noises was noticeable also. From birth the child was used to the noises of the street, which rarely disturbed him. In the eleventh week he was taken to the country where, during eleven weeks he heard no noises similar to those of the city. In the twenty-second week he returned to town, and when laid down to sleep in a room which was not directly on the street, it was quite impossible for him to rest. Although he was tired and many times composed himself to sleep, some passing vehicle invariably aroused him. At the end of two days he had become somewhat accustomed to the noises of the street, and by the tenth day they no longer exerted a disturbing influence. In the twenty-third week hammering in the next room did not arouse him.

The acquirement of an insensibility to certain classes of sounds would seem to have been as important in development as the increase of sensibility. There was not, however, a history of growing indifference to the influence of all sounds. The striking of the clock, a sound which arrested the child's attention on the twenty-fourth day, interested him repeatedly during that part of the two years which he spent at home, and long after all ordinary noises of the street had ceased to be remarked, he would pause to listen to the striking of the clock.

It has already been stated that sudden noises often startled the child and caused him to cry violently. This was especially true of noises which disturbed him while sleeping or eating. The effect produced by sounds at such times seemed to depend, not so much upon quality and pitch, as upon abruptness. Even a low voice addressing the child when he was attentively looking at something, often caused him to start violently.

After the ninety-fourth week he evidently appreciated the rhythm of poetry, for he greatly liked to hear the Mother Goose melodies. Dr. Bolton's studies on rhythm[1] suggested to me the advisability of ascertaining whether any particular rhymes were more agreeable to the child than others. I began by repeating ' Baby Bye, here's a Fly, ' etc. At first he did not like it, and once he cried when, thinking to please him, I began to say it. This was in the eighty-eighth week. Some days later he, of his own accord, asked for the rhyme which he had not in the meantime heard. Once in the ninety-fourth week I heard him repeating it to himself. He had the rhythm correct, but not all of the words. Nonsense syllables took the places of the words omitted. He would not at any time listen to poetry which contained no familiar words. After a few stanzas his interest flagged, and if the poetry continued he became impatient, and ordered it to be stopped. On the other hand, he often sat quietly listening to some simple rhyme or poem whose repetition he demanded from five to fifteen successive times. He had some favorites among the rhymes and jingles, but I could not discover that his choice of them as such depended upon a peculiarity of the rhythm.

If he had an appreciation of melody he never showed it. He learned to recognize tunes without the words of the songs which they accompanied; but he did not care for songs containing no familiar words, and in the ninety-eighth week he cared most for those of which he could understand the most.

[1] *American Journal of Psychology*, Vol. VI., No. 2.

No reactions whatsoever pointed to an inborn ability to localize sounds, and to judge of the distances they traversed. Simply to look at an object from which a sound issued was the first step towards localization. This the child did on the fourth day, in looking at a person speaking to him. As the localization of sound was not established till somewhat after the child had formed the habit of turning the eyes and head in order to see, a connection in development may have existed between the two acquirements. It is certain that the eyes had many times followed noiseless movement, and movement accompanied by sound, before the accurate localization of the direction of sound was established. On the twentieth day the child turned his eyes twice to look into the face of a person who spoke to him. On the thirtieth day he began to turn his head in the direction whence sounds proceeded. By the eighteenth week he could locate very well sounds coming from objects within the visual field. In the twenty-sixth week he seldom cried at sounds which startled him ; but was curious as to their source. In the twenty-seventh week, when he could sit, it was found that he could not localize sounds which came from behind him, but looked for their sources in front. This was true especially of sounds made near the middle of the back of the head. In the thirtieth week he for the first time drummed on the upright piano, and was surprised that the noise issued from the piano case instead of from beneath his hands. He looked up at the piano and down at his hands repeatedly.

Some experiments in playing 'hide and seek' made in the forty-eighth week showed how well the ability to judge of the direction whence sounds proceeded was established. Some one hid while the child was out of the room. When he crept in she made some low noise to serve him as a guide. The experiment was repeated a number of times, but he invariably found her without a mistake, wherever she was concealed. When the voice came from the closet he seemed puzzled for a moment, and paused to look about before starting and on his way towards the door. Nevertheless, he went without deviation to the right place.

He had no perception of the distance traversed by the sound

in reaching him. In the eighteenth week this was well shown in an experiment with an organ. The child lay in his bassinet eight or ten feet away from the organ. A person sat on a chair between him and the organ, yet not obstructing his view. Upon hearing the tones of the organ he looked in surprise at the person in the chair, accepting the noise as from her. When taken on the lap of the person playing he looked at the organ in astonishment.

In the fifty-fourth week in calling to a dog at some distance he scarcely raised his voice above a whisper. He was over two years of age before he recognized the fact that people at a distance could not hear him unless he raised his voice. It was quite certain that ideas of distance and pitch were not generally associated with sounds before the close of the second year.[1]

Probably the first sound recognized by the child—the first one assimilated with past experiences of a like nature—was that of the human voice. By the nineteenth day the sound of the voice was distinctly associated with pleasant experiences, so that he smiled when addressed.

On the forty-sixth day he began to respond to sound by sound, crowing when someone talked to him.

Recognition, in the case of the young infant, did not necessarily involve discrimination, but was rather a preliminary to discrimination. It did not depend upon diversity of experiences, but upon repetition of them. The bases of the first recognitions of sounds were to be found in some elements of experience other than sound itself. This was clearly shown in the case of footsteps. After the eighteenth week, if the child wakened crying, footsteps on the stairs at once quieted him, for these he had learned to associate with the relief which followed the appearance of his mother. In the seventeenth week he was interested in one of the kindergarten action songs, and looked repeatedly from the face to the moving fingers of the singer. In the twenty-eighth week, having heard this song frequently, he recognized the tune alone, and amidst a medley of other tunes. From the twenty-second to the twenty-seventh weeks

[1] Nor have such ideas become elements in the perception of sounds at 2 yrs., 7 mo.

the child might have heard trains passing at almost any moment of the day, yet the noise of the shrill whistle was the only sound of the trains to which he responded. In the twenty-seventh week he was taken on a journey, during which he was interested in the passing trains. A few moments after his return a train passed along the neighboring tracks. He heard this at once and looked about for it. Such cases might be multiplied almost indefinitely; but those cited illustrate sufficiently the statement made above.

The sounds first recognized were those which had been heard by the child many times. Later his memory for sounds developed, and he often recognized those which were comparatively new.

He became familiar with a wide range of sounds, and could, after the ninety-eighth week, refer each instantaneously and correctly to its source. All the noises of the house, whether loud or low—footsteps, coughing, rustling garments, objects falling, fire crackling, kettle boiling, etc., etc.—were remarked upon by him; and each experience seemed to have for him its auditory accompaniment. The sounds of nature also interested him greatly, from the noises of insects, birds and beasts, to the whistling of the wind, and so forth.

When his memory for sounds, was once established, the child often alluded to a sound if the circumstances upon which the recognition was based occurred without it. In the forty-third week he gave some evidence of an ability to recognize a sound absolutely. One day his mother snapped her fingers. He listened attentively to the noise produced thereby. Then he clicked with his tongue against the hard palate, and the result was a sound almost exactly like the one produced by the fingers.

It must not be supposed that the child could discriminate nicely when able to recognize so many sounds. On the contrary, he was easily thrown into confusion if similar sounds, which he was able to recognize singly, were used together. This was true especially of words sounding alike. The development of the ability to discriminate was noticeable during the acquirement of language. As a first step towards discrimination there was babbling—a separation of the sounds of the voice from other sounds. Then a few sylables were distinguished. Words often appeared in babbling before the child could use any words intelligently, which showed that certain combinations of sounds had been singled out for reproduction from the many which greeted his ear. Frequent repetition of such syllables occurred about the forty-second week. Many of these were parts of words from the conversation of his elders which did not relate personally to the child.

It was not uncommon, especially when he first began to speak, for him to confuse words sounding somewhat alike. This I have spoken of under Language and have there shown how it affected the acquirement of the correct pronunciation. If, however, he knew what the pronunciation should be, yet failed to achieve it, he was quick to detect the mistake and always paused to correct himself. The perception of differences in spoken words no doubt depended somewhat upon the movements and positions taken by the mouth-parts in framing the sounds; he was, however, often able in the second year to detect by the ear alone individual differences in the pronunciation of other persons.

Regarding his interpretation of sounds, enough has been said in the discussion of recognition to show that well nigh all the sounds perceived came to be so associated with experiences involving other than auditory sensations, that the instantaneous reference of a sound heard to one of these experiences was inevitable. All early meanings attached to sounds were naturally of a personal nature, and the first sounds interpreted were those associated with the comfort or discomfort of the child himself.

When his intelligence had moved beyond the stage of purely personal reference, and he had begun to be interested in things for themselves, a new and wider circle of interpretations was formed (close of the first year). Then it was that the child, while rightly recognizing sounds, fell into errors of interpretation. Such errors became more numerous with the passage of time. His accurate memory for past experiences led him constantly to reconstruct upon the basis of a single element, and to demand repetition when there was no liklihood of its occurrence. One example will illustrate. In the sixty-eighth week a little boy in the neighborhood used a tin horn to celebrate the Fourth of July. The sounds of the horn came to us from across the road at frequent intervals for a week, and the baby often looked from the window at the little boy, who went away at the end of the week. Three weeks later a tradesman announced himself by means of a similar horn. The child who was playing on the floor, looked towards the window and called his little playmate.

It was pointed out in the part of this work devoted to Vision that the observer had some means of judging of the relative intensities of sensations. It was possible to learn more of the intensities of visual than of auditory impressions. The reason for this is obvious. The vast majority of auditory sensations of the little child did not stand alone, but were associated with objects perceived at the same time through the medium of another sense or senses. It was not for themselves that the interest of the child was excited; but rather in their relation to objects did they have a value for him. It was therefore difficult to isolate in one of these complex experiences his reaction to the auditory element alone. It often happened that he seemed not to hear a sound which he afterwards recognized unfalteringly. Hence the effect upon him of one sound after another was not so readily to be noted as the effect of one visual sensation after another; and it was far less apparent to the observer that they did influence him in such varying degrees.

The notes record but few instances of sounds which, unaccompanied by other stimuli, engaged and held attention, in proportion to the number of such examples relating to vision; and they give but comparatively few cases in which sounds induced the reactions attendant upon excitement. But the early auditory sensations were often the means by which intensely unpleasant feelings were produced. There is certainly no example recorded in which a purely visual sensation was unpleasant enough to cause crying. Even the direct rays of the sun upon the eye did not do that; and the necessity of focusing the eyes upon the object, together with various protective adjustments, of iris, lids, etc., excluded the possibility of shock, from which the discomforts of hearing resulted.

On the nineteenth day he began to smile when spoken to,

and the sound of the voice in singing and speaking afforded him pleasure. In the eighteenth week the tones of the parlor organ, and the whistling of the wind induced pleasurable excitement. In the thirteenth week he evidently derived pleasure from noises made by his own voice. In the thirty-eighth week and later, noises made by himself in hammering and screaming, however discordant and loud, did not annoy him. These noises were tolerated or enjoyed, not only because they were associated with his own activity, for it was clearly shown in other cases, that such loud discordant sounds did not affect him unpleasantly. One day towards the close of the second year he went under a bridge over which a heavy freight train was passing with tremendous clatter and vibration. It did not seem to affect the child unpleasantly. On the ensuing day, as he passed beneath the same bridge, he bewailed the absence of the train. In the fifty-first week he began to cry when for the first time he heard muslin torn, but laughed when the noise was repeated. Something has been written above of his susceptibility to the qualities of auditory sensation. It remains for me to record the influence upon him of a few sounds of fixed quality. On the twenty-fourth day the striking of the clock began to affect him. On the same day, when someone chirped to him, he started violently. On the forty-sixth day the sound of rattling spoons interested him. It was observed from the sixty-first day that the voice of his father had a more subduing effect than the voice of his mother. In the fifty-ninth week the music of a street band of wind instruments afforded him evident enjoyment. The ear of the child would appear to have been sensitive to a wide range of auditory sensations; but the principle which governed the increase of the range of sensibility to visual sensations, was active in extending the range of sensibility to auditory; namely, the development of perceptions which took place as a consequence of the direction of attention to sounds. The stages of the development of hearing may be described briefly as follows:

1. Sensation.
2. Recognition and distinction.
3. Discrimination.

Interpretations occurred along with recognitions and discriminations.

SECTION III.—TOUCH.

If in the foregoing discussions of sensations I have made one generalization clear, it is now understood that any sensation which had an observable effect upon the child was followed by some form of motor reaction. It has also been shown that the forms which should be assumed by reactions differed in quality according to the sense stimulated. The reactions which were associated with sensations of the skin consisted of movements of the body as a whole, or of its members, and in the most primitive stage of reactions these were further the movements of the parts which lay near, or were closely connected with the portion of the surface stimulated; such, for example, as a twitching of the muscle beneath an area of skin subjected to tickling (nineteenth week), and licking in response to the feeling of milk flowing over the lips (third day). Some touch movements belonged to the class earlier described as instinctive, others to that of reflexes. By means of such reactions one of two possible ends was accomplished, either the body (or some portion thereof) was withdrawn from an unpleasant contact, or it was brought into closer union with a pleasant one. When voluntary movements had become possible the members could be brought into contacts not actually present to the skin, but thought of, or suggested by some one of the train of circumstances in which the contact was first felt as agreeable. There were then two distinct forms of action which figured as reactions to sensations of contact; namely, the inherent and the voluntary. Reactions of the first kind, by inducing changes in consciousness, made the child aware of those gross areas of his body which responded in a fixed way to definite qualities and quantities of stimulation. If we bear in mind the great number of inherent reactions, their distribution to nearly all parts of the body, and that each was called forth by the stimulation of a definite portion of the skin, and, except in rare cases, by the stimulation of no other area, the method by which the child came to

TABLE I.—TOUCH RECORDS.

DATE.	CONTACT.	TEMPERATURE.	PAIN.	LOCALIZATION.
Day 1st	He ceased crying a number of times when a hand was laid upon his body.			
2d	He felt the touches of calipers upon his head.			The touches of the calipers upon the head were responded to by attempts to withdraw the head. He turned his head toward the cheek touched.
4th	He felt the touch of a finger upon the cheek. Full immersion in a warm bath was agreeable to him, and when water from a sponge trickled over his head and face he seemed to like it.			He pressed his hands against his mother's breast while suckling—the beginning of localizing sensations of touch in the palmar surface of the hand.
6th		To be soiled or wet at once caused the child to cry.		
17th			An irritation of the skin caused restlessness and irritability.	
20th				When water was poured over his head he closed his eyes and mouth.
36th				When his mother washed out his mouth he put his hands up to hers.
38th				He grasped his mother's forefinger and carried it towards his mouth.

TABLE I.—TOUCH RECORDS. *Continued.*

DATE.	CONTACT.	TEMPERATURE.	PAIN.	LOCALIZATION.
Day. 39th Week.				
11th	Active feeling of what came to his hands.	....	....	He objected to having his hands covered. He began to finger and to feel objects.
12th	He perceived the difference between flannel and muslin. Gentle rubbing of the head caused the child to stop crying.	....	An arm, very sore because of vaccination, seemed to cause him little or no discomfort.	....
14th	He began to feel his own body when undressed.	....	....	He began to feel of the various regions of his own body when undressed.
16th	....	....	He struck his head hard against the chin of another person; he looked surprised and then began to cry. When scratched in the leg by a pin, he cried.	He began to play with his own fingers.
18th	He liked to have his body and limbs rubbed.	....	....	He sometimes used the feet to feel with.
20th	He sometimes used the feet to feel with.	....	....	He rubbed his eyes when soap suds accidentally got into them.
22d	....	....	....	Covering on the feet became distasteful to him.
24th	....	....	For two days he frequently struck himself forcibly on the mouth and face, but he seemed to feel no pain.	....
26th	....	....	....	He located tickling on the ear, which organ he scratched.

TABLE I.—TOUCH RECORDS. *Continued.*

DATE.	CONTACT.	TEMPERATURE.	PAIN.	LOCALIZATION.
Week 27th	Active touching with hands, feet and lips. Flies wakened him if they walked on his face.	. . . . .	. . . . .	He felt objects with hands and feet, and then put them to his mouth.
30th	. . . . .	. . . . .	. . . . .	He localized quite accurately the touch of a finger tip upon various parts of the head, evincing his ability to do the same by reaching after and grasping the finger.
35th	A blanket, laid over the child during his sleep and nowhere touching the skin, was often the means of waking him; as it disturbed him before he had had time to feel a change of temperature, he must have felt the pressure.			
33d to 46th	After the 33d week touch was cultivated by handling a variety of simple objects—balls, clothespins, spoons, celluloid and rubber "gum-rings," a palm-leaf fan, paper, cubical blocks, boxes, a little doll, a string of buttons, books, bread, etc., each of which he felt of and looked at.			

TABLE I.—TOUCH RECORDS. *Concluded.*

DATE.	CONTACT.	TEMPERATURE.	PAIN.	LOCALIZATION.
Week 38th	Solid food in the mouth was objectionable to him.			
39th				The forefinger tip used to feel small objects.
46th	In trying to hold three un-like things in one hand, one always slipped away, yet he did not miss it till he had looked in his hand.			
52d				He localized pain well, put-ting his hand on the hurt.
69th	He walked into the water, but drew back half frightened when the wavelets washed against his legs.	He seemed oblivious to the difference of temperature be-tween the sand and water of the shore of Vineyard Sound.		
101st		In this week he began to use 'too hot' to designate what was either hot or cold.		Internal pain he localized on the surface of the body near the organ affected. During the latter half of the second year he was inter-ested to learn the names of the parts of his body. It was easy for him to separate the various members and fea-tures, but not to make dis-tinctions which rest upon internal divisions, such as the abdomen, thorax, etc.

know those areas of his body which were, so to say, mapped out by sensations and movements, becomes clear to us. But from the repetition of the inherent reactions he could learn nothing further than this. In the attempt, however, to reproduce the movement and to regain a contact, there entered the element through whose agency the adjustments and distinctions were developed which were essential to progress.

There are three ways in which the reproduced movements affected development:

1st. By recurring at the suggestion of similar and practically identical circumstances they brought about a result practically identical with the original one. Older experiences were thus defined and older impressions renewed and intensified.

2nd. By recurring at the suggestion of similar, but not identical circumstances they produced a result which varied somewhat from the original one, and in which new sensations of contact were given and new adjustments obtained.

3rd. By recurring at the suggestion of similar circumstances they produced a result entirely unlike the original one, in which material for contrast was furnished. In early infancy, the child could not use such material, hence totally dissimilar experiences entered but little into the woof of the mental fabric during some six months.

The reactions which have been described as instinctive actions and reflexes[1] showed that localization of sensation to certain areas of the skin existed soon after birth. This localization must not be mistaken for a conscious appreciation of the parts stimulated. The fact that the child was able to remember and to reproduce an action upon the recurrence of the conditions which had first induced it, showed that a sensation had been consciously felt. There was, however, absolutely no evidence of the ability to locate such a sensation in a part of the body which he recognized; but the evidence showed sensations in general to be experienced and confused. The slow and laborious process was apparent by which the mental separation and differentiation of the bodily parts and surfaces were developed. The steps by which one portion after

[1] Part I, Movements.

another of the surfaces of the members was separated from its surroundings, and used through the agency of movement to obtain sensations, were recorded and have been spoken of under Movements.[1]

Therefore, whether we agree with those writers who claim that the so-called local signs depend upon some quality of the end organs themselves, or with those who believe them to be associated movement elements, or with those who find in the varying thicknesses of epithelial layers, or in muscle tensions, or in the number of end organs excited, sufficient explanation of their existence, it must be admitted in the present case, that they were not inherent or primitive; and that they were mental, the results of syntheses of sensations; and that the sensations out of which these syntheses were constructed were primarily of two kinds, pressure and movement. It is a question whether movement sensations alone were sufficient to give a local coloring to dermal sensations. Considering only the sensations of the skin proper, it must be admitted that the movement element was the one *essential* to the development of localization. It may, however, be argued, that if the slow differentiation and mental gaining of part by part were pursued as described above, years instead of weeks would have been required in development. But it was the first steps, and the first syntheses which required time for their completion, and it may be laid down as a law, that neither the time nor the experience was necessary for a succeeding related synthesis which had been required in obtaining the elements out of which its predecessor had been constructed.[2]

Pressure caused by a hand resting upon his body was soothing to the child from birth. The gentle patting of the back had a soothing effect also. He was at first the passive recipient of pressure stimuli. By the sixth day his open hands often rested upon surfaces of various kinds, and thereafter he slowly acquired the habit of feeling objects—or, rather be it said, the surfaces of

[1] Movements, pp. 21-23.

[2] For illustration consult Hand and Arm Movements, comparing the acquirements of the first twenty-seven weeks with those of the nineteen weeks following; also Observations on the Development of Visual Perceptions of the first sixty days with the period included by the nineteenth and twenty-seventh weeks.

objects—till by the time grasping was possible to him (twelfth week), he had experienced many touch-sensations.

Sensations of touch were obtained not only from the surfaces of the hands, but from the lips, tongue, soles of the feet and toes. Indeed the lips and the tongue were the first organs of active touch, the hands were next used, and lastly the feet. In the twenty-seventh week he used all three sets of organs, grasping an object in the hands, feeling it with the soles and toes, then putting it up to his mouth. Long after he had ceased to use his feet for touch, the lips still supplemented the hand.

It may be stated in a general way that his sensibility to impressions of contact increased with the development of active touch. Prior to the sixteenth week he was content to suck his own thumb when hungry, the feeling of milk in the mouth was, therefore, not an essential element in the feeding-complex. But in the thirty-eighth week it undoubtedly was; for he then at once spat out the thickened cream of sterilized milk.

In the twenty-ninth week he perceived the presence of salt or sugar in the mouth, acting as one does who finds his mouth filled with sand. His first objections to solid food were evidently founded upon the novel touch sensations which it aroused in the mouth.

In the eleventh week the hands distinguished between flannel and muslin.

In the fourteenth week, when rubbing his hands over a face, he encountered a handful of hair, and was surprised thereby.

After this the sensations of the skin of the hands became so closely associated with movements that, having made no experiments upon skin sensation only, I cannot separate the development of the one from that of the other.

In the nineteenth week flies walking on the face of the child caused his muscles to twitch; but when on the hands they seemed not to annoy him.

In the twenty-seventh week flies on his face became unpleasant to him, and caused him to waken if they crawled upon him during sleep. Beyond this I do not know whether he was sensitive to tickling or not.

From birth he objected to a wet or soiled diaper. It seems probable, since a bath of proper temperature was agreeable to him, that the warmth suddenly suffused over a considerable area of the skin was the cause of his displeasure. About the thirty-ninth day it was observed that he frequently cried when returned to the bassinet at night after having been taken out to receive the necessary attentions. If a hot water bag was laid in the child's place during his absence, and he was then laid upon the spot so warmed, he never cried, but at once went to sleep. The temperature of the sleeping room did not not at this time fall below 66°F.

In the sixty-sixth week he frequently stepped barefooted from the warm sand of the beach to the cool water of Vineyard Sound, without seeming to notice a difference in temperature. In the eighty-second week he liked to hold his head under the spigot, and it was apparently a matter of indifference to him whether warm or cold water flowed therefrom over his head and face. He liked to be washed in cold water less than in warm.

In the one-hundredth week he objected to the introduction into his arm pit of the bulb of a thermometer. This objection may not have been based entirely upon the temperature of the bulb.

In the early weeks the child gave no evidence of an ability to localize pain. Indeed, he did not localize pain till he was able to localize other dermal sensations. This was in part due to the imperfect use of his hands, for he could not have been expected to place the hand upon an injured part before he was able to place it voluntarily upon an object.

This peculiarity of the growth of the ability to localize sensations of pain would seem to be accounted for by the explanation which considers the localization of pain to be dependent upon the localization of touch sensations, and the result of the association of sensations of pain with those of contact. A further proof of the correctness of such a view was found in the manner of localizing internal sensations of pain, which he referred to some portion of the surface of the body near the internal part from which the disturbance originated. Distress in the throat he localized on the neck, and pain in the bowels in the naval.

By the fifty-second week he was able to locate pain on the surface of his body with considerable accuracy. During the first year he displayed the comparative insensibility to pain which is said to be characteristic of early childhood. On the twenty-first day he suffered not a little from an attack of colic. In the eleventh week, however, he had as the result of vaccination, a very sore arm, which seemed to give him little or no discomfort. He often knocked his head against that of a person holding him with force enough to hurt the adult, yet he apparently felt no pain. In the sixteenth week he struck his nose in this manner, and surprise at the result was after an interval succeeded by crying. During the fifth and sixth months he kicked the bassinet repeatedly with force enough to hurt the soles of bare feet, yet it was doubtful whether he was ever hurt.

In the twenty-ninth week, when trying to get on his hands and knees he bumped his head and nose severely; but this did not deter him from persisting in his efforts to creep. Nor did hurts long cause discomfort, even though the bruises and cuts in which they originated remained. Upon several occasions during the second year the child fell while running and cut his upper lip badly, so that it bled profusely, and afterwards swelled and looked extremely sore, yet after the first outcry he never referred to it. Quick sharp blows, cuts, and the one insignificant burn which he received did hurt him. In the eighteenth week he cried long and loud when scratched on the leg by a pin point. About the thirty-fourth week he sometimes scratched his scalp with his own finger nails, breaking the skin, which caused him to cry.

It was always possible to destroy the effect of an ordinary bruise by distracting his attention from it; and later by suggestion. To have the hurt kissed was more efficacious as a cure than to have some medicinal remedy applied.

It was a difficult matter to judge of the comparative intensities of sensations of touch. The occurrence of movements along with contact presented a difficulty which it was hard to get over without assistance from experiment. Then too the employment of sight in addition to touch began to add complications at an early date.

The recognition of sensations of touch was not as a rule based upon the association of touch with touch sensations; but upon the association of touch with movement or vision. The eye saw many objects in proportion to a few felt by the hand.

The eye might rest upon a pleasing thing, return to it, become familiar with it, inculcate its aspects into experience; for months the hand felt only what came or was given to it, so that the most pleasing of sensations might have been forgotten before it could be repeated. Hence the development of the perception of objects of sight was considerably in advance of the development of the perception of objects of touch, which began to assume noteworthy proportions only after the child could see (carry into his visual field) that which he handled.

SECTION III.—TASTE AND SMELL.

The records which I gathered upon the sensations of taste and smell were very meagre. I was unwilling to experiment upon the sense of taste, since substances introduced into the mouth must inevitably have found their way, as a whole or in part, to the stomach, whose normal processes might thus have suffered disturbance. From the first, water was given to the child daily; this he seemed to enjoy.

On the twenty-first day some soda mint in hot water was administered. He swallowed it, as he did water, giving no evidence of having experienced a different flavor. Thereafter until the twenty-ninth week milk and water were the only food substances which passed his lips. In the thirty-sixth week he received his first meal of artificial food, consisting of sterilized cow's milk slightly sweetened with cane sugar, and this he seemed to like.

In the thirty-eighth week his objection to solid food in the form of sugar, and thickened cream from the sterilized milk, was very strong.

In the forty-sixth week he refused bread and milk, probably because it too was solid, but was extremely fond of cow's milk alone. In the forty-seventh week he learned to suck a crust of bread, and doubtless in this way got its flavor. Thereafter he liked bread greatly and soon learned to swallow it.

In the fiftieth week he was given in water some medicine having a saline taste, which he liked. In the fifty-second week he was given some of the juice of an orange, which he liked at once, and of which he soon became exceedingly fond. In the fifty-eighth week he objected to a bitter medicine, even when sweetened and mixed with orange juice. In the sixty-fourth week he ate crackers and grew to like them very much. He ate also a little potato, bread and butter, broths, custards and boiled egg, each of which he seemed to like when first given to him, but no one of which tempted him when it appeared a second time. Indeed he often refused a food which had at first seemed agreeable to him. It would seem that the different flavors were not severally disagreeable to him, but they were not sufficiently pleasing to create a desire for the articles to which they belonged.

By the seventy-sixth week he liked salt greatly, and would have eaten it by the spoonful; sugar he refused to eat, but he liked to play with it. Throughout the second year he continued to like juice of oranges, grape fruits or lemons (the last in lemon jelly), also apples and grapes. He did not care for sweets,[1] but continued to demand salt. Milk, bread and butter, and fruits constituted the staple articles of his diet; other plain foods he sometimes took and sometimes refused.

From the above scattered records it may be learned that certain simple tastes were pleasing to the child in themselves, and at least one, bitter, was disagreeable to him; but that the flavors of the mixed foods were responded to with indifference.

SMELL.

During two years the child gave no evidence of a great sensibility to the influence of odors. But by the end of the first month the odor of milk was undoubtedly one of the signs by which he recognized the near presence of his mother. From the second month until complete weaning had been accom-

[1] In the third year he liked pure cane sugar and maple sugar.

plished proximity to his mother suggested feeding. Early in the third month the experiment was made of holding close to the child a cloth moistened with milk. He began at once to act as if hungry. The experiment was so arranged that smell must have been the only sense to which an appeal was made. If sweetly scented flowers were held close to his nostrils during the fourth month and later, his face often wore an attentive expression. Of course he never inhaled the perfume as adults do, and it is not even certain that he perceived it.

In the eighty-sixth week he began to ask to have flowers given him to smell, and leaves also. When his mother's hand, wet with coal oil was offered to him to smell, he smelled it and seemed pleased, wanting to repeat the performance many times. He also insisted upon smelling the cosmoline as soon as the bottle appeared.

In the twenty-third month he opened an old box in which some rose perfume yet lingered. This he at once perceived. It would seem that odors had not for him the distinctness and individuality which they have for older people. He did not learn to inhale properly, therefore, it is probable that he did not experience to the fullest, the sensations of smell.

PART III.—IDEAS.

SECTION I.—MENTAL DEVELOPMENT.

In the parts devoted to the consideration of movements and sensations, evidence has been brought forward to show how these are the forerunners of all mental development. But sensations and reactions alone are not sufficient to account for mental progress. A great expanse existed between any sensation, or group of sensations, and an idea. What united the ends of such a series? By what processes was an idea built up from one, or from many sensations?

Sensations and reactions heaped one upon another never could have developed an idea. The processes by which ideas were built up were after all not so many, nor so complicated, as we are accustomed to suppose. It is not too great a claim, as a result of these observations, to maintain that idea formation rested upon a few simple processes, easily recognized and leading to a progressive series of planes of mental development.

Sensations and reactions furnished the materials of all ideas, providing an immense number and variety of elements. Some of these elements were gathered around limited sets of experiences. Whenever this was the case, associative links were formed uniting sensations, movements and experiences into fixed connections. The formation of such associative links was a first step towards mental development. The earliest manifestations of memory were given in such associated connections. During the first months of life I saw no evidence of memory except as presented in series of associations whose recall was initiated by suggestions.

The memory of the young child may be said to have shown tself in the ability to record. In a last analysis memory coincides with habit, memory being the making of a record of what had been experienced; habit, the tendency to act again as he

85

had acted before under similar circumstances. Both rested ultimately upon a common foundation and found no differentiation in the young infant; for, given the recurring conditions as a suggestion, and there was in either case recall and action.[1] If we arbitrarily separate the association series from the action series, we shall find in the former the first expression of an individual memory; but in making such a division we must not for a moment lose sight of the fact that no such severance actually occurred.

The chief factor in the development of apperception and in the organization of apperception masses was found to be the qualitative connection of experiences. When examining into the development of the perception of things seen and heard I have, in a measure, forestalled and outlined this position in regard to apperception. I have there pointed out that every variety and combination of sensation was not, at a given time, possible to the child; but that the sensations which he might then experience were dependent upon the stage of development of the sensory apparatus, the use made of previous experiences, and the power of the stimulus to engage attention. I have shown that a sensation utterly disparate from all perceptions previously obtained, did not receive the share of attention which was necessary in order to impress its effects upon the mental organization. No experience took its place in the mental life of the child which did not fall into the line of connections by which past and necessarily somewhat similar experiences were united.

Apperception was the assimilation *in continuity* of the new and similar in experience with the old; and apperceptive masses were the associated groups of experiences. The paths along which apperception might be effective, and the limits within which apperception masses might accumulate, were fixed by the laws of sensation and movement, and by the order and succession in which the sensory apparatus became instrumental as a means for the acquirement of perceptions. If the reader will recall that portion of the introduction which told of the periods

[1] For illustration consult Movements, pp. 17 and 18, 1st to 49th days.
[2] See Sensation, pp. 58–60.

of development and activity within the various territories of sensation[1], he will be aided to a better understanding of the meaning of these statements. He is also referred to Touch, p. 82, where it was shown in part why sight succeeded in attaining to a higher plane of development than touch during the first of the periods described.

One more reference to facts already established will make clear how close we stand to the central point from which lines of mental development diverge. In treating of vision[2] I have endeavored to explain the method by which the range of perception became increased. If the reader will now refer to the statements there made, the close relationship of perception and apperception will become apparent.

When the simplest memory is regarded as the retention of the impressions of experience; when personal memory is seen to be the retention of definite and interrelated series of experiences; when habit is found to be the tendency to repeat an act upon the recurrence of conditions which suggest it; when perception is admitted to be the reference of sensations before experienced to stimuli whose effects have been felt before; when apperception is found to be the assimilation of new material with what has been obtained through experiences in the past; when memories, habits, perceptions and apperceptions are understood to rest upon sensations and movements, and upon the ability to establish connections among the mental representatives of the same, we find ourselves on a vantage ground of comparatively simple manifestations from which to view the paths of departure that lead to the so-called faculties of the mind.

One question has doubtless presented itself to the reader as a stumbling block in the way of the acceptance of the above analytic simplification. The part played by attention in the scheme of development has been everywhere noted, in particular receiving consideration under vision. What is attention, and among what class of activities does it belong? Attention is to be regarded as an adjustment to the influence of the stimu-

[1] Introduction, pp. 4–6.
[2] Sensations, pp. 58–59.

lus;[1] thus it is cast into the class of inherent reactions. It differed from the inherent reactions of the special senses in this, that under the necessary conditions it could be called forth by the stimulations of any sense. In common with other inherent reactions the course of its development was towards its final (but not complete) subjection to voluntary control.

It is often stated that the ability to attend increases with age, and that the little child is quite unable to settle himself to the contemplation of one thing for any length of time. I do not know how true this may be of children in general. I am prepared to deny the truth of such a statement in the case under consideration. No doubt the ability to attend voluntarily does increase with age—of this I cannot as yet speak—but the power to attend involuntarily was established immediately after birth, and was manifested whenever the sensory apparatus was employed.

An older child could not do more to evince attention than to lie gazing at a patch of light or a moving object during a period varing from fifteen to thirty minutes. As he became older the same things did not interest the child in the same way. After touch had been developed through handling, he often occupied himself for an hour or more with a single object. In such cases a factor entered which was not found with the earlier sensations; namely, the continual changes which the child himself induced in the object, as a result of which he perceived it in new situations which were in truth like so many changes in stimuli, each requiring a fresh adjustment of the attention. Hence the infant when older amused himself for a longer period and seemed to attend for a longer time. It is true, the attention of the child daily became subject to a greater number and variety of diversions as he became, through his developed perceptions, sensitive to a wider range of influences which he was not able, nor did he will, to shut out. This fact alone might lead to the assumption that his attention could not, under any circumstances, remain fixed for more than a few moments —an assumption not borne out by the full evidence.

[1] As such it is regarded by Wm. James, Psychology, Vol. I., Chap. on Attention.

Concerning the emotional factors determining the mental survival of experiences, it is to be noted that there were at first no evidences of emotion other than those of comfort and discomfort. The sensations first assimilated were connected with bodily feelings of well being—the satisfaction of hunger, dryness, warmth, etc.[1] On this purely personal foundation all subsequent development was built up. Along with intellectual evolution there occurred a differentiation of emotions. In so far as those degrees and complexities of feeling and thought to which we are accustomed to refer as the emotions, were severally called forth by the situations in which the child was placed, they became instrumental in determining lines of activity and of survival. As the child became acquainted with things an interest in them was developed which became the chief determining influence of survival.

We have now seen: (1) The point from which the lines of mental activity diverged; (2) the means by which the mental outlook was expanded; (3) the connection of the successive view points or apperception masses; and (4) the motive of such connection.

The processes of mental elaboration remain to be described.

Reactions have already been so fully treated under movements and sensations that from this point I shall omit all special consideration of them, giving them only incidental mention where necessary. Suffice it here to make the general statement that reactions were to be found corresponding to any plane of development upon which the child stood. There was a graduated series of such reactions extending along the pathway from sensation to idea.

Sensations, as I have pointed out, were developed around certain centers. These centers were objects of the environment acting in various ways as stimuli. When a given center with its associates stood out in consciousness from other centers and clusters, which were all the while forming, that particular center was distinguished. Intermediate between sensations and such distinctions there were perceptions and recognitions. It is not

[1] It has already been shown that the first movements to be developed were connected with the attainment of comfort. Movements, p. 43.

possible to ascribe a fixed time limit to each stage of development, because when a stage was once reached, necessary and useful gains either continued to appear in their original form, or led to further progress through a series of transitional changes; yet a rough time estimate may be made for each period. Thus the child may be said to have been in the sensation stage during the first month; in the perception stage during the next three months; and at the beginning of the stage of distinction with the entrance into the fourth month. That he was always in a stage of association must not be forgotten, for the continual formation of associations was one of the very noticeable features of infancy.

In speaking of distinctions I do not wish to convey the idea that discrimination, or the perception of analogy, were involved in this separation of object from object, which (separation) was based upon recognitions[1] akin to such as have been described under hearing.[2] When the child was in the stage of distinction the objective reference of sensation was fairly well established. In this stage he looked for the source of stimulation outside of himself and found it in some object whose qualities were associated as they influenced him and were fused into his personal idea of the object. Such ideas were necessarily incomplete. At first they dealt with comparatively few objects, but the circle widened by degrees. As he became able to sit, to creep and to walk he was brought into fresh contacts and was enabled to form new distinctions. This he constantly did.

In discussing sensation, movement and association I have used the expression 'mental representative' without having attempted to explain what the nature of a mental representative was. Such an explanation I cannot make without entering a field of conjecture. That the mental representatives of the early weeks were the forerunners of true mental images or representations there can be no doubt. Early mental images did not deal with objects as wholes. Each was the result of a mental synthesis of feelings derived from particular contacts. Some of the later ideas were the outcome of experiences with objects

[1]For illustration of recognitions see appended table.
[2]Sensation, pp. 67–68. Of this part.

perceived as wholes. A study of the desires of the child gave some insight into the nature and number of his representations. When the child could by the use of language show that he wished to have an object not present to sense we may conclude that he possessed a representation of the object complete enough to be associated as a central figure with feelings of pleasure. Some representations had undoubtedly been formed by the ninth month, but it was not till the second year that the child showed himself to be possessed of a number of fairly complete images. In Part I.[1] it was shown that the child came to be practically at the mercy of such images, which through suggestion exercised the controlling influence upon his activities. It was apparent that his memory images were not bound to the the terms of one sense. That the child belonged to one of the so-called types I have never been able to ascertain. A study of his recognitions pointed to the conclusion that he was not of determined type. Up to the close of the first year the representations or memory images were of a very primitive kind. Whatever may have been the number of sensation elements which had entered into the formation of one of these memory images, and however complete a representation of an object such an image might have been, it was nevertheless not associated with other images or representations in such a way that one was able to call up another. Memory images were not associated with one another independently of objective suggestion before the second year.

It is easy to understand why comparisons and discriminations were rarely made before the second year, for how could one object be measured against another which it had not the power to call up? And in the case of the perception of similarity, how could that occur before one mental image could call up another? During the second year, and especially during the second half of this year, associations were gradually formed connecting mental image with mental image. Thus chains of images, of acts, persons, words, etc., were formed and the mental life became far more complex.

But even at the end of the first year the child had practi-

[1] P. 31.

cally no mechanism of voluntary recall. In order to recall anything it was necessary to reach his memory for it through the suggestive influence of recurring circumstances, some of which must be the same, or very similar, to those which had formed the original setting of that which was to be recalled; for example, the child, having laid down and left a toy for a time, was not afterwards able to recall its whereabouts, though he desired greatly to find it. If, however, he happened to find himself in the place in which he had previously left the article, he at once remembered about it, and demanded it if it were no longer there.

In the second year his natural retentiveness was remarkable. The time during which the accurate memory of an incident was preserved was a frequent source of surprise to his elders. Yet his memory images were not held in words, nor had the child himself any evident control over them.[1]

Beginning in the twenty-first month, I made a few experiments in order to learn something of the nature and duration of these memories. The following facts were revealed: When the memory image did not fuse with a class idea it could persist distinct and full as to its details for from six to eleven weeks (eleven weeks was the experimental, not the real time limit); where it did fuse with a class idea it lost its distinctness and individuality in a period of time which varied in length according to the stage of development of the class idea with which it fused. If the class idea was in process of formation and rested as yet upon but few representatives of the class, each of those few was naturally more distinct than it would be at a later day, when many representatives had contributed towards the making of the class.

Thus far I have everywhere spoken of associations simply as such, without pausing to define the kind of association with which we were dealing.

I now wish to show, first, that what is commonly called association by similarity is as fundamental a type as association

---

[1] During the third year the feats of memory became more noteworthy; it was a matter of daily occurrence for the child to refer spontaneously to events which had taken place three, six, nine and even twelve months earlier.

by contiguity, even though it be a somewhat less primitive one; second, that association by similarity led to (*a*) the perception of analogy (*b*) discriminations (*c*) inference; and third, association by contiguity lay at the foundation of (*d*) reproduction, and (*e*) reconstruction.

It has been said that the representations and ideas of the child were formed by the union of diverse elements. It has further been stated that there was in each representation a central or principal element around which the others were clustered. Upon such foundations there occurred two forms of association which may be somewhat approximately designated as association by contiguity and association by similarity. In the form first named the series of connected memories was called forth by the repetition of the leading circumstances—it was that form which depended upon the existence of identity. In the second form we have the series of connected memories called forth by something (either object or experience) not identical with the center to which the cluster belonged, but enough like it in one or more particulars to be effective as a means of recall. There were a few rare instances of confusion of identity, the second suggestion resembling an earlier one closely enough to bring this about. Associations of simple contiguity predominated at all times. In the ninety-eighth week I found every act of the child during the greater part of a day to be connected with such associations. Associations of similarity began to occur about the fortieth week. They were the descendants of recognitions, and began, not in the association of like object with like object, but in the power of certain elements to suggest a well known experience. They began in the suggestive power of elements forming the bases of recognitions; but as object became separated from object, and experiences became multiplied, these associations grew to consist in the suggestion of an image by a similar object.

Association by similarity and association by contiguity met in an undifferentiated process at a time when objects were not recognized as wholes, when the child responded to features of the environment and not to things perceived as such.

Elements always continued to be suggestive; in fact, they

became more suggestive as time went on, but the suggestion of object by object was not of common occurrence before the seventy-first week.   Through association by similarity the mental juxtaposition of like objects was brought about, as a result of which the perception of analogy was developed.   It will now be seen in what manner the ability to discriminate was genetically related to association by similarity.   There was an opportunity for the development of discrimination only after an object present to sense could call up the representation of one not present.

The perception of likeness and of difference are often spoken of as though they were separate aspects of the same thing.   In the present case the perception of likeness was not the reverse side of the perception of difference.   As a matter of fact, it was developed while discriminative power was in its infancy.   Both belong to the third, rather than to the second year.

The study of many cases of childish inferences reveals these characters to be common to all.   Each was based upon past experiences.   The premises from which the conclusion followed were elements common to both past and present experiences, and both premises and conclusion fell within the ' apperceived system ' of the child.[1]

In Language it is said that the extension of the meanings of words depended upon inferences of a crude form.   This is the form to which I there referred.   Likewise all errors and all spontaneous interpretations of phenomena were inferences based upon the suggestions of similar elements.

What is familiarly known as imagination was the reconstruction and rearrangement of what was already at hand.   In its most primitive form, that in which associations by contiguity were involved, chains of experiences were reproduced in the order in which they had been met; but as the child became able to perceive likenesses and differences, and true internal associations became possible, one representation could suggest another quite independently of original contiguity arrangement.

[1] "Inference cannot possibly take place except through the medium of an identity or universal which acts as a bridge from one case or relation to another. * * * * Ultimately the condition of inference is always a system." B. Bosanquet, The Essentials of Logic, pp. 139-140.

Thus reconstructions involving a greater number of processes began to occur about the close of the second year.

A few points remain to be mentioned before the subject of mental elaboration is laid aside. The first of these is concerned with the nature of the child's ideas. Had he class ideas resembling our own? During the second year he undoubtedly had some, but not a great many, and those that he possessed had grown up as the result of an extended series of experiences with the objects which we are accustomed to designate by class names (dogs, cats, men, women, children, dishes and chairs are a few of them).

His words, as a rule, had a definite content, a fixed relation to the object or phenomenon to which they applied. The fact that they were rarely used just as we use words, and with the meanings which we are wont to attach to them, might lead to the error of supposing that the meanings which the child himself attached to his words were vague. It has been shown that abstract words did not occur in the vocabulary; had I space in which to do so I could show by a citation of special cases that he had no abstract ideas pertaining to his concrete words. A close observation of the meanings attached by the child himself to his words showed that those which had not reference to some one occurrence or object related to one or more aspects of experience upon the basis of which things possessing these in common were designated by a common name. For example, the verb *to spill* meant voluntarily to tip the mug or glass and pour some fluid therefrom, while the verb *to find* referred to the act of appearance under the greatest variety of circumstances.

All ideas of the first year were not connected with words. The ideas of the second year were formed along with the learning of words and were modified accordingly. The formation of ideas did not depend upon words, but upon perceptions. obtained directly from the world without the child. Nearly to the close of the second year language belonged to the apperceived system, and was not in its beginnings a prime factor in the development of thought. Late in the second year language became a channel for the conveyance of thought.

Special care must be taken not to fall into the error of as-

cribing indefiniteness to the ideas of the child—an error which
has arisen out of the custom of measuring his ideas by the
standards of our own. When a representation had been
evolved it was concrete and limited. It is true, it did not represent the whole object together with its uses in the sense in
which we conceive of a thing, but it did represent very definitely
the object in its relations to the child himself. In the second
year was it indefiniteness which compelled him to perform day
after day the same round of actions? Not at all, for it was the
circumscribed and closely knit groups of associations which
controlled the direction of motor discharge, and which in a
given case was only finally broken up by the interpolation of a
new product of experience.

It has already been stated[1] that in no case did a subsequent
synthesis require an amount of time for its construction equal
to that which had been consumed in gathering the materials
and building the first synthesis of a series of related ones.
The ability of the child to form such syntheses increased with
practice till it became habitual to him to form them. What the
process was by which the mental synthesis of the associated
representatives of sensations was accomplished I cannot say.
Yet it was certain that after the fourth month some cluster of
associations daily passed through the transforming process and
became the mental representative of a thing. The history of
childish generalizations and of so-called errors showed that
representations were often formed upon incomplete experiences;
namely, a few sensations, incorporating material drawn from
memory. In early infancy errors rarely occurred, and it was not
till many associations had been established that errors arose. In
early infancy each synthesis was based directly upon sensations
connected by contiguity; while in later infancy new experiences
did not stand alone, but were instantly placed, as if by necessity, in some arrangement with those of the past. Such an arrangement might or might not correspond to the objective one.
If it did not so correspond the resulting incongruity might be
designated an error. What I have called a necessity was the
mental habit according to which it was so placed.

[1] Touch, p. 78.

Inference was not the only form of reasoning of which there was evidence. Generalization and induction[1] also occurred, and if they were less conspicuous than inference it was because a longer time was required for their accomplishment. It seems to me that an embryonic induction was manifested when the child refused to reach for an object whose distance from him was greater than the length of his arm; for, whatever the mental terms in which a knowledge of distance was given, it is certain that he had the knowledge, and that it was a permanent measure which had been given to him out of the common element of innumerable separate trials. The same might be said of his ideas of magnitude, depth and direction. A good example of induction occurred in the second year. About the one hundredth week the child became impressed with the 'againness' of experiences, and constantly remarked upon it with surprise. On coming to the table he looked at the various dishes, viands, etc., exclaiming at each, "Here it is again!" Likewise if a member of the family returned after an absence he never failed to notice the reappearance in a similar manner. After some two weeks of this he acquired a confidence in reappearance and recurrence—derived a principle, as it were—and began to state in a positive manner that such was to be expected. When he had gotten to this stage he cheerfully saw his mother go away, asserting that she would come again, whereas before he had been loth to have her leave him.

Under voluntary movement[2] I have spoken of an influence exerted by reason in determining the course of a discharge as early as the forty-sixth week. But I did not show what we are now in a position to observe; namely that the higher forms of thought were developed with the more complicated movements and existed in embryo before abstraction was to any extent possible, and that inference, induction, generalization and reconstruction were mental habits in the same sense that sitting, creeping, etc., were habits, and that each mental habit was developed by a method similar to that found in the development of a bodily

[1] "Really induction is only a popular name for such inference as deals with numbers of instances." H. Bosanquet, op. cit., p.163.
[2] Part I., Sec. 2.

habit, becoming fixed as an active factor in mental life and the means of further acquirement very much as each habit of the body did.   Thus we find two systems of habits developing side by side and mutually dependent.   And with them two systems of ideas, to the first of which belonged those derived from experiences with things, and to the second those resulting from the use made of experiences according to the habits or processes of mental integration and elaboration.

A careful examination of the two tables which are herewith appended will facilitate the understanding of the statements that have just been made.   These tables will be found to be self explanatory, and need not detain us longer here.   I shall therefore proceed to sketch in outline the course of this development of an idea which is added, with the tables, in the hope of giving definiteness and clearness to the above exposition. The idea selected for the sketch had its beginnings in the most primitive experiences of the child.   This was the idea of his mother; it was, in fact, the only idea that referred to an object which was not a part of himself, and which yet was an ever present factor of his environment.   From my notes I have selected a few of the salient points in the growth of this idea.

In the beginning the child sucked whatever was put into his mouth, whether this was his own finger, the nipple or the corner of a pillow.   He usually suckled with his eyes closed.   On the fifty-fifth day he began to keep his eyes open while suckling, letting them wander over the dress, breast and sometimes the face of his mother.   Through seeing her face so frequently in other situations than this he became independently familiar with it, and began to associate the sight of her face with his own comfort.   But it was not till the thirteenth week that he identified the face above the breast with the one familiar in other circumstances.

In the tenth week he began to notice his mother's dress, being at once attracted by a change in it.   In the fifteenth week she wore a dress at which he often looked, yet three weeks later, lying on the floor beside the chair in which she sat he was at first interested in the dress, then became lonely, beginning to worry as if though she were away, and finally was surprised when he chanced to discover her face just above him. It was not till about the twenty-seventh week that he began to connect a skirt, moving or at rest, with a face above it. As early as the tenth week he was dissatisfied if his mother sat near him with her face averted, and only ceased to worry when she altered her position, yet in the fifteenth week it startled him to see her face alternately with the back of her head. In the fourteenth week he often felt her hair, but it was not till the forty-fourth week that he was interested in watching her put it up, and it was late in the second year before he understood that it could not be taken off of her head and given to him.

By the thirty-eighth week the satisfaction of hunger had become so closely associated with his mother that, although nourished better by artificial food, he refused it from her hand, while he accepted it readily from his father if his mother were not in sight. In the thirty-eighth week he recognized his mother's hand as similar to his own, and later other parts of her body and portions of her clothing. Such recognition, however, did not extend to parts of which he did not have experience, for in the one-hundred-and-third week he insisted that her neck, which he saw between the ends of her collar in front, was her back. In the sixty-sixth week he was distressed to see her in an unusual attitude, her arms outstretched above her head. By the eighty-third week her clothing had become so completely involved in his idea of her person that he was shy with her when for the first time within his recollection she appeared dressed for a social event. In the forty-first week he showed a decided preference for his mother over other people. In the forty-eighth week he began to regard her as exclusively his, and resented attentions shown her by anyone else. In the second year he did not like to have her attention engrossed by other people and things. About the ninety-seventh week he began to understand that other children had mothers of their own, but it was difficult for him to grasp the idea of one mother for two children.

TABLE II.—DEVELOPMENT AND RELATION OF RECOGNITION, INFERENCE AND RECONSTRUCTION.

SIMPLE RECOGNITION BASED ON EXPERIENCE.	RECOGNITION CONNECTED WITH EXPECTATION.	INFERENCE, THE HABIT OF BASING CONCLUSIONS UPON ANALOGOUS ITEMS OF EXPERIENCE.	RECONSTRUCTION:	
			EITHER A SIMPLE REORGANIZATION OF EXPERIENCE;	OR, A REORGANIZATION INVOLVING AN INFERENCE.
5th week: He recognized the human face.	21st week: He recognized hands extended to him and expected to be taken up.	24th week: He tried to take the hand of his own reflection in the mirror.	81st week: He threw his baby doll on the floor and ran into another room calling "Bye, bye, baby!" Then exclaiming, "Poor baby cry!" he ran back and picked it up.	66th: He found on the floor a bit of black wool about the size of a fly, which he at once called a fly. He picked it up, carried it to the window and stuck it on the screen. Then pointed to it, exclaiming, "fly! fly!" a number of times.
7th week: The sounds of the voice.	22d week: The spoon, and prepared to receive water.	25th: Seeing a visitor wearing a hat he evinced delight; when she went out and did not take him he was distressed.		
9th week: He recognized the breast when he saw it; and the face of his mother.	23d: His mother's hat, expecting to be taken out when she wore it.	59th: Seeing a cow for the first time the child called her a bird.	He laid the doll on the bed springs and worked them up and down, giving the doll a ride as his grandmother rode him.	
12th week: His own hand.	27th: He recognized a tune, and expected it if he saw the movements which accompanied the song.	64th: A caterpillar he called a fly.		
16th: His thumb; the nipple.	35th: Repeatedly threw his spoon on the floor and looked after it; sometimes he held out his hand as if to receive something, seeming to expect it to come to him.	83d week: In the afternoon the child walked in the station with his parents and rode in the street car. In the evening he and his mother went back to the station alone. When the child found himself next to a man in the street car he called him papa, and insisted upon getting up	93d: Upon going into the bath room he asked for a large empty bottle which was often given him to play with. Having received it he said, "Mamma, neck." His mother, who was busy, did not heed him. Then he said, "Mamma, hand!" and taking her hand he got her to sit	
17th: He recognized his ball at a distance of some feet.				
18th: Footsteps on the stairs.				
24th week: He recognized his grandfather, whom he had not seen for two weeks.				

TABLE II.—DEVELOPMENT AND RELATION OF RECOGNITION, INFERENCE AND RECONSTRUCTION.—*Continued.*

SIMPLE RECOGNITION BASED ON EXPERIENCE.	RECOGNITION CONNECTED WITH EXPECTATION.	INFERENCE, THE HABIT OF BASING CONCLUSIONS UPON ANALOGOUS ITEMS OF EXPERIENCE.	RECONSTRUCTION:	
			EITHER A SIMPLE REORGANIZATION OF EXPERIENCE	OR A REORGANIZATION INVOLVING AN INFERENCE.
34th: Changes in the facial expression of people.	44th: His father was accustomed to take him from his chair every evening after dinner. When the child saw his father fold his napkin, he was delighted, expecting to be taken up.	on his lap, all without having looked in the man's face. In the station he ran after a man who walked a little in advance, calling him papa. When the man turned his face, the child at once saw that he was not his father.	down beside him. He then went through the performance of tipping the bottle as if pouring something out on his hand with which he afterwards rubbed his mother's neck as his had been rubbed with oil some three weeks before.	103d: One day, while out, the child saw a man standing in the midst of a flock of chickens. He was too far away to see what the man and the chickens were doing; but
43d: He recognized and imitated a number of sounds.	44th: When he saw his mother brush her hair (an operation usually performed before donning her hat) he expected to be taken out.	87th: He called a watch a clock.	101st: Ke put the scissors on a book and said they were riding on horseback.	
56 h: The child liked to stand on a chair and look out of the window. If his mother moved the chair towards the window, calling him to come, he hastened towards the window; if she spoke the words without moving the chair, or adjusted the chair without addressing him, it meant nothing to him.	46th: His mother was accustomed to sit in a certain chair. One day the child saw his mother in the room, but while he was playing she took her seat in another chair. He soon looked at her chair, and not seeing her	95th: A picture was shown to the child. It represented a girl standing on a road in front of a fence. Her shadow lay on the ground behind her. He was asked to point out her shadow. He looked on the fence for it and could not find it, neither could he on the next day satisfy him-	103d: He lost a pin which fell down a crack. When he complained that it was gone his mother asked him where it was. He replied: "Gone to church; gone a sleigh ride." He saw	
75th: A little playmate who had been away for four weeks was upon				

TABLE II.—DEVELOPMENT AND RELATION OF RECOGNITION, INFERENCE AND RECONSTRUCTION.—*Continued.*

SIMPLE RECOGNITION BASED ON EXPERIENCE.	RECOGNITION CONNECTED WITH EXPECTATION.	INFERENCE, THE HABIT OF BASING CONCLUSIONS UPON ANALOGOUS ITEMS OF EXPERIENCE.	RECONSTRUCTION:	
			EITHER A SIMPLE REORGANIZATION OF EXPERIENCE	OR A REORGANIZATION INVOLVING AN INFERENCE.
his return immediately recognized. He was seen for the first time in his wonted surroundings.	there began to worry as if alone, looking repeatedly at the chair. At last he chanced to perceive her, was satisfied and began to play again. Soon he looked up at her chair again, and, evidently having forgotten where she sat, behaved as at first. After having a second time discovered her he remembered where she was. Nor did he on the next or following days have trouble in remembering where in any part of the room she sat.	self as to the shadow which he sought to find on the fence. 95th: He went with his mother to a strange house. He ran about the rooms examining everything. Of a large standing lamp he said: "See the big tree;" of the books behind glass doors: "See the books in the window!" 98th: In the forenoon he saw a neighbor sweeping snow. In the afternoon when questioned as to her whereabouts he replied that she was sweeping the snow (he had not in the meantime seen her). 100th: Seeing his mother tacking down an oil cloth on the kitchen	'bizz' (his own moving shadow) on the floor and watched it. When asked what 'bizz' was doing he replied that 'bizz' was eating a big apple.	was told that the man was feeding the chickens. The next day he described to his mother what he had seen, adding that the man fed the chickens with beef tea from a cup.

Table II.—Development and Relation of Recognition, Inference and Recon-struction.—*Concluded.*

Simple Recognition Based on Experience.	Recognition Connected with Expectation.	Inference, the Habit of Basing Conclusions upon Analogous Items of Experience.	Reconstruction: Either a Simple Re-organization of Experience.	Or, a Reorganization Involving an Inference.
		floor he exclaimed that the kitchen was broken (he had seen things mended with hammer and tacks.) 101st: The corner of his napkin bent up against his face, and this he attributed to the wind which blew under his cape and raised it in a similar manner. 103d: He broke the petiole from the blade of a leaf and asked his mother to mend it. She replied that she could not do so. He sat as if thinking for a few moments, then looked up and said, "Mamma mend(ed) the sofa; mamma mend(ed) the rabbit."	104th: The child gave his mother a pin; then offered one to his aunt (not present) and to many other persons whom he called by name, extending his hand now here, now there, as if giving the same pin to each in turn.	104th: His grandfather showed him the picture of a bunch of grapes, and promised that when the child visited him he should pick grapes. In a few weeks his grandfather went home. Thereafter the child in telling about his grandfather always represented him as picking grapes.

TABLE III.—ASSOCIATIONS.

EARLY ASSOCIATIONS.	CONTIGUITY ASSOCIATIONS.	TRANSITIONAL FORMS.	SIMILARITY ASSOCIATIONS.
4th day: Turning the head towards the cheek touched. 17th day: Rolling the head from side to side with open mouth when in discomfort. Turning the head towards the breast against which he happened to lie. 30th day: Turning the head to the side from which sounds came. 33d day: Turning the head in order to follow with the eyes. 35th day: Sucking the backs of the hands he associated with sucking the thumb. 36th day: Grasping was associated with hand contacts. 38th day: Holding with grasping. Balancing the head with looking. 55th day: Being held on the arm with feeding. 59th day: The sight of the breast with feeding.	38th week: The word mamma was associated with uncomfortable feelings (hunger, wetness, etc.). 46th week: He connected a certain chair with his mother, and looked for her there. 50th week: If his mother said, "here comes papa," the child stopped his play, listened for his father's footsteps, then hastened towards the door. 64th week: Having twice seen the cracker jar and received crackers from it, the child expected them when he saw it approach. 72d: When the child saw his mother sit down on the floor to put on her shoes, he took them to her, and, saying "da! da!" handed first one and then the other. 77th week: A certain fur rug was sometimes laid over the door step. Upon several occasion a cracker had been given to the child to eat while sitting	30th week: The child had been drumming with a ring or spoon upon the table of his little chair. When for the first time he drummed with his hands upon the upright piano he was surprised that the sound did not come from beneath his hand. 33d: When given an orange to play with he handled it without awkwardness, evidently applying to it movements and adjustments acquired in playing with his balls, which were considerably smaller. 70th week: In this week the child developed a method of going downstairs which he applied to inclines. Face towards the step and feet downward he slid from step to step. When going down a terrace he slid from top to bottom. 84th: When the child pulled his mother's hair she cried out; when next she brushed his hair he made a similar exclamation.	71st week: The child was given a hen's egg of the size, shape but not color of a darning egg which he had not seen for two weeks. He at once tried to separate the two halves as he had done those of the wooden egg. 87th week: A watch suggested to him a clock, and he so named it. 92d week: A copy of the Sistine Madonna, measuring $18\frac{3}{4}$in. $\times 13\frac{1}{2}$ in...in the sitting room was a picture which often attracted notice and comment from the child. One day, in looking through an art catalogue, he came upon a small copy of this picture, $2\frac{1}{2}\times 4$ in. He regarded it intently, then turned and looked at the large picture as if comparing them. This he did several times. 94th week: The stopper of the bath tub he called a cork. He called a ten pin a bottle

TABLE III—ASSOCIATIONS.—*Concluded.*

EARLY ASSOCIATIONS.	CONTIGUITY ASSOCIATIONS.	TRANSITIONAL FORMS.	SIMILARITY ASSOCIATIONS.
10th week: His mother's face with his personal comfort.	on this rug. Thereafter when he found himself upon it he was accustomed to call for a cracker. He called for a cracker also when he heard a tin box rattle.		and played at giving his doll a drink from it.
12th week: The appearance of his mother was connected with the satisfaction of hunger. The sight of his mother unfastening her dress with the satisfaction of hunger.	83d week: One day his mother, after blackening her own shoes, seated the child on a chair and blackened his. Ten days later he entered the room while his mother was blackening her shoes, climbed on a chair and held out his feet to have his done.		He called a filbert nut an egg. 99th week: Little pieces of wood shaped very much like books and about half an inch square the child named books.
16th week: Waking at night with being fed.	93d week: When he saw someone lift off the shade to light the lamp he called by name the person who was accustomed to remove the shade to fill the lamp.		100th week: Some one gave the child a small oval box containing turtles whose limbs and heads trembled. Some artificial flowers and leaves occupied spaces about the turtles. The whole was covered with a piece of glass secured to the margin of the box. He named the turtles flies and said the flies were taking a bath in the bath tub. Wishing to have the glass removed he asked to have it cut off.
17th week: The palm of the hand with grasping.	96th week: If the child was told to call his uncle, he called instead his aunt, whom he always saw with his uncle,		
18th week: Her voice with his mother.	97th week: The postoffice and a letter were so connected that if he heard one mentioned he was sure to speak of the other.		104th: The top of the sewing machine lay on the floor inverted. The child threw in a paper (the nearest thing at hand) exclaiming, 'Paper, take a bath!'
Pulling himself into a sitting position with being held by both hands.			
The sight of a cup with a drink of water.			
19th week: Movements seen with a song heard.			
The thumb stall with the inhibition of sucking.			

SECTION II.—TIME.

The experiences underlying the perception of time may be divided into two classes. To the first class belong those experiences which had to do with periodicity; to the second those which formed sequences. The experiences of periodicity related to the functions of the body—sleep, nutrition, etc.—and came to consciousness in the form of recurring wants. No time regularity in the recurrence of these wants was established previous to the sixth week. In the case of nutrition this was owing to several causes, the most significant of which were the susceptibility of the child to fatigue and the long hours of unbroken sleep, which operated against the methodical apportionment of the day. By the fourth month the child became hungry and sleepy at regular intervals and at fixed hours. The regularity of the recurrence of the feeling of hunger was most marked; for it was a matter almost of certainty that he would awake within a few moments of the hour for feeding, though it had never been customary to arouse him for this purpose. From the second to the sixth month intervals resting upon periodic functional performance were the time data. That consciousness was aware of each of these recurrent experiences was clear. It was through the acts, feelings and perceptions which accompanied it that each was known.

The intervals between the satisfaction of the physiological requirements gradually became filled with successions of daily experiences, so that from morn till night there was a chain of major events each of which suggested its next in order. In the eighth month the child became cross and refused to be satisfied if at the usual time he was not taken for his daily airing; and this was because he recognized the events which usually preceded his going out, and not because he perceived the time. That an abstraction such as we are wont to designate as time resulted directly from this periodic and serial arrangement of experiences, I am not prepared to maintain. Late in the second year his daily performances became associated with the clock through the references which he had heard to the hour in connection with what was about to be done. Thus his own intervals were brought to bear upon the acquirement of that human concept—the idea of time.[1]

SECTION III.—DISANTCE, DIRECTION AND MAGNITUDE.

The perceptions of distance, direction and magnitude, involved as they are with the conception of space, rightfully belong to this portion of the work which treats of ideas. The development of these perceptions could not, moreover, have been classified with any one subdivision of sensations and movements.

By the 31st day[2] the child was able to fixate and to follow, with the necessary accommodations to distance, an object which moved from directly before him slowly to a distance of ten feet. On the same day his eyes followed the slow movements of the carpet sweeper over the floor, as it approached and receded in front and from side to side of the sofa upon which he lay. That the eye had an appreciation of distance derived from its own adjustments independent of those of other sets of muscles seems possible; but it is certain that measures of distance were obtained from data furnished by movements other than those of the eye muscles.

Sensations from the eye and those of movement from another part of the body began to be used together in the recognition of distance about the fifty-seventh day. Shortly before this date it became apparent that the child perceived the breast by sight. Then he learned to reach for the nipple with his head when he chanced to lose his hold upon it. It is uncertain whether the distance thereto was correctly perceived by the eye or not. Inasmuch as accommodations to changing distances were already established, it is posible that he had some percep-

[1] In the third year the child used the phrase ' after a while' intelligently, and invented 'big after a while' to indicate a longer period. All past, immediate or remote, he referred to a yesterday, and a future less fixed than ' after a while' as Sunday. ' Now' meant at once.

[2] Vision, p. 56.

tion of the distance, although the axes of his eyes converged somewhat more than an accurate adjustment would have required. The peculiarity of the reaches with the head was not that they deviated markedly to one side or to the other of an imaginary straight line uniting the position of the child's mouth with that of the object to be grasped; but that they fell short of the mark. In the beginning they did not always become successively longer, and it therefore often happened that no one of the attempts had a fortunate termination. By the fourteenth week success invariably attended the first effort.

The initial attempts at reaching with the hand bore one resemblance to those of reaching with the head; for while the eye plainly perceived what the hand should have touched, there was no accurate adjustment of the arm movements to the distance at which the the object stood. Now there are four ways of explaining this want of adjustment:

1. The eye may not have perceived the distance at which the object stood; or

2. The eye may have perceived the distance and the difficulty have rested altogether upon the arm movements; or

3. Both eye and arm may have been at fault; or

4. The want of adjustment may have been due to a mental gap in the associative connection, as a result of which (gap) eye distance and arm distance failed to combine. By the expression 'arm distance' are meant feelings of movements which correspond to various degrees of extension. The study of arm movements has brought out the fact that arm distance was at this time somewhat established and we have seen above that the eye had received some training in the perception of distance. Therefore the fourth explanation is probably the correct one.

The child was next (thirteenth week) seen to reach for what was within the range of his arm, and not to try for that which was beyond. Here the distance of the arm and that of the eye had combined to form the first concrete measure of distance. A little later (sixteenth week) he did reach for objects beyond the arm range, at the same time leaning towards them or moving his body in their direction. The eye must have

recognized this distance as longer; for the body, as yet un-
tried, had not given an indication of its range. This knowledge was not fully developed till the thirty-ninth week. After
the sixteenth week the perception of distances was developed
slowly and very gradually, involving on the one hand eye movements and the observation of things seen, on the other the development of the perception of magnitudes gained through hand
contacts. It must be remembered that there was a time when
the child could not handle what he reached after, when he did
not know how to hold what came to him, unless the hand could
close over and clasp it. After grasping, reaching and holding
had become possible to him his experience was extended from
object to object by dint of much practice with each. When he
could sit erect and look at what he held, the sensations from eye
and hand were at last systematically and not occasionally induced
by the same object. In the early days of sitting erect there occurred some illustrations of the process by which the separate
perceptions were used to the accomplishment of a common end,
and thus made to contribute towards the development of ideas.
One of these illustrations is here quoted from the journal:

While the child was sitting in his crib a glass dumb-bell
(long diameter four in.), with cut facets was laid in his lap
close to his body. This he had not before seen. He held a
napkin ring in his right hand. During the performance about
to be described his gaze remained fixed upon the dumb-bell in
his lap. This he tried to strike with the napkin ring. The
blow fell too far out. The attempt was repeated three times
with a similar result for each trial. He then with the left hand
felt the dumb-bell, after which he struck it successfully once
and many times.[1]

Within a few weeks after sitting alone had become habitual
the child had acquired some working knowledge of form and
size which enabled him to handle objects with more certainty
and ease, and here the perception of small distances was developed. By the forty-first week the hand and arm made move-

[1] As I did not watch the child during the time he continued to play thus, I
do not know whether any unsuccessful attempts alternated with the successful
ones or not.

ments which corresponded to small distances perceived by the eye.   In the twenty-ninth week the child began to roll over the floor and so to get himself from one place to another.   When he began to creep (forty-sixth week) and later to walk he was already familiar with the lengths to be traversed and had no difficulty in accommodating himself to them.   But in the sixty-first week he moved with his parents to a new home, and instead of one room in which to exercise his powers of locomotion, he had now the freedom of two.   Much, though not all, of the furniture in these rooms was already familiar to him, but the floor spaces between the individual pieces were considerably larger.   His distance measures did not fit the new surroundings at all and for two days the child was like one out of his element.   All his efforts at going from place to place ended in disaster.   On the third day his accommodation to the new surroundings was well established.   Within ten days thereafter a second change was made, and on being taken to a third house the child did not show again the same difficulties of adjustment.

It is probable that the experiences of going towards objects, and of seeing them approach and recede, had an influence all along in the development of the perception of what may be called the horizontal distance.   But the effects of such an influence were not obvious to the observer in the way that those of other influences were.   The child had a better estimation of horizontal than of vertical distances; but whether this was the result only of the greater number of experiences with them, or also of a second factor such as I have pointed to above, it is impossible to say.   He had some perception of height in the forty-seventh week, and this distance was measured by himself, as reaching up, standing, etc.   He seemed to have no perception of distance below himself, or depth, before the sixty-eighth week; for though he could go up stairs and inclined surfaces, he would have walked off of platforms, porches and flights of steps with the movements of one who walks upon a plane surface. In the seventieth week he learned to go down stairs, and afterwards recognized at once places in which this method was to be applied, starting upon one occasion to back down from a platform raised more than six feet above the ground.   His estimation of heights beyond those measured by experiences with his own body was always inaccurate. After he had found (eightieth week) that he could sometimes get objects by the aid of a chair, he climbed up continually to try to get what was beyond his own reach, or that of an adult.[1] Thus it would seem that the development of the perception of distance did not depend upon sensations of the adjustments of any one set of muscles; but upon the establishment of concrete measures of distance.

To return to the perceptions of magnitude. After these had been developed according to the method described above, it was noteworthy that he was not impressed by the comparative sizes of things. His ideas of size during the greater part of the second year were absolute rather than comparative. He was repeatedly trying to fit large objects into small places and committed many other blunders of a like nature which showed a failure to grasp the size relations of things. The words ' big ' and ' little ' did not refer to nice discriminations of magnitude. Things which he called ' big ' were strikingly so of their kind, and so of those which he called ' little.' He did not use adjectives to describe intermediate sizes, and if questioned concerning them he would give no reply.

Direction is the relation of an object to the surface of the body. The recognition of direction would seem to have been a matter of association and was evidently established along with the development and use of the sensory apparatus.[2] It was the necessary concommitant of all sensations which lay at the foundation of the perception of distance; but was not so involved with this perception as to be inseparable from it.[3]

Observations revealed the fact that his memory for direction and for distance was not extremely accurate. To quote an observation of the eighty-ninth week in illustration: In playing with a blue stick (the shape of a match stick one inch in length) the child dropped it on the rug, three feet from the border and about midway between the sides of the room. As he was about to pick it up (having seen where it fell) he was called to

[1] At two years, nine months he asked me to get a star to hand to him, saying: "I can't reach It; you can reach It."

[2] Consult Hearing, p. 66; also Vision on the direction of the gaze.

[3] For Illustrations consult Hearing, p. 66; also Touch on Localization.

a person who sat nine feet away.   In a moment he returned to get the stick and ran beyond it some three feet (till he reached the end of the rug) before stopping to pick it up.   Not finding it there he walked back and forth across the rug several times looking for it all the while.   At last he gave up the search.

SECTION IV.—SOME NOTES ON THE RECOGNITION AND INTERPRETATION OF PICTURES.

Fifty-third Week.—When the leaves of a magazine were turned for the child pictures of people induced expressions of pleasure; but he took no notice of pictured animals and of very small figures.   From this week he often looked at pictures, but his interest continued to be centered upon illustrations representing people.

Seventy-fourth Week.—He designated all pictures by one name (little girl) without regard to contents.

Seventy-seventh Week.—He called the photograph of a baby, baby; any man, papa; any woman, girl.

Eighty-seventh Week.—A barefooted, scantily-clad damsel, standing near a cupid, the child called Mamie, he said nothing about the smaller figure.   Among pictures of a number of men he called only one who had a mustache, papa.

Eighty-eighth Week.—The Sistene Madonna interested him frequently.   He would look at it and exclaim: " A baby !   A mamma !   A man !   A girl !"

Ninety-first Week.—Of a small picture of a girl (figure 1 ½ inches in height) sitting with her head buried in her hands, he said: " Girl cry."

Ninety-fourth Week.—He had an attachment for an exaggerated caricature of a cat which he called ' pussy cat.'

He now liked pictures of any description, but especially the small ones among the advertisements in the backs of magazines. He was interested in pointing out and naming conspicuous features of pictures.   He got the relations of the various parts quite well, and had some appreciation of the perspective of some pictures.

Ninety-fifth Week.—Seeing for the first time a picture representing a naked child sitting on a bench in the water and holding with one arm a large pen, he said : "A little boy, sit down, boat."

Ninety-seventh Week.—Of a shepherdess and sheep he said : "See dogs, see dogs, mamma!"

Ninety-eighth Week.—Of pictures of men he always recognized Mr. Darwin, M. Charcot, M. Pasteur. A picture of a mountain he called a lady. When told to point to the members of her body he said of each in turn that it was gone, ending by explaining that only her dress was there. If only a part of the body was depicted (the head and trunk, for example) he described the picture as that of a person broken. Of a woman sitting on a chair lashed to the bowsprit of a vessel he said : "Lady, sit down a chair, water, boat." He recognized at once a great variety of pictured boats, which was noteworthy, as twenty-two weeks had elapsed since he had seen ocean or boat, and the pictures were unlike any which he had in the meantime looked at.

Ninth-ninth Week—In this week some experiments were made on the interpretation of simple pictures. I shall not here stop to enumerate the difficulties besetting the experimenter. As I cannot give the pictures, it is only necessary to say that the number and variety of objects and relations correctly apprehended by the child was very large.

One Hundredth Week.—Some cuts of sections of the brain he called 'baby frog' (his name for pictures of embryos). The marbled paper on the inside of a book binding he called flowers.

One Hundred and Third Week.—In this week the meaning and movement of pictures rather than the simple contents began to impress the child, and thereafter he described them, wherever possible, in terms of action. Very little has been said about his recognition of pictures which he had seen before. In the ninety-first week a book of animals was given to the child in which at least fifty individuals were portrayed. The familiar domestic animals he knew at once, and by the afternoon of the next day he could point out nearly all the other animals if they were named for him. The pages of this book were soon scattered and lost.

In the one hundred and second week someone gave the child a little book containing six full-page illustrations and a number of smaller pictures, in all some eight pages of illustrations and text. He looked it through several times, both alone and with another person. This was on March 5th. On March 6th he described to his mother, from memory, each of the full-page illustrations. He spoke of them in the sequence of the book.

One of those memory tests elsewhere mentioned was made with a picture. It was selected from a book with which he was thoroughly familiar. The illustration in question was entitled The Monkey's School, and represented a large monkey wearing a gown, glasses and cap, sitting in the midst of a class of young monkeys also dressed and engaged in various pursuits. All were so disguised that he did not himself recognize them as monkeys. When his grandfather showed him this picture he often repeated a rhyme in which the word monkey occurred. The child himself was most impressed by the school mistress, which he called 'Mamma monkey,' and was accustomed to point to her glasses, cap and book (slate). This picture was abstracted from the book and put away. During six weeks and six days he did not see it; but he saw other pictures of normal monkeys, and sometimes recalled the rhyme when playing with a monkey made of rags. When the picture was restored to him (103d week, the book in the meantime having undergone disintegration) he at once recognized it, called out the rhyme and named the contents according to his former method.

PART IV.—LANGUAGE.

SECTION I.—SOUNDS.

The first sound which the child made was the short, expiratory ă, uttered only in crying. By the twentieth day he evinced a decided interest in sounds. By the thirty-third day he would watch attentively the face of a person speaking to him, and three days later, when being talked or sung to, he began to move his lips and to make some sounds. Ten days after this responsive sounds were habitually made. Then what is familiarly known as ' crowing' began to occur with frequency when the child, lying alone and in comfort, made many and various sounds.

The voice, at first weak, gradually became strong, but prior to the eighteenth week no fixed method of using it was developed. At different times all qualities of tone, from the deep chest tones to the strongly nasal ones, were heard. After the eighteenth week the variation in tones slowly disappeared and the voice gradually settled into a clear falsetto.

By the twelfth week he had begun to use his tongue, which had hitherto moved but little in his mouth. Thereafter there was a rapid increase in the number and variety of sounds made by the child in crying and babbling. It is very difficult for one not practiced in the detection and recollection of sounds to hear and to note accurately all those which a little baby may make in its rapid and continuous babbling.

At the close of the fourth month it was my impression that the child had made well-nigh all the sounds which occur in the language. Yet I had the exact record of but few which had been pronounced as isolated sounds, or as short syllables, and so distinctly as to render their identification easy and certain.

The following is a list of the principal sounds and syllables heard and noted between the twelfth and fortieth weeks:

In crying :

eng	dă	ŭ	mä–mä–ä
mä–ä–ä, explosive â		ĕ	nĭn nĭn

In babbling :

ĕng	z	gr–r–r	bō wō
ăng	diddle, diddle, ē ē	ing	bow wow
d	ĕ	ŭ–ŭ ŭ	bä
t	th	ŭdn	pop–pä–pä–pä
bä	dth	ŭdŭ	bob–bä
â	ûm gô	good	mom–mä
ô	ă gô	ō	ĕ dä
ŭr–r–r	ä mä	â dä	tä tä
s	hadn	mä	tduck

In the thirty-sixth week he acquired the habit of repeating a sound of his own upon hearing it uttered by another person. In itself this practice may not have been of great moment, but as an intermediate process, leading to the conscious imitation of sounds not his own, it was of importance; for by conscious imitations he got the pronunciations of his words.

In the thirty-eighth week he began to associate a few words with persons and objects. In the fortieth week the associations became established in the case of one word—*papa*. In the forty-second week conscious but unintelligent imitation of words became habitual, and syllables thus acquired occurred afterwards in babbling. These syllables were strung together and uttered with great rapidity, producing a chatter which in its tones and inflections bore a striking resemblance to conversation.

Though so many sounds were uttered with fluency during the months which preceded the acquirement of language, not a word of those which formed the first vocabulary, with the single exception of the word *mamma*, was phonetically an exact reproduction of the word-copy. Each of 238 of the 475 words in the vocabulary passed through one or more transitional phonetic changes before its final form was attained. Table V. illustrates some of these changes; it shows the alterations actually undergone by twenty-six words. The several headings; namely, omission, introduction,, addition and substitution explain the processes by which these changes were wrought. There is also a column in which is to be found the last recorded pronunciation of the word, and a further column in which, under the caption 'nucleus,' are placed those sounds which belonged to the word-copy and afforded a definite phonetic point around which later changes might take place. Alterations by omission of sounds and of syllables were very common, as is shown in Table VI.

But four instances are recorded of the introduction of extra sounds or syllables into words, and but one case of the addition of a final sound. Alterations by substitution occurred frequently, sometimes alone in the word, sometimes accompanying omissions. When the child had learned but a few words, alterations in pronunciation were often caused by confusion, for example the word *papa*, at first correctly pronounced, became appa when ama (grandma) had been acquired, paba (bä bä= baby) and papē (bē bē=baby) after baby was added. Out of the confusion the word *papa* finally emerged and was thereafter correctly pronounced.

The acquirement of a new sound in a new word frequently preceded its introduction into words wherein it had not before been used; thus, after the child had learned to pronounce w in wash (wass) and woman, w was introduced as a substitute for r. A new sound, once acquired, was likely to crop out repeatedly, in the word in which it had been learned, in other words, and in unintelligent babbling. The occurrence of sounds not in the language was by no means rare. These consisted of gutterals, ch, rs, and the indescribable one which I have tried to express by the h'h in bottle, but which any letters, alone or combined, must fail to convey, and in the German ö (written oe in the tables to avoid confusing with ö).

After having examined Tables IV. and V. the following questions would naturally present themselves and demand a reply before it should be possible to perceive the direction of development :

1. Did the nucleus become larger as the child became older?

2. Were the words seen to pass through fewer changes towards the close of the record?

3. Did omissions and substitutions tend to become habitual—
or to state it otherwise, were certain sounds regularly omitted,
or replaced by more or less fixed substitutes?

4. How were the habitual alterations broken up and finally
replaced by the correct sounds?

If, in order to obtain an answer to the first question, the first
ten words of the vocabulary are compared with ten words acquired at the close of the second year, 48.7 % of all the sounds
of the first word-copies are found to have been correctly pronounced, and 70.5 % of the sounds contained in the second list
of words ; 62.9 % of the sounds of twenty words acquired at
the close of the second year were correctly pronounced.   It may
be said that the first ten words might have contained a preponderance of phonetic elements especially difficult to the child.
This is to some extent the case, as they contained four sounds
which he had not used even at the close of the second year,
against one such sound in the second list (these were f, j, nk,
ï and ch).   The selection of ten additional words eliminated
the difference and reduced the average of later words to 62.9 %.
The fact remains that the child was able to pronounce a word
more correctly by 14.2 % of sounds at the end of a year of
practice.

As said above, each of the early words passed through one
or more transitional changes.   For the first ten words (excepting *mamma*), the average number of changes was 2.8, while
five of them had each four transitions.   In the ten words taken
from the last of the list, there was a maximum of two transitions, one being close to the average.[1]

In looking over Table V. the reader will be struck by the
variety of substitutions for each sound.   While Dr. Tracy
has found the principle of replacement to be that of the substitution of an easier, related sound for the difficult one,[2] we can
scarcely, in the face of such diversity of sounds and substitutes,
look to his as the *only* principle upon which the apparently law-
less replacement of sounds rested.   It is doubtless true that

[1] It was impossible to obtain a perfectly correct average for the second list,
as at the present time some have yet to undergo a final alteration.

[2] Psychology of Childhood, 2d ed., p. 150.

Dr. Tracy's principle is the underlying one—indeed, the evidence I have at hand lends proof in a general way to his main conclusions. There are, however, other principles, also fundamental, active at different times and in varying degrees. One of these has already been noticed; namely, the confusion of sounds resulting from the acquirement of new words somewhat similar to those already in use. This confusion is more likely to occur in the early stages of learning to speak. Errors in the recognition of sounds were a second and fertile source of imperfect reproduction.

Tables V. and VI. do not afford a full reply to the third question. In glancing at the multiplicity of substitutes recorded in Table V., one would find many cases in which there was apparently no fixed substitute. When pursuing through their changes the courses of the various words, the following facts were found to be true concerning the alterations of sounds; habitual substitutions were evolved in a special word and in the vocabulary as a whole, but habitual omissions were common prior to habitual substitutions. A fixed substitute was not, as one might suppose, always developed with the repeated occurrence of the sound. It appeared sometimes early, sometimes late in the history of a word sound. There can be no doubt, however, that in many cases the addition to the vocabulary of a number of words which contained a certain difficult sound influenced the substitution of a sound. This was the case with the substitution of *oe* for *ir*, six words in which *ir* is found, having been added about the same time. Fixed substitutions were broken up in several ways; by the introduction of a second substitute; by the influence of new phonetic combinations in new words; but chiefly through persistent efforts of the child to correct his mistake, and the consequent approximation of the pronunciation to that of the word-copy.

Yet another question now arises—why was the child unable to reproduce in words, sounds which he had made repeatedly alone and in combination, when babbling before he had learned to speak (trilling l and r; and th, etc.). No doubt the incomplete subjection of the apparatus of speech to the centers of voluntary control had much to do with his imperfect pronunciations.

They may further be traced to faults in perception. What the child did perceive of the spoken word or word-copy were the sounds and syllables emphasized; these he reproduced before he fully distinguished the phonetic elements. In words of more than one syllable he was plainly seen to have been impressed by the rhythm of the syllables as the following lists will show:

E′dith	A′dith	crack′er	ka′ka
grand′ma	a′ma	car′pet sweep′er	gah′luck′n
bot′tle	bot′n	flow′er	bă′loo
Al′len	A′na	thermom′eter	mä′teh
night gown	gi′gown	grand′pa′pa	pa′pa′pa

When the child did distinguish the phonetic elements in a word he did not reproduce it as his own earlier sound (with which he probably failed to identify it), but as a new sound, his articulation of which was controlled on all sides and rendered difficult by his articulation of other sounds in the word.

SECTION II.—WORDS.

Writers who have studied the acquirement of language describe the process by which children learn to speak essentially as follows: The infant perceives an object or action and at the same time hears a certain combination of sounds. Each time the object is brought before him the sounds are repeated, till he comes to associate the sounds with the object, so that when he hears them a memory image of the object is rung up, and upon seeing the object the sounds are called forth. Thus he gets to associate object by object with word by word.

At first he does not attempt the articulation of the words, understanding merely names, simple commands, etc. A little later he essays to reproduce the words, the success of the result being variable. In this manner the vocabulary has its beginning; it undergoes further increase by the same method.[1] My

---

[1] See article by Professor Sully in Pop. Sci. Mo., for February, 1895.

observations have led me to consider an associative process such
as I have briefly described above as the chief underlying process, active throughout the whole period during which language was being acquired.   It accounted for the multiplication
of speech forms, which, however, was not the only feature of
language development.   For in addition there was the increasing ability to use more complicated constructions, and the peculiarities of mental activity which were effective in producing
the changes in the use of language which were observed at intervals during the second year.   These additional features in
turn are but different aspects of the process by which the child
comes, by a method of successive approximations into the
power to use, in common with other persons, a language which he
finds prepared for him.

As early as the twelfth week certain sounds were associated
with the expression of fixed states of feeling; for the child cried
" eng " when hungry, and " Mä-ä-ä " when hurt or in sudden
distress.   A great variety of sounds, as I have elsewhere stated,
occurred when the child was babbling in comfort and contentment; but at such times no one sound was used exclusively.
Nevertheless the voice was clearly expressive of pleasure, interest and excitement.

In the twenty-sixth week a peculiar, ' singing' noise was
made when the child was contented.

Twenty-ninth Week.—Bob-ba indicated comfort and good
feeling.   Mom-ma, indicated hunger and other discomforts.

For two weeks, beginning with the thirtieth, he always said
' tä-tä,' after having satisfied his hunger.

Fortieth Week.—' Nin-nin,' indicated hunger.

In the forty-second week *papa* and *mamma* were associated,
though not exclusively with his parents.

In this week the child, while playing on the floor at feeding
time, suddenly looked up and said, ' mamma, nin nin,' thus indicating that he wished to be fed.   He associated ' don't suck'
with having his thumb taken out of his mouth so that he removed the thumb upon hearing the command.   After this he
learned rapidly to understand many words and some phrases.
The word *papa* became a proper name for a special individual,

but as late as the fifty-second week *mamma* had been used only under the following circumstances :

1. When his mother had gone.
2. When she reappeared.
3. When he was hungry.

It was two months later when he began to use the word freely in designating his mother, though if the word *mamma* were used in his hearing he immediately looked about for her.

The phrase ' here it is' came into use in the fifty-second week, accompanying the presence of something pleasing, and the act of giving. No similar phrase was acquired prior to the eighteenth month.

The words next added to the vocabulary were those indicating persons and individual things in which the child was especially interested.[1] Dogs had often been pointed out to him and he was familiar with three of quite different appearance, but he used the word *dog* first in speaking to a black mongrel which played around his carriage during an afternoon walk. On the day following he pointed out as a dog a St. Bernard and a small black nondescript. After this the word *dog* fell into complete disuse. It did not reënter the vocabulary till six months had elapsed.

All the above examples, with the exception of one, are instances in which a simple form of association by contiguity controlled the reappearance of sounds and words. Under conditions as similar as possible sounds were repeated as similar as possible to those before uttered. In the exceptional example, that in which he designated as dog two very different representatives of the type, the selection of a name depended upon his familiarity with four other and dissimilar dogs, one of which had only the day before impressed the child exceedingly.

In the fifty-eighth week that period was ushered in during which each word (except some proper names) was given every day a more extended application. Table VII. gives the history of fifteen words which were made of service in many situations. Other writers have discussed the tendency—which seems to be

[1] Upon referring to Table V. it will be seen that all words in the vocabulary at the close of the first year were proper nouns.

common among children—to widen the application of every word,[1] but have not, it seems, found this tendency to be characteristic of a limited period of language development. By some the tendency has been attributed to other causes than the one herein described. I regard it as the outcome of a crude form of inference. In the part of this work devoted to the development of ideas I have endeavored to show what the nature of this inference was.[2] Here I shall not digress from the subject in hand; but shall try to show that the extension of the application of a word did not *necessarily* rest upon (1) an uncircumscribed concept of the thing named, or upon (2) comparison and the perception of analogy.

This period extended from the fifty-eighth to the eighty-fourth week. During that time the child acquired but fifty-three words, yet he was familiar with many objects and could point them out when he heard their names. This shows that his perception of things exceeded considerably his use of words. Though he called all men ' papa' for a short time, he never met a stranger upon the same footing of familiarity as he did his father; and though he called all little girls ' Dorothy,' he never danced with glee at their approach, unless at a distance they bore a striking resemblance to his friend of that name. He always called a cat ' bird,' yet when he heard a voice calling ' cat! cat!' he looked about for the animal exclaiming ' bird! bird!' In these cases it was clearly shown that he did not confuse the individuals comprised by his class name. Whatever the quality of his concept of each of the things named, it was not sufficiently vague to permit of a fusion of individuals. We are, therefore, not justified in assuming such a fusion to be the basis of the class names used by the child. If we look to his concept of the meaning and use of words we shall find the real explanation of this peculiarity; for it will then be seen that he by no means understood the necessity of a separate name for each thing, and that at this period his words were used like so many exclamations by which he announced the presence of what was interesting.

[1] See Tracy, Psychology of Childhood, 2d ed., pp. 78–9, also Baldwin, *op. cit.*, p. 325.

[2] Part III., p. 94.

We may well ask what influences controlled the selection of the word for a wider application. Why, for example, did the child call a cow ' bird,' instead of ' dog,' both of which words were known to him? In the early days of language development each word, whose faulty pronunciation had been laboriously acquired, replaced for a time the old words which for several days were scarcely heard. The child practiced the new word when the object to which it referred was not present, and it entered largely into his babbling ; *it had an interest of its own.* The words first spoken were the names of things which had excited a great interest in the child, so that they with their circumstantial setting were in the best position to be remembered. The word whose application was extended was either the most recent addition to the vocabulary, or an old word about which fresh interests centered.

The child saw a cow under circumstances very similar to those in which he had seen birds and dogs ; but bird experiences were more recent, bird word fresher, and thus the elements of similarity called up the bird series, rather than the dog series ; but the cow, as the central figure, was substituted for the bird, and the child chirped to her, exclaiming ' bird !' Usually the jump from one object to another designated by the same name was not so great as that from bird to cow. The application of the word was extended slowly and by degrees. It depended upon internal association of a very primitive form, and not upon the perception of similarity.

If we regard the tendency to extend the application of words as due to the recall of sounds previously used under conditions of greater or less similarity, we are at once relieved of the necessity of postulating a perception of analogy as a fundamental human faculty. In Part III.[1] we have seen that the perception of analogy was a phenomenon of development depending upon the formation of internal associations, and the consequent mental juxtaposition of like objects, and that it was rudimentary, not to say unformed, during the greater part of the second year. We are therefore not at liberty to invoke the perception of analogy as a means of explanation here.

[1] p. 94.

With the entrance into the eighty-second week the child began to give a name to each object with which he came in contact. If he did not know or recall the name given to it by others he invented a name. A few of the coined names remained in use for several months; others were used once or twice and forgotten. The following lists give:

1. Names invented and retained in use:

lum = a cat.

bizz = his own shadow on the bathroom wall.

bahdiz = a figure on the ceiling of a bedroom.

Alah = a little girl, frequently seen from across the street.

2. Words invented, used only in one conversation and forgotten:

babax = a hinge.

blebs = a very small ledge on the piano.

piece it = to break a piece off, to break into pieces.

3. Often, finding it necessary to have a name, he babbled some jumble of sounds, as it were, gathered together for the occasion and soon forgotten.

bane,

sug,

fē sō back ō are examples of these.

The custom of naming each thing is of course inconsistent with that of classing many things under one name; therefore as the former habit grew the latter diminished, and the classes became smaller by the successive subtraction of object after object. At the close of the second year the child invariably asked the name of a new object, and was familiar, as is shown in Table VIII., with the names of most common things.

By the ninety-fifth week his vocabulary having grown considerably, the child came to a better understanding of the uses of words. The method of acquiring language then underwent a radical change. It became an imitative process. He imitated not only words, but phrases and sentences whose meaning he caught from observation of the actions of his elders. It was shortly after this that he began to be interested in rhymes; at first those containing familiar words as landmarks, then any nursery rhymes or poetry, which he quickly learned to reproduce.

During this preëminently imitative period, what he said expressed no reflections. Unintelligent imitation was rare though it sometimes occurred.[1]

The words that he used stood for visual percepts and memory images; his sentences represented observations on the actions of others, or a running commentary on his own performances.

A little later, ninety-seventh to ninety-ninth weeks, he frequently expressed outlines of actions proposed for himself and other persons, thus: "Say, mamma, Anna git a li' poon Wahn Moh" (Mamma shall say, Anna get a little spoon for Warren Moore), or defined his own intentions before beginning some performance. In the last three weeks of the second year the child began to use language to give the results of his reflections.[2] Language now assumed the function of an instrument with which to marshal and construct concepts.

We have now briefly reviewed the processes by which words were first connected with objects, then used to signify them, and lastly as symbols, substituted for the reality. Let us now turn our attention to the vocabulary itself, to inquire how many words and what classes of words were used by the child, and what the order of acquirement was.

If the reader will refer to table VIII. he will see that all words belonging to the first year were proper nouns—the names of persons (and of his doll)—known and of especial interest to the child. Nor did the acquisition of proper names become less prominent later. The child was always profoundly interested in people, whether real or portrayed in pictures. He quickly learned a name, and remembered it even after the face was forgotten. Many of the proper names in the vocabulary pertained to pictures. After the first proper nouns had been mastered a few common nouns were learned.

From the fifty-second to the eighty-second weeks words were added very slowly to the vocabulary. Though the child

[1] As in the reproduction of rhymes not fully understood; but here the rhythm was doubtless a point of interest.

[2] In the first weeks of the third year he reflected upon many things and was asking for explanations continually: Where were the chickens' hands? Where had the clouds gone? etc.

talked a great deal he made a few words, chiefly nouns, useful within extended limits. After the eighty-second week the acquisition of nouns proceeded at a rapid rate. In the one-hundred-and-fifth week there were 306 nouns in the vocabulary, of which 48 were proper nouns. The others were the names of common objects; for of abstract nouns there was not one.

In the sixty-fourth week the first verb made its appearance, *gone* doing duty for all sorts of disappearance. The verbs in use before the eighty-ninth week differed plainly from action words. They might more fitly be called substantive verbs than verbs proper. Four examples will make my meaning clear. Gone = disappeared, not the act of disappearance, but the phenomenon. See = a word used in calling attention to something perceived through the agency of sight or of touch. Hark = a word used in calling attention to a noise. Come = I wish it to be in this place. *Bye-bye* was the nearest approach to a word designating action; it was a term of vigorous dismissal by which the child signified refusal to obey, or his desire that an extremely distasteful thing should go away.[1] In these substantive verbs, which also partake of the character of interjections and may justly be called interjectional substantive verbs, we have what is really a transitional form.

In the ninetieth week the first action word proper came into use, and was in the succeeding weeks followed by other words unmistakably verbs. These verbs were used in the imperative form—' sit down'! (you sit down) ' brush (my) hair !' etc.—or in describing something performed or experienced by the child himself, as ' fell down' (I fell down). These two forms of verbs (exclamatory and imperative) did full justice to the quality of the child's mental attitude during the period extending from the ninety-first to the ninety-eighth weeks, during which no distinction of tense was made, any form of a verb which had been acquired being used without change. With these two forms he was able to make known his wants and to express his observations.

In the ninety-seventh week he made his first distinctions of

[1] After bye-bye had acquired this secondary meaning the child would never use it to a departing friend whom he wished to remain.

tense; ' I got'=I have got, and ' I get'=I shall get. Thereafter
he slowly acquired the ability to use the several forms of the
verbs and some of the auxiliaries, *did* being the member of the
last mentioned class most frequently heard.   Of course he made
many blunders in attempting to transform the present tense into
the past, usually the common one of adding *ed* to verbs of the
old conjugation.   In the vocabulary noted in Table VIII. the
parts of certain verbs are put down as separate words; this is
because they were learned and used as such before the child
had caught the practice of using one word under several aspects.

A few interjections also were used.   Such as *helloa!* and
'da ! da ! (indicating something).   Representatives of the class
of interjections were among the earliest words in the vocabulary.

Adjectives, ranking third in numerical importance, were
fifth in the order of acquisition.   The adjective first in use was
the numeral two (ninety-first week), which was in the beginning
correctly employed to designate two things, but later became
a plural form signifying any number more than one (still just 2
also).   Some of the adjectives of quality were at first used in
connection with respective special substantives (awful cough
and round O, for example), from which they were separated
and endued with a meaning which transformed them into true
quality words; others were added to the vocabulary by a process quite the reverse of this, functioning as quality words from
the beginning.   This was the history of *big* and *new*.   An adjective was never used in any but the positive degree.[1]   Things
were compared and contrasted thus : " This is a dirty napkin."
" This is a clean napkin."[2]   Color adjectives were the last to be
added.   Between the ninety-first and ninety-fourth weeks occurred the first numeral (two), the first pronominal (another)
and the first undoubtedly intelligent use of an adjective of quality.   I could not determine the exact order of acquisition, because sporadic instances of the use of each had previously been

[1] At twenty-eight months he understood the uses of the degrees of comparison.

[2] At twenty-eight months comparison and contrast became a favorite exercise in which the child indulged much.   For example he would say : " That's a
moth.   A very little moth.   Not a great big one, just a very little one."

recorded, from which it was impossible to conclude anything as to their meaning to the child.

Adverbs of place occurred early in the phrases, ' here it is' (fifty-second week) and ' where gone?' (seventy-sixth week). The word *here* in the former phrase had no separate adverbial meaning, but the whole phrase, used as a single word was, as I have pointed out, interjectional in character. Later, however, (ninetieth week) *here* was used as a separate word and as a true adverb of place. Thus the adverbs, though far outnumbered by the nouns, verbs, and even by adjectives, antedated all classes of words but interjections, nouns and verbs, albeit the manner of use was difficult to define in its early stages. ' Hard' was by the child himself applied to difficulty in performance.

As early as the eightieth week he was able to distinguish between *mine* and *yours*, and *you* and *I*. It was not till the ninety-sixth week that he began to use them. In the ninety-seventh week he substituted *I* for *Warren* (his name), and later learned to speak of himself as *he*, probably because he heard himself thus spoken of. At first he always substituted *mine* for *your* (*i. e.*, mine coat for your coat), but this error he soon corrected. He did not confuse the genders of the personal pronouns *he* and *she*, and they were usually put in the right case.

As they had been acquired after the imitative period[1] had been initiated, this is not surprising.

Of the remaining parts of speech, classed under ' others' in the table, there is but little to say.

The indefinite article made its appearance in connection with the word *fly* as early as the sixty-fourth week, and was afterwards (from ninety-fifth week on) used before nouns, both plural and singular, and before many verbs, producing a curious effect in sentences, thus: '' Little Warren a turn a pages'' (Little Warren turns the pages). The definite article had not come into use at the close of the second year.

The copula *and* was used rarely but correctly during the latter part of the second year.

Prepositions were acquired late. The first use of one was recorded in the ninety-fifth week. Though occasions were not

[1] See above p. 125.

wanting upon which a preposition might easily have been used, the relation of object to object was, except in rare instances, expressed by the approximation of substantives, thus—a woman stands a door.   At the closing of the record, *in, on, under, by* and *beside* were frequently used, though not always correctly placed in the sentence.[1]

Yes and *no* were rarely heard.   In replying to a question the child used a full statement, either of affirmation or of negation.

We have now to determine, before we leave the subject of words, the actual number of words in the vocabulary of the child, and the proportional relations of the parts of speech therein contained.   Table VIII. gives the vocabulary in full. Some other words had been used for a time and relinquished ; these have not been recorded in what is to be considered a working vocabulary.   At the close of the second year the child had in use 475 words.   Of these

$$306 \text{ or } 62.3 + \% \text{ were nouns.}$$
$$92 \text{ or } 19.3 + \% \text{ were verbs.}$$
$$38 \text{ or } 8 \quad \% \text{ were adjectives.}$$
$$14 \text{ or } 2.9 + \% \text{ were adverbs.}$$
$$11 \text{ or } 2.3 + \% \text{ were pronouns.}$$
$$14 \text{ or } 2.9 + \% \text{ were } \begin{cases} \text{prepositions.} \\ \text{interjections.} \\ \text{conjunctions.} \end{cases}$$
$$\overline{475} \quad \overline{98.6 +}$$

In the percentages of nouns, verbs and adjectives in the vocabulary of the child there is a close agreement with the results obtained by Dr. Tracy.   I have said that the proportion of verbs to nouns varied at different times.   I shall again recur to this variation in proportion when discussing the development of the sentence.   In the one-hundred-and-second week I endeavored to note everything said by the child during a single day.   At this time he used sentences almost exclusively, no longer expressing himself in single words.   150 different words entered into the construction of the sentences. Of these

[1] This will receive further notice under the sentence.

71 or 46.6 % were nouns.

40 or 26.6 % were verbs.

13 or 8.6 % were adjectives.

8 or 5.3 % were pronouns.

7 or 4.6 % adverbs.

11 or 7.3 % other parts of speech.

———

150   99.0

Here in the conversation of the child there existed a larger percentage of verbs in proportion to all the words in use and to the nouns than in the vocabulary as a whole. The following tables show the differences between the order of acquisition and that of the numerical importance of the classes of words in the vocabulary.

Order of acquisition:	Order of numerical importance:
1. Nouns.	Nouns
2. Interjections.	Verbs.
3. Verbs.	Adjectives.
4. Adverbs.	Pronouns.
5. Adjectives.	Adverbs.
6. Articles.	Prepositions.
7. Pronouns.	Interjections.
8. Prepositions.	Conjunctions and articles.
9. Conjunctions.	

SECTION III.—SENTENCES.

The first sentence was uttered in the sixty-sixth week. It contained but two words, 'papa gone,' and was the product of much previous practice on the part of the child, who had made many trials before he was able to pronounce successively the sounds therein contained. The simple assertion, exclamatory in character, was composed of subject and predicate; it was typical of all early sentences. Between the sixty-sixth and seventy-ninth weeks the sentences were either assertions or interrogations. Three verbal forms sufficed for all. For the in-

terrogative form the expression 'rsh' (where is he, she, it?)
was used in this way: 'Ama rsh?' (grandma, where is she?)
In announcing the presence of something to which he wished
to call attention, the child said 'h'r's' (here is) the object named.
Thus the child announced something, exclaimed at its disappearance, inquired concerning its whereabouts. These simple
sentences were fairly complete—that is to say the omissions, an
article or an auxiliary verb, were not essential parts of the sentence. But when the child had acquired a larger vocabulary,
he broke away from the bondage of his early copies and launched
freely into word combinations. The errors which he then committed were still those of omission, and the most glaring of them
was the omission of the verb.

In the eighty-sixth week the imperative sentence made its
appearance, and about the same time the affirmative or assertive
sentence became more common. The interrogative sentence
persisted, altered somewhat in form, but retaining the meaning.
The one interrogative form which the child used when inquiring about some absent person or thing was often heard, and to
the one hundred and second week remained the only form of
question put by the child. After the eighty-sixth week sentence-
formation pursued two paths of progress; the one leading
towards a more complete expression of the results of his observations of things, the other towards the issuance of many and
varied commands. As he was observing what people *had*,
rather than what they were *doing*, it was natural that his sentences should have contained a larger proportion of nouns and
a smaller proportion of verbs. The use of the emphasis as
well as word forms in the expression of certain meanings was
very common with the child. He could by its means convey
the idea of something having taken place before he could
change a verb into its past tense, for example: " Mamma
wash it, all dirty" (his hand). "*Mamma* wash it, all dirty"
(washed). The imperative sentence invariably contained the
verb.

Many of his verbs were accompanied by a gesture, attitude,
or the act which they signified; for example, when he said,
'bye-bye come' (meaning do not come!) he waved his hand

in dismissal; if he said 'back!' (meaning carry me on your back) he put himself in an attitude of readiness; and when, after a meal, he said 'pull napkin' (take off my napkin), he accompanied the command by a steady pull at the article in question. The accompaniment of a sentence by an action of some sort was the rule till about the ninety-eighth week. In the recitation of past experiences and in those speech forms by which he gave expression to the results of his reflections, gestures were not introduced. During the utterance of the sentences in which the child proposed some course of action for himself he maintained the attitude of one who is ready to act the moment he has finished speaking. Here we come upon an illustration of that intimate relationship of mental to bodily activity which is so apparent in childhood.

Leaving the first simple sentences constructed upon a few unaltered models, and coming to that period in which the sentence became more varied, we find it necessary to frame some definition of a sentence before it is possible to pursue the history of its development. Words were combined in such a variety of ways, so utterly without parallel in the usages of syntax, that I was oftentimes at a loss when trying to get these combinations into a system of classification which should place them in line with adult speech constructions.

I have taken as my definition of a sentence any combination of words whatsoever, beyond the simple naming of an object of sense. This definition allows of the inclusion of those transitional sentence forms which are intermediate between the stages of naming and of describing. The following series of sentences will illustrate my meaning. The child perceives his mother sitting down reading a book; he exclaims:

   1. Book.
Later 2. Mamma book.
 " 3. Mamma sit down, a book.
 " 4. Mamma sit down, read a book.
 " 5. Mamma is sitting down, reading a book.

Now No. 2 could not, according to the rules of English grammar, correctly be termed a sentence; yet I have ventured to call it such, because it represents a complication of thought from which springs a more complex expression than the one used by the child when, by a name, he indicated the presence of an object.

To recur, however, to the construction of the sentence, we may ask what formed the predicate in those sentences from which the verb was omitted. The sentences consisted of nouns so arranged as to express some striking relation between the objects to which they referred. One of the nouns was the subject; by the others was made known the connection in which the subject at the time was seen to be. They therefore constituted the predicate. Examples of such sentences are:

'Man, cow' (a man on a horse). 'Mamma, a man, bottle!' (Mamma, see the man with bottles).

The child often expressed his observations in sentences without verbs, and in those beginning with the word *see,* thus: 'See biscuit mamma hand' (see the biscuit in mamma's hand).

In the ninety-seventh week there was a rapid increase in the number of verbs corresponding to a close watchfulness of the actions of other persons and the growing habit of translating these into such language as he could command. In sentences constructed at this time one and two verbs often occurred. There was also some attempt at producing an agreement of tense and person. Qualifying words made their appearance; some were adjectives qualifying the subject; some were adverbs assisting in the predicate.

The qualifying words first introduced (excepting adverbs of place) were adjectives used to qualify the subject, such as: 'There goes two little boys.' 'Warren's apple is good.' Before the ninety-fifth week the sentences were all very simple, each containing only one statement; but in the ninety-fifth week he began to make some attempts at compound sentences containing two statements or two commands. The second statement of the compound sentence might or might not contain a verb. An example of these first compound sentences is, 'Mamma sit down, rubbers on,' (mamma sit down, put your rubbers on). The example contains one subject who is to perform two separate acts. A sentence sometimes occurred in which there were two subjects and two predicates. Such a one was composed of two simple statements, sometimes, but rarely, united by the copula *and ;* sentences did not become more complex than this during the second year.

He never used one of the responsives alone in reply to an interrogation.[1] His replies to all questions consisted in a statement, usually a complete repetition of the question cast, by the emphasis upon certain words, in an affirmative or negative form. Towards the close of the second year he began to use yes and no in connection with the full statement, as : ' Yes, I did go for a walk.' ' No, I can't find my pencil.' In the ninety-ninth and one-hundredth weeks the frequent introduction of adjectives, adverbs and prepositions began to give to the sentence the appearance of being more complete.

Of the position of the various words in the sentence there is but little to be said. Such words as the sentence contained were almost invariably in the proper sequence, though the omission of the many small words brought about some unusual and awkward effects due to the proximity of those parts of speech which we are not wont to hear together. There was, however, a peculiarity of construction in which the preposition figured as the chief agent of modification. It has elsewhere been said that before the introduction of the preposition the relation of object to object, which should be expressed by the interposition of a preposition between the names, was indicated by the juxtaposition of the names. When the preposition was introduced, instead of being placed between the two nouns, it was tacked on to the end of the sentence. This happened particularly to the prepositions *in* and *on.* ' See little cup dish on' is an example of the construction. In this example the verb *see* occurs; but a further peculiarity of his use of the preposition was the omission of the verb from the same sentence, as if the preposition stated all that was necessary concerning the nouns. ' Mamma, monkey glasses on,' and ' little hand hole in,' are two illustrations. *In, on* and other prepositions were also used in the customary manner, which gradually superseded the odd construction of which, in the one-hundred-and-fifth week, I found no trace.

[1] The use of the responsives became customary in the twenty-eighth month.

Averages obtained from numbers of sentences noted at different periods indicate some few points well. 163 sentences, each typical, and the whole forming a progressive series which began in the sixty-sixth and ended in one-hundred-and-fifth week contained in all 661 words,[1] an average of 4.05 + words to a sentence. 43.4 % of the 661 words were things talked of, or nouns or pronouns. This allows an average of 1.82 + nouns and pronouns to a sentence. 24.8 + % of the words were verbs, giving an average of 1.06 + verbs to a sentence, considerably more than half the number of nouns. The proportion becomes a striking one when compared with percentages of nouns, pronouns and verbs in the vocabulary as a whole; for we then perceive that the number of verbs at the child's command was less than one-third the number of nouns and pronouns, but when it came to a question of use, the number of verbs employed rose to more than half the number of nouns and pronouns employed. A similarly striking proportion occurs in favor of adverbs, which comprised 9.5 + % of the 661 words, or an average of 0.38 + adverbs to a sentence, as compared with a percentage of 2.9 representing the adverbs in the vocabulary. With adjectives the proportional relations are somewhat different, for they constituted but 7.4 % of the words (8 % of the vocabulary) and averaged 0.28 + to a sentence; 3.7 % of the words were prepositions. The remaining 11.8 % consisted of the indefinite article, a few interjections and an occasional conjunction.

On a certain day in the ninety-sixth week I noted 124 of the primitive sentences, and once again in the one hundred and second week 138 sentences were noted. In Table IX. the results of a study of these sentences are arranged in a form to facilitate comparison. It will be seen that many of the tendencies are here illustrated which have been referred to above in the discussion of the development of the sentence, and of the gradual introduction of classes of words used in forms of construction. It will be seen that the verb came rapidly to the front as a factor in the sentence-formation. There is also a pronounced increase in the average number of words to a sentence, traceable

---

[1] Not 661 *different* words.

to the introduction of words of all classes, but especially to that free use of the indefinite article which has already been noticed.

From this table we shall learn, also, that the percentage of words of a class contained in the vocabulary is but an indifferent index of the frequency with which representatives of the class are brought into active service. This was made clear in the case of prepositions, whose number, five, is equal in the two vocabularies, while the sentences of the one-hundred-and-second week contained a proportional increase of 44% of prepositional constructions. The indefinite article furnishes a further illustration of this point; for in the sentences of the one-hundred and-second week its employment was found to have made a proportional increase of 45% over the sentences of the ninety-sixth week.

TABLE IV.—TABLE ILLUSTRATING CHANGES IN THE PRONUNCIATION OF WORDS THROUGH.

THE WORD.	OMISSION.	INTRODUCTION.	ADDITION.	1ST SUBSTITUTION.	2D SUBSTITUTION.	3D SUBSTITUTION.	4TH SUBSTITUTION.	LAST PRO-N'NC'TION.	NUCLEUS OF WORD.
Edith	1. Dith	3. Ădădith	2. Dithă		4. Ădith	Tdss	Dits	Ădith,	Dith
Jinks				Tsn	Dz			Dits	I
dog	dŏ							dŏ	dŏ
bird	bir			bürd	boed	băd		băd	bd
horse	1. h 2. orse							orse	orse
bye				bă				bye	bye
papa				ăppă	păbă	păpă		papa	papa
fly				hlă	lă	hly	ly.	lily	ly
grandma				ămă	gŏmmă	gămă	gwămă	gwămă	gămă
gone				gong				gone	gone
kitty	ki							ki	ki
baby				băbă	băbĕ			baby	baby
Allan				Ădl	Ană			Ană	Ană
cracker				kăkă				kăkă	k k
down				dŏn	Ill			down	down
little				Ită		lă	ittle	little	little
bath				bă				bath	bath
see				zĕ				see	see
bottle				bŏtn	bŏttĕ	bŏktĕl	bŏh'hle	bŏh'hle	bŏ l
cry	ky			ky	kwy			kwy	c y
light				lich(gutt'ral)				light	light
garter				gărker				gărker	gar'er
car				căh				căh	ca
nightgown				gi gown				gigown	i gown
pull	pû			pû				pû	pû
stool	tool			tool				tool	tool

The words are arranged in the order in which they were acquired, except where the serial numbers occur to indicate the order of acquirement.

TABLE V.—SUBSTITUTION OF SOUNDS.

Letter	Substitutes		Letter	Substitutes
A	ā 2 ĕ ă		P	3 b
	ă 5 ä ī ă		Q	k
	ä ă ĕ ŭ â		R	19 w l y ŏ
	â		S	z h n f
B			T	ch (gutteral) 2 k g w l
D	2 y p w 2 m u		U	ū ŭ ŏ
E	ĕ 3 ă ă ä			ŭ 3 ä ŏ û ă
	ĕ 5 ă 2 ă 2 ŭ ĕ ī ow			û ŏ
F	4 h 2 w K., s			ŭ 2 ī
G			V	2 b w
H			W	4 v pf f
I	ī 3 ă 2ä ĕ		X	2 k 2 ks ts
	ĭ 10 ĕ ĕ ä 3 ă 3 ŭ oe ow		Y	
	ÿ ŭ ă oe ŏ		Z	2 s
J	4 d 2 dz ts tds z		th { soft	2 l k f ä
K	4 t 2 g p		{ hard	z
L	8 ŏ 2 w d g n		sh	7 s 2 h l
M	n		ch	2 t 2 ts d s
N	2 ng m g d t		ow	ŏ
O	ō 2 ŏ oe		oi	y
	ŏ ow ī		ir	5 oe ă ŏ
	ô û		ing	oin
	ŏ ŭ ï oe			

TABLE VI.—SOUNDS OMITTED AND MISPLACED.

	WHEN INITIAL.	WHEN MEDIAL.	WHEN FINAL.	PRESENT BUT MISPLACED.
A	3	2		
D		2	4	
E	1	3		
F	2	1		
G				
H	2		1	
I	9			
K	2			
L	2	7	8	1
M	1	1		
N		8	5	2
P	2	1		
R		27	21	
S	17		1	
T				
U	1	5	5	
V		1	1	
Y			1	
th	2	1	1	
sh	1			

TABLE VII.—ILLUSTRATING EXTENSION OF APPLICATION OF WORDS.

The Word.	Its First Use.	Second.	Third.	Fourth.	Fifth.	Sixth.	Sev'nth.
Papa	his own father.	any man					
Dog	a certain dog.	two other dogs	dogs	cats	any animals not 'flies'		
Bird	sparrows,	a cow				crumbs of bread	a toad
Horse	a horse	a horse and wagon					
Fly	fly	specks of dirt	bits of dust	all small insects	his toes		
Gone	said of an article dropped	any disappearance	go away!				
Little girl	a special little girl	a picture of a little girl	any picture				
Down	anything which fell or was thrown down	up					
Poor		broken	sorrowful or unfortunate				
Chair	a rocking chair	any chair					
Bye bye	good-bye	go away!	take it away!	do not come!	something has ceased or gone		
Mamie	a young lady in neighboring house who look'd from a window	any lady in any house at the window					
Clock	a clock	a watch					
Cork	a cork	the stopper of the bath tub					
Baby frog	a certain picture in his father's book[1]	any picture in any book of his father's	some parallel curves and lines	any picture in any book which he cannot interpret			

[1] The picture in question illustrated an embryo.

TABLE VIII.—WORDS IN VOCABULARY AT CLOSE OF FIRST AND SECOND YEARS.

Proper Nouns.	Common Nouns.	Common Nouns.	Common Nouns.	Verbs.	Verbs.	Adjectives of Quality.	Pronouns.	Adverbs.	Oth'rs.
Allen	apple	beef tea	cough	am	find	awful	he	asleep	a
Ada	apron	bit	cat	are	found	big	him	away	and
Allie	aunt	block	comb	bye-bye	fix	beautiful	it	again	along
Audubon	bird	bubble	cap	brush	give	clean	I	down	by
Anna	bread	bell	corner	bring	gave	cool	me	fast	beside
Blowing Rock	baby	bureau	cover	blow	go	dark	my	hard	for
Bunker	bath	breakfast	carriage	bark	goes	dear	mine	how	in
Charcot	bottle	button	corn	belongs	going	dirty	that	here	on
Catherine	bowwow	blanket	case	bounce	gone	dry	this	now	to
Dahma	box	chicken	collar box	brought	get	empty	them	out	under
Dicky	bahdiz	cracker	cushion	boil	got	funny	you	ready	please
Dorothy	bizz	chair	chin	cry	get up	good		till	good-bye
Darwin	basin	car	collars	crying	hark	great		there	yes
Emerson	bed	cart	ducka	cut	hurt	hot		up	no
Frank	book	cow	duck	call	hang	little		where	
Faure	butter	coat	dish	can	hide	Merry Xmas			
Grandma	beans	clock	dirt	can't	help	new			
Grandmamma	back	cup	door	climb	has	poor			
Grandpapa	boys	carpet-sweeper	dog	cover	have	pretty			
Grandpa	biscuit	cake	doctor	comes	kicks	round			
Gault	basket	cocoa	dinner	coming	knows	red			
Gorman	body	cork	drink	drink	keep	smooth			
Glazer	boat	crow	desk	did	left	warm			
Gerty	bag	can	dough	doing	like	windy			
Humboldt	belt	cold-cream	dressing-gown	don't	lay	another			
Josephine	brush	coffee	drawers	drop	lost	all			
Katy	bundle	cuffs	dust-pan	dance	let	any			
Kathleen	ball	clothes	dust-brush	excuse	mend	both			
Luella	blotter		dress	eats	must	more			
Langtry	bicycle			fell	make				
Edith									
Grandma									
Jinks									
Mamma									
Papa									

TABLE VIII.—WORDS IN VOCABULARY AT CLOSE OF FIRST AND SECOND YEARS.—*Concluded.*

PROPER NOUNS.	COMMON NOUNS.	COMMON NOUNS.	COMMON NOUNS.	VERBS.	VERBS.	ADJECTIVES OF QUALITY.	PRO. NOUNS.	ADVERBS.	OTH'RS.
	polywog	soap	tree						
	pie	shaddock	tooth brush						
	petticoat	sheet	tin pail						
	pencil	shirt	train						
	pages	smoke	towel						
	post office	shoes	thermome-ter						
	people	stick	trousers						
	pocket	stocking	thumb						
	parasol	slippers	tack						
	plant	sugar	toe						
	pease	scissors	top						
	package	saque	uncle						
	potatoes	string	umbrella						
	purse	shoe-buttoner	veil						
	quilt	somebody	water						
	rose	skates	wrapper						
	rocking-chair	snake	wind						
	ring	sneeze	watch						
	rain	sleeve	woman						
	rubbers	stomach	wagon						
	room	sofa	window						
	rag bag	sail	wings						
	ribbon	shutters	walls						
	red ball	strap							
	rabbit	sunlight							
	sterilizer	sun							
	stool	teeth							
	shadow	tongue							
	spoon	table							

TABLE VIII.—WORDS IN VOCABULARY AT CLOSE OF FIRST AND SECOND YEARS.—*Continued.*

PROPER NOUNS.	COMMON NOUNS.	COMMON NOUNS.	COMMON NOUNS.	VERBS.	VERBS.	ADJEC-TIVES OF QUALITY.	PRO-NOUNS.	ADVERBS.	OTH'RS.
Maggie	elephant	berries	mouth	muss	wash	some			
Mamie	eye	heart	milk	open		this			
Marjory	ear	hiccup	music	pull		that			
Maidie	eraser	hole	money	push		what			
Napoleon	fly	ice	mug	put on		one			
Percy	foot	Indian	mittens	put away		two			
Pasteur	feet	juice	medicine	play		three			
Porter	fur	jacket	machine	play peep		five			
Rubenstein	flower	kitty	nightgown	ride		six			
Stanley	finger	kiss	nose	run					
Shaw	fish	kitchen	napkin	see					
Suche	frog	kangaroo	nail	sit					
University	fork	knife	neck	shut					
Warren	floor	kettle	necktie	singing					
Wylie	flour	knee	needle	sweep					
Wayne	gloves	light	noise	say					
Yorke	girl	lum	orange	spill					
	garter	ladder	piano	sew					
	goose	lady	picture	show					
	gate	leaves	pin	stop					
	glasses	lap	paper	set					
	grapes	letter	pan	stay					
	hat	leg	plants	stick					
	hand	leaf	plate	stand					
	house	lid	pimple	take					
	head	leggins	piece	turn					
	horse	man	pussy	throw					
	handker-chief	men	pot	tied					
	holly-	monkey	pig	torn					
		meat	pillow	untied					

TABLE IX.

NINETY-SIXTH WEEK.	ONE-HUNDRED-AND-SECOND WEEK.
124 sentences containing 384 words.	138 sentences containing 570 words.
Vocabulary — 118 words.	Vocabulary — 150 words.

NUMBER AND PERCENTAGE OF WORDS OF A CLASS CONTAINED IN:

	THE SENTENCES.		THE VOCABULARY.			THE SENTENCES.		THE VOCABULARY.	
	No.	Percentage.	Number.	Percentage.		No.	Percentage.	Number.	Percentage.
Nouns and Pronouns.	200	52.0	72	61.5	Nouns and Pronouns.	267	46.8	78	52.
Verbs.	82	21.3	22	18.6	Verbs.	131	22.9	40	26.6
Adjectives	29	7.5	11	9.3	Adjectives	37	6.4	13	8.6
Adverbs	26	6.7	5	4.2	Adverbs	46	8.0	11	7.3
Prepositions	13	3.3	5	4.2	Prepositions	21	3.6	5	3.3
Others	34	8.8	3 (art. 1, Interj. 2)	2.5	Others	68	11.9	3 (art. 1, Interj. 2)	2.0

Average number of words to a sentence — 3.02
" " nouns and pronouns[1] — 1.6
" " verbs — 0.6
" " Adjectives — 0.23
" " Adverbs — 0.2
" " Prepositions — 0.10
Percentage of sentences containing no verb — 33.8 %

Average number of words to a sentence[1] — 4.1
" " nouns and pronouns — 1.9
" " verbs — 0.9
" " adjectives — 0.27
" " adverbs — 0.3
" " prepositions — 0.15
Percentage of sentences containing no verb — 7.2 %

[1] Read " to a sentence" after all but first and last lines.

TABLE X.—TABLE ILLUSTRATING THE DEVELOPMENT OF THE SENTENCE.

	THE SENTENCE.	ITS MEANING.
66th week.	Pāpē gong	Papa is gone.
	Āmä rsh?	Grandma, where is she?
70th week.	Papa, h'r's itta gur.	Papa, here is a little girl.
79th week.	Ama er gong?	Where is grandma?
	Bēbē ky.	The baby is crying.
82d week.	Poo' Deekëy down.	Poor Deeky has fallen down.
86th week.	Poo' bowwow ē down	Poor bowwow fell down.
89th week.	HI down!	(You) sit down.
91st week.	See two by.	See two boys.
93d week.	Heh come cŭ	Here comes a car.
	Mamma, see book lap	Mamma, see this book, and take me on your lap to look at the pictures.
95th week.	Lil by sit down, a boat.	A little boy is sitting down, and a boat.
	Papa, come on, see vind, vind b'ow	Papa come on, see the wind; the wind blows.
96th week.	Wahwon's dess cawnah	Warren's dress is in the corner.
	Caw Anna	(You) call Anna!
	Mamma dis vay	Mamma, put the dish away.
97th week.	Ee goes two men	There go two men.
98th week.	Fin' It, a lil pitser	Find a little picture.
100th week.	Play mamma	Play with mamma.
101st week.	Mamma, Wahn git down, sō gahmpa zussahs	Mamma, Warren will get down to show grandpa the scissors.
103d week.	See Percy papa doing.	See what Percy papa is doing.
	Wahn a goyn a Bowling Wock	Warren is going to Blowing Rock.
	Percy papa come home, Wahn give im a butn	When Percy papa comes home Warren will give him a button.

INDEX.

A

Abstraction 29, 97, 106
Action, accompanying speech . . 132
Actions, habitual 9
    "   voluntary 27
    "   renewal of 44
    "   survival of 44
Activity 42
Adaptations 9, 59
Adjustments 77
Adjectives . . . 111, 128, 130, 134, 136
Adjustment, of eye muscles, see
    eye.
Adverbs 129, 130, 136
Analogy 90, 93, 94, 123
Anticipation 53
Apperceived system 94, 95
Apperception 86, 87
    "   masses 86
    "   and perception . . . 87
Arm movements, see grasping,
    etc.
Articles 129, 131, 137
Assimilation 86, 87
Association . 20, 21, 28, 30, 48, 69, 85
            91, 92, 108, 116, 120
    "   contiguity . . 93, 94, 122
    "   internal 94, 124
    "   similarity 92
Associations, series of . . . 52, 86, 96
Associative links 44, 85
Attention 45, 52, 54, 59, 86 87
Attitude, fœtal 21
Attitudes . . . .
    "   pre-natal 20
    "   post-natal 20
Auditory sensations 63, 70, 71
Automatism 10, 29
Awakening 40
    "   day of 6

B

Babbling 68, 115

C

Choice 30
Clasping 20, 21
Color 46, 53
    "   sensations 53
Comfort 15, 43
Comparison 91
    "   and contrast 128
Concepts 29, 123
    "   and language . . . 123, 126

Confusion of sensations . . 14, 58, 77
    "   of sounds 69, 119
Conjunctions 130
Contact, sensations of 20
Contrast 77
Consciousness 43, 44, 72, 89
Convergence, see eye.
Coördinations 55
Copula 129, 135
Creeping 5, 7, 25, 90

D

Deliberation 30
Depth 97, 110
Desire 28, 29, 43
Development 2, 43
    "   individual . . . 44, 52
    "   movement and direc-
            tion of 4
    "   periods of 4, 90
Differentiation of sensations . . . 22
Direction 97, 107, 111
    "   of the gaze 57
Discomfort 15, 43
Discrimination . 14, 53, 68, 71, 91, 93
    "   and perception . 53, 68
Distance 97, 107
    "   estimation of 49
    "   and pitch 67
    "   and sound, see sound.
Distinction 69, 71, 77, 89

E

Ear 71
Emotions 37, 89
Emphasis 132
Environment 44
Error 94
Errors in interpretation 69, 96
Excitement in pleasure 37
    "   in displeasure . . . 37
Experiences . . . 85, 86, 87, 89, 93
Experimentation 2, 82, 92
Expression, emotional 10, 37
Expressive actions 30, 31
Eye, adjustments 51, 55, 56
  " convergence of axes 45
  " focus 45, 56
  " movements 45, 55, 58

F

Facial expression 40
Faculties 87
Falling, fear of 33, 42

Feeling 4, 22, 78
" and sounds 121
Feet, use of 17, 22
Fixation 56
Focus, see eye.
Following with the eyes 45
Food 79, 82
Functions 44

G

Generalization 96, 97
Gestures 30
Grasping 16, 20, 79

H

Habit 2, 10, 12, 21, 29, 85, 87
" mental 96, 97
" personal 12
Hand and arm movements . . . 15
Hearing, development of 71
" observations 60
Hedonic element 15
Height 110
Holding 20

I

Idea 22, 28, 85, 90, 93, 98
class ideas 92, 95
" development of an . . . 85, 98
" formation 85, 95
Ideas and words 95
Identity 93
Imagination 94
Imitation, conscious. 23, 30, 32, 116, 125
Indirect vision, ... 52, 53, 55
Individual development, see development.
Induction 97
Inference 30, 93, 94, 123
Inheritance 44
Inhibition 32
Insensibility to sounds 61, 63
Instinct 55
" definition of 9, 43
" race 9
Instinctive acts 43, 44
Intensities, relative of sensations . 51
54, 70, 81
Interest 45, 89
Interjections 127, 128, 130
interpretation of sounds 69
Interpretations 72, 94

L

Language 95, 115
Language, understanding of . . 121
Light sensations 51, 53
Local signs 78
Locality 50
Localization of sound 66
" and touch 77

M

Magnitude 97, 107, 111
Melody 65
Memory . . 53, 69, 85, 87, 92, 111, 114
" of sounds 68
" images 91, 126
" personal 86, 87
Mental activity 89, 121, 133
" correlatives 44
" development 85
" elaboration 89, 98
" image 90
" integration 98
" representative . 28, 87, 90, 96
" survival 89
" synthesis 78, 90, 96
" type 91
Method, of observation 2
Motor discharge 96
" impulse 55
Movement, sensations, see touch.
Movements, ... 8, 85, 97
" accessory to seeing . 56, 57
" automatic . . . 8, 35
" development of . . 8
" of expression . . . 37
" of eyes, see eye.
" impulsive 8
" inhibitory 8, 32
" instinctive . . . 8, 59
" habitual 8, 35
" range and direction of 44
" rapid 34
" reflex 8, 10, 42
" reproduced 77
" selection of . . . 9
" spontaneous . . . 8, 9, 40
" survival of 11
" transformation of . 11, 31
" voluntary . . 8, 23, 35, 72
Muscular sensations 20

N

Names 95, 121, 123
Nervous system 44
Nouns 126, 130, 134, 136

O

Objects 44, 58, 90, 96
Observations 126
" method of 2
Observed 1
Observer 1

P

Pain 80
" localization 80
" sensibility 81
Perception . 21, 28, 51, 55, 58, 88, 67, 89
" see discrimination.
" and apperception . . . 87

Perception of distance 107
" of direction 107
" of the hand, etc. 21
" history of 59
" requisite of 59
" and sensation 58
" of things seen . . . 45, 58
" of small objects 55
Perceptions of sight and touch . . 82
Periodicity 106
Persistence 30
Personal memory, see memory.
" habit 12
Perverseness 27, 31
Pictures 50, 60, 112
Pitch and distance 67
Pleasure 43, 54, 91
Prepositions 129, 135, 136
Pressure 78
Progress, rate of 6
Pronouns 129, 130, 136
Pupils of eyes 45

R
Rate of movement 11
Reaching 16, 97
Reaction time 11
Reactions 51, 85, 89
" inherent 72, 88
" and sensations . . . 51, 54, 58
" and touch 72
Reason, see inference, etc.
Recall 86, 92, 124
Recognition 52, 71, 89, 93
Recognition of sounds 67, 119
" of a tune 67
Recognitions of touch 82
Reconstruction 93, 94
Reflections 126
Reflex movements 42
Repose 35
Representation . . . 29, 90, 91, 93, 96
Reproduction 93
Response 130, 135
Restlessness 42
Retentiveness 92
Rhymes 65, 125
Rhythm 65

S
Satisfaction 28, 43
Seeing near and far 56
Sensation, auditory 63
" and distinction . . . 89
" pleasant and unpleas-
ant 70
" quality of 51, 71
" relative intensities, see
intensities.
" and reactions, see reactions.

Sensation, simple 52, 58
" visual 45, 53
Sensations . . 52, 53, 55, 58, 85, 96
Sensibility to sounds 64, 71
Sensory apparatus 86
Sentence, the 126, 130, 131
" compound 134
Sequence 106
Sight, see vision, etc.
Sit 90
Size, see magnitude.
" estimation of 49
Sleep 35, 64
Smell 82, 83
Smile 40
Sound and distance 66
" and habit 64
Sounds 68, 115, 121
" conscious imitation of . . 116
Space 107
Speech forms, multiplication of .
Spontaneous movements . 11, 40, 44 56
Stages of mental development . . 89
Stimuli susceptibility to influence
of 58
Structures, ... 44
Substitution of sounds 118
Sucking the thumb 12
" " variations . . 13
" " effects 13
Suckling 64
Suggestion . 30, 35, 77, 81, 85, 91, 94
Survival of actions 44
" movements 44
Synthesis, see mental.

T
Taste 82
Tear secretion 37
Temperature 80
Tickling 79
Time, perception of 106
" reaction 11
Tongue, movements of 115
Touch 72
" and movement sensa-
tions 20, 79
" organs of 79
" sensations and reactions . 72
" sensibility 79
Transformation, see movements.

V
Verbs 127, 130, 136
Visual coördinations 9
Vocabulary 7, 116, 120, 126
Voice 38, 40, 115, 121
Volition, see voluntary movements.
Voluntary movements, see move-
ments.

Voluntary movements, classes of . 29
     "   "   observations
                             on . . . 23
     "   "   stages of . 29

W

Walking 6, 26, 90
Words 95, 116, 120, 136
  "   application of 94, 122
  "   coined 125

Monograph Supplement.　　　　No. 4, January, 1897.

THE
Psychological Review

EDITED BY

J. MARK BALDWIN
PRINCETON UNIVERSITY

AND

J. McKEEN CATTELL
COLUMBIA UNIVERSITY

WITH THE CO-OPERATION OF

ALFRED BINET, ÉCOLE DES HAUTES-ÉTUDES, PARIS; JOHN DEWEY, UNIVERSITY OF
CHICAGO; H. H. DONALDSON, UNIVERSITY OF CHICAGO; G. S. FULLERTON
UNIVERSITY OF PENNSYLVANIA; JOSEPH JASTROW, UNIVERSITY OF WIS-
CONSIN; G. T. LADD, YALE UNIVERSITY; HUGO MÜNSTERBERG,
HARVARD UNIVERSITY; M. ALLEN STARR, COLLEGE OF PHY-
SICIANS AND SURGEONS, NEW YORK; CARL STUMPF, UNI-
VERSITY, BERLIN; JAMES SULLY, UNIVERSITY
COLLEGE, LONDON.

A STUDY

OF

KANT'S PSYCHOLOGY

WITH REFERENCE TO

THE CRITICAL PHILOSOPHY

BY

EDWARD FRANKLIN BUCHNER, Ph.D.,

Professor of Descriptive Psychology in New York University,
Instructor in Pedagogy and Philosophy in Yale University.

PUBLISHED BI-MONTHLY BY

THE MACMILLAN COMPANY,

66 FIFTH AVENUE, NEW YORK; AND LONDON.

Es ist schwer, den Menschen ganz abzulegen.

—*Kant.*

Es kann nicht etwas erkenntnisstheoretisch wahr und psychologisch falsch sein.

—*Carl Stumpf.*

PREFATORY.

Most studies of the Critical philosophy proceed historically, logically, or metaphysically. They trace the external influences upon it, and its development in Kant's mind; or, they inquire into its consistencies and test its strength from its own principles; or, taking it as truth-expressing, they search its metaphysical validity. In this way there has accrued during the past century a large amount of psychological material in Kantian criticism, turning chiefly on the two points, whether the critical method is psychological, and, the scope of Criticism falls within psychology. Most of these helpful, many-sided interpretations have been necessarily omitted in the following study, owing to the limitations of time. A like cause is responsible for the unsatisfactory treatment given in chapter IV., as, also, for the non-elimination of various discussions.

Citations in Kant's writings are made by volume and page from Hartenstein's 'chronological' edition, excepting the *Critique of Pure Reason*, where the two-volume translation of Max Müller is followed.

E. F. B.

NEW HAVEN,
    June, 1893.

TABLE OF CONTENTS.

CHAPTER I.

INTRODUCTORY: THE IDEA OF PROPÆDEUTICITY AND KANT'S
PSYCHOLOGICAL PROBLEM 1–12
Threefold relation of nature and reason, 1. The idea of
propædeuticity, 4. The services of psychology to philosophy,
4. Unity and sketch of metaphysical problems, 8. Kant's
general problem, 11.

CHAPTER II.

PSYCHOLOGY IN KANT'S CONCEPTION OF ' WISSENSCHAFTLICHE
ENCYCLOPÄDIE '...13–35
Value and difficulties of Kantian psychology, 13. The
sources of Kant's psychology, 15. Kant's doctrine as to the
nature of science, 17. *A priori* knowledge and philosophical system, 19. The mathematical elements, 21. Psychology
and metaphysics, 23. Psychology and logic, 26. Psychology
and ethics, 30. Psychology and æsthetics, 33. Conclusion,
35.

CHAPTER III.

KANT'S POSITIVE CONCEPTION OF PSYCHOLOGY AND THE FORM
OF THE CRITICAL PHILOSOPHY 36–87
Further difficulties in Kant's psychology, 36. Empirical *vs.*
rational psychology, 38. Empirical psychology *vs.* anthropology, 43. Psychology and scientific method, 47. Kant's
negation of scientific psychology, 49. Its influence in the
critical philosophy, 52. Mathematics in psychology, 54.
Physiology and psychology, 56. Their relation to theory of
knowledge, 58. The conscious and unconscious, 59. The
doctrine of faculties, 62. History of Kant's division of the
faculties, 63. Kant's meaning of the faculties and their interrelation, 67. Influence of the faculty doctrine upon the form
of the critical philosophy, 71. The true value of the so-called
faculties, 75. Kant's emphasis of the feelings, 78. His defective theory as to the relation of the three faculties, 79.
Kant's *principium divisionis* found in psychology alone, 85.

vii

CHAPTER IV.

EMPIRICAL PSYCHOLOGY AND THE CONTENT OF THE CRITICAL
PHILOSOPHY 88–134
The relation of form and content, 88. Kant's idealism, 91.
The nature of sense-perception, 94. Kant's views as to the
nature of sensation, its qualities, and classes, 95. Perception
of space, 98. Sensation, perception and knowledge, 99. Sensibility and understanding, 110. Imagination in the critical
philosophy, 114. Memory, *ditto*, 117. Understanding, *ditto*,
120. The 'oberen Erkenntnissvermögen' and their scientific
import, 122. Reason and reasoning, 124. The psychological
certification of knowledge, 129. The psychological character
of Kantian skepticism, 133.

CHAPTER V.

RATIONAL PSYCHOLOGY IN THE CRITICAL PHILOSOPHY........ 135–208
Relation of rational psychology to the critical system, 135.
Analysis of the four Paralogisms, 140. The source of the
rational psychology which Kant criticised, 147. A criticism
of Kant's criticism, 149. The value of rational psychology
for critical philosophy, 153. Kant's doctrine of the *ego*, 160.
The ideality of time, 162. External and internal sense and
apperception, 164. Kant's unpsychological theory of a fourfold *ego*, 167. Kant's defective conception of judgment, 179.
Epistemological bearings of psychology, 183. Philosophy of
mind, 186. Reality of mind, and views of Lotze, 188. Unity
of mind, 195. The psycho-physical relation, 196. Diagrams
of the faculties, 206.

CHAPTER I.

INTRODUCTORY: THE IDEA OF PROPÆDEUTICITY,
AND KANT'S PSYCHOLOGICAL PROBLEM.

Nature rushes onward to intricacy, while reason pushes backward for simplicity. Life and its complexity surround us, but we satisfy ourselves only in constant reductions. All history, whether manifold in being or thinking, is one grand comment on these antithetic endeavors of mind and reality. The infinitude of numerical quantities and spatial forms are the rational multiplex of primal digits, points and lines, and a minimum of equalities. The surging spectacle of a mechanical universe is simplified in the physicist's quanta of force and mass. The discommoding dust and the beautiful crystal, the blooming plant and the psychosating cell are phantasmagoria coming from nature's adjustment of elemental atoms in their infinite valencies. Protoplasmic specks are the last insight into that power which differentiates into the moving, seething masses where nature crowns herself with the phenomena of life. That evanescent and never-to-be-recovered sensational bit given to a unifying *actus* is the primordial fact at the core of this incomparable complex that we ourselves are. What atoms are to chemical nature, and cells to life, such is the valency of feeling in the last work of all life and being.

But reason itself is an item occurring in nature's inventory. It too is a complexity. Its characteristic search for a unitary somewhat comparable with the data of any phenomenal group has come out of manifold experiences. Intellect, in the beginning, does not believe in the reality of whatsoever it may endeavor to simplify. Only as it has struggled over frequent frustrations in infantile attempts to relate things in a truth-expressing manner does it come to the attainment of 'scientific' knowledge. While all history reveals the great forth-putting that nature is, and the essence of reason as persevering with the complication of all reality, it contains no less the fact that reason becomes reason only as it is natural, an evoluting of that unique synthesis of adjusting an explanation to a phenomenon. The separation of any sense-element in a childish perception is logically at one with that act which posits great, yet determinable stellar orbits, or finds a supreme reality implicated in a most obscure sand in the desert. But the mind that knows the *rationale* of experience is as psychologically and really unlike the transitory psychosis that pathetically calls for infantile sustenance, as being is unlike knowledge. The difference between the Newton telling us of great truths and the Newton prattling his gleeful tale, is obviously the difference of time and growth which all education is. But reason in its becoming feeds on the pabulum of knowledge. Instruction is the empiristic term admirably expressing the relations in question; so that, however the evolving of the complexity of being, nature, or ultimate reality, may be expressed, the development of reason from the primal discrimination of the babe to the analysis and synthesis of him who contends with the enigmatic, can be formulated only in terms of the knowledge that is its product.

The unfolding of reason, as indicated in this difference, is explicable in the biological principle of growth. It is merely the way the organism is helped to its full development. But, to be of any service, the principle must be rendered into terms comparable with the nature of the object. It is thus that we get 'the morphology of knowledge' as an expression indicating what happens to reason when it is considered as subject to the process of all nature. This phrase, however, is highly complex and becomes intelligible in an analysis relating it to a variety of elementary views which may be taken of that knowledge.

Probably three points exhaust the features characterizing reason set in the flow of nature, wherein it is finally brought to an attainment of its right as searching for causes or reducing to simplifications. *Psychologically*, everything depends upon the degree of maturity which reason has attained at any one time. It has no right to abide the judgments of youth. The philosophy of the world's childhood is swept away by the developed reflections of its manhood. The mind of the boy does not operate with the surety that may characterize it when all sides of his being are stored with experiential pabulum. Everything that makes for attainments depends upon the comparative age. *Logically*, (and this is the objective aspect, as it were, of that which is given subjective recognition in the psychological consideration) the full and complete activity of reason is conditioned by the concatenation of knowledges. No 'royal pretender' can here usurp the rational throne. There obtains such a descent in its activities that reason goes against itself in attempting to make a leap for which it is not properly prepared. To be warrantable, any act of relating demands a certain amount and quality of known facts. Physics presupposes its mathematics, biology its chemistry, physiology its anatomy. This logical feature is just that great law that is valid in all developments where knowledge is at stake, viz. : to pass from the known to the unknown. The every-day questions inquiring as to what must be in hand before acts can be performed, or, as to what and how much knowledge is presupposed by any subject that is made an ideal for future acquisition, merely express obeisance to this necessity of all mental life.

But these two facts remain isolated, except they be united in a third. That the activity of the subject is conditioned upon his own ripeness as well as upon the logical sequence of the object-matter is meaningless without a teleological fusion. It is *pedagogically* that the development of reason, as it hurries on to the time when it shall seek the elementary, has a unified significance. Agreeing that the biological principle is expressive of the way reason comes to itself, we at once meet the profound relation wrapped up in the term 'method.' This is the logic of education and metaphysic of pedagogy. Method is always the arrangement of thought with reference to some end. But this has meaning and can be set into reality only as it is an experiential expression of the principle of becoming, at the basis of which lie two conditioning facts. Only as the fact of change is characteristic of reality can we orientate ourselves with reference to an ideal attainment, whether intellectual, ethical or aesthetical. Were this a static universe, method in any form whatsoever could never have come, even as an idle dream. Were it also a chaotic universe the facts in question would have no *a priori* possibility. So far as law is not a mere fiction, so far can we, as rational beings, institute a proceeding. Without the fact of uniformity we can have no assurance of what would follow upon our endeavors. This thing of certainty, however, is the great point in all method. Orderliness throughout changing relations, but subject to progressive discovery, is the great presupposition here. Changing causality, then, reducible to formulæ, is a term of reality that gives deeper meaning to the common phrases, growth of mind and development of reason.

But it appears that the foregoing analysis has arrived at the idea of propædeuticity. It is properly a pedagogical conception, and the very etymology of the term might have suggested the same treatment. We, too, are philologically wise in having received into our language, from the ancient Greeks, the essential word of that side of human knowledge and endeavor which had its genuine rise among them. Προ-παιδευειν is its original, and means to give instruction beforehand with reference to what may follow. It is a dealing with knowledge having reference to some rather ultimate form of the same. As soon as there is a dim awareness of the fact of mental development, of a correlation between bodies of knowledge that may have a close affiliation with the apprehending mind, then is there possible the rise of the idea that certain knowledge is a fit, natural and necessary introduction to what may follow. The notion that a certain procedure is necessary in the discovery of truth, and that instruction in that truth follows a method comparable with the mode of discovery, is true logic, real psychology and genuine pedagogy.

The idea of propædeuticity has been traced in the foregoing manner that it may be turned to account in estimating the relation of psychology to philosophy. We affirm that psychology is the true propædeutic to philosophy, and that in this instance there occurs the highest and ultimate application of this pedagogical conception. By psychology, one can mean only that body of scientific truths expressing the phenomenal relations of the individual human consciousness as attained by all those methods of research applicable to such phenomena. By philosophy, one may understand that sum of the attainments of reflective analysis and synthesis, pertaining to reality, however expressible, as it sweeps over 'the facts of life.' The one is rational and feels a satisfaction when it has accounted for all that is contained in experience; the other employs the scientific mind and fairly completes its task when an explanatory adjustment has been made between known facts and any group of obscure psychical phenomena. Just as all knowledge is variously yet closely related, so is all knowledge reciprocally helpful. But between these two endeavors there obtains this propædeutical relation that has not its like in any other phase of human activity. For it is intimately related to the conceptions of nature and reason that have preceded. Nature is the one great enigma upon which philosophy feeds. Its life is enriched in proportion as the former is revealed in a progressive complexity. But the attainments of philosophical inquiry as to the constituents, or 'nature' of nature, are merely the utterances of reason in its advancing efforts to reduce that complexity to the elementary in terms of the real. Herein appears the psychological proximity of the particular science to the rational discipline. The chief method of psychology is the analysis carried on by a developed consciousness, while the one mode of resolving philosophical problems is reflective analysis. Yardsticks and measures are of no aid in either. But the analysis of the latter only comes out of the former. One reasons as to reality when he has first come to a recognition of self and to that belief which has won its way through the strata of adolescent doubt. The proceedings in the two instances are so closely related that the one easily shades into the other. It is this stage in the development of reason that has psychological pertinence to both endeavors.

Though it is the same reason that develops the science and puts forth a philosophy, it approaches the problems of nature in a somewhat characteristically different manner. The ends to be attained in the respective instances are different: the one is individual, phenomenal; the other is universal, noumenal; the one correlates appearances; the other posits a reality. But in their content the two products stand logically related. This is the vital point in the propædeuticity of psychology. Its considerations lead to and shape the solutions of reason. Indeed, there is no philosophical problem that does not take its rise in the science of mind. It is not that we would have a philosophy 'of consciousness' from the start; but no inquiry, as to what reality is, can advance a little way without encountering on every hand the question of what a thing is as it appears to us men. The orientation about the self is the unique feature common to psychology in its latter stages and philosophy in its initiation. When we have analyzed mere processes we naturally press on to ultimate inquiry. It is well-nigh impossible to refrain from raising these problems. Such are 'content-wise' considerations which indicate the logical relation between psychology and philosophy as is expressed in the introductory character of the former. What are the various phases of this relation may appear to some extent throughout the ensuing study.

Just as matter and form never have meaning in separation, so the logical and psychological aspects of the dependence of ultimate inquiries, and their solution of one's knowledge of self, are fruitless for a systematic endeavor. They are significant when solidified and intermingled in the pedagogical relation of propædeuticity. Here the philosophical value of psychology becomes *real.* Whether in the original discovery of metaphysical truths, or in their impartation to a developing mind, the essential relation is not changed. It comprehends all the anterior relations in which the pursuit of philosophy stands, thus deepening the conviction that we place methodical certainty on the one basis possible for us men as we endeavor to make intelligible the intricacy of nature.

The service of psychology for philosophy is not exhausted in the foregoing relations. This handmaid of reason not only makes an open way and conducts her into her domain, but also can turn guard and repel all civil assault. Against any freak of scepticism or absolutism true philosophy has a safeguard. This protective service of psychology is a truth than which none other is more plainly revealed in the ebb and flow of human confidence. To the far-seeing observer the path of philosophy is winding and ledgy. Now it has lain in broad, unbounded fields where the eye had no Polaris, and eager feet would lose their way only to wander in cusps. Again it has led to ledgy heights where reason's vaunting self would be dangerously near to a precipitating doom. Now it is a path of onward movement and unfaltering step; then a time of rest in distrust. Now a dubious reconnaissance is the safeguard to a conquering attack on the real, or the preliminary of a withdrawal from the field of the unknown. As reason casts a furtive glance at her past, there echoes to the historic ear her repentant loreley :

> Prone to wander, oh, I feel it,
> Prone to leave the truth I seek.

The optimistic faith is, indeed, not left to meagre sustenance. As often as there was a wandering, there came a quickened recognition of it. The individual subjectivism of the Greek Sophists repelled the Socratic ' demon' to call men to knowledge and moral insight. Their later frivolity died away in the serious calm of Platonism, revealing the purity and reality of archetypal ideas, whose universality is cognitive, and whose purity is expressive of the perfect, ethical good. The Pyrrhonean sceptic selfishness that would secure peace of mind in withholding judgment and esteeming everything indifferent, was avenged in the Plotinean Platonism which brought back the ideal ' nous' and its supportive relation to the sensible soul who has been estranged from this ῎εν χαι αγαθόν. Cartesian doubt is summarily displaced by Cartesian dogmatism. Hume's halting (a scepticism without a motive) is unpegged in the painstaking Scottish realism and the long withheld Critical philosophy. Kant endeavored to sweep away his own limitations of the sensible by the reëstablishment of the practically super-sensible, and was seconded by the unique faith of Jacobi, the realism of Herbart, and the conservatism of Lotzean idealism.

No less is the truth instanced in reason's reaction against dogmatism and absolutism. It has found virtue in the demand of Criticism that dogmatism shall first render an account of man and his powers to know and act.   Her abhorrence of absolutism still lingers in our ears.   Is it not Lotze and Schopenhauer who recall Hegelianism to a more empiric study of man?   Thus, speculation may be cautious in its doubt, or wild with its un-limited possibility of converting thought into reality.   From either snare, protection lies in a rational self-knowledge.   In every instance where reason has gone astray she has harked back to truth with a psychologic call.   When her 'proneness' has become pathological, a draft for the *materia medica* is made upon her own realm of consciousness.   Now it is with an in-stinctive feeling for the right composition; then, a purposive, long-wrought-out formula whose administration is designed to be effective.   Psychology, as it were, brings man back to his senses.   The Critical philosophy is a supreme instance of this unique, protective service of the analysis of consciousness for that later rational synthesis which is the sole and distinctive right of philosophy.

Man's rationality and the unity of metaphysics are the absorbing themes of philosophical discipline.   These are the keystones let into the arch resting on the butments of Socratic wisdom and Hegelian dialectic.   The history of reflective thought is rather a chronology of the sublimation of these truths into rational consciousness than a record of developments in the way of accretions to the various departments forming philo-sophical discipline.   'Eras' and 'epochs' in philosophy thus become the times when the strength of some minds was focused upon particular speculative problems.   The accuracy herein attained and the limits set to the problems give characteristics to the ramifying developments within the respective periods.

Ancient philosophy, true to the psychologic age of its re-flective mind, spent its force upon the *cosmos*.   Its 'world wisdom' comprised a theoretic knowledge of that which was posited as 'external.'   Nature, as the subject-matter of 'physics,' and man, whose objectivity manifesting itself in the state, as the subject-matter of 'politics,' were the great facts of experience which appealed to the speculative mind in antiquity.   Those principles were sought which were thought adequate to rationally account for that which was *presented* in man's experience. Unable to overcome that ' warmth of feeling' which attaches itself to any stream of consciousness, early philosophy is marked by its emphasis of the real, of that which is ' here and now.'

The departure from 'the here to the h ereafter,' the rejection of the natural and the acceptance of the supernatural, marks the second great period in the unfolding of speculative reason. Epicurean and Stoic dogmatism found reactions in 'the Pyrrhonic form of doubt' and the milder scepticism of the so-called Middle Academy. A second reaction of the historic mind restored reason's self-confidence. The influx of Jewish and Oriental ideas, precipitating attempts to blend Judaism with Hellenism, resulted in that mystical tendency of the Theosophists prior to the rise of Christianity, and in the development of Gnosticism succeeding the establishment of Apostolic churches. After running the gauntlet of revived Platonism and 'orientalized Pythagorism,' Christianized reason emerges under the wavering form of scholasticism—now as an attempt to fuse religion and reason, then as an effort of the one or the other to maintain a speculative superiority. In spite of the rapidly moving lights and shades of these arid attempts to unite philosophy and theology, there is, indeed, a common object found as the subject-matter of the thinking of this period. Religion, theology and ethics were searched by ' unpractical students' in order to arrive at a systematic, formal knowledge of *God*. In marked contrast with antiquity, the historic mind in mediæval philosophy filled its repository of ' theological wisdom' by brooding over the ideal.

Thus, philosophy in its two main branches—the real, as comprehended under the speculative use of reason, or the philosophy of nature, and the ideal, as that which relates to what ought to be, or the metaphysic of morals—had repeated the process of development, maturity and decay. By means of a dialectic not unknown in the empiric employment of reason, and still more valid in the objective progress of mind, there is to be recorded of the latter an attempted synthesis of the content of the earlier periods.

Modern philosophy contents itself with the 'knowledge of man.' It finds him a *microcosmus* and a *microtheos*. Noëtics and metaphysic, ethics and æsthetics, all center in man as the content of philosophic pursuit. From this mosaic of the real and the ideal, reason, under the garb of religion, reaches up to the Ideal-real—the supreme object of all rational discipline. The scholastic spell was broken by the philosophic doubt and 'cogito' of Descartes. From him issued those myriad insular and continental streams of speculation that eddy about the *ego*. But the keynote of our era was not sounded until, from an outpost of Germanic civilization, there was raised the cry: '*Was ist der Mensch?*' This question not only 'unites in a systematic whole' the Critical philosophy itself, but also serves to link the speculative past with its present. "For a survey of all philosophical investigations," says Lotze, "one must classify the questions to which one seeks answer." The systematic answers given by Kant to his supreme question, justify Rosenkranz in likening the Criticism of Reason to the head of Janus in the temple of philosophy—fusing all preceding truth in its own conquests, and signaling the points of attack in all future attempts. They comprehend critical investigations, not only of cosmology, the essence of ancient philosophy, and of theology, the essence of mediæval philosophy, but, also, of psychology, which forms the essence of modern philosophy. Thus, while man's rationality finds its highest expression in the latter, the unity of metaphysic is discernible in the two former. How these stand related in that ultimate unity, which philosophy claims to be real, is only to be discovered in the execution of that discipline itself. In this historic attestation to the unity of reason, it has been seen very briefly how reason must take up the same problems in its progressive endeavors.

The development of philosophic pursuit in the individual, as well as the progress of speculation itself, is conditioned upon the multiplicity of problems raised, and the clearness with which they are defined. Doubt in the individual is convertible with a recognition of problems. Dogmatism marks no progress. It only treasures past attainments. When the spirit is grieved with misgivings, and turns with critical boldness upon threatened tenets, then becomes possible that which makes for speculative advance. It is his hearty recognition of great problems that links Kant with the past, as, on the other hand, it is the profound thoroughness of his solutions that binds us to him.

'What is man?' is the comprehensive inquiry to which the Critical philosophy was wrought out as an answer.[1] To have set a greater goal was impossible. This question draws all others to it. Their answers contribute to and are lost in the ultimate reply permitted to this most profound problem. "The whole interest of my reason," says Kant, "whether speculative or practical, is concentrated in the three following questions: 1. What can I know? 2. What should I do? 3. What may I hope?" These three express the last reduction to which the field of philosophy is possible.

The value and completeness of this classification of the questions which confront reason is seen both from what should be the guiding impulse to speculation and from the basis and content of the discipline itself. Speculation that is wild by reason of a conspicuous absence of any goal to be reached rightly loses its title as a rational endeavor. As Lotze approves, a recognition of ends "keeps a firm and vivid recollection of the needs for the satisfaction of which all speculation is undertaken." Speculation, too, that pushes forward to its goal in utter disregard of the life of man must likewise be banished from among those efforts which undertake to satisfy the philosophic instinct. Philosophy, in its objective content, as it were, possesses naught else than 'the facts of life.' It must not only remain in touch with practical, every-day experience as found in the life of conduct and feeling, but it must also go down into the haunts where certified knowledge of fact and formulæ are kept. This two-fold appeal to the nature and con-

[1]That this is the *real* question uppermost in Kant's mind, is to be inferred from the relative position given to the concepts of God and Immortality, and the function they serve as speculatively practical tenets. Though he insists (*Werke* V. 487) that God, Freedom and Immortality are the real problem of metaphysics, yet the position left to God—to realize in a mechanical manner the *Summum Bonum* dictated by the 'Categorical Imperative,' and how perfunctorily a future state is to admit of this realization, throw a dark shadow over Kant's assertion.

tent of speculation yields to Kant a warrant for claiming that the chief duty of philosophy is to answer man's self-centered question : what am I?

In this glance at the historical setting of Kant as a philosopher, there appeared a statement of the comprehensive problem to whose solution he turned the patient reflections of a clear intellect.   First and foremost, his answers are philosophical.   He labored to unearth the structure of knowledge in its dealings with reality.   The problem thus became, how are possible certain judgments, given in experience, yet, utterly unlike the ordinary associations of concepts which merely explicate what is acquired in various empirical ways?   "How are synthetic judgments *a priori* possible" as to the knowledge of things and selves, as to the reality of ethical relations, and as expressing the objectivity of unique feelings in which we lose ourselves in contemplating the beautiful and sublime?   The resolution of these enigmas was Criticism's gift to the world.   But, back of its solutions, developing in its progress, and consciously explicated at its close, lies another problem implicated in the inquiry, 'What is man?'   Critical philosophy is metaphysical in a rigid sense, but does not cut loose from 'our' reason, 'human' reason.   In that it *does* build upon experience to satisfy its problems, there appears its psychological problem, viz., so to make an empirical analysis of man as shall best harmonize with the explication of metaphysical needs.   'What is man?' centers the empirical and rational sides of Criticism, which fuse in such a way as to shape and color the latter.   To what extent these influences interact and how far the conclusions of Criticism may be justifiable, it is the chief purpose of the ensuing study to estimate, leaving the development of points to the progress of the discussion.

CHAPTER II.

Psychology in Kant's Conception of 'Wissenschaftliche Encyclopädie.'

Whatever may be said for the exhaustiveness of any search for first principles, it cannot be maintained that the field of empirical knowledge is closed. Nowadays, it is the fashion to cast obloquy on 'the old, traditional psychology.' It knew not the rights of science, nor grasped the value of methods. It was filled, we are constantly reminded, with 'crude observations,' and these were thrown into severely 'speculative moulds.' It is not designed to challenge any seeming affront to the historic foundations of psychology as it is now rapidly striding to the rank of a 'natural science.' Her devotees may wrangle over her methods and assumptions. The present task is to inquire how far this charge is true against Kant. If he be guilty of purloining the heritage and rightful power of psychology, then it must be determined how far and in what particular points. The unity and extensity of modern 'scientific' knowledge of the mind warrants the assurance that the entirety of any historic doctrine can best be traced by this comparative vision. Herein lies the value of a detailed study of Kant's psychology. Taking as given and allowed much that can be proved only by special investigation in the respective departments of psychology, we merely propose in general to submit Kant's views to the test of psychology as it is now generally agreed upon, inquiring at the chief points their relation to philosophy and the sciences involved. It is not intended that on this basis there shall be a reconstruction of the Critical philosophy. It is only hoped that there will be laid an admitted ground from which some of the chief defects in Kant's analysis and synthesis may be appreciated.

The students of Kantian psychology encounter serious difficulties. Some are individual, biographic; others are impediments characteristic of his age. As perhaps with no other thinker, his periods of development and the various phases of his maturity have introduced variations into his products, spread consternation among his critics, and given rise to antithetic extensions of his influence. Though there were ends reached, the patient tracing of the windings through the 'scientific,' 'speculative,' and 'practical' periods begets a useless weariness.[1] Neither at all times is there a fixity of tenets. The asseverations of one epoch are swept away by the long-nursed reflections of a succeeding period. The dogmatism of youth was perfected in the criticism of manhood, and revealed in the ethical exotericism of old age. Yet, with all the multifarious content of his thinking, and the chameleonized forms it was led to assume, there runs through it all a common trait. The attitude to the problems is ever taken from one general point of view. The tenor, even, is quite always the same; the 'critical awakening' from dogmatism being no exception. Kant is *par excellence* the psychologic philosopher, and Criticism is imbued with the same spirit. It is such a fact that invites and encourages the study here undertaken, and counteracts the difficulties arising from the vagaries in the developing of Kant's own mind; while the variety of successive tenets only invokes a constant cautiousness.

There remains another source of perplexities more appalling. Kant wrote no distinct treatise on psychology, though he, more than any other philosopher of the eighteenth century, has profoundly influenced that science since his time. This lack of avowed psychological material is what we miss.[2] Yet, he often makes an introspective whisk and lands out some psychologic catch. Now he heaps weighty criticism against attempts to pry into the nature of the soul, or mitigates his speculative prowess by collecting anthropological observations, or turning out witty aphorisms. Empirical observation is at times held in distrust, and he despairs of any hope for a scientific knowledge of mind. But he does not remain true to his opinions of this science's

[1] Hastie, *Kant's Politics*, tr. p. X.
[2] *Cf.*, Drobisch, *Empirische Psychologie*, p. 309.

weakness. His psychology in many respects (and this is true of the initiation of all psychology) is only pious and witty reflections on his own life and mind.[1] He was faithful to the doctrine of subjectivity, but frequently pleads the atttainment of universality. Sully's observation with reference to Schopenhauer,[2] "that philosophers no less than other men, have their intellectual conceptions most powerfully influenced by the facts of their own personal experience," finds a truth in that element of suppressed melancholy in Kant's temperament which was so conducive to the introspection goaded on by incessant physical pain. Indeed, his psychologic spirit finds an autobiographic bit when he writes in the 'Anthropologie'[3] of the emotions of wonder and astonishment: "Ein Neuling in der Welt verwundert sich über alles." It is this factor of intellectual curiosity turned inward that is one of the sunken piers on which psychology rests; it too was a passion with Kant, expressing itself in the profound inquiries as to the possibility of *a priori* judgments, or in the passing empiric phenomenon of the 'Eigenlicht.'[4]

Kant, also, did not engender a closet psychology. He linked himself to his predecessors, and by academic means helped tide over this science's experience during his career, lecturing on psychology either from such handbooks as Baumgarten's 'Metaphysik' and Meier's 'Logik,' when empirical psychology was 'peculiarly the metaphysical yet experiential science of man,'[5] or on 'Anthropologie,' a mixture of studies on human nature. It was this pedagogic interest which laid the foundations for the literary forms into which he variously cast his opinions and reflections.

Of course, the chief writings to be considered as sources are those embodying the Critical philosophy. The three Critiques abound in psychological material, and particularly the first, which is preëminently psychologic in a non-Kantian sense.

[1] Stuckenberg, *Life of I. Kant*, pp. 106 ff., 219.
[2] *Pessimism*, p. 436.
[3] *Werke*, VII., 582.
[4] *Werke*, VII., 428.
[5] *Werke*, II., 316; Erdmann, *Reflexionen Kants zur Anthropologie*, Lpzg. 1882, p. 63.

Among the pre-critical writings there are principally the essays
'Beobachtung über das Gefühl des Schönen und Erhabenen
(1764), 'Träume eines Geistersehers erläutert durch Träume
der Metaphysik' (1766), 'Versuch über die Krankheiten des
Kopfes' (1764), and the two important Latin dissertations
(1756, 1770). The post-critical essays and treatises are such
as are explanatory of the critical views, or contain the empirical
tenets on which they rest, and frequently embody the materials
gathered during a life-time, but published by his academic
friends; such are the 'Beantwortung der Frage; was ist Auf-
klärung?' (1784), 'Muthmasslicher Anfang der Menschen-
geschichte' (1786), 'Ueber Philosophie überhaupt zur Einleitung in die Kritik der Urtheilskraft' (1794), 'Zu Sömmerring : über das Organ der Seele' (1796), the later ethical and
political treatises, 'Der Streit der Facultäten' (1798), the
'Anthropologie in pragmatischer Hinsicht' (1798), 'Logik'
(1800), 'Ueber Pädagogik' (1803), 'Die wirklichen Fortschritte, die Metaphysik seit Leibniz und Wolff's Zeiten in
Deutschland gemacht hat' (1804), and Poelitz's posthumous
'Vorlesungen über Metaphysik' (1821). His correspondence
is also invaluable in tracing the growth of certain psychological tenets.

In addition to the difficulties that may appear throughout the
study, it must be remembered once for all, that any attempt to
gather Kant's psychological views must beware of distorting
doctrines and their mutual consistency, rendered possible so
easily because of the various character of the sources. It will,
however, be found upon inquiry that there is presented a fair
unity of tenets, though one must ever regret that 'that great
observer of the pathology of the human soul,' as Herder called
him, did not take enough interest in empirical psychology so as
to articulate its ascertained truths into a science.

No inquiry can proceed a brief way without encountering
cross-purposes, unless there are at least provisional conceptions
which shall indicate the results desirable and provide limits to
the undertaking. "Definitions," says one, "are fatal; they
make good back-doors only." The mere playing with them is
a very hazardous manner of appreciating sciences and their in-

ter-connection. Nevertheless they are handy and bind down aimless feet. Indeed, definitions must be taken as the counters of students. Upon these they justly light as the linguistic necessities of developed rationality. Yet, the variations remain so constant, that what is lost in one point is gained in another. Thus, in a study of this kind the inquiry must be raised at the beginning : What is Kant's conception of psychology—its nature, aims and method? An answer cannot be given directly. It must be felt for, and in a round-about way. Psychology with Kant does not stand alone, but is severly linked to conceptions wider and architectonic. It requires a determination of his view of science and a presentation of philosophic system, in which will be found the position given to psychology by its separation from metaphysic and logic on the one hand, and from ethics and æsthetics on the other. This, however, yields only his *negative* conception of psychology.

Kant's opinion as to the nature of science is bound up with his speculative verdict as to the fate of knowledge, either experimental or systematized. His earliest and pre-critical expression[1] gives a broad extension to scientific knowledge, classifying it as either the work of the historic or the mathematical understanding. There appears, however, a clear-cut sentence as to the nature of science only when Criticism had completed its task and investigated the highest certainty as to knowledge itself. In the preface to the 'Metaphysische Anfangsgründe der Naturwissenschaft,'[2] he says : "Eigentliche Wissenschaft kann nur diejenige genannt werden, deren Gewissheit apodiktisch ist; Erkenntniss, die blos empirische Gewissheit enthalten kann, ist ein nur uneigentlich so genanntes Wissen. Dasjenige Ganze der Erkenntniss, was systematisch ist, kann schon darum Wissenschaft heissen, und, wenn die Verknüpfung der Erkenntniss in diesem System ein Zusammenhang von Gründen und Folgen ist, sogar rationale Wissenschaft. Wenn aber diese Gründe oder Principien in ihr, wie z. B. in der Chemie, doch zuletzt blos empirisch sind, und die Gesetze, aus denen die gegebenen Facta durch die Vernunft erklärt werden, blos

---

[1] *Werke*, II., 314; *cf.* VIII., 72.
[2] *Werke*, IV., 358.

Erfahrungsgesetze sind, so führen sie kein Bewusstsein ihrer Nothwendigkeit bei sich (sind nicht apodiktisch-gewiss), und alsdenn verdient das Ganze in strengem Sinne nicht den Namen einer Wissenschaft, und Chemie sollte daher eher systematische Kunst, als Wissenschaft heissen."

Certainty must characterize the knowledge that would aspire to a scientific claim. Experiment and observation can never be reduced to universality. The practical phases of ' natural philosophy' result in an *Unding*, rather than science.[1] The clear articulation of a body of truths, whether of *Körperlehre* or *Seelenlehre*,[2] can never come by way of testing and the defence of hypotheses.[3] Science, as such, demands ' einen reinen Theil' from which must spring its certainty. Only so far as science is applied mathematics can it be recognized. Quantitative estimations alone go for any worth. " Ich behaupte aber, dass in jeder besonderen Naturlehre nur so viel eigentliche Wissenschaft angetroffen werden könne, als darin Mathematik anzutreffen ist."[4] By this conception Kant held fast. Though it were hard to explain what should properly come under science,[5] or to demand that the nature of science requires the careful separation of the empirical from the rational part[6] and the determination of its method, which is something other than mere ' *Manier*,'[7] the former resting on certain principles that make the content of the *modus logicus*;[8] there is no departure from the demand that the *Wissenschaft* (that etymologically comes from *Wissen*[9]), and is to become *Wissen* in the thorough-going meaning of the term, must come to it by way of the *a priori* constitutiveness of the understanding that puts forth those bodies of knowledge. And in those sciences which are to contain nothing but the *a priori* there can be no ' Wissen' under the

[1] *Werke*, VI., 377.
[2] *Werke*, IV., 357.
[3] *Critique*, II., 659 ff.
[4] *Werke*, IV., 359–360.
[5] *Werke*, VIII., 22.
[6] *Werke*, IV., 236, 113–119.
[7] *Werke*, V., 157.
[8] *Werke*, V., 329.
[9] *Werke*, VIII., 72.

spurious form of 'Meinen.' "Denn es ist an sich ungereimt, *a priori* zu meinen."[1]

This opinion did not stand alone, but, as was said above, is closely connected with his speculative verdict on knowledge in which the conception of the *a priori* plays a great role.[2] Its function and the estimation of 'rational knowledge' articulate science and philosophical system with Kant, and furnish him with the clue to an encyclopædia of the sciences. The distinction, made in 1770, between the sensible and the intelligible worlds,[3] and the doctrine of noumenality, which Schopenhauer[4] justly applauds as Kant's greatest service, both have their basis in the discernment of the *a priori.* Phenomena and noumena are the objectification, as it were, of this difference between empirical and rational knowledges. The distinction also enters into the favorite tripartition of 'criticism,' 'doctrine' and 'science.'[5] 'Criticism' is the ferreting-out by an analysis of mind, of those concepts whose totality constitutes the circle of *a priori* knowledge.[6] When these concepts have been so far treated as to yield principles which are guiding in systematic knowledge, a body of truths is had which make up 'doctrine,' *e. g.*, such knowledge as it is possible to have of the æsthetic judgment. Wherever experience, or facts of nature, may be subsumed under the *a priori* certainty, which is possible only from the complete admixture of mathematics and a consequent reduction to measurement, then 'science' is possible. Such are the fruits ripened on the well-tilled distinction of the *a priori* and *a posteriori.* The pedagogically well-meant expressions, that reason was to be tested standing alone, "when all the material and assistance of experience is taken away, etc.,"[7] have always borne a mystifying

[1] *Werke*, VIII., 67.
[2] *Werke*, VII., p. 451, Sec. 6: In true science "bedarf es wissenschaftlicher Principien a priori;" in most knowledges "aber können es auch Erfahrungen, d. i. Urtheile sein, die durch Versuch und Erfolg continuirlich bewährt werden." *Cf.* VI., 121, note.
[3] *Cf.* Letter to Herz, *Werke*, VIII., 688, et al.
[4] *Sämmtliche Werke*, I., p. 534 f.
[5] *Werke*, VI., 400; v. Vaihinger, *Comm. zu Kants K . d. r. V., Stuttgart*, 1881, I., ii., pp. 534 f.
[6] *Cf. Werke*, VI., 43, 491 f, VIII., 32, 548 f.
[7] *Critique*, II., p. XXIV.

sense, and especially when the treatment of reason is to provide an '*a priori* possibility.'[1] But knowledge *a priori* and the cognitive satisfaction of reason are one and the same.[2] And rational knowledge is the mere knowledge of principles which results from the analysis of concepts,[3] not concepts that come by way of intuitional construction, but an analysis carried on by abstraction and reflection, and 'known immediately through self-observation.'[4]

Philosophy consists in the analytic treatment of reason, deducing the principles of science from those rational concepts which subsume themselves under that which is and that which ought to be. Thus understood, logic and metaphysic, ethic and æsthetic (so far as the latter can lay any claim to a unifying relation between the others) compose the philosophical system. Nature, art and morals are the experimental products which rest on the submerged *a priori* principles of 'legality,' 'purposiveness,' and a 'purposiveness that is at once a law or obligation,' respectively, and whose sources are the rational faculties.[5] It is not in place to justify, nor in our present disposition to quarrel with this conception of philosophy and the perfect articulation of all rational knowledge into such a system where " every science must have its place in the encyclopædia of sciences."[6] The former is beyond our limits, and the latter would involve an analysis which can be pointed out only later. What remains in question, though it does stand in such intimate relation to the speculative whole, is the conception of science, as such, and from this point to estimate Kant's view of psychology.

Whatever may be the intrinsic warrant to be found in the nature of science by which Kant remanded it to the severe treatment which it must receive at the hands of philosophy, we fancy that much that enters into his opinions is a splash from

[1] *Critique*, I., 398 ff.

[2] "Vernunfterkenntniss und Erkenntniss *a priori* ist einerlei." *Werke*, V., 12; *cf.*, VIII., 23.

[3] *Critique*, II., 611.

[4] Meyer, *Kant's Psychologie*, Berlin, 1870, p. 129.

[5] *Werke*, VI., 399 ff., V., 204.

[6] *Werke*, V., 429; *cf.*, VIII., 14, 43f, 49.

his age. It must be stoutly maintained that science cannot
render an account of itself when brought before reason's legitimate question as to the warrant of scientific procedure and the
nature of that proportion of ultimateness in answering problems
which such solutions may have. Science is not the last step in
rational inquiry, and only transcends its proper function when
it would have the inquirer be satisfied with its discernments.
The 'nature' of things and events is omitted in the proper task
of noting their behavior and succession. And in so far as Kant
demands that science shall truly resolve the former questions,
he is in the face of what *has been* the essence of scientific
knowledge. On the other hand, he is perfectly defensible in
maintaining that scientific principles—those stepping-stones of
empiric explanation—are of metaphysical origin, though exception may and must be taken to certain forms of his treatment of them.

It is at that point, however, where he demands certain
features of scientific knowledge, that a protest must be entered.
All science must be exact, mathematical. From this outlook
Kant's complaint against psychology, that it is not an exact
science, is logical. As long as science remains the mere application of number to causation, a science of consciousness is impossible. 'Retain causation in consciousness,' says Hodgson,[1] 'and you make psychology illusory (since causation by
consciousness is incalculable).' On the ground of his speculative doctrines Kant was justified in placing physics first in
preference to psychology; for 'the former,' as Meyer says,[2] 'requires the thoroughgoing application of the space and time
forms, the latter not,' it being subject to the intuitive form of
time only. These limitations, however, are undoubtedly mere
splashes from his contemporaries, and the spirit of his time is
guilty of recognizing only one form of scientific knowledge.
The rigid exclusion of all unmathematical formulæ is a petrified
pulse throbbed by the elation from the cosmological triumphs of
physics. The success of the mechanical sciences appealed to
Kant. His first view of metaphysics (1747) saw it ' nur an der

---

[1] *Philosophy of Reflexion*, London, 1878, II., 65.
[2] *Op. cit.*, 288; *cf.*, *Werke*, IV., 361.

Schwelle einer recht gründlichen Erkenntniss;'[1] and in 1764 he
attained the conviction that " die ächte Methode der Metaphysik
ist mit derjenigen im Grunde einerlei, die Newton in die Naturwissenschaft einführte und die daselbst von so nutzbaren
Folgen war." In 1787, with the second edition of the *Critique*[2]
it appeared in rational consciousness that Criticism was the
adoption of this method.[3]

Kant is culpable only in so far as he accredited the opinion
of the day, and linked with it his insight into the nature of
science, and circumscribed it far within the limits to which this
form of knowledge has been extended by the intervening century's developments. Kant's limitation holds good of only one
form of science (and indeed a small portion, the chief of which
is abstract mechanics). "If science," says Bosanquet,[4] "meant
exclusively the sciences which grow out of the one-sided forms
of measurement, then we should rightly deny that there is a
science of history, and, for the same reasons, that there is a
science of art, of political form, or of religion." However priceless may be the rigid formulæ to which ' partially unified knowledge' aspires, it must remain true that science seeks a generalized expression of the facts " of the world as our human modes
of consciousness reveal it to us; a knowledge of the laws of objective existence as that existence appears to man......ex-
pressed in general terms."[5] Demonstrativeness is a mark of a
portion of such knowledge *only in so far as* the realities considered find themselves immersed in those forms which are susceptible of quantitative treatment. Science lurches a metaphysical
right when it advances the Pythagorean claim that in phenomena
reside the principles of number, and denies the ' scientific' reality
of such groups of facts as are not reducible to those principles.
"It is the systematizing of experience......by explaining
the different groups of phenomena through the discovery and
the verification of the existing uniform relations."[6] Science, as

[1] *Werke*, I., 29.
[2] *Preface*, I., 370 f.
[3] *Cf. Werke*, Dieterich, *Kant und Newton* Tübingen, 1876, pp. 2, 72 ff., et
al; cf., *Werke*, II., 288, 294 f.
[4] *Logic*, Oxford, 1884, I., 277.
[5] Hodgson, *Phil. of Reflexion*, I., 80.
[6] Ladd, *Introduction to Philosophy*, New York, 1890, p. 66.

such, is to be satisfied when the heterogeneity of isolated phenomena has been converted into the homogeneity of a law which
expresses the uniformity of their behavior.

Such a conception, however, did not prevail with Kant; and
psychology, far from being a science, was given only a *negative* significance in the philosophical system. As 'Seelenlehre,'
it fell within the precincts of metaphysics, where the course of
Criticism brought it under the ostracizing ban, expelling it from
any legitimacy as an object for human research.[1]

The attainment of Kant's conception of psychology requires
a further elimination. The admitted sciences, logic, metaphysic, ethic (and æsthetic) were so closely articulated under
the idea that 'alle Erkenntnisse stehen unter einander in einer
gewissen natürlichen Verknüpfung,'[2] and so firmly bound with
the ligaments of philosophic architectonic,[3] that they need dis-
secting and an estimation of his separation of psychology from
these three respectively.[4]

With the growth of Kant's insight, there appears an increasing extension of the domain of metaphysics, while there remains a tolerably constant element as to what constitutes the
particular task before it. In ·1764[5] 'die Metaphysik ist nichts
Anderes, als eine Philosophie über die ersten Gründe unserer
Erkenntniss.' A more specific determination that 'die Metaphysik ist eine Wissenschaft von den Grenzen der menschlichen
Vernunft'[6] appears in 1766. While in the important dissertation (1770) the chief element of *a priority,* or a purity from all
empirical dross, appears in the conception that 'Philosophia
autem prima continens principia usus intellectus puri est Meta-
physica.'[7] When Criticism had matured we find metaphysic to

---

[1]Notwithstanding, there is a sense in which 'die Psychologie......ist ein
Theil der philosophischen Wissenschaften, zu denen die Logik die Propädeutik
sein soll.' *Werke,* VIII., 18–19. What significance this has, will appear shortly
when the relation of psychology and logic are treated of. Philosophy, however,
merely remains as 'Metaphysik und Logik.' *Werke,* VII., 426; cf. IV., 236.

[2] *Werke,* VIII., 49.

[3] *Werke,* VII., 27, 49.

[4]Vide *Critique,* II., 714–730.

[5] *Werke,* II., 291.

[6] *Werke,* II., 375.

[7] *Werke,* II., 402.

be 'in reality nothing but an inventory of all our possessions acquired through pure reason systematically arranged.'[1] When this 'inventory' has been tabulated, "metaphysic, in the more limited sense of the word, consists of *transcendental philosophy* and the *physiology* of pure reason. The former treats only of understanding and reason themselves in a system of all concepts and principles which have reference to objects in general, without taking account of objects that *may be given:* the latter treats of nature, *i. e.*, the sum of given objects, and is therefore *physiology*, although *rationalis* only." The principles of metaphysic having been wrought out, there followed an application of them to objects, resulting in "the whole system of metaphysic: 1. Ontology, 2. Rational Physiology, 3. Rational Cosmology, 4. Rational Theology. The second part contains two divisions, viz., physica rationalis, and psychologia rationalis."[2] Additional passages, of which there are many,[3] merely explicate in more detail the already noted definition of metaphysic—chiefly in determining 'the objects' which properly belong to it, or in delimiting the field of metaphysical knowledge from that empiric sort which is gone over by psychology. The chief passage[4] which maintains the deviation of metaphysic from psychology, has special reference to the source of the data of which each science treats. Again, in the *Critique,*[5] in circumscribing the limits of metaphysic, the ejection of psychology is more cruel. "Empirical psychology must be entirely banished from metaphysic, and is excluded from it by its very idea." Yet it does not stand

---

[1] *Critique*, II., p. XXIX.

[2] *Critique*, II., 725-727.

[3] Briefly told, metaphysic investigates "die Möglichkeit der Erkenntniss *a priori.*" VIII., 454. *Cf.* Kant's own excellent commentary notes scattered throughout his essay entitled ' *The Progress of Metaphysic since Leibnitz and Wolff*,' VIII. *cf.* 520, 524, 576, etc.,

[4] "Was die Quellen einer metaphysischen Erkenntniss betrifft, so liegt es schon in ihrem Begriffe, dass sie nicht empirisch sein können. Die Principien derselben (wozu nicht blos ihre Grundsätze, sondern auch Grundbegriffe gehören), müssen also niemals aus der Erfahrung genommen sein; denn sie soll nicht physische, sondern metaphysische d. i. jenseit der Erfahrung liegende Erkenntniss sein. Also wird weder äussere Erfahrung, welche die Quelle der eigentlichen Physik, noch innere, welche die Grundlage der empirischen Psychologie ausmacht bei ihr zum Grunde liegen. Sie ist also Erkenntniss a priori, oder aus reinem Verstande und reiner Vernunft." IV., 13.

[5] II., 728.

an isolated body of 'artful' knowledge. "It has its place by the side of applied philosophy, to which pure philosophy supplies the principles *a priori;* thus being connected, but not to be confounded with it." The complete disregard for psychology, even as then developed, could not be more pathetic than when he suddenly reinstates it, doubtless influenced by an under current of cherishing memory of his earlier academic programmes.[1] "We shall probably have to allow to it (though as an episode only) a small corner in metaphysics, and this from economical motives, because as yet, it is not so rich as to constitute a study by itself, and yet too important to be banished entirely and to be settled in a place where it would find still less affinity in metaphysic." One can scarce suppress the regret that Kant so underestimated the value of psychology in the solution of metaphysical problems as he understood them. "Fortunately," says Hodgson,[2] "we possess a genuine *a posteriori* experimental psychology, a true science, which is daily yielding results of the highest value to many able and distinguished investigators. Fortunately for the world, and fortunately also for metaphysic, for metaphysic will derive from that psychology an independent support and verification." Yet that regard should be seasoned with a remembrance of the facts that those very problems, whose difficulties melt away as psychological theory advances, were first raised by Kant himself; and the meagreness of a true psychological doctrine was one source of his difficulties; and, on the other hand, that this 'genuine *a posteriori* psychology' as 'a true science' is to be regarded as an offspring of Criticism itself.[3] Still, after all is said, one feels disposed to muse, whether even an indefinite extension of 'modern experimental' psychology will ever clarify the speculative obscurity of those 'metaphysical' problems which take their rise in psychological phenomena. We wonder.

Kant is, also, as stringent in his demand that there shall be

---

[1] *Werke,* II., 316f; Erdmann, *Reflexionen Kant's zur Anthropologie,* p. 63; cf., Carl du Prel, I., *Kant's Vorlesungen über Psychologie,* Leipzig, 1889, pp. 5-6, 12-50.

[2] *Phil. of Reflexion,* I., 227.

[3] *Cf.,* A. Classen, *Ueber den Einfluss Kants auf die Theorie der Sinneswahrnehmung u. d. Sicherheit ihrer Ergebnisse,* Leipzig, 1886, *passim.*

a wide gap between logic and psychology. Indeed, on the former disparateness of psychologic 'opinion' and 'metaphysical' science rose the whole structure of Criticism itself; while the divergence of logic from psychology provided the foundations of that edifice on the former science. Having once determined what the 'sure' science of Criticism required, Kant looked about for some corner stone which should have the inherent potency of shaping the structure, and not merely the kindliness of a propædeutic. Accordingly, this was to be had in the logic of Aristotle which 'has not had to retrace a single step; so that to all appearance, it may be considered as completed and perfect.'[1] Logic, in itself, deals with the 'necessary rules' of the understanding. It answers the question, not how we *do* think, but how we *must* think.[2] General logic is either 'pure or applied,' 'analytic or dialectic,' 'elementary logic or an organon' of a particular science. In a passage recommending certain rules to logicians there is expressed the specific difference between logic and psychology: "1. As general logic it takes no account of the contents of the knowledge of the understanding nor of the difference of its objects. It treats of nothing but the mere form of thought. 2. As pure logic it has nothing to do with empiric principles and borrows nothing from psychology (as some have imagined, *i. e.*, of the influence of the senses, the play of imagination, the laws of memory, the force of habit, the inclinations, and, therefore, the sources of prejudice also), because psychology has no influence whatever on the canon of the understanding. It proceeds by way of demonstration and everything in it must be completely *a priori*."[3] The transformation of this general logic into absolute universality gave the 'Transcendental Logic' whose explication resulted in the medley of philosophical divisions which the *Critique of Pure Reason* really presents.

Thus it is seen that psychology has as little to do with the logical foundations of metaphysic as it has share in the latter science. And, while Kant is so careful in eliminating all psy-

---

[1] *Critique*, I., 364-5.
[2] *Werke*, VIII., 14, 16; II., 318; *Critique*, II., 46-54.
[3] *Critique*, II., 46-7.

chological elements in transcendental logic, he is also aware of a pretty close and definite relation between general logic and psychology.[1] No less is he lenient with the defects of psychology, and allows it a possible value; but he remains in agreement with former sublimations of logic as the true propædeutic to philosophical inquiry.

While the first duty is to explain our author and to note his own inherent consistency, criticism has no birthright in this preliminary work, much less to foist upon him the developed conceptions of a century later. Of all the empirical sciences—and logic must be classed as such—logic, no doubt, was the one having a most finished form in the time of Kant; and for his purposes he was right in drawing the fixed line we saw him to have marked between it and the vagarious psychology then in vogue. Notwithstanding, the impulse to turn aside and briefly consider the relation of these two sciences cannot be withstood.

Perhaps no more serious debate—though less verbose—has been carried on during the century than that which has engaged psychologists, logicians and epistemologists as to the functions of their respective disciplines. Logic, in the fixed Aristotelian form, has suffered considerable breaking up since Kant's time. A most recent " conception of logical science is that of an unprejudiced study of the forms of knowledge in their development, their inter-connection and their comparative value as embodiments of truth." Logic is no longer the abstract, rigid rules for the attainment of truth, but is 'the morphology of knowledge.'[2] Psychology does not only describe and classify the facts known by introspection, but it must now dip down into 'the genesis' of every conscious state. Noëtics, too, is out of harmony with the empirical sciences from which it gathers its data, unless it gives due cognizance to the forms of ideation, processes of cognition, etc.

All this change in viewing the various knowledges has come about by admitting into the sciences, and 'working it for all its

[1] *Reflexionen*, etc., p. 70, No. 24; *Werke*, VIII., 14; VIII., 18–19; cf., *Critique*, I., 365; VII., 445, note.
[2] Bosanquet, *Logic*, 1884, Title page, and Preface, p. V.

worth,' that very conception of which Kant was one of the
earliest defendants. He, himself, did a great service (though
disputed by the friends of Laplace) to modern cosmogony by
weaving in this conception in an explanation of the origin of
the stellar universe.[1] He also made a somewhat fanciful, yet
partially defensible psychological application of the same hypothesis in his 'Muthmasslicher Anfang der Menschenge-
schichte.'[2] It is the conception of evolution, whose 'doctrine
he enunciated, if he did not formulate.'[3] Standing as he does,
at the source of that doctrine, which has been at least one of
the greatest factors in recent scientific developments, it would
be an unpardonable injustice to turn a flaw-searching glance
even upon his tenets which were developed long after his success in applying the conception and formulating a satisfactory
doctrine.

As to the self-sufficiency of logic, or its subsumption under
psychology, there has been no little contention. There has
been reached, however, a tenable agreement as to the proper
relation which neither detracts from the historic virtue of the
Aristotelian form, nor shelters any disparagement to the worthy
attempt of this science to progressively establish an organon of
truth. In one sense, logic is a propædeutic to every science.
In their procedure, and as forth-puttings of the understanding,
they must go to logic for their vindication. Logic has confessedly to do with thinking; and wherever thoughts are arranged with reference to an ideal, as the attainment of particular or general truths, there is logic's proper domain, whatever
may be the content of that logic. In this (limited) meaning,
logic is propædeutic to psychology, but the exact character of
that propædeuticity must be established by aid from the psychologist. This, however, is only a formal relation, and is
unproductive of advance within logic itself or in any other department of knowledge. In so far as Kant's separation of logic

---

[1] *Cf., Werke,* II., 207-345, *Allgemeine Naturgeschichte und Theorie des Himmels,* 1755.

[2] *Werke,* IV., 313-329.

[3] *Cf., Werke,* IV., 188, V., 432 f, VI. 340; also Dieterich, *Kant u. Rousseau,* Tübingen, 1879, p. 26 f, 98; Bax, *Kant's Prolegomena,* etc., London, 1883, p. LXX; Bernard, *Kant's K. of Judgment,* London, 1892, p. XXVIII.

from psychology, with reference to philosophical system itself, is made from this formal standpoint, he is right. For, in this formal aspect, philosophy, from the days of Thales to the hour of 'the final philosophy,' could never even step within its rightful domain, if psychology were the introduction. But a defensible exception might be taken to Kant's emphasis of 'form' over 'matter.'

Fortunately, there remains another side to the relation between these two sciences. It has reference to the material with which they deal respectively. This, we take it, has been 'the bone of contention,' and, wherever philosophical investigations have grown up from the acceptance of one view or the other, they have invariably been diametrically influenced by that credence. With respect to its content logic is dependent upon psychology. We must, as it were, have gone through psychology, before logic has any right to appear. What is it to think? What are the processes involved in thinking? are the preliminary questions to which psychology must, in the first instance, return any answer. By a description of the variations which occur in the so-called thinking processes, logic receives a contribution which it treats in its unique manner. Logic is regulative of the forms of cognition of which it learns in psychology. In so far as logic is regulative, or " deals with the correct method of discovery and verification in the particular sciences, it is but an apartment of applied psychology."[1] And Kant is certainly in error in wielding his cleaver so forcefully on this relation as to deny[2] that even logic is responsible to psychology for its material. For the moment granting a special character to logic, one must say with Porter,[3] " it is through psychology that we reach the very sciences to which psychology is subject and amenable."

There yet remains a third possible relation, directly from which springs philosophical systems either as logical or psychological. In reality it is a fusion of the two already mentioned, with a metaphysical claim added. Logic often appears, *e. g.,*

[1]Ladd, *Introd. to Phil.*, p. 99.
[2]*Werke*, VIII.,14.
[3]*Human Intellect*, New York, 1884, p. 15.

in Kant, as treating of cognition in the forms of the universal, or, with metaphysical reference, as in Hegel. Now the special task of theory of knowledge is to investigate the problem of knowledge with respect to its reality. Logic has also reference to the validity of cognitions, *i.e.*, objectively, but only with reference to their formal truthfulness. Psychology deals with knowledge and the processes of cognition subjectively.[1] It is this relation of their respective intent, or purport of the treatment which each provides. But, as Baldwin says,[2] " as a formal skeleton or framework of thought, logic misses the meaning, the motive which is alone valuable to psychology." Here is Kant's error, since the content of Criticism or philosophy proper was received directly from logic.

So far the cognitive aspects of psychology and those sciences which confessedly deal with cognition and the real, have been considered as to the distinction Kant makes between them. Psychology also treats of impulses and actions—which Kant will soon be seen to have recognized—and there is a 'science' which treats of them in their 'objective' aspect; while psychologic emotions have their philosophic correlative in æsthetic. A brief mention of the disparity placed between these by Kant will permit us to come to a more definite and empiric conception of psychology and to the divisions he made.

In conformity with the effective idea of *a priority* as it was carried out in metaphysic, separating the pure from the empirical-psychological logic, Kant introduces the same division in the ethical sphere. The first passage showing the influence and possible outcome of Criticism expressed doubt as to a pure rational treatment of ethics. " Although the highest principles of morality and their fundamental concepts are *a priori* knowledge, they do not belong to transcendental philosophy, because the concepts of pleasure and pain, desire, inclination, free will, etc., which are all of empirical origin, must here be presupposed. . . . . Everything practical, so far as it contains motives, has reference to sentiments, and these belong to empirical sources of knowledge."[3] Only when the Critical doctrines confront the

[1]*Cf.*, Sully, *The Human Mind*, London, 1892, II., 350 f.
[2]*Handbook of Psychology*, New York, 1890, I., 271.
[3] *Critique*, II., 13.

persistent Antinomies does the difference between psychological and transcendental freedom emerge.[1] In the 'Grundlegung zur Metaphysik der Sitten' it appears as the special problem of ethics to establish this transcendental freedom as a function of rational beings.[2]

The practicality of such a reason must lie in the possibility of will being law-giving, unhampered by the empirical conditions and processes of motivation. Since 'empirische Principien taugen überall nicht dazu, um moralische Gesetze darauf zu gründen,'[3] it becomes needful to separate 'Ethik' like 'Logik,' 'wiewohl hier der empirische Theil besonders praktische Anthropologie, der rationale aber eigentlich Moral heissen könnte.'[4] Ethics, as such, deals with the concept of freedom *a priori*. "Vorausgesetzt, dass ein Wille frei sei; das Gesetz zu finden, welches ihn allein nothwendig zu bestimmen tauglich ist."[5] Such a principle Kant will find without any reference to empirical principles of morality.[6] It is in this will itself that the determinative quality of an end and action is to be found. On *a priori* grounds, in so far as it is seen that 'reine Vernunft ist für sich allein praktisch, und gibt (dem Menschen) ein allgemeines Gesetz, welches wir Sittengesetz nennen,' is it possible to derive the objectivity of the law. "Handle so, dass die Maxime deines Willens jederzeit zugleich als Princip einer allgemeinen Gesetzgebung gelten könne."[8]

With great passion Kant defends ethics from any admixture with psychology and appears not a little jealous of the self-sufficiency of *a priority*. Psychology, however, has ethical bearing and significance when the rule of pure ethics would be set in the causal, phenomenal life of man; that is, when the 'Moralische Anthropologie' would formulate 'Rechtslehre' and 'Tugendlehre.'[8]

[1] *Critique*, II., 388 f., 417 f.
[2] *Cf.*, *Werke*, IV., 237, 294 ff., V., 3 f.
[3] *Werke*, IV., 290.
[4] *Werke*, IV., 236 ff., *cf.* 275.
[5] *Werke*, V., 30, Sec. 6.
[6] *Cf.*, *Werke*, V., 43 f., 21 ff.
[7] *Werke*, V., 32, 33.
[8] *Werke*, V., 98-99; *Reflexionen, etc.*, p. 70, No. 24; *Cf.*, VII., 12-18; VI., 395, 'Die Sittenlehre verlangen von den Psychologen,' etc.,V., 9, foot-note, gives

Natural science, or 'Physik' in the broad sense as dealing with that which is, is science only so far as it is mathematical; from this it gains that certainty which is universal. Ethics, however, obviously admits of no mathematical treatment, though "man kann also einraumen, dass, wenn es für uns möglich wäre in eines Menschen Denkungsart, so wie sie sich durch innere so wohl, als äussere Handlungen zeigt, so tiefe Einsicht zu haben, dass jede auch die mindeste Triebfeder dazu uns bekannt würde, imgleichen alle auf diese wirkenden äusseren Veranlassungen, man eines Menschen Verhalten auf die Zukunft mit Gewissheit, so wie eine Mond-oder Sonnenfinsterniss anrechnen könnte."[1] Yet 'pure ethics' is claimed to have that same universality which belongs to the speculative half of metaphysics. The discovery of the moral law by the critical method finds attached to it the quality of being 'categorical,' which makes its unconditional universality. When this is found to be its *a priori* element, the 'science' ceases to be metaphysical and must drop to an empiristic level.

In this relation of psychology to ethics Kant has overlooked the true relation between them. The former must first bring to our cognizance the ethical elements of consciousness. The origin and individualistic nature of the conception of an ideal which is recognized as good and worthy, and desirable over and above that which is actually existent, needs first to be traced. The moralist vitiates his science when he erects an ideal in utter disregard of what are the common sentiments of mankind. Their approval of actions and ethical relations does not stand aloof from the character given it by its development. No ethics, not even Kant's, carries itself a little way without calling in psychological discussions on the possession and comparative quality of those sentiments and motivations which contribute in the realization of the ideally good. Ethics, on the other hand, becomes distinct only as it takes these unique sentiments and their inter-developments as revealed in psychology,

---

an excellent statement as to what psychological presuppositions enter into ethics, and their limits, viz., the definitions of the ethical faculties, the conceptions of good, pleasure, etc.

[1] *Werke*, V., 103 f.

and tries to determine the validity of their empirical claims. To find their 'objective import' is quite a different thing from noting their rise. What they mean, however, can never be told with contempt for what they are.[1] Even the 'Imperative' can be shown to be a generalization from ethical experiences in which many of the truly 'ethical data of feelings and judgments' are not taken account of.[2]

The sum of true philosophy, according to Kant, is found by adding 'metaphysic' and 'ethics.' When this point is reached the 'scientific' content of metaphysic is at an end. Yet the Critical philosophy comprehends a third critique. But æsthetics is not a 'science.' It is merely 'the criticism of taste.' The attempt to bring 'the critical judgment of the beautiful under rational principles and to raise its rules to the rank of a science is a vain endeavor.[3] For, 'weil alle Bestimmungen des Gefühls blos von subjectiven Bedeutung sind (and never can be elevated above their empirical origin), so kann es nicht eine Æsthetik des Gefühls als Wissenshaft geben, etwa wie es eine Æsthetik des Erkenntnissvermögens gibt.'[4] Judgment, or æsthetics, however, possesses a principle *a priori*, but it is only subjective.[5] Hence this lack of 'objectivity' proscribes its share in the transcendental philosophy. It is a subsumption of the particular under a universal, but a universal that has its essence in the feelings, either of the beautiful or the sublime. "So kann es mir erlaubt sein in der Bestimmung der Principien eines solchen Vermögens, dass keiner Doctrin, sondern blos einer Kritik fähig ist, etc."[6]

Æsthetics, nevertheless, has a unique relation in the system of the sciences of pure reason. Unity is the constant aim of philosophy, and the hierarchy of the 'sciences' is wont to express the relations the bodies of truth hold to the knowing mind. But understanding (cognition) stands separated from reason (morals). The phenomena of causality have been so dirempted

[1] *Cf.*, Sully, *op. cit.*, II., 362 f.
[2] *Cf.*, Ladd, *op. cit.*, p. 187; Meyer, *op. cit.*, pp. 188 ff.
[3] *Critique*, II., 19 note.
[4] *Werke*, VI., 387 f.
[5] *Cf.*, *Werke*, V., 192, 271, 417; VI., 380, 389 ff.
[6] *Werke*, VI., 400.

from the realm of freedom that there appears an impassable gulf between the sensible and the super-sensible. Criticism can only complete her task in endeavoring to span this chasm and make possible this realization of the ideal and intelligible in a real and sensible world. It searched for that 'Erkenntniss-vermögen' which shall unite all rational elements.[1] In the judgment is found the unique 'faculty' dealing with the subjective feelings of beauty. Though, as here intimated and as will appear fully in the sequel, æsthetic deals with a 'faculty' of empirical origin, Kant has yet vigorously maintained his attack upon all attempts to introduce empirical elements which would spoil the 'purity' of all the principles. This is likewise the case in the psychological basis of the æsthetical feelings.[2] Psychology can never assume the function of testing the *a priori* validity of whatever consciousness may apprehend as having reference to the beautiful. This requires special philosophical criticism.

The relation of philosophical æsthetics to psychology is about the same as that which obtains between it and ethics. In fact, the working out of any theory of the beautiful constantly runs back to the explanation offered for the rise of such phenomena. Psychology answers the very same questions which appear before an æsthetical theory, *viz.*, what are the distinguishing marks of æsthetic pleasure, etc.? The latter inquires as to the 'objective' nature of beauty: what is it really to be beautiful? But the only way of coming to the beautiful is through the æsthetic delight which we experience. Thus, no philosophical account of that which is pleasing to us, and has an agreeableness common to all, can be adequate without closely linking itself to the analysis and genetic account of those states of consciousness which are uniquely pleasurable. Kant is to

[1] "There must be a ground of the unity of the super-sensible which lies at the basis of nature, with that which the concept of freedom practically contains; and the concept of this ground, although it does not attain either theoretically or practically to a knowledge of the same, and hence has no particular realm, nevertheless makes possible the transition from the mode of thought according to the principles of the one to that according to the principles of the other." V., p. 182, Sec. ii. (Bernard's trans.)

[2] V., 274; *cf.* VI., 395.

be seconded in denying to any account of *how* I happen to have a 'beautiful' feeling or a cognition of the sublime, the character of philosophical explanation. But metaphysical æsthetics lies much nearer the despised psychology than he is wont to admit. Even his own æsthetical theory has adequacy only as he invokes the psychological data accessible in this department of mental science.

Thus, it is seen, by 'wissenschaftliche Encyclopädie,' Kant means the hierarchy of philosophical truths as they are contained in the three 'sciences' of metaphysics, ethics and æsthetics, and not such a coördination of the empirical sciences as has been attempted since his time. Metaphysics is to be the 'matron' who apportions to each of them the principle or principles which are to guide research in experience. In attaining positively the 'scientific' elements in philosophy according to Kant's views, we have also found that psychology is pushed out on every hand, virtually yielding the negative aspects of this forlorn body of truth. In its scientific limitations, both as respects its function as a propædeutic to philosophical system, and its inherent virtue claiming for it a distinct place within the system of the science of pure reason (though we shall find a certain aspect of psychology does come within the limits of rational science), or even a right entitling it to a sector within the encyclopædia of the sciences—*on these three points Kant was firm in the negative.* To what extent he was justifiable is appreciable in the light of the general handling which psychology received previous to him. Whether the relations he affirms between psychology and philosophy can remain unquestioned may be seen in the course of this study.

CHAPTER III.

KANT'S POSITIVE CONCEPTION OF PSYCHOLOGY AND THE FORM OF THE CRITICAL PHILOSOPHY.

It was comparatively easy in the previous chapter to arrive at Kant's notion of what constitutes 'science,' and to exhibit what he means to comprehend in philosophical system. In so doing there were half-furtive, half-heedless glances cast towards psychology, or again, a passionate vigilance in keeping off surprises from the begging empiricism which constantly appeared under the cognitive or affective aspects of psychological doctrines. Now careful inspection must be the prelude to an answer. Kant always entertained psychological interests, but he never developed them into a literary form. What he meant by a knowledge of the soul, what its scope and how far subject to methods, all this is to be gathered in the bits and crumbs scattered throughout the active half century after 1755. What that means has already been estimated. The nature of the data makes it necessary that, even in a search for positive results, there be a remanent examination of what has preceded.

The determination of Kant's idea of what constitutes psychological inquiry is further embarassed by a two-fold encounter. First, and what must ever be a source of apprehension as to the adequacy of these representations, and of misapprehension of the data to be gone over, modern psychology poses as a definite science. It assumes, as Sully says,[1] 'the modest title of Empirical Psychology,' because it draws inferences respecting the laws of the analyzed facts which fall within its domain, and properly separates from itself and hands over to another department of human activity the consideration of such ultimate problems as the nature of mind, its relation to the world of

[1] *Op. cit.*, I., pp. 3 f.

reality, etc. This is a demarcation that must be accredited to the developments in recent psychology (though it ought to be confessed that its devotees have not always endeavored to maintain it in their discussions). The difficulty here becomes a tendency to interchange Kant's and present-day notions of psychology.

The second difficulty grows out of the first, but has a larger historic background, *viz.*, the confusion of the two or three aspects of psychology. It was after the precedent set by Wolff, says Meyer,[1] that psychology considers two separate disciplines, *viz.*, empirical and rational. This division was accepted by Kant in the form into which it had been modified by the various phases of the Wolffian school. But Kant does not rest the distinction upon what we may call a 'scientific' basis. The division appears to take its rise in his general theory of knowledge.[2]

In general, rational psychology has to do with the 'logical *ego*, the subject of apperception,' and empirical psychology with the 'subject of perception, the psychological *ego*.'[3] There appears a further separation of empirical psychology from anthropology, the latter being 'eine Lehre von der Kenntniss des Menschen, systematisch,' etc.[4] A consideration of these interrelations and separations must first be made. We have, then, two couplings; 1, Empirical Psychology and Rational Psychology; 2, Empirical Psychology and Anthropology.[5]

---

[1] *Op. cit.*, p. 207.

[2] The constant epistemological character of Kant's opinions, as they here, *e. g.*, appear on the surface, is worthy of far more than a way-side note. For the most part Kant actually fails to maintain a distinction between the psychological and epistemological aspects of any question, a distinction which it is so difficult to keep above 'the threshold of consciousness.' Many scientific and philosophical considerations are valuable only in proportion as this vital relation is constantly in mind. The absence of it in Kant—and he is not blameworthy, for it is chiefly through him that there is the possibility of this relation being discerned—is one of the greatest, if not the greatest, inherent difficulty continually assailing the integrity of this study. So far as possible and necessary, it is aimed that the discussion shall be aware of this double-faced aspect of many of the salient points with which it must deal.

[3] *Werke*, VIII., 531.

[4] *Werke*, VII., 431.

[5] This latter separation has been overlooked by Meyer (*op cit.* 267) though he has, as we shall see, Kant's own expressions for their identification.

Coupling first is 'Empirical Psychology *vs.* Rational Psychology.' The first distinct mention Kant is found to make of psychology is rather an anomaly. It is quite a mixture of psychological and noëtic implications turned to a fanciful account. It has chiefly a biographic value in showing how completely, in one sense, Kant changed his opinions (though no rare thing for the immature man). Here is expressed not only the complete dependence of the soul on the body; but even the mental life is a forth-putting of the force in the universe. " Es ist aus den Gründen der Psychologie ausgemacht . . . . . dass, mit der Lebhaftigkeit des Leibes, ... die Hurtigkeit des Gedanken, die Klarheit des Vorstellung, die Lebhaftigkeit des Witzes und das Errinnerungsvermögen werden kraftlos und erkalten." The imperfections of man "findet sich die Ursache in der Grobheit der Materie, darin sein geister Theil versenkt ist, in der Unbiegsamkeit der Fasern, und der Trägheit und Unbeweglichkeit der Säfte welche dessen Regungen gehorchen sollen," and even " nach dem Verhältniss der Abstandes ihrer Wohnplatz von der Sonne." The value of rational consciousness as a means for the study of animate beings, especially man, and the genesis of that consciousness and its various contents, which is the chief problem of the psychologist, are estimated when he says : "Der Mensch ist dasjenige unter allen vernünftigen Wesen, welches wir am deutlichsten kennen. Des unendlichen Abstandes ungeachtet, welcher zwischen der Kraft zu denken und der Bewegung der Materie, zwischen dem vernünftigen Geiste und dem Körper anzutreffen ist, so ist es doch gewiss dass der Mensch, der alle seine Begriffe und Vorstellungen von den Eindrücken her hat, die das *Universum* vermittelst des Körpers in seine Seele erregt, sowohl in Ansehung der Deutlichkeit derselben, als auch der Fertigkeit, dieselben zu verbinden und zu vergleichen, welche man das Vermögens zu denken nennt, von der Beschaffenheit dieser Materie völlig abhängt, an die der Schöpfer ihn gebunden hat."[1] Such were the views of Kant, *the scientist*, trying to understand the universe from the standpoint of matter and force. Psychology is made amenable to astronomical mechanics.

We shall not meet such expressions again. The next time

[1] *Werke*, I., 333 f., 337.

(1765) there appears a suffusion of those metaphysical explications which were beginning to brew in the awakening Kant. There is a separation of the two parts of psychology, but both fall within metaphysics.[1] Empirical psychology always fell within metaphysics during his pre-critical lectures, as Erdmann says,[2] and only diminished in importance as he built up material for anthropology. He writes to Herz[3] (1778): "Empirische Psychologie fasse ich jezt kürzer nachdem ich Anthropologie lese." In the already quoted passage in the *Critique*,[4] empirical psychology is allowed to have 'a small corner in metaphysic,' but only 'from economical motives.'[5]

After the critical epoch, empirical psychology is sharply severed from rational psychology and can never pass within the *a priori*.[6] They have a common basis laid in that experience which expresses itself thus: "Ich bin mir selbst bewusst;" but they begin to diverge in so far as there advances a treatment of the 'Ich' in 'der erstern' or 'der zweiten Bedeutung.'[7]

But psychology, *i. e.*, empirical psychology,[8] in its positive aspect (for we shall see later that rational psychology is a science, but only in a negative sense), can never be a science. It can never be more than 'blose Meinen.' If psychology cannot be a science and contains nothing *a priori*, what can it be and of what does it treat? An answer to this question is found, among others, in a long passage in the preface to the 'Metaphysische Anfangsgründe der Naturwissenschaft.'[9] It contains his views

[1] On which his lectures for that year and following were to begin 'nach einer kleinen Eintheilung, von der empirischen Psychologie an, welche eigentlich die metaphysische Erfahrungswissenschaft vom Menschen ist; denn was den Ausdruck der Seele betrifft, so ist es in dieser Abtheilung noch nicht erlaubt, zu behaupten, dass er eine habe." II., 316.

[2] *Reflex.*, p. 63.

[3] *Werke*, VIII., 706-7.

[4] II., 728.

[5] In Kant's *Vorlesungen über Psychologie*, reprinted by du Prel, 1889, almost half of the treatment of 'Psychologie' is bestowed on empirical psychology.

[6] *Cf.*, *Werke*, V., 274, VIII., 547.

[7] *Werke*, VIII., 530-531.

[8] *Cf.*, *Werke*, VI., 395: 'Psychologie-darunter man immer nur die empirische versteht.'

[9] *Werke*, IV., 361.

on the problems of psychology, its relation to the sciences, its standpoint with reference to its material, and the nature and limitation of the modes of inquiry (points to which we shall refer shortly), that it must be quoted at length. "Noch weiter aber, als selbst Chemie, muss empirische Seelenlehre jederzeit von dem Range einer eigentlich so zu nennenden Naturwissenschaft entfernt bleiben, erstlich, weil Mathematik auf die Phänomene des inneren Sinnes und ihre Gesetze nicht anwendbar ist, man müsste denn allein das Gesetz der Stetigkeit in dem Abflusse der inneren Veränderungen desselben in Anschlag bringen wollen, welches aber eine Erweiterung der Erkenntniss sein würde, die sich zu der, welche die Mathematik der Körperlehre verschafft, ohngefähr so verhalten würde, wie die Lehre von den Eigenschaften der geraden Linie zur ganzen Geometrie. Denn die reine innere Anschauung, in welcher die Seelenerscheinungen construirt werden sollen, ist die Zeit, die nur eine Dimension hat.[1] Aber auch nicht einmal als systematische Zergliederungskunst oder Experimentallehre kann sie der Chemie jemals nahe kommen, weil sich in ihr das Mannigfaltige der inneren Beobachtung nur durch blose Gedankentheilung von einander absondern, nicht aber abgesondert aufbehalten und beliebig wiederum verknüpfen, noch weniger aber ein anderes denkendes Subject sich unseren Versuchen, der Absicht angemessen, von uns unterwerfen lasst, und selbst die Beobachtung an sich schon den Zustand des beobachteten Gegenstandes alterirt und verstellt. Sie kann daher niemals etwas mehr, als eine historische, und, als solche, so viel möglich systematische Naturlehre des inneren Sinnes, *d. i.*, eine Naturbeschreibung der Seele, aber nicht Seelenwissenschaft, ja nicht einmal psychologische Experimentallehre werden. . . . . "

Psychology treats "von dem Erstehen der Erfahrung, sondern nicht von dem, was in ihr liegt. Das Erstere würde selbst auch da, ohne das Zweite, welches zur Kritik der Erkenntniss gehört."[1] It "erklärt das was geschieht, und beschäftigt sich mit Gemütskräften."[2] It considers the nature of cognition in its

[1] *Cf.*, *Werke*, VI., 395.

[1] *Werke*, IV., 52, Sec. 210a.

[2] Erdmann, *Reflex.*, p. 70, No. 24.

genesis and resources, and the conditions under which it is modified;[1] the source of the various feelings and emotions and how they are affected by the developments in the individual and in society;[2] and "die Handlungen und Bedingungen des menschlichen Wollens überhaupt."[3] Psychology, then, with Kant merely describes 'unseren Vorstellungen des inneren Sinnes,' going back to the genesis of experience and classifies its various products as they appear, in the one intuitional form of time,[4] to that observation which marks out the 'Stoff zu künftigen systematisch zu verbindenden Erfahrungsregeln sammeln, ohne sie doch begreifen zuwollen.' Such is 'die einzige wahre Obliegenheit der empirischen Psychologie.'[5]

Yet both empirical and rational psychology bear a common fate. They suffer the noëtic verdict estranging them from genuine knowledge, *i. e.*, science. In the one case, there *lacks* the *a priori* element, which leaves it *far behind*, arising from the inherent impossibility of the subject-matter being treated that way; while in the other, there is the well-known criticism that it *steps beyond* the limits of true knowledge, arrogating the attainment of truth respecting a certain portion of the supersensible.

Rational psychology, however, differentiates itself from empirical observations as to its method, its content and its aims. It at least wins for itself a claim to be considered as a 'science' by the method with which it proposes to deal with its subject-matter. "In der rationalen Psychologie wird die menschliche Seele nicht aus der Erfahrung, wie in der empirischen Psychologie, sondern aus Begriffen *a priori* erkannt."[6] Observation, or mere appearance, counts for nothing here. Every step is to be apodictically secured by the *a priori* analysis of concepts; and the science is to be made up of '(transcendental) propositions which are synthetical knowledge acquired by reason according to' such concepts.[7] That is, by means of her syllogisms, reason shall

[1]*Critique*, II., 48; *cf.*, VIII., 18.
[2]*Werke*, VI., 395.
[3]*Werke*, IV., 238.
[4]*Werke*, IV., 361, VI., 395.
[5]*Werke*, VI., 396.
[6]*Vorlesungen*, p. 52.
[7]*Critique*, II., 619.

determine a totality of phenomena as they are rendered in that unconditioned which bears 'a relation to the subject.'[1]

The aim in all this is to ascertain "wie viel wir von der menschlichen Seele durch die Vernunft erkennen könne...." But, "die einzelnen Sätze der rationalen Psychologie sind hier nicht so wichtig, als die allgemeine Betrachtung der Seele von ihrem Ursprunge, von ihrem zukünftigen Zustande und der Fortdauer;"[2] or, as the *Critique* puts it, its assertions "can only be of any value in so far as it enables me to distinguish the soul from all matter, and thus to except it from that decay to which matter is at all times subject."[3]   To reach this end it is proposed to apply this method to its conceptual content. Whatever theoretical or practical aims they may have in common, the two branches of psychology fall asunder in so far as one is limited and the other capable of any indefinite experiential extension of its method and content.   For rational psychology can deal only with 'cogito' or 'ego cogitans.'   "The term *I*, as a thinking being, signifies the object of psychology which may be called the rational science of the soul, supposing that we want to know nothing about the soul except what, independent of all experience, can be deduced from the concept *I*."[4]   There must not creep in any empirical element, "because the smallest empirical predicate would spoil the rational purity of the science and its independence of all experience."   There is, however, a certain relation to experience which this conception bears. "We take nothing from experience beyond what is necessary to give us an object of the internal sense. ... This is done through the concept of a thinking being (in the empirical internal representation I think)."[5]   This concept is the only one possible, and is selected, "because this inner perception is nothing more than the mere apperception, I think, without which all, [even] transcendental concepts would be impossible."[6]   Although the object of rational psychology is of empirical extrac-

[1] *Ibid.*, 280, 290.
[2] *Vorlesungen*, 52.
[3] II., 310.
[4] *Critique*, II., 298.
[5] *Ibid.*, II, 728.
[6] *Critique*, II., 298.

tion, " it must be observed, that if I have called the proposition, I think, an empirical proposition, I did not mean to say thereby that the *ego* in that proposition is an empirical representation; it is rather purely intellectual, because it belongs to thought in general."[1] The almost infinitesimal proximity of the two branches of psychology is seen in the caution that " the smallest object of perception (even pleasure and pain), if added to the general representation of self-consciousness, would at once change rational into empirical psychology." Nothing is left but the ' I think—the only text of rational psychology out of which must evolve all its wisdom."[2]

The limitation of rational psychology is further seen in the fact that the ' psychological idea' is never given in any experience as such, but is born of pure reason.[3] Treating only of the ' *ego* of apperception',[4] it can go no farther than to exhibit the concepts of the immateriality of a thinking substance, its changes, and the identity of the person within these changes. It necessarily remains a small science.[5] It remains to be said that it is only a pretended science. "There is no rational psychology as a doctrine, furnishing any addition to our self-knowledge, but only as a discipline, fixing impassable limits to speculative reason in this field, partly to keep us from throwing ourselves into the arms of a soulless materialism, partly to warn us against losing ourselves in a vague, and for this life, baseless spiritualism."[6]

A critical consideration of empirical psychology we shall pass over until the second couple has been noticed, while the relation of the two branches of psychology with a study of Kant's conception of the same will be taken up when we come to treat of the latter.

Our second coupling was ' Empirical Psychology *vs.* Anthropology.' Its significance is not so great as that of the former

[1]*Critique*, I., 503 note.
[2]*Critique*, II., 299.
[3]*Werke*, IV., 97.
[4]*Werke*, VIII., 531.
[5]*Werke*, VIII., 547.
[6]*Critique*, I., 502; *cf. Werke*, IV., 110; V., 475.

couple.[1] But the difference goes for something, though Kant
is vacillating in his expressions of the distinctions he made.
These cannot be taken entirely as they stand, but must be appreciated in the light of the historical developments attending
Kant's anthropology, which have been painstakingly traced
by Erdmann.[2]

In his early 'scientific' period, Kant engendered a taste for
physical geography which developed throughout his life, resulting in the cosmopolitic anthropology of old age and bearing with
it distinct traces from each successive epoch in his own mental
development.   When he began lecturing on anthropology is not
well made out.   In 1793[3] he writes Stäudlin that these lectures
have followed annually more than twenty years; and in 1798
he appended a note to the preface of the then published work
in question, saying that for 'more than thirty years' he
lectured on anthropology and physical geography in the
summer and winter semesters respectively.[4]   However that may
be, his physical geography had been assuming such proportions
during the three preceding decades that in 1773-4 it is
divided and a portion is given the name 'Anthropologie' for
the first time.   'Out of moral and political geography sprang
this new science,' which, as he wrote Herz (1774),[5] he wished
to make a regular academic study.   And, in fact, Kant was
the first in Germany to raise anthropology to an academic rank.
The true object of anthropology is not man as an individual,
who merely represents the species, but, as a member of the
totality of the human race.   Man, writes Kant (1775),[6] should
be studied not as he is, *i. e.*, as an object singly regarded—for
of this treats empirical psychology; but he must be considered

---

[1] Yet one can say, from an experiential point of view, that Kant's anthropology is a sort of a self-erected center pole, around which hangs what is truly
Kantian. *Cf.*, Bastian, *Die Vorgesch. d. Ethnologie*, p. 62 note, on the relation
of anthropology to metaphysic and philosophy.

[2] *Reflexionen*, etc., pp. 37-61.

[3] *Werke*, VIII., 791.

[4] Emil Arnoldt in *Altpreuss. Monatschr.*, 1890, pp. 97-110, makes out that
B. Erdmann (*Reflex.*, I., i., p. 48) is in error when saying Kant began to
lecture on anthropology in 1773-74, it being rather in 1772-73.

[5] *Werke*, VIII., 696.

[6] *Werke*, II., 447.

'cosmologically,' 'in ihr Verhältniss im Ganzen.' This gave
the new science an indefinite extension, and there was no problem in psychology, logic, æsthetics, ethics, pedagogy, juris-
prudence, etc., which did not have its value in this totality. As
here hinted, anthropology is entirely 'pragmatical'; but it grew
up out of the physical and political elements which enter into
that world which is 'das Substrat und der Schauplatz auf dem
das Spiel unserer Geschichlichkeit vor sich geht.'[1] It is only in
its architectonic form that it is 'physical-political-moral,' *i. e.*,
pragmatic. What this new science was to Kant, that was to
contain 'die Kenntniss des Menschen,'[2] is best expressed by
Erdmann:[3] "Dieselbe ist ein Kind von Kant's geseeligen An-
lagen und seines früh entwickelten psychologischen Beobach-
tungstalentes, gross gezogen unter der Vorsorge der physischen
Geographie, spater hin vor allem ausgestattet mit den Mate-
rialien der empirischen Psychologie für die Kant sonst wie
bekannt keinen rechten officiellen Platz hat."

Such an opinion, as just expressed, in regard to the fate of
empirical psychology, is no doubt true in one sense, and justly
finds support in what Kant wrote to Herz in 1778.[4] On the
other hand, Meyer's conclusion,[5] that Kant threw empirical psychology overboard into the great sea of anthropology, is properly based on numerous expressions.[6] Erdmann[7] also attempts
to reduce them to an equivalency; so far as their methods are
concerned, 'wird anthropologisch gelegentlich gleich bedeutend
mit empirisch.'[8]

Notwithstanding these reductions, it must be maintained
that there is a wide distinction made between anthropology and

[1] *Werke*, VIII., 153.
[2] *Werke*, VII., 431, VIII., 151.
[3] *Op. cit.*, 52.
[4] "Empirische Psychologie fasse ich jetzt kürzer nachdem ich Anthropologie lese." VIII., 706 f.
[5] *Op. cit.*, 213 f, 267.
[6] *E. g.*: "Psychologie sei blos Anthropologie des inneren Sinnes," etc.,
V., 175; "Alles Uebrige [*i. e.*, everything excepting *rational* psychology] aber
empirische Psychologie, oder vielmehr nur Anthropologie ist," etc., VIII., 547,
cf. 570.
[7] *Op. cit.*, p. 51, note 4.
[8] And wishes several distinctions in the *Critique* to be so interpreted. *Critique*, II., 722, 729, etc.

empirical psychology, on the one hand, and rational psychology on the other. In the former instance, Erdmann is quite right in identifying them; but he can be justified only to the extent of *method*, when Kant makes the sweeping distinction between *a priori* and *a posteriori*. This one point of agreement, however, is not sufficient to sink one into the other. From the standpoint of essentials, those which make them even empirical sciences, they stand far apart. They differ as to the limits within which they must circumscribe themselves, and as to the ends for which their respective knowledges are systematized. Psychology treats of the individual solely. Anthropology considers the totality of the race. Psychology has reference to the course of ideas as consciousness reveals their three-fold variety. Anthropology's "Absicht ist durch dieselbe die Quellen aller Wissenschaften, die der Sitten, der Geschichlichkeit, des Umgangs, der Methode Menschen zu binden und zu regieren, mithin alles Praktischen zu eröffnen."[1] Psychology is satisfied when observation as to what takes place in the 'innere Sinne' has been duly recorded. The difference between them could not be more manifest. That empirical psychology crept into anthropology is easily seen in the fact that its results are data which the latter must properly gather up, and are helpful in historic explanations, as *e. g.*, Kant attempts in his own description of psychologic evolution of human history from animal instinct.[2]

In the second instance, anthropology stands far from rational psychology, both as to method, content and avowed aims. The former is empiric, world-wide, pragmatic. The latter is a small, *a priori* science, beating back 'soulless materialism' from the one standpoint of the logical *ego*.

Gathering up results, which will aid in sorting the material,

[1] *Werke*, VIII., 696, *letter to Herz*, 1774; *cf.*, II., 447, VII., 474, VIII., 151, 570, 706 f.

[2] *Werke*, IV., 313 f. With all this difference it is still a fact that 'Anthropologie' is one of the chief sources of his empirical psychology. But such an unkindness to psychology, as such, induces a hesitation in taking a detailed review of Kant's conception and treatment of psychological material. The significance of Kant's treatise on anthropology, which was very popular, but temporarily, in the historic foundations of that science, is much less than its academic influence in German universities. *Cf.* Bastian's *monograph*, pp. 7 ff., Topinhard, *Anthropology, trans.*, pp. 1 f., 15 f.

we can say, rational psychology is a (pretended) science that endeavors to know the nature of the soul through reason alone. Empirical psychology is the (impossible) science of the phenomenal mind as it is given in the stream of consciousness. Anthropology is the empirical knowledge of man set in a physical and social universe.

"Psychologisch beobachten mithin Stoff zu künftigen systematisch zu verbindenden Erfahrungsregeln sammeln, ohne sie doch begreifen zu wollen, ist wohl die einzige wahre Obliegenheit der empirischen Psychologie."[1] The intrinsic scope of psychology is fairly well recognized by Kant. It endeavors to unify ' der Lauf unseren Vorstellungen' by a systematic reduction to laws, 'unseren Vorstellungen' taken in the meaning pregnated by the developments of the Leibnitzian monadology, later to break forth in the Herbartian psychology. But Kant stands in historic disagreement and mistakes the function of psychology when he pronounces upon its relation to the physical sciences and characterizes the methods to which it is limited.

The relation of psychology to the other sciences finds its basis laid in the 'nature' of psychologic things. Those phenomena by whose peculiarity "the psychologist is forced to be something of a nerve physiologist,"[2] exhibit the fact that man is set in a mass of relations not of a psychic sort. This gorgeous variety that surges upon consciousness is recognized 'not to be of itself.' The demand that a science shall be, so far as possible, explanatory, not merely descriptive, means that causation has been the fertile factor in the modern developments, and shows that psychology can go but a little way ere it invokes the biologic results of the physical sciences. In one sense, that *is* physical science, the manipulation of causation among phenomena. And psychology has been persistent in its efforts to realize in its own equipment its mutuality with the physical sciences. The extent

[1] *Werke*, VI., 396. It scarcely needs be pointed out, that Kant did not and could not mean 'observation' in the methodized sense in which it prevails to-day. *Cf.*, " aus der Psych. d. i. aus der Beobachtungen über unseren Verstand," (VIII., 14), or (V., 388), "welche methodisch angestellt wird und Beobachtung heisst."

[2] James, *Psychology*, New York, 1890, I., p. 5.

to which this impulse goes is generally to call upon physiology and neurology. The supposition of some sort of relation between bodily conditions and ' mind states,' either *a parte ante* or *a parte post*, yields a warrant. And we shall find Kant, the empiricist, or ' the cool, psychological realist,' as Dieterich calls him, maintaining a ' thorough-going, blank unmeditated correspondence' between brain states and bodily conditions, and the course of ideas and feelings; but not in any such manner as the since-developed biological sciences permit. This, however, is not to his detriment, nor should it be a prejudice to his age.

Kant, however, in making the essence of science to be mathematics, denies such a development to psychology. With him it is separated from the sciences in a far different manner than is done nowadays. The subject-matter of psychology, in a general way, is quite as easily distinguished from that of the material sciences as are the boundaries of any of those among the latter.

But to point out the specific differentiations between psychology and the natural sciences is not quite the easy task so generally supposed, as appears from Ward's discussion of ' the standpoint of psychology.'[1] The distinction involves not only the integrity of the science, but, also, and to a very determinative extent, limits the methods applicable in psychological research. Physics, in the general sense, confessedly deals with objects of the external sense. They have space relations, as *e. g.*, the weight is *in* the balance. The psychological objects are sometimes spoken of as 'in' or 'out,' as the idea of a tree is in my mind, but never in the sense of spatiality. They are objects of the inner sense, *i. e.*, are subject to time only, are merely before or after. This is a wide-reaching and 'negative' distinction, which, as we shall see, was the psychological stumbling block to Kant.

Besides the distinction of external and internal, which Ward criticizes as inadequate for its purpose, there is a positive feature belonging to its phenomena which serves to mark out the field of psychology. It is by the way of this characteristic that the former is made possible. When we speak of an internal object,

[1] *Art. Psych.*, Encyc. Brit., 9th ed., Vol. XX., pp. 37 ff.

we refer to some one in a series which goes by the name of conscious experience.   A feeling never occurs alone.   Nor is a thought separated and handled, tossed to the way-side to lie until the remanent psychologist examines it.   On the contrary, they are set in a series, a series that is not arranged from without, as books on a shelf.   But a series with all its infinite variety that is grouped in some hap-hazard way by a consciousness to which they belong.   Not only is his range of objects limited by the need that they must ' be regarded as having place in or as being part of some one's consciousness, '[1] but also '' the first fact for a psychologist is that thinking of some sort goes on, '' with every 'thought' tending to become a part of a personal consciousness.[2]   Into this stream of consciousness the psychologist must plunge and from it return with whatever sort of a science he may, he can define it only as the science ' of the states of human consciousness, as such. '[3]

To Kant, with whom '' die Psychologie ist eine Physiologie des innern Sinnes oder der denkenden Wesen, ''[4] these facts appeared in a negative sense entirely.   Whether it should relate itself to the physiological sciences, as foreseen by Alcmæon,[5] or actually carried out by Fritsch and Hitzig and others,[6] or to physics, as the changes conditioned by the introduction of its data and reduced to numerical measurement; or, even whether it could stand alone by that method which is its peculiar birthright, *viz.*, 'introspection' in either its subjective or objective forms, it was all the same.   There could be no science of psychology.   And, since the relation it might bear to other departments of knowledge depends upon the reduction of the data to a common form; and also, since Kant has always stood the great champion of the valuelessness of introspection and nullity of exact method in their application to the inner sense, we shall briefly consider the data and method which are at the psychologist's hand.

[1]Ward, *loc. cit.*, p. 38, col. 2.
[2]James, *op. cit.*, I., 224 f.
[3]Ladd, *Outlines of Phys. Psych.*, p. 3.
[4]*Vorlesungen*, 6.
[5]*Cf.* Siebeck, *Gesch. d. Psych.*, Gotha, 1880, I., 1., pp. 89 f., 103 f.
[6]*Cf.*, Ladd, *Phys. Psych.*, pp. 253 f.

As a finished product, psychology presents us with a typical mind, something that is never realized in experience; otherwise it would descend into mere biography. Nevertheless, psychology in the first instance is 'individualistic,' and the chief method of collecting its data must come by the way of that 'standpoint from which these experiences are viewed, *viz.*: some one's consciousness' (Ward). This material is ever at first hand; we know our feelings and our efforts immediately. So far as the psychologist is concerned, "the phenomena inwardly apprehended," as Brentano[1] says, "are true in themselves. As they appear, so they are in reality." The mere having of these 'inward phenomena' is not introspection. Their 'immediacy' is not enough. Still it is their 'immediacy' which makes adaptable that method on which "we have to rely first and foremost and always."[2] It is the inflexion at a late stage of that consciousness which from the very beginning had the tendency to become 'a personal consciousness.'

Kant denies adequacy to this method. In the above quoted preface[3] he maintains that "the manifold of internal observations is only separated in thought, but cannot be kept separate and be connected at pleasure again. Even the observation itself alters and distorts the state of the object observed." These are objections that did not perish. They have been urged since, *e. g.*, by Auguste Comte and Dr. Maudsley, growing into debates as to psychological methods. Such objections are true, but paradoxical, demanding of every one that he be fit for a psychologist's leap. The mere fact of a reflective consciousness, however, is no more the accoutrement of a psychologist than mere star-gazing constitutes an astronomer. They are objections that would reduce psychology to mere autobiography which would, in any attempted analysis, belie its very title. But in this individualism of its data lies the superiority of the method over that of the physical sciences. Its data can be only

[1] *Psych.*, bk. II., chap. III., sec. 2, cited by James, *op. cit.*, I., 187. This view should not be taken in the same sense as is to be understood by Beneke's guiding thought 'that through self-consciousness we know ourselves psychically just as we really are.' Ueberweg, *Hist. of Phil.*, II., 281.

[2] James, *op. cit.*, I., 185.

[3] *Supra*, p. 40.

in a consciousness.   On the other hand, it is true that introspection is not absolute.   It, too, is subject to disturbances, as Sully
points out in his work on 'Illusions' (Chap. VIII.) ; though
its "errors are numerous, yet are all too slight to render the
process of introspection as a whole unsound and untrustworthy."
James' unearthing of 'the psychologist's fallacies' meets Kant's
second objection, while the first finds its counterpart in that
'stream of thought,' the treatment of which is always difficult
and fallible.

  "Still less," adds Kant, "is another thinking subject
amenable to investigations of this kind." Pure introspection
could never take us outside our own thoughts and feelings.
Moreover, while psychology is of an individualistic origin, and
must necessarily be of the same type for a longer or shorter
way, it cannot remain there.   Just as psychology cannot stop
when it has concluded a graphic consideration of neural tremors,
so it must enlarge its field beyond that of mere introspective
manipulation.   It must transcend its certain morbidity, crack
its shell, and become 'objective' in a generous meaning of the
term.   Consciousness is to be regarded as 'an object,' and not
merely as belonging to a me, over which I must brood.   Even
here, Kant consistently denies the possibility of a psychology.
For the comparative method of collecting psychological data
can never pass beyond the validity and reach of introspection.
It is a varied and later form of the latter.   It comes in auxiliarly, and essentially is the anthropomorphism of the introspective method (as Baer[1] demands it must be in anthropology).
"We watch the manifestation of mind in others, and interpret
these by the aid of our own conscious experiences."[2]   But the
treatment psychology gives is not of consciousness as of the
individual, but 'as such.'   It must roam amongst its manifestations not only in the infant's mind, in the exceptional or abnormal minds, but also into that 'collective mind,' where our
historic foundations are entombed, even into that of the animal
consciousness.   No doubt Kant is right in complaining that
none of this is quantitative.   Yet we estimate by instituting

[1] *Cf.*, Bastian, *op. cit.*, p. 54.
[2] Sully, *op. cit.*, I., p. 18.

comparisons between experiences of the like kind, never passing from one group to another.

Kant spurned psychology not so much, it seems, from the fact that the use of the only method possible produces disturbances in the data. For he himself makes use of the 'observation' which he elsewhere [1] recommends to it, not only making some additions, but also accepting them as foundations on which the whole Critical philosophy and its articulation into a system rest. In the nature of the subject and its incompatibility with quantity is to be found the real source of his condemnation. From the general tone that prevails, it seems that this condemnation would best be understood as a desideratum, while he may secretly wish, with Herbart,[2] that psychology might yet find her Newton.

On the other hand, Kant laid emphasis and insists throughout on the 'negative' features of the data of psychology. That is, the distinction between external and internal sense, the latter being consciousness, plays a great *rôle*, often to the production of havoc. He would have science conform itself to his metaphysics of apperception. " Still farther even than chemistry," he might be heard to say, as the last and chief objection, " must empirical psychology be removed from the rank of what may be termed a natural science proper; because mathematics is inapplicable to the phenomena of the internal sense and its laws, unless, indeed, we consider merely the law of permanence in the flow of its internal changes; . . . . for the pure internal intuition in which psychical phenomena are constructed in time has only one dimension." This was after the *Critique* had been thought out. " It can never therefore be anything more than an historical, and as such, as far as possible, systematic natural doctrine of the internal sense, *i. e.*, a natural description of the soul, but not a science of the soul, nor even a psychological experimental doctrine."

In so far as the content of a science can be consequentially effected by its method, this opinion as to the possibilities of psychology relates itself in a two-fold way to the Critical philoso-

[1] *Werke*, VIII., 14.
[2] *Werke*, Vol. VI., p. 463.

phy. Anticipating possible results of our study, it must be said
that the drift of Kant's speculations goes against that very materialism, which was then so rampant, and which Kant undoubtedly thought would be the outcome of any psychology that
would be quantitative, *i. e.*, as a 'science' that would have its
'pure part,' which meant, "Metaphysik der Natur, d. i., Principien der notwendigkeit dessen, was zum Dasein eines Dinges
gehört, beschäftigen sich mit einen Begriffe, der sich nicht con-
struiren lässt, weil das Dasein in keiner Anschauung *a priori*
dargestellt werden kann."[1] As Kant himself worked this out,
there resulted matter as characterized by force and motion. He
even purposed to treat 'Seelenlehre' in the same manner ; so he
wrote Schütz in September, 1785. The fate of his intention is
clearly seen in the above quotations from the preface of the work
as it appeared the following year.

It also has its bearings in a positive way with the Transcendental Æsthetic, which provided the only possible form of all
qualification, *viz.*, that in which motion becomes a mark of the
permanent. Duration, simply, cannot suffice. In a negative
aspect, this is inconsistent with one of the principles in the
'Analytic,' *viz.*: "The anticipation of perception, whose principle is : 'In all phenomena sensation, and the Real, which corresponds to it in the object (realitas phænomenon), has an intensive quantity, that is, a degree.'" A "sensation by itself[2] is no
objective representation; and, as in it the intuition of neither
space nor time can be found, it follows that though not an extensive, yet some kind of quantity must belong to it. . . . That
quantity must be intensive and corresponding to it, an intensive
quantity must be attributed to all objects of perception so far as
it contains sensation." It is not true, however, as Weber's law
indicates,[3] that sensations rise gradually with the 'quantity' of
the stimuli, nor that sensations, subjectively considered, have
this gradually changing quality which Kant calls 'degree.'
The phenomena of the rhythm of consciousness, as *e. g.*, in
the ebb and flow of the perception of the barely audible ticking

[1] *Werke*, IV., 359.
[2] As the 2d ed. explains, I., 465–466.
[3] Ladd, *Phys. Psych.*, pp. 365 f.

of a watch, shows that there is a periodicity in sensations whose
rise and fall are best indicated by the steps of a stair.

It also is curious that the nature of psychology as it was seen
in 1786 did *not* have a *corresponding* influence on the second
edition of the *Critique*. As Itelson[1] calls attention to it, there
remains this inconsistency between the possibilities of psychology
and the principle on which the judgment is permitted to construct the rules of all perception.

In cutting off this last resource, as it were, of the science of
psychology Kant does not critically anticipate the modern developments which have come about mainly by the adoption of
experimental methods of gathering its data. Speculations were
then rife concerning the possibility of a psychometry. Wolff
already[2] said, "theoremata haec ad *Psychometriam* pertinent
quae mentis humanae cognitionem mathematicam tradit et ad
huc in desideratis est.....Dari etiam mentis humanae cogita-
tionem mathematicam, atque hinc *Pyschometriam* esse possi-
bilem." Bernoulli (1738) had discovered the dependence of
the *fortune morale* on the *fortune physique* (which was in some
sense an anticipation, as Fechner says, of Weber's law), and was
further developed by Laplace and Poisson. Euler (1739) had
treated of the relation of the sensation of tone-intervals to the
rate of vibrations.[3] Against this brewing of experimental psychology in the middle of last century, as foreseen in Wolff's expression,[4] "monuimus, Psychologiam empiricam Physicae experi-
mentali respondere," Kant remained steadfast, not however in
the sense that experimentation results, as he says,[5] in an 'Unding,' which might be transformed by an arrangement about
metaphysical principles; but from a transcendental standpoint he
negated the possibility of the science. The objections raised

[1]*Cf., Archiv für Gesch. d. Phil.,* 1890, p. 286., *cf., Werke,* IV., p. 55, Sec. 24.

[2]In his *Psychologia Empirica* (1732),Sec. 552. Wolff's opinion is also echoed
in Baumgarten's *Metaphysik* (Sec. 552), with which Kant was familiar, since
he used it as the basis of his lectures. *Cf., Werke,* II., 316, 43.

[3]*Cf.,* Fechner, *Elemente d. Psych. Physik,* II., 548 ff; Külpe, '*Anfänge und
Aussichten der Exp. Psych*'., in *Arch. f., Gesch. d. Phil.,* 1892, Bd. VI. H. 2
p.170 ff.; Itelson, *loc. cit.*; Sommer, *Grundzüge einer Gesch. d. deutsch Psych.
etc.,* Wurzburg, 1892, p. 3 f.

[4]*Op. cit.,* Sec. 4.

[5]*Werke,* VI., 377.

by Kant undoubtedly interfered, as Külpe surmises, with the growth of those investigations carried on by the surging Wolffian and eclectic schools of those decades.

However far this objection against the unsatisfactory condition of psychology at that time is of an architectonic origin, it is now a fact that psychology rightfully undertakes the measurement of psychical phenomena as to time, intensity and extensity or their voluminousness. As to the validity of psychophysical methods, it must be said that the psychologist profits by them only in so far as they extend his horizon and present him carefully selected data. Beyond this, or when he becomes lost in his experimentation, he forfeits his scientific birthright. Methods of gathering data do not solve psychological problems. In all its departments the science is, as Prof. Ladd maintains for the physiological portion, 'first experimental and then speculative.'[1] The variations in methods come with the variations in the character of the activities, data concerning which are to be ascertained. Experimental psychology is not psychology by virtue of its methods. They are an elastic garb that only covers up those real processes which ferret out explanations. Thus, then, Kant is right in maintaining that psychology is not and cannot be demonstrative. But far be it from us—the admission that psychology remains an 'Unding.'

It has already been seen how Kant's philosophy limited itself to the foundations of science as they appeared in logic and physic. From the view as to what is possible to psychology from the standpoint of method, we can now affirm with Hegler,[2] that "Kant's ganze Erkenntnisstheorie ist auf die Wissenschaft der Natur zugeschnitten, die Psychologie ist von Anfang an nicht gleichberechtigt." An explanation for this is ventured here, which may appear clearer farther on, that Kant, while really contributing much to noëtics—and we would not undervalue nor diminish the fame of his services in this regard—only attempts, or at most, only makes out a theory of perception so far as external objects are concerned. His difficulties can be understood from this point of view, and the metaphysical foun-

[1] *Phys. Psych.*, p. 12.
[2] *Die Psych. in Kant's Ethik*, Freiburg, 1891, p. 33.

dation of science finds its extension to objects in the objective sense of that term. The struggle with ' objectivity ' and a disregard for psychology send out reciprocal influences.

Inquiries relating to the physical basis of mind life admit of two kinds of considerations; one, of what sort and of what extent is the phenomenal relation that may obtain between the body and its concatenating nervous systems, and the flow of consciousness? the other, what shall be the answer to the ultimate question : what is this relation, and how shall it be resolved? The one problem disappears before the scalpel and a pricking pin, by strenuous determination and a rage of anger. The other goes beyond the length of observation, and begins with the consistent adjustment of conceptual facts. The one confronts us in empirical psychology ; the other conducts us into philosophy itself when the nature of the real, so far as it concerns mind, is to be wrought out.

This distinction is made by Kant. Of all psychological points that are confessedly two-sided, this is probably the one where Kant appears properly as the empirical realist and a metaphysical idealist when required. He recognizes the length to which empiricism can go, and demands that at that point the problem be taken up by metaphysics.[1] Beyond this statement we can hardly go, except for the sake of historical curiosity. It is not to be expected that he speak of the correlation of mind and brain with any such explicitness as the theory of localization of cerebral functions now permit us. He must needs confine himself to the crude state in which were the chemical and anatomical sciences. Our inquiry is satisfied when it is discovered that he, as a psychologist, has consulted the physiological knowledge of his day, and an investigation into the question, as to how far *he* consistently adopted this knowledge, is useless here.

There are, however, a few points which should be mentioned. At times he speaks as a medical psychologist,[2] writing a tract on the diseases of the head ; again as a physiognomist,

[1] *E. g.*, *cf.*, his letter to Herz, *Werke*, VIII., 696.
[2] It might be mentioned that, when still a youth, the medical profession was inviting to him.

giving more or less credence to the phrenological theory then
formulating by the German physician, Gall. Many of these
opinions are full of that humor in which Kant delighted, or
contain biographical material.[1] It is as a psychologist that he
details these relations in a manner and to an extent interesting
to note in comparison with present tendencies. It is not merely
the intelligence, but the whole mental life of man, that stands
in connection with the body. "Die Gemeinschaft ist die Verbindung wo die Seele mit dem Körper eine Einheit ausmacht;
wo die Veränderungen des Körpers zugleich die Veränderungen
der Seele, und die Veränderungen der Seele zugleich die Veränderungen des Körpers sind. Es geschehen im Gemüt keine
Veränderungen, die nicht mit der Veränderungen des Körpers
korrespondirten. Ferner so korrespondiert nicht allein die
Veränderungen, sondern auch die Beschaffenheit des Gemüts
mit der Beschaffenheits des Körpers. Was die Korrespondenz
der Veränderungen betrifft, so kann in der Seele nichts statt-
finden, wo der Körper nicht ins Spiel kommen sollte."

This is detailed in the various ways of thinking, volition, emotions and passions, and the modifications of external origin
through the senses. "Die Seele affiziert gar sehr das Gehirn
durch das Denken." "Also ist das Gehirn die Bedingung des
Denkens." "Das Wollen affiziert unsern Körper noch mehr,
als das Denken." "So wird der Körpers auch sehr affiziert
wenn der Menschen in Affeckten und Leidenschaften gerät."
"Auch die äusseren Gegenstände affizieren meine Sinne . . . .
durch diese Affecktion der Nerven geschieht das Spiel der
Empfindung in der Seele, etc."[2] Over against this *naïveté* in the
sort of correspondences, appears the plodding course of physiological psychology which carefully passes from the physiology
of the senses to the more doubtful localization of the 'higher'
mental activities.

Or, again, Kant admits a reciprocal action between the soul
and body. The former is as much temporally responsible as to
what occurs to a certain extent in the latter,[3] as *vice versa*.

[1] As, *e. g.*, "Der Streit der philosophischen Facultät mit der medicini-
chen," VII., 409–428.
[2] *Vorlesungen*, p. 47 ff.
[3] *Cf.*, also *Werke*, VI., 457, VII., 409 f.

Nowadays it is at times maintained that the brain is responsible for all, and a mechanical conception is made to do the service of both science and a metaphysic.[1] Kant, however, constantly expresses a doubt as to the complete carrying on of this reciprocal action, which we shall notice when we come to the imagination. As a scientific doctrine, it would be unjust to pit Kant with more modern formulæ, as was said above. And so far as it is given a metaphysical interpretation, it must be reserved until we take up rational psychology, where will appear an estimation of what seems to be the relation between the philosophical and physiological aspects of psychology, and also as this relation appears in Kant.

So far there has been a general elimination, or a comparison of psychology with other departments. The circumscription gained from a general preliminary view is the safeguard when approaching details. The separation of psychology as a science, and the pointing out of some causal, or, at least, temporal relation between the mind and the neural substrate, does not complete the possibilites. The psychologist deals with the facts of consciousness, in which every fact seems to be linked to a body. But it soon appears that this consciousness in the individual is not continuous, but either is periodically intermittent, or can be interrupted extraneously. So, for psychology there appears the third general consideration of consciousness, its varieties and possible negations.

This distinction appeals not only to the physiologist objectively, as a general and variable concomitancy of mental manifestation, but he gives it a subjective turn when he invokes the aid of assimilative tendencies, or unconscious natural synthesis, to the perceiving of an object. The whole doctrine of sensibility, as it stands in the forefront of the science, is affected by the recognition of the possibility of some sensations being ' unattended to.'

The distinction is of no less importance in a theory of knowledge, or at least has been made so. Constructiveness (as preeminently Kant) in the knowledge of things, or in the being of things as known (Lotze), is flatly vitiated by mere con-

---

[1] As, *e. g.*, partially appears in James's *Psychology*.

sciousness when it says, "I merely perceive this or that." A constructiveness it must then be which is of some mystic sort, unknown except by rational positing, and incurring the objection from James,[1] that the notion of such an internal, hurly-burly machine-shop is shocking. And not only in a theory of knowledge is the distinction helpful or treacherous; but the difference is one turned to the account of metaphysics, where it repays by calling the Schopenhauerian world a blind, unknowing, unconscious will; or, as in his disciple, the essence of the universe or absolute finds its remarkable expression in the unconscious. On the other hand, its opposite is made to be the real, as the monads of Leibnitz, or the conscious souls of Lotze.

Indeed, the great problem in all philosophy is how consciousness can or does come from the unconscious. And the facts which appear early in psychology, as the distinguishing marks of its data, have their bearing throughout the course of philosophical discipline, and grow in importance when the nature of consciousness is sought in order to carry over the scattered tenets of its analyses into the ultimate synthesis which it is the constant effort and special right of philosophy to attempt. Schools of philosophy begin to part way when they enter upon their respective treatment of consciousness. For inquiries into the nature of consciousness take us back to beginnings. But beginnings are always profound. When a thing is 'realized,' we appreciate its reality and think we understand it when we are finally compelled to defer one question, *viz*: how did it become? Still, Lotze's frequent musing that we do not completely understand what a thing is by describing how it came to be, may have its full truth. Yet, when we wish to pronounce upon the ultimate nature of the world-ground we can defensibly do so in no other terms than are warranted by our psychological analysis of consciousness. We must be at least so anthropomorphical as to affirm of reality no less than what we find in ourselves, but affirm by the special right of a rational defense.

This variety of uses to which the distinctions between the conscious and unconscious is put, indicates the elemental psy-

[1] *Op. cit.*, I., 363.

chologic variation which must be differentiated, at least for preliminary treatment. Not only is it a factor in the conceptions of the psychologist, but he must at once proceed to establish, in some tenable manner, the mind's relation to other things by answer to a question so variously prominent since Locke: "Are we ever wholly unconscious?" It emerges when he sets out on his way by equipping his science with those general characteristics of mind among which attention, as conscious selection, appears. How far consciousness figures in those sensations which are attended by perceptions, whether there is necessary the distinction of the form of being conscious of something, or conscious of it through remembering; how far ethical tenets may require imputability of my actions, if habits are 'unconscious' modes of my being, etc., etc., are only preliminary empirical questions which culminate in the highest form of the consciousness of life. When the empirical laws of the mind's synthetic activity are being discovered, the same distinction presents itself in the form of what is ordinarily called mere representation or feeling, against which reasoning must force a positing of submerged activities, or technicalize it and think it sufficient to pass under the name of apperception. Here it passes into one's theory of knowledge and the query becomes, what function has it in that synthesis which must make for cognition and reality? In affirming a perduring unity, the philosophy of mind appeals to it in some way as ramifying all the infinite variation we actually find in sensuous elements, and expects of it a potency that makes for an *ego*, yesterday, to-day and forever. Finally, when philosophy ceases with 'the facts of life' and passes to its 'unitary conception of the world,' it must *a fortiori* weave into its last words the great facts of 'the psychic half over which it dare not draw the pall' in its empirical advance, and adequately account in reality for all that pervades *our* life and without which there could not have been one jot of that experience which urges us on to the riddles of existence. Consciousness is the great fact, and only grows in importance and acquires an ontological momentum as we pass from the survey of the silent fact of awakening from deep sleep, to the conclusion, that, that surveying consciousness is itself set in a unified Reality of which he can be scarce more than a sympathetic sensation.

But we must hasten to say that the nature of consciousness is not to be dwelt upon here, nor can there be tested the implications of a psychological doctrine in a philosophical discipline. On the contrary, here is properly indicated the place of those psychological considerations which assume varied forms in the mental life, and to mark out where Kant appears in the scheme, limiting the discussion to those sections where he properly belongs. Kant does not go to the length of this matter, especially in the first stages of its empirical side, as the results of recent psychical and natural research now require. Nor does he appear to treat it in its proper psychologic forms, except in a very general way in perception and in the consciousness of the empirical self. The philosophic implications are profoundly drawn out, as is well known, in his deduction of the categories; and the possibilities of consciousness, *i. e.*, tenets in regard to personality, etc., are negated in the rational psychology. Of course his sceptical outcome gave him no right to attempt a weaving-in of the factor of consciousness in reality. In a general way it will become us to test the legitimacy of his claims as to the impossibility of extending positive inquiries as to the nature of the individual mind and of what may be beyond.

It must suffice here to point out that Kant recognizes not only the antithesis of the conscious and the unconscious, but also makes much of the latency of, or degrees in consciousness. This was only a historic reflection from Leibnitz's doctrine of monads and their representations.[1] After Locke's discussion and Leibnitz's theory, consciousness and its characteristics became of special interest. Accordingly, we find Kant speaking[2] of representations of which we may be unconscious, though "darin scheint ein Widerspruch zu liegen;" or again, recognizing 'degrees' both in consciousness and in the knowledges which it throws off.[3] We find him even going to the length of giving the distinction a positive significance in his theory of the categories, saying, "that synthesis, the faculty of imagination, is a blind but indispensable function of the soul, without which

---

[1] *Cf.*, Duncan's trans. of Leibnitz's *Philosophical Works*, p. 218 ff.
[2] *Werke*, II., 298, 346 note, VII., 445 f.
[3] *Cf.*, *Critique*, I., 497 f., *Werke*, IV., 55, 438; VIII., 65.

we should have no knowledge whatsoever, but of the existence of which we are scarcely conscious."[1]   Indeed one feels, at times, disposed to take the very conception of the *a priori* and the whole system of transcendentalism as a most acute parody on the unconscious.

The first thing needful in scientific inquiry is the analysis of material.   Methods merely supply data, which, being submitted to that process, begin to assume scientific function.   Since psychology first began its career under the hands of Aristotle, this duty of classification was recognized and became crystallized in his classification of the various souls and their forces (δύναμεων).

The necessity of such analytical procedure has not yet disappeared.   Indeed, one might say that the analysis of mental functions constitutes the very definition of psychology and truly comprehends the whole task of such inquiry.   It is of these that psychology treats, and such a division can have meaning only when the work of the psychologist has been accomplished. Moreover, one dare not present a scheme and then endeavor to fill in with observations.   If psychology is to be empirical, it must by all means distinguish itself from that scholastic procedure which began, as Drobisch says,[2] with such expressions as "Ich verstehe unter Vernunft, unter Verstand, etc., das und das."   One may overlook such attempts when men confine themselves to speculation as yielding the truths of nature.   We may find traces of this very spirit in Kant himself.

The division of the faculties has had its great *rôle* in the history of philosophy.   Cartesianism recognized reason and will as the chief characteristics of mind and sought to weave from them such philosophical doctrines as should somehow allow for the explanation of other elements of human nature, *e. g.*, the passions.   English thinking, as clearly expressed in

---

[1] *Critique*, II., 69; *Cf., Crit.*, II., 92. "This consciousness may often be very faint, etc." But he also denies total unconsciousness, saying, "to sleep and to die were one and the same, if dreaming were not added." "Man kann aber wohl für sicher annehmen, dass kein Schlaf ohne Traum sein könne, und wer nicht geträumt zu haben wähnt, seinen Traum nur vergessen habe." *Werke*, VII., 505, 506.

[2] *Emp. Psych.*, p. 302.

Reid, swung about the 'intellectual' and the 'active powers.' A still more famous instance of how psychology in this way *has* been the starting point in philosophy—at times so unconsciously —we will find in our own author. Whether this is *the* service that psychology can and dare render to reason in her attempts to understand the world may constantly appear throughout the study.

The remark must here be made that more or less confusion has entered into the analysis of mental functions, especially the meaning which it can have. Now it is undertaken in a purely psychological spirit. Then, again it has savored of ontology, where the reconstruction of hard and fixed faculties into a doctrine of the simplicity of the soul to which they belong has found its great historic culmination in that rational psychology which Kant attempted to pierce through. It must be borne in mind that 'mental faculties' serve a psychological purpose, but assume another aspect, which should be clearly distinguished, when the attempt is to make a philosophical use of them. It is not comparatively easy to keep this distinction in view, and we shall find Kant groping in the same darkness.

A study of Kant's psychology and philosophy has, as R. Quäbicker says,[1] 'to satisfy itself before all else with the rational psychology and the doctrine of the faculties of the soul.' In this sense, and truly, his empirical psychology comprehends the detailed examination of the faculties and their relation to Criticism *ab ante*, and, rational psychology in its relation *ad post*, as being an application of the principles of Criticism. We shall first trace the development of the division of the faculties within Kant's own mind; then gather the special divisions whose ramifications lead us into the particular consideration of empirical psychology; with a remaining inquiry as to the fact and an estimation of the formal relation of Kant's psychology and the Critical philosophy.

According to Meyer,[2] the first mention made by Kant of the elemental powers of the soul is found in 1764 (?; 1763); but, in the treatise on "Der einzig mögliche Beweisgrund, &c.,

---

[1] *Phil. Monatsheft*, Bd. IV., p. 116.
[2] *Op. cit.*, p. 41.

für das Daseins Gottes," appearing in the year preceding that in which was issued the work mentioned by Meyer, Kant says: "die Eigenschaften eines Geistes sind Verstand und Willen,"[1] and turns the statement to his immediate ontological purpose. In 1764 he did his psychologizing on ʻdas Gefühl des Schönen und Erhabenen,' but later in the same year considers the relation of the faculties, first as explanatory necessities, and secondly as to the ultimate nature of our reduction when we have ʻrun down' a faculty, as it were.[2]   In the same writing[3] he approves of the psychological progress, saying: "Man hät es nämlich in unseren Tagen allerest einzusehen angefangen, dass das Vermögen, das Wahre vorzustellen, die Erkenntniss, dasjenige aber, das Gute zu empfinden, das Gefühl sei, und dass beide ja nicht mit einander müssen verwechselt werden." Not only a partial expression of the inner relation of the faculties, but also of their relation as to philosophical distinctions, is implied in his musing "ob lediglich das Erkenntnissvermögen oder das Gefühl (der erste innere Grund des Begehrungsvermögens) die ersten Grundsätze [der Sittlichkeit] entscheide."

This was Kant's own first conquest over the variety of internal states.   The distinction between knowledge and feeling already lay deep when the effect of scepticism began to seethe within him.   Then he writes to Herz[4] of his psychological discovery and his philosophical intention.

Here it appears that Kant made a distinction within the realm of what had heretofore, in modern psychology, been considered as the ʻBegehrungsvermögen' or ʻactive powers.'   In so far as the feelings are recognized, he has introduced a new element in psychological explanations, but not without precedent. But what it meant to him both psychologically and for Criticism, appears in the foot-note in the ʻCanon of Pure Reason.'[5]   "All practical concepts relate to objects of pleasure or displeasure, that is, of joy or pain, and therefore, at least indirectly, to ob-

[1] *Werke*, II., 131.
[2] *Werke*, II., 288.
[3] *Werke*, II., 307–8.
[4] Feb. 21, 1772. *Werke*, VIII., 688.
[5] *Critique*, II., 687.

jects of our feelings.[1]   But as feeling is not a faculty of representing things (Vorstellungskraft der Dinge), but lies outside
the whole field of our powers of cognition, the elements of our
judgments, so far as they relate to pleasure or pain, ... do not
belong to transcendental philosophy which is concerned exclusively with pure cognitions *a priori.*"

Here also appears for the first time, and with considerable
integrity, what we shall find more fully developed and completely recognized in later years, namely, that 'metaphysik'
could proceed only with regard to the faculties of the soul.[2] That
Kant was working with faculties which he presupposed, as Drobisch hints, as already adequately determined, is also seen in the
remarkable statement a decade later,[3] to make which he had not
yet given himself the teleologic right. "Everything that is
founded in the nature of our faculties must have some purpose
and be in harmony with the right use of them."

As we approach the close of the critical maturing, we find
the expressions more decided and the conviction grown firm,
that the mind appears under these sorts of activities, for it
had cost twenty years' painful reflection to adjust the psychological matter-of-fact into a philosophical interpretation.   In the
preface of the *Critique of Judgment* (1790)[4] he writes more
explicitly than he had expressed himself to Reinhold three
years previous.[5] " Denn alle Seelenvermögen oder Fähigkeiten
können auf die drei zurückgeführt werden, welche sich nicht

[1]That the separation of the feelings from will, or pleasure-pain from desire,
required time on the part of Kant, appears in a comparison of these earlier expressions with one in 1788 (V., *Practical Reason* preface, p. 9, note): "Man
konnte mir noch den Einwurf machen; warum ich nicht auch den Begriff des
Begehrungsvermögen, oder des Gefühls der Lust vorher erklärt habe." But so far
as Criticism is concerned these are ' in der Psychologie gegeben;' for the critical method applies itself to "Begriffen die aus der Psychologie entlehnt werden.'
Strange that Kant should now affirm psychology to be the peculiar basis of
philosophy, when we saw in the previous chapter how thoroughly it was denied
any such relation, and know that he yet goes in the face of it!

[2]How much this is due to the bent of his philosophical genius, that it preyed
continually on that one fact of *knowledge*, and how he tried to bring all philosophy within the precincts of noëtics, may be estimated later on.

[3]*Critique*, II., 551.

[4]*Werke*, V., 183.

[5]*Cf.*, letter to Reinhold, Dec., 1787, *Werke*, VIII., 739.

ferner aus einem gemeinschaftlichen Grunde ableiten lassen:
das Erkenntnissvermögen, das Gefühl der Lust und Unlust, und
das Begehrungsvermögen." Or, again, in the treatise 'Uber
Philosophie überhaupt, etc.' (1794), the trichotomy of mental
powers, with an admixture of what each faculty represents, is
defended with Kantian jealousy.[1] Finally, in 1798, the psychological 'Anthropologie' appears, whose first part treats "von
Erkenntnissvermögen, von Gefühl der Lust und Unlust, und
von Begehrungsvermögen" in three books respectively.[2]

Kant, then, recognizes three ways of viewing the mental
life.   But he does not overlook attempts to reduce them to one.
In the posthumous 'Vorlesungen über Psychologie,'[3] he turns an
interestingly critical eye towards a Leibnitzian development.
It has been questioned " ob alle Kräfte der Seele vereinigt, und
aus einer Grundkraft können hergeleitet werden, oder ob
verschiedene Grundkräfte anzunehmen sind um alle Handlungen
der Seele daraus zu erklären? *e. g.*, Wolff nimmt eine Grundkraft an und sagt, die Seele selbst ist eine Grundkraft, die sich
das Universum vorstellt."   But, to call the soul a fundamental
power is false ontology.   Power (die Kraft) is not a particular
principle, but only ' ein respectus der substanz zum Accidenz.'
Furthermore, to reduce the powers to one, because the soul is a
unit, raises a far different query.   This unity of the soul amidst
the diversity of activities must take care of itself.   In empirical
psychology we must account for the classified varieties of
phenomena, and find accordingly, " das wir verschiedene
Grundkräfte annehmen müssen, und nicht aus einer alle Phänom-
ena der Seele erklären können ; demnach sind das Erkenntnissvermögen, das Vermögen der Lust und Unlust und das Begehrungsvermögen Grundkräften."   They have a peculiar but
limited service " um die empirische Psychologie desto syste-
matischer abzuhandeln."[4]

Before inquiring what Kant intends to comprehend under
each 'faculty' respectively, it is well to note what the recogni-

---

[1] *Werke*, VI., 379.

[2] *Werke*, VII., pp. 437, 548, 571.

[3] Pp. 50 ff.

[4] This has special interest in a historical comparison with the Herbartian
developments in psychology.

tion of faculties can really mean. Reason in its *a priori* function possesses three principles which are regulative of the understanding in its observation of nature, *viz.:* manifoldness, variety and unity, which have their application to the facts of the inner sense as seen in this psychological doctrine of the faculties.[1] But what could be meant by those principles of homogeneity and specification, as they apply to the various groups of conscious states, is happily told us in a magazine article appearing in January, 1788. Not only does he here enunciate a consequence which may condemn his own conception of the faculties later on; but his interpretation of all this facultization is a weak, lone pulse of that new life coming out of scholasticism. Elemental powers mean no more than this: upon the observation of activities which can be grouped, there is to be a (metaphysical) positing of some substratal power that may assume the name given to that class of phenomena. When we have reached these fundamental powers human insight is at an end. We are forced to accept them, for their possibility cannot be understood by any means.[2] But only in the very popular essay on 'Philosophie überhaupt' does Kant become the true metaphysician, and express the real function of the so-called faculties that may not only be reduced to one, but even increased to four. After all "muss man doch gestehen dass es mit psychologischen Erklärungen, in Vergleichung mit den physischen, sehr kümmerlich bestellt sei das sie ohne Ende hypothetisch sind, und man zu drei verschiedenen Erklärungs-gründen gar leicht einer vierten, ebenso scheinbaren erdenken kann;"[3] and this in the self-same treatise that gives almost his ultimatum on the question of mental powers and their relation to Critical philosophy.

There now issues the more difficult task of answering the inquiry, What does Kant mean by the cognitive, affective and conative faculties, and how do they relate themselves to each other? It is difficult, since, in the first instance, Kant though extremely systematic, was not fond of hard and fixed defini-

[1] *Critique*, II., 567; *cf.*, Meyer, *op. cit.*, p. 44.
[2] *Werke*, IV., p. 492 and note.
[3] *Werke*, VI., 395 f.

tions. He always defines himself as may be suitable for his immediate purpose. Secondly, because it is no whit less true in psychology than in philosophy, that 'the definition,' as Kant himself says,[1] 'in its complete clearness ought to conclude rather than begin our work.' But it is desirable, though extremely difficult, to construct a proper definition.

In general, Kant means by the respective faculties something like what follows: "Erkenntnissvermögen (facultas cognoscendi) ist das Vermögen des Gemüths das Daseyn und das Veränderungen der Gegenstände zu bestimmen."[2] It is a unique faculty whose activity consists in carrying on the mechanism of 'Vorstellungen,' a mechanism into which enter both a receptivity and a spontaneity, and representations that have objective reference. Feeling is something *toto cælo* different. "Man nennt die Fähigkeit Lust oder Unlust bei einer Vorstellung zu haben, darum Gefühl weil beides das blos Subjective im Verhältnisse unserer Vorstellung, und gar keine Beziehung auf ein Object zum möglichen Erkenntnisse desselben (nicht einmal dem Erkenntnisse unseres Zustandes) enthält."[3] Conation is variously represented; yet all expressions may agree in these: now it is will in its highest critical meaning; "Man kann den Willen durch das Vermögen der Zwecke definiren indem sie jerseit Bestimmungsgründe des Begehrungsvermögens nach Principien sind;"[4] then it is the empirical activity of desire, as "das Vermögen durch seine Vorstellungen Ursache der Gegenstande dieser Vorstellungen zusein."[5] What sort of passivities and activities is included under each is most briefly and graphically seen in diagrams which gather up about all there is to be found on his special divisions of the faculties.[6]

Next to the division and the conception of the faculties, the most important point in Kant's psychology that has influence on the form, and even on the content of Critical philosophy, is his

[1] *Critique*, II., 626 and note.
[2] Mellin's *Encyc. Wörterbuch d. Krit. Philosophie*, 1797, II., I., p. 384.
[3] *Werke*, VII., pp. 8 f.; *cf.*, V., 62; *Vorlesungen*, etc., pp. 31 f.
[4] *Werke*, V., 62; *cf.*, VII., 10.
[5] *Werke*, VII., 8; *cf.*, V., 9, note.
[6] *Cf.*, *infra*, at end of study.

notion of what are the relations between the various fields of mental activities. Indeed this feature of his opinion, as to the empirical nature of mind, may be said to stand second to none in its influence on transcendental philosophy. All others become appreciable only when Criticism had exhausted itself in the three *Critiques*. But this is the great fact which fashioned the articulation of the three parts, and gave coloring to the treatment each 'higher cognitive' faculty received. Eliminate this psychological influence, and Criticism could never have ripened a speculative scepticism, the moral law with its intellectual austerity would have vanished before the affective conditions of ethical needs, and in the æsthetical judgment there would have been introduced an objectivity as categorical in its demands, that the ideal of beauty shall be realized in an 'intelligible' world, as is the ethical imperative, that I shall find my complete manhood in the perfection of myself in terms of the ultimate good.

Kant's utterances on the point in question are not exceedingly numerous, yet they come with no uncertain sound whose sonority is intensified as we introduce the implications easily to be read in that huge commentary which the whole of Criticism is. The general view taken may be summed up thus : "Die Verknüpfung zwischen dem Erkenntnisse eines Gegenstandes und dem Gefühle der Lust und Unlust an der Existenz desselben, oder die Bestimmung des Begehrungsvermögens, ihn hervorzubringen, ist zwar empirisch erkennbar genug."[1] When expressed in detail it must include such views as these. Reason (cognitive) is the special and great activity which throws off knowledge, as it were. It can never be replaced by faith, or belief, which is some sort of feeling, and this is directly opposed to knowledge.[2] Though there be feeling in all sensuous elements,

---

[1] *Werke*, VI., 379.

[2] "Aller Glaube ist nun ein subjectiv zureichendes, objectiv aber mit Bewusstsein unzureichendes Fürwahrhalten ; also wird er dem Wissen entgegengesetzt." "Die Vernunft fühlt ; sie sieht ihren Mangel an, und wirkt durch den *Erkenntniss-trieb* das Gefühl des Bedürfnisses ;" *i. e.*, orientation in reflection starts from a subjective means which is nothing more than a strange 'Gefühl des der Vernunft eigenen Bedürfnisses' (which Kant thinks peculiar to intellect alone, but is really an affective accompaniment of all acts of discrimination,

and pleasure-pain may be an accompaniment of perceptions,[1] yet it is subordinate to all ideational determinations and cannot reflect backwards over the intellective processes, except as strong emotions interfere with the activity of attention or mutilate the formation of concepts.[2] An object being once determined through the senses, its possible psychical history is not completed until it has stirred the desires and motivated the will through those feelings with which it is particularly connected. Desire always has at its basis that class of feelings which appreciate the continued presence of an object.[3] Yet all feeling does not rest on the will. This converse does not hold. Even if this be the natural history of the will, the metaphysic of morals can find no principle based on feelings; for with whatever sort we may begin, 'vom pathologischen oder dem rein ästhetischen, oder auch dem moralischen Gefühl,' we can never get beyond the 'physical' character which belongs to feeling, because of its initiation.[4] The will, however, as it actualizes itself in the ethical life, is the source of any amount of feeling.[5] Reason still stands alone, howsoever feeling and desire may be mixed up. Much less than the affective faculty does the will have any legitimate or constructive influence on the intellect. To the question, 'ob das Wollen einer Einfluss auf unsere Urtheile habe?' an affirmative answer cannot be given; 'dies wäre auch sehr ungereimt.'[6] Thus knowing, feeling and willing are distinct activities not influencing one another so as to promote rational life, and the Critical method proposed to itself to see what could be known by each faculty alone.

so much so that one might say the whole cognitive life is based on the one motive of interest). IV., pp. 342, ff.; *cf.* the famous antithesis between 'knowledge' and 'faith' as clearly brought out in the second edition preface. *Critique,* I., 380. *Cf., Werke,* VIII., 72 f., belief *vs.* knowledge, etc.

[1] *Werke,* V., 210 f. 297, 388.

[2] *Werke,* VIII., 37 f., VI., 379.

[3] *Werke,* VII., 8 f.

[4] *Werke,* VII., 178 f.; *cf.,* V. 26.

[5] *Werke,* V., 76 f.; *cf.,* VI., p. 380.

[6] *Werke,* VIII., 74: "Hätte der Wille einen unmittlebaren Einfluss auf unsere Ueberzeugung von dem, was wir wünschen [mere whim or desire is thus confused with will as an executive determination], so würden wir uns beständig Chimären von einem glücklichen Zustande machen und sie sodann auch immer für wahr halten. Der Wille kann aber nicht *wider* überzeugende Beweise von Wahrheiten streiten, die seinen Wünschen und Neigungen zuwider sind."

This leads at once to the inquiry, how Kant turned these psychological tenets to the account of Critical philosophy. Even here we are not left to a mere inference of what may be implicated. He himself becomes explicit when it was finally discerned that reason had been carrying on, not merely an investigation of the formal, but also of matters that have specific relations to the mind analyzed, and is then ready to say:[1] "hiemit endige ich also mein ganzes kritisches Geschäft." The articulation of the system ('aggregate') has already been indicated; here it must be seen what basis he found for it in human nature.[2]

From the very start Kant announces his position as antithetic to scholasticism. It is 'human reason,' '*our* reason,' not angelic or divine rationality, that is to be submitted to the tests of the proposed methods. The humanness of his inquiry he has even further explained. The earliest expression of this, with which I am familiar, is near the close of the year 1787. He writes to Prof. Reinhold that he is struggling to unearth the elements of knowledge and to trace them back to their elemental powers.[3] Three years intervened, when the last *Critique* appeared, filling in a lacuna 'in der Familie der oberen Erkenntnissvermögen.'[4] That this triplicity, however, was not taken with psychological intent, is seen in the footnote[5] replying to the surprise and dubitancy that philosophy always appears threefold. "Das liegt aber in der Natur der Sache . . . . . . So muss, nach demjenigen, was zu der synthetischen Einheit

[1] *Werke*, V., 176.
[2] This relation has a manifold interest as Kant carried it out: 1st, In his attempt to break away from 'dogmatism,' which meant the scholastic procedure of saying, 'by this, I understand such and such, etc.,' and then proceed to develop concepts expressive of reality; 2d, That it has been the most potent expression of the anthropological modernism in philosophy. Inquiries as to reality are to be settled first by an appeal to man and his capabilities. This was the call of Criticism; 3d, How, while this very Criticism first founded itself on formal logic, it required only a decade and within the maturity of its patient founder, to run its own development into psychology—that anthropological branch of knowledge most helpful to him who would think out the truth of experience.
[3] *Werke*, VIII., 739 t.
[4] *Werke*, V., 183.
[5] *Werke*, V., 203.

überhaupt erforderlich ist, nämlich (1) Bedingung, (2) ein Bedingtes, (3) der Begriff der aus der Vereinigung des Bedingten mit seines Bedingung entspringt, die Eintheilung nothwendig Trichotomie sein." What view of the various faculties is to be taken, and what portion of their activities are to be regarded in Criticism are told us when that was wrought out.[1] In these explanations it appears that philosophy, in general, treats only of the 'higher' faculties, the 'lower' being subject to such treatment as they might receive in psychological anthropology.   That is, a threefold division of each faculty is made: first, the lower or empirical, are those which are thrown into the medley mechanism of experience; second, the higher or rational aspects, where activity is the chief mark. It is on these that Criticism builds itself. When it demands an analysis of man's power to know, and an inquiry as to the respective constituents of his moral and aesthetical natures, there abides this constant elimination of what is empirical; thirdly, there occasionally appear allusions to transcendental faculties, those discovered by Criticism, as *e. g.*, the pure apperception of the *ego*, a 'transcendental faculty' in rational psychology.

The more general or extensive psychological substrate of Kantian philosophy is detailed in the specially written essay.[2] The system of all the faculties of the human mind gives the triplicity of powers and shows their empirical relation. Kant had treated 'understanding' (knowledge) and 'reason' (ethical relations) 'objectively,' but they stand so far apart. There is no transition from mechanism and nature to man and freedom.   All experience, being given as a series in time, falls in the clutches of casuality. Practical reason revealed a rational spontaneity as law-giving and eliminated all empiricism. A great gulf abides between these two precipices erected by metaphysic. Somehow the chasm must be spanned. But the material for such a possibility can be sought only in the system of the faculties.[3] Feeling, in its entirety, is not represented in the Critical system. The large mass lies below metaphysical par.

[1] *Werke*, V., 183-185.

[2] *Ueber Phil. überhaupt, zur Einleitung in d. K. d. Urtheil.*, 1794, *Werke*, VI., 373-404.

[3] *Werke*, VI., 380.

It is always 'physisch,'[1] and its very essence as 'sensible'[2] brings it within the limits of subjective sensitivity. It remains ever individualistic, and, *a fortiori*, can never enter the holy grounds of Criticism. This deals only with what falls within "das System der reinen Erkenntnissvermögen durch Begriffe."[3] ·The possibility of the admission of aught within this circle, lies in the claim, that it carries on transactions with 'objectivity' in one way or another. It is the pleasure of 'taste' or the enjoyment of the beautiful, which requires some representation within the mechanical side of human nature, and yet links itself with that ideal spontaneity which freedom is, thus coordinating the three *Critiques* with the cluster of mental faculties.[4]

The three external divisions of philosophy not only grow out of the psychological triplicity, but the very treatment within each is also traced back to the same source. "Dass es drei Arten der Antinomie gibt, hat seinen Grund darin dass es drei Erkenntnissvermögen: Verstand, Urtheilskraft und Vernunft gibt, deren jedes seine principien *a priori* haben muss, etc.*"* As Kant thus tries to work out an intimate relation between much of the Critical philosophy and the content of the human mind (and this was his special and necessary right in view of his great problems), there constantly appears the attempted *schmelzung* of formal, abstract logic, and concrete, living psychology. The former was the starting point, the latter the conquest of the critical development.[6]

---

[1] *Werke*, VII., 179.

[2] *Werke*, V., pp. 80, 95, 123.

[3] *Werke*, VI., 400.

[4] *Werke*, VI., 388 f., 401 f.

[5] *Werke*, V., 356.

[6] This, as well as the immediate points of contact between the results of psychological analysis, the faculties which fall within Criticism, the transcendental principles it discovers, and the facts of experience to which they are metaphysically related, clearly appears in the following table abridged from V., 203 f.; VI., 402 f:

Erkenntnissvermögen,   Gefühl der Lust und Unlust,
                    Begehrungsvermögen

are the three elemental faculties. But their "Ausübung liegt doch immer das Erkenntnissvermögen [rational treatment?] obzwar nicht immer Erkenntniss

That Kant thought himself to have covered all the facts of
experience and given them a complete philosophical interpretation, we must take him to mean, and he seems also thus to clinch
the system of transcendentalism to 'the facts of life,' when he
says :[1] "So entdeckt sich ein System der Gemüthskräfte, in
ihren Verhältnisse der Natur und Freiheit; deren jede ihre ei-
genthümlichen bestimmenden Principien *a priori* haben, und um
deswillen die zwei Theile der Philosophie (die theoretische und
praktische) als eines doctrinalen Systems ausmachen, und zugleich ein Uebergang vermittelst der Urtheilskraft, die durch ein
eigenthümliches Princip beide Theile verknüpft, nämlich von
dem sinnlichen Substrat der erstern zum intelligibilen der zweiten
Philosophie, durch die kritik eines Vermögens (der Urtheilskraft), welches nur zum Verknüpfen dient und daher zwar für
sich kein Erkenntniss verschaffen." We see then that Kant did
go to considerable length in empirical psychology, in recognizing empirical faculties, in ascribing a large content to them, and
in so doing, pronounced upon the influence he supposed to obtain between them. We see, also, that he developed a consciousness of the substratal relation of this empirical psychology to the

zum Grunde." The 'higher cognitive' faculty, therefore, as shown by the
course of Criticism, that stands alongside of

Erkenntnissvermögen	is	Verstand;
Gefühl der Lust und Unlust	"	Urtheilskraft;
Begehrungsvermögen	"	Vernunft.

The metaphysical principles which correspond with the faculties and lie in the
higher forms of cognition respectively, are:

Gesetzmässigkeit,	Zweckmässigkeit,	Zweckmässigkeit, die zugleich Gesetz ist—Verbindlichkeit.

Finally, a table that associates the products of the various mental factors, how
Criticism works among them, products whose fusion, we might fancy Kant
saying, makes up the totality of experience:

Gemüthsvermögen:	Obere Erkenntnissvermögen:
Erkenntnissvermögen,	Verstand,
Gefühl der Lust und Unlust,	Urtheilskraft,
Begehrungsvermögen.	Vernunft.
Principien Apriori:	Products:
Gesetzmässigkeit,	Natur,
Zweckmässigkeit,	Kunst,
Verbindlichkeit.	Sitten.

[1] *Werke*, VI., pp. 401–404.

Critical philosophy, on all of which it now remains to gather up an estimation.

When we consider the variety of aspects from which the stream of our mental life can be regarded, we find that they all cluster about three groups. It is a general agreement, with some notable historic exceptions, that we can view consciousness from three view-points; or as Ward says,[1] we find we can make three statements in reference to ourselves: "I feel somehow, I know something, I do" somewhat. As long as our psychology is to be, as it were, a natural history of the soul, that is about all we can say. Taking some object, or any stepping-stone in the flow of consciousness, substantives of mental life, I somehow cognize, or properly, I recognize it. With this apprehension of it there is some shade of concomitant feeling; it is not merely the proper cause of some pleasure or pain, but there is a tonic ingredient. Some form of feeling attends me. I am also said to make some effort, either a purpose striving or 'an involuntary act of will' somehow appears, or there are inhibitions, negative efforts as well as positive strivings. The complexity of adult mental life is merely the developed fusion of the infinite terms which come in the growth of such a consciousness.

But when psychology becomes some form of psychical dynamics it passes beyond to something which we cannot truly admit as psychology. Nor is it the psychology that has been struggling under biologic influences to assume the rank of a natural science. It includes these in a more or less absorbent way, but its roots lie confessedly elsewhere. Not only on 'Erfahrung' and 'Mathematik,' but also 'auf Metaphysik,' is this science 'neu gegründet.'[2] Empirical psychology is to be reconstructed from a metaphysical standpoint. The historic precedent in English and French thought since Locke is set aside. Metaphysic does not have psychology as its foundations. The rather psychological analyses are to start from the metaphys-

[1] *Loc. cit.*, p. 39; or as perhaps better put by Drobisch (*Emp. Psych.*, p. 36), some of the states of consciousness appear only 'in uns zu geschehen'— Vorstellen; others 'mit uns vorzugehen,' so that we suffer—Fühlen; and finally others 'aus uns hervorzugehen—Streben.'

[2] Herbart's *Psychologie*, 1824-25.

ical postulate, that the soul, like all other realities, is of a simple
nature and quality and of spaceless essence. Its real nature
is that of ' self-preservation,' and when affected neurally it acts
in opposition. "Every such act of self-preservation on the
part of the soul is an idea." Feeling is the consciousness of the
process of 'Vorstellen;' *e. g.*, if the relation of 'Vorstellungen'
is such that the process of 'Vorstellen' is characterized by conflict, then there is a painful feeling. To will there is denied
any independent nature. Such was an epoch-making psychology—a metaphysical ' Mechanik and Statik' of ideas,[1] from
which the course of mental life was to be deduced. It was a
' realism' that rose in opposition to idealism, and was the most
signal reaction for the science of psychology.

Kant's position in the history of the division of mental functions is a most prominent one. As we have already seen, modern
tendencies before Kant were to regard merely two functions of
mind, or to posit some realistic simplicity, as in Wolff, etc.,—influences coming from the doctrine of monads. It is only in
recent times that the tripartite classification has been taken up.
We find its beginning among the German psychologists, *e. g.*,
Mendelssohn and Tetens.[2] It was Kant's acceptance and authoritative defense of the trichotomy of powers that has made it
modern psychologic orthodoxy. Herbart, as Harms says,
merely developed a tendency in Wolff's psychology which first
represents all spiritual activities as merely modifications of ideating powers. The triplicity of mental function was completed
when feeling had been declared to be a primal element. The
late recognition given to it in psychology is probably due to the
fact that feelings are rather obscure, inaccessible and marvel-

---

[1] Harms, *Phil. seit Kant*, Berlin, 1876, p. 548 f.

[2] *Cf.* Mendelssohn's *Schriften*, II., 294 f. '*Morgenstunden*,' ch. VII.:
"Man pfleget gemeiniglich das Vermögen der Seele in Erkenntnissvermögen
und Begehrungsvermögen einzutheilen, und die Empfindung der Lust und
Unlust schon mit zum Begehrungsvermögen zurechnen. Allein mich dünkt,
zwischen dem Erkennen und Begehren liege das Billigen, der Beifall, das Wohl-
gefallen der Seele, welches noch eigentlich von Begierde weit entfernt ist," etc.
Cf. Teten's *Phil. Versuche*, etc., I. p. 625.: "Ich zähle drey Grundvermögen der
Seele: das Gefühl, den Verstand und ihre Thätigskeitskraft." *Cf.* Ziegler's
Erkenntnisstheorie Tetens in Beziehung auf Kant, pp. 58 f.; Sommer's *Grund-
züge einer Gesch.*, etc. pp. 291 ff.

ously fantastic, and, as Kant indicates in his 'Anthropologie,' were generally considered physiological functions having no place in psychology proper. On the other hand, that the feelings should have been recognized in Germany first is, no doubt, in some way to be associated with the rise of modern æsthetics in the labors of Baumgarten and Schiller.[1]

Closely associated with this are recent psychological attempts to reduce the aspects of consciousness to one element and develop the others from it—not to mention metaphysical attempts, such as Schopenhauer's, who would reduce all to will. Lotze[2], who champions the trichotomy of faculties in his vigorous criticism of Herbart, seems in the end to make feeling the primordial element in consciousness, and by its presence sees, in the consciousness of any grade whatever, the power to differentiate itself from its environment. It is Horwicz[3], however, who not only recognizes feeling as an independent mental function, but stands the chief representative of the attempt to reduce feeling to the primordial type of mental manifestation.

Will has also been the point of psychological reduction of the faculties. Wundt[4] seems to find in 'Trieb' that which constitutes the fundamental aspect of consciousness. Höffding[5] finds it in will, "if any one of the three species is to be regarded as the original form." James[6] secures in 'purposive action' the trait which is to characterize the phenomena that may come within the scope of psychology, thus virtually agreeing with Wundt and Höffding.[7] But attempts to find the essence of self-consciousness in other terms than that itself, leads us beyond distinctive psychological considerations; and, indeed, we need not be surprised to find in Kant a metaphysical

[1] *Cf.*, Sommer's *Grundzüge, etc.*, pp. 2, 277, 297.

[2] *Phil. of Rel.*, tr., p. 61 ; *Microcosmus*, Eng. trans., I., 247, 250.

[3] *Cf.*, Bobtschew, *Die Gefühlslehre von Kant bis auf unsere Zeit*, Lpzg., 1888, p. 83 ff.

[4] *Phys. Psych.*, II., ch. XXIV., Sec. 2.

[5] *Outlines of Psychology*, tr., pp. 99–100, 308 f.

[6] *Psych.*, I. pp. 5–11.

[7] Fortlage also shares the opinion with Schopenhauer, that 'Wille oder Trieb,' in general, is the fundamental aspect of the empirical *ego;* even, that impulse is the foundation of that phenomenon ordinarily called 'consciousness.' *Cf.*, *System der Psych.*, 1st. Th., Vorrede XIX.

reduction of the soul to rational will. In one sense he has anticipated many of the developments since his time, whereas, as Harms says[1], he had predecessors only in Augustine and Dun Scotus.

It is of importance, however, to note that Kant's greatest service here to psychology is his constant clamor for the feelings as a distinct type of mental life, as well as recognizing the disparity between the other two forms. Bobtschew[2] points out another merit in Kant's conception of the feelings in that they were particularly regarded as of purely subjective nature. But it can hardly be conceded that Kant considered the feelings as a tone quality of representations in the same way as they are now regarded as one of the qualities of the sense element which enters into the ideational processes.

While Kant's service to modern psychology is great in this respect, he fell into the scholastic error of abstract entities being indicated by faculties. It is a difficult task even for professed psychologists to free themselves from the same error, notwithstanding their constant efforts to do so. They warn themselves against partitioning off mentality into faculties, but straightway their discussions require us to believe them viewing presentation, memory, thought, feeling, etc., as so many separate entities which come up with consciousness. It is no metaphysical leap which permits one to point out that faculties, as such, are no original mental possession. The natal consciousness has no faculties and knows none. Faculties, if anything, only come with the development of adult consciousness. And then there can be meant nothing more than the attainment of certain aspects of that development. The fundamental fact is that ' some sort of thinking goes on,' that consciousness is on the march, and cannot be impeded or split up in any other way than by its own activities, which we find clustering about its substantives. It is Herbart's brushing away all the abstract talk about faculties, to which this tendency in psychology must be attributed. But on the other hand, he subverts the truth, that "every psychic act requires for the expression of its full con-

[1] *Gesch. d. Psych.*, p. 346.
[2] *Op. cit.*, p. 19.

tent three acts: discriminative, affective, conative; though any one of these aspects may be emphasized, possibly at the expense of the others, but all depending on the given amount of psychic energy at disposal."[1] That Kant laid the basis for leaving to musty shelves all scholasticism about 'faculties' as mental apartments into which one might put anything and then proceed to demonstrate by the articulation of such conceptual pack-horses, but on the other hand appears to fall into the same fault, will appear more clearly in considering the psychological basis for his divisions of philosophy.

For psychology then, in its formal aspect, Kant is of great historical value. And one could almost agree with Harms[2] in saying that with Kant psychology entered a new era in setting off the phenomenal realm of consciousness, had he not called men away from scientific psychology in denying its mathematical possibilities, and showing the uselessness of building up any 'rational' system concerning the soul.

In his analysis of consciousness, Kant must receive psychology's approval. But when he characterizes the inter-relations of the so-called faculties, the same science must take him severely to task. He not only announced a false psychology, but makes it the empiric basis for his conception of *a priori* cognition, and took from it the coloring matter that suffuses, not only his sceptical tenets, but gives the entire tone to his ethics and æsthetics. So important is this point with Kant that one can conceive of nothing else, except his wilful and persistent disregard for the influence of one form of consciousness on the others, that made possible the very conception of the transcendental itself. Unlike the scholastic adage that something might be true in philosophy and false in theology, *we cannot concede for a moment Kant's implication that something may be true for psychology but useless for philosophy.*

The relation of the faculties to each other is, in Kant's view, about as hard fixed and far apart as they appear in a diagram. Curiously enough, there are two aspects to this relation, one empirical, the other transcendental. In the former

[1] Prof. Ladd.
[2] Harms, *Gesch. d. Psych.*, p. 339.

Kant allows (and, as it seems, it is an echo from the *Recherche de la Verité* and its unique method) only a relation of hinderance between the faculties. The ideating powers are distorted in their primary functions when the appetitive feelings enter.[1] Emotions, requiring a pulsating heart, detract from cold-blooded reflection. The will is helpless in its true desires when it falls within the clutches of the all-prevading passions. Rational beings are irrationalized in the contemplative, subjective moods where the beautiful and the sublime yield forth no object. An answer to ' What is truth?' based on the empirical nature of man, only shows us ' of what crooked material he is made,' and from which nothing perfect can come.

But the faculties must be viewed from a critical point. What is, either in knowledge or in reality, we may fancy ourselves to hear Kant say, can be got at only as we transcend trammeling experience, and find what each faculty can do for itself. The cognitive powers must be examined in themselves. The will must submit to a treatment when all the vagaries of motivation have been swept away. Feeling of the ' pathological ' sort has such a vast amount of what constitutes the nature of ' der Pöbel' that it can never be granted an introduction into the enthroned sanctum of pure reason. Each faculty in its ' oberen aspects, only, belongs to philosophy.

Kant's attempt to smudge psychological facts for the sake of speculation is classic, and stands as an example of a host of philosophers,[2] who proceed on the assumption that ' pure thought' is a possibility unattended by the ' baser' elements of human nature. Psychology was not cultivated among them for its own sake. It could proceed only with an admixture of ethics. And with our author naught else but pietistic convictions give permission for moral judgments only when activity and its affective conditions were in question. Thus, and as we have seen, the influence of the ' faculties' was of a negative, moral aspect. Psychological observation was carried only far enough to assure the religious sentiment that the hindering and inhibitory

---

[1] *Cf.*, *Werke*, VII., 451 f., 575 f.; Erdmann, *Reflexionen*, 70 ff.

[2] *E. g.*, Hegel and Hamilton. " Consciousness is knowledge." " Pure apperception is fundamental."

results of feeling exhausted them; or, where noëtic activity was in dispute, there frequently appeared citations of the supposed fact that 'reason' and the 'passions' were in conflict, and struggled for a supremacy; consequently, philosophy must view 'pure reason' alone. Will, movement, strivings were properly conceived of as flowing from affective impulses, but these again contaminated ethical purity.

Such ethical psychologizing appears erroneous from the fact that not only are the feelings inhibitory on the presentative activity of the conceptual sort, and thus lodging in the feelings the mass of conservatism that pervades human nature; but also the feelings are helpfully influential in the processes of cognition, while ideas can no less be severed from the development of the feelings. It must here suffice to point out one or two instances of such inter-dependence, in order to show how the failure to provide for such psychological facts influenced Kant's formal divisions of philosophical discipline, and wherein the *principium divisionis* resides in knowledge in its widest sense, and lastly, to estimate the formal aspects of his philosophy from a psychologic point of view.

It is one of the conquests of recent psychology in heeding Lotze's[1] imploration that "we must above all wean ourselves from the habit of looking on the feelings as subsidiary events that sometimes occur in the succession of our internal states, while the latter for the most part consist of an indifferent series." Since this reaction against the tick-tack play on dry, abstract thought in order to call the attention of the absolute to the way of dialectic, as we find it in this philosopher's 'musings from his æsthetical perch in Göttingen,' whither Aristophanic facetiousness has placed him, psychologists have been wont to inquire into the nature of feelings, not to say, philosophers build on them. Not only do associations form themselves between ideas, as such; but, "every idea connects itself also with the momentary tone which characterizes our universal vital feeling, or the general feeling of our whole state at the instant when the idea appears."[2] Nay, more, cognitions do not only fall along

[1] *Micr.*, I., 242-3.
[2] Lotze, *Metaphysics*, Eng. trans., II., 229.

side of the feelings, but the growth of the latter is inextricably bound up with the ideational attachments which give characteristics to the core of feeling. In a certain sense there is an evolution in the life of feeling which comes from their fusion of elements. Even in Spinoza there appears a recognition of the fact that "feeling naturally enters into an association with the idea of that which played as the apparent or real cause" of the joy or sadness. He, too, is guilty of the attempt of abstracting pure feeling and pure cognition, overlooking the fact most patent to any one observing his own mental life, that ideas are *structural* in the life of feelings, in that, through their sense and perceptive elements, they contribute to the very possibility of feeling coming into reality. For, "the most important crisis in the development of a feeling is when its object is removed out of the sphere of sensation and perception into that of ideation and memory."[1] Psychology finds the possibility of an adult feeling laid in the fact that the germs of the affective life differentiate only as they become "directed through ideas which fuse with it, to definite objects." Again, the association of feeling does not belong to affective retentiveness and control, but undoubtedly is subject to the connection of the ideational elements fused in each emotive state.[2] This affinity of the representative factors is a biologic necessity, nor dare its importance be lessened when the unitary life of mind is sought in contradistinction to the variety so apparent on all its sides.

The relation of cognition to feeling is still farther seen in the dependence of the latter on the former. Feelings are often found to be regarded as effects whose causes appear in a previous idea. The changes in the flow of feelings no doubt contribute to this as exhausting, or being the chief point in the nature of feeling. Cognitions could go singly, but feelings take their rise in ideas. "We never find," as Ward says,[3] "that feeling directly alters, *i. e.*, without the intervention of the action to which it prompts—either our sensations or situations, but that regularly these latter with remarkable promptness and certainly

[1]Höffding, *Outlines of Psychology*, London, 1892, p. 254.

[2]As Höffding quite clearly shows, *op. cit.*, p. 239 ff.; *cf.* also Lotze, *Metaphysic*, II., 314.

[3]*Encyc. Brit.*, XX., 40.

alter it. We have not first a change of feeling, and then a change in our sensations, perceptions, and ideas; but, these changing, change of feeling follows." This relation was taken by the psychology underlying Criticism, as the sum of the whole matter.[1] Accordingly we find Kant consistent in making his divisions follow the order of facts as they appeared to him. We shall see in a moment, that the opposite is just as true, that change of feeling changes the course of ideation.

Had this been all of the matter, Kant could be justified in his formal aspect of philosophy. But, profounder than the relation of cognition to feeling, is the influence of feeling on ideation. Not only in the mechanism of mental life so far as psychology is interested in depicting it, but the very nature of reality itself, as we look to metaphysic for its analysis, cannot be faithfully regarded with an utter neglect of this deep influence of feeling on cognition. Neither can philosophy in its formal and material aspects disregard this fusion of primitive elements, and, in so far as the initiative separation and final articulation of the three *Critiques* hang upon the oversight of these facts, so far is the Critical philosophy blame-worthy. The development within the Critical philosophy, as seen in the order of the appearance of its parts, and as Kant explains their concatenation,[2] indicates that an ethical judgment was pronounced on the play of the faculties, whereas we now demand a psychological judgment. Not only is it true as Kant chiefly recognizes, that the feelings may have a hindering effect upon the combination of ideas, but the phenomena of what is called 'the expansion of feeling'[3]—wherein the principle is, that "all strong feeling struggles for the sole control in the mind, and give a coloring to all its mental activities;" but it is just as true that "the simplest and apparently driest notions are never quite destitute of an attendant feeling."[4] Nor is there a chance rela-

[1]*Cf.*, *Werke*, VI., 380, V., 123.

[2]That there is a development within the Critical philosophy is one of the rather recent attainments of Kantian criticism; *cf.* Caird, *The Crit. Phil. of I. Kant*, II., pp. 406, 643; Bernard's *trans. of K. of Judgment*, pp. XIV., ff.; Kant's letter to Reinhold, VIII., 738.

[3]Höffding, *op. cit.*, 298 ff, 303 f.

[4]Lotze, *Micr.*, I., 243.

tion between the strength of an idea and its feeling. Just as it may be contended philosphically that knowledge is not without conviction,[1] so it must be maintained that the phenomena of strained expectation, as in spiritualism, or in the common-place experience of desiring aught, demand that we find in the feelings an anticipation and realization of ideas; whereas, one does not only find that for which he seeks; but, also, the very reality of any finding, even ordinary percept-having, goes along with some anticipating interest. This is as much as to say, with Ward,[2] that "feeling leads the attention to concentrate on its object."[3] Even profounder yet is the relation of feeling to what was formerly thought to be a purely discriminative act, *viz.*, apperception, or self-consciousness.

The mutual influence of will among the other sides of consciousness was inadequately conceived by Kant. All favorable influence proceeds forwardly from ideas through feelings to movement and choice. A retrograde working, other than pro-motive, was denied. That would be 'absurd.' It is true that ideas and feelings are the motives of the will. But it is no less a fact that volition enters into the structure and course of ideas at first involuntarily, when nature steps in to help us in our helplessness, and later in the conscious activity of attention. This reaction of will upon cognition is quite as important as the feelings; for, by it we *work* our way through states of dubitancy and matters of delusion up to certainty and reality.

In the mechanism of ideas and feelings, the will acts not only indirectly, but immediately in the sometimes-thought closed circle of the nature of mind. It is an 'augur, boring' sluices

---

[1] *Cf.*, Ladd, *Introd. to Phil.*, pp. 186, 198 f.

[2] *Loc. cit.*, p. 43.

[3] Kant himself is an excellent illustration of this very psychological principle. Popularly thought to be a sordid philosopher writing only dry books, he is, on the contrary, subject to the most intense feelings, so little known to those who thus judge him. As a psychologist one might say the whole Critical philosophy has its reality and actualization in that 'pedagogic primness' which is its constant passion. The desire to make a *formaliter* exhibition of rationality is undoubtedly the sunken pier on which rests the conviction that the *a priori* and its ramifications are its *materialiter* expression. It is without question that this interest was the psychologic affinity which caused the transcendental philosopher to precipitate a whole series of *a priori* scientific principle from the menstrum of cosmological knowledge he had gathered in early years.

for the flow of ideas and feelings.[1] The will itself is no less subject to its own reactionary influences. Volition is not a voluntary affair, but becomes a habit which expresses the highest form of mental fusion that comes with development. One does not even have the priceless self-consciousness without a persistency in attention that is not born of the moment, a fact showing that subjective idealism needs to resubmit itself to what transpires in the developing mind, which is not always made up of 'logical' *a priority*.

It also appeared that Kant did not clearly distinguish between the conative and affective elements in the mental life. And, no doubt, he thought the work of speculation was completed when it had gone through the practical aspects of life. This vacillation had its disturbing effect upon the apportionment of the formal and material aspects of his philosophy. For the *Critique of Judgment*, in its formal articulation, had its basis laid in a mental content, while its matter is subjected to an attempted formal reduction of speculative logic.

We were at last compelled to touch upon psychology so far as it affects the content of philosophy in order to hint at some *principium divisionis*. The brief venture also illustrates the difficulties which attend the division of philosophy, and that the ground must be gone over again. There is a reciprocal relation of this sort both in psychology and philosophy. One cannot partition off their problems and be done once for all with their treatment. Kant's *principium divisionis* is to be found in whatever may have led him to distinguish between fact and reason, sensibility and intelligibility. This conception remained. It appears, and seemingly in a manner to justify the procedure Criticism has taken, in his classification of mental faculties. In the first *Critique*, logic, as dealing with knowledge of that which is, gave him the guiding lines. When the field of conduct, as known, is to be inquired into, some principle is wanting, and he at once attacks the rational voluntary faculty. When the circle has been completed we still find the treatment restricted, to what may be known; but it is now with reference to the faculties whose activities throw off the respective pro-

---

[1] Goldschmidt's figure quoted by Höffding, *op. cit.*, p. 331.

ducts. Finally, it is vigorously maintained (by Kant himself)
that the (knowing) faculties have supplied the *principium* all
the way. Now, from the way in which Kant worked out his
conception of philosophy and the manner in which he relates it
to the human mind, we must say, with some provision to be
noted in a moment, that *the basis of his division of philosophy
lay in the psychological division of the mind.* The formal aspects of the former grew out of the formal aspects of the latter.

It is to be gathered from the preceding mention of the relation of the faculties, that psychology is concerned with the tracing out the mechanism of what may be called knowledge in its
most liberal meaning. It dare not estimate the value of the
various elements, for then it becomes ethical; nor can it pronounce upon the ultimate facts and their inherent worth, for
then it becomes philosophical. Processes only are the goal of
psychological inquiry. The impulsive queries which go beyond these must find satisfaction in the answers rendered by
philosophy. So close do they lie, they are difficult to separate.
One begins where the other ends. Thus knowledge and its
manifold implications are to be submitted to the eye of reason;
and the breaking up into problems depends, not on the 'faculties' which have contributed to that knowledge, but on the way
in which that knowledge may be broken up. There first
emerges that broad distinction which Kant recognized and is
fundamental, *viz.*, between that which is, and that which ought
to be. The former falls within knowledge in its more limited
sphere, and breaks up into the dirempted products of consciousness, affording the subject knowing and the object known.
The latter provokes inquiry into the nature of the objective object and subjective object the me and not-me. The second
broad distinction finds unique implications in manifold ways,
which philosophical analysis must bring to light. Such are the
ideals we feel reality somehow ought to realize.

In raising his profound inquiry, what is knowledge? Kant
truly apprehends both the data and formal basis of philosophy.
And in this psychologic age there is a sparkle of wisdom in the
'return to Kant' which seeks to enter the domain of philosophy by the only possible gate. Here Kant was concrete, liv-

ing. But as he worked it out, it appears that his appreciation was entirely of the abstract, and he at times becomes truly speculative in a scholastic sense. This is the attempt to fuse the initiative, formal logic with the ultimate, living psychology. But the confusion sprinkling it throughout indicates that Criticism found no other pedagogic demand than to satisfy the formal faculties of the mind. Its problems corresponded to these. Moreover, it was a Criticism of transcendental faculties —faculties unknown to psychology. The formal aspect only multiplies the abstractness as we see it carried back. The success of it withal, lay in an inconsistent, but defensible departure from these formal demands. Kant's harking back to scholasticism is seen in this, while his vigorous break with 'angelic' speculation appears in his invitation to men to examine human reason as it is.

CHAPTER IV.

EMPIRICAL PSYCHOLOGY AND THE CONTENT OF THE CRITICAL PHILOSOPHY.

It is a very treacherous procedure to attempt to split up the Critical philosophy and view it from the two aspects of form and content. It has its precedent in Kant himself.[1] The 'Transcendental Æsthetic' and the 'Transcendental Analytic' rest on a violent separation of the form and matter of knowledge. Indeed, the very *raison d'être* of the Critical philosophy itself is found in the possibility of that asseverated distinction. And when a study of it would force it to the same treatment, it must *a fortiori* find itself doubly abstract and still farther removed from a foothold in experiential or rational realities.

It is a precedent only, not a model. It constantly appeared in the preceding chapter that any attempt to carry out the diremption is futile. We cannot pass beyond its mere expression. The two 'aspects' have naught else than a conceptual reality. It is the peculiarity of all species of philosophical inquiries, that how they shall express themselves is inextricably wrapped up in the nature of that which shall constitute the expression. *Sie sind wechselseitig.* And, if we admit that there obtains a qualitative series of such inquiries, this mutuality advances *pari passu* with the relative importance of the respective inquiries. Kant's system does not half complete itself before it begins to struggle with the difficulties arising from its illegitimate sublimation of the bare whirling machinery that is to turn out the fine grist of reality. The necessity of pitting speculative and practical reasons in order to champion reality, however near it may approach hyperbolization in transcendental phraseology, and, the ultimate insight that it all needed a rounding out by a Critical appeal to the most subjective subjectivity, are supreme

[1] *Critique*, II., p. 18 f.

parodies on the conviction that fostered the first nursling of pure reason, and warnings to him who in his search for truth must run the gauntlet of the facts of life.

The distinction of form and content, however, is only a convenience for this study. Psychology underlies Criticism in more ways than one; nor in an entirely negative manner. The conception of psychology and its preliminaries very properly enters into its relation with the formal nature of Criticism. The more serious and difficult task remains—an estimation of the tenets arrived at by Criticism, from a psychological point of view. So much presupposition and implication from this empirical science is wrapped up in Criticism, it was the original purpose of this study to inquire into the extent of the influence it feels from all psychological principles and reach conclusions from a detailed systematic study. But the limitations of time require that an exhaustive treatment be replaced with a condensed consideration of three or four of the most important psychological problems so far as they enter into philosophical doctrines.

In the introductory chapter it was affirmed that psychology and philosophy are two distinct, yet closely, uniquely related, and, consequently often confused endeavors. The truth of this appears even in all forms of sceptical thinking. For in general, their scepticism is due, either to an imperfect psychology; or, their philosophy is only a psychology under a different name, and makes of it an unwarrantable application to problems which do not concern it. Psychology always leaves us with an X and processes. It has also been hinted all along that Kant's was an intensified psychological age that expressed itself in 'Orientations' and 'Aufklärungen,' under whose rational countenance of free-thinking there was a fermenting psychologic spirit only to break forth in the *Critique of Pure Reason* and its supplementary treatises. It must be said the Critical philosophy is the best and natural expression of its age, basing itself on the concatenating unity that man furnishes and thus being an answer to all forms of modern speculation—at one stroke rebuking empiricism and materialism, and checking every variety of dogmatic spiritualism. The preceding chapter

saw how far psychology was Kant's guide, notwithstanding his
utter repudiation of such an impure, empiric matter-of-fact
science as he conceived psychology to be.   From the general
content which he allowed to that psychology, it was seen how
closely he links Criticism to a knowledge of mind life.   There
has also been indicated the substance of Kant's answer to his
great question—his sceptical solution—and how he proceeds at
once to build an ethical metaphysic on the ruins of a speculative structure once erected by the same reason, and to fuse the
positive, empirical limitations of the one with the transcendental
possibilities of the other by a critical examination of subjective,
i. e. æsthetical, judgments.   This provides at least three chief
problems—the nature of knowledge and certainty, and man's
ethical and æsthetical being.   These, in terms of brevity constitute philosophy.   Even Kant says as much with some apparent incongruity with the contents of the first *Critique.*[1]   It is
not proposed to investigate the integrity of Kant's philosophy—
though this has been one of the most obvious points of attack in
the history of Kantian criticism, and may appear so far as desirable in a study of this kind.   Nor is it proposed to inquire
entirely into the legitimate employment Kant made of his own
psychology in his theory of knowledge and rational ethics.
This would partially approach the above problem, and would
also encounter that serious and irremovable difficulty, that, up
to the time of Critical philosophy, we have its psychology only
in implications.   And a doubtful attempt it would be to gather
the involved psychological facts as they appear to any student.
And furthermore, Kant's psychology, while not in dissonance
with his time, was given to us mainly after his philosophical
reflections and with their speculative coloring.   On the basis of
man's self-knowledge, with which the Critical philosophy first
spent itself, did it afterwards attempt to build up a doctrine of
philosophical knowledge—both scientific and moral.

Now philosophy, as a whole, is a progressive doctrine.   It
renews its attacks on ' the riddles of life' from the sometimes

---

[1] "Ich habe gelernt, dass Philosophie eine Wissenschaft des Menschen, seines
Vorstellens, Denkens und Handelns sei; sie soll den Menschen nach allen seinen
Bestandtheilen darstellen, wie er ist und sein soll, etc." *Werke,* VII., 386 f.

clearer vantage ground afforded it by a deeper scientific insight
into the entirety of nature. Yet some of its tasks are perennially
concerned 'with the same old problems.' Philosophy as a
discipline must somehow render an account to reason of its in-
gress into its 'inquiry after ultimate reality,' either by halting
first at this universal fact of knowledge and endeavor its solution, whether man can know reality, as Kant has done ; or with
Hegel 'learn to swim by at once proceeding into the water.'
Notwithstanding Lotze's objection that the orchestra never comes
to music by a constant tuning of the instruments, the music, if
it is to be defensible, must come only after the fitness of the instruments has been ascertained. And it is this very problem of
philosophy—an analysis of knowledge, that receives least help
from the advancement of the empirical sciences. However
much knowledge may be increased, the problem of knowledge
remains the same. Reflective analysis must here go over the
same ground from thinker to thinker, and with the aid of processes and elements acquired by empirical induction, the conviction of an ultimate solution may be increasingly confirmed.[1]
It is this fact, coupled with Kant's claim that he had said the
last word on the nature of knowledge, that makes inviting a
consideration of Kant's results with the results of empirical psychology, as it may have advanced.

Kant is an idealist, as the phrase has philosophical vogue ;
but of what sort, has been the great question from the very first
among his critics. He himself labelled his position in the first
edition of the *Critique,* and later expressions are mere vindica-
tions of his original doctrine. By 'idealist,' Kant understands
one who teaches the doctrine of the doubtful existence of external objects, of which there " are two kinds : *dogmatic,* who denies the existence of matter, and the *sceptical* who doubts it, because he thinks it impossible to prove it."[2] In the popular
'*Prolegomena*'[3] is found the expression of what *he means* by
'idealism," which "besteht in der Behauptung, dass es keine
andern als denkende wesen gebe." His idealism "betraf nicht

[1] *Cf.,* Ladd, *Introd. to Phil.,* pp. 181 ff.
[2] *Critique,* II., 318, 327.
[3] *Werke,* IV., 37, Anmerkung II; 42 Anmerk. III.

die existenz der Sachen . . . . denn die zu bezweifeln, ist mir niemals in den Sinn gekommen, sondern bloз die sinnliche Vorstellung der Sachen, dazu Raum und Zeit zuoberst gehören."

Again, his idealism is the critical kind which subverts the dogmatic idealism of Berkeley and the sceptical, problematical idealism of Descartes.[1] This 'transcendental idealism' was still the bone of contention among his critics when the second edition (1787) appeared, whose only alteration or addition was 'the new refutation of psychological idealism.'[2] Such emendations were more unsatisfactory than any previous, inviting such perverse aud unethical criticism as is notably that of Schopenhauer, that these latter refutations were the cowering utterances of the 'verältende' Kant. Instead, 'the new refutation' is plainly sarcastic; and while the second edition is less confident in its tone, there is undoubtedly a thorough-going adherence to the same doctrine of transcendental ideality, which, when taken in connection with the doctrine of noumenon,[3] is utter scepticism in the critical sense of that term. 'Objects' are such only for the active understanding whose principle of causality has no validity beyond the mere series of temporal events as they are dirempted in the two forms of consciousness. This noëtic conclusion was reached by the transcendental process which neither finds an auxiliary in psychological data, nor is it a psychological procedure.

But Kant has left an excellent loop hole in which the psychologist can thrust his inquiries with a disposition to question the validity of his psychological implications. While there is not a little psychology thrown up as a bulwark behind which Criticism takes its refuge, we must concede to Kant that his fixed armament is philosophical. "We have declared ourselves from the very beginning in favor of transcendental idealism." "The transcendental idealist is an empirical realist and allows to matter, as a phenomenon, a reality which need not be inferred, but may be immediately perceived." "If then we are asked whether dualism only must be admitted in psychology, we

[1] *Werke*, IV., 122 f.
[2] *Critique*, I., 386 f., note, 475-479.
[3] *Critique*, II., 205 ff.

answer certainly, but only in its empirical acceptation."[1] Such passages, though removed in the second edition, are most excellent psychological texts for the Kantian student.

An objection must first be raised against Kant's persisten utterance, that he was dealing only with the 'oberen Erkenntnissvermögen.' Not only does he obviously pass beyond these, but he is compelled to make heavy drafts upon the powers he placed among the lower or sensible—*e. g.* imagination, so important in the transcendental deduction and in the doctrine of schematism. But he swept away the ground on which the Wolffian distinction of higher and lower faculties rests, and which was made with reference to the cognitive activity of mind. "The distinction between confused and well-ordered representation," says Kant, criticizing the psychology of Leibnitz and Wolff,[2] "is logical only and does not touch the content of our knowledge." He replaces this logical by a transcendental distinction, and at once goes farther away from any allowance granted by psychology. The impossibility of his working out his problem on the line of psychological 'purity' is seen in the necessity of his constant invocation on something other than 'pure reason.' It alone could not spin out the knowledge into whose nature he made inquiry. While his conclusions justly entitled him to say,[3] "einem jeden Vermögen des Gemüths kann man ein Interesse beilegen, d. i. ein Princip, welches die Bedingung enthält, unter welcher allein die Ausübung desselben befördert wird," he also found himself compelled to abide with the principle, announced in 1770,[4] that sensations excite mental activity.

As an idealist, Kant is in perfect consistency and truth when he affirms the 'reality' of the facts of experience.[5] Dualism

---

[1] *Critique*, II., 321, 322, 328.

[2] *Critique*, II., 38. It was largely this distinction which aided Kant in coming to the insight of sensibility *vs.* intelligibility. *Cf.* 1770 *Disser. Werke* II., 402 ff; *cf.*, *Vorls. üb. Psych.*, p. 26, where Wolff's position is more clearly repudiated; *cf.* also on the distinction between 'æsthetischen' and 'logische Deutlichkeit.' *Werke* VI., 391 note.

[3] *Werke*, V., 126.

[4] *Werke*, II., 413.

[5] Although the very core of criticism is to see what reason can do without all experience, whence that very shallow criticism that the *a priori* of the

in psychology is a healthy sign of the right sort of an idealism. It leaves unquestioned the reality of things given by the immediacy of consciousness, and comes to us as an answer to those inquiries which press beyond the bare is-ness of things and confronts the mystery of their nature.[1] Here is where realism and idealism as ontological doctrines begin to part ways, the former affirming the independent reality of a world of related things which we know, while to idealism is given the defensible right of maintaining a mentality in, or behind this reality.

Here, also, appears clearly the relation of psychology to either form of metaphysics. They pronounce upon the ultimate nature of the known things as real, while to psychology is incumbent a delineation of the processes whereby a knowledge of those things, *as real*, arises. Both presuppose psychological investigation and plant themselves upon it. They cannot cut loose from it. For the sake of consistency, realism must be realistic and idealism must be idealistic, because each has adopted certain empirical laws as summing up psychological truth. Moreover, in so far as each harks back to the way this knowledge of things as real comes about, they lose their philosophical birthright and drop down to the level of psychological empiricism. But this is satisfied when the manner of acquiring a knowledge of things and the attainment of other forms of developed consciousness has been recited.

The first great and fundamental problem in psychology is the process and nature of sense-perception. These are states of consciousness having the mark of objectivity, and make the first and enduring appeal to the conscious activity. It expresses itself in such terms as, "I see this, here or there; or that, then or now, etc." It affirms itself to be knowing things in space

elements of understanding is of a very doubtful kind, since Kant himself must have been *in* experience in order to have the problem suggested to him. *Cf.*, Lange, *Hist. of Mat.*, II., 190 n., represents them as fruits of an 'inductive process.' Meyer, *op. cit.*, pp. 7, 129 ff., represents it a 'ssteadfast, constant reflection.' Fischer, *Gesch. d. n. Phil.*, V., reduces the method of Criticism as 'psychological empiricism.' Cohen, *Kant's Theorie d. Erfahr.*, pp. 105-107, finds the mode of discovery in "der Reflexion, der psychologischen Besinnung über der Erfahrung."

[1] *Cf.*, Watson, *Journ. Spec. Phil.*, 1881, p. 337 ff., "The Critical Philosophy in its relations to Realism and Sensationalism."

and time, things that are distinguished from that consciousness which knows; (and more significant yet) things (which are not fantastic creatures) that are given to it, oblivious of what theoretic importance the past may have for the being of that which is given. Here psychology steps in with its atomic sensations. It invokes all the scientific resources to which its position, as at the head of the biological sciences, entitles it, to aid it in its explanations, or rather in constructing a satisfactory theory of perception. Here, too, is where the choicest work in psychology has been done, and from this quarter comes the imputation that Kant, in his denial of the possibility of a scientific form being attained by psychology, does nothing more than work crude observations into a speculative form. Only so far, however, as the mechanical manipulation of sensations is concerned can this charge be allowed. For when this much has been accomplished, orthodox psychology links itself to the authoritative classification of Kant.

Sensations are taken as the simplest and original of the facts of consciousness, but as data which the developed consciousness is unable to separate from that fused complex which it must regard as 'presentation.' These simple elements modern psychology[1] regards in three chief aspects: the quality, or what-sort-ness, the quantity, or how-much-ness, the tone or the felt-ness. Its investigations, especially of the first two marks of sensations, have been its chief success and rightly entitles it to its claim of scientific character. Kant also recognized three such qualities of the sense elements. The quality of sensations are classified not according to the kinds of sensations that may appear in consciousness, but rather on the basis of the variety of the organs of sensation.[2] There was that broad and common distinction between 'the vital' or bodily sensations and the special or 'organic' sensations. The former are connected with the emotions and passions; and, furthermore, are to be distinguished from the feelings, *e. g.*, 'of delight and disgust,' and from 'the internal sense,' which is considered as the mind's mode of affecting itself and an observation

---

[1] *Cf.*, Ladd, *Phys. Psych.*, pp. 306 f., 356 f., 509 f.
[2] *Cf.*, *Werke*, VII., 451 f., 465 f.

of these affections. The special or 'organic' senses are the five : sight, hearing, touch, taste and smell. The sensations of 'heat and cold, smoothness and roughness' belong to the 'vital' sense. The sense of touch 'gives *form* only and immediately.' Vision is a mediated perception and gives the 'image' of an object. Indeed, it is 'the highest form of pure intuition of the immediate representations.'[1] Hearing, which is 'merely mediated perception,' does not give the '*form*' nor '*image*' of an object. For the most part it is a 'vital sense;' it is the 'musical sense,' and gives rise to feelings. Taste and smell are closely related to each other as, *e. g.*, one who has no smell has a coarse taste, etc.

The first three senses are of mechanical origin, the others are of chemical.[2] The first three are the perceptive senses. Their sensations are more objective than subjective, thus contributing chiefly to the cognition of external objects. The second set are the purely hygienic, organic senses of enjoyment, their sensations being more subjective and contributing less to the knowledge of objects. Seeing and hearing seem to be held to be 'acquired,'[3] while perception or 'cognitions' come only with a fusion of touch (form) with sight (image) and hearing (which is partially concerned with the location of noises in space). Vision is most closely associated with touch, and has 'least sensation' but 'most perception.' With this is closely associated the law of relativity which exists between sensation and perception; for Kant made the distinction, and psychologists generally attributed the first statement of it to him.[4] In the first three senses, an increase of sensation diminishes the perception and (internal) pain ensues. Even the fact is general that 'the more strongly affected the senses feel themselves to be, the less they teach.'

Very closely associated with this relativity of the effective

---

[1] A remark that may be of significance to him who finds all idealists 'eye minded' thinkers, *Werke*, II., 468; *cf.*, V. 13.

[2] A statement not borne out by the facts of later discoveries in the case of sight, whose physiological origin resides, probably in the photo-chemical changes that occur in the retinal visual purple, etc., *cf.*, Ladd, *Phys. Psych.*, pp. 179, 184.

[3] *Werke*, VII., 487.

[4] *Werke*, VII., 470; *cf.* Höffding, *op. cit.* 129.

and perceptive elements in sense cognition, is the psychological principle which Kant raises to the rank of *apriority* in his 'Analytic of Principles.'[1] "In all phenomena sensation, and the real which corresponds to it in the object, has an intensive quantity, *i. e.*, a degree." Strangely enough, this very principle stands in contradiction with the possibilities of psychology allowed by Kant in the preface passage already dwelt upon in the previous chapter. Nor was it removed or essentially modified in the second edition. In truth, it is some such a presupposition which lies at the basis of modern psychophysics. It assumes some quantitative relation between a sensation and its stimulus, and attempts to measure it, as, *e. g.*, Weber's law[2] summarizes the relation (whether it be physiological or psychological in its character is scarcely pertinent here); while the determinations of the kinds of sensation is chiefly of the physiological psychological sort, more strictly speaking.

Kant enumerates[3] several conditions on which the quantity of sensation depends, though they contain admixtures of higher psychological principles and can doubtless be reduced to items which concern the interest accompaniments of attention. They are: 1, *contrast*, where sense intuitions are placed side by side, under one and the same conception (chiefly the principle of the comic, as he expands it); 2, *novelty* increases the degree of our sense perception because of the newly involved acquisition; 3, *change* refreshes our senses, while monotony results in atony; 4, *intensification*, where the maximum is the turning point, towards which the influence is reviving, beyond which it is exhausting. But such are semi-popular classifications of everyday observation, that there is not a like intensity attending our sense experiences, and has had no real consequence in the history of psychology.

There is also a sharp distinction of what is now known as the sensation and its tone of feeling.[4] It is a wide-reaching psychological principle, and was especially fundamental in that

---

[1] *Critique*, II., 147 ff.
[2] *Cf.*, Sully, I., 88 f.
[3] *Werke*, VII., 475 f.
[4] *Cf.*, *Werke*, V., 195 f, 210 f, 296, 311; VI., 388; VII., 8 f.

it was the psychological fact on which the last and unifying *Critique* planted itself.   Sensation is an affection of the mind, and as known in consciousness, includes at least two elements, *viz*: 1, the cognitive or objective; 2, the æsthetical or subjective.   A pleasure or pain is 'combined' with sensation and perception.   The fusion of a rational element (judgment) with the form of sensibility gave Kant his warrant for finding in the *Critique of Judgment* the investigation which should close the circle and unite sensibility (knowable experience) with reason (a law-giving morality) in the totality of a system.   Whether psychology may permit him this conclusion cannot be inquired into here.

Modern psychology also undertakes the measurement of the 'extensity' or 'voluminousness' of sensations.[1]   This sensational 'quale of spatiality' was not an unknown psychological tenet in Kant's time.   It had been developed by Condillac, and even yet finds acceptance in some psychological quarters. Kant, speaking with his speculative intent,[2] has denied the extensive or spatial quality of sensations.   "Sensation being that in the phenomenon the apprehension of which does not form a successive synthesis progressing from parts to a complete representation, is without any extensive quantity."   "As sensation by itself is no objective representation, and as in it the intuition of neither space nor time can be found it follows that an extensive quantity does not belong to it, etc."

Now Kant did not go into the perception of space as a psychological problem, and only occasionally do there occur allusions to this process.   In 1766 a passing reference[3] is made to the fact that the localization of an object in space conforms with the direction whence comes the rays of light which enter the eye, within which is the *focus imaginarius*.   Again, and with more physiological reference, he finds[4] the principle to be

[1] Ward, *loc. cit.*, 46, 53 f.

[2] *Critique*, II., 148, I., 465-6.   A passage (*Crit.*, II., 145) says, " every phenomenon, as an intuition, must be an extensive quantity."   Here, however, the ' intuited phenomenon ' is plainly the product of perceptive synthesis.

[3] *Werke*, II., 352 f.

[4] In the essay 'Von dem ersten Grunde d. Untersch. d. Gegenden im Raume' [1768]. *Werke*, II., 387 f.

of a physiological-psychological character.   The relation of objects is expressed in judgments which at first have distinct reference to the characteristic feeling of being in the body and distinguishing one side of it from the other.[1]   Absolute space, however, is already discerned to be not an object of external sensation, but a primal concept (Grundbegriff), which makes all else possible (*i. e.*, as objects).   This same physiological basis of the judgments is again referred to almost twenty years later.[2]   Beyond this Kant did not go.   There was discerned no problem of space perception, and much less was there felt the need of positing 'local signs,' towards which his fragmentary expressions can hardly be likened.

What distinction Kant makes between sensation, perception and knowledge it is difficult to conclude, and especially so in regard to the first two.   For in them is wrapped up that great element in Criticism, *viz*: 'that which is given.'   Between this and 'knowledge' the distinction is apparently broad.   Now, representations are perceptions which become sensations or knowledge, according to the direction into which we turn our reference to them either subject-wards or objectively.[3]   Again, sensation is represented as the groundwork of perception, and a psychological reality in the latter is conditioned upon the presence of the former.[4]   Or, sensation is no 'intuition' (perception),[5] and can become 'representation' only with the attachment of 'consciousness,' *i. e.*, perception is the consciousness of an empirical intuition.[6]

As to the nature of this perception there is quite as much vacillating vagueness.   A tone time[7] 'perception is the given element' after which there comes that cognifying, transcendental

---

[1] " Die beiden Seiten des menschlichen Körpers, ungeachtet ihrer grossen äusseren Aehnlichkeit, durch eine klare Empfindung genugsam unterscheiden." *Ibid.*, 389.

[2] *Werke*, IV., 340 f.

[3] *Crit.*, II., 278.

[4] *Ibid.*, II., 196.

[5] *Werke*, IV., 55.

[6] *Werke*, VI., 33, 22; *Critique*, II., 327. On sensation *vs.* perception, *cf.*, also *Crit.*, II., 105 note, 102.

[7] *Crit.*, II., 105, 44.

synthesis; at another,[1] perception is immediate consciousness of a representation in which there is no inference, for a perceptual reality is immediately given. But in his empirical expressions we saw a vague mediacy and immediacy given to the various senses in their activity. Again,[2] neither 'sensations' nor 'ideas' are knowledge. It presupposes both while they are yet in need of 'the synthetic unity of apperception' in order to become cognitions. Indeed, these 'representations' are represented as being the material which understanding synthesizes.[3] With this confusion, we may safely conclude that, with Kant, sensation is the affection of a passive mind (Gemüths),[4] which somehow is yet dormant in the 'ideas,' 'representations' (Vorstellungen), concerning which are given those 'judgments of perception' from which knowledge and experience flow pursuant to a later intellective activity.[5]

Thus we can have scarce any ground on which to rest an answer to the inquiry whether perception with Kant is 'mediate,' or 'immediate.' He certainly makes a broad, generous distinction between perception and knowledge, the latter being in chief the core of judgment around which the fantastic variety of sensibility clings, and does not represent knowledge as a datum given to us—a diametrical criticism of strong currents of sensationalism that eddied about him. It was 'knowledge,' not mere perception, which was his absorbing theme. Yet perception was a phase of his problem, if we make the unsubstantiable supposition that by 'object' and objectivity he means the constructive, perceptive activity of mind. Here appears how closely the content of Criticism borders upon psychology and yet has in it a savoring that differentiates it from the empirical science. It could not have been perception, as such, that Kant is explaining. *He presupposed the work of psychology as completely done and accepted in certain forms the doctrine of ' Vorstellungen' then regnant in psychological circles, but combats the empiricism which attempted to bring knowledge out of these*

---

[1] *Ibid.*, 327, f, 322.
[2] *Werke*, VIII., 34, 527, 529; VIII., 537.
[3] *Crit.*, II., 44; V., 222.
[4] *Crit.*, II., 17; *Werke*, VIII., 689.
[5] *Werke*, IV., 47 f., 499; V., 296 f., 300, 222.

ideational images.[1]   For ideation is not a knowing judgment.[2]   Yet perception, as such, with Kant is an immediate act of consciousness, and he does not hesitate in subverting the 'representative' theory that had obtained such Cartesian vogue. But if we grant an extensive meaning to perception, then this 'immediacy' is confronted by that famous and frequently employed phrase of Criticism,[3] the 'correlative' or that which 'corresponds' to an object. Even yet, perception remains an immediate spontaneity; for such expressions treasure up what Reid might have been struggling with, but in Kant are connected with the doctrine of noumenon, which concerns the *knowledge* of the (causal) reality of that which lies in our (phenomenal) representations. Still, allowing the generous meaning to be given to knowledge and perception, the immediacy of perception remains, even if Kant's analysis of the

---

[1] Schopenhauer (*Fourfold root, etc., tr.,* 94) with a characteristic feeling, criticises Kant's views of perception. 'He simply identifies perception with sensation,' and 'is therefore obliged to leave the genesis of empirical perception unexplained.' As to the first point, S. is wrong. Wherever else K. may have failed, he does not fail to make the distinction between sensation and perception (*cf., Crit.,* II., 278, 196, 327; *Werke,* IV., 55, 47, 499; V., 195, 300; VI., 33; VII., 46 f. ('Sensation' is here identified with perception only, and so far agrees with S.) 470; VIII., 529, 527, 537; Erdmann, *Reflexionen,* I., i., p. 79, No. 66, etc). Cf., Meyer, *op. cit.,* 268. As to the second point there are serious difficulties as to K.'s real purpose. But we think the text indicates these and at the same time discriminates his accepted doctrine of percepted 'representations,'—'accepted,' because K., presumably, was not concerned with the problems of 'empirical perception,' as such, but struggled with the obscurities of 'judgmental' knowledge, if it might be so expressed. If, on the other hand, he was attempting an explanation of the 'objective' ideational states of consciousness, then S. may be in the right. We admit the confusion possible, but can hardly conceive of K. attempting to parody psychological analysis with his sublime philosophical reflexions. It does seem that the 'problem of perception' did not confront him. K. even intimates that ideation is something mysterious; *cf.,* VII., 34: 'Ideas cannot be explained; for this always requires another idea.'

Again K. does not question the validity of perception, such as is frequently done by idealists. 'For perception is the representation of a reality' (*Crit.* II., 324), and the two sorts of realities given in perception, external and internal things, so-called, and feelings, thoughts, etc., come by way of the diremptive process of consciousness, for everything is at first given in that consciousness, internally as it were. *Cf., ibid.* 322, 324, 88, 128, 428, 326, 156, 167-8, 196.

[2] *Cf.,* VIII., *Werke,* 34, 526, 584; *Crit.* I., 492, II., 45, etc.

[3] *Cf., Critique,* II., 26, 92, 219, 333, 429; I., 386-387, note, 487; *Werke,* IV., 84; VIII., 526, 580, 585 f., etc.

nature of knowledge was intended to be an account of perception. In either case there must be a synthesis *somewhere*,
which Kant places in mental spontaneity rather than in the
' corresponding' relatedness of objects which stamps itself upon
us.

From what has been said above (p. 95 f.), which is about all
that Kant has given us for the explanation of perception, it is seen,
not how disrespectful he might have been of empirical efforts, but
how ultra-psychological were his investigations. One must
mourn this want of psychological material, or find stupendous
implications in the most psychological portions of the *Critique*.
We, of course, allude to the problems of perception as they find
themselves united in that supreme problem of the 'perception
of space.' How comes about the knowledge of what, in the reflective period, leads one to give to *that* an independent reality?
And that portion of the Critical philosophy, which has special
bearing on the nature of spatial perception, stands at its threshold and really gives to transcendentalism its great wedge for
driving asunder the knotty, antinomistic problems which arise
in the course of the natural, metaphysical procedure of reason.
It is the Transcendental Æsthetic—its first part. It gives the
whole drift to speculative reason, and virtually forces Kant to
push his inquiries into the moral, intelligible world for the
nature of reality.[1] It also is one of the first of the critical tenets
with which psychology, as since developed, finds itself closely
related. It is likewise the psychological problem on whose
solution realistic and idealistic metaphysics partially base themselves. The wise ontologist will consult the myriad facts entering into our ideas of space. Thus an intense significance is attached to the respective answers given by the associational
school (Spencer), the sensational, empiristic school (Ward,
James), and the nativistic school of 'psychical stimulists'
(Lotze, Ladd), to the psychological problem of space-percep-
tion.[2] These are instances where respective philosophical

---

[1] His doctrine of space is the ground.of his idealism, while his scepticism is
undoubtedly due to the ideality of time which swept away all reality to what
may be given in mind-life. *Cf. Werke*, V., 105 : ' Our capital supposition of the
ideality of time.' *Cf.*, in following chapter on time-consciousness and the *ego*.

[2] Wundt divides the theories of space perception into ' Nativistic ' and ' Gene-

views of mind *do* condition the acceptance of certain scientific views. Natural logic, in the name of consistency, invites this close affiliation of psychology and metaphysics, though their respective tasks are by far unlike.

Now Kant's doctrine of space is that of its ideality; it is an empty *a priori* form of the mind which must be filled with the material of intuition, or rather sensation. From the manner in which Kant leaves it, his students are justified in thinking of it as an abstract form. And some psychologists have attempted to weave that interpretation into a scientific theory, giving such views as that of Müller's, the physiologist, 'nativism.'[1] The view of Prof. James as to the 'voluminousness of sensations' would class him among those who agree with Müller's speculations; but he repudiates any affiliation with that 'machine shop' that appears thoroughly 'mythological' to him. For 'the essence of the Kantian contention is that there are not *spaces*, but *space*—one infinite continuous *unit*.' He concludes with the general agreement that 'it is a notion,' an abstract form and could possibly be 'no intuition.'[2] James is with the throng, and we too must admit that the Kantian space is apparently the space of abstraction—something unknown in the perceptive consciousness. As a speculator, this may be vouchsafed to Kant; but where he speaks with reference to psychological realities[3] we must not forget such passages as, *e. g.*, 'space consists of spaces only,' etc., which James has apparently done. Moreover, Kant does fight 'abstract space.' When on the threshold of the critical period he contends that 'absolute space' is no object of the senses, but much rather a 'Grundbegriff' which makes possible the *totality* of experience.

In a curiously obscure foot-note[4] occurs a passage which

tic,' and affirms himself as adhering to the latter. Now his classification is really unfortunate. All psychologists are 'genetic' nowadays. Their points of difference lie in what is implied in the terms employed above, *viz*: 'Nativistic,' 'Empiristic,' 'Associational.' *Cf.*, Ladd. *Phys. Psych.*, p. 389, James, *op. cit.*, II., 277, Helmholtz, *Phsy. Optik.*, 435, Wundt, *Phys. Psych.*, II., 23.

[1] *Critique*, II., 371; *cf. Crit.*, I., 437, note.
[2] Sully, *op. cit.*, II., 332.
[3] *Op. cit.*, II., 273 f.
[4] *Crit.*, II., 149. Though in the same paragraph time and space are spoken of as 'quanta continua.'

seemingly makes against that very abstractness of space on which rest the antinomies (among which it occurs). "Empirical intuition is not a compound of phenomena and of space (perception and empty intuition). The one is not a correlate of the other in a synthesis, but the two are only connected as matter and form in one and the same empirical intuition.[1] If we try to separate one from the other, and to place space outside all phenomena, we arrive at a number of empty determinations of external intuition, which, however, can never be possible perceptions, etc." Nothing could be more plainly a refutation of that interpretation of Kantian space which has been significant in the development of some 'nativistic' theories regarding the perception of space. Of course, Kant was satisfied with the vague expression 'pure *a priori* form of external intuition;' in fact, he seemed to stick in it. Nor does he give more than rare psychological reference to it anywhere. Gathering together the analyzed bits, we may affirm psychologically that Kant denies any spatiality, or 'extensiveness' to sensations, but space still remains a mental form.[2] How then might these be fused, or, speaking more in accordance with the facts of consciousness, how does it happen that 'objects are external or outside ourselves?'[3] We can reply only by taking an implication of his theory of knowledge, *viz:* the synthetic activity of mind (Gemüth), which is so fundamental with Kant.[4] The 'manifold' must be submitted to mental constructions before they become affirmable realities 'to ourselves.'

In this connection there should be noted a psychological principle which Kant adopted. It lends its coloring to all that portion of the *Critique* which relates to the genesis of knowledge, the subsumption of the manifold, and the construction of the schema, and doubtless enters into his negative conception of

---

[1] Note that 'intuition' is not exactly equivalent to sensation, but rather to the 'representations' of sense.

[2] These two are in opposition in Prof. James's theory, but not because of the 'unconscious machine shop' *he* has not.

[3] *Crit.*, II., 20.

[4] *Cf. Crit.*, II., 144. "Every phenomena as an intuition must be an extensive quantity, because it can be known in apprehension by a successive synthesis only (of part with part)"—a statement of psychological import.

self consciousness and his ideality of time. The acceptance of the principle is certainly to be associated with his one-sided conception of memory, at whose expense he exalted imagination (as we saw in the preceding chapter). He believed in the fact so firmly that it is sublimated into an *a priori* principle, in fact, *the* ' axiom of intuition,'[1] *viz:* " All phenomena are, with reference to their intuition, extensive quantities." Its foundation resides in his view that consciousness has no span, but is necessarily limited to one point, or moment only ; for the (synthetic) imagination ' must first necessarily apprehend one of these manifold representations after another.'[2] Even this sort of ' going through,' which belongs to the nature of consciousness, is subtly connected with the idea of ' synthetic' judgments. This is a view not common with Kant alone, but it was a favorite in all forms of rational psychology where the soul was considered as a unit and in its attentive powers was unable to ' attend to more than a single object at once,' as Hamilton[3] expresses it.

Though Kant gives this a significance wherever possible, it is a question not admitting of speculation. Only experiments can properly arrive at a conclusion. Bonnet, *e. g.*, before Kant, and Hamilton since, have concluded that the ' circuit of consciousness' could embrace six or seven impressions.[4] This possibility also enters into a theory of perception, and, indeed, provides the conscious basis of that fusion which all psychologists somehow recognize as entering into spatial perception. Its possibility lies in the simultaneity of impressions coming upon moving organs, etc.[5]

Beyond this the lack of any attempt on the part of Kant to solve the special problem will not permit one to go. However he might turn the conception, he still holds fast to the opinion that ' space itself exists within me only, ... and is nothing outside our sensibility.'[6] There only remains to point out what

[1] *Crit.*, II., 143 f.
[2] *Ibid.*, 88, 91, 114.
[3] *Lectures on Metaphysic*, 165 f.
[4] In recent times Dietze has undertaken to ascertain the facts and found the variations in the ' span of prehension' to be between 15 and 40. Ladd, *op. cit.*, p. 494 f. ; *cf.* James, I., 405 ff.
[5] *Cf.*, Sully, *Human Mind*, I., 223, 238.
[6] *Crit.*, II., 325.

validity modern psychology may allow to such a conception of space.

Whatever judgment metaphysic may pronounce on the nature of space, psychology can regard it only as a mental form of some sort, and not an independent object, a knowledge of which is built up in the usual manner. This appears in the inky discussions of the various modern views on the nature of this form of perception. Whether ' nativistic,' in the sense that space is a mental form peculiarly such and not to be had or given in the jumble and associative assortment of sensations, or 'empiristic' in the contrary meaning, that space is an original form, not of the mind, as it is said,[1] but of the sensations themselves, and is a necessary quality of them, is the chief point of difference. In some way the spatial element is a given factor in consciousness. Their divergence of views widens as they both become ' genetic.' Neither view can now dispense with that development which enters as a potent, transforming process. They all are geneticists and must look to experience for that native constructiveness which rounds out the deficiencies in any theory. In the one view the serious task encounters growing difficulties as it attempts to satisfy the explanation of the process whereby the mental form develops into the spatial series. Its analysis of the qualities of those sensations which enter into such a synthesis must needs be searching, and then only partially accomplishes its task by calling in some sort of ' local signs' which differentiate in consciousness those elements which successively enter the fields of simultaneous perception. The other view has an apparent triumph in the slight necessity of merely throwing the original sensational *quale* into arithmetical computations in order to satisfy theoretically that which is given in adult consciousness, but drags in the scientific absurdity that in the primal datum there is the mysterious fact of space. In one sense, nativism and empiricism do not lie far apart, and are each closely related to and suffused with that philosophy of mind with which they furnish their psychology. In another sense, as psychological theories, they are antipodal ; the difficulties of one are matters of scientific fact and their consistent ad-

[1] *Cf.*, Bain's ' *massiveness*,' Ward's ' *extensity*,' James ' *voluminousness*.'

justment, while the other is compelled to defend itself from the possible absurdity that mingles in its assumption of a 'big extendedness' (James). The one is disburdened at the very point at which the other becomes encumbered.

There has been briefly and intentionally expressed the comparative value of the two rival theories, hinting the validity which it is believed either view can rightly claim. As a psychological theory the empiristic or sensational view bears the *onus probandi.* It mistakes scientific function. The mere statement of facts is not explanation. No brilliancy, however versatile, can be left unmolested in the assertion that the limit of the possibility of conceiving, reachable by 'matter-moulded forms of expression,' is to be posited as the elemental affair.[1] The atomic sensation posited by the psychologist is a subjective affair, and only in adult consciousness do things appear 'out and spread out' in space. The gap is as wide as the extremities of a maturing experience, and it becomes psychology to adjust a theory to its presuppositions and the inductive facts which have accrued from that patient analysis of sensations and perceptions which are now its possession.

It is thus indicated that Kant's conception of space agrees with that of psychology, in that he maintained it as a mental form; but disagrees with the one view that it belongs to sensation as such, and throws its suggestive influence with the opposite view that the manifold of sense receive spatial character only by a synthesis of apprehension.[2] He omitted the numerous details of fact, and reached on theoretic grounds the conclusion

---

[1] James, *op. cit.*, II., 31 f. Höffding, *op. cit.*, 190 f. Ladd, *Phys. Psych.*, 385 ff. and art. 'Psych. as so-called Natural Science,' in the *Phil. Rev.* Jan., 1892, p. 24 ff.

[2] This fact must never be lost sight of : that, in the first instance, Kantian space is mathematical space (showing how his analysis of ' knowledge ' emerges out of mathematical conceptions) ; and that the space of psychology is utterly unmathematical. It is, as Sully somewhere says, that sort of room that seems to be felt as out a little way in front of us ready to vanish as we orientate ourselves. The mathematical space is much rather the space of non-sensuous imagination —that which flits beyond the horizon of our accustomed perceptions. The confusion of interpretation and source of general objection when K. speaks of space as a ready-made form or mould into which sensations must get themselves synthetically arranged, may thus be obviated. The *real* space that we *know* is built up, but not in that way.

which it has taken the patient search of half a century to verify in its discovery of details involved in the psychological processes.

This compatibility is that possible consonance which is of an hereditary origin, for it is true, doubtless, that Kant's speculations have shaped empiric investigations, and the psychology of space perception can be pointed out as showing one of the streams of influence issuing forth from the *Critique*.[1] But it should not lead one to overlook the fact that it does not indicate any accordance between his views of perception and those which are now defended by psychology. ' The mere having of ideas ' was the vogue psychology of the two preceding centuries. Kant's doctrine of the representation of the object (Vorstellung) is, in some confused sense, ' the given element,' with which Schopenhauer charges Kant as smudging over the problem of perception. ' Representations ' are given, and then the understanding broods over them in its categorical forms.[2] The phenomena become cognitions, realities, only when brought under other than sense forms. These are conceptual realities, whose becoming and the grounds of whose perdurance Kant is describing. Perceptual realities are the facts of experience which come with the immediacy of consciousness. The problem of ideation and percept-making could not have occurred to him.[3]

The facts of experience were never submitted to doubt.[4] " It cannot be denied that phenomena may be given in intuition without the functions of the understanding."[5] Schopenhauer[6] is right in objecting to Kant in taking causation and understanding out of perception ; right, since it left room for his own ' dis-

---

[1] *Cf.*, Classen, *op. cit., passim.*

[2] *Cf., Crit.*, II., 80, 105, 137.

[3] It may be an interesting speculation to inquire how many questions Kant had to wade through before he could have put himself in a position to answer the problem of the *Critique ;* but such attempts are fanciful, such, *e. g.*, as that of Münz (*Die Grundlagen der Kant'schen Erkenntnisstheorie*, Breslau, 1882), who puts K. through the process of answering such questions " How is perception possible?" "How is representation possible?" As his solution stands, such queries did not arise, for his real task was the supervision of an affirmative answer to the question, " May not our knowledge be an illusion?" See *Mind*, VIII., 142.

[4] *Werke*, IV., 41 f.

[5] *Crit.*, II., 80.

[6] *Loc. cit.*

covery' of the rational character of perception; right, since it does not hit the mark, for Kant is not dealing with perception.

The relation in question must be insisted on. Psychology is utterly unconcerned with the validity of knowledge. Logic has need of psychology, but forfeits its right as a philosophical propædeutic, or even as a part in a system of philosophy, by the fact that its supreme interest is bound up in *truth* and its human expression. A theory of knowledge, mingling with primal elements in those two sciences,[1] has its essence laid in inquiries into the *validity of knowledge* and *its reference to reality*, thus dirempting itself peculiarly from them as well as from a metaphysic which analyzes the *nature* of reality, or, 'works over those conceptions' which make their appearance in psychology, when it treats of the thinking consciousness, and in a theory of knowledge, when it depicts the inweavings of the forms of thought. Philosophy has had painful struggles before it has come to the clear recognition of the close relations in which its own departments stand with reference to each other and to the sciences of mind life. Nor has she been long in receiving this lesson; but severe has been the punishment as she has been stubbornly harking back to the abstract form in which 'thought' is to be her content, or wantonly selling her rational primacy for the vapory pottage of empiricism. A brief century has been the lesson's hour, but how packed have been the instructions of her master! With Kant began the tutoring that philosophy is an exercise not to be swallowed with one pedagogic gulp. What success attended that supreme effort of reason to clean the metaphysical board at one sweep, we may yet see. Hegel shrivelled this throbbing world into the frigidity of dialectic. 'Logic' was to be the 'first, last, and altogether' of truth and reality. 'Blind will' that has no hope and reality, struggles for reason's diadem and sceptre, but comes clad in the dust and tatters of the mob. Lotze, to whom psychology and philosophy are so greatly indebted, apparently banishes psychology and embosoms logic. But the nature of the Real comes with the

---

[1] *Cf.*, Höffding, *op. cit.*, p. 355-6; "Psychology is a special discipline, which presupposes the general principles of our knowledge, but cannot explain their validity."

mental unit of consciousness, and a healthy agnosticism ultimately emerges from that 'system of philosophy' modestly
coming up out of logic. And the Insular mind? Ah! Reason,
confined to the lever and balances of force, or thrust out among
the cold facts of 'bodies,' shook the sands of British shores and
flew to a balmier clime and warmer hearts. Philosophy must
note these evoluting pulse-beats and find in them nature's admonition that rational provender for continued life must be
sought elsewhere than in an unanalyzed mixture of ideal abstractness and vanishing phenomena.

But we must return to the inquiry which comes up out of
the Transcendental Æsthetic, as it expresses itself in the nature
of the presentations of sense, and gradually emerges into the
problem which finds its supreme answer in the first book of the
Transcendental Analytic. How is knowledge possible? and
what is the nature of experience? To all appearances, Kant
unwarrantably separates the matter and form of knowledge,
sense and understanding. The former is disposed of in the
Æsthetic, but we hear strangely reverberating echoes of the nature of sense knowledge (from the psychological point of view)
away over in the Fourth Paralogism of Rational Psychology.
How these 'phenomena,' in the getting of which the mind is
passive,[1] become 'cognitions,' 'objects' and 'objective,' Kant
proceeds to show by an analysis of understanding, but links it
backward to sense in the doctrine of 'the Synthesis of Apprehension in Intuition,'[2] so that he justly entitles his exposition to the
worthiness of a comment issued late in life.[3]

It is true, that while his idealism admits only 'denkenden
Wesen' as realities, he yet fails to bring about any unification of sense and understanding. It indicates, on the one
hand, that the unity of knowledge was lost in his view, and he

---

[1] *Cf., Crit.,* II., 17 f.; *Werke,* V., 300; VII., 451 f.; VIII., 689.

[2] *Crit.,*II., 88 f.

[3] "Verstand und Sinnlichkeit verschwistern sich, bei ihrer Ungleichartigkeit,
doch so von selbst zu Bewirkung unserer Erkenntniss als wenn eine von der
anderen, oder beide von einem gemeinschaftlichen Staunne ihren Ursprung
hätten; welches doch nicht sein kann, wenigstens für uns unbegreiflich ist, wie
das Ungleichartige aus einer und derselben Wurzel entsprossen sein kann."
Werke, VII., 492.

was unable to free himself from the real thought of his task, and what was the real nature of its solution, *viz:* an abstractness which comes with the criticism of mere faculties. On the other hand, the longing for such a unity, as a philosophical tenet, appears in the development of absolute idealism where sense becomes sublimated into understanding. In a very true sense, Kant had the principle which serves to unify the disparate elements from which he could not charm his thinking, *viz:* in that knowledge itself.[1] And the opinion that sense and understanding have no common ground is the fruit of his sceptical outcome, but in opposition to " the central idea of the *Critique*, that knowable objects exist only in relation to intelligence."[2] This disparateness, that is affirmed to the last, shows both Kant's disregard for psychology as having any value for philosophical reflection, and the need any constructive philosophy has of the results of psychology. As a philosopher, Kant takes the world as already here. It is the 'given datum.' Whatever that may be, this world of *ours* is an intelligible world permeated by the 'rule-giving understanding.' He saw the need of a foundation for a philosophical system, found it in that ' given datum,' and proceeded at once to examine the structure among its upper stories, as it were. Indeed, sensations go for everything in experience (excepting only the idea ' des Zusammengesetzten;[3]) and he is thus led to agree, in an initiatory sense, with Lotze,[4] that all knowledge begins with sensibility and must come back to that.

Kant's theoretic emphasis of ' sensibility' has been taken up by inductive psychology until its greatest progress has been in that very department of mental life. Of course, every philoso-

[1] Lange (*Hist. of Mat.*, II., 196 ff.,) is quite right in saying that ' the physiology of the sense organs' has brought out the fact that many ' thought-processes' are correspondingly involved in perception; *Cf.*, Sully, *Human Mind*, I., chs., VI. and VII. Processes of mental elaboration of the sense data, etc., initial forms of intellection are apparent in the early stages of perception. These are empirical facts that render assistance to the epistemologist who is working out his problem on the Kantian line.

[2] Watson, *Kant and his English Critics*, p. 332.

[3] *Werke*, VIII., 536–7.

[4] *Werke*, IV., 339, *Cf.*, *Microcosmus*, I., 563. Kant, of course, with sceptical intent, while Lotze gives it a positive significance.

phy that comes within human experience must and will recognize a 'given datum.' The material aspects of this world lie heavily on its hand. Even scepticism itself owes its stumble to the fact of 'the given object.' The sense element does come in. But here is where a philosophy links itself to the facts of the world vision and finds in psychology's account of the nature of this so-called sense element the starting point for the subversion of those two antagonistic functions of mind (as supposed by Kant). For in perception is assured the mentality of all elements; "only mental factors can be built into mental products,"[1] and in its unity is typified the unifying activity that comes with the presence of the subject.[2] Moreover, as psychology progresses in tracing the acts of mental complexity, it finds not only the submergence of sense data in a flood of mentality, but also, that sense, intellection, yea, all the activities and forms of the subject bound up in that perception which feels its reference to realities and is fit to assume the profounder name of knowledge. Sensations become not only percepts or ideas which relate themselves to a mere outwardness; but, in the transforming power of concepts and judgment they generalize and objectify themselves [*cf.* the German word ' *Gegen*-stand'] as cognitions. It is this product whose genesis psychology traces in a progressive manner, irrespective of its validity and possible implications of either formal or material reality, and which epistemology takes up, going through it both forward and backward with the explicit philosophic intent to hunt down any implications of a reality given, or of its nature as known. Whatever certification of reality noëtics may find in the facts of knowledge, either positively or negatively, philosophy as a system will accordingly drift and shape itself. In accordance with its views on the nature of knowledge, a philosophy either proceeds to construct a metaphysic or to end in scepticism. Kant is famous for his inconsistent jumble of both. That valuable sentence,[3] without which Criticism would not be

[1] Ladd, *op. cit.*, 383.

[2] Even in the Kantian theory no fact receives more emphasis, nor is of greater importance. *Cf.*, *Crit.*, II., 103 note, I., 435 note.

[3] *Critique*, I., 380.

half so precious to the world, expresses it in its entirety: " I had, therefore, to remove *knowledge* in order to make room for *belief.*" This knowledge in the Kantian sense has its positive, limited, and its negative, unlimited aspects.

One terse paragraph[1] sums up the entire constructive results of the analysis of pure reason: "The whole of our perception rests on pure intuition (if regarded as representation, then on time, as the form of our internal intuition), their association on the pure synthesis of imagination and our empirical consciousness of them on pure apperception, that is, on the permanent identity of oneself in the midst of all possible representations."

Herein Kant concluded that he had attained *a priori* certainty, a synthetic necessity which gave to philosophical knowledge the apodicity of mathematical constructiveness. It was an answer to the problem as more analytically stated in the second edition,[2] a statement more truly in accord with the nature of the solution itself, as it limits metaphysical apodicity to the bounds hemming in sensibility. Nor less attributable to the model which is constantly before pure reason is the elimination of non-rational factors as participant in that synthetic activity, and the pruning of sporadic attempts which have no immediate reference to the starting point of all knowledge. Kant was too faithful an imitator of mathematics to have served philosophy in the ultimate service of attending reason's last call as to the nature of knowledge. The whole lesson of the historical reaction is that reason cares not for geometrical formulæ. Mathematical certainty and the path that leads to it as its goal are now placed in philosophy's trinket bag. Noëtics must seek *rational* necessity, such as comes to the demands of man's thinking. Other realities, either epistemological or metaphysical, are illusory of the genuine sort, and the need of the philosophic age, as it has come up out of Kantian scepticism, is an ontology which shall accord with reason and life. 'Back to Kant' can be a heeded cry only as it indicates an attempt to raise, on the foundation of a reconstructed theory of knowledge, a metaphysic which shall quicken this finite reflex of reality into a yet more

[1] *Critique*, II., 102.
[2] *Cf., Critique*, I., 398–412.

serious realization of that goal which lies enshrouded in the ground of the world.

Granting the validity of a distinction between the presentations of sense—as chiefly expressive of the synthesis that ' runs through the manifold '—and preception as inclusive of the intellective processes, and chiefly in its most highly developed form as given in self-consciousness, *i. e.*, perception as correlative with psychology's account of ' knowledge,'[1] we then have a dividing principle which yields a constant service in separating the content of speculative Criticism so far as it has psychological bearings on the elemental and developed forms of perception; and, of course, a principle that arranges the faculties engaged in the various sorts of mental products (Kantian) : sense, intuition, and cognized ' object,' for it is a criticism of the faculties that is undertaken.

The first ' faculty ' which comes to view by this partition is the imagination (' Einbildungskraft.') It is an empirical and a transcendental faculty, which, from a *psychological* point of view, is the most important fundamental power of the mind. On its presence depends the constructive character of positive Criticism, while on a confusion of its limitations hangs the sceptical outcome of the *Critique.* It is the ' go-between ' of sense and understanding. Kant's reflective genius might have ferreted out the truth that "thoughts without contents are empty, intuitions without concepts are blind," but could never have shown its legitimacy in the Transcendental Deduction had "this faculty of empirical imagination remained buried in our mind as a dead faculty."[2] That Kant found a unity of sense and understanding ' unbegreiflich ' is due to the fact that he viewed knowledge backwards, faculty-wise, and failed to appreciate the supreme function of this ' blind, but indispensable ' imagination which presses forward and brings unity in the product knowledge. In it lies the *a priori* possibility of

[1] A caution must be borne in mind *pari passu:* any ' rigid demarcation of the spheres of sense and thought '—such as is common among speculative masters who build on logical forms—subverts the psychic truth that the mental life has a continuity in its movement that finds its best figure in the flow of a stream. *Cf.*, Sully, *op. cit.*, I., 212 ; James, *op. cit.*, I., 224 ff.

[2] *Critique*, II., 89.

knowledge, whose *nature* and *content* arise from the ingredients of understanding and sense. For it is the one faculty which is found in both the divisions of higher and lower.

At this point Criticism works up a warm feeling for psychology in spite of the careful sifting which thought itself to conclude in its selection of a logical basis. Nor does the function of the faculty appear in the Transcendental Deduction alone. It, in reality, promotes that synthesis in the Æsthetic, which secures the manifold as given in 'intuition' or 'representation.' For 'phenomena,' as such, 'bedarf der functionendes Denkens in keiner Weise.'[1]

Not only is it the 'faculty of synthesis' in the Æsthetic, and not only does it assume transcendental proportions in the Deduction, but it is the activity, under guidance of the understanding, whose product is the Schema.[2] It is also an element in the Transcendental Unity of Apperception which figures in the legitimacy of the categories, and likewise is the 'transcendental faculty' in the Rational Psychology which it attempts to subvert; it is the synthesis which produces the Antinomies and manufactures the Ideal which is naught else than the anthropomorphic absolute. Imagination is thus a mighty current in Criticism, pushing reason to the extremity of metaphysical confusion. It is just as true that 'the *a priori* necessity' and 'natural illusion' might be replaced by a corresponding *need* or *act* of *imagination* and much of the '*a priority*' in 'pure reason' would find rather the matter-of-fact statement of what constitutes the syllogistic need and procedure of mind.

No less is the significance of the imagination in the *Practical Reason*. Indeed, the whole moral law is the appeal of an ethical ideal to the rational imagination. True, Kant does not introduce the faculty, and seems to deny its activity when he ostracises all empirical deductions of the supreme categories of freedom and the imperative. These are given a deduction, but what a demand is made on the ethical imagination! They are never given in any experience. They transcend the world of sense. Their reality lies in a postulated faith—a vigorous de-

---

[1] *Critique*, p. 123, second ed. *Cf.* II., 80.
[2] *Critique*, II., 124 f.

mand of Criticism that the rational imagination shall be turned
loose in the fields of the supersensible where the ideal of humanity is a kingdom of free selves.[1]   The possibility of the
Critique of Judgment lies in the freedom which must characterize the æsthetical taste as, in its judgment, it roams over the
free purposiveness of organic nature.   It is a draft upon the
imagination when the judgment subsumes a ' particular ' under a
concept.[2]   We would not for a moment attempt to depreciate
the ' rational ' character of the Critical philosophy, but here is a
truly psychological object—the imagination—which increases in
relative importance as the system advances towards its close.
It is seen at a glance that psychology stands not only round
about Criticism, giving to it the defense that comes in its virtue
of having reflected the rational unity of man, but also passes
through it all, sporadic almost, in the infinite ramifications which
everywhere carry with them the stamp of the humanness of
Criticism.

The detailed characteristics of this faculty need scarce detain us here.   Its general feature is the ' intuition of an object
without its presence,'[3] and is either producive—as phantasy, or
the imagination which precedes all experience ; and reproductive—plainly empirical in that it merely brings back to the
mind ('ins Gemüth zurück bringt') some intuition we have
already experienced.   It is a wanton, active power, and knows
no limits, both in its effect on the mind and on the body.   It,
but not understanding, may be forgiven if it dreams.   With all
its varieties it is not so ' creative ' as one is ready to suppose.   It
cannot go beyond what is given it in sensations ; these it cannot create, nor can it conceive of a rational being with any
other than a human form ; whence the anthropomorphism in
the knowledge of God.   Thus its activity has its fantastic field
hemmed in by the influx of sensations and by the ultra limits
of sensibility.

[1] *Cf.*, Frohschammer, *Ueber die Bedeutung der Einbildungskraft in der
Kant'schen Philosophie*, München, 1879, p. 84–91.

[2] *Cf.*, further Frohschammer, pp. 91–114, Mellin's *Wörterbuch, etc.*, II.,
222 f; *cf.*, also *Werke*, V., 246, 257, 277; Dieterich's *Kant und Rousseau*, p. 150.

[3] *Critique*, I., 449; *Werke*, VII., 481; Kant is not steadfast in the *Critique*
in what he means by imagination.   Now it is itself; and now it is understanding, spontaneity.   *Cf.*, I., 457 n., 449.

The imagination is thus given a very comprehensive scope. And Kant is doubtless right in holding to its generic sense, for representation in all its forms deals with 'images'; and in classifying reproduction as voluntary and calling it memory, and production as imagination proper. This alone contributes to (Kantian) knowledge and is limited to dealings with space and time associations. To his views on the former (memory) exception must be taken. Remembrance comprises merely retention and recall, with retention of three sorts, *viz.:* mechanical, ingenious, judicious, a classification of the kinds of memories whose pointedness has scarce been excelled.[1] On yet another point Kant is to be commended, not for his truthfulness, but for his refusal. The law of association is that of repeated continguity.[2] His refusal is to accept no physiological explanation of this phenomenon; even to demand such 'is idle.' It is now maintained that the basis of retention *is* laid in the cerebral nervous system, and psychologists differ not in their analyses of memory, but chiefly as they accept or modify the physical basis of memory.[3] But the chief point in the phenomenon of memory lies not in retention and recall. These are, as it were, the mere initiation of the 'object.' Over and above these is recognition—the essential thing in an act of memory. This is a complex feature and must be drawn out, as including (a) reference to the *past*, wherein memory differs from expectation or prevision, as Kant readily allows; (b) explicit reference to *my* past, with more or less definite localization with reference to that past; (c) lastly and supremely characteristic, 'the feeling of belief in this peculiar complex object.'[4] This last element Kant overlooks not only here, but seems purposely to exclude it in a still wider field of cognitions—whose consequence may appear in subsequent consideration of self-consciousness.

[1] *Cf.*, Lindner, *Empirical Psychology*, p. 103.

[2] " Empirische Vorstellungen die nach einander oft folgten, bewirken eine Gewohnheit im Gemüth, wenn die eine erzeugt wird, die andere auch entstehen zu lassen." VII., 490; *cf.*, Porter, *Human Intellect*, p. 282.

[3] *Cf.*, Ladd, *Phys. Psych.*, p. 545 ff; James, *op. cit.*, I., 653 ff.

[4] James's own words, which appear to antagonize his physiological explanation. *Cf.*, Rabier, *Leçons de Psych.*, pp. 176 f; importance of definite localization in the past.

Kant recognizes[1] memory as yielding a body of knowledge, but objective, *viz:* such historical knowledge as is *ex datis* and gives it a subjective turn so far as it carries a memoriter impress. But his general oversight of memory, as a distinct form of mental activity, is doubtless the cause of one's not finding its forthputtings mentioned as some form of knowledge subjectively considered, or as a stage in the development of knowledge. It has also an influence on his theory of knowledge. It abstractness is accounted for in that he misses that definiteness to reality within a particular subject, which memory as a noëtic function compels one to admit; and, by throwing all the stadia or developments of knowledge into the transcendental imagination, he analyzes the knowledge of no one that psychology can be aware of.

To this it might be objected, that the individualistic reference which is implicated in knowledge, Kant fully recognizes in the necessary activity of the apperceptive consciousness which gathers all in the unity of experience. To which it must be replied, that Kant's self-consciousness is, again, something which never comes by way of psychic experience. The self as an object of knowledge does not come through the vague indefinite representation which imagination is. On the contrary, it is the moment of memory which makes for the development of one-self consciousness.[2] The states of one time must be permeated with the 'my' which is referable, *either with certainty or with doubt,* to the ' my ' which was found implicate in preceding, remembered states.[3] In some such way does this defect of Kant's doctrine of memory creep into his negative conclusions regarding the met-empirical identity of the *ego* and the nature of personality. He would seem to have in rational psychology a fixed faculty of self-consciousness, springing in the full armor of a diremptive and concatenating power, from

---

[1] *Crit.*, II., 717.

[2] *Cf., Crit.*, II., 103 n ; the relation of the empirical self-consciousness in the becoming of knowledge.

[3] Even a so-called false memory is just as significant for a theory of knowledge, as a so-called accurate memory, though it may not be useful in perception. Here the order of experience is unloosed and the individual is the victim of a pathological consciousness.

the mysterious depths of our being. But memory essentially and imagination non-essentially enters into that form of life in which the *ego* unifies itself in its own discriminative diremption.

Since Kant it has been customary to distinguish between productive and reproductive imagination. But we cannot agree with him[1] in consigning the latter to the limbo of psychology and assigning the synthetic function of understanding to the former, for psychologic falsity is noëtic error. But, granting him his meaning of imagination, it is not only a worthy merit of the Transcendental Deduction that it finds in conscious thinking the nature of knowledge (logically a higher activity of mind than sensation,[2] and "logically a subjective point of view is deeper than the objective"), and in a fusing representation, the mechanism of that knowledge ; but also it must be specially mentioned that Kant calls the attention of psychologists to the fact that imagination is a factor in preception.[3] Kant is right in finding in imagination something underneath the ordinary estimation that it is only a phantastic power that promotes romantic pleasures. Imagination is an indispenable faculty and has its uses in gathering up vague images and fusing them with discriminated sensations into the percept so often thought of only as a presentation by the senses.[4] But, in overlooking the virtues of empiric memory and ascribing the mediatory function to the imagination, he takes all reality out of knowledge, and psychology must continue to clamor for a revision of his theory at those points where particularity accompanies knowledge. There is no knowledge in general. His treatment of imagination leads one to think his theoretic knowledge is such.

Moreover, imagination appears important not only in the

[1] *Critique*, I., 449 f.

[2] *Cf.*, Ladd, *Introd.*, p. 193, Höffding, *op. cit.*, p. 68.

[3] "Dass die Einbildungskraft ein nothwendiges Ingrediens der Wahrnehmung selbst sei, daran hat wol noch kein Psychologe gedacht. Das kommt daher, weil man dieses Vermögen theils nur auf Reproductionen einschränkte, theils, weil man glaubte, die Sinne lieferten uns nicht allein Eindrücke, sondern setzten solche auch sogar zusammen und brächten Bilder der Gegenstande zuwege, wozu ohne Zweifel ausser der Empfänglichkeit der Eindrücke noch etwas mehr, nämlich eine Function der Synthesis derselben erfordert wird." *Critique*, 1st *ed.*, Erdmann's *Ausgabe*, p. 607.

[4] *Cf.*, Sully, *Human Mind*, I., p. 212.

positive, constructive aspects of Criticism; it is essentially concerned with the negative limits set by that same Criticism. In the doctrine of hypotheses,[1] it is the imagination that is chiefly at work, and where it 'dreams with the concepts of things' there knowledge ceases and reason becomes subverted in mere opinion, which, in reference to realities, is always an absurdity. We can 'think' many things also, but this, too, is nothing other than imagination active in the field of judgment. The negative possibilities of both 'thinking' and 'opining' rule out all that rich field of scientific knowledge to which inductive logic does give validity. The theory of hypotheses is entirely wrong, for it attempts to draw a fixed line between reason as a categorical activity in experience and imagination as a sensuous faculty ursurping the perogative of rationality. Psychology finds in judgment itself a large amount of representation, and particularly so in its most recent advances, where the old-time 'concept' is being more accurately displaced by the 'Gesammt-bilder,' which form the stepping stones over which the relating and universalizing activity of judgment passes, as intellect carries on processes whose material is already laid in the representative sensuousness of knowledge.

This, however, approaches a higher psychological activity. Understanding is the second, and, according to Criticism, the last cognitive faculty which appears upon adoption of the principle pointed out above. It is one of the triad,—sense, imagination and apperception, each one being an irreducible faculty of the soul and conditioning the possibility of experience. It is the cognitive power in the soul's triplicity of faculties, the others being feeling and desire. In the hierarchy of 'oberen Erkenntnissvermögen,' it stands chieftain at the gateway of Criticism; but for the sake of reality it is the weakest of man's possessions. In the history of Kant's influence, understanding, its positive and negative functions, has been given the precedent, but, in the architectonic of the *Critiques*, its *a priority* pales before the solar light of the law-giving reason.

Sense and mere synthesis do not constitute knowledge. They provide only raw material under blind handling. Ex-

[1] *Cf., Crit.,* II., 659 f., *Werke,* VIII., 81 f.

perience *is* an orderly affair. Whatever this world may be in
itself, its seeming is to us something of reality and sequence.
These are the features of the knowledge that comes to us.
Whence those touches of noëtic beauty ? and what the constitu-
tive function that makes the little we have that which it is ?
Says one, ideas are innate, and the whole world is a sort of
Platonic reminiscence of monadic souls ; another, sensualism
finds entire passivity in knowledge, for things come to us ; and
scepticism (Hume) reaches a higher psychological stage and
sees the nature of experience lie in the habitual association of
ideas, but sees certainty falling to the zero point of constant
doubt. Logically more profound, and psychologically higher,
Criticism unites what is found in all other systems, and, re-cast-
ing it in the psychologic mould, finds knowledge in sense,
imagination, *and* understanding. These three, and these three
only, make for cognitions objective. They are a forthputting of
intelligence, a discernment of relations ; and the nature of
knowledge, or its form, partakes of the essence of that principle
which lies at its core—judgment. Knowledge ? Its content
comes from sense ; its possibility lies in imagination ; its nature
is of judgment—these three and no less ; it lies in the nature of
the thing.[1]

What Kant proposes to do with 'understanding' as a cognitive faculty, and also as a treatment mediating between scepticism and dogmatism, is more manifest in his elaboration of its
functions than in his definitions of this faculty. To take him
as he speaks means confusion for us. To say that knowledge
involves mind, *is* mind, leaves a vagueness inadequate to distinguish it from that dreamy pageantry which must answer to
the description of sensationalism. To take him as he presumably means, we may find clearness. For, in that meaning he
banished the inadequate vagueness which comes with the
affirmation that knowledge is the minding of things, and is explicit in the analysis of that understanding whose functions it
is to give that nature to knowledge which it has.

[1] As a psychologist, Rabier well expresses Kant's historic advance : " C'est
le grande mérite de l'école criticiste d'avoir mis en relief l'originalité et l'importance de cette fonction intellectuelle ; c'est le grand défaut de Hume et de toute
l'école empiriste de l'avoir confondue avec des fonction sensitives de la simple
appréhension on de l'association des idées." *Leçons de Psychologie,* p. 277.

We have Kant's own word for the looseness of his definitions: "We have before given various definitions of the understanding, by calling it the spontaneity of knowledge (as
opposed to the receptivity of the sense), or the faculty of thinking, or the faculty of concepts, or of judgments." But he also
fixes on a comprehensive and explicit formula that is more in
accordance with the totality of the Transcendental Analytic in
its notions of *a priority*. "All of those explanations, if more
clearly examined, come to the same; it is the faculty of rules.
This characteristic is more significant and approaches nearer to
the essence of the understanding."[1] Yet it is a faculty that applies its rules in various ways. Now it is a synthetic activity
endeavoring to unite and fuse the particular, or manifold, in
the objective legitimacy of the universal or categories, giving
us an 'object' or a judgment of experience; then it is the subsumption of things according to a rule, but not concepts,[2]
whereby we come to æsthetical objects, (for this is a judgment of taste); finally, the vigorous struggle to get an enlarged
concept over the totality of any class of experiences results in
the unconditioned totalities—the desired predicates of metaphysical judgments. (Ethical judgments do not properly fall
within the Critical philosophy. They appear in 'Tugendlehre;'
but in 'Sittenlehre' something vastly more *a priori* and less
susceptible of a diversity of forms can occur).

Here is the proper place to mention the famous tripartition
of the 'oberen Erkenntnissvermögen,' an analysis of which it
was Criticism's special aim to complete, as was seen in the preceding chapter. The separation of 'lower' from 'higher' was
not a new division of human faculties; but one thoroughly in
vogue, and with which Kant agreed.[3] It was a century when
faith in 'reason' was almost a religious tenet. But the faith
had become so rational that Kant frequently calls it 'the age of
criticism.' Criticism itself was a child of reason, and the
greatest work of the age was the *Critique of Pure Reason.*

[1] *Critique*, II., p. 110.
[2] *Werke*, V., 200.
[3] *Cf.*, Baumgarten, *Meta.*, Sec. 383, 462, 510; Hegler, *op. cit.*, p. 106 f.;
Kant, *Werke*, IV., 145-6, 243, 490; VII., 388; V., 214, 478 n.; *Reflex.*, 108, 113;
Dieterich, *Kant u. Rousseau*, 30, 125 f.

The influence of such external data is to beget a doubt as to the psychologic intent of the title which Kant adopted. What he apparently meant by 'reason' as a 'higher faculty' is also partially explained by the general conception then attached to the term. Man is always the metaphysical egoist, ever ready to set himself off in terms of reality from all forms of animal life below him. No less was he thus rationally selfish last century, when attributing 'reason' to himself, whereby he supposed the merely 'apprehensive,' apperceptionless animals to be peculiarly separated from himself. Animals have only instinct. The understanding is man's peculiar possession which gives human reality to the passions.[1] It is the opposite of instinct, and constitutes the humanity of man.

Another suggestion[2] not only clears the way to an appreciation of his treatment of reason, but lends coloring to the conception of the faculties in the preceding chapter and to the existence of the mind as undertaken by rational psychology. It is this. To all appearances Kant endeavors to avoid all metaphysical implications. In psychological passages, 'Gemüth' is the term of his choice, while 'Vernunft' is the great encyclopedic cart of philosophical entities. In empirical psychology we cannot speak of a 'Seele' or 'Geist.' The admonition is, psychologize without a soul.[3] 'Gemüth' has a vague, indefinite meaning, limited only to the states of consciousness. After these have been adequately considered by the corresponding science, one may be positivistic or spiritualistic, just as he choses. 'Vernunft' is also a favorite term with Criticism, whose inherent difficulties are made more difficult by the obvious effort to leave out all psychological presuppositions, either as to the nature or the existence of the soul. These two points have validity only when the psychological attainments of Criticism can be existentialized by a trustworthy metaphysic of mind. Is it not a worthy supposition to fancy Criticism saying, we can and do reason or philosophize, no matter whether we *be* matter

---

[1] *Werke*, VII., 590.

[2] Lange, *op. cit.*, II., 191, note 23.

[3] *Cf.*, the very recent effort to make psychology 'non-metaphysical.' James, *op. cit.*, I., 182, 350.

or spirit? This, in turn, is a point upon which there must be reasoning. From such a view-point it appears that the investigations of Criticism are quite largely psychological, *viz:* in so far as it engages in describing the functions discovered in that reason; but, more metaphysical, as it posits their reality as *a priori* necessities of all experience, whether cognitive, ethical or æsthetical.

No more convenient term than ' reason' is at philosophy's command. It is ever large enough to pour forth the creative categories of absolute being, or so contractile as to be reduced to a minimum capacity, holding only an ever dubitable principle of habitual association as the binding link of all experience. The use of the term is a psychological necessity with philosophy; nor can it be wisdom to clamor for a discontinuance of its employment. But when philosophy persists in giving a highly specialized content to that reason, so as to have validity in the life of a self, then psychology is invited forthwith to inspect the ' rational' importations. This is what Criticism has done. It has ascribed a manifold individualistic content to reason, even introducing diametrical variations in the meanings assigned to it, so that no point in the Critical philosophy is more factually vexing than the diversified attributes of reason. Now it is the supreme quality of intelligence and constitutes the special domain of philosophy; here it is inclusive of all the ' higher cognitive faculties.' Again, it is ' speculative' reason that exhibits a spontaneity towards representations and makes for the ' objective' reality known things have; but is to be separated somehow from ' practical' reason that is a spontaneity in the function of self-determination—a separation that renders possible the antithetical foundations of Criticism and desiderates the appendant unification in subjective Æsthetics. No less is it reason standing in opposition to sense whose intellective realization comes about through the former. It is likewise the aspiring logical reason, making spuriously syllogistic advances on totalities that really are but function-wise distinguishable from the ethical, yet modest metaphysical reason intuiting its own implied reality in the consciousness of a relentless duty. Or, it is the genuinely psychological, but critically delusive reason laboring to know realities that are syllogistically implied in the things and selves which are the 'critical' creatures of a self-apprehensive understanding that appears to be the faculty of positing cognitive particularities. Now it is an understanding whose judgment is the fusion of sensible and intelligible forms into *a priori* rules, determinative of the categories to phenomena; or it is a judgment, natural and uneducable, synthetic and subjectively universal, fusing an ideal of beauty with a construction of apperception by which we experience a 'pleasurable purposiveness' as we contemplate nature and find our æsthetical 'Wohlgefallen' in pronouncing this judgment of taste.

This great variety in conceptions is allowable to philosophy. Its interpretation of the world always predicates a chosen content to 'reason.' But when reference is made to pure speculation, which equals psychological intellection, then psychology modestly presents its request that the ratiocinative processes be properly indicated. The psychology of thought comprehends the treatment of generic terms, their adjustment in affirmations or negations, and the manipulation of their consequent judgments so as to arrive at some new truth. The concept, judgment and syllogism are psychical processes and products, an analysis of which completes a description of that ideational development from primitive discrimination and comparison that results in cognitions or perceptual realities. There is no 'thing' for any consciousness without an explanation of the possible relations inherent in its antecedent image. The copulizing of a related predicate need not necessarily be a complete and well-rounded-out grammatical expression. A thought psychosis may be realized without the propositional formality. The only point is, that 'ideas' are products, not impressions, constructions, not presentations. And modern psychology very properly refuses to call that consciousness cognitive which has not predicated somehow. A mere sensational reaction or a returning image must ever be denied the positedness which 'things' have. An ideational state does not become what we adults all recognize it to be, without a judgment-wise execution of a percepted discrimination. Things are not known, unless, in some manner, we make them to be known. This is the Anglo-Saxon of Leibnizian 'apperception' and of the ' transcendental synthetic unity' of Criticism. It merely expresses the fact that in every knowing consciousness there is a relatedness mingled with the content. But psychology fails to find a necessity of limiting this relatedness to a physiological consciousness. That would omit what is patent to all observation, that there is a psychical fusion of specific with conceptual images (as in a proposition), and, *also* of concepts of perception and experience with chosen concepts, as in the syllogism. The one mode of synthesis is not unlike the other, of which it is only a developed form. Judging and syllogizing are psychologically not the widely separated processes nor differentiated products as Criticism's treatment of them would have one believe.[1] Syllogism, in fact, is the judging process turned at a later period upon the judgment product. The process of relating propositions does not enter into the judgments of experience. (*E. g.*, the knocker announces some one's presence without. I rely upon my friend's promise to confer with me at an appointed time; and, upon suggestion by contiguity, I recognize this as the appointed hour. There ensues a fusion of chosen elements, as a result of which mental activity I refer, by numerous abbreviated syllogisms, the presence of my friend without.) What are the modes of the fusion which beget affirmations is seen in an analysis of the various products.[2] Propositions may be the association of concepts, one of which is experientially given in the other and essentially enters into its previous formation; as, *e. g.*, flowers have petals. Such are analytical judgments which merely explicate the (logical) intensiveness of the subject concept. But when I affirm that the paper is the cause of my present sense-experience of grayish white, I am proceeding in a characteristically different manner. I am fusing an extensive and chosen concept with a given experience. I pronounce a synthetic judgment, and add to the concept of experience. What these various forms of synthesis are, cannot be answered except by special investigations. Suffice it to say

---

[1] *Cf.*, the ' Analytic' with the ' Dialectic' as to their psychological basis.
[2] *Cf.*, Sully, *op. cit.*, I., 439 ff; Baldwin, *op. cit.*, I., 292 ff.

that these modes of fusion are the categories which have been so famous in the history of philosophy. *What* they are, must be answered by metaphysic as it investigates the constituents of reality. *Why* I use them in my experience, this way or that, it is incumbent on a theory of knowledge to inquire. *How* I do proceed in their application throughout experience, psychology must testify in reporting on the psychical transactions which it is constantly observing.

The foregoing are, in general, the psychological processes called reasoning, and the faculty is intellect or reason proper. It is but a mere speck in that multitude of rational activities, so-called by Criticism. Its term for the discriminating and ratiocinating consciousness is ‘ understanding ’ over against which is set ‘ speculative reason.’ Now, so far as the psychology of speculation is concerned, it can find no other processes in the intellective consciousness. These must be employed by every philosopher in his contribution to man's attempt to come to a more perfect *rationale* of experience. Thus the distinction between understanding and reason, as cognitive, is unwarrantable and Critical scepticism is not an *a priori* necessity as seen by an examination of pure reason alone. This separation of the higher cognitive faculty is also the source of the epistemological defects and ethical excellencies of Criticism. Knowledge, so delusively limited, is the three by four (the grouping of the categories) of the *a priori* forms of judging, and has a *quid juris* only so far as this present sensuous consciousness is concerned. Nor does Criticism win psychological approval in attempting to identify pure and practical reasons, if process and contents are to be the truth of names.[1]

Thus the great constructive portion of the *Critique* is, as it were, a prophet of psychology. The latter finds it impossible to separate widely between the process of perception and the process of conception. But more pertinent in its vindication of Criticism is the general agreement that conceptualizing and re-

---

[1] On the *antithesis* of ‘ Verstand ’ and ‘ Vernunft,’ *cf.*, beside the *Critique, Werke,* VII., 449 f. 515, 390; V., 53, 413 f.; *Vorlesungen,* 51; on the *unity* of the two reasons *cf.*, V., 125 ff., in which Green attempts to vindicate Kant : *Phil. Works,* II., p. 111 f. Schopenhauer critizes Kant's separation of Verstand and Vernunft, and with much justice ; *op. cit.,* pp. 551 f.

lated activities are psychical processes that round out into a percept and a cognition, those discriminated and assimilated sensations of psychic beginnings. Thus, while it may be a serious defect in the Transcendental Logic that it endeavors to separate the above processes, it is its chief value in having contended that judgment is knowledge.[1] Whether reason and understanding are one and the same,[2] or whether they are separated and constantly antagonistic in the manufacture and attempted ultimate interpretation of experience, experience can be as it is for us men only as we exercise those powers we have by virtue of being rational, thinking beings, and let 'knowledge rest on Verstand.' Sensations or ideas empirical-wise, thinking or mere thought are not knowledge.[3] So far Criticism remains psychological; but it pilfers the mind of a valid activity when it affirms that we can be said to 'know' when we have categorized the 'stuff' of sense by the one discriminative form of judgment. Our intellective activity, as it develops with the continuity of sensuous life, does not merely relate concepts. Inferences in all directions coöperate with lower ideational functions to bring assimilated sensational factors to the order of objective or real things. The syllogism does not remain the distinctive instrument of the old rational sciences. It has a psychological validity in perceptual realities, that varies inversely as the amount of clearly discriminated sense and image factors.[4] Indeed, this whole rational activity is at least given play in the large amount of 'thinking' that appears and rounds out, as it were, the perceptual consciousness into the 'scientific' mind. So far as the psychical processes are concerned in either instance they are one and the same. It is the material elaborated by each which differentiates the world of things and their varieties from the world of hypothesized atoms and unseen forces. Thus it is that Criticism permits cognitive, objective validity to only certain judgments, its scepticism cutting off all

---

[1] This may be partially questioned; *cf.*, the distinction between, and relation of 'Wahrnehmungsurtheil' and 'Erfahrungsurtheil' mentioned in the next chapter.

[2] *Werke*, II., 66.

[3] *Cf.*, VIII., 34, 584, 526; VII., 512, 545 f.; *Critique*, I., 492, II., 67.

[4] *Cf.*, Baldwin, *op. cit.*, p. 301.

this mass of 'thinking' which passes as inference and hypothesis, *etc.*; but for its famous limitations it can find no suggestive warrant in an introspective explication of the respective processes. Here it appears to a certain extent that the conclusion of the preceding chapter is true of the intellective processes: Kant either supposed the work of psychology as already complete when he began the metaphysical reflections, or used terms into which he put chosen material, rather than such as appears empirically.

Almost inextricably wrapped up with Criticism, and appearing in connection with the great purpose which was its speculative goal, is the question as to the degree of certainty attending our knowledge of reality. Kant wished to place metaphysic on a sure foundation, to give it a sub-structure which should be as unshakable as the piers on which rested the triumphs of mechanical science in formulating the space and time of our universe. It was certainty that Kant was desiderating. Philosophy had degenerated to a weakling where any dubitating breath, fragrant with literary perfume, might toss it about in the scene of experience. With a mathematical model, he plunges into the *a priori* and discovers the sources of primitive synthetic judgments. It was their possession and the (highly fictitious) schema under the guidance of pure apperception which gave certainty, reality, as they were applied to objects. When once the forms of judgment had been discovered, all was secured. The difficulty became, how these forms were applied. It is the deduction of their experiential legitimacy that is the grave concern.[1] With their application to 'Vorstellung,' sensationalism is denied, rationalism rebuked, and an assured answer given to the great problem of certainty, but a certainty limited to phenomena. Only in a use of the categories do we know objects and by an application of the *a priori* principles into which they are somehow fashioned by a static, uneducable judgment,[2] do we come to reality. Indeed, these principles are the *via media* of the categories.

Since these forms belong to some consciousness, and a

[1] *Critique*, II., p. XXVI.
[2] *Critique*, II., 117, *Vorlesungen*, p. 29.

degree of certainty is no less a feature of cognitive psychoses
psychology has its descriptive word as to the application of the
categories and the source of conviction that suffuses that intellection which predicates reality as its content. In the preceding chapter,[1] there were generalized some of the facts for which
psychology must adequately account in expressing the interrelation of the faculties. Such are, also, facts which make
against Kant's great claim that it is understanding to which all
cognized experience is attributable. Pure discrimination and
relativeness are mental functions setting the categories adrift
among sense-elements in such a manner as to make up the
legality of experience. But psychology finds no empirical
guarantee for the doctrine that mere comparison adjusts *a priori*
forms to the idea as it has passed its way up through the lower
cognitive faculties.[2] In the first place, and as apparent
throughout the study, Criticism really overlooks the significance
of the patent facts of growth and fusion which contribute to that
judging consciousness. Whatever else may be said as to the
nature of adult consciousness, no consideration of it which includes processes can be competent without regarding the way
in which it has become. And a theory of knowledge, if it
desires, as it ought in every instance, to introduce judgment as
a conditioning process, cannot subvert psychologic truth.
This may encroach upon the cherished purity of philosophy,
which was Kant's passionate ideal, leading to the exclusion of
all empirical dross.[3] But the truth of experience, expressed in
terms of rationality, should be the great aim of all inquiry basing
itself on the self-confidence of reason. Secondly, and what is
an outgrowth of the first, the categories 'get applied,' not by a
non-empirical, apperceptive unity, but only in the frequent re-
buffs which primitive attention and motor consciousness receive
at the hands of that cruel, violent congeries which surge in upon
infantile beginnings. The stubborn refusal to abide the warning disappointments, the pleasure that accrues in the successful
issue of petty strivings, and the determination to be self-assertive

---

[1] *Vide supra*, pp. 79 ff.
[2] *Cf.*, Lang, *op. cit.*, II., 197, note 26.
[3] *Vide supra*, pp. 17 ff.

and rebut the imperiousness of things are of great moment in the obscure and often under-valued forthputtings that posit things as realities. Thus psychology's word on the categorization is brief, but comprehensive in that every psychic nerve is quivering that the mental discriminativeness may realize itself in this varied world of things and selves. One must admit that differentiation, as a cognitive process, essentially belongs to intellect. But, in his vigorous attempt to explicate the intelligibility of the world, Kant has sublimated understanding into such a spontaneity that the question becomes extremely pertinent: How much will has been clandestinely introduced into that ' faculty' whose forthputting is knowledge and experience? It is not a psychological impossibility that a ' synthesis,' a 'fusion,' an ' activity,' should be the supreme characteristic of that which pierces the obscurity of the unrelated. If Kant's ' understanding' is the faculty of *human* knowledge, then it must invoke that impulse which goes along with all intellection, and is properly called will, but not that ' free, voluntary' activity which strives to set into reality a purpose and choice; that can appear only as a product of a highly complex development. If will means anything in the life of mind, it does mean the actualization of ' *a priori* forms.' As a condition of experience this striving in its worth with the power of relatedness is so important that one could say, without the conative inherency of cognition, there would not be any knowledge that is knowledge (and we must, on the whole, take Kant's answer to his specialized question as being an account of the nature of knowledge, and not merely a logical treatment of certain forms of *a priori* judgments).

In Criticism's discovery and application of the categories lay another deep-seated, genuine purpose, namely, to find a certification of knowledge in its dealings with reality.[1] Some truths come to us claiming greater validity than mere habitual association seems possible to grant. We make affirmations or negations, positing them as true for all time and absolutely necessary in the experience of every rational being. What are the grounds on which rest these features of our knowledge? or, what is the evidence that ' our' knowledge is dealing with re-

[1] *Cf.*, *Critique*, II., pp. XXV, 1, 94; *Werke*, V., 12 f.

ality? Kant answers this question in no less an *a priori* manner than the problem of the intelligibility of experience. In
fact the two problems are answered in the same solution. Kant
did not distinguish them, but makes the famous discovery of the
categories whose various validity solves, *mutatis mutandis*, all
the difficulties of known realities encountered not only by transcendentalism, but by all philosophy. While sensuous objectivity and cognitive reality are conditioned by the *a priori* concepts and the manifold that is given, certainty, or necessity, rests
upon the one 'transcendental faculty' which makes possible the
fusion of the two widely various factors in knowledge, namely,
pure apperception, or the synthesis of one consciousness.[1] But
experimental certainty is limited to phenomena only. What
we construct in intuition is the only 'object' which properly belongs to the noëtic acquisitions of pure reason. Reality, however, or noumenal determinations, are implicated in our ethical
being. The moral law demands 'faith,' and brings truly 'objective' realities. But reason can 'know' only a little way.
When knowledge is to stand alone it ends with experience, revealing the cognition of phenomena. Thus it is that there is a
critical scepticism. We can know things only as they 'are
given' and elaborated by understanding. This 'faculty,'
though it is the corner stone of all nature, limits its truth-expressing activity to only that which has 'sensual content.' Realities elude our cognitive grasp. They are for us only as we
pass beyond the positing of relations to a credence in ethical
being. Thus in Criticism, knowledge and certainty are given
in a consciousness that explicates relations, while reality and its
paramount certification come with the feeling that 'the ought'
is somehow valid even in the phenomenal series into which we
are set. 'Knowledge' ends in scepticism and the universality
of *a priori* forms concludes in the transcendental dream of sensuous phantasmagoria—a pleasing play in which we all are de-
luded. 'Faith' ends in the attainment of true reality, and the
imperativeness of the inner self brings us real being, set in manifold ontological relations with existences not ourselves, whose
natures are likewise indicated by the reciprocity of 'the ought.'

[1] *Critique*, II., 93-94.

Even more than Jacobi is Kant the ' faith' philosopher. Critical philosophy in its entirety is idealistic realism, but a ' known' realism that lies outside cognizing activities. It ventured as sceptical idealism, but when the circuit of its purposes was run, it became an ethical realism founded on the former. The later explication of the reflective, æsthetical judgment does not modify its foregoing essential conclusions.

The scepticism of Criticism does not rest merely upon this separation of belief and knowledge. It also has its roots in an unpsychological view of the ratiocinative processes whether dealing with perceptual things or with the self of consciousness, which have been considered elsewhere.[1] Yet the famous antithesis between faith and knowledge, as clearly expressed in the preface to the second edition of the *Critique,* is the great objective point towards which Kant is constantly working. If Criticism be true, then the point of orientation in all rational life is faith, belief, conviction, feeling, a purely subjective condition which has its universal validity in the ethical experiences of each one who posits self and selves and finds them binding each other down to the fulfillment of an obligation that will not cease its clamorings, though it be persistently denied that gratifying experience which comes in the satisfaction of duty done. Criticism seems to say that there is no belief, no feeling in knowledge, as such; but in certain super-sensuous relations there obtains ' critical' validity of this inner impulse that comes up as the content of a conscience.[2]

So far as the scepticism of Criticism rests upon the elimination of the affective factors in the cognitive consciousness, it remains without psychological warrant. All intellection is suffused with the element of belief. Judgments proceed with the conviction that they are dealing with somewhat real. In its speculative aspects, Criticism unpsychologically considers mere intellection. Though there is yet dispute among writers whether ' belief' is intellectual or affective, there is no doubt

[1] *Cf., supra.* pp. 125 f.

[2] At times a moral 'sense,' or conscience, is denied: *cf., Werke,* II., 307, V., 122 f., VII., 19, IV., 290, 308; at others it is partially recognized as a valid psychical faculty: *Werke,* V., 41, 80, 102 f., VII., 178 f., 204 f., 257, VIII., 609 f.

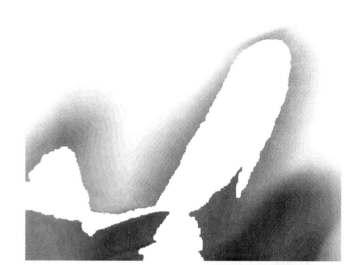

CHAPTER V.

RATIONAL PSYCHOLOGY IN THE CRITICAL PHILOSOPHY.

Empirical psychology relates itself in various ways to the positive or constructive aspects of Critical philosophy, and especially to that portion which treats of speculative reason. The theory of knowledge and the system of *a priori* principles represent the experiential side of Criticism. Rational psychology, on the other hand, is the first realm of supposed knowledge against which Criticism hurls itself with destructive force. Empirical psychology relates itself to the Analytic in its making, while the results therein attained are turned upon the rational science. Thus psychology relates itself to Criticism in two ways: 1. in building itself up; 2. when it struggles to clear the ground, that room and defense may be had for its own standing. Kant himself, however, would doubtless deny such relations, especially the former; for Criticism, basing itself on logic, was (supposedly) far removed from psychology—that anthropology of the inner sense.

What Kant means by rational psychology, and how it separates itself from, as well as approximates the empirical science, we have already seen.[1] The requirement here is merely to state what that discipline contained and to estimate the famous criticism of it.

Rational psychology is one of the three metaphysical sciences which erect themselves upon the ground of reason alone. This is a faculty of principles which has nothing to do with objects directly, much less any concern with intuitions.[2] It is sharply distinguished from understanding in the Critical philosophy, and from Kant's notorious attempt to split them off from each other came not only many of the essential psychological tenets which suffuse Criticism, but also, many of the criticisms against Kant

[1] *Supra*, pp. 38 f.
[2] *Critique*, II., 258–262.

himself for this procedure, take their point of orientation here, especially that of Schopenhauer.[1] Kant did not make the distinction first in the *Critique* nor in the important *Dissertation* of 1770; but yet a decade earlier is found the first distinction between 'Verstand' and 'Vernunft,' which he attempts to do away with, in that both are 'Grundfähigkeiten' whose effort is 'deutlich zu erkennen' and 'Vernunftschlüsse zu machen.' As he advanced in his thinking, however, there came the noteworthy recognition that perception, or knowledge, involves immediate activities of the understanding. Its functions alone make experience, and certainty is confined to this. As he attempts to define reason on the basis of this acquisition, he began 'to feel considerable misgiving.' Whereas understanding is the faculty of the mind immediately concerned with objects and the rules of nature, reason tries to reach the unconditioned and is distinguished as a faculty of principles. Understanding works with judgments of twelve kinds; but the syllogism is the instrument of reason. It arranges judgments so as to bring out of them a new judgment, which is properly called 'a conclusion of reason.' Of these syllogisms there are as many kinds as there are possible relations expressed in the major propositions. Categorical, hypothetical, and disjunctive judgments are the three and no more, which express the relation of knowledge in the understanding, and accordingly there are three kinds of syllogisms differing from each other as those judgments.[3]

Reason manipulates bare concepts through the machinery of these syllogistic forms until it attains those bodies of rational knowledge known as psychology, cosmology, and theology. The various 'Ideas' of reason are appropriate to the respective syllogisms; why, nothing but his 'pedagogic primness' can explain,[4] so that the categorical syllogism finds the unconditioned

[1] *Loc. cit.*

[3] *Werke*, II., pp. 52–68, especially 66–67.

[3] *Critique*, II., 263, 289, 343.

[4] Since existence is given us in three different ways, *viz.*: change under the law of causality *within us* as internal phenomena; a spatial and temporal series of existence *without us*; and an existence *in general*, a clue to the explanation of the applicability of the several syllogisms to the respective existence may be found in such facts as these. Assertory propositions may be made concerning ourselves, the phenomena of mind are given immediately (*cf.* Kant's utterance

synthesis in a subject; the hypothetical, the ultimate synthesis of the members of a series; the disjunctive, the ultimate synthesis of the parts of a system.[1] The first comprehends our knowledge of the nature and destiny of our soul; the second presents us with the limits of the world and the character of its events, while the third contains the final relation of all things and beings to the Ultimate Being.

These presumed triumphs of reason, Kant says, are illusions through and through. They rest on sophisms that belong to the very nature of reason and can no more be dispelled than many of the illusions known in optics. It is the duty of dialectic to expose the falsity that lurks within the grounds on which one rests his conviction that he does know aught of any unconditioned.

It is not merely the impulse of architectonic which added the Transcendental Dialectic. The adoption of pure logic as the basis of the larger portion of the *Critique* merely contains the formal demand that a dialectic should be appended. But the very content of the Critical philosophy in its speculative half demanded that a dialectic be given. In the Æsthetic was laid the broad basis whereon the Copernican reform was to plant itself and from which a reconciliation between the opposing developments would be effected. Empiricism and scepticism have their severest criticism in the Analytic where it is shown that reason *has* a modicum of knowledge given only in experience, but not coming out of experience in the ordinary sense. Only half the task of Criticism is here accomplished. Dogmatism and superstition might still be rampant in their flights to-

on the nature of perception, of the two sorts). Of external existence we must be more doubtful, since it is farther out in the fringe of consciousness, so to speak. While the existence in general, or absolute being, is still less intimately given in the immediacy of consciousness, *i. e.*, the respective syllogisms thus depend on the degree of mediacy in our so-called knowledge of the objects. On the other hand, a general objection might be raised with the query, whether reality is to be given by mere reason as a logical form, a presupposition which has had a mighty commentary within this century. Kant seems to confound metaphysic from the very start when he affirms that it is the work of reason which has to *construct* the unconditioned by a *deductive* process in order to get at it.

[1] *Crit.*, II., 280, 290.

wards the supersensuous. But the Dialectic appears with its harsh and almost conceited rebuke, checking the asseverations of those who would not 'taste of criticism.'[1] They went headlong in gathering *quod-est-demonstrandum* 'trash,' while critical dialectic brought them to a sudden halt in showing how illusory is any possible knowledge of God, the soul, and the world.

Dialectic was also demanded by the peculiar tenets of Criticism within itself, besides the exoteric attempt to reconcile contending teachings. Its great doctrine up to this point was that knowledge has significance only as it comprehends intuition and thoughts. Judgments alone, nor mere sensations, were not knowledge. But even back of this, we might say, for it is the chain binding all parts of Criticism into a systematic whole, lies the distinction between phenomena and noumena of which transcendental idealism is its expression, both positive and negative. He first tells us what knowledge is and how it comes about, and then proceeds to point out its insular limitations. The phenomenality of knowledge is announced already in the Æsthetic when it is maintained that those things which become 'objects' for us receive their characteristic forms from the sensing mind. Kant, however, did not propose to remain a dogmatic idealist; and the statement that objects are not things in themselves, but are only as they appear to us—obviously reclining on some doctrine of representativism—would not suffice. It remained to show in detail why such is the truth, culminating in the affirmation that nature is a creature of understanding. All the while there are volcanic tremors, now near the surface, then receding into the depths which supported Criticism. Only when the Analytic had completed its task were the pietistic bands loosed and the nursling of Criticism broke forth in the retarded chapter 'On the Ground of Distinction of all subjects into Phenomena and Noumena.'[2] Kant is the model of patience. He can maintain a speculative coolness and withhold metaphysical clamorings until reason's 'patient search and vigil long' have ended in the demand for some philosophic assent.

[1] *Cf., Werke*, IV., 113.
[2] *Critique*, II., 205 ff.

Then, with the powerful sweep of a speculative conviction, he clears the field of dogmatism by his elaboration of the doctrine of phenomenality. With the demarcation of the *negative* concept of noumenon, so far as it struggles to creep into experience, he at once turns to expose that immense mass of misconceived opinion.

If, then, the interpretation be true and dialectic and noumenon are synonymous terms, much of Kant's own vagueness will be cleared away, when for ' the unconditioned ' there is substituted ' noumenon ' or ' transcendental object.' Kant's criticism of the three spurious sciences really means so much, and the fancifulness he exhibits in referring each science to a corresponding syllogism really comes to light; and queries as to the legitimacy of such references disappear as it is learned that all the legality is derivable only from Kant's utter disregard of psychology as suggesting the problems which philosophy considers, and accepting logic as the organon of transcendental truth. Kant was true to his propaedeutic. He discovers truth, but lets go reality. For truth and reality are not one and the same for philosophy, Hegel notwithstanding. Though Kant disheartens reason by revealing in the Analytic that knowledge, such as falls to our lot, deals only with phenomena, manufactured articles, and not with those bearing the stamp of pristine reality; yet, in his careful examination of the dialectical sciences, Kant gives an expression of his obeisance to what is ' natural ' to man, and therein shows the sincerity of his wish to best serve the philosophic mind. The verbosity of the third section of the *Critique* reveals, as nothing else, the humanness of Criticism and its readiness to step from the realm of transcendental insight to cast its attainments in a pedagogic mould.

Rational psychology can no longer erect itself with logical legitimacy. It always has an essential defect, not in its content, but in its former faultiness. It is paralogistic. In its constructive attempts its procedure vitiates its character as truth expressing, by being peculiarly fallacious, and brings itself to that bar of applied logic where fallacy and dilemma are shown up in their true character. What Kant means by the mistaken logic which rational psychology applies he tells us in his

Logik.[1] As a correlative of this form of logical fallacy, there is also 'the transcendental paralogism' which leads a subjective, rational necessity to formally false conclusions. That is, rational psychology arises from inevitable, yet entrapping snares.[2] Though the illusion is transcendental and inherent, his placing it under dialetic shows that it is not irresolvable, at least, in the Kantian sense.

We have already seen that rational sciences deal with concepts, and not objects in experience, and psychology can draw out its wisdom from only one concept, *viz.:* 'I think.' This does not appear in the formal exhibition of the categories; nevertheless, it partakes of their nature as a necessity of possible experience. It even passes beyond them in value, for it is the 'concept' or 'consciousness' which must attend them all.[3] And, of course, since any knowledge, true or false, must be an embodiment of the categories, rational psychology puts the 'purely intellectual intuition' into the categorical hopper, and receives in open bag the grist of supersensible knowledge. Thus is possible that arrangement which gives 'the topic' of this science which begins with 'relation,' since it is a thing or substance which is given in this *cogito:* 1. (relation) the soul is *substance;* 2. (quality) as regards its quality, *simple;* 3. (quantity) as regards the different times in which it exists, numerically identical, that is *unity* (not plurality); 4. (modality) it is in relation to *possible* objects in space.[4]

Kant's discussion hints also at a fifth 'topic'—a class of facts relating themselves to the paralogism which expresses the commerce of body and soul. It would properly come under the group of 'relation,' either as 'causality,' or 'community.' But he had already exhausted 'relation' on the substantiality of the soul and his architectonic would not allow him

---

[1] *Werke*, VIII., p. 131, § 90. "Ein Vernunftschluss, welcher der Form nach falsch ist, ob er gleich den Schein eines richtigen Schlusses für sich hat, heisst ein Trugschluss. Ein solcher Schluss ist ein Paralogismus, insofern man sich selbst hintergeht • • •." He distinguishes it from the Sophism, which is of the same character, but 'mit Absicht.'

[2] *Cf., Critique*, II., 296, 256 f.

[3] *Crit.*, II., 297; *cf.*, I., 434-440, 450 f.

[4] *Crit.*, II., 300.

to find room for it in the topic. In the first edition the relation in question is discussed under the fourth paralogism as an appendix; while in the second edition it is banished from psychology as an improper task.[1]

Such is the elemental reduction of rational psychology into terms of the Analytic, which is always Kant's point of orientation. The science which combines these elements attempts to secure, with *apodicity*, a series of conclusions regarding the subject-matter, such as its immateriality, incorruptibility, and personality which fuse in the conception of spirituality; and furthermore, to set the soul free from a dependency on matter as the ground of life, and thus secure immortality. Kant, thus epitomizing this psychology, exhibits four syllogisms as expressive of its entirety, and sends the sun's ray of criticism through them, which causes this body of supposed knowledge to lift and float away like morning mists.[2]

First paralogism: That which is represented as the absolute subject [metaphysical or real substance], of our judgments, and cannot be used, therefore, as the determination of any other thing, is the substance [metaphysical or real].

I, as a thinking being, am the absolute subject [logical substance, not as inherent thought, nor as the object of thought] of all my possible judgments, and this representation [predicate] of myself can never be used as the predicate of any other thing.

Therefore, I, as a thinking being [Soul], am [metaphysical or real] substance.

Substance is not a metaphysical core belonging to things, as dogmatical realism would have it; but substance as a reality may be either noumenal or phenomenal. "What applies to a thing by itself * * * does not apply to what is called substance as a phenomenon. This is not an absolute subject, but only a permanent image of sensibility, nothing in fact but intuition, in which nothing unconditioned can ever be met with.'[3] If phenomena were independent objects we would never be able to

---

[1] *Cf., Critique*, II., 334, I., 506; Erdmann, *Kant's Kriticismus, etc.*, p. 58 f.; Krohn, *Die Auflösung der rational Psych. durch Kant*, p. 70.

[2] What follows is a summary of *Critique*, II., pp. 303-350. The bracketed phrases help indicate Kant's meaning.

[3] *Critique*, II., 454.

judge how the series of the manifold in time is connected with those objects.   But we have always to deal with intuitions only, which are related in a changing, temporal series that demands something permanent which ' is the substratum of the empirical representation of time itself.'   This permanent is the object itself,[1] or the permanent is a concept having validity only as intuitions are given on which it can rest.

Now the only substantial element of the *ego* of which rational psychology can make use is that permanence of a logical sort, which is inherent in all thoughts and makes them possible internal objects; but it itself is an epistemological substrate which is never an intuition.   It must be distinguished from the ' empirical *ego*,' which ' cannot be admitted as a thing by itself because it is under the condition of time, a form that can never be the determination of anything by itself.'[2]   Thus psychology gives itself no demonstrative right to speak of the substantiality or existence of the soul.   Its proof must use the middle term paralogistically, *if they are to have any meaning.*

Second paralogism: Everything the action of which can never be considered as the concurrence of several acting things is simple.   Now the soul, or the thinking I, in such a thing; therefore, the thinking I is simple.

This is ' der Achilles ' of rational psychology—invulnerable, except at one spot.   Dogmatists have great plausibility in maintaining the symplicity of the soul, since the necessity of the unity of the subject seems implicated in that varied whole which thoughts are.   But the *nervus probandi* of this cardinal proposition of psychology lies in the statement that in order to constitute a thought the many representations must be comprehended under the absolute unity of the thinking subject.   This is impossible of proof, for it is not an analytical proposition; nor does a deduction from concepts *a priori* avail.   Identity in compositeness is a synthetic concept having concern with that which is presented in sensibility.   Only as we have reference to ' objects ' can we properly speak of a permanent simple which inheres in

[1] *Critique*, II., 160 f., 167.
[2] *Ibid.*, II., 427; *cf.*, 94 f., 108, 304, 305, 310, 315, 318, 331, 344, 347; I., 492., 502 f.

that whose action is referable to a unit, but not a unity of intuition.

The *ego* here, as in the first proposition, is intended to have metaphysical meaning. Herein lies the subtilty of the syllogism. Dogmatism would be secure in its pretensions if it were possible to use ' simple thing ' in the minor with the same meaning as in the major. But here it must relinquish its claims, for the only possible meaning that can be put into this *ego* is that it is the logical subject, a verbal impersonation, a necessity of thought throughout. This so-called intuition of simplicity does not give ' the real simplicity of my subject,' but only the identity of that unity of transcendental apperception. ' I am simple ' is the immediate expression of this apperception and truly means an absolute, non-manifold subject, but logical only, and as a proposition is tautological. If the empirical *ego* were the logical *ego*, much less the transcendental *ego*, then rational psychology would stand, but the whole teaching of phenomenalism would fall to the ground. Simplicity in the subject is no datum of the inner sense, and psychology can in no other way know the transcendental object of the internal sense.

Third paralogism: Whatever is conscious of the numerical identity of its own identity at different times [that it is always one and the same *ego*], is in so far a person. Now the soul is conscious, *etc.* Therefore, the soul is the person.

This syllogism is much like the first, in that it builds itself upon some permanent that is given in consciousness. The permanence is not that which I am to myself; but the permanence that I, as an object for another consciousness, am given by him as though I were an object of his external intuition. Thus only can be found any metaphysical meaning in the numerical identity of a consciousness! This is, my identity within several times depends upon the functioning of the observer's understanding according to the first Analogy of Experience,[1] which finds in his temporal apprehension of me the necessity of some permanent which is the measure of and comparable with the flow of the manifold he perceives.

Now the minor seeks to put that meaning into the conscious

[1] *Cf., Crit.,* II., 160 ff.

identity of the soul, but surreptitiously. For, it is true that I do have an identity in my consciousness, but an identity that is not at all like that which comes with the perception of myself *in* time. It is only the numerical identity of the 'I think' which is a formal condition of my thoughts and their inherence. Identical apperception is always given first; but from it we cannot infer the personality of that *ego* which is given in time. Thus the statement of the numerical identity of the real *ego* becomes only the tautology of the transcendental or formal unity which is always nothing but a pre-condition of any synthetic judging.

Fourth paralogism: That, the existence of which can only be inferred as a cause of given perceptions, has a doubtful existence.

All external phenomena are such that this existence cannot be perceived immediately, but we can only infer them as the cause of given perceptions.

Therefore, the existence of all objects of the external sense is doubtful.

The fault in this paralogism[1] turns upon the expression ' outside us.' It involves an inevitable ambiguity which Criticism alone has been able to resolve. The major regards the objects ' outside us' in a transcendental sense, and dogmatic idealism posits things as occurring in a space of independent existence. Thus our perceptions are merely effects of something which the understanding calls their cause as corresponding to them. But the minor takes ' external *phenomena*' to be of the same character; and, overlooking the second meaning possible in the ' outside us' which recognizes objects as empirically external, leads psychology to the conclusion of problematical idealism.[2] The conclusion of this argument is false, because it *fails* to take this ambiguity in its genuine possibility and *to make itself paralogistic*. It is criticised because it is *not* guilty of some formal fault, but for another reason very curious in connection with the method of Criticism.

---

[1] *Crit.*, II., 323 f.

[2] It is difficult to represent the paralogical fault of this syllogism, for Kant's criticism of it has taken a very surprising turn, as we shall see later.

Such is the exhibition and treatment of the chief psychological doctrines as found in the first edition. Whatever may have been the inducements, Kant issued the second edition which has caused so much confusion and often been the source of misinterpretation. No doubt, the tone of the revision is considerably changed, the general doctrine of transcendental or sceptical idealism is less palpable, and many passages seem to contradict flatly the earlier conviction which accompanied the negation of 'the unknown X.' Schopenhauer, after Jacobi, performed a service to the philosophical world in calling its attention to those changes and modifications, but surely enlarges his data when he accuses Kant of retrenching. Possibly, Kuno Fischer[1] expresses more truly the relation of the two editions and the influences operating upon them when he writes that the first is the work of Kant and the second and following that of the Kantians.

Rational psychology was one of the two sections which received the greatest revision (the other being the Deduction of the Categories).[2] It is notably shortened, the logical formulæ of the syllogisms are omitted, and the running criticism attempts, in each of the four instances, to reduce the paralogisms into terms of the great problem as it is stated and analyzed in the 'Introduction' to that edition,[3] *viz.*, 'How are synthetic judgments *a priori* possible?' The possibility of such judgments lies 'in the consciousness of a determining self'—a definite expression of that concept *cogito* which lies at the basis of the science. ut the dogmatists seek by an analysis of the determinable self, which forms the object, to attain metaphysical knowledge. They fail, however, in that their conclusions are based on propositions that are identical or analytical, and are thus an analysis of thought in general. This *sophism per figuram dictionis* is resolved as it is seen that the science employs no synthetical *a priori* propositions, but mistakes its logical analysis of thinking in general for a metaphysical determination of the object.

[1] *A Commentary on Kant's Critique of Pure Reason*, p. 174. *Cf.*, Drobisch, *Kant's Dinge an Sich*, etc., p. 30; Erdmann, *Kriticismus*, p. 203, 223.

[2] *Crit.*, I., 492.

[3] *Cf.*, *Crit.*, I., 408 f.

How completely the refutation of rational science rests on the Transcendental Deduction will be readily granted, as Kant rests 'the whole of our critique' on his denial of a possible scientific conception of personality. The only objection to it can come through an *a priori* proof that thinking beings are simple substances. Herein he is right in so far as the logical *ego* is the keystone of the whole Analytic and the key that solves the mysteries of noumenality. The long excursus in the first edition on transcendental idealism and its agreement with psychological perception is replaced in the second by two widely separated passages : one, the famous note in the preface,[1] and the addition in the text on the 'Refutation of Idealism.'[2] There is also added a refutation of Mendelssohn's proof of the soul's permanence, and a clearer recognition of a possible *fifth* paralogism. With this brevity of treatment and these additions, there is yet no change so far as psychology is concerned. There is no rational psychology as a *doctrine*, furnishing any addition to our self-knowledge, but only as a *discipline* fixing impassable limits to speculative reason in this field.[3] If there be any change, it is only the growing recognition of the articulation of the first two *Critiques*, the second of which was soon to appear, and *whose speculative basis is laid in the criticism of transcendental dialectic.* The rational sciences must be removed before an ethical noumenality could be established. But for psychology and speculation it remained the same. Thus ended the great tragedy of Criticism whose first act was performed so many years before when its undogmatic doubt fell on the world's great clairvoyant. About spiritual beings 'kann man vielleicht noch allerlei meinen, niemals aber mehr wissen.' "Lasst uns demnach alle lärmende Lehrverfassungen von so entfernten Gegenständen der Speculation und der Sorge müssiger Köpfe überlassen. * * * Es war auch die menschliche Vernunft nicht genugsam dazu beflügelt, dass sie so hohe Wolken theilen sollte, die uns die Geheimnisse der andern Welt aus den Augen ziehen ; * * * denn es wohl am rathsamsten sei, wenn sie sich

---

[1] *Critique*, I., 280–281.
[2] *Ibid.*, 475–479.
[3] *Ibid.*, 502.

zu gedulden beliebten, bis sie werden dahin kommen. 'Lasst uns unser Glück besorgen, in den Garten gehen, und arbeiten.'"[1]

It has been a mooted question as to the sources of the rational psychology which Kant criticizes. Since Kant, as is well known, was no thorough student of philosophy in its historical development, being much rather an independent discoverer in the field of speculation, it becomes a doubly important query in the history of philosophy itself in so far as his criticism was epoch-making in its own realm, and also stimulating in that of the positive sciences.

Kant, as a student, was nurtured in the Leibnizo-Wolffian philosophy which was regnant throughout German universities. These methods and doctrines were accepted for the most part until the influence of materialism and scepticism awakened him to original and profound inquiries. As Criticism was developed, it appeared against dogmatism, and especially against its method.[2] And where the knowledge of reality was claimed, he subverts the doctrines of dogmatism. In the preface to the second edition however, Wolff is highly estimated and his method is given great value.[3] It was also Wolff who rational-ized voluminously in the two departments into which he divided psychology, *viz.* : empirical and rational. Thus it would naturally seem that Kant was representing Wolffian tenets and arguments. That this is *not* what Kant had in mind, will be seen from what follows. In the *Psychologiæ rationalis prolegomena*, (sec. 3) is briefly stated what Wolff understands by that science and the sources of its proofs : " Anima humana cum actu existat (sec. 20, *Psych. empir.*), in numero entium est (sec. 139, *Ontol.*) consequenter ad eam tanquam speciem applicari possunt, quae de ente in genere demonstrata sunt (sec. 360, 361, *Psych. empir.*). Quamobrem cum in Ontologia demonstrentur, quae de ente in genere praedicanda veniunt (sec. 1, *Ontol.*) ; in Psycholgia rationali principia demonstrandi petuntur ex Ontologia." Wolff, as a psychological idealist, arrived at most of the conclusions which Kant exhibits, but by a far different

[1] In 1776, *Werke*, II., 359, 381.
[2] *Crit.*, I., 383; *Werke*, VI., 43 f., 491 f; VIII., 84.
[3] *Crit.*, I., 384.

method. It was through ontology that certain essential conceptions were deduced and with them fused *ex notione privativa*
of the soul, thus reaching the conclusions which are chiefly
given in sections 44 ff. of the *Psychologia rationali.* The soul
is an immaterial, simple substance to which the properties of
material things are repugnant. By means of the body, the soul
is able to express its essence, which consists in the representation
of the universe (sec. 62, 66). It is hardly possible that Wolff
is Kant's model ; the former developed his proofs so differently
from the latter. Scarce can Baumgarten have been the immediate source. His *Metaphysik* Kant selected for the basis
of his lectures because of its ' scientific wealth and precision ;'[1]
but the popular work does not depart from the author's master
in metaphysic.[2]

It has been suspected that under the title of ' rational psychology,' which had been swung with scholastic triumph for
half a century, Kant places tenets which had a much greater
warmth in his consciousness by reason of their nearness in time,
place and friendship. Martin Knutzen, the one among Kant's
university teachers, who could influence his genius,[3] is the first
who has been mentioned as the one having had most influence
in erecting some form of psychology against the materialism
which was prevailing at that time.[4] Reimarus, of whom Kant
says,[5] his work has not yet been superseded, secures[6] the coveted
tenets of rational psychology, but not *per viam ontologiae*, and

---

[1] *Werke,* II., 316, 43.

[2] *Cf.,* Baumgarten's *Meta.; Die vernünftige Psychologie,* sections 547, 558,
560, 576 f., *etc.*

[3] Reicke, *Beiträge zu I. Kant's Leben und Schriften,* pp. 7, 31, 48.

[4] *Cf.,* Meyer, *op. cit.,* pp. 222-228. Knutzen's work appeared in 1744 with
the title *Phil. Abh. von der immateriellen Natur der Seele, etc.* I have not
been able to see this work. *Cf.,* Ueberweg, *Hist. of Phil.,* II., 174 ; Krohn, *op.
cit.,* 70 note 4 ; B. Erdmann, *Martin Knutzen und seine Zeit,* p. 145 ff, contends
with Meyer, Ueberweg, Bergmann and Jahn, that the question can have no pertinence, either as to the form or content of Criticism, for (p. 148) ' die allgemeine Färbung seiner Darstellung, ihr wesentlich psychologischer Character,
ist durch die erkenntnisstheoretischen Entwicklungen, die zu ihr führen, von
selbst gegeben.' *Cf.,* Lange's *Hist. of Materialism,* II., pp. 124 ff, 153 ff.

[5] *Werke,* V., 491.

[6] In his work, *Abhandlungen von den vornehmsten Wahrheiten der natürlichen Religion,* 1754, 5th ed., Tübingen, 1782.

leaves off the scholastic dress of the syllogism. On the principle that ' niemand kann sein Bewusstsein verläugnen,' he affirms the simple substantiality of our soul that is given us immediately in consciousness. 'Allein, die Seele, das Wesen in uns, das sich bewusst ist, kennet sich innerlich;' and, ' ist also keiner blosse veränderliche Beschaffenheit eines andern Dinges, sondern eine Substanz.' 'Dergleichen Substanz die eine Bewusststein besitzt, ist in jeglichen einzelnen Menschen nur eine.'[1] Mendelssohn, also, receives special recognition from Kant, who gave his arguments for the continuity of our soul life a special section in the second edition.[2] The logical and enlightened Jew justly deserved this acknowledgment. In his *Phaedon, oder über die Unsterbichkeit der Seele* (1767), he argues for the simplicity of the soul on the grounds of the contradiction which inheres in the proposition that thought is the result of compositeness, using the exact figure which Kant reproduced fourteen years later.[3] ' Es gibt in unserm Körper wenigstens eine einzige Substanz,' whose nature is arrived at by deduction from that which is given in consciousness. Basing his ' whole proof' on the dilemma of compositeness in the permanent, he puts his opinion in the questioning words of Socrates : " Diese einfache Substanz die unausgedehnt ist, Vorstellungsvermögen besitz, die vollkommenste unter den denken Substanzen ist, die in mir wohnen, und alle Begriffe, deren ich mir bewusst bin, in eben der Deutlichkeit, Wahrheit, Gewissheit u. s. w. in sich fasset, ist diese nicht meine Seele?—Nichts Anders."

It can hardly be agreed with Erdmann that Kant is all the while trying to strangle an effigy of his own pseudo-exaltation. That would be casting back into Kant's deeply-rooted intention an insincerity, which Erdmann, least of all, would think of doing. Nor does his explanation of the ' Färbung' of the exhibition sufficiently harmonize matters. Yet, it is true, the famous paralogisms are to be found no where else. But this does not

---

[1] *VIth. Abhandlung vom Menschen und dessen Seele,* secs. 4-6.

[2] *Crit.,* I., 497 f ; *cf., Werke,* IV., 343 f. note, where the method of Mendelssohn is approved as over against the dogmatism of the Wolffian school.

[3] *Cf.,* Mendelssohn, *Gesammelte Schriften,* II., 155, 158, 194, and *Crit.,* II., 306, I. 497.

deny that the criticism of them finds Wolff and all the others reprehensible in their metaphysical attempts.   Wolff is attacked in so far as the form is concerned, for his method is reducible to that of the syllogism, and rebuked in spoiling the purity of the rational science by invoking all sorts of ' unsinnliche und abstractesten Begriffe'[1] to reach its conclusions.   The later psychologists who were contending against the varied forms of materialism, receive indeed the edge of the criticism.   They took only the data of consciousness and from it evoked all their wisdom, thinking all the while that the *ego* which came with every moment or thought, was the *ego* of reality—that which conditioned all the phenomena of the internal or external senses. The whole criticism turns upon this very point, that an error in the supposed fact introduces the fault in the syllogism.   They employ a presumable empirical *ego* which turns out to be the *ego* of apperception.   Thus, in agreement with Meyer, it appears that the psychology Kant exhibits and criticizes, is that which was prevalent in his hour.   Still one must admit, with Erdmann, that the solitariness of the paralogisms comes from the touches of Kant's own hand.   But this can only mean that to him and his purpose, it was privileged to so exhibit what was rampant, in a form suitable to the limits of his space and conformable with the logical basis of Criticism.

In his meta-critique of Kant's rational psychology, Herbart[2] contends not only that Kant misrepresents the Leibnizian doctrine of the monads or spiritual substances, but, also, that the errors of rational psychology cannot be clothed in paralogistic form, and the fault in Kant himself lies in his conception of the *ego*.   It has already been seen how much truth can be admitted in Herbart's first objection.   Nor is the second objection valid. Rational psychology, as understood by Kant, was not guiltless in its proofs.   The old metaphysicians had somehow wandered far away from psychical reality.   Their tenets could be properly presented by the paralogisms.   Meyer also confuses matters in his criticism[3] that Kant's errors lie in ' the form ' given to the para-

---

[1] Baumgarten, *Metaphysik*, sec. 1.
[2] *Psychologie als Wissenschaft, etc.*, Sämm. Wk., V., 249 f.
[3] *Op. cit.*, p. 228 f.

logisms. It is not necessary that the syllogisms be rearranged, for in the Kantian sense of substantiality, *etc.*, the conclusions, excepting one, are properly drawn to show the illogical nature of the science.

But this does not say that Kant's criticism is faultless. He believed in the conclusiveness of his objections and felt a triumph over the rational giant. On the contrary, the criticism has not logical perfection, and curiously lacks harmony with the Critical method. For instance, the paralogism of substantiality is itself guilty of a *petitio principii.* According to his own conception of this fallacy,[1] the major premise is condemned. The substantiality of the subject is the very thing demanding proof which the paralogism purports to give ; whereas, the major makes an affirmation of that which itself stands in need of proof.[2] It involves an existential proposition in order to get over from the given subject to its permanence. But such propositions are either 'nothing but a miserable tautology,' or, 'as every sensible man must admit, synthetical.'[3] For the concept of a thing tells us nothing of its possible existence. Kant falls into the same error in his refutation of Mendelssohn's argument. The latter seeks to prove the soul's permanence by showing the impossibility of the soul being liable to a 'vanishing.' From the Critical standpoint, Kant must maintain that 'the permanence of the soul as an object of the internal sense, remains undemonstrated and undemonstrable,' and, from the same standpoint, he dare not attempt to prove the opposite, *viz.*, that the soul, as a simple being, can be changed into nothing through 'elanguescence.' But to attribute an intensive quantity to the soul,[4] and to affirm of consciousness that it has degrees of reality, without a presupposition from experience, is to fall into the same error of which he accuses rational psychology—that it hypostasizes phenomena.

Again, the formal procedure of Criticism must be questioned

---

[1] *Werke*, VIII., 131, sec. 92 : "Unter einer 'petition principii' versteht man die Annehmung eines Satzes zum Beweisgrunde als eines unmittelbar gewissen Satzes, obgleich er noch eines Beweises bedarf."

[2] *Cf.*, Meyer, *op. cit.*, 229 f ; Krohn, *op. cit.*, 29 f.

[3] *Crit.*, II., 513 f ; *cf.*, 196 f.

[4] *Crit.*, I., 497 f. II., 147 f. I., 465.

as it occurs in the fourth paralogism, not so much as to the
consistency of the paralogism (?), but whether Kant has remained true to the method which he elsewhere champions as
the new step taken by metaphyic.   " All objections may
be divided into dogmatical, critical and sceptical.   The
dogmatical attacks the proposition, the critical the proof of
the proposition. • • • The critical objection, as it says
nothing about the worth or worthlessness of the proposition, and attacks the proof only, need not know the object itself
better, or claim a better knowledge of it.   All that it wants to
show is, that a proposition is not well grounded, not that it is
false."[1]   Kuno Fischer[2] goes so far in his vindication of Kant's
criticism, as to say that it " is not dogmatical.   It is far removed
from asserting the reverse of the doctrine of the soul held by
metaphysicians, or even favoring such a reversal. • • •
When Kant refuted rational psychology in all its details, his
objections were neither dogmatical nor sceptical, but merely critical."   That the historian's opinion needs modification appears
from a consideration of the criticism of the fourth paralogism,
which begins thus :   ' We shall have to examine the premises.'[3]
What follows is *not* a criticism of the *proofs*, but an examination
of the *worth* of the propositions, and especially of the minor
premise.[4]   Thus is offered an opportunity to present the doctrine which had been clearly expressed once already, and the
criticism becomes the *second* exposition of what transcendental
idealism teaches.   The minor affirms that ' external phenomena '
cannot be ' perceived immediately,' for they are something
extra-mental which are said to underlie our perceptions.   Descartes is justified in affirming that immediate perception is of
that only which is within me.   Psychology clings to this doctrine of ' representative perception ' and becomes unable to know
the existence of things.   In the first three paralogisms there
was shown the logical defect of *quaterni terminorum*, and the

[1] *Crit.*, II., 336.
[2] *Op. cit.*, p. 196.
[3] *Crit.*, II., 319.
[4] *Cf.*, Hippenmeyer, Art. in *Zeitschrift für Phil. und phil. Kritik*, vol. 56,
p. 114; Krohn, *op. cit.*, p. 69 ff.

conclusion is false because of the absence of the complete identity of the middle term in its two uses. So far Kant is true to his purpose, and he remains strictly critical. But the minor of the fourth is *false*. For it was irrefutably shown in the Æsthetic that space and time dwell in us as forms of our sensuous intuition, and objects are only empirically external, whose reality is given immediately in that perception. Thus something real in space always corresponds with our intuitions, and the strictest idealist cannot demand a proof from us that objects are out in space. The criticism allows to psychology a dualism, but such as must say that the existence of objects is given immediately in the sensations which beget their reality. Kant has become ' dogmatic' in his criticism—dogmatic after his own definition. The syllogism remains as to form ; for as we saw above, it could not be illogical, and the impossibility of psychology at this point lies in the falsity of its premises. There is no Kantian criticism of the last paralogism. It is displaced by an exposition of Critical idealism so far as its content relates to perception and the reality of its objects.

There has already been intimated the relation which the criticism of rational psychology holds to the Critical philosophy, chiefly in its speculative half. Metaphysicians, especially the Scholastics, had long played with psychological doctrines. *De Animæ Natura* was the frequent theme of learned disputations. When that new race of scientific minds had sprung up, there rang out the jubilee through England and the Continent that the mathematical formulæ of forces would explain all that might be given in consciousness, and surely that which empirically underlay its manifestations. Materialism became rampant. But in the German mind it was current with many a fluctuation. The home of the Reformation was still too fond of religious ideas to admit the strange guest. Materialism did take root early in Germany, but chiefly in connection with medicinal and scientific inquiries. There came the reaction, and a versatile Leibnitz would banish it all with the one stroke of a genius. Instead of his pre-established harmony marking no progress in psychology,[1] his whole philosophy is much rather only psy-

[1] Hippenmeyer, *loc. cit.*, p. 88.

chology.[1] And the determinations of the monadological principles comprehended psychologic insight into the universe :—
for all substances are souls.   From this center radiated the reaction which contended against the adoption of scientific empiricism, until the lines of divergence led to points so antipolar as
are baseless pneumatism and soulless materialism.

The spirit of the Enlightenment expressed itself in the metaphysic of psychology.   The constant wrangle was over truly
disputable points.   Criticism, in shaping its problem, had an eye
to the philosophic needs of the day, and maintains that on the
basis of what is given in experience and its rational or *a priori*
implications, neither party is given any right to defend its case
before the bar of man's reason.   A philosophy of mind is impossible.   Experience limits us to phenomena.   Nor is it permitted us to *know* possible reality.   For metaphysic can never
be constructed on *a priori* ground.   The limit of reason is self-
knowledge—to know that it cannot know.   Even the polymathic
Faust soliloquizes not only the outcome of speculative criticism,
but also sees what must be its relation to the ethical life :

> " What we know not, is what we need to know;
> And what we know we might as well let go."—*Blackie's Tr.*

Men would know the ground of immortality and sought to
refute materialism, not leaving the idea of a somewhat beyond
on the slippery foundation of a faith.   We cannot know the
nature of the thinking being ; but *that* knowledge, it seems, is
our need.   No, replies Criticism, enough ground is yet left for
practical purposes.   Indeed the value of dispelling ' the idle
dream' of self-knowledge is to turn us within and seek ' the
consciousness of righteous,' an inconsistency in the face of
which Criticism blindly thrusts itself.   Whereas it sought to let
go, yea, even pass beyond that which we do know (Kantian),
that questions concerning our own being are not to be answered.

Thus the refutation of rational psychology bears a three-fold
relation to the Criticism in which it stands as a link.   The age
did not care for God.   He was thrust out as far as possible

---

[1] *Cf.*, Kirchner, *Leibniz's Psychologie*, p. v, 3, *et al*; *cf.*, Sommer, *op. cit.*,
pp. 4, 50, 213 f., 252, 439, NO. XXX.

from the world of experience. Even Kant abides the tendency, and his God is merely the last link in that chain which anchors in the individual for whom its sole and degraded function is in securing happiness for him who has respect for the moral law.[1] It also relates itself to the age in so far as it enters into Kant's solution of the problem which he proposed to himself—a solution he intended as a reconciliation. Moreover, the refutation, and that which it concerns in the lives of men, is most important for Criticism. The Analytic was possible itself only with the insight that reason has faculties which contribute to cognition. From the positing of activities it was but a psychologic step, which we have already seen as receiving Kant's recognition, to seek into the nature and source of those activities. From those early assumptions, based on logic, came the refutation based on that self-same Criticism which grew up out of the former.

But only as the rational science of the soul was removed, could there be erected those postulates of the psychological world of morality. Did we know the nature of that being which thinks within us, there could be no need of passing on to those practical needs which find sufficient ground in a silent disinterestedness in the possibilities of knowledge as it pries into the secrets of psychical life. Kant did not care for cosmology. He is triumphantly humorous in so armoring the giant physicists, that when one strikes the other equals his blow. He is liberal with theology; but a God is not his chief concern. Experience is possible without Him, as is well-nigh the moral law. In that infinite series, beginning with the non-moral, mechanical rise of ' experience,' to its consummation in the perfection of the ideal of humanity, He is given a modicum of reality in that now mysterious condition of how the *summum bonum* is to be realized in accordance with the mandates of the categorical imperative. On the other hand, What is man? is the chief question before Critical philosophy within which rational psychology and practical reason are the negative and positive allowances. They are the points of orientation, both of which swing on the pivot of 'the psychological idea.' For this Kant entertains a kindly feeling. When

[1] *Cf., Crit. of Prac. Reason*, bk. II., ch. II., sec. V., "The existence of God a postulate of pure practical reason."

156   *EDWARD FRANKLIN BUCHNER.*

comparing the three rational sciences he throws his opinion to
the favor of the first and third. "There is no such antinomy
in the psychological and theological ideas." But the former
yet has the precedent. "The transcendental paralogism caused
a one-sided illusion only. * * * * All advantage is on the side
of pneumatism."[1] While he remained dissatisfied with his
criticism of rational psychology,[2] he abides with its outcome;
but maintains rightly, in spite of all the objections and limitations which attend the applicability of regulative principles to
experience, that 'nothing but good can spring from such a psychological idea.'[3] He is rather lenient, on the whole, with
rational psychology, not because it has a firm basis—on the
contrary, it has only an apparent one; but rather, in that it embodies the 'psychological idea' which has a firm basis, as is
seen in the fundamental postulate of the moral reason. The
soul must be left over in some way. He would need it in the
practical law which expresses the essence of man. Thus the
criticism of rational psychology, while containing the essential
entirety of the *Critique,* is a negation with that large and mental
reservation which is later to break forth in the ethical noumenality where freedom is the great goal to be reached, in the race
for which the 'critical' reality of 'the psychological idea' is the
first laurel whose attainment cheers Criticism on throughout
the course.[4]

Empirical psychology was denied any authority in shaping
the conclusions of philosophy. Rational psychology, with the
whole of metaphysic, has been swept into the lumber room of
transcendentalism. What shall we think? Is Kant's criticism
irrefragable? Has he merely restated the problem of psychology, affirming, from the standpoint of 'a fair but severe criticism,' its insolubility? Must it be agreed with him that we cannot know ourselves, and with *that* knowledge heap condemnation upon an irrational experience! Can we no more attempt
to *know* in the name of rational necessity ($=a\ priori$) the 'na-

[1] *Crit.,* II., 711, 352, 577.
[2] *Werke,* IV., 129.
[3] *Crit.,* II., 585.
[4] *Cf., Crit.,* II., 340; *Werke,* V., 4, 6.

ture' of that being which thinks within us? Has Kant said the last word that may be uttered with rational confidence (=knowledge)? Or, allowing full value to the refutation, may we not still seek to harmonize the facts of psychical experience, not only in a body of scientific explanations, but also so enable us to entertain theoretical views on the *Träger* of inner experience, as that we may build up a philosophy of mind? Such are the questions which confront the conclusion of our study. The opinions of such thinkers of the order to which Kant belongs should be treated with profound respect. It becomes an ethical maxim, based on the sincerity of their reflections and the value of their service to speculation, that deference be paid to their intellectual wares. Not only should these be shown in good light, but the mathematics of their perspective and the mixture of their primal pigments should be formulæ attending the exhibition. Still, we way say of the criticism of rational psychology, as Hume said of Berkeley, 'it is irrefutable, but it does not produce conviction.' The instinct to let philosophy draw back 'the pall' which science 'pulls over the psychic half,' is too strong, and we yet seek—yes, let it be 'transcendentally'—conclusions which the 'natural science' of psychology refuses to give. Nor is it merely theological interests as of old that lead us on. Rather do we seek to know ourselves by reason of that metaphysical impulse, which is larger and broader, engulfing all other unique goods. "The creed of a man," says Schopenhauer,[1] "is, that I must have a metaphysic." We all seek to go back of that which appears, to a somewhat comparable in its nature with the character of the appearance. The old psychology gave no less an expression to this impulse, but perverted it with theological squints.

It appeared in the exposition that Kant's criticism is not faultless. Even more defects might be pointed out. Yet it must be admitted that his attempt is successful. He did overthrow the old rational psychology—the psychology as he understood it, and from the arguments which in his time were generally adopted. They held that in consciousness there is an envisagement of an atomic simplicity and identity of the soul.

---

[1] *Op. cit.*, II., 184.

They sought physical symbols, but so applied them to mind that it was conceived as an inert *thing* living through the ages. Adjectives they were, which might have had significance in molecular physics, and would fain have attached themselves to our own *ego*. We are substances. We have a core of permanence around which the ebb and flow of the restless inner experience clings. We are one—such an one that no edge of the physicist's or materialist's tools can affect us. We have atomic simplicity. It is a sort of psychic atom that we are, which has a consciousness that harks back to former experiences in which the same simple was found. Our personality is the conscious continuity of a potent 'mathematical point,' which the mechanical affinities of a chemical universe are unable to destroy. The relation of this psychic atom, with its essence *in vi repraesentativa universi*, to material extended atoms—that is the insoluble problem from Descartes downward. Dogmatic and sceptical idealism, or empirical idealism, is the only resource psychology leaves us as it plays tricks with our queries.

All this, says Kant, is floundering. Such terms have meaning 'in experience.' Only 'objects' can give validity to the categories. 'Ideas' are beyond their reach. The latter remain regulative principles. He made a psychological inquisition, banishing all except 'the logical *ego*.' This it is, says he, which the science is guilty of using. Into these abstract terms it tries to put experiential meaning. The impossibility of enlivening this highest of all the categories, since it must accompany them all throughout, is glaringly seen in the illogical nature of the argument brought forward in support of the conclusion 'that the soul is a simple, substantial personality.' They, says he, are dealing with abstractions, for the mind as known by itself is not a fit term in a syllogism of this sort. And that term which is used can never be an object of knowledge. His criticism is invincible, as he understood the science. And we have seen how great was his right to the form given it and the one fact on which it could rest. It is invincible by reason of two things: the form into which it was cast, and the basis of his argument, which he very properly drew from the Analytic. The glaring inconsistency that sprang from these roots make us desist. But what must be given up? We have lost our perfectly demonstrable argument of the old theological science. No more may we deduce natural immortality by a series of concepts. Reason dare no more syllogize over what may be given in consciousness. Have we lost all? Has metaphysic been so refuted that we must not attempt again a philosophy of mind? No. Kant's criticism of rational psychology is perfectly harmless to a metaphysic of mind. Kant's criticism is invincible—the postulate of a soul and an effort to find out its nature is still our right— let it be paradoxical; it may be such only in appearance.

"Es kann gar nicht zugegeben werden," says Herbart, "das Kant den Begriff des Ich richtig gefasst habe."[1] While the great modern realist may object to Kantian psychology, he is no better off in the end than the critical idealist. The latter maintains by his criticism that we are not to vex ourselves with the insoluble problem of the nature and essence of the mind, now and then, however, hinting at some sort of a spiritual monism. The former maintains that " das einfache *Was* der Seele ist völlig unbekannt, und bleibt es auf immer; es ist kein Gegenstand der speculativen so wenig, als der empirischen Psychologie."[2] There is a manifest difference between the treatment psychology received at the hand of the great Königsberger and that given by his successor of a few years later. The one attempts to destroy, while the other started influences which have been greatest in the modern psychological world. Hence, their is undoubtedly a great difference in what may be their agreement or disagreement on central psychological questions. But both have been potent in their ways—one, the last of the scholastics, because he denied scholasticism; the other, the first of the moderns, because psychology was to be 'founded anew on mathematics and experience.' Herbart's criticism, however, will serve as an excellent starting point.

Kant's refutation is invincible, and removed the apodicity of the science of the last century. It does not produce conviction and is perfectly harmless to a philosophy of mind. The former was accomplished from the standpoint of that psychology which Kant

[1] *Werke*, V., p. 251.
[2] *Op. cit.*, p. 109.

himself adopts unwittingly in the Transcendental Analytic, chiefly his principle of 'pure apperception,' which gave him the clue to the paralogisms, the detection of which allowed him to make the formal exhibition. The latter is the outcome of the whole matter. Modern psychology cannot abide with Kant's doctrine of the *ego*, and the functions which it served for him, do not affect in the least any attempt to purify a metaphysic of the soul.

We will not give Kant the rejoinder, as is often done,[1] that in negating psychology, he has brought in an almost complete system of that science. It has already appeared frequently that psychology lies close to his undertaking. The solution of his problem could be carried no great way without dependence on psychological principles. He is not dealing with a description and the sequence of mental phenomena. He must be granted that much.[2] Although he is constantly exhibiting the contents of the mind under the *a priori* laws of their function and appearance, his is truly a psychological task. This retort, however, would never permit such a critic to construct a metaphysic of mind. His 'psychology' would be the very negative of that. The repartee might be a scholastic pleasantry, but helps not one jot towards the existence and nature of that which is the supporter of this inner play of states. Indeed, the kernel of the whole *Critique*—the Analytic—is one stupendous hypothetical judgment; and Kant himself has withdrawn that portion of empiricism from which he can select the butments which are to keep the theory of knowledge from tottering.

Kant's strength against the psychologists lay in his ' logical *ego* of apperception,' and in that same weapon is lodged the inapplicability of his criticism to present day attempts. It is thus we allow validity to *all* his psychological strictures except the content of his argument, or the epistemological foundation to which he constantly refers it. Here is the great sin of Kant. He did a service in the history of psychology by frightening away to their death the scholastic ghosts of abstraction. He turned upon them in the same unearthly shroud, and by the most figur-

---

[1] *Cf.*, Porter, *Human Intellect*, p. 59; Cousin, *Hist. of Mod. Phil.*, Vol. I., p. 245 ff.

[2] *Cf.*, Bax, *Prol., tr.*, p. lxxvii.

ative abstractness in the logical *ego* cleared the vanguard of modern mental science from the harassing brigands that hid in Neo-Aristotelian caves. But in his splitting up of the *egos* we cannot follow him. There is so much psychological slag about Kant, that the present day charge against the old psychology, that it cast everything into severely speculative moulds, is too true at this point. In the two preceding chapters we saw much that shows Kant's effort to get away from positive schemes into which the mental facts were to be fitted as if in the Procrustean bed. But in rational psychology he himself is guilty of hypostasizing figurative expressions, and in the criticism he is wont to let steel cut steel, abstraction meet abstraction. At this point modern psychology must rightly refuse to allow his claim. The psychological coins of transcendentalism are spurious and the arrest of their philosophical circulation must follow forthwith.

Any criticism of Kant's refutation can have its validity established only in some theory of knowledge. It must meet him on his own ground. His denial of metaphysical science is grounded in the Analytic and Æsthetic. Those dealers in theoretical knowledge who will not send noëtic merchandise through the straits of Criticism are contrabandists and their polemical wares must be confiscated. It is not necessary, however, that a whole campaign be struggled through in order to gain a height whose outlook grants a detection of the opponent's weaknesses. This can be mounted at once, surreptitiously to all appearance, but really with the manifold presuppositions of hard won conquests. And criticism demands only so much. Still, Kant is right. Pure reason is such a perfect unity that it stands or falls together.[1] The completeness is so interdependent that a flaw at one point injures the whole.

Kant makes fearful havoc of man when he comes to the nature of consciousness and self-consciousness. *His doctrine*, rather doctrines, *of the ego is the pernicious tenet of the whole criticism.* This we indicate as the chief defect of the entire analysis. The nature of necessity, the necessary machinery that is to grind it out, the dependence of ' Nature ' on understanding, the demand

[1]*Crit.*, II., p. xxiii, I., 494.

that science shall finally submit itself to the keen analysis of metaphysic, that fact that so much naïvete prevails as to produce a 'natural delusion' which philosophy must seek to remove, the whole outcome that ours is an intelligible world whose expression finds adequacy only as ethics becomes the complement of metaphysic—all this and more may be granted to Criticism. But that ideality which was consequential in its absolute scepticism, the readiness to expunge the mind because the knowledge of it could not be reduced to the same formulæ expressing the cognition of a thing, the denial that we are entitled to a rational conviction as to the nature of our own being, the getting away from so-called reality and the prepositing of an unknown X, whose confusion becomes worse confounded on later explanations—these are the logical attachments of Criticism which show how far it has wandered from an expression of reality, to what length its adherence to logic has led it astray, and how defective were the psychological implications whose rectification entitles us to eliminate its unworthy results.

We repudiate the scepticism of Criticism and maintain our right to a metaphysic of mind, on the ground of its ideality of time and unpsychological doctrine of the *ego*; but not on the immediate basis of such conceptions that in consciousness we have an envisagement of 'objective' reality—for Kant allows so much.[1]

Objection against Kant's ideality of time is not taken because we conceive time to be some sort of an independent thing which gets perceived or empirically intuited like things. 'We have no primary and proper perception of time at all,' says Lotze,[2] in protest against the view which has prevailed since Kant, of regarding time as 'an intuition.' Kant himself, however, is not guilty of regarding time in that fashion. It is merely the 'order of relation' in which internal determinations must be represented.[3] He makes the distinction between the psychological and ontological question of time, but confusion of interpretation came because he uses epistemological phrases

---

[1] *Cf.*, Stäh04lin, *Kant, Lotze and Ritschl, tr.*, p. 44; *Crit.*, II., 320–329, I., 475 f.

[2] *Meta.*, I., 315.

[3] *Crit.*, II., 20, 88.

with reference to the latter. Whatever else time may be, it is certainly a mental form. It has reality only as a relating consciousness sets the flow of events under the temporal cover. Even the reality of change, which comes as an objection, need not deter us from some sort of an ideality to time. Change is real, but its reality comes in the reality of time. Change is significant, however, only in a knowing consciousness. Change the fact, and time the condition, have no deeper reality than that which can come out of what contains the one and posits the other.[1] It must be admitted, however, that Kant has employed unhappy expressions in expounding his ontology of time. The sceptical confusion which confounds the first and second ' Analogies of Experience,' and the proof and counter-proof of the first ' Antinomy,' are the ripe fruits of his inapt language.

Of more value at present is his psychological use of time in the perception of a self. As to his ontological time, it must be objected without further debate that he places it so far out of reach that when it attains an experiential expression, it must always be dubbed phenomenal. We mean to say that Kant's conception of the ' internal sense ' is faulty and with it *that* ideality of time which took its empirical rise from the former. The point in question is thus rather a medley of the two considerations of time which should be separated—and Kant has done this, but not in the doctrine of inner sense.[2]

The division between the external and the internal sense is an old one.[3] It is also one of the first to spring up in the untutored mind. We have sights, sounds and touches that correlate themselves through the special senses to the ' objects ' that are without us. There are, on the other hand, thoughts and ideas, images, feelings, desires and strivings that spring up seemingly out of and are related to ourselves only. These belong to the internal sense. The mind, they say, is affected some way, and

[1] *Cf.*, *Crit.*, II., 32; Ladd, *Introd.*, p. 253; *cf.*, Lambert's letter to Kant, Dec., 1770, *Werke*, VIII., p. 667, where the writer insists on the reciprocal character of ' time ' and ' change.'

[2] *Cf.*, *Werke*, VII., 453 f., 473, 550; VI., 365; *Reflex.*, 82 f.

[3] Locke (*Essay*, etc., II., 1, sec. 2 ff.) was the first to give philosophical expression to this sense; *cf.*, also Vaihinger, *Commentar*, II., 126 f; Volkmann, *op. cit.*, II., 180 ff.

what it perceives are these various forms of consciousness. Kant makes this distinction, but carries with it much of the old-fashioned belief that the mind is affected—that something ' is given ' from which, by the constructive and recognitive activity of ' understanding,' it builds up the phenomena of the inner sense. He proceeds *ab extra* to get the principle whereby he classifies the two forms of sense :[1] objects which come to affect the body, and the mind which affects itself. But psychology, as it is feeling the influences of evolutionary theory and looks upon the development of consciousness, must seek elsewhere the basis of a division. So far as psychology is concerned, it regards consciousness as dirempting its own states into those belonging to selves and those belonging to bodies or objects, things. (Of course, cerebral psychology will look for the principle of division in the direction of nervous currents, whether peripherally or centrally originated.)

What Kant means by ' inner sense ' is not easily determined.[2] Without squeezing the text on this point, Kant gets at the internal sense by way of analogy with the external, and means by it a special faculty of perceiving the changes that go on in ' empirical consciousness ' where we have an *ego* of apprehension, which is the *object* of this inner perception and contains a manifoldness of determinations which make possible (the content of) an inner experience. It is also to be sharply distinguished from the apperception, either of an empirical or transcendental nature. The latter is the pure understanding which makes the very concept of succession (time) possible, or produces it ' by affecting the internal sense.'[3] The analogy is carried so far as to make the mind *passive* in the internal sense as well as in the external. On both sides it is the victim of something that preys upon it, while it is the mere gazer upon what may arise. Hence, one reason why time, as a form of sensibility, is put in the Æsthetic.

---

[1] *Cf.*, *Werke*, VII., 465, sec. 13; also *Reflex.*, 1, NO. 70.

[2] *Cf.*, Greene's *Phil. Works*, II., pp. 65-71, 252-257; *cf.*, Vaihinger, *Commentar*, II., 480.

[3] *Cf.*, *Crit.*, I., 434-437, 450-453, a passage aiming to make the distinction clear between ' the internal sense ' of the Æsthetic and the logical apperception of the Analytic; *cf.*, *Werke*, IV., 361; V., 62; VII., 444 f. note, 452 f., 465, 473 f. ; *Reflex.*, 87 ff.

Kant also represents himself as instituting this distinction between internal sense and apperception. "'The founders of the systems of psychology have preferred to represent the internal sense as identical with the faculty of apperception, while we have carefully distinguished the two.'"[1] The probable fact is that this doctrine of internal sense, with its very close accompaniment, was taken from the psychologist Tetens, whose book[2] was very pleasing to Kant and was often seen lying open on the latter's table.[3] The consequence or accompaniment of this theory of the internal sense is, in Kant's own words,[4] that the internal 'sense represents to consciousness ourselves not as we are by ourselves, but as we appear to ourselves, because we perceive ourselves only as we are *affected* internally.' How closely allied Kant's view is to that of Tetens is seen in the passage quoted.[5] Tetens means to say that we never are conscious of ourselves in a state of thinking or feeling, but what we *do* catch is something that lingers in memory which represents the former given experience. We are dealing with 'Nachempfindung.'[6] An excellent theory from which the ideality of time might spring! We never get a consciousness with any immediacy, but we always find it in a change, passing various states in view, which, when settled in the form of a representation (memory image), become the empirical *ego.* As we know things as we are af-

[1] *Crit.*, I., 450.
[2] *Phil. Versuche ueber die menschliche Natur und ihre Entwickelung*, 2 Bände, Leipzig, 1777.
[3] *Cf.*, Erdmann, *Geschichte der Phil.*, II., p. 356.
[4] *Crit.*, I., 450.
[5] *Op. cit.*, vol. I., p. 50: "Wir haben Empfindungsvorstellungen von den einzelnen Thätigkeiten unsers Denkens, in eben dem Verstande, wie wir solche von den körperlichen Gegenständen haben, die auf unsere äussere Sinnglieder wirken. Hier befindet sich das selbsthätige Princip des Denkens, von dem die Seele modificiert wird, *in der Seele* selbst, bey den äussern Empfindungen kommt die Modificatione von einer äussern Ursache. In beiden Fällen aber wird die neue Veränderung aufgenommen, gefühlet und empfunden; in beiden bestehet sie, und dauert einen Augenblick in uns tort, und muss wenigstens alsdenn fort dauern, wenn sie bemerkbar seyn soll. Diese macht eine Nachempfindung, oder die erste Empfindungsvorstellung aus. In diesem Stande kannsie gewahrgenommen, mit Bewustseyn empfunden, mit andern verglichen und von andern unterschieden werden." *Cf.*, *Vorrede*, p. xvii, and Sommer, *op. cit.*, p. 283 f.
[6] Compare Kant's and more modern objections against introspection as a psychological method.

fected by a possible transcendental x, so we know ourself only as we find an affection 'im Gemüthe gegeben.' Our self-consciousness rests entirely on this affection. It and the mental forms lie between what is known internally and 'das Was' which corresponds in the temporal connection of a causal sequence. It would, without doubt, be a true substitute and adequately express Kant's own psychological meaning, if, wherever he says we know ourselves only as we appear to ourselves (and this is the keynote to the whole Critical philosophy), we should read, we know ourselves only as we remember ourselves to have been affected—a position even worse than that famous one of Hume's, that in looking inward he always found himself with some perception or feeling. Against all that view, however, it must be maintained that, unless consciousness and its content come with an immediacy, there is no possibility whatever of a 'Nachempfindung' rising up in memory claiming a reference to a recent past which was once a state of that same consciousness to which the memory is a part.[1]

This strange psychological doctrine and its consideration really belong to the empirical chapter; but from its intimate association with and influence upon Kant's conception of the *ego*, it was left over to this point. Kant accepts the thesis from Tetens and moulds it into the internal sense which gives us only a subjective 'Blendwerk'—including sensations and feelings. These we have already seen Kant to maintain as subjective, non-cognitive, hence expelled from the special province of Criticism. It is concerned with 'die Erkenntnissvermögen.' But there can be no 'objective' character to the knowledge of a self; and the whole critical analysis, as is often justly claimed, becomes nothing more than an attempt to reduce the knowledge of sense-things to a universal formula. Whatever cannot be fitted to this, is exiled, 'removed' from knowledge. This empirical notion of the inner sense is undoubtedly the source of that *a priori* principle called the 'Anticipation of Perception.'

---

[1] This, however, permits full credence to the results of recent investigations that a measureable time is involved in getting sensations above the threshold of consciousness, and that the temporal factor conditions the variations possible between mere precept-having and clear apperception.

That consciousness has degrees, is a cardinal Kantian doctrine which is often called upon in a refutation of systems which teach the reality of the conscious *ego*. But the internal sense is important in Criticism, since it contains all representations. Even external phenomena in the last analysis fade away into a temporal series,[1] and all experience must be qualified by ' my.' Thus time, a universal form of cognition, must go into Criticism, as well as the ' my' to which every representation must be referable. In this manner the internal sense contributes two of the most important objects upon which the Critical method settles itself. From its analysis of both spring that scepticism which is its outcome.

The internal sense, the subjective, illusory knowledge of empirical phenomena, and time, the one pervading form of all experience, have their highest development in the doctrines of the *ego*. This likewise is the high-water mark reached by Criticism.[2] ' Pure consciousness' is Criticism's best word in its explanation of the world. But back of that, as the psychological scaffolding by which it may have mounted to the copestone of the Critical edifice, are the various conceptions of the *ego*. Some seem to have been the presuppositions on which Criticism rests, while others appear to be the accomplishments of its profound task. Altogether they are yet the sources of those differentiations which make Criticism the idealism that it is. And in the second edition the distinction between a ' pure consciousness' and the indefinite ' internal sense' is more rigidly drawn, especially in the revised 'Deduction.'[3]

On the basis of the inner sense Kant, at first sight, makes a distinction between two *egos*, or affirms a ' doppeltes Ich,' the empirical *ego*, that which appears, and, that which has a noumenal correspondence to this experience. This has been the general acceptance.[4] The ' Ich als intelligenz 'and ' Ich als ge-

---

[1] *Cf., Crit.*, II., 88, 128, 156, 167 f.

[2] *Cf., Crit.*, II., 94 f.; I., 434 f.

[3] A fact which should be given full weight in estimating the character and idealistic bearings of the changes made by Kant in 1787, especially the ' Refutation of Idealism ;' *Cf.*, Cohen, *op. cit.*, p. 149 f.

[4] *Cf.*, Krohn, *op. cit.*, p. 35 f.; Vaihinger, *op. cit.*, II., 125 ff., 477 f.; Volkelt, *Kant's Erkenntnisstheorie*, pp. 118 ff.

dachtes object' would be the generous characterizations of the two species of the *ego*—alone enough to incur a psychological condemnation. But it appears, on the other hand, that Criticism regards at least *four* kinds of *ego*.[1] There is the *empirical ego* which is 'lediglich das Bewusstsein,' and must be carefully distinguished from the *ego* of experience or the phenomenal subject. It is that broad substrate, as it were, of the whole of experience—the 'Schauplatz' of all that occurs, whether mere phenomena, conditions of knowledge, or the possibly inherent noumena.[2] It is the one characteristic which must be possessed by any element, process or product of which psychology or philosophy takes account. Secondly, there is the *Ich als Erscheinung*. This is the psychological subject, the true object of inner experience, and ' nur Bezeichnung des Gegenstandes des inneren Sinnes."[3] This is often taken as *the* reality of the subject and thus becomes the source of confusion in empiricism and paralogistic dogmatism. Without criticism, we are wont to hypostasize this which is ' given us' from ' the inner sense,' but becomes an object of perception only under the aspect of change. That which is the *a priori* kernel of such an object, is the mental form of time. This is the *ego* known in experience, from which Kant most commonly distinguishes the transcendental *ego*.[4] Psychologists usually called it 'empirical apperception,' from which he widely separates *the ego* which is most potent in Criticism. Thus far Kantian students are justified in interpreting Criticism as recognizing only two subjects or a ' doppeltes Ich.' The third *ego* which figures in Criticism is the 'transcendental subject' or the *logical ego*. The appellations vary so that at one time it may mean the extra-mental reality, or at another the epistemological condition of any *ego*. It is the latter sense in which it is taken here. It is ' transcendental apperception,' the '*ego* of pure apperception,' 'the original synthetical unity of apperception,' 'the one consciousness of permanent identity,' ' the *objective* unity *versus* the subjective

[1] *Cf.*, Mellin, *op. cit.*, III., 367 f., art. *Ich*; B. Erdmann, *Kant's Kriticismus, etc.*, pp. 52-58.
[2] *Crit.*, II., 103, 105.
[3] *Werke*, IV., 82.
[4] *Cf.*, chiefly the 'Deduction' in both editions and the 'Paralogisms.'

unity of consciousness,' the 'I think,' 'the pure understanding itself.'[1] This is the logical *ego*, the one self-consciousness which is the very foundation of all our knowledge, in that its logical possibility rests on a necessary relation to this apperception.[2] It is the transcendental consciousness which consists merely in 'der Vorstellung des Ich.' It is neither an intuition, (for all intuition belongs to 'sensuous' condition, as shown in the Æsthetic; there is no 'intellectual intuition'—a psychological defect which appears glaringly in the epistemological necessity that falls upon Kant, of representing at least three working *egos*), nor a concept (Begriff), but the bare form of consciousness, the supreme category which is no longer a true transcendental category and does not appear in 'the apostolic band' of the Deduction—since it must accompany *each* one of them, and thus sublimates all representations into knowledge. It is the proposition, *I think*, and must accompany every possible judgment of the understanding as the only vehicle that passes on the highway to knowledge.[3] Its representation cannot pass beyond that of the grammatical subject of all predicates ($=x$).[4]

From a comparison of the 'empirical and transcendental' *ego* of the Analytic with the 'phenomenal' *ego* and the *ego* 'an sich' of the Æsthetic, there comes an intimation of a fourth

[1] *Crit.*, II., 94, 108; I., 434, 435, 440.

[2] *Crit.*, II., 103 note.

[3] *Crit.*, II., 302 f, 310, 315, 331.

[4] Kant's meaning would have remained much clearer if he had not made such wayside expressions as these: "Wäre die Vorstellung der Apperception, das Ich ein Begriff, so würde es auch als Prädicat * * * * gebraucht werden können." Rational psychology would then be justified in its syllogisms. The empirical *ego* would be one and the same with the logical *ego*. But, 'es ist nichts mehr als Gefühl eines Daseins'—only a representation to which all thinking has a 'relatione accidentis'(IV., 82 note). "Das Erste, was ganz gewiss ist, ist das: dass ich bin, ich fühle mich selbst, ich weiss gewiss, dass ich bin." "Ich bin, das fühle ich, und schaue mich unmittelbar an." (The posthumous *Vorlesungen über die Metaphysik*, 1821, quoted from Krohn, *op. cit.*, p. 34.) The expression 'Gefühl eines Daseins' undoubtedly means something which is made nowise intelligible by any explanation found in the *Critique*. Erdmann conjectures that it intimates a view that this apperception is no longer the pure and highest category; for, then it becomes absurd. (*Kriticismus &c.*, p. 96). The expression, however, in so far as it attempts to describe this pure apperception, is a flagrant contradiction of the whole attempt of Criticism to expunge from its data all that has subjective reference. *Cf.* above, discussion on Kant's negative conception of psychology, pp. 21 ff., 49 ff.

ego.   Mere consciousness is not the condition of experience objective and universal.   For this the express synthetic unity of the logical *ego* is necessary.   But the logical *ego* of the Analytic is not the empirical or phenomenal *ego* of the Æsthetic.   This is a manufactured article bearing the impress of the pure understanding under the form of time.   It is a moment in this unsubstantial pageantry which all experience is.   But Criticism in these earlier stages implies a somewhat of reality which is not included in the logical and the phenomenal *ego*.   The latter is opposed to the *ego* in itself.   What we know of ourselves is a representation of some object which 'corresponds' to our internal perception.   The *ego* 'an sich' appears in a negative manner in the refutation of rational psychology.   This science supposed itself to know the soul as it *is*.   Experience, however, gives the soul as it *appears*, and the refutation reveals that the science was dealing with a logical subject—the transcendental *ego* as the *condition* of all knowledge.   Thus the noumenal *ego* is negatively recognized in the *Critique*.   We can make no metaphysical determination of this object of the inner sense.[1]   In the *Practical Reason*, however, this 'Ich an sich' is the first attainment by way of the moral law.   That is, the imperative demands freedom; but freedom becomes an absurdity without the postulate of the metaphysical correspondence of the object of the inner sense.   Omitting mere consciousness, Kant has, then, *three working egos*.   The one, the self we all know, but always undergoing mere kaleidoscopic changes, varying with those infinite permutations that are possible from the three primal elements of knowing, feeling and desiring.   The second is the self that is substantial, simple, an identical unity and the correlate of existence.[2]   The third is the speculatively negated

[1] *Crit.*, I., 494.

[2] *Crit.*, II., 303 f., 308 f., 313, 347.   Here appears one of the distinctions between the logical or 'transcendental' (conditioning, determining) *ego*, and the *ego* an sich, or noumenal.   To the latter *none* of the categories are applicable.   These modes of the understanding's functioning are limited only to sensible objects—and as Kant develops his doctrine of substance, they are applicable only to the presentations of sense.   *Cf.*, *Crit.*, I., 482 f.   This is the great teaching of Criticism, notwithstanding the doubtful interpretation that Criticism presupposes a multiplicity of noumena.   *Cf.*, *e. g.*, Krohn, *op. cit.*, p. 53.   But to this logical *ego* there is applicable at least *two* particular categories, *viz*: reality,

'transcendental object of the internal sense,' which has its ontological reality established in the *a priori* determinations of a will that is law-giving. The first is the subject matter of anthropological psychology. The last is relegated to practical philosophy. While metaphysic proper considers only the second or logical *ego*—the central point in the subjective conditions of knowledge. This logical *ego* must do the whole business of Criticism. It is the monster engine that drives the machinery turning out experience. It is not only the highest category which contains all the categories of understanding, recognizing them through itself[1] and thus supporting the grounds of truth and certainty ;[2] but even space and time, the forms of intuition, are based with all their ' necessity ' in the inmost nature of this ideating subject.[3] *On his supposition of the psychological presence of this logical ego, Kant refutes sensualistic scepticism. When he wishes to check the rationalists, he rushes back to the Deduction for the logical ego—a condition of knowledge which can never come within knowledge.*[4] It is the constructive climax of his theory of knowledge. What precedes it can only be understood in the light of this ' unity of apperception.' When once attained, he uses it as the weapon of defence keeping back all psychological speculations from the limits of experience. In the first instance it is opposed to the empirical apperception. In the second, or dialectical instance, it is op-

---

a species of ' quality,' which conditions its simplicity ; for it is ' single in all respects.' *Crit.*, II., 350. It also claims to be ' applicable to all thinking beings ' and expresses itself as ' I am.' This, however, implicates the category of existence—' Wirklichkeit '—for it is the correlate of all existence, even of the categories themselves. *Crit.*, II., 308, 347 ; I., 454 note. And yet, this 'highest' of the categories must have even its theoretic and abstract validity established in such a contradictory resort to those very forms of mental life whose activity it supports. Kant's criticism against rational psychology, that it becomes absurd in trying to take a ' condition' of knowledge for knowledge itself, might, it seems, be turned on Kant himself, since this plays with him the trick in the same way, as his ' Refutation of Idealism' juggles with the imposition of problematic idealism. *Cf.*, Erdmann, *Kriticismus, &c.*, p. 54 f.

[1] *Crit.*, II., 347.
[2] *Ibid.*, 109, f.
[3] *Ibid.*, 95, 97.
[4] *Cf.*, *Crit.*, II., 301, 302 f., 305, 310, 315, 318, 331, 334 ; 1, 492, 502 f.

posed to the 'Ding an sich' which corresponds to the object given in the internal sense.[1]

The mere exposition and an apprehension of Kant's doctrines of the internal sense and its objects are almost sufficient to understand the psychological errors which underlie doctrines so vital to speculative Criticism and which were doubtless suggestive when transcendentalism began its constructive undertaking with the practical reason. Psychology recognizes no such intermediary form of internal perception as the 'inner sense' seems to demand. Whatever may be the metaphysics of consciousness, psychology must regard the having of states, or the possession of ideas which succeed each other and become related, as the general equivalent of consciousness. It is not susceptible of a definition. And when Kant defines consciousness as 'the idea that we have an idea,'[2] he has wandered far away from the right given him by his own frequent æsthetical and sensational observations that consciousness is to be known only in its possession. The attempt to pattern consciousness, even self-consciousness, after the model of the physiological conditions of certain so-called external forms of that consciousness, is to supplant a whole by a part, and mistake the essential element which makes external senses what they are. Psychological inquiry must regard individual things or objects as no more than factors or events belonging to the constant activities of a consciousness.[3] To designate a certain class of these states as coming by way of an

[1] There are times, however, when this logical *ego* is represented as the real subject of inherence, and is taken as the name for the noumenal soul, that transcendental object of the internal sense. (*Crit.*, II., 313, 305.) It would doubtless afford an interesting parallelism to trace the corresponding expressions in the progress of the *Critique*, in reference to 'things' and *egos*. With reference to the source of 'that which is given,' the phrases vary as 'Ding an sich,' 'transcendental object,' and 'Dinge überhaupt,' in the three sections of the *Critique*, respectively. As to the *egos* we find 'Ich an sich,' 'das logische *Ego*,' and 'transcendental Ich.' This, however, would lead into a consideration of Kant's doctrine of noumena and thus carry us beyond the limits of our study. There would be no special gain as to interpretation, for beyond this the correspondence is fanciful, unless one concludes that Kant theoretically posits noumena in their various phases. *Cf.*, Drobisch, *Kant's Dinge an sich, &c.*, pp. 28, 38, who denies, and Krohn, *op. cit.*, p. 353, who affirms such an interpretation.

[2] *Werke*, VIII., p. 33.

[3] *Cf.*, Ladd, *Phys. Psych.*, p. 599, sec. 12.

internal sense which intimates itself as being some cerebral or psychical precondition of certain subjective or reference-to-self-alone states of consciousness, is bad psychology and worse metaphysic. Whatever may be the manifold mysteries connected wtth the rise of consciousness and its succession of states, psychology takes it as the given datum ; and, relying solely upon the method of introspection, proceeds to sort things and minds according to the grouping which comes through the dirempting development of that consciousness. In some such manner it must be indicated that the internal sense is a psychological fiction which had its pernicious effects upon Criticism. Philosophy, too, instead of starting with the individualities thrown up by that consciousness as its own qualitative states, takes the datum of the unity of consciousness—a self-reference from state to state. So far forth the Transcendental Æsthetic becomes philosophical in an unpsychological manner. That consciousness *may* be called the internal sense should never be so misunderstood as to imply that in its self-perception it ' must experience *quasi*-sensations.'[1]

The consequence of this sublimation of a ' sixth sense ' is the degradation of consciousness, and especially in its developed forms. This was the accompaniment of Kant's disregard for psychology, and out of it came that metaphysical gradation of *egos* for which psychology can never give warrant. It is true, psychology does recognize a variety of selves.[2] There is ' the material self,' ' the social self,' ' the spiritual and pure *ego*.' But these have been rightly called the ' constituents of the self.' The self which psychology seeks and attempts to account for is the spiritual self—' the self of selves.' It is on the search for that central principle, or datum, around which all else clings, to which all else becomes referable. It is that unity of consciousness in the circle of which all other forms of self come to have meaning. This is the psychological starting point which it is the business of a metaphysic of mind to accept and properly account for in its way.

This duty of psychology as a science appears in its definition as having to do with the states of consciousness, as such, or

---

[1] *Cf.*, Porter, *Human Intellect*, p. 85 f.

[2] *Cf.*, James, *op. cit.*, pp. 291 ff.

phenomenally considered. It starts with these and gets to the
individual things and selves that every-day practical life regards
as individual and classifiable, not because of their inherent likenesses or unlikenesses ; but, because the phenomena are 'plainly
classifiable.'   We all compare and group our psychical states
without disputing the right.   We do it in immediacy, as it were.
But the classification of these states, as undertaken by psychology, can proceed on no 'other foundation than the simple one
of how I, the conscious subject, am affected.'[1]   Only groups
acquired from that principle consider 'the phenomena as to what
they really *are*.'

Now Kant admits this principle in one sense, and finds in the
consciousness of one's self the basis of all phenomena.   Even
the characteristic of the 'immediate awareness' of the states of
consciousness, is the key to his whole criticism of the fourth
paralogism.   The determinations of our own apperception, or,
what is found in our perception can be perceived immediately.[2]
But this is the trick transcendental idealism plays against problematical idealism.   It is the humor of the moment and not the
cardinal psychology of Criticism.   Against it rises up the curious
doctrine of the internal sense which was so influential as to strike
the one key note which perdures in the strain, 'I am conscious
of myself, neither as I appear to myself, nor as I am by myself.'[3]
This was the extreme to which Kant went in his opposition to
'intellectual intuition' which posited a knowledge of ourselves
as we really are.   We do not propose to replace Kant's 'internal sense' with this 'intellectual intuition.'   He is right as to
the latter.   We have no intuition of a punctual simplicity which
is to be called an *ego*.   But between these two extremes lies a
mean which more nearly expresses the psychological truth in
regard to the *ego*.   We do have an awareness of a self which
finds itself to be the subject of all its states.   This is the unique
characteristic of the subject-matter of the science of psychology.
Only as there is a reference to a one consciousness is their possible any psychical series whatsoever.   Even in the weird phe-

[1]Ladd, *Phys. Psych.*, 601 f.
[2]*Crit.*, II., 318 ff.
[3]*Ibid.*, I., 453, 'Deduction,' 2nd. *ed.*, sec. 25.

nomena of double personality, which bring many lacunæ into the life history of the individual, the doubleness has a significance only as there is attained a unity of consciousness in either series of states, as A, A_1, A_2, A_3, or B, B_1, B_2, B_3. Either series does not pass over into the other, does not destroy the integrity of the unity which is characteristic of each series, and even makes it such a series.

With the foregoing remarks there has been in mind the view which modern psychology has arrived at respecting the nature of self-consciousness and the evolution of the *ego* in the life of the individual. The *ego* is not a 'primitive notion' such as the old rational psychologists would have it. It is not a static unity of metaphysical intuition. On the contrary, the *ego* is a product. Selfhood is an acquisition. Its presentation is not a datum of sense, and the objections of metaphysicians that the logical simplicity of the *ego* defies any analysis, is an instance of a psychological fallacy.[1] This conception of a self which is so necessary a condition of all representations and is underivable from other elements, may be an attainment of a long psychological unfolding. The most abstract notion is often the last result of a complex development. "The idea of the *ego*," says M. Taine,[2] "is a product; many variously elaborated materials concur in its formation." Not only are abbreviated memories, a chain of recollections, and the ideas of a cause, a power, and 'a stable within,' intellectual factors entering into this product;[3] but the growth of the emotional, and active, struggling sides of mind life enter into and promote the acquisition of the conception of self. All of the states of consciousness in their progressive development contribute to that ideal product of reflection, the central point around which the whole of the intellectual life swings. Not only is the basis of its unity laid in the facts of memory, but the function of apperception, as provoked by the varieties of feelings, brings it into an empirical prominence which finds its culmination in the feeling of self-control over

[1] *Cf.*, Ward, *loc. cit.*, p. 83, note 4.

[2] *On Intelligence*, II., p. 110.

[3] These are all that M. Taine recognizes; James, *loc. cit.*, Sully, *Human Mind*, I., 475 ff., Ward, *loc. cit.*, Höffding, *op. cit.*, p. 136 f., call attention to the value of other factors that contribute to the growth of the conception of self.

the muscular adjustments and chiefly in conduct as imputable to an 'inner self.'[1]

Kant recognizes the complexity which enters into the *ego* of experience. With him, too, it is a slow product. Maturity is necessary before 'das Ich' is properly recognized by the faculty 'Verstand.'[2] But, according to the psychological presuppositions of Kant's criticism, 'Ich' is not merely an experiential product as psychologists now recognize it to be; but, rather, a *quasi*-sensational 'Vorstellung' that is constantly changing. For it comprehends the relations of the determinations of the inner sense only as they occur in time. As implied in the Analytic, apperception is the ingredient not only of a cognition of objects, but also of selves.[3] Had he not succeeded this claim by his commentary on the apperceptive *ego* in the refutation of rational psychology, much would be in his favor. Apperception is the act of mind common to its treatment of all psychical data. It is the relating activity of attention, a synthesis which constructs the material into higher relations and is the last stage in the development of that unique life whose mysterious beginnings lie in the physiological unconscious.[4] But Kant's view is guilty merely of a limitation. He represents the one activity as doing it all; whereas we saw above that all the primal psychic elements enter, even much more than the mere data out of which the *ego* arises. *E. g.*, it was seen in the previous chapter how the phenomena of memory were slighted (of course, imagination is the comprehensive term which stood for all that representation which is necessary to knowledge). But in the very fact and nature of memory, as referring over lapses of times to a past which *is my* past, is given the primal basis out of which the intellectual character of a unitary consciousness can arise. He also leaves out the specially characteristic elements, other than bare cognitive consciousness, which make empirically for the *ego* of experience. We are the phe-

[1] *Cf.*, also Baldwin, *Senses and Intellect*, pp. 66 f., 143 f.

[2] *Werke*, VII., 438, *Anthropologie*, sec. 1.

[3] *Cf.*, 'Deduction,' 2d *ed.*, I., p. 453, note 3, where 'every act of attention gives us an instance' of our internal perceptions as we are determined by the spontaneity of the understanding.

[4] *Cf.*, Baldwin, *op. cit.*, p. 63 ff.

nomenal, kaleidoscopic *ego* that we are, not because time is a form of the inner sense into which the relating activity of attention, as it is *a prioristically* determined by the possible categorical forms, constructs the feelings and sensations that come out of nothing, into the object; but, in that, consciousness emerges *pari passu* with the integration of the three classifiable variations of its own states as knowing, feeling and willing. The psychological oracle reveals the impossibility of a purely cognitive consciousness, and philosophy does well with the reality it seeks, if it abides this finite wisdom, remaining partial to none of the so-called superior faculties of man.

But the fault of limitation, which attends a possible interpretation of Kant's views of the nature and development of self, becomes an error as we turn to what seems to be Criticism's last word on the nature of the *ego* which is to have in it the self-sufficiency of knowledge. The former might have been permissible in view of the state of psychology in his time, when it was considered as a department of natural history. Even the discovery of apperception as conditioning the knowledge of self as well as of things, is commendable in so far as the Critical method proceeds psychologically in order to refute sensationalism.

Kant, however, aggravates our confusion as he gives his own commentary to the Analytic in the Dialectic, and in his criticism of rational psychology adds foot-notes, as it were, explanatory of his conception of the *ego*—a subject of thinking which signifies the pure apperception. These explanations take all the life out of us, if we ever had any. The transcendental *ego* is absolutely nothing. In the Analytic we thought we were getting to the very root of the matter only to find ourselves implicated in it all. The reality of a cognition of 'objective' things turns upon the unifying *actus* of a-to-itself-relating activity which wandered among the manifold that comes to us because of our psycho-physical organization, but coming out of nothing. Here in the Dialectic, however, where the *ego* is pruned and all hindering growths are removed that it may stand out in its own integrity against all the prevalent notions of the self, it becomes woefully reduced. *There* we learned that the unity of a one consciousness was the determining element in the orderly array which experience is, and makes it so different from ' the whole crowd of phenomena that rush in upon us.' It is the intense activity of an agent,[1] which gives coloring to the whole of experience. But *here* it is nothing more than the ' vehicle' of what is thrown over the manifold. In the intellectualism of Criticism it withers into a logical *ego*. The pure apperception becomes a ' cheap and second' edition of the spontaneity of mind. The agent of the Analytic is the head of a constructive operation. The *ego* of the Dialectic is the preexistent, unpredicable condition of that which the old psychologists supposed was in their possession. It is a logical presupposition which can never be turned to the content of a judgment. It is a static form, absolutely given.[2]

If the foregoing reduction of the Critical *egos* remains justifiable, there is obvious at least two errors in the notion of the logical subject which can never become a predicate. First, this *ego* is represented as given absolutely; *i. e.*, it is a formal condition attending all cognitive consciousness. Without it we can never judge; and in attempting to categorize its nature, we constantly turn in a vicious circle—it always remains a preposited ' representation.'[3] Now, whatever may be the epistemological mysteries concealed in the rise of a cognitive consciousness, it is a psychological fact that the logical *ego* is a

[1] "As regards the soul * * * the whole drift of Kant's advance upon Hume and sensational psychology is toward the demonstration that the subject of knowledge is an *agent*." G. S. Morris, *Kant's Critique of Pure Reason*, second edition, p. 244.

[2] The difficulty of throwing a search light on Kant's benighted expressions concerning the various phases of the logical and psychological *egos*, is seen by comparing the Analytic and the Dialectic with the following foot note found in his *Anthropologie*, VII., p. 445. After distinguishing the respective subjects of the perceptive and apperceptive consciousness (and noting that the distinction is an apparent contradiction), he says: "Die Frage ob bei den verschiedenen inneren Veränderungen des Gemüths der Mensch, wenn er sich dieser Veränderungen bewusst ist, noch sagen können; er sei *ebenderselbe* (der Seele nach), ist eine ungereimte Frage; denn er kann sich dieser Veränderungen nur dadurch bewusst sein, dass er sich in den verschiedenen Zuständen als ein und dasselbe *Subject* vorstellt, und das Ich des Menschen ist zwar der Form (der Vorstellungsart) nach, aber nicht der Materie (dem Inhalte) nach zwiefach."

[3] *Crit.*, II., 301.

product of that very experience which Kant claims it to condition. Whatever may be its ontological simplicity as a logical notion, it is a late development in the mental life and bears with it all that complexity which characterizes the products which come in with the unfolding of the intellective processes. Only as the fundamental traits of mind, such as attention, discrimination and comparison, develop into the thought aspects, which are no special faculty or power, and result in such products as the concept or universal image, the judgment or the perceptual aspect of comparison which develops into one of the highest ideals of rational thinking, *viz.* : the principle of identity, which harks back and claims to underlie all conscious activity and thus is truly the universalized form of comparison—only in such an evolution, we affirm, can there arise that concept which is the corner-stone of all absolute idealism, the laying of which is so ceremoniously performed in the chief psychological sections of the *Critique of Pure Reason.* Such an *ego*, however, only plays the lie with our metaphysical instincts. From it we can get a formal reality only. Kant was right in repudiating, from his foundations, the claims of the dogmatists. But he slurs over the principle of becoming and squashes the postulates which *do* integrate even into our so-called abstract conceptions. This is only another instance of how illusory is the propædeuticity of logic and the necessity which constrains philosophy to turn to psychology when it would fain understand even what *is*. As elsewhere, Kant is logical in the inconsistency of his presuppositions.

Furthermore, there is another deficiency in the logic, or psychology—call it what you please—of Kant's conception of judgment. An error here has been magnified into a grievous falsity in the psychological scepticism into which Criticism developed. There is a failure to distinguish properly two sorts of judgments, and he starts out with the old-time notion of the function of a judgment and the source of its materials. It is not the distinction between analytic and synthetic judgments, which is so fundamental to Criticism, that is here in question. Since all judging is a developed synthesis, a unification, psychology very properly considers this aspect of the thinking process not, however, with reference to the validity of the comparison and integration, but with distinct reference to the individual, its growth and relation to his previous knowledge.[1] But back of these logical judgments lie the psychological judgments. The former are 'secondary and artificial.' They deal with concepts. Their comparisons are apparently not of things. Were this all that might be said of judgment, the supposition of an ever non-predicable subject would be the only possible view, and one would needs be shut into the Kantian conception of the *ego.* So long as such judgments are true to their function, we are left in abstractness, for no intuition is permitted among them. They are regardless of reality and deal only with ideal thought products. Kant's treatment of the judgment implies so much. But there are other judgments, ' primary and natural. These are they by which concepts are formed' and are known' as the psychological judgment.[2] On such previous acquisitions in the individual are founded the abstract, comparative judgments with which logic deals. The *quid juris* of the logical judgment has apparently been overlooked by Kant. It was taken as the ultimate expression of the nature of understanding, or the apperceptive process grown big under that grave name.

And yet, the entire right of comparing concepts as though they were things, is derivable from the psychological judgment, or that integration of perceptive images developed into a totality which becomes the representative of a group.[3] Concepts are not ready-made stuffs which are woven into the fabric of experience. Nor does Kant mean as much, even though in the *Critique* he circles about in the astounding phrase of the transcendental *a*

---

[1] *Cf.*, Sully, *Human Mind*, I., 438 f., 452 ; Baldwin, *op. cit.*, pp. 272-275, 292 f.

[2] Porter, *Human Intellect*, p. 432.

[3] Kant has recognized two sorts of judgments which bear the real distinctions which are noted in the text. *Cf.* his very important distinction between ' Wahrnehmungsurtheil' and ' Erfahrungsurtheil'—the former arising first in the individual, and out of which come the latter objectively-referring judgments. *Cf., Werke,* IV., 46 f. ; V., 296 ; VIII., 110 f. ; Watson, *op. cit.*, 63 ff. Thus Kant might be said to acknowledge the psychological implications which attend all his treatment of judgments ; but when he comes to the synthetic *a priori* judgment concerning the subject, he passes beyond those empirical implications and treats it with utmost abstractness, from which his scepticism might be said to take its rise.

priority of the categories.[1] Concepts are formed, even the *a priori*, out of the perceptual bits on which the unfolding thought process expends itself. Kant does not claim that the categories are 'innate,' but are 'erworbenen' in the process of experience. But the *Critique* seemingly overlooks the great fact of development and pronounces categorically upon the peculiar forms of thinking. Though there be a multitude of 'synthetic judgments *a priori*,' they all must come in with that struggling unfolding, which psychology is compelled to describe. That *a priori* concepts are not ready-made, but are mysterious psychological acquisitions, does not detract in the least from their critical purity.

These natural, or psychological, judgments are the point where 'sense' and 'understanding' really fuse. They are the go-between of ideation and intellection. It is true that ideation is only one species of cognitive activity of which intellection is the more comprehensive term. There is no proper image or idea without its net of relations. But the adjustment of these relations to sense data is made by the natural judgments. Concepts, anyway, are nothing except as they have come up out of representative materials.

Here it is where Kant seems to depart from the psychological nature of judgment. Our concepts are conditioned upon percepts. Since judgments are said to deal with concepts only, it is easily seen what relation perception and conception hold. Subject and predicate do not stand in quite the same logical relation as Kant's logic would have them. "Our perception of what (an object) is," says Mr. Hodgson, "and what its relations are, as a precept, determines our choice of the predicates; is their *conditio existendi* as predicates; while conversely their application as predicates is the *conditio cognoscendi* in our logical or reasoning cognition of (the object)."[2] This is particularly true of objects and thoroughly in harmony with the Kantian view of our knowledge of things. "Thoughts without intuitions are empty." But it must be maintained that this log-

---

[1] *Cf.*, his popular exposition of how 'die reinen Verstandesbegriffe in den Kopf kommen.' *Vorles. üb. Psych.*, pp. 18 f., 24 f.

[2] *Op. cit.*, 386.

ical and psychological reciprocity is just as true of the subject which is perceived in every psychical state. There can be no percept without a referableness to a 'my,' to the perceiving 'thought,' or whatever name any species of psychology may offer as a substitute for the supporter of psychoses. That is the unique character of consciousness. Out of the multitude of these subject-wise perceptions, concerning which Kant may be allowed his view, that this is no 'intellectual intuition' revealing an atomic subject—there arises the notion of a self. Psychology knows no 'pure-thought' *ego*. The conceptual *ego* which we all recognize has its varied sources laid in the bits of a transitory experience. Unless there is some discrimination of a subject in every conscious, presentative state, the grammatical *ego* could never have come. This interrelation between the perception and the conception of the subject is also expressed by Hodgson, whose statement is especially apt against Kant, since the latter refers rational psychology to that very species of judgment which the former has analyzed. Every categorical proposition begins with a percept changed into a concept, and ends with a concept which can be changed into a percept again. The first of these is the subject and the last the predicate of a proposition.[1]

Thus the 'logical *ego*' of Criticism is a highly complex

---

[1] *Op. cit.*, I., 332. Kant's attempt to draw a hard and fixed line between 'intuition' and 'concept' incurs psychological disapproval. The very function of the psychological judgment shows, that, with reference to the activities of the individual mind, they almost indiscernibly shade into each other. In the essay, *Ueber Phil. überhaupt*, he says, "Anschauung und Begriff unterscheiden sich von einander specifisch; denn sie gehen ineinander nicht über, das Bewusstsein beider und der Merkmale derselben mag wachsen oder abnehmen, wie es will." (VI., 391, note). The fact is, the discovery of the categories after the guiding principle of the logical judgment was too good a thing, and Kant really overworks them. Yet, when he comes to the most difficult of his problems, *viz:* how the categories get applied, he tones down the rigid demarcation which the discovery sets up . These modifications come in those passages where the Deduction is ejected, passages other than that which occurs under that special title. *Cf.* the whole 'Doctrine of the Schematism' and the 'Analytic of Principles.' In a little essay of 1786, he begins, "Wir mögen unsere Begriffe noch so hoch anlegen und dabei noch so sehr von der Sinnlichkeit abstrahiren, so hängen ihnen doch noch immer bildliche Vorstellungen an, etc." IV., 539. *Cf., Logik*, VIII., 33 f.; *Ueber die Fortschritte der Metaph.*, etc., VIII., 584 f.

product, though no more than a rational figment which contains more or less of the content that may be given in perception. Its psychological history demands that it be a subject which *can* become a predicate. It is a concept made up of many perceptions, in whose *empirical* reality are found transcendental or ontological implications which it is the privilege of a philosophy of mind to explicate. The conceptual self, thus 'naturally' derived, is the *ego* of reflection, and becomes the logical subject which is given in every cognitive or propositional consciousness. It cannot, however, be admitted with Kant that it is the *a priori*, static subject. While it is the rational self in the fullest meaning, it becomes enlarged, as it were, in every additional state of knowing, feeling and willing. A metaphysic of mind is thus permitted to develop itself, only profiting by the warning which Criticism has given. It is not to hypostasize highly abstract terms, nor is it to find in any rational or logical development a sceptical negation of the metaphysical virtue given in every perceptual reality.

Our consideration of speculative Criticism, as it centralizes itself in rational psychology, has led us far from that apodictic science. This necessity has its valuable indication in showing that rational psychology is not so widely separated from empirical psychology as Kant would have us believe.[1] Philosophy aids us in coming to rational views—concepts, if one pleases; but concepts that are to have their vindication in the facts of experience. Rational psychology does not build itself on concepts alone, but is related to the empirical science as the very next link in the chain of causal and ultimate explanations of what is given as the phenomena of consciousness. The one begins where the other ends. Kant might be heard to say that an infinite logician could have a rational psychology. Out of his tutorial Criticism has come the modest opinion that only man, as he has a multiplex psychical experience, can come to a rational science of the perceptual self which is his constant attendant. Rational psychology no longer cares for the necessities of the logician, but endeavors to satisfy, in terms of reality, the belief of every common man that in his feeling and willing, as well

[1] *Cf.*, Meyer, *op. cit.*, 293 ff.

as in every cognition, there is a being which shares in those phenomenal occurrences, and whom he calls himself.

The purposes of this study feel satisfied when the criticism of rational psychology has been reviewed in its relation to the Critical philosophy, the question of its historic right has been inquired into, and an indication of its vulnerable points has been given. The general significance of the whole can be quite adequately designated by noting its bearing on two of the problems which properly fall within the inquiries of theoretical psychology, *viz.*, a conception of the mind as a real being, and the vexed question which has provoked all sorts of ingenious attempts at solving the relation of mind and body. When defensible conclusions on these two points are in the hands of a philosophy of mind, it can very safely supplement its speculative knowledge of that being with an insight into ethical and æsthetical influences which help to determine its relations to other finite beings, and finally, reach the goal of all inquiry by constructing in philosophical fashion the relation of this finite reality to the being whose reality it implicates. They are problems which any school of philosophy must take up, and in their tendencies, they are the realism which posits the physical and ends with explanations turning on forces and laws, or the idealism which posits the reality of the ideating subject and finds in it a microtheos. This is the peculiarity of philosophical discipline, of whatever tendency, that the execution of its departments surge with a common, wave-like motion, and no conclusion is left to its own seclusion, but is caught up and carried away in the multitude of rational convictions crowning speculative inquiry. On one problem Kant is not altogether faultless. On the second problem it may appear that the last word of Criticism and its occasional outstretching intimations have been only a re-statement of the real question.

The relation between psychology and philosophy has been constantly re-appearing, either as a caution under some historic instance, or at particular points where the empirical notion may be said to completely mould the philosophical conviction. The most obvious point of contact in these scientific and rational endeavors is at the theory of knowledge. The empiric investigation re-

sults in a description of the rise of knowledge and hands over
to epistemology the problem whose presence in the philosophical consciousness is the *raison d'être* of that department of philosophical inquiry which had its beginning in the *Critique of
Pure Reason*. Noëtics is called upon to validate, in the terms
of rational analysis, that product whose constituents are ex-
hibited in the science of mind. To remain rational it cannot
present some factor or relation as true which is psychologically
false. They are, as it were, two forces emerging into their new
resultant. It is one of the splendid acquisitions of recent philosophy that it is recognizing the partnership of observation and
experiment on the one hand, and reflective analysis on the other,
whose great struggle is to increase the capital stock of human
reason in its unending competition against the 'riddles of life'
that hedge our ways.

It is not only to this philosophical equipment that psychology
specially relates itself. Certain phenomena which the science
considers under the one leadership of the causal sequence have
the universal significance, which entitles them to the analysis of
philosophy, as it ventures to sweep over the world for its factual
material. Psychology can be a 'natural science' only to feel
the burden of problems insoluble so long as it struggles to keep
back in the company of physicists and physiologists. Up to
that point where such a psychologist believes in the reality of
the unique elements upon which he must make heavy drafts for
explanations, and where he refuses to give answer to interro-
gated relationship, the remaining whole of psychological considerations become philosophical. The reality of mind and its
phenomena are *posited* by the scientist. They are his working
hypotheses, employing which he feels content in articulating
groups of facts to their phenomenal antecedents. The conclusions to which he comes, as well as his prepositings, are also
material for the analysis of him who feels oppressed by the
mysteries of real being.

Thus psychology becomes one of the special departments of
philosophy, as well as being the proper propædeutic in all fields
of ultimate inquiry. It comprehends a unique class of facts
which are objective to science and belong to the real, which

forms the content of metaphysic.   The world, or nature, and
minds or selves, comprehend all that experience yields to which
ontological principles must be fitted for rational explanation, yet
not in such a manner as to distort the 'facts' as they are given.
Those principles, however, as taught us by the history of metaphysic, are none other than mental forms which are regulative
of all that we know as real.   It is from this upper story of the
psychology of intellect that metaphysic derives its material.
Thus the philosophy of mind comprehends a class of phenomena
whose ultimate problems have been suggested by psychology,
and the epistemological terms into which philosophy attempts to
convert the knowledge of the object of that science are discov-
erable in that self-same science of mind.   Psychology, in its
rational stages, is not entirely progressive, but constantly returns
to the experience whence all mysteries take their rise.   It must
also submit itself to the metaphysical judges of the categories,
whose existence it first reveals, but whose validity leads beyond
its proper domain.   The alpha and omega of such psychology
are the conception of the soul's substantiality and the physical
basis of mental activity.   Between the discovery of some notion
of the soul's unitary being and the philosophical reduction of
'mind and body,' are articulated the peculiar ascertainments of
this science.

     Kant's criticism of the old-time theory of the substantiality
of the soul apparently rests upon his ideality of time, the peculiar internal sense, and the limitations of the judgment.   We
tried to show the defective source whence Kant drew his criticism, and to free psychology from the inadequate rebuke he attempted to give.   But it really implies a negation of the adequacy
of self-consciousness to get at the real being whose substance is
called mind.   The illusoriness of Kantian self-consciousness is
not due to the non-psychological interest on the part of Criticism;
but, rather, is to be accounted for in its too naïve conception of
substance, notwithstanding its being made a category, and to
the insufficient theory of knowledge which affirmed a cognition
of 'things' only.

     According to Criticism, thinking can have 'necessity' only
as representations are given in *both* space and time.   The

soul has no spatial relations—position being the only extensive adjective attributable to it.   Hence, whatever may be given
in time cannot be 'known.'[1]   We can know the permanent—the
substantial core which corresponds to our 'concept'—only as
we have 'external intuitions.'   "In order to give something permanent in intuition, we require an intuition in space, because
space alone can determine anything as permanent, while time,
and therefore everything that exists in the internal sense, is in
a constant flux."[2]   Criticism would pattern the knowledge of
self after the model given in the knowledge of things, whereas
the truth may appear that the knowledge of things is patterned
after that of selves.   'Substance' was an *a priori* figment, since
in his application of it to experience, there goes with it an implication of the common sense view that things are substances—
masses which cannot be known since the 'qualities' are in the
way of immediate intuition.[3]   It was the metaphysic of a molecular age when things were given supreme reality.   The heritage of Criticism as it has been nurtured in this psychological
age is, that, substance is what Criticism would have it—a concept which we externalize, as it were, in our natural but metaphysical perception of things—a mode of our thinking which
attempts to reduce the infinitely various behavior of things to
some limitation which becomes a law regulating the 'nature' of
that which behaves.

Kant, however, believed in a soul—a being which is the
subject of our inner experience, but on moral grounds.   It was
only an implication of the categorical imperative that gives us

[1] On this very ground it might be shown that Criticism labored in vain—for
the modicum of knowledge it left to reason rests on an inconsistency.   Space is
not time—but there are instances where Kant is on the verge of reducing every
form of representation to the Heraclitic principle of ceaseless change and becoming.   *Critique*, II., 88: "All our knowledge must finally be subject to the formal condition of that internal sense, namely, time."   *Cf.*, the 'Schematism' and
its one form of time, pp. 126 ff; 'the third necessity which makes possible all
synthetical judgments,' p. 137; the function given to time in the first and second
'Analogies of Experience,' pp. 160 f., 167 f.

[2] *Critique*, I., 482 f.

[3] The doctrine of noumena is not quite so thoroughly idealistic if one considers in connection with it the 'category' of 'permanence' and the treatment
Criticism gave it.

a critical right to a mere faith in our own existence.   This shifting of the philosophical ground on which the existence of a one
real being could rest, was intended by Kant as a real service to
cultured reason as it attempts to systematize its body of truths.
Against this necessity as Criticism exhibits it, we must cry out
with all *its* vehemence against 'psychological idealism,' and
slightly changing the famous sentence which was thrust at
Jacobi and threw Fichte into indignant consternation, let it read :
It remains a scandal to philosophy, and to human reason in
general, that we should have to accept the existence of *that
thing within* us on faith only, unable to meet with any satisfactory proof an opponent who is pleased to doubt it.[1]   In order to
prove the existence of things, Kant searches the principles of
conscious thinking and the nature of representations.   But the
existence of a self finds a so-called proof ($=$ the warrant for a
transcendental postulate), in a non-empirical law—the chief
point in the intelligible, but unknowable world.   In all this
Kant cannot be vindicated except as we take him in reference
to the cosmological metaphysics which preceded 'the age of
criticism.'   Unless philosophy can find in some other fact, given
in the totality of rational experience, a ground of proof for the
unitary being of what is the metaphysical confidence of every
man, then, indeed, sceptical idealism does remain a scandal.

Now it is the peculiarity of the metaphysic of psychology
that the ground of belief in the reality of mind cannot be sought
elsewhere than in consciousness.   The proof for the existence
of the objects of other knowledge may be a long chain of circumstantial evidences.   Realism may even appeal to the existence of objects as the ground of proof that our ideas of them
are real.   But the philosophy of mind can proceed by no other
means than the datum of self-consciousness.   Psychology, as a
science, ventures consciousness as the one mark of its data.
When it comes to affirm the reality of the soul, no round-about
way of evidencing its postulate will suffice.   Psychology is so
metaphysical a science that it must find implicate in a one consciousness the proof (?) of the being whose consciousness it is.
With one grasp, as it were, it endeavors to secure the substan-

[1] *Critique*, I., 386 note.

tial simplicity of the *ego* for the acquisition of which Kant represents two paralogisms, or one-half of rational psychology, as necessary.

In modern times, it is Hermann Lotze in particular, who has found in the unity of consciousness the fact from which is argued the unitary existence of the being called mind.[1] According to Lotze, it is ' the unity of consciousness' which compels any explanation of the mental life to find some immaterial form of being as the subject of the phenomena. Without this decisive fact of experience the total of our internal states could not even become an object of self-observation.[2] Now, no tenet of psychology has been more abused than the conception of self-consciousness. It was a violent and unwarrantable use of this against which Kant contended. But when it is said that Lotze has ' revived' the old argument of the existence of the soul from the data of self-consciousness,[3] there is a culpable failure to appreciate Kant's objection to the employment of self-consciousness, and to realize the shifting of the ground when

[1] The views of Lotze were submitted to several restatements, each modified to harmonize with the immediate discussion before him. In his popular exposition of the *Microcosmus*, (I., pp. 143–167 and other corresponding sections) it appears essential in his description of the little being which is a little world in itself; in the *Metaphysic*, (II., 163–198) the considerations of theoretical psychology are presented in their metaphysical connections; *cf.*, his *Medicinische Psychologie*, pp. 9 ff., 135–151; *Outlines of Psychology*, pp. 91 f., 119 f.; *Outlines of the Phil. of Rel.*, pp. 58–66, *etc.* Though starting from other presuppositions, Ulrici has come to the same conclusion as Lotze; *cf.*, *e. g.*, the following : "Die Einheit des *Bewusstseyns* ist nicht zu verwechseln mit dem Bewusstseyns *der* Einheit unseres Wesens." " Die Einheit des Bewusstseyns, d. h. die Thatsache, dass wir nur *Ein* Bewusstseyn und nicht mehere neben oder nach einander haben, lässt sich schlechterdings *nicht* leugnen und bestreiten." Out of this identity which we all recognize, ' sobald wir darauf reflectiren,' "folgt allerdings, dass auch das Wesen, welches seiner selbst und des Bewusstseyns sich bewusst ist, ein einiges, mit sich identisches seyn muss." *Leib und Seele,* 1866, pp. 314 f.

[2] *Microcosmus*, I., 152. Kant has an important statement of nearly the same import : " Only because I am able to connect the manifold of given representations in one consciousness, is it possible for me to represent to myself the identity of the consciousness in these representations." *Crit.*, I., 435. Yet *wie himmelweit* are the ' unities' in these instances it is hardly necessary to show. That they differ completely is merely to express the difference between modern metaphysics of mind and the psychology of Criticism.

[3] Meyer, *op cit.*, 250 ff., 310; Krohn, *op. cit.*, 38.

Lotze makes an appeal to the apprehension of self for the proof of his belief in the existence of the mind.   What Kant criticises is not what Lotze invokes.   This sober worker in the field of philosophy was acute enough to heartily enter into Kantian criticism and to keep shy of reproducing the arguments of Knutzen, Reimarus and Mendelssohn.   Kant, so far as there is discernible any taint of a rational psychology to his critical scepticism, seems to believe, in common with his time, that the soul has being which afterwards comes to be observed or known.   If only the mind could *be*, as the substance deeply hidden within the phenomenal appearance of consciousness — that was the one admitted ontological principle upon which Criticism sets an epistemological limit.   We may *be* five hundred substances.   Yet, while it is inconceivable how a unity of one experience can arise from the interaction of a plurality of elements,[1] we cannot even know of them so as to permit us to affirm the simple identity of our soul.

In Lotze's treatment, however, there disappears the presupposition of a psychical molecular unity, where the problem is, how such a pre-existent object can be known in the terms of self-consciousness.   That he really abandons this old-time view is implied in his protest against a possible misconception of his position, saying: "I do not mean that our consciousness of the unity of our being is in itself, by what it directly reports, a guarantee of that unity."[2]   "I repeat once more, we do not believe in the unity of the soul because it appears as unity."[3]   In these statements, in which he guards his own views, appears also a second point of difference between the Lotzean 'revival' of the Kantian off-cast of psychology, namely, the nature of self-consciousness as to the existence of the being which it purports to envisage.   These changes entitle Lotze to reconsider anew the basis of that argument which Criticism showed to be faulty (but from entirely different psychological grounds).   Kant had to struggle against the monster of an ontological psychology.

In the modern view of self-consciousness the aim is to har-

---

[1] *Cf.*, the Second Paralogism.
[2] *Microcosmus*, I., 156.
[3] *Metaphysic*, II., 176.

monize a mental experience with a psychological metaphysics, and the problem for argumentation becomes : Can we infer from the unity of our consciousness the unity of a real being conscious of itself? or, Given the unity of human consciousness, can we argue to the degree of metaphysical demonstration (not mathematical) the reality and unity of the soul? To the question of introspection, whether the beholder in each state of so-called self-consciousness really gazes upon that substantial unity which is the creator and supporter of all states of consciousness, a negative answer, undoubtedly, must be given. This, we take it, is the point of Kant's criticism, but not the nerve of Lotze's argument. Kant, however, is psychologically culpable in apparently passing over that indescribable feeling which expresses itself in the trite phrase, 'Ich bin hier und jetzt.' This is the point of departure in the modern conviction of the soul's being one. A necessary distinction must not be overlooked as is frequently done in what might be called realistic psychology (Herbart excepted).[1] This felt-cognition of selfness is mistaken for an atomic envisagement; whereas it, too, is a unique conscious state and must be treated as all other states in the stream of consciousness. Its uniqueness properly entitles it to the appellation of self-consciousness, and is the basis of the argument. Herein appears the distinction that must be made between consciousness and self-consciousness. States of consciousness are not *referred* to a unitary subject in every such state. The common assertion that in consciousness we have given the immediate reality of the subject knowing and the object known, passes beyond the psychological warrant of any psychosis. These states are never simple, but emerge into each other so that the current of mental life at any one point partakes of a kaleidoscopic complexity. This succession of complex fields are not referred to a perduring subject, but they *are* conscious states only in their virtue of being *referable* to a self. Even in the beginnings of mental life, where the most incautious would hesitate to affirm a consciousness of self, there is not

---

[1] *Cf.*, Porter, *Human Intellect*, p. 95, ff. : "Of the *ego* itself we are also directly conscious. The states we know as varying and transitory. The self we know as unchanged and permanent."

given, as a fact, any sensation or perception without a subject.[1] Any psychosis is inconceivable without there being a somewhat which has it. This, however, is far from affirming that in the infantile, or even adult state, there is also given that whose state it is. But in this consciousness there lies a possibility of an immediate awareness of its present reality which expresses itself as 'Ich bin hier und jetzt.' This acquisition of the mental life gathers up all that is implied in the subject-ward referableness of all the states which are attributable to the self. But the 'bin hier und jetzt' no more explains the 'Ich' than the subject apprehended in other states, and is *itself* only referable to a subject. This is all that can be meant by any self-consciousness. It does not intuite a unitary being. Even the most successful, determined effort to shut out all sensuous content of consciousness in order to open the way for the immediate intuition of a self as it is in itself, gets no farther in its possessions than a conscious state, however free of objective content, which in turn becomes referable to a subject whose state it is. This merely adds another instance vouching for the unity which consciousness has, and brings us around to the datum on which any argument for the soul's unity can base itself. The problem remains: What do we mean by 'Ich'? and what is there in the phenomenal expressions concerning itself which warrants metaphysic to affirm the substantial unity of that which becomes conscious of itself as the subject of all its states? This aspect of the question Kant's criticism does not affect, and herein is found Lotze's real advance and right in 'reviving' the old time argument of the unity of consciousness.[2]

In the foregoing statement of what appears to be the real nature of the problem and the material with which the metaphysician can deal, there comes to view the necessity of bringing in other clarified conceptions, whose considerations profoundly affect the conclusion of rational psychology. Any completely intrenched speculative decision as to the unitary ex-

---

[1] *Cf.*, Lotze, *Metaphysic*, II., p. 169, sec. 241.

[2] *Cf.*, Prof. Ladd's reply to Mr. G. F. Stout's strictures on his argument 'from the unity of consciousness to the existence of a real unitary being as the subject of consciousness,' (as briefly presented in pt. III., ch. IV., of his *Phys. Psych.*), *Mind*, vol. 13, p. 627 ff. Mr. Stout's criticism, *Ibid.*, p. 466 f.

istence of a being called mind is not acquired until we agree with ourselves as to what we shall mean by 'unity' and by 'being.' The intuition of a permanent, identical existent by the realistic consciousness overworks the to-a-self-referable phenomena. "We can never envisage any unity or being." Were perceptual apprehension the mark of reality, the human mind would never have conceived the need of a metaphysic. Aristotle could not have ventured the foundations of a τά μετά τά φυσικά were the Berkleian tenet of 'Esse est percipi' true. But this itself is a naïve, unsubstantiated metaphysics and vaults into a conclusion that may come only as the conceptions of a 'prima philosophia' are fitted to the facts of experience. Thus our psychological adjectives can have no meaning until we have analyzed ontological conceptions, and, as it were, got them ready for some meaning. None other than the inadequacy of mere intuition can be the intent when Browning says:

"Whether after all, a larger metaphysics might not help our physics."

Lotze's belief in the soul's unity 'rests not on our appearing to ourselves such a unity, but on our being able to appear to ourselves at all.'[1] It is not what it may appear to us to be. But back of all appearance lies a synthesis integrating any manifold, in which is found proof (?) of a one being. "The mere fact that, conceiving itself as a subject, it connects itself with any predicate, proves to us the unity of that which asserts this connection."[2] The mere ability to manifest itself in *some* way, not necessarily in that formal unity which Kant implied and demanded, is a sufficient guarantee for the existence of the mind. Whereas, Lotze at times labors in the interest of this view as though it were a proof, a demonstration, he yet intimates that, like all explanation of whatever sort, it is a mere juxtaposition of facts. "The fact of the unity of consciousness is *eo ipso* at once the fact of the existence of a substance."[3] And if we are 'a substance' it is just such a factual existence that we desire, and not an inscrutable perdurance which has its ideal

[1] *Microcosmus*, I., 157.
[2] *Metaphysic*, II., 176.
[3] *Meta.*, II., 175.

reality far away in the mysteries of mathematical demonstration.

What we are, is not told us in this guarantee of the existence
of a somewhat that appears. It is the fact of this seeming and
not the fact our consciousness directly reports the unity of
our being, on which Lotze has justly based his inference to the
existence of the being which appears in all its states. To stop
here, however, is to loose all that has been gained in this re-
statement of the validity of the unity of consciousness. It must
be supplemented by some meaning being put into ' reality ' and
' unity.' But what I am, can have no meaning unless reference
is again made to the self-same consciousness. Now the only
what-ness that any of us care for, is just such as we appear to
ourselves to be. Unless I thus am the subject of all my states,
no substance behind all the states can affect me in the least.
I am just such a being as knows itself as apprehending, as
striving, and moved by feelings. That, indeed, is the highest
meaning that can be put into the words ' being,' ' substance,'
' reality.' That soul *is* which shows itself in any mode of being
affected which psychology may reveal. ' Being ' other than for
my self-apprehension, is the substance for which the child is
searching when he seeks back of the mirror for what appears in
it, but remains something always out of his sight. It is only
' being for self,' says Lotze in another place,[1] that is ' reality.'
It is not their possession of ' a core ' of reality which make
things have being ; but they are substantial and belong to the
existent only as they in such a manner appear to us to have a
substance present in them. " To ' be really,' and to be the one
permanent subject of changing states are but different ways of
expressing the same truth."[2] What things are, is told in an
enumeration of their attributes ; but to look for a somewhat is to
hypostasize a query and to forget what one already has. The
same is true in regard to the mind. What it is, is told in no
less a manner than the expression of the modes of its appearance. And for myself really to be, is to be myself as remembering, as suffering, as perceiving, and all those various states

[1] *Outlines of Metaphysic*, p., 138.
[2] Ladd, *Phys. Psych.*, p. 679.

with whose description psychology is replete. Criticism did not overlook such an *ego*, but mistook the meaning of reality when it implies that there is a psychical thing by itself—existing in the solitary blessedness of unknowability.

With the assurance of the substantial existence of the mind, there is also desirable an answer to the question of its numerical qualities. The old psychology thought the soul is one because it perceives its identity, and also on account of the incompatibility between a plurality of substantial elements and the unity in the subject which is reported upon in self-apprehension. Modern psychology also finds a multiplicity of modes of mental affections, each referable to one of three great groups, yet each one of us affirms his own identity—apparent let it be. To be, to be substance, to be self-apprehensive, and to be a unity are one and the same with Lotze. The unity of consciousness is the great fact to which he appeals for the guarantee of them all. But such a unity needs farther explication. I am not one because I am an identical somewhat back of knowing, feeling and willing. Much less am I one because I had a physical, atomic identity before I became conscious of the unity that I now attribute to and affirm of myself. But I am one only as I make myself one. Unity is not for me except as I am one to myself. Much rather of its unitary, than of its substantial being, can it be said that such is a mental achievement. The unity of the atom is a unit conceived *ab extra* by the physicists, and then only as a unity in multiplicity. Such, too, is the only unity Kant would allow to the soul, (as implied in the subjectivity of the categories of quantity.) But the only unity it would be a hardship to forego is just such a unity as I make good to myself in all my conscious states. Such is ' the most indivisible unity there can be.' One ' does not care whether he be reckoned as one, or more than one, according to the reckoning employed by the student of physics in counting up his atoms, or of the housewife in counting up her things. Thus to be a unitary being (if it were possible) would be no boon.'[1] Nor is an *a priori* identity any advantage to my integral reality. For only as I can fill up all the interstices of my conscious existence by inference

[1] Ladd, reply to Stout, *loc. cit.*

and an effort of memory to connect my present with yesterday
and a past of representations, and believing in my identity on the
morrow, have grounds for a hope in the future of an experience
that shall be amenable to the my which now is one to itself—
i. e., only as I have a conscious empiristic unity, is it a simplicity attributable to that self existent as the subject in every
state of consciousness.   Moreover, the *ego* is just our own
natural way of analyzing our states of consciousness.   That we
recognize a self is an attestation to our metaphysical nature
whence springs that postulate that we are.   It is not merely
an ethical postulate, but a product of cognitive faith which
Kant attempted to rule out.   Without feeling a belief in our
reality, we could never have come to such a cognition.   The
logical ego and the moral *law* are supreme instances of how
metaphysical Criticism is, but naïvely.   Both are hyposta-
sizations—impersonations of late developments in the rational
life.

   With such an interest in our unitary substantiality, we could
affirm that Kant's refutation of rational psychology was harmless to rational views on the nature and being of mind.   What
he criticised and the implications he carried into his criticisms,
though bearing the same linguistic stamps, do not effect the
meaning we hold in honor.   Yet it would be an unkindness,
coming out of historical ignorance, not to say that Kant's
trenchant criticism really prepared the way for such opinions
which the modern philosophy of mind attempts to vindicate for
itself.

   The second problem need not detain us so long.   The relations of body and mind have given rise to no little dispute.   Indeed, the belief that the body or brain, is *the* reality, has been
so common, that materialism has now a history almost as volu-
minous as any other form of scientific doctrine.   We do not
propose to go into a scientific consideration of the issue.   The
entire achievement of physiological psychology, and especially
in its highly specialized modern developments, is that the interaction of body and mind really is the causal modes of their behavior.   It must affirm that mind and body are tied both ways.[1]

   [1] *Cf.*, Ladd, *Phys. Psych.*, pt. III., ch. III., especially p. 667.

If this is materialism, well and good. Nevertheless it is the scientific conclusion warrantable by the facts of experience.[1]

There remains, however, a rational reduction of the relation in question. As a philosophical consideration it is one of the most interesting problems, if not *the* most, connected with a meta-empirical analysis of the *real*, and is the high-water mark of philosophy's attainments wherein it deals with the facts of life. In its solution is comprehended not only all of noëtics and metaphysics, and the earlier conclusions of rational psychology regarding the nature and being of the mind; but, from the solution offered to this question stream out influences that will, *must*, profoundly affect our consideration of *all* the ideal phases of the great problem of reality. It is so significant, embodying the choicest work in the philosophy of the real and reaching up to the first factor wherein is given intimations of the ideal, that it can be called the point of orientation in any system of philosophy.

Whatever may be the result of 'scientific' explanation—and there can be no doubt as to that—the problem changes entirely when brought before philosophy. Not only does it become the query as to the 'seat' of the soul, and *how* the brain and mind

---

[1] What can be meant by a 'causal relation' between body and mind, is something mysterious. We express it by such terms as 'connection,' 'seat,' 'organ,' *etc.* Such expressions do not clear up matters. I do not know by any special, immediate intuition that such a relation exists. I know nothing whatever in the act of vision that certain occipital centers are specially active; nor in hearing that the conditions include the neural activities of certain centers of the convolutions of the temporal lobe most adjacent to the Sylvian fissure. So long as we persist in retaining such terms and their empiric meaning, neither psychology nor philosophy explain matters. That the brain and its organs are given functions in our sentient life is a most pleasing instance of how metaphysical we are, and by a series of inferences seek to fill up gaps in the explanation of our experience.

In this connection it should be noted that Kant admitted the causal relation of brain and conscious states in that crude way in which the state of physiology and anatomy permitted him (*cf.*, *Werke*, II., 217, 224, 'Condition of the mind dependent on the body;' V., 387, 'Union of the soul with matter;' VII., 390 f., *Vorlesungen*, 47, 71 f., 'Commercio of the soul and body;' Erdmann's *Reflex.*, 92, 122, 128, 222). It also appears that Kant would banish the problem from psychology and anthropology; *Critique*, I., 506 f., VIII., 696: how the body is united with thought not to be answered by anthropology; *cf.*, also, the criticism of the fourth paralogism where the question is taken out of the hands of the dogmatic psychologists.

It is also interesting to compare Kant's empirical view of regarding the

are related;[1] for this is still a point of physiological import, or must be banished to the limbo of unwitted speculation. But when it has reached the point of a rational reduction, the question has been so transformed as to have lost all significance. Long before the relation in question is submitted to reason, one party has become a materialist out and out, and the other confirmed in his spiritualism. The one has negated the independent reality of brains, and the other has seen no need of asserting anything else but the 'epi-phenomenal' reality of consciousness. *The literal question has no meaning;* the materialist has nothing *in reality* to be juxtaposed; and the spiritualist has nothing with which the mind can have a spatial relation. With the reality of matter, or the ideality of space, neither party can contend as to the views of the other. So far, then, Kant is right. " The question is no longer as to the possibility of an association of the soul with other known and foreign substances

brain as the seat or organ of the soul with the conclusion of physiological psychology as it has made such rapid achievements in this century. In his special communication to Sömmerring, ' Über das Organ der Seele,' (which the latter so honored in his book, appearing under that title, as to crown his ' Arbeit mit seinen [Kant's] eigenen Worten,') he says, in effect, that after all else has been attempted, the special problem is not solved; nor is it merely physiological, for there yet remains ' die Einheit des Bewusstseins seiner selbst,' which must be made representable or imaginable in a spatial relation of the soul to the organ. This, however, is not only an insoluble problem which is properly ' eine Aufgabe für die Metaphysik;' but it is also contradictory in itself. To apprehend self-consciousness under some relation to its physical organ is to give it a spatial significance and try to make it an object of the external sense. Nor less is it that this problem of the place of the soul ' führt auf eine unmögliche Grösse $(\sqrt{-2})$,' VI., 456–461; *cf.*, Kant's letter to Sömmerring, August 10, 1795, VIII., 800. *Cf.*, Ladd, *Physiological Psychology*, p. 544 f. : ' As to a special organ of consciousness in the brain, it is not proper to speak.' ' If the question is pressed as to the *physical basis* for the activities of self-consciousness, no answer can be given or even suggested.' ' From its very nature, * * * it can have no analogous or corresponding material substratum.' It must also be noted that Kant not only empirically recognizes a dependence of the mind on the brain, but the causal relation works in the opposite direction, *cf.*, V., 471, 342 f., VII., 409 ff. : ' Power of mind over bodily feeling and diseases,' summing up autobiographic experiences. *Cf.*, corresponding topics in the *Anthropologie*, VII., 518 ff., II., 211 ff.

[1] *Cf.*, these phases of the question in the seventeenth century philosophy, *viz.* : the ' physical influence 'of Descartes, the ' divine mediation ' of Malebranche, the ' occasionalism ' of Geulincx, the monism of Spinoza, and the ' pre-established harmony ' of Leibnitz.

without us."[1] Up to this point, Criticism has thrown its influence in favor of the spiritualist. The 'coarse dualism' which science follows in its affirmation of a causal relation between brain and mind has been removed. It was an achievement of the Transcendental Æsthetic.

Yet we are not out of the difficulty. The facts of experience out of which the problem takes its rise are not removed. There persists this feeling of 'being in the body,' an in-ness so unique that it is utterly unlike the spatial meaning implied in the saying, our soul is not in a tree. There constantly surges upon us those waves of sensations—some highly specialized, others more massive and of an organic sort—which we fabricate into the objects of our knowledge, but constantly reminding us that things are as if there were real afferent nerves and real cortical centers. The problem of objects and apprehensive minds still remains. We have the data of so-called senses and the constant flow of cognitive experience. It is at this point, we affirm, Kant has *restated* the famous problem of the body and mind.[2] The question is no longer that which confused

[1] *Critique*, II., 334.

[2] Mention must be made of an apparent monistic reduction of body and mind which appears at times in the Critical philosophy. By 'monistic' we mean the attempt to harmonize the two orders of phenomena, giving them each equal validity. Such is the monism of substance. "No doubt I, as represented by the internal sense in time, and objects in space outside me, are two specifically different phenomena, but the foundation of external phenomena, and the other which forms the foundation of our internal intuition, is therefore neither matter, nor a thinking being by itself, but simply an unknown cause of phenomena that supplied to us the empirical concept of both." (*Crit.*, II., 329.) "If we consider that both kinds of objects thus differ from each other, and that possibly what is at the bottom of phenomenal matter, as a thing by itself, may not be so heterogeneous after all as we imagine, that difficulty (of the community of soul and body) vanishes, and there remains that one difficulty only, how a community of substance is possible at all." (I., 507, 2d ed.; *cf.*, II., 311, 332, 341, *Werke*, IV., 439 f., V., 182, VIII., 570 f., Bernard's *trans.* of *Crit. of Judgment*, Preface xxxviii f., Bax's *trans.* of *Prolegomena*, xci f., Höffding, *op. cit.*, 69.) With this intimation of the 'identity-hypothesis,' there was scarce any acceptance of it, unless we take his comparison of the mechanism and the teteology of nature as maintaining that 'all nature is the mere development of freedom' (*cf.*, V., pp. 417–423). If, on the other hand, we look to the whole drift of the *Critique*, Kant found no necessity of a substance-wise identification : Matter is only a hypostasized form of representation. He taught that idealism which 'besteht in der Behauptung dass es keine andern, als denkender

the seventeenth century philosophy and disturbs the modern mind because of the convictions of scientists; but is now as to the possibility of the 'connection of the representation of the internal sense with the modification of our external sensibility, and how these can be connected with each other according to constant laws, and acquire cohesion in experience.' "The notorious problem comes to this, how external intuition, namely that of space, (or what fills space, namely, form and movement) is possible in any thinking subject."[1] How can 'sensibility' and 'understanding' be united, or from the receptive beginnings of sentient life, how can it be that a knowledge of things arises? This is Kant's psychological innovation and must be awarded philosophical merit in having removed the old meaningless question, replacing it with the real point at issue.

Rational psychology thus ends in epistemology.[2] But the *crux metaphysicorum* has been as little solved by Kant as by his perseverant predecessors. "To this question no human being can return an answer."[3] Criticism had edge keen enough, however, to hew this Gordian knot of the dogmatists, *i. e.*, how to untie the knot from their view point was an insoluble problem. His criticism of the fourth paralogism removed the insoluble aspect presented to his age, but left the knot *in itself* as

Wesen gebe,' though he repudiated such a scepticism, and maintained on the contrary, 'es sind uns Dinge als ausser uns,' but only as phenomena, (IV., 37). At any rate, Spinozism produced rather a weird effect on Kant, who is careful to differentiate the methods of substantial monism and idealistic scepticism. "Die Kritik beschneidet dem Dogmatismus gänzlich die Flügel in Ansehung der Erkenntniss übersinnlicher Gegenstände, und des Spinozismus ist hierin so dogmatisch, dass er sogar mit dem Mathematiker in Ansehung der Strenge des Beweises wetteifert." (IV., 349 f., note; *cf.*, II., 118; IV., 465; V., 106, 404, 434; VI., 367, for the general estimation of the doctrine of a one substance.) If the ideality of space and time is not adopted, nothing remains but the Spinozistic mysticism. With the change in methods there comes different results, so that the identification of soul and body in one transcendental substance is nothing more than a wayside obstacle which Criticism sweeps away, passing on to that ulterior reduction of the problem as stated in the text.

[1]*Critique*, II., 334, 339 f.; *cf.*, VI., 67; IV., 81, 85.

[2]Kant distinctly removes the problem from psychology: "The difficulty of explaining the (apparent) community of the soul with the body is not the business of psychology to solve." The analysis of the Analytic shows it to be an insoluble problem. *Critique*, I., 506 f.

[3]*Critique*, II., 340.

firm as ever. Sceptical idealism prevents us from the attempt by removing the *crux* out of our reach.

In the same sentence, Kant seems to forget the significance of his own work in the Analytic. He goes back to his cosmological metaphysics and supplements his theory of knowledge with that weird ontology that is constantly reappearing in the doctrine of the extra-mental realities. "Instead of attempting to fill this gap in our knowledge, all we can do is to indicate it by ascribing external phenomena to a transcendental object as the cause of this class of representations, but which we shall never know, nor be able to form any concept of." If Kant means to interpret the problem as inquiring *why* it is that things have being, or more pertinently, *how* it is that anything can be, and *how* it is that 'thinking beings' know some spatial realities at all, he is right in regarding it insoluble. Human reason is not to struggle with the problem of creating a universe. The task of philosophy is to so understand the juxtaposition of primal elements as to make the rise of experience intelligible and to get at the meaning of the course of the world. No one has emphasized this more than Lotze who conducts us far into the intelligible order and value of all experience. "*How* things can exist and can manifest themselves anyhow, is the universal enigma."[1]

But if Kant reduces 'the notorious problem' to the questions: Why is it that our knowledge is partly of so-called objects? and, What is the *rationale* of that illusion which leads the scientific psychologist to affirm a causal relation between a brain and an ideating consciousness? then he must be represented as outwitted by a confusion of 'dogmatic' psychology with absolute speculation, and as failing to appreciate his own labors in the Æsthetic and Analytic which were 'to supply the key to the solution of every metaphysical problem.'[2] It is hardly a mark of wisdom to charge Kant with such turmoil and forgetfulness when the doctrine of phenomenality always furnishes the key to the solution of every 'natural' illusion, yet the whole criticism of the fourth paralogism savors of just such embarrassments. For us men, however, an insight into the enigmatical relation of

[1] *Microcosmus*, I., 192.
[2] *Critique*, II., XXIII.

body and mind, or the more pertinent implications in the rise
and nature of knowledge, of which the former is a complex and
highly developed phase—can come only by way of some such
procedure which was first brought to the world by Criticism.
Through an analysis of knowledge, we do come to a satisfactory
solution of why it is that we 'know' things as they appear to be
and 'posit' those relations of them which come back to us as
consternations through their hypostasization by science. When
the form or the conditions of knowledge are traced back to the
subject, as well as the materials or content-wise factors are seen
to be mental factors, then does it dawn upon us that 'experience' is one great mental product. It is not as we stand aloft
and watch, as it were, the epistemological unfolding of mind,
but only as we go and toil within that knowledge, do we have a
right to assure ourselves of the validity of our analysis, and know
in the name of rational coherence, that just such an analysis is
adequate for the interpretation of experience.

The ancient saying, 'That art thou,' is true; and what appears to be set over against thyself is nought else than an unfolding of thine own being. But it is not as overthrown with
the veil of *Maya* that we must affirm this unity of experience
and the apparent sublimation of all that belongs to sensibility.
It is only in the reality of experience that thou art thyself. The
enigma of the union of sensibility and understanding is solved
by the very fact of knowledge itself. *A priori forms*, synthetic *acti*, and the data of sense are the alluring snares of the
metaphysic of a theory of knowledge. We must draw back
the hand of Criticism when it holds up the *crux* of how 'space
is possible in any thinking subject.' We can press on yet a
little farther. If knowledge is made up merely of 'space' and
'thinking,' then there remains an insoluble residuum that must
be labeled transcendental object. But Criticism cannot be justified. It put the epistemological residue in an influential reality,[1] and omitted a large psychological remainder. Only one-

[1]We do not here have in mind such facts as those on which Prof. James
bases his criticism of Kant. "In the function of knowing there is a multiplicity to be connected, and K. brings this multiplicity inside the mind. * * * We,
on the contrary, put the multiplicity with the reality outside, and leave the mind
simple." *Op. cit.*, I., 363.

third of mental life has been given any noëtic virtue. Knowledge, however, *is*, only as it is the *developed reflex* of the *whole* of mind. Mere intellection, the discrimination and positing of relations is not experience. The mere envisagement of dirempted spatial form (if it were in any wise possible) is not intuition. But the whole being of mind is put into the fabric of experience. What activities *and* their products are to the psychologist, such is 'knowledge' to the epistemologist. We do not objectify things because space is a mental form, or *because* we have an external sense. We do not know ourselves as *egos* *because* we are *egos*. But we do have objects and are selves only as we struggle in a motor consciousness, or will ourselves to be. Without voluntary movement there is no world of perception, and if we never willed or felt a sense of innervation, we should never have awakened to the dignity of self-hood. In these widely dirempted products there is yet no disparity. The world of things, the range of non-*egos* is just as much mine as we figuratively express the possession of one's earned wage. The highest meaning that can be put into 'is' and 'mine,' is just such meaning as the diremptive activity of a developing consciousness puts into things and selves. Both are mine by the eternal right of a cognizing creation; I am not except as I am in them. 'That art thou.'

Some integrity can be gained in attempting the solution of the problem as Kant restated and left it. He stopped where his scant psychology brought him to the difficulty of how space is a form—an *a priori*, intuitive integer of thinking beings— such beings as we popularly designate by 'myself'—this varied course of ideas that is located in the head. Such distinctions, however, must be passed over, at least a little way. How space belongs to me as a reflective being is told by my own activity and passivity in coming into a possession of what constitutes experience. But if we lop off, as it were, those springs of discrimination and categorization, as Kant has done in the psychological aspects of Criticism, then philosophy is utterly unable to make intelligible any *rationale* of the speculative conviction: I am what I see, and in the totality of experience is found the progressive activity of myself whose product is Knowledge.

In the foregoing identification of self and the so-called world
of things, which seemed to Kant to be an unreachable conclusion, it has not been thought that all the mysteries have been
solved.   Had 'the Child of Pure Reason' pressed on his way
with greater integrity, he, too, might have found warrant for
removing the grounds of explaining spatiality and its content
from the unknowable x and placed them in the transcendental
faculty of cognition.   'That art thou,' is a truth which finds
complete guarantee in the facts of psychology and the necessities of noëtics.   But there must be drawn back the veil of *Maya*.
The conviction, that all is meaningless delusion, sins against the
metaphysical postulates no less than does the scepticism of Critical idealism.   In the 'That art thou,' lie implications of reality
which give even seeming content to 'That.'   In the 'Thou' and
in all that enters into self-apprehension are tokens, as it were,
of a somewhat that makes for the experience whose phenomenal
totality makes the circuit of self.   This is saying no more than
can be meant if one says, " all the truth we know must be found
in the primary facts of knowledge, in perception and self-consciousness."   Both orientalism and speculative transcendentalism belie the conviction of reality.   The one does not go far
enough in the mysteries of knowledge, and cuts off a grasp for
reality in its insufficient analysis on which it attempted to deny
any identification of that which is, with that which is known.
The other mistakes the one for the all, the individual for the
whole, but rushes on to an identification of knowledge and being.   The one was the careful treading of scientific demonstration, which wins for itself the true name of philosophy.   The
other is the groping of a religious instinct, springing from the
smart of unending pain.

Though everything is given in that mighty forthputting of
the individual which can most generously be called knowledge,
yet the whole of reality is not therein contained.   Absolutism
and scepticism both err in either brushing aside, or not giving
full weight to that conviction which is embedded in all experience that it is dealing with somewhat real.   It is the acceptance
of this incohate demand of a real, manifesting itself in various
forms all the way through experience, but seems most impera-

tive in all those states of consciousness having objective reference—which entitles reason to such an emboldened analysis of
what may be the constituents of such a reality, as expressed in
her choice off-spring, metaphysic.   Here is not the place to
explicate what interpretation reason shall best give of this vague
message that comes, as it were, from another far distant world,
but only to intimate the basis, there may be, of any right on
our part to speak of a world ground.   Admitting this claim of
all life, that there is a reality known and a truth that may be
expressed—both of which are the very core of any attempted
reduction of the relation of body and mind—reason has left to
itself a modicum of knowledge which it may progressively enlarge.   But what shall be our final answer to the question Kant
has left open, we cannot say.   Under an elaborate analysis of
knowledge it is found that the way in which Kant stated the
question is not pertinent.   The very life of knowledge itself
shows *how* ' space is possible to a thinking being.'   Yet, as the
final problem of rational psychology is seen to emerge into a
point for epistemological explication, the *crux metaphysicorum*
becomes, *why* is it that we are so related to the world-ground
as to give ourselves the peculiar reality that we do?   *This* is
the gap in our knowledge which cannot be filled.   What corre-
spondent relation the elements of our experience may have in
the absolute, we do not know.   Philosophy can do no more
than take as given the so-called elements attained by its analyses.
These can be given a rational coherence so as to make experience intelligible.   Thus Kant's question finds its answer in the
very knowledge which he so profoundly analyzed.   But *why*
we are as we are, *why* we develop such a self, such an unity of
experience as we do, that is the ultimate enigma.   This is the
outcome of all explanation—to bring us to the unexplained.
The recognition of the mysterious at some point is the profound-
est result of an interpretation of nature.   Whether philosophy
may sometime have an insight into the *why* of experiential
factors, or the *how* of the being of things, it is not for one to
say.   Let us return to the broad fields of experience, saying,
with the spirit of Criticism :

"Lasst uns unser Glück besorgen, in den Garten gehen, und arbeiten."

DIAGRAM OF THE FACULTIES, cf., p. 68.

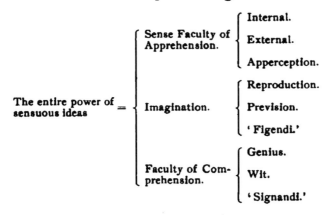

The following diagram represents what might be called the more anthropological view and division of the knowing faculty in which Kant takes empirical delight.

The entire power of sensuous ideas =

- Sense Faculty of Apprehension.
  - Internal.
  - External.
  - Apperception.
- Imagination.
  - Reproduction.
  - Prevision.
  - 'Figendi.'
- Faculty of Comprehension.
  - Genius.
  - Wit.
  - 'Signandi.'

[1] It is interesting to note that Kant avoids, we might almost say, all metaphysical implication in his empirical terms. 'Gemüth' may mean any state of mind, possibly corresponding to our 'consciousness as such.' In his psychological passages, he employes 'Gemüth' instead of 'Seele' or 'Geist.' This same effort to be non-metaphysical as far as possible, is apparent in the *Critique*, where he prefers 'Vernunft;' *cf.*, *supra* pp. 123 *f.*

[2] The 'lower' are involuntary and against the will; the 'higher' are voluntary, are under 'free' will, *Reflexionen*, p. 70 *f.* The diagrams refer to the following citations: *Critique*, II., 109, 115; VII., 451 *f*, 465, 473, 481, 489, 512, 515; *Reflexionen*, 59, 65, 80 *ff*; *Vorlesungen*, 12 *f.*

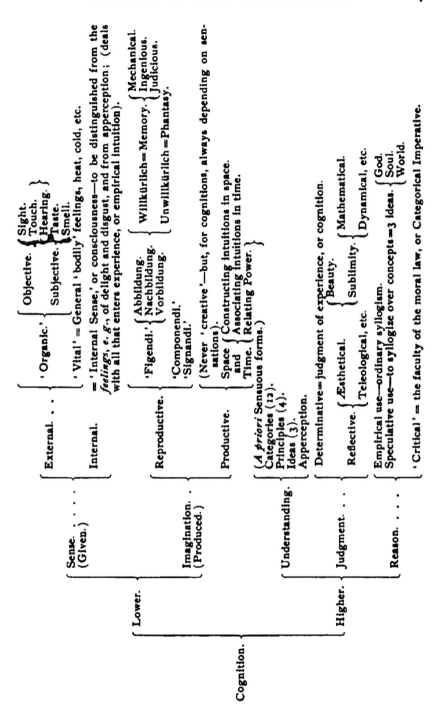

Cognition.

Lower.

Sense. (Given.)

External . . { Objective. { Sight. Touch. Hearing. Taste. Smell. } Subjective. }
    'Organic.'
    'Vital' = General 'bodily' feelings, heat, cold, etc.

Internal. = 'Internal Sense,' or consciousness—to be distinguished from the *feelings*, *e. g.*, of delight and disgust, and from apperception; (deals with all that enters experience, or empirical intuition).

Imagination. (Produced.)

Reproductive.
    'Figendi.' { Abbildung. Nachbildung. Vorbildung. }
    'Componendi.' 'Signandi.'
    Willkürlich = Memory. { Mechanical. Ingenious. Judicious. }
    Unwillkürlich = Phantasy.

Productive.
    (Never 'creative'—but, for cognitions, always depending on sensations).
    Space and Time. { Constructing Intuitions in space. Associating Intuitions in time. Relating Power. }

Higher.

Understanding.
    (*A priori* Sensuous forms.)
    Categories (12).
    Principles (4).
    Ideas (3).
    Apperception.

Judgment. . .
    Determinative = judgment of experience, or cognition.
    Reflective. { Æsthetical. { Beauty. Sublimity. } { Mathematical. Dynamical, etc. } Teleological, etc. }

Reason. . . .
    Empirical use—ordinary syllogism.
    Speculative use—to syllogize over concepts = 3 Ideas. { God. Soul. World. }
    'Critical' = the faculty of the moral law, or Categorical Imperative.

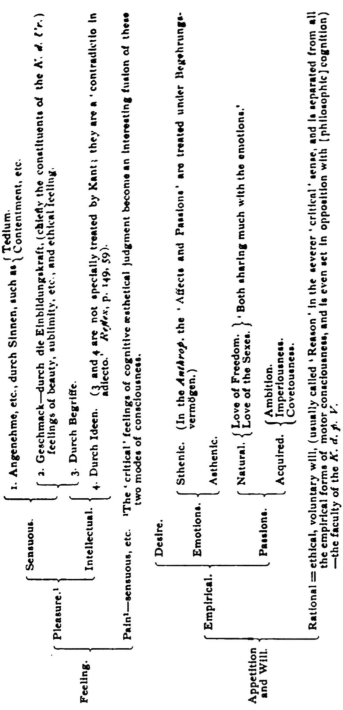

Feeling.

Pleasure.[1]

- Sensuous.
  1. Angenehme, etc., durch Sinnen, such as { Tedium. Contentment, etc.
  2. Geschmack—durch die Einbildungskraft, (chiefly the constituents of the K. d. U'r.) feelings of beauty, sublimity, etc., and ethical feeling.
- Intellectual.
  3. Durch Begriffe.
  4. Durch Ideen. (3 and 4 are not specially treated by Kant; they are a 'contradictio in adiecto.' Reflex, p. 149, 59).

Pain[1]—sensuous, etc. 'The 'critical' feelings of cognitive æsthetical judgment become an interesting fusion of these two modes of consciousness.

Appetition and Will.

- Empirical.
  - Desire.
  - Emotions.
    - Sthenic. (In the Anthrop. the 'Affects and Passions' are treated under Begehrungs-vermögen.)
    - Asthenic.
  - Passions.
    - Natural. { Love of Freedom. Love of the Sexes. } 'Both sharing much with the emotions.'
    - Acquired. { Ambition. Imperiousness. Covetousness.
- Rational = ethical, voluntary will, (usually called 'Reason' in the severer 'critical' sense, and is separated from all the empirical forms of motor consciousness, and is even set in opposition with [philosophic] cognition—the faculty of the K. d. p. V.

One thing chiefly noticeable is, that the effectiveness of Kantain psychology falls away as it approaches the close of the analysis of consciousness. Its force was spent in validating the analysis of cognition or intellective consciousness.

ST

To avoi
or

FEB 25

CPSIA information can be obtained at www.ICGtesting.com
Printed in the USA
BVOW011811041011

272795BV00005B/13/P